D0001788

Practice, Engage, Apply and Develop Employability Skills with MyLab Operations Management

86%

of students said it helped them earn higher grades on homework, exams, or the course

*Source: 2016 Student Survey, n 523

MyLab™ Operations Management is an online homework, tutorial, and assessment program constructed to work with this text to engage students and improve results. It was designed to help students develop and assess the skills and applicable knowledge that they will need to succeed in their courses and their future careers.

See what more than 25,000 students had to say about MyLab Operations Management:

"It helped me get a higher grade on my exams because it offered a lot of practice and explained different steps to me when I became confused."

— Luke Piercy, Illinois State University

Operations Management Simulations give students hands-on experience in **real-world roles**, helping them to link course concepts to on-the-job application. Using real-life situations, students evaluate information and then engage in **decision-making** and **critical analysis**. By receiving real-time, dynamic feedback from stakeholders, students see the actual impact of their choices and can gauge their performance against individual, peer, and system metrics—with results recorded in the MyLab Gradebook.

"I like how MyLab Operations Management provides step by step instructions that also stimulates your thinking in working through the problems."

—Helen H., University of Washington - Bothell

Question Help offers a number of tutorial tools and learning aids that give students the help they need when they need it. Exercises provide step-by-step instruction, input-specific feedback, and hints, and may link to spreadsheets, sample problems, or the exact spot in the eText that addresses the learning objective of the problem.

89% 95% 95%

eText Study Plan Dynamic Study Modules

% of students who found learning tool helpful

Dynamic Study Modules help students study chapter topics effectively on their own by continuously assessing their **knowledge application** and performance in real time. These are available as graded assignments prior to class, and accessible on smartphones, tablets, and computers.

Pearson eText enhances student learning—both in and outside the classroom. Take notes, highlight, and bookmark important content, or engage with interactive lecture and example videos that bring learning to life (available with select titles). Accessible anytime, anywhere via MyLab or the app.

The **MyLab Gradebook** offers an easy way for students and instructors to view course performance. Item Analysis allows instructors to quickly see trends by analyzing details like the number of students who answered correctly/incorrectly, time on task, and median time spend on a question by question basis. And because it's correlated with the AACSB Standards, instructors can track students' progress toward outcomes that the organization has deemed important in preparing students to be **leaders.**

89% of students would tell their instructor to keep using MyLab Operations Management

For additional details visit: www.pearson.com/mylab/operationsmanagement

INTRODUCTION TO

FIFTH EDITION

OPERATIONS AND SUPPLY CHAIN MANAGEMENT

Cecil C. Bozarth

North Carolina State University

Robert B. Handfield

North Carolina State University

 Pearson

New York, NY

Vice President, Business, Economics, and UK Courseware: Donna Battista

Director of Portfolio Management: Stephanie Wall

Editorial Assistant: Linda Siebert Albelli

Vice President, Product Marketing: Roxanne McCarley

Senior Product Marketer: Product Marketer: Kaylee Carlson

Product Marketing Assistant: Marianela Silvestri

Manager of Field Marketing, Business Publishing: Adam Goldstein

Executive Field Marketing Manager: Field Marketing Manager: Nicole Price

Vice President, Production and Digital Studio, Arts and Business: Etain O'Dea

Director of Production, Business: Jeff Holcomb

Managing Producer, Business: Melissa Feimer

Content Producer: Yasmita Hota

Operations Specialist: Carol Melville

Design Lead: Kathryn Foot

Manager, Learning Tools: Brian Surette

Content Developer, Learning Tools: Lindsey Sloan

Managing Producer, Digital Studio and GLP, Media Production and Development: Ashley Santora

Managing Producer, Digital Studio: Diane Lombardo

Digital Studio Producer: Regina DaSilva

Digital Studio Producer: Alana Coles

Digital Content Project Lead: Courtney Kamauf

Project Management: Thistle Hill Publishing Services

Interior and Cover Design: Cenveo® Publisher Services

Cover Art: Oscar Sanchez/EyeEm/Getty Images

Printer/Binder: LSC Communications, Inc./Willard

Cover Printer: LSC Communications, Inc./Willard

Microsoft and/or its respective suppliers make no representations about the suitability of the information contained in the documents and related graphics published as part of the services for any purpose. All such documents and related graphics are provided "as is" without warranty of any kind. Microsoft and/or its respective suppliers hereby disclaim all warranties and conditions with regard to this information, including all warranties and conditions of merchantability, whether express, implied or statutory, fitness for a particular purpose, title and non-infringement. In no event shall Microsoft and/or its respective suppliers be liable for any special, indirect or consequential damages or any damages whatsoever resulting from loss of use, data or profits, whether in an action of contract, negligence or other tortious action, arising out of or in connection with the use or performance of information available from the services.

The documents and related graphics contained herein could include technical inaccuracies or typographical errors. Changes are periodically added to the information herein. Microsoft and/or its respective suppliers may make improvements and/or changes in the product(s) and/or the program(s) described herein at any time. Partial screen shots may be viewed in full within the software version specified.

Microsoft® and Windows® are registered trademarks of the Microsoft Corporation in the U.S.A. and other countries. This book is not sponsored or endorsed by or affiliated with the Microsoft Corporation.

Library of Congress Cataloging-in-Publication Data

Names: Bozarth, Cecil C., author. | Handfield, Robert B., author.

Title: Introduction to operations and supply chain management / Cecil C. Bozarth, North Carolina State University, Robert B. Handfield, North Carolina State University.

Description: Fifth edition. | New York, NY : Pearson, [2019] | Includes bibliographical references and index.

Identifiers: LCCN 2017050841| ISBN 9780134740607 (hardcover) | ISBN 0134740602 (hardcover)

Subjects: LCSH: Management. | Production management. | Business logistics.

Classification: LCC HD31.2 .B69 2019 | DDC 658.5—dc23

LC record available at https://lccn.loc.gov/2017050841

2 18

ISBN 10: 0-13-474060-2
ISBN 13: 978-0-13-474060-7

To Andrea, James, and Philip

C.B.

To Sandi, Simone, and Luc

R.H.

Cecil Bozarth is Professor of Operations and Supply Chain Management at the Poole College of Management at N.C. State University, where he has received awards for teaching excellence at both the undergraduate and graduate levels. He is a former chair of the Operations Management Division of the Academy of Management, and in 1999 was recognized by APICS as a subject matter expert (SME) in the area of supply chain management. His particular areas of interest are operations and supply chain strategy and supply chain information systems. Cecil's consulting experience cuts across a wide range of industries, including such companies as BlueCross BlueShield of North Carolina, Daimler-Benz, John Deere, Duke Energy, Eisai, Ford Motor Company, GKN, IBM, GlaxoSmithKline, Milliken, Patheon, Sonoco, and others. For thirteen years, Cecil was an associate editor for the *Journal of Operations Management*; he now serves on the journal's editorial advisory board. Cecil has also served as a guest editor for the *Academy of Management Journal*, as well as the *Journal of Operations Management*.

Robert Handfield is the Bank of America Professor and a Distinguished University Professor at N.C. State University. Handfield has consulted with over 25 Fortune 500 companies, including Biogen Idec, Caterpillar, John Deere, GlaxoSmithKline, Boston Scientific, Delphi, Chevron, British Petroleum, Chevron Phillips, Bank of America, Sensata, Honda of America, KPMG, Conoco Phillips, Federal Express, SAP, and others, and is a world-renowned expert in the areas of purchasing and logistics. Rob is the former editor-in-chief of the *Journal of Operations Management* and has written several books on SCM topics, including *Introduction to Supply Chain Management* (Prentice Hall, with Ernest L. Nichols; translated into Japanese, Korean, Chinese, and Indonesian), *Supply Chain Redesign* (Prentice Hall Financial Times), and *Purchasing and Supply Chain Management*, 5th edition (South-Western College Publishing, with Robert M. Monczka, Larry C. Giunipero, and James L. Patterson).

BRIEF CONTENTS

CONTENTS

5 Managing Quality   108

6 Managing Capacity   142

6S Advanced Waiting Line Theory and Simulation Modeling   175

PART III

Establishing Supply Chain Linkages   189

7 Supply Management   189

15 Developing Products and Services 451

When we set out to write the first edition of this book, we wanted to create an introductory text that provides an integrated and comprehensive treatment of both operations *and* supply chain management. That goal has remained the same through this, our fifth, edition.

NEW TO THIS EDITION

PROFESSIONAL PROFILE

MANDY ALTHOFF, METLIFE

MetLife is a well-respected financial services company that provides life insurance, annuities, employee benefits, and asset management services. Whenever MetLife issues an insurance policy, it takes on some financial risk in exchange for the premiums paid by the customer. Sound business practice and regulatory requirements dictate that MetLife keep enough cash reserves to pay off expected claims by the customers. In some instances, it makes good business sense for MetLife to outsource bundles of existing policies to another insurance company who "reinsures" the policies and takes the financial risk, while MetLife, in some cases, continues to provide service support to the customers.

Reaching an outsourcing agreement that is a win-win for MetLife, the reinsurer, and the final customer is a complicated task. While actuaries and underwriters perform much of the financial analysis, someone has to help manage the actual negotiation process (see Chapter 7). Enter Mandy Althoff, a Senior Sourcing Consultant at MetLife. As Mandy puts it, "The idea of having someone from sourcing involved in helping arrange these outsourcing agreements is relatively new—these agreements used to be purely finance driven." Mandy continues: "The business leadership team has been open to my creative approach to negotiation, allowing me a unique seat at the table. It all goes back to my undergraduate sourcing class."

PROFESSIONAL PROFILE

DWIGHT HENDRICKSON, CATERPILLAR

Throughout this book, we have made the point that supply chains cover everything from sourcing-to-producing-to-delivering the final product or service. Furthermore, supply chain *management* takes place at the strategic planning level, looking years into the future, down to the execution of day-to-day activities.

In over 20 years at Caterpillar, Dwight Hendrickson has experienced all of this firsthand. He has been a commercial purchasing analyst and a lead buyer; a general operations supervisor and certified Six Sigma black belt; and a logistics manager and product program manager. In fact, Dwight's experience is so comprehensive that outside professional organizations regularly look to him for his expertise and leadership. He currently serves on the North Carolina District Export Council (NCDEC), which is made up of professionals who act as consultants to small- and medium-sized businesses that want to export products into markets outside of the United States.

be like? Since the demand for building construction products is tightly tied to the overall health of the world economy and other geopolitical factors, Dwight has to make sure Caterpillar is ready to increase volumes dramatically when the economy is strong and scale down activ-

With this new edition, we have continued our strategy of providing detailed coverage of important SCM topics while still maintaining a trim, integrated book. One of the most notable changes is the **professional profiles** found in selected chapters. These half-page profiles focus on individuals working in the operations and supply chain area—their company and industry, experiences and responsibilities, and their advice to others entering the field. These professional profiles are positioned to coincide with the relevant chapter topics so that readers can make the connection between what we are talking about in the book and how this plays out in practice.

We also added a section in Chapter 1 discussing the various employability skills that students can develop by studying the course and incorporating the learnings from this book into their daily lives. We have also updated Chapter 1's discussion of long-term trends to include the concepts of agility.

Chapter 3 now includes a discussion of 3D printing, also known as additive manufacturing. Long used in prototyping new products, 3D printing promises to change the volume/variety trade-offs for many manufactured items. Last, we have updated the opening case study in many of the chapters to reflect the changing business conditions and challenges facing operations and supply chain managers.

SOLVING TEACHING AND LEARNING CHALLENGES

The Six Sigma Methodology

Of all the various approaches to organizing for business process improvement, the Six Sigma methodology arguably best represents current thinking. It certainly is popular, with many top companies, such as GE, Motorola, and Bank of America, citing it as a key element of their business strategy. Six Sigma has its roots in the quality management discipline. (Quality management is such an important topic to operations and supply chain managers that we have devoted Chapter 5 to the subject.) The term *Six Sigma* refers to both a quality metric and a methodology. In *statistical terms*, a process that achieves Six Sigma quality will generate just 3.4 defects per 1 million opportunities (DPMO). As a *methodology* for process improvement, Six Sigma has a much broader meaning. Motorola[10] describes the **Six Sigma methodology** as:

Six Sigma methodology According to Motorola, a business improvement methodology that focuses on an organization on understanding and managing customer requirements, aligning key business processes to achieve those requirements, utilizing rigorous data analysis to understand and ultimately minimize variation in those processes, and ... rapid and sustainab...

A business improvement methodology that focuses an organization on:

- Understanding and managing customer requirements
- Aligning key business processes to achieve those requirements
- Utilizing rigorous data analysis to understand and ultimately minimize variation in those processes
- Driving rapid and sustainable improvement to business processes

Let's consider this definition for a moment. The first two points reinforce the idea that busi-

5.4 STATISTICAL QUALITY CONTROL

At the start of the chapter, we noted that organizations must:

1. Understand what dimensions of quality are most important to users.
2. Develop products and services that will meet the users' requirements.
3. Put in place business processes capable of meeting the specifications driven users' requirements.
4. Verify that the business processes are indeed meeting the specifications.

Statistical quality control (SQC) is directly aimed at the fourth issue—making sur business's current processes are meeting the specifications. Simply put, SQC is the app of statistical techniques to quality control. In this section, we describe some popular SQ cations and illustrate how basic statistical concepts can be applied to quality issues.

Instructors teaching operations and supply chain management face several challenges. The first is helping students **make the connection** between the needs of the business and the tools and techniques operations covered in the book. A second challenge is deciding exactly *what* tools and techniques to cover, especially in an introductory course. Finally, some of the more quantitative tools can be quite complex, requiring a variety of learning approaches to help students master them. This book addresses these challenges in the following manner:

- The book contains **comprehensive coverage** of the tools and techniques in the traditional OM areas (quality, capacity, queuing, forecasting, inventory, planning and control, and project management), *as well as* the purchasing and logistics areas.

Decision Trees

Decision tree
A visual tool that decision makers use to evaluate capacity decisions. The main advantage of a decision tree is that it enables users to see the interrelationships between decisions and possible outcomes.

A **decision tree** is a visual tool that decision makers use to evaluate capacity decisions. The main advantage of a decision tree is that it enables users to see the interrelationships between decisions and possible outcomes. Decision trees are particularly good at helping users visualize complex *series* of decisions and outcomes.

The basic rules for using decision trees are as follows:

1. Draw a tree from left to right, starting with a decision point or an outcome point, and develop branches from there.
2. Represent each *decision point* with a square, with the different branches coming out of the square representing alternative choices.
3. Represent *outcome points* (which are beyond the control of the decision maker) with circles. Each possible outcome is represented by a branch off the circle. Assign

14.3 PROJECT MANAGEMENT TOOLS

Practitioners and academics have developed a host of tools to aid organizations in their project management efforts. Project management tools are used to plan, measure, and track a project's progress. In this section, we introduce two well-accepted tools: Gantt charts and network diagrams. These tools help managers understand what activities need to be completed, who is responsible for various activities, and when the activities should be completed. These tools also allow managers to track the time it takes to complete activities as well as costs. With the proper planning and control information, managers can take corrective actions when necessary to meet project objectives.

- Tools and techniques are always introduced **within the context** of the OM and SCM issues at hand. For example, we show how sales and operations planning (Chapter 10) can be used to coordinate activity *across* supply chain partners, as well as in its traditional role as an intra-firm planning approach.
- In addition to the extensive use of solved problems, students are shown how tools and techniques can be applied using **Microsoft Excel spreadsheets.** Learning is reinforced through homework problems that provide the students with a template and hints for checking their answers.
- An **Enhanced eText,** available in **MyLab Operations Management,** gives instructors and students the ability to highlight the text, bookmark, search the glossary, and take notes. More importantly, the eText provides a new way of learning that is particularly useful to today's students. Students are able to review animations of figures, indicated by **MyLab Operations Management** Animation, and videos of solved problems available on MyLab Operations Management with a simple click of an icon. Visit www.pearson.com/mylab/operations-management for more information.

Tools and Techniques Integrated Throughout

TOOLS AND TECHNIQUES	SOLVED EXAMPLES	HOMEWORK PROBLEMS	EXCEL EXAMPLES/ PROBLEMS
Chapter 2: Operations and Supply Chain Strategies			
Value index	✓	✓	✓
Chapter 3: Process Choice and Layout Decisions in Manufacturing and Services			
Service blueprinting	✓		
Line balancing	✓	✓	
Assigning department locations	✓	✓	
Chapter 4: Business Processes			
Performance measures (productivity, efficiency, cycle time, percent value-added time)	✓	✓	
Process mapping	✓	✓	
Six Sigma methodology and DMAIC process	✓		
Continuous improvement tools (root cause analysis, scatter plots, check sheets, Pareto charts)	✓	✓	
Cause-and-effect diagrams	✓		
Chapter 5: Managing Quality			
Process capability ratio	✓	✓	
Process capability index	✓	✓	
Six Sigma quality	✓	✓	
X and R charts	✓	✓	✓
p charts	✓	✓	✓
Acceptance sampling	✓		
Chapter 6: Managing Capacity			
Expected value analysis	✓	✓	✓
Decision trees	✓	✓	
Break-even analysis	✓	✓	✓
Indifference point	✓	✓	✓
Learning curves	✓	✓	
Theory of constraints	✓		
Waiting lines (queuing analysis)	✓	✓	
Little's Law	✓	✓	
Simulation analysis	✓		✓
Chapter 7: Supply Management			
Total cost analysis	✓	✓	
Weighted-point evaluation system	✓	✓	✓
Profit leverage	✓	✓	
Spend analysis	✓	✓	
Chapter 8: Logistics			
Shipment consolidation	✓	✓	✓
Perfect order calculation	✓	✓	
Landed costs	✓	✓	
Weighted center of gravity model	✓	✓	✓
Optimization modeling (assignment problem using Excel Solver function)	✓	✓	✓
Chapter 9: Forecasting			
Moving average model	✓	✓	✓
Exponential smoothing model	✓	✓	✓
Adjusted exponential smoothing model	✓	✓	✓
Linear regression	✓	✓	✓
Seasonal adjustments	✓	✓	✓
Multiple regression	✓	✓	✓

(Continued)

TOOLS AND TECHNIQUES	SOLVED EXAMPLES	HOMEWORK PROBLEMS	EXCEL EXAMPLES/ PROBLEMS
MAPE, MAD, MFE, and tracking signal	✓	✓	✓
Chapter 10: Sales and Operations Planning (Aggregate Planning)			
Top-down sales and operations planning	✓	✓	✓
Bottom-up sales and operations planning	✓	✓	
Cash flow analysis	✓	✓	
Load profiles	✓	✓	
Optimization modeling (top-down sales and operations planning using Excel Solver function)	✓	✓	✓
Chapter 11: Managing Inventory throughout the Supply Chain			
Periodic review systems	✓	✓	
Economic order quantity	✓	✓	✓
Reorder points and safety stock	✓	✓	✓
Quantity discounts	✓	✓	
Single-period inventory systems (newsboy problem)	✓	✓	
Pooling safety stock	✓	✓	✓
Chapter 12: Managing Production across the Supply Chain			
Master scheduling	✓	✓	
Material requirements planning (MRP)	✓	✓	
Job sequencing rules	✓	✓	
Distribution requirements planning (DRP)	✓	✓	
Chapter 13: JIT/Lean Production			
Kanban sizing	✓	✓	
Linking MRP and kanban	✓	✓	
Chapter 14: Managing Projects			
Gantt charts	✓	✓	
Activity on node (AON) diagrams and critical path method (CPM)	✓	✓	Microsoft Project example
Project crashing	✓	✓	
Chapter 15: Developing Products and Services			
Quality function deployment (QFD)	✓		

MyLab Operations Management

Reach Every Student by Pairing This Text with MyLab Operations Management. MyLab is the teaching and learning platform that empowers you to reach *every* student. By combining trusted author content with digital tools and a flexible platform, MyLab personalizes the learning experience and improves results for each student. Learn more about MyLab Operations Management at www.pearson.com/mylab/operations-management.

Deliver Trusted Content. You deserve teaching materials that meet your own high standards for your course. That's why we partner with highly respected authors to develop interactive content and course-specific resources that you can trust—and that keep your students engaged.

Empower Each Learner. Each student learns at a different pace. Personalized learning pinpoints the precise areas where each student needs practice, giving all students the support they need—when and where they need it—to be successful.

Teach Your Course Your Way. Your course is unique. So whether you'd like to build your own assignments, teach multiple sections, or set prerequisites, MyLab gives you the flexibility to easily create *your* course to fit *your* needs.

Improve Student Results. When you teach with MyLab, student performance improves. That's why instructors have chosen MyLab for more than 15 years, touching the lives of over 50 million students.

DEVELOPING EMPLOYABILITY SKILLS

This book covers many skills that hiring managers identify as important to success in a variety of business settings, including small and large firms, nonprofit organizations, and public service.

Critical Thinking

Critical thinking involves purposeful and goal-directed thinking used to define and solve problems, make decisions, or form judgments related to a particular situation or set of circumstances. This book is filled with dozens of useful frameworks that managers regularly use to support problem solving, including the Six Sigma methodology (Chapter 4), decision tree analysis (Chapter 6), sourcing portfolio analysis (Chapter 7), and project management tools (Chapter 14). It is not an exaggeration to say that critical thinking and fact-based decision making are built into the DNA of the operations and supply chain discipline.

Collaboration

Many key operations and supply chain activities require close collaboration with participants from other areas, such as marketing, engineering, and finance. Throughout this book, we will emphasize the importance of cross-functional collaboration as well as collaboration with outside supply chain partners. Forecasting (Chapter 9) and inventory management (Chapter 11) are just two areas in which collaboration is essential for the process to work. Chapter 10, in fact, is devoted to sales and operations planning, an approach to planning that depends entirely on collaboration and negotiation between operations, marketing, finance, and human resources in order to succeed.

Knowledge Application and Analysis

Knowledge application and analysis is defined as the ability to learn a concept and then apply that knowledge in another setting to achieve a higher level of understanding. Put another way, understanding is more than just memorizing formulas and cranking out answers. As such, this book seeks to move students "beyond the formulas" by illustrating how the concepts can be applied in a wide range of settings, using both extended examples and in-chapter case studies.

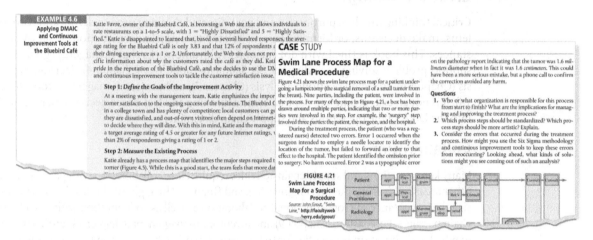

Information Technology Application and Computing Skills

Finally, information technology application and computing skills are defined as the ability to select and use appropriate technology to accomplish a given task. This book covers this skill set in a couple different ways. First, the book includes numerous, detailed examples of how Microsoft Excel can be used to carry out the various calculations covered in the text. Second, we have devoted the Chapter 12 supplement to understanding supply chain information system needs and reviewing recent trends in the area.

TABLE OF CONTENTS OVERVIEW

I. Creating Value through Operations and Supply Chains

Ch. 1: Introduction to Operations and Supply Chain Management	Introduces basic concepts and definitions that lay the groundwork for future chapters
Ch. 2: Operations and Supply Chain Strategies	Discusses operations and supply chain strategies, including what they are, how they support the organization's overall strategy, and how they help a firm provide value to the customer

II. Establishing the Operations Environment

Ch. 3: Process Choice and Layout Decisions in Manufacturing and Services	Describes the manufacturing and service processes that firms put in place to provide products or services
Ch. 4: Business Processes	Introduces the topic of business processes, which can be thought of as the "molecules" that make up all operations and supply chain flows
Ch. 5: Managing Quality	Provides an overview of the different perspectives on quality, as well as some of the tools and techniques companies use to improve and monitor quality levels
Ch. 6: Managing Capacity	Discusses capacity and introduces several tools that managers use to evaluate capacity choices, including expected value analysis, waiting line theory, and Little's Law

III. Establishing Supply Chain Linkages

Ch. 7: Supply Management	Describes the broad set of activities carried out by organizations to analyze sourcing opportunities, develop sourcing strategies, select suppliers, and carry out all the activities required to procure goods and services
Ch. 8: Logistics	Discusses the physical flow of goods throughout the supply chain and covers such areas as transportation, warehousing, and logistics decision models

IV. Planning and Controlling Operations and Supply Chains

Ch. 9: Forecasting	Discusses the different types of forecasts firms use, and covers the most common quantitative forecasting methods
Ch. 10: Sales and Operations Planning (Aggregate Planning)	Describes S&OP process and major approaches to developing plans. Additional topics include cash flow analysis and linking S&OP throughout the supply chain
Ch. 11: Managing Inventory throughout the Supply Chain	Discusses the critical role of inventory, and tools and techniques for managing it
Ch. 12: Managing Production across the Supply Chain	Introduces some of the systems manufacturers use to manage production and to coordinate these activities with their supply chain partners
Ch. 13: JIT/Lean Production	Introduces the just-in-time (JIT)/Lean philosophy, and provides coverage of kanban production techniques

V. Project Management and Product/Service Development

Ch. 14: Managing Projects	Describes how organizations manage projects, and covers common project management tools, including network-based models
Ch. 15: Developing Products and Services	Addresses the product and service development process, with an emphasis on how these decisions directly affect choices in operations and supply chain management

INSTRUCTOR TEACHING RESOURCES

This program comes with the following teaching resources.

SUPPLEMENTS AVAILABLE TO INSTRUCTORS AT WWW.PEARSONHIGHERED.COM/BOZARTH	FEATURES OF THE SUPPLEMENT
Instructor's Solutions Manual, authored by Geoff Willis from UCO College of Business	• Detailed solutions for all end-of-chapter Discussion Questions, Problems, and Case Study questions • Solutions of the Excel problems available on the Data Download page
Test Bank, authored by Geoff Willis from UCO College of Business	More than 1,500 multiple-choice, true/false, short-answer, and graphing questions with these annotations: • Difficulty level (1 for straight recall, 2 for some analysis, 3 for complex analysis) • Type (Multiple-choice, true/false, short-answer, essay) • Keywords (The term or concept the question supports) • Learning outcome • AACSB learning standard (Written and Oral Communication; Ethical Understanding and Reasoning; Analytical Thinking; Information Technology; Interpersonal Relations and Teamwork; Diverse and Multicultural Work; Reflective Thinking; Application of Knowledge)

(Continued)

SUPPLEMENTS AVAILABLE TO INSTRUCTORS AT WWW.PEARSONHIGHERED.COM/BOZARTH	FEATURES OF THE SUPPLEMENT
Computerized TestGen	TestGen allows instructors to: • Customize, save, and generate classroom tests • Edit, add, or delete questions from the Test Item Files • Analyze test results • Organize a database of tests and student results
PowerPoints, authored by Dr. Kathryn A. Marley from Duquesne University	Slides include key Excel figures, graphs, tables, and equations in the textbook PowerPoints meet accessibility standards for students with disabilities. Features include, but not limited to: • Keyboard and Screen Reader access • Alternative text for images • High color contrast between background and foreground colors
Excel Problems	Instructors can create different homework problems for different class sections and even different students. This feature is ideal for instructors teaching large sections of an introductory operations/supply chain course. With these homework problems, professors have an extra measure to guard against plagiarism in homework assignments. Here's how it works: 1. Students go to the Multimedia Library in MyLab Operations Management or to the Data Download page at www.pearsonhighered.com/bozarth and open an Excel spreadsheet listed under the chapter of interest. 2. Students type their name and a four-digit number chosen by the instructor into the spreadsheet. The four-digit number creates new parameters for the problem. 3. Students print out their customized homework sets and solve the problems. 4. The instructor uses an Excel-based key that uses the same four-digit number to generate the correct answers.

If assistance is needed, our dedicated technical support team is ready to help with the media supplements that accompany this text. Visit **support.pearson.com/getsupport** for answers to frequently asked questions and toll-free user support phone numbers.

ACKNOWLEDGMENTS

We would like to thank the following reviewers of the previous editions:

R. C. Baker, University of Texas at Arlington
David L. Bakuli, Westfield State College
Gregory L. Bier, University of Missouri
Terrence M. Boardman, East Carolina University
Kimball Bullington, Middle Tennessee State University
David T. Cadden, Quinnipiac University
Cem Canel, University of North Carolina at Wilmington
Sohail Chaudhry, Villanova University
Christopher W. Craighead, University of North Carolina at Charlotte
Richard E. Crandall, Appalachian State University
Barry A. Cumbie, University of Southern Mississippi
Sime Curkovic, Western Michigan University
Eduardo C. Davila, Arizona State University
Kenneth H. Doerr, University of Miami
Matthew J. Drake, Duquesne University
Ike C. Ehie, Kansas State University
Lawrence P. Ettkin, University of Tennessee at Chattanooga
Jared Everett, Boise State University

Kamvar Farahbod, California State University, San Bernardino
Donavon Favre, North Carolina State University
Geraldo Ferrar, University of North Carolina at Chapel Hill
Bruce G. Ferrin, Western Michigan University
Gene Fliedner, Oakland University
Tom Foster, Brigham Young University
Ram Ganeshan, University of Cincinnati
Janet L. Hartley, Bowling Green State University
Ray M. Haynes, California Polytechnic State University, San Luis Obispo
Lesley Gail Scamacca Holmer, The Pennsylvania State University
Seung-Lae Kim, Drexel University
Timothy J. Kloppenborg, Xavier University
Terry Nels Lee, Brigham Young University
Binshan Lin, Louisiana State University in Shreveport
Rhonda R. Lummus, Iowa State University
Daniel S. Marrone, State University of New York Farmingdale
Mark McKay, University of Washington
Mohammad Meybodi, Indiana University Kokomo
Philip F. Musa, Texas Tech University
Joao S. Neves, The College of New Jersey
Barbara Osyk, The University of Akron
Fariborz Y. Partovi, Drexel University
Charles Petersen, Northern Illinois University
Carl J. Poch, Northern Illinois University
Robert F. Reck, Western Michigan University
Richard A. Reid, University of New Mexico
Shane J. Schvaneveldt, Weber State University
V. Sridharan, Clemson University
Mahesh Srinivasan, The University of Akron
Harm-Jan Steenhuis, Eastern Washington University
Joaquin Tadeo, University of Texas at El Paso
V. M. Rao Tummala, Eastern Michigan University
Elisabeth Umble, Baylor University
Enrique R. Venta, Loyola University Chicago
Y. Helio Yang, San Diego State University

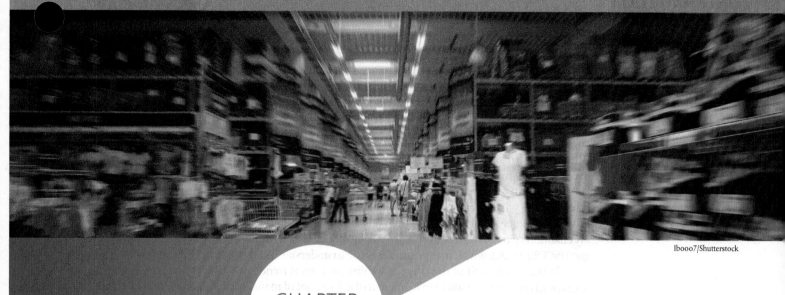

Ibooo7/Shutterstock

CHAPTER
one

Introduction to Operations and Supply Chain Management

CHAPTER OUTLINE

Introduction

CHAPTER OBJECTIVES

By the end of this chapter, you will be able to:

- Describe what the operations function is and why it is critical to an organization's survival.

- Describe what a supply chain is and how it relates to a particular organization's operations function.

- Discuss what is meant by operations management and supply chain management.

- Identify some of the major operations and supply chain activities, as well as career opportunities in these areas.

- Make a case for studying *both* operations management and supply chain management.

INTRODUCTION

Let's start with a question: What do the following organizations have in common?

- **Walmart,** which not only is a leading retailer in the United States but also has built a network of world-class suppliers, such as GlaxoSmithKline, Sony, and Mattel
- **FedEx,** a service firm that provides supply chain solutions and transportation services
- **Flex Ltd.,** a contract manufacturer that assembles everything from plug-in electric motorcycles to LCD and touch displays
- **SAP,** the world's largest provider of enterprise resource planning (ERP) software

While these firms may appear to be very different from one another, they have at least one thing in common: a strong commitment to superior operations and supply chain management.

In this chapter, we kick off our study of operations and supply chain management. We begin by examining what operations is all about and how the operations of an individual organization fit within a larger supply chain. We then talk about what it means to *manage* operations and supply chains. As part of this discussion, we will introduce you to the Supply Chain Operations Reference (SCOR) model, which many businesses use to understand and structure their supply chains.

In the second half of the chapter, we discuss several trends in business that have brought operations and supply chain management to the forefront of managerial thinking. We also devote a section to what this all means to you. We discuss career opportunities in the field, highlight some of the major professional organizations that serve operations and supply chain professionals, and look at some of the major activities that operations and supply chain professionals are involved in on a regular basis. We end the chapter by providing a roadmap of this book.

Operations management and supply chain management cover a wide range of activities, including transportation services, manufacturing operations, retailing, and consulting.

1.1 WHY STUDY OPERATIONS AND SUPPLY CHAIN MANAGEMENT?

So, why should you be interested in operations and supply chain management? There are three simple reasons.

1. ***Every organization must make a product or provide a service that someone values.*** Otherwise, why would the organization exist? Think about it. Manufacturers produce physical goods that are used directly by consumers or other businesses. Transportation companies provide valuable services by moving and storing these goods. Design firms use their expertise to create products or even corporate images for customers. Software firms develop apps that consumers use on their smartphones. The need to provide a valuable product or service holds true for not-for-profit organizations as well. Consider the variety of needs met by government agencies, charities, and religious groups, for example.

   The common thread is that each organization has an operations function, or *operations*, for short. The **operations function** is the collection of people, technology, and systems within an organization that has primary responsibility for providing the organization's products or services. Regardless of what career path you might choose, you will need to know something about your organization's operations function.

   As important as the operations function is to a firm, few organizations can—or even want to—do everything themselves. This leads to our second reason for studying operations and supply chain management.

2. ***Most organizations function as part of larger supply chains.*** A **supply chain** is a network of manufacturers and service providers that work together to create products or services needed by end users. These manufacturers and service providers are linked together through physical flows, information flows, and monetary flows. When the primary focus is on physical goods, much of the supply chain activity will revolve around the conversion, storage, and movement of materials and products. In other cases, the focus might be on providing an intangible service. For example, automobile insurance companies like Progressive Insurance depend on cellular phone networks and Internet service providers (ISPs) to support the data flows that allow customers to upload photos of accident damage and receive settlement checks electronically.

   Supply chains link together the operations functions of many different organizations to provide real value to customers. Consider a sporting goods store that sells athletic shoes. Although the store doesn't actually make the shoes, it provides valuable services for its customers—a convenient location and a wide selection of products. Yet, the store is only one link in a much larger supply chain that includes:

   - Plastic and rubber producers that provide raw materials for the shoes.
   - Manufacturers that mold and assemble the shoes.
   - Wholesalers that decide what shoes to buy and when.
   - Transportation firms that move the materials and finished shoes to all parts of the world.
   - Software firms and ISPs that support the information systems that coordinate these physical flows.
   - Financial firms that help distribute funds throughout the supply chain, ensuring that the manufacturers and service firms are rewarded for their efforts.

   So where does this lead us? To our third reason for studying operations and supply chain management—and the premise for this book.

3. ***Organizations must carefully manage their operations and supply chains in order to prosper and, indeed, survive.*** Returning to our example, think about the types of decisions facing a shoe manufacturer. Some fundamental operations decisions that it must make include the following: "How many shoes should we make, and in what styles and sizes?" "What kind of people skills and equipment do we need?" "Should we locate our

Operations function
Also called *operations*. The collection of people, technology, and systems within an organization that has primary responsibility for providing the organization's products or services.

Supply chain
A network of manufacturers and service providers that work together to create products or services needed by end users. These manufacturers and service providers are linked together through physical flows, information flows, and monetary flows.

Dmitri Maj/Shutterstock

Athletic shoes at a retailer represent the last stage in a supply chain that crosses the globe and involves many different companies.

plants to take advantage of low-cost labor or to minimize shipping cost and time for the finished shoes?"

In addition to these operations issues, the shoe manufacturer faces many decisions with regard to its role in the supply chain: "From whom should we buy our materials—the lower-cost supplier or the higher-quality one?" "Which transportation carriers will we use to ship our shoes?" The right choices can lead to higher profitability and increased market share, while the wrong choices can cost the company dearly—or even put it out of business.

Operations Management

Let's begin our detailed discussion of operations and supply chain management by describing operations a little more fully and explaining what we mean by operations management. As we noted earlier, all organizations must make products or provide services that someone values, and the operations function has the primary responsibility for making sure this happens.

One way to think about operations is as a *transformation process* that takes a set of inputs and transforms them in some way to create outputs—either goods or services—that a customer values (Figure 1.1). Consider a plant that makes wood furniture. Even for a product as simple as a chair, the range of activities that must occur to transform raw lumber into a finished chair can be overwhelming at first. Raw lumber arrives as an input to the plant, perhaps by truck or even train car. The wood is then unloaded and moved onto the plant floor. Planing machines cut the

FIGURE 1.1
Viewing Operations as a Transformation Process

Inputs	Transformation Process	Outputs
• Materials	• Manufacturing operations	• Tangible goods
• Intangible needs	• Service operations	• Fulfilled needs
• Information		• Satisfied customers

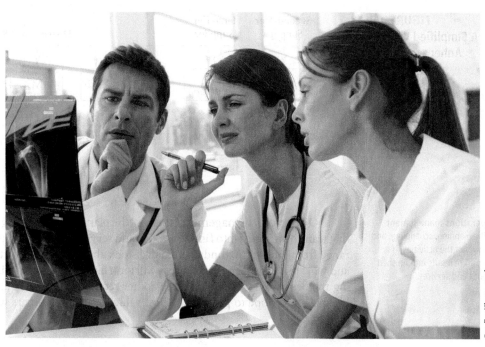

Health care services use highly skilled individuals as well as specialized equipment to provide physiological transformation processes for their patients.

lumber to the right thickness. Lathes shape pieces of wood into legs and back spindles for the chairs. Other machines fabricate wood blanks, shaping them into seats and boring holes for the legs and back spindles.

In addition to the equipment, there are people who run and load the machines, conveyors, and forklifts that move materials around the plant, and there are other people who assemble the chairs. Once the chairs are finished, still more people pack and move the chairs into a finished goods warehouse or onto trucks to be delivered to customers. In the background, supervisors and managers use information systems to plan what activities will take place next.

The operations function can also provide intangible services, as in the case of a law firm. A major input, for example, might be the need for legal advice—hardly something you can put your hands around. The law firm, through the skill and knowledge of its lawyers and other personnel, transforms this input into valuable legal advice, thereby fulfilling the customer's needs. How well the law firm accomplishes this transformation goes a long way in determining its success.

Figure 1.1 makes several other points. First, inputs to operations can come from many places and take many different forms. They can include raw materials, intangible needs, and even information, such as demand forecasts. Also, operations are often highly dependent on the quality and availability of inputs. Consider our furniture plant again. If the lumber delivered to it is of poor quality or arrives late, management might have to shut down production. In contrast, a steady stream of good-quality lumber can ensure high production levels and superior products. Second, nearly all operations activities require coordination with other business functions, including engineering, marketing, and human resources. We will revisit the importance of cross-functional decision making in operations throughout the book. Third, operations management activities are information and decision intensive. You do not have to be able to assemble a product or treat a patient yourself to be a successful operations manager—but you *do* have to make sure the right people and equipment are available to do the job, the right materials arrive when needed, and the product or service is completed on time, at cost, and to specifications!

FIGURE 1.2
A Simplified View of Anheuser-Busch's Supply Chain

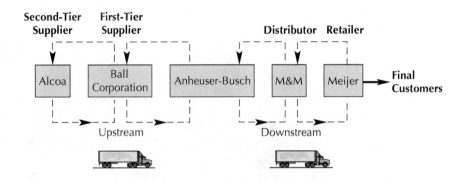

FIGURE 1.2
A Simplified View of Anheuser-Busch's Supply Chain

Operations management
"The planning, scheduling, and control of the activities that transform inputs into finished goods and services."

Operations management, then, is "the planning, scheduling, and control of the activities that transform inputs into finished goods and services."[1] Operations management decisions can range from long-term, fundamental decisions about what products or services will be offered and what the transformation process will look like to more immediate issues, such as determining the best way to fill a current customer request. Through sound operations management, organizations hope to provide the best value to their customers while making the best use of resources.

Supply Chain Management

Upstream
A term used to describe activities or firms that are positioned *earlier* in the supply chain relative to some other activity or firm of interest. For example, corn harvesting takes place upstream of cereal processing, and cereal processing takes place upstream of cereal packaging.

Downstream
A term used to describe activities or firms that are positioned *later* in the supply chain relative to some other activity or firm of interest. For example, sewing a shirt takes place downstream of weaving the fabric, and weaving the fabric takes place downstream of harvesting the cotton.

First-tier supplier
A supplier that provides products or services directly to a firm.

Second-tier supplier
A supplier that provides products or services to a firm's first-tier supplier.

The traditional view of operations management illustrated in Figure 1.1 still puts most of the emphasis on the activities a particular organization must perform when managing its own operations. But, as important as a company's operations function is, it is not enough for a company to focus on doing the right things within its own four walls. Managers must also understand how the company is linked in with the operations of its suppliers, distributors, and customers—what we refer to as the supply chain.

As we noted earlier, organizations in the supply chain are linked together through physical flows, information flows, and monetary flows. These flows go both up and down the chain. Let's extend our discussion and vocabulary using a product many people are familiar with: a six-pack of beer. Figure 1.2 shows a simplified supply chain for Anheuser-Busch. From Anheuser-Busch's perspective, the firms whose inputs feed into its operations are positioned **upstream,** while those firms who take Anheuser-Busch's products and move them along to the final consumer are positioned **downstream.**

When the typical customer goes to the store to buy a six-pack, he or she probably does not consider all of the steps that must occur beforehand. Take cans, for example. Alcoa extracts the aluminum from the ground and ships it to Ball Corporation, which converts the aluminum into cans for Anheuser-Busch. In the supply chain lexicon, Ball Corporation is a **first-tier supplier** to Anheuser-Busch because it supplies materials directly to the brewer. By the same logic, Alcoa is a **second-tier supplier;** it provides goods to the first-tier supplier.

The cans from Ball Corporation are combined with other raw materials, such as cartons, grain, hops, yeast, and water, to produce the packaged beverage. Anheuser-Busch then sells the packaged beverage to M&M, a wholesaler that, in turn, distributes the finished good to Meijer, the retailer. Of course, we cannot forget the role of transportation carriers, which carry the inputs and outputs from one place to the next along the supply chain.

As Figure 1.2 suggests, the flow of goods and information goes both ways. For instance, Ball Corporation might place an order (information) with Alcoa, which, in turn, ships aluminum (product) to Ball. Anheuser-Busch might even return empty pallets or containers to its first-tier suppliers, resulting in a flow of physical goods back *up* the supply chain.

Of course, there are many more participants in the supply chain than the ones shown here; Anheuser-Busch has hundreds of suppliers, and the number of retailers is even higher. We could also diagram the supply chain from the perspective of Alcoa, M&M, or any of the other

[1] J. H. Blackstone, ed., *APICS Dictionary*, 15th ed. (Chicago, IL: APICS, 2016).

FIGURE 1.3
The Supply Chain
Operations Reference
(SCOR) Model

participants. The point is that most of the participants in a supply chain are both customers and suppliers. Finally, the supply chain must be very efficient, as the final price of the good must cover all of the costs involved plus a profit for each participant in the chain.

While you were reading through the above example, you might have thought to yourself, "Supply chains aren't new"—and you'd be right. Yet most organizations historically performed their activities independently of other firms in the chain, which made for disjointed and often inefficient supply chains. In contrast, **supply chain management** is the *active* management of supply chain activities and relationships in order to maximize customer value and achieve a sustainable competitive advantage. It represents a conscious effort by a firm or group of firms to develop and run supply chains in the most effective and efficient ways possible.

But what exactly *are* these supply chain activities? To answer this, we turn to the **Supply Chain Operations Reference (SCOR) model.** The SCOR model is a framework that seeks to provide standard descriptions of the processes, relationships, and metrics that define supply chain management.[2] We will explore the SCOR model in more detail in Chapter 4, but for now, Figure 1.3 provides a high-level view of the framework. According to the SCOR model, supply chain management covers five broad areas:

1. *Planning activities*, which seek to balance demand requirements against resources and communicate these plans to the various participants.
2. *Sourcing activities*, which include identifying, developing, and contracting with suppliers and scheduling the delivery of incoming goods and services.
3. *"Make," or production, activities*, which cover the actual production of a good or service.
4. *Delivery activities*, which include everything from entering customer orders and determining delivery dates to storing and moving goods to their final destination.
5. *Return activities*, which include the activities necessary to return and process defective or excess products or materials.

Finally, notice that Figure 1.3 shows the supply chain management task extending from the company's suppliers' suppliers, all the way to the customers' customers. As you can imagine, coordinating the activities of all these parties is challenging.

To illustrate, let's consider Walmart, one of the earliest proponents of supply chain management.[3] What Walmart was doing in the late 1980s and early 1990s was nothing short of revolutionary. Individual stores sent daily sales information to Walmart's suppliers via satellite. These suppliers then used the information to plan production and ship orders to Walmart's warehouses. Walmart used a dedicated fleet of trucks to ship goods from warehouses to stores in less than 48 hours and to replenish store inventories about twice a week. The result was better customer service (because products were nearly always available), lower production and transportation costs (because suppliers made and shipped only what was

Supply chain management
The *active* management of supply chain activities and relationships in order to maximize customer value and achieve a sustainable competitive advantage. It represents a conscious effort by a firm or group of firms to develop and run supply chains in the most effective and efficient ways possible.

Supply Chain Operations Reference (SCOR) model
A framework developed and supported by the Supply Chain Council that seeks to provide standard descriptions of the processes, relationships, and metrics that define supply chain management.

---

[2]SCOR Framework, **www.apics.org/apics-for-business/products-and-services/apics-scc-frameworks/scor.**
[3]G. Stalk, P. Evans, and L. E. Shulman, "Competing on Capabilities: The New Rules of Corporate Strategy," *Harvard Business Review* 70, no. 2 (March–April 1992): 57–69.

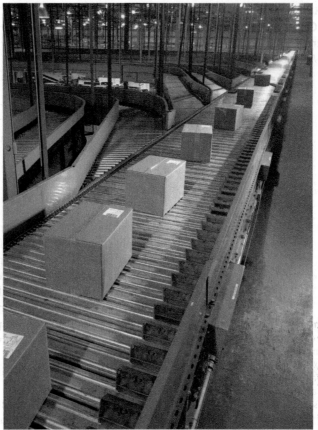

Walmart was an early proponent of superior supply chain performance. Other companies have now adopted many of the practices Walmart pioneered in the 1980s.

needed), and better use of retail store space (because stores did not have to hold an excessive amount of inventory).

Walmart has continued to succeed through superior sourcing and delivery, and many of the practices it helped pioneer have taken root throughout the business world. In fact, many retailers now make *multiple* shipments to stores each day, based on *continuous* sales updates. To illustrate how widespread supply chain management thinking has become, consider the example of Panera Bread in the *Supply Chain Connections* feature.

Supply chain management efforts can range from an individual firm taking steps to improve the flow of information between itself and its supply chain partners to a large trade organization looking for ways to standardize transportation and billing practices. In the case of Walmart, a single, very powerful firm took primary responsibility for improving performance across its own supply chain. As an alternative, companies within an industry often form councils or groups to identify and adopt supply chain practices that will benefit all firms in the industry. One such group is the Automotive Industry Action Group (AIAG, **www .aiag.org**), whose members "work collaboratively to streamline industry processes via global standards development & harmonized business practices."[4] The Grocery Manufacturers of America (GMA, **www.gmaonline.org/**) serves a similar function. Other organizations, such as APICS (**www.apics.org/apics-for-business**), seek to improve supply chain performance across many industries.

---

[4]Automotive Industry Action Group (AIAG), **www.aiag.org/about.**

SUPPLY CHAIN CONNECTIONS

PANERA BREAD: "A LOAF OF BREAD IN EVERY ARM"

If you live in the United States or Canada, there is a good chance that you have either heard of or visited a Panera Bread bakery-cafe. Panera Bread is a specialty food retailer that has built its business on providing consumers with fresh artisan bread products served at strategically located, distinctive bakery-cafes. As of December 2016, Panera Bread had over 2,100 company- and franchise-operated bakery-cafes.[5] Financial results have been equally impressive: for 2015, revenues from $2.68 billion, with an operating profit of over $240 million.[6]

But consider for a moment the upstream supply chain activities that must take place to ensure that these bakery-cafes receive the fresh dough needed to fulfill the company's mission statement, "A loaf of bread in every arm." In the case of Panera Bread, the operations and supply chain team has responded by putting in place a network of 24 fresh dough manufacturing facilities that produce more than 300 million pounds of dough annually. To ensure the freshest product possible, this dough is delivered 7 days a week, 365 days a year, to the bakery-cafes. Panera's operations and supply chain team also controls the distribution system for the retail bakery-cafes and supports the company's baking activities. In effect, the team is responsible for everything that comes through the back doors of Panera Bread bakery-cafes.

Even in this short description, we can see how Panera Bread's supply chain activities cover everything from sourcing to production to delivery. It's a safe bet that Panera Bread's interest in effective supply chain management will continue to "rise" along with its products.

Judith Collins/Alamy Stock Photo

[5]Reuters, Profile: Panera Bread (PNRA.O), **www.reuters.com/finance/stocks/companyProfile?symbol =PNRA.O**, April 6, 2017.
[6]Panera Bread Company, 2015 Annual Report to Stockholders, **www.panerabread.com/content/dam/ panerabread/documents/financial/2016/pbc-annual-report-2015.pdf.**

1.2 IMPORTANT TRENDS

As we shall see, operations management and supply chain management are as much philosophical approaches to business as they are bodies of tools and techniques, and thus they require a great deal of interaction and trust between companies. For right now, however, let's talk about three enduring trends that will continue to attract the attention of operations and supply chain management professionals for the foreseeable future:

- Agility
- Information technologies
- People

Agility

Agility
The ability to recalculate plans in the face of market, demand, and supply volatility and deliver the same or comparable cost, quality, and customer service.

As customers become more demanding and globalization expands the number of competitors in any marketplace, many businesses have found it increasingly important to develop agile operations and supply chains. *Supply Chain Insights* defines **agility** as "the ability to recalculate plans in the face of market, demand and supply volatility and deliver the same or comparable cost, quality and customer service."[7]

For example, in the past it might have taken *months* for a manufacturer to increase or decrease production levels in response to market demands. This is no longer a viable option—today's customers will not wait months for products when demand is going up, and investors will not tolerate excess inventories when demand is going down.

Of course, quickly adjusting production levels is just one example of agility. Agility can also include the ability to quickly respond to interruptions in the supply chain, reconfigure the supply chain to include new partners, or even the ability to launch new products and services based on changing market conditions, all while simultaneously minimizing negative impacts on operational and financial performance. Agility depends in large part on sophisticated information technologies that give a firm "visibility" into how operations and supply chains are performing, as well as supply chain professionals who know how to use these systems, two trends we discuss next.

Information Technologies

Electronic commerce
Also called *e-commerce*. "The use of computer and telecommunications technologies to conduct business via electronic transfer of data and documents."

Over the past 25 years, no area has had a greater impact on business than information technology, most notably the Internet and electronic commerce. **Electronic commerce,** or e-commerce for short, refers to "the use of computer and telecommunications technologies to conduct business via electronic transfer of data and documents."[8] Progressive Insurance, which we mentioned earlier, is just one example of a company that has built its business around e-commerce. Another is Netflix, which first used the Internet and advanced software applications to help subscribers order DVDs but now uses the Internet to stream content to its customers.

As you will see in the chapters that follow, information technology affects everything from the execution of day-to-day operations activities to the development of long-term plans. For example, in the opening case study for Chapter 5, we discuss how Delta Air Lines is using radio frequency identification (RFID) to precisely track the location of millions of bags in real time. At the other extreme, companies are using sophisticated decision support systems to develop long-term business plans. We explore the operations and supply chain impacts of information technology—including such topics as cloud computing and the Internet of Things (IoT)—in more detail in the Chapter 12 supplement.

People

The last trend concerns people; specifically, the current shortage of talented operations and supply chain professionals and the importance of relationship management. With regard to the talent shortage, Sue Doerfler from *Inside Supply Management* puts it this way, "Unlike agility with its growth potential, the talent shortage presents more of a dilemma going forward for the supply management profession. There is a diminishing senior leadership labor pool as baby boomers reach retirement. Conjointly, a new talent shortage predicament is emerging as the profession becomes more technological."[9]

---

[7]Supply Chain Insights LLC Research Report, "How S&OP Drives Agility," March–April 2012, **http://supplychaininsights .com/research-reports/agility-report/**.

[8]Blackstone, *APICS Dictionary*.

[9]S. Doerfler, "Now Trending!," *Inside Supply Management*, November–December 2016, 16–19, **http://magazine.ism .ws/wp-content/uploads/2016/12/16-19-now-trending**.

But agility, information technology, and a talented pool of professionals are not enough to guarantee a firm's success. Any efforts to improve operations and supply chain performance are likely to be inconsequential without the cooperation of other firms. As a result, more companies are putting an emphasis on relationship management.

Of all the activities operations and supply chain personnel perform, relationship management is perhaps the most difficult and therefore the most susceptible to breakdown. Poor relationships within any link of the supply chain can have disastrous consequences for all other supply chain members. For example, an unreliable supplier can "starve" a plant, leading to inflated lead times and resulting in problems across the chain, all the way to the final customer.

To avoid such problems, organizations must manage the relationships with their upstream suppliers as well as their downstream customers. This can be quite difficult when supply chain partners are geographically distant or when there are cultural differences. In the case of high-tech firms, many components can be purchased only from foreign suppliers who are proprietary owners of the required technology. In such environments, it becomes more important to choose a few, select suppliers, thereby paving the way for informal interaction and information sharing. We will discuss the challenges of relationship management more in Chapter 7.

1.3 OPERATIONS AND SUPPLY CHAIN MANAGEMENT AND YOU

At this point, you might be asking yourself, "If I choose to work in operations or supply chain management, where am I likely to end up?" The answer: Anywhere you like! As the Professional Profiles for Mandy Althoff and Stuart Williams show, operations and supply chain professionals are found in virtually every business sector.

Salaries and placement opportunities for operations and supply chain personnel also tend to be highly competitive, reflecting the important and challenging nature of the work, as well as the relative scarcity of qualified individuals. In fact, each year the Institute for Supply Management (ISM) publishes a salary survey broken down by job position, work experience, and education level.[10]

You also might be asking yourself, "What would my career path look like?" Many operations and supply chain managers find that over their career, they work in many different areas. Table 1.1 lists just a few of the possibilities.

TABLE 1.1
Potential Career Paths in Operations and Supply Chain Management

Analyst	Uses analytical and quantitative methods to understand, predict, and improve processes within the supply chain.
Production manager	Plans and controls production in a manufacturing setting. Responsible for a wide range of personnel.
Service manager	Plans and directs customer service teams to meet the needs of customers and support company operations.
Sourcing manager	Identifies global sources of materials, selects suppliers, arranges contracts, and manages ongoing relationships.
Commodity manager	Acquires knowledge in a specific market in which the organization purchases significant quantities of materials and services. Helps formulate long-term commodity strategies and manage long-term relationships with selected suppliers.
Supplier development manager	Measures supplier performance, identifies suppliers requiring improvement, and facilitates efforts to improve suppliers' processes.
International logistics manager	Works closely with manufacturing, marketing, and purchasing to create timely, cost-effective import/export supply chains.
Transportation manager	Manages private, third-party, and contract carriage systems to ensure timely and cost-efficient transportation of all incoming and outgoing shipments.

---

[10]ISM's 2016 Salary Survey, **http://magazine.ism.ws/wp-content/uploads/2016/12/16-23-Salary-Survey-May16.pdf.**

PROFESSIONAL PROFILE

MANDY ALTHOFF, METLIFE

MetLife is a well-respected financial services company that provides life insurance, annuities, employee benefits, and asset management services. Whenever MetLife issues an insurance policy, it takes on some financial risk in exchange for the premiums paid by the customer. Sound business practice and regulatory requirements dictate that MetLife keep enough cash reserves to pay off expected claims by the customers. In some instances, it makes good business sense for MetLife to outsource bundles of existing policies to another insurance company who "reinsures" the policies and takes the financial risk, while MetLife, in some cases, continues to provide service support to the customers.

Reaching an outsourcing agreement that is a win-win-win for MetLife, the reinsurer, and the final customer is a complicated task. While actuaries and underwriters perform much of the financial analysis, someone has to help manage the actual negotiation process (see Chapter 7). Enter Mandy Althoff, a Senior Sourcing Consultant at MetLife. As Mandy puts it, "The idea of having someone from sourcing involved in helping arrange these outsourcing agreements is relatively new—these agreements used to be purely finance driven." Mandy continues: "The business leadership team has been open to my creative approach to negotiation, allowing me a unique seat at the table. It all goes back to my undergraduate sourcing class."

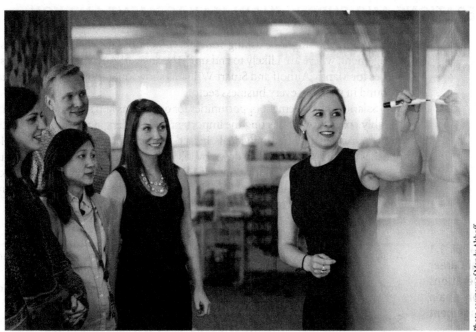

Photo courtesy of Mandy Althoff

Professional Organizations

If you decide to pursue a career in operations or supply chain management, you will find a number of professional organizations willing to help you. These organizations have certification programs that establish an individual as a professional within his or her particular area. Most organizations also have regular meetings at the local level, as well as national and international meetings once or twice a year. We highlight some of these organizations here.

APICS—APICS (**www.apics.org**) describes itself as "The Association for Operations Management." It is a widely recognized professional society for persons interested in operations and supply chain management. APICS currently has more than 67,000 members and 250 chapters throughout the United States and its territories.

ISM—The Institute for Supply Management (ISM, **www.ism.ws**) provides national and international leadership in purchasing and materials management, particularly in

PROFESSIONAL PROFILE

STUART WILLIAMS, MARSH FURNITURE COMPANY

Stuart Williams has had an interesting career path. After graduating with an undergraduate degree in Education, Stuart went back to school and received his MBA in Finance and Supply Chain Management. After working for Carquest, where he honed his inventory management skills, Stuart took a job as Supply Chain Manager for Marsh Furniture Company, a 110-year-old manufacturer of kitchen cabinets located in High Point, North Carolina.

As Stuart puts it, "The immediate reaction of many people is, 'How hard can it be to manufacture kitchen cabinets?' But there are quality specifications and manufacturing tolerances to consider, a wide variety of sizes and styles, and material flows and production levels that must be planned and coordinated. The level of complexity is higher than you might think."

When Stuart arrived at Marsh Furniture Company in 2013, one of his first jobs was to get a better handle on the flow of parts and raw materials coming into the assembly plant. This included working closely with key suppliers and improving inventory accuracy. Stuart also worked with others in the company to move from a batch style manufacturing process to a paced production line process (see Chapter 3) and to put advanced planning and control information systems in place (Chapter 12). Thanks to these efforts, Marsh has improved cash flows and is positioned for another one hundred years of success.

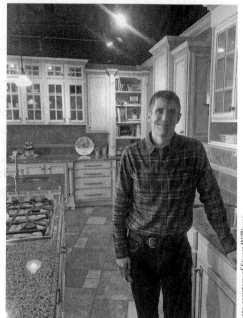

Photo courtesy of Stuart Williams

When asked what advice he would give students entering the workforce, Stuart says, "Do the task on hand. Immerse yourself in details." He also suggests that students take the advice of Cal Newport, a Computer Science professor at Georgetown University—"Be so good they can't ignore you."

the areas of education, research, and standards of excellence. Established in 1915, ISM has grown to more than 40,000 members.

CSCMP—The Council of Supply Chain Management Professionals (CSCMP, **www.cscmp.org**) seeks to be the preeminent professional association providing worldwide leadership for the evolving logistics profession through the development, dissemination, and advancement of logistics knowledge.

ASQ—The American Society for Quality (ASQ, **www.asq.org**) is a leader in education and all aspects of quality improvement, including the Baldrige Award, ISO 9000, and continuous improvement activities.

If you are a student, it is not too early to start thinking of joining one of these organizations. In fact, many of them provide scholarships for college education and can help defray education costs.

Cross-Functional and Interorganizational Linkages

Even if you decide that a career in operations and supply chain management is not for you, chances are you will still find yourself working with people in these areas. This is because *none* of the major operations and supply chain activities takes place in a vacuum. Rather, these activities require the input and feedback of other functions within a firm, as well as suppliers and

TABLE 1.2
Major Operations and Supply Chain Activities

OPERATIONS AND SUPPLY CHAIN ACTIVITY	PURPOSE	KEY INTERFUNCTIONAL PARTICIPANTS	KEY INTERORGANIZATIONAL PARTICIPANTS
Process selection	Design and implement the transformation processes that best meet the needs of the customer and the firm	Engineering Marketing Finance Human resources IT	Customers
Forecasting	Develop the planning numbers needed for effective decision making.	Marketing Finance Accounting	Suppliers Customers
Capacity planning	Establish strategic capacity levels ("bricks and mortar") and tactical capacity levels (workforce, inventory).	Finance Accounting Marketing Human resources	Suppliers Customers
Inventory management	Manage the amount and placement of inventory within the company and the supply chain.	IT Finance	Suppliers Customers
Planning and control	Schedule and manage the flow of work through an organization and the supply chain; match customer demand to supply chain activities.	Marketing IT	Suppliers Customers
Purchasing	Identify and qualify suppliers of goods and services; manage the ongoing buyer–supplier relationships.	Engineering Finance Marketing	Suppliers
Logistics	Manage the movement of physical goods throughout the supply chain.	Marketing Engineering	Suppliers Customers

customers. Table 1.2 lists some major operations and supply chain activities, as well as some of the key outside participants. Look, for example, at process selection. Engineering and IT personnel help identify and develop the technologies needed, while human resources personnel identify the people skills and training programs necessary to make the system work. Involving marketing personnel and customers will ensure that the process meets the customers' needs. Finally, finance personnel will need to be involved if the process requires a substantial investment in resources.

1.4 EMPLOYABILITY SKILLS

Throughout this book, we will cover many skills that hiring managers identify as important to success in any variety of business settings, including small and large firms, nonprofit organizations, and public service. These skills are important, even if your career path takes you outside the operations and supply chain discipline.

Critical Thinking

Critical thinking involves purposeful and goal-directed thinking used to define and solve problems, make decisions, or form judgments related to a particular situation or set of circumstances. As you will see, this book is filled with dozens of useful frameworks that managers regularly use to support problem solving, including the Six Sigma methodology (Chapter 4), decision tree analysis (Chapter 6), sourcing portfolio analysis (Chapter 7), and project management tools

(Chapter 14). It is not an exaggeration to say that critical thinking and fact-based decision making are built into the DNA of the operations and supply chain discipline.

Collaboration

As we showed in Table 1.2, many key operations and supply chain activities require close collaboration with participants from other areas, such as marketing, engineering, and finance. Throughout this book, we will emphasize the importance of cross-functional collaboration as well as collaboration with outside supply chain partners. Forecasting (Chapter 9) and inventory management (Chapter 11) are just two areas in which collaboration is essential for the process to work. Chapter 10, in fact, is devoted to sales and operations planning, an approach to planning that depends entirely on collaboration and negotiation between operations, marketing, finance, and human resources in order to succeed.

Knowledge Application and Analysis

Knowledge application and analysis is defined as the ability to learn a concept and then apply that knowledge in another setting to achieve a higher level of understanding. Put another way, understanding is more than just memorizing formulas and cranking out answers. As such, this book seeks to move you "beyond the formulas" by illustrating how the concepts can be applied in a wide range of settings, using both extended examples and in-chapter case studies.

Information Technology Application and Computing Skills

Finally, information technology application and computing skills are defined as the ability to select and use appropriate technology to accomplish a given task. This book covers this skill set in a couple different ways. First, the book includes numerous, detailed examples of how Microsoft Excel can be used to carry out the various calculations covered in the text. Second, we have devoted the Chapter 12 supplement to understanding supply chain information system needs and reviewing recent trends in the area.

1.5 PURPOSE AND ORGANIZATION OF THIS BOOK

Now that we have defined operations and supply chain management, it's time to discuss the purpose and organization of this book. Simply put, the purpose of this book is to give you a solid foundation in the topics and tools of *both* operations management and supply chain management. This is a significant departure from most other operations management textbooks, which are dominated by internal operations issues and treat supply chain management as a sub-discipline. Our decision to emphasize both areas is based on two observations. First, organizations are demanding students who have been exposed to traditional supply chain areas such as purchasing and logistics, as well as more traditional operations topics. Students who have had a course only in operations management are seen as not fully prepared. Second, our years of experience in industry, education, and consulting tell us that supply chain management is here to stay. While a strong internal operations function is vital to a firm's survival, it is not sufficient. Firms must also understand how they link with their supply chain partners. With this in mind, we have organized the book into five main parts (Table 1.3).

Part I, *Creating Value through Operations and Supply Chains*, introduces some basic concepts and definitions that lay the groundwork for future chapters. Chapter 2 deals with the topic of operations and supply chain strategies, including what they are, how they support the organization's overall strategy, and how they help a firm provide value to the customer.

Part II, *Establishing the Operations Environment*, deals with fundamental choices that define an organization's internal operations environment. Chapter 3 deals with the manufacturing and service processes that firms put in place to provide products or services. Chapter 4 is devoted to the topic of business processes, which can be thought of as the "molecules" that make up all operations and supply chain flows. Chapter 4 will also introduce you to some of the approaches companies use to design and improve their business processes, including the Six Sigma methodology. Quality control is a particularly important part of process management, and so we devote Chapter 5 to the topic. In Chapter 6, we discuss the concept of capacity: How much and what types of capacity will an organization need? In the supplement to Chapter 6, we also offer a more advanced discussion of capacity from a process perspective. The topics covered here—including queuing theory and simulation modeling—are particularly relevant in service environments where capacity decisions can have a direct impact on customer waiting and processing times. Chapters 3 through 6 together set clear boundaries on what an organization can do and how the operations function will be managed. As such, we address them early in the book.

Part III, *Establishing Supply Chain Linkages*, turns the spotlight away from the internal operations function to how organizations link with their supply chain partners. Through sourcing decisions and purchasing activities, organizations establish supply chain relationships with other firms. In fact, nearly all firms play the role of upstream supplier or downstream customer at one time or another. Chapter 7 describes the broad set of activities carried out by organizations to analyze sourcing opportunities, develop sourcing strategies, select suppliers, and carry out all the activities required to procure goods and services, while Chapter 8 deals with the physical flow of goods throughout the supply chain and covers such areas as transportation, warehousing, and logistics decision models.

Part IV, *Planning and Controlling Operations and Supply Chains*, focuses on core topics in planning and control. These topics can be found in any basic operations management book. But in contrast to more traditional books, we have deliberately extended the focus of each chapter to address the implications for supply chain management. Forecasting, covered in Chapter 9, is a prime example. By forecasting downstream customer demand and sharing it with upstream suppliers, organizations can do a better job of planning for and controlling the flow of goods and services through the supply chain. In Chapter 10, we discuss not only how firms can develop tactical sales and operations plans, but also how they can link these plans with supply chain partners. In Chapter 11, we don't just cover basic inventory models; we discuss *where* inventory should be located in the supply chain; *how* transportation, packaging, and material-handling issues affect inventory decisions; and *how* inventory decisions by one firm affect its supply chain partners. Similarly, in Chapters 12 and 13, we don't just cover basic production planning topics; we show how such techniques as distribution requirements planning (DRP) and kanban can be used to synchronize the flow of goods between supply chain partners.

The last part of the book, Part V, *Project Management and Product/Service Development*, covers two topics that, while not generally considered part of the day-to-day operational activity of a firm, are nevertheless important to operations and supply chain managers. Chapter 14 describes how organizations manage projects, such as new product development efforts or capacity expansions. Chapter 15 addresses the product and service development process, with an emphasis on how these decisions directly affect choices in operations and supply chain management.

The chapters in Part I provide the foundation knowledge, while Part II deals with fundamental choices that serve to define the capabilities of a firm's operations area. Sourcing and logistics—the topics of Part III—establish linkages between a firm and its supply chain partners. Finally, through the planning and control activities described in Part IV, firms and their partners manage the flows of goods and information across the supply chain.

CHAPTER SUMMARY

Operations and supply chains are pervasive in business. *Every* organization must provide a product or service that someone values. This is the primary responsibility of the operations function. Furthermore, most organizations do not function independently but find that their activities are linked with those of other organizations through supply chains. Careful management of operations and supply chains is, therefore, vital to the long-term health of nearly every organization.

Because operations and supply chain activities cover everything from planning and control activities to sourcing

and logistics, there are numerous career opportunities for students interested in the area. Trends in e-commerce and global competition, as well as the growing importance of maintaining good relationships with other supply chain partners, will only increase these opportunities. Fortunately, there are many professional organizations, including APICS, CSCMP, and ISM, that cater to the career development of professionals in operations and supply chain management.

KEY TERMS

Agility 10	Operations function 3	Supply chain management 7
Downstream 6	Operations management 6	Supply Chain Operations Reference (SCOR) model 7
Electronic commerce 10	Second-tier supplier 6	Upstream 6
First-tier supplier 6	Supply chain 3	

DISCUSSION QUESTIONS

1. Consider the simplified Anheuser-Busch supply chain shown in Figure 1.2. Is Alcoa really the first entity in the supply chain? What other suppliers would Anheuser-Busch have? What information should be shared among companies in the supply chain?
2. One of your friends states that "operations management and supply chain management are primarily of interest to *manufacturing* firms." Is this true or false? Give some examples to support your answer.
3. In this chapter, we defined a supply chain as a network of manufacturers and service providers that work together

to create products or services needed by end users. What are some of the different supply chains that support a product such as the Apple iPhone? How does Apple manage the supply chain that allows users to download various software apps to their iPhones?

4. Early in the chapter, we argued that "every organization must make a product or provide a service that someone values." Can you think of an example in which poor operations or supply chain management undercut a business?

PROBLEMS

Problem for Section 1.1: Why Study Operations and Supply Chain Management?

1. Draw out the transformation process similar to Figure 1.1 for a simple operations function, such as a health clinic or a car repair shop. What are the inputs? The outputs?

Problems for Section 1.3: Operations and Supply Chain Management and You

2. Visit the Web sites for the professional organizations listed in this chapter. Who are their target audiences? Are some more focused on purchasing professionals or logistics professionals? Which of the careers listed at these Web sites are mentioned in the chapter? Which ones sound appealing to you?

CASE STUDY

Supply Chain Challenges at LeapFrog

Introduction

A supply chain consists of a network of companies linked together by physical, information, and monetary flows. When supply chain partners work together, they are able to accomplish things that an individual firm would find difficult, if not impossible, to do. Few cases illustrate this better than the situation faced by LeapFrog in August 2003.[11,12]

LeapFrog, which describes itself as a "leading designer, developer and marketer of innovative, technology-based educational products and related proprietary content,"[13] had just introduced a new educational product called the LittleTouch LeapPad. The distinguishing feature of the LeapPad, whose target market was toddlers, was that it combined high-tech materials and sophisticated electronics to create an interactive "book" that made appropriate sounds when a child touched certain words or pictures.

While LeapFrog was confident the toy would be popular, no one—including the retailers, LeapFrog, and Capable Toys, the Chinese manufacturer who had primary responsibility for producing the LeapPads—knew for sure what actual consumer demand would be. Such uncertainty, which is typical for the toy industry, can be particularly problematic because the demand for toys is concentrated around the November and December holiday season, giving supply chain partners little time to react. Furthermore, toy companies planning for holiday sales have traditionally had to place orders many months in advance—in February or March—to allow enough time for products to work their way through the supply chain and to retailers' shelves. In effect, toy companies had *one chance* to get it right. If a toy company ordered too few copies of a particular toy in February or March, customers in November and December went away disappointed, and the toy company lost significant revenues; if a toy company ordered too many, the result was leftover toys that had to be sold at a steep discount or loss.

By 2003, however, LeapFrog had developed a new approach that used sophisticated forecasting systems, fast information flows and cooperation between supply chain partners, and a flexible manufacturing base to improve the responsiveness of the toy supply chain. Here's how it happened.

E-commerce, Relationship Management, and Forecasting

The first inkling that the LittleTouch LeapPad was a hit came in early August 2003, when major retailers such as Target and Toys "R" Us showed sales of 360 units during the introductory weekend. In previous years, these retailers might have hesitated to share such detailed sales information with a toy company. By 2003, however, retailers realized that sharing sales information in real time with LeapFrog would increase the toy company's odds of meeting surging market demand. The result was that by the Monday following the introductory weekend, LeapFrog knew about the weekend sales figures.

While 360 units might not seem like a lot, LeapFrog's forecasting models indicated that if the trend continued, holiday demand for LeapPads would be approximately 700,000, more than double what LeapFrog had requested be produced by Capable Toys. LeapFrog and its manufacturing and logistics supply chain partners would have to find a way to produce another 350,000 LeapPads and move them to retail stores, all within a few months.

Supply Chain Constraints

Within days of developing the revamped demand forecast, LeapFrog started to work with Capable Toys to identify what steps would need to be taken to increase production levels. They found that several constraints had to be resolved:

- **Production molding constraints.** To manufacture the required plastic parts used in the LeapPad, Capable Toys had designed and built two sets of mold tools capable of producing the equivalent of 3,500 LeapPads each day. If these mold tools were run for 60 days, they could produce only $3,500 \times 60 = 210,000$ additional units—far short of the quantity needed.
- **Material constraints.** Capable Toys and LeapFrog faced a limited supply of key components, including custom-designed electronics and Tyvek, a special water- (i.e., drool-) proof paper.
- **Logistics constraints.** Even if Capable Toys was able to produce the additional toys required, LeapFrog had to consider how best to get those units from China to U.S. retail shelves. Traditionally, toys produced in China traveled by ship. Although this option was relatively slow, it kept down costs. But with production creeping into September and October, LeapFrog had to consider other, more expensive, options.

How did LeapFrog and its supply chain partners resolve these constraints? First, Capable Toys put its in-house engineers to work designing two additional mold sets. The third mold set, which went online in October and improved on the design of the earlier two sets, allowed Capable Toys to increase its production of LeapPads from 3,500 to 6,300 units per day, an 80% increase.

At the same time, Capable Toys called on its first-tier suppliers to help identify additional sources for the specialized chips, membranes, and other electronics used in the LeapPads. Finding a source for the Tyvek paper was a little bit trickier; to gain access to this key material, LeapFrog had to contract with a U.S. company for the printing. While this added to the product's costs, LeapFrog management felt this was a better alternative than running out of units and alienating retailers and their customers.

With the production capacity and material constraints resolved, LeapFrog had one final problem—getting the units

---

[11]UPS, *Maximizing Your Adaptability—Surviving and Winning the High Tech Supply Chain Challenge*, 2005, **www.ups-scs.com/solutions/white_papers/wp_maximizing_adaptability.pdf.**

[12]G. A. Fowler and J. Pereira, "Christmas Sprees: Behind Hit Toy, a Race to Tap Seasonal Surge," *Wall Street Journal*, December 18, 2003.

[13]LeapFrog Enterprises, Inc., *About Us*, **www.leapfrog.com/en/home/about_us.html.**

to the stores in time for the holiday season. Because of the short lead time, LeapFrog was forced to use air shipping and special fast shipping, which added $10 to $15 to the cost of each LeapPad. These additional costs ate into the profit of the LeapPad, which sold for $35, but as with the Tyvek paper, Leap-Frog management felt that the long-term satisfaction of retailers and customers outweighed the additional costs.

In the end, the decisions LeapFrog made to respond to the surging demand for LeapPads turned out to be the right one. While LeapFrog struggled financially in recent years, in 2013 the company made $84 million on sales of $553 million.[14] And the company has used its success with the LeapPad product line (discontinued in 2008) to launch a wider range of educational toys that incorporate even more sophisticated electronics.

Questions

1. Draw a map of the supply chain for LeapFrog, including the retailers, Capable Toys, and suppliers of key materials (i.e., Tyvek). Which supply chain partners are upstream of LeapFrog? Which are downstream? Which partners are first-tier suppliers? Second-tier suppliers?

2. What data ultimately led to LeapFrog's decision to increase production levels of the LittleTouch LeapPads? Where did these data come from? How long after interpreting these data did LeapFrog start talking with Capable Toys about increasing production levels—was it days, weeks, or months?

3. What part of the production process limited output levels at Capable Toys? How did Capable respond to the challenge?

4. What were some of the material sourcing challenges LeapFrog and Capable Toys faced? How did they resolve these problems?

5. What type of logistics solutions did LeapFrog use to get the toys to the stores on time? What are the strengths and weaknesses of these solutions? If it had been August rather than December, what other options might Leap-Frog have used?

6. In the chapter, we described agility as an enduring trend in operations and supply chain management. In your opinion, did LeapFrog and Capable Toys demonstrate agility in responding to the new market demands?

REFERENCES

Books and Articles

Blackstone, J. H., ed., *APICS Dictionary*, 15th ed. (Chicago, IL: APICS, 2016).

Fowler, G. A., and J. Pereira, "Christmas Sprees: Behind Hit Toy, a Race to Tap Seasonal Surge," *Wall Street Journal*, December 18, 2003.

Gorton, L., "Fresh Ideas," *Baking and Snack*, December 1, 2004.

Stalk, G., P. Evans, and L. E. Shulman, "Competing on Capabilities: The New Rules of Corporate Strategy," *Harvard Business Review* 70, no. 2 (March–April 1992): 57–69.

Internet

American Society for Quality (ASQ), **www.asq.org.**

APICS, **www.apics.org.**

Automotive Industry Action Group (AIAG), **www.aiag.org/about.**

Doerfler, S. "Now Trending!," *Inside Supply Management*, November–December 2016, 16–19, **http://magazine.ism.ws/wp-content/uploads/2016/12/16-19-now-trending.pdf.**

Federal Reserve Bank of Dallas, *Supply Chain Management: The Science of Better, Faster, Cheaper*, 2005, **www.dallasfed.org/research/indepth/2005/id0501.html.**

Grocery Manufacturers of America (GMA), **www.gmaonline.org/.**

Institute for Supply Management (ISM), **www.ism.ws.**

ISM's 2016 Salary Survey, **http://magazine.ism.ws/wp-content/uploads/2016/12/16-23-Salary-Survey-May16.pdf.**

LeapFrog Enterprises, Inc., *About Us*, **www.leapfrog.com/en/home/about_us.html.**

LeapFrog Enterprises, Inc., *2010 Annual Report & 2011 Proxy Statement*, **http://media.corporate-ir.net/media_files/IROL/13/131670/2010AR/HTML2/leapfrog_enterprises-2011_0003.htm.**

Panera Bread, *Investor Relations*, **www.panerabread.com/en-us/company/investor-relations.html.**

SCOR Framework, **www.apics.org/apics-for-business/products-and-services/apics-scc-frameworks/scor.**

Supply Chain Insights LLC Research Report, "How S&OP Drives Agility," March–April 2012, **http://supplychaininsights.com/research-reports/agility-report/.**

UPS, *Maximizing Your Adaptability—Surviving and Winning the High Tech Supply Chain Challenge*, 2005, **www.upsscs.com/solutions/white_papers/wp_maximizing_adaptability.pdf.**

---

[14]LeapFrog Enterprises, Inc., *2013 Annual Report*, **www.leapfroginvestor.com/phoenix.zhtml?c=131670&p=irol-reportsannual.**

CHAPTER
two

Operations and Supply Chain Strategies

CHAPTER OBJECTIVES

By the end of this chapter, you will be able to:

● Explain the relationship between business strategies and functional strategies and the difference between structural and infrastructural elements of the business.

● Describe the main operations and supply chain decision categories.

● Explain the concept of customer value and calculate a value index score.

● Differentiate between order winners and qualifiers and explain why this difference is important to developing the operations and supply chain strategy for a firm.

● Discuss the concept of trade-offs and give an example.

● Define *core competencies* and give an example of how core competencies in the operations and supply chain areas can be used for competitive advantage.

● Explain the importance of strategic alignment and describe the four stages of alignment between the operations and supply chain strategy and the business strategy.

TESLA MOTORS

Since Tesla Motors introduced its first roadster in 2006, the company has followed a business strategy designed to ultimately position it as one of the leading manufacturers of electric-powered vehicles. Tesla has purposefully moved toward more affordable models, including the Model S, which was launched in early 2012 and topped 100,000 in total sales by the end of 2015. Tesla's newest offering is the "entry-level" Model 3, which will sell for $35,000, and is scheduled for delivery to customers by the middle of 2017. Yet Tesla's future is far from certain.[1] To succeed, Tesla will need an operations and supply chain strategy that matches its business strategy. Here's how it intends to do it:

Manufacturing and After-Sales Service Strategy

Tesla Motors currently assembles its vehicles in Fremont, California, at a site originally opened by General Motors (GM) in the 1960s. From the start, Tesla management understood that while a few early adopters would buy the cars simply to have access to the "latest" technology, the company would need to build high-quality, reliable vehicles and provide top-notch customer service in order to sway customers that might otherwise buy a vehicle from a more-established make. So far, Tesla has met the challenge, achieving high marks for build quality and after-sales service.[2]

Upstream Sourcing Strategy

While its electric drivetrain is radically different from traditional gas-powered vehicles, the Tesla shares many components, such as brakes, suspension, and steering systems, with other vehicles. This helps hold down costs and provides Tesla with access to the best technologies available. Nevertheless, the availability, quality, and performance characteristics of the battery packs, which power the cars, are critical to Tesla's long-term success. Tesla therefore made the decision to build the batteries it needs rather than outsource them. In 2014 Tesla broke ground on its futuristic battery plant, known as Gigafactory 1, near Sparks, Nevada. By 2017, the plant was producing the battery cells needed to support Tesla's assembly operations.[3,4] Tesla ultimately expects the plant to "be able to turn out more lithium-ion batteries than all the battery factories in the world today."[5] By developing a *core competency* in battery manufacturing, Tesla hopes to simultaneously improve battery performance (i.e., more miles per charge) while driving down costs.

Ink Drop/Shutterstock

Downstream Strategy

Finally, Tesla could build the best electric vehicle in the world but still fail. Why? Simply put, many consumers are hesitant to buy a vehicle whose top range is 265 miles, even though the vast majority of car trips are under 30 miles. To address this concern, Tesla is building a network of supercharger stations in the United States that will allow owners to charge their vehicles in as little as 20 minutes. As of April 2017, Tesla had put in place over 800 supercharger stations with more than 5,000 superchargers.[6]

But will it all work? As one expert noted, "I don't see how they can reduce the [battery] cost more than 20%. . . . We are already reaching the limit on the energy density you can get in the lithium-ion battery. Next-generation battery chemistries, such as lithium air, are another 25 years away from commercialization."[7] And Tesla's competitors are not holding still: Toyota, for example, is pushing hydrogen-cell technology.[8] A more serious threat in the near-term are hybrid vehicles, which combine the benefits of an electric vehicle and the convenience of a backup gas-powered engine. But one thing is certain: If Tesla *does* succeed, it will be because it made investments in manufacturing, after-sales service and technology that are consistent with its goal of being a leading manufacturer of electric-powered vehicles.

[1]M. Pento, "Tesla Is a Hot Mess–There Is No Path to Profitability," CNBC, May 3, 2016, **www.investopedia.com/news/will-tesla-make-profit-2017-tsla/**.

[2]J. Goreham, "J.D. Power Study Proves Why Tesla and the Model S Are So Popular," *Torque News*, January 16, 2014, **www.torquenews.com/1083/newest-jd-power-and-associates-study-proves-why-tesla-and-model-s-are-so-popular**.

[3]F. Lambert, "Tesla Gigafactory Reaches over $1 Billion in Construction Costs as Battery Production Ramps Up," *Electrek*, February 7, 2017, **https://electrek.co/2017/02/07/tesla-gigafactory-construction-costs-battery-production/**.

[4]"Gigfactory 1," **https://en.wikipedia.org/wiki/Gigafactory_1**.

[5]Y. Chernova, "Are Tesla's Plans for a Giant Battery Factory Realistic?," *Wall Street Journal*, May 18, 2014, **http://online.wsj.com/news/articles/SB10001424052702303647204579546060181430456**.

[6]Tesla Motors, **www.teslamotors.com/supercharger.**

[7]Chernova, "Are Tesla's Plans for a Giant Battery Factory Realistic?"

[8]D. Baker, "Hydrogen-Fueled Cars Face Uncertain Market in California," *SFGate*, June 1, 2014, **www.sfgate.com/news/article/Hydrogen-fueled-cars-face-uncertain-market-in-5519890.php**.

INTRODUCTION

Discussing operations or supply chain management without someone mentioning the word *strategy* is almost impossible. But what does that term really mean? What constitutes an operations or supply chain strategy, and how does it support a firm's overall efforts? In this chapter, we will describe how businesses actually create strategies and how operations and supply chain strategies fit within the larger process.

The second half of the chapter is devoted exclusively to the topic of operations and supply chain strategy. We will discuss the three main objectives of operations and supply chain strategy and consider some of the decisions managers face in developing and implementing their strategies. Throughout this discussion, we will stress the key role operations and supply chains play in creating value for the customer.

2.1 ELEMENTS OF THE BUSINESS

Structural element
One of two major decision categories addressed by a strategy. Includes tangible resources, such as buildings, equipment, and computer systems.

Infrastructural element
One of two major decision categories addressed by a strategy. Includes the policies, people, decision rules, and organizational structure choices made by a firm.

Before we begin our main discussion, let's take a moment to consider the business elements that, together, define a business. These elements include structural and infrastructural elements. **Structural elements** are tangible resources, such as buildings, equipment, and information technology. These resources typically require large capital investments that are difficult to reverse. Because of their cost and inflexibility, such elements are changed infrequently and only after much deliberation. An excellent example would be the new battery plant for Tesla. In contrast, **infrastructural elements** are the people, policies, decision rules, and organizational structure choices made by the firm. These elements are, by definition, not as visible as structural elements, but they are just as important. In Chapter 4, for instance, we will discuss the Six Sigma approach to improving business processes. As we will see, the success of Six Sigma depends on highly skilled people, top management support, and a disciplined approach to problem solving. Organizations that adopt Six Sigma will probably make very different infrastructural choices than will firms that don't follow such an approach.

To make these ideas more concrete, think about the business elements at a typical university. Structural elements might include the classrooms, laboratories, dormitories, and athletic facilities. On the infrastructure side, there are people who handle everything from feeding and housing students, assigning parking spaces, and building and maintaining facilities to performing basic research (not to mention teaching). Another part of the infrastrucure are the university's policies and procedures that guide admissions and hiring decisions, tenure reviews, the assignment of grades, and the administration of scholarships and research grants. Some schools even have policies and procedures that guide how students get tickets to football and basketball games.

For a business to compete successfully, all these elements must work together. Because some of these elements can take years and millions of dollars to develop, businesses need to ensure that their decisions are appropriate and consistent with one another. This is why strategy is necessary.

2.2 STRATEGY

Strategy
A mechanism by which a business coordinates its decisions regarding structural and infrastructural elements.

Strategies are the mechanisms by which businesses coordinate their decisions regarding their structural and infrastructural elements. As Harvard Business School professor Michael Porter puts it, "Strategy is creating fit among the company's activities. The success of a strategy depends on doing many things well—not just a few—and integrating among them."[9] Strategies can be thought of as long-term game plans. What is considered *long-term* can differ from one industry to another, but generally the phrase covers several years or more.

---

[9]M. Porter, "What Is Strategy?," *Harvard Business Review* 74, no. 6 (November–December 1996): 61–78.

FIGURE 2.1
A Top-Down Model of Strategy

As Figure 2.1 suggests, most organizations have more than one level of strategy, from upper-level business strategies to more detailed, functional-level strategies. (When organizations have *multiple* distinct businesses, they often distinguish between an overall *corporate* strategy and individual *business unit* strategies.) The **mission statement** explains why an organization exists. It describes what is important to the organization, called its *core values*, and identifies the organization's domain.

Much has been written on what a business strategy should accomplish. To keep things simple, we will focus on the parts of a business strategy that are directly relevant to the development of successful operations and supply chain strategies. In this vein, the **business strategy** must:

- Clearly identify the firm's targeted customers and broadly indicate what the operations and supply chain functions need to do to provide value to these customers.
- Set time frames and performance objectives that managers can use to track the firm's progress toward fulfilling its business strategy.
- Identify and support the development of core competencies in the operations and supply chain areas.

The concept of core competencies deserves special attention because of the implications for operations and supply chain strategies. **Core competencies** are organizational strengths or abilities, developed over a long period of time, that customers find valuable and competitors find difficult or even impossible to copy. Honda, for example, is recognized for having core competencies in the engineering and manufacture of small gas-powered engines. Those core competencies have helped Honda conquer numerous markets, including the markets for motorcycles, cars, lawnmowers, jet skis, and home generators.

Core competencies can take many forms and even shift over time. IBM used to be known as a computer hardware company. Today, IBM's core competency is arguably its ability to provide customers with integrated information solutions and the consulting services needed to make them work. In some cases, the ability of a firm to manage its supply chain partners may in itself be considered a core competency (see *Supply Chain Connections: Apple iPod*).

Functional strategies translate a business strategy into specific actions for functional areas, such as marketing, human resources, and finance. An operations and supply chain strategy might address the manufacturing or service processes needed to make a specific product, how suppliers will be evaluated and selected, and how the products will be distributed.

Mission statement
A statement that explains why an organization exists. It describes what is important to the organization, called its core values, and identifies the organization's domain.

Business strategy
The strategy that identifies a firm's targeted customers and sets time frames and performance objectives for the business.

Core competency
An organizational strength or ability, developed over a long period, that customers find valuable and competitors find difficult or even impossible to copy.

Functional strategy
A strategy that translates a business strategy into specific actions for functional areas such as marketing, human resources, and finance. Functional strategies should align with the overall business strategy and with each other.

SUPPLY CHAIN CONNECTIONS

APPLE iPOD

A firm's ability to manage its supply chain partners may in itself be a core competency. This has certainly been true for Apple. Consider Apple's iPod, which at one time dominated the market for portable media players. Figure 2.2 shows the sales history for the iPod.[10] As the numbers suggest, iPod demand consistently showed large seasonal "bumps" in the fall of each year. These bumps can be attributed to the introduction of new generations of products combined with the holiday shopping season.

As the iPod comes to the end of its life cycle, it is fair to say that not only has the iPod been a marketing success, it's been a supply chain success. This is because Apple put in place a supply chain strategy that addressed both physical flows and information flows. Consider:

- On the upstream side, Apple partnered with suppliers capable of providing both the *quantity* and *quality* of components Apple needs to assemble the iPod. These suppliers are located around the globe and include Samsung, Wolfson Microelectronics, Sigma-Tel, and Hitachi. Having suppliers that can respond quickly to new requirements is crucial for products with short life cycles and variable demand levels, such as the iPod.

- On the downstream side, Apple worked with a wide range of logistics service providers and retailers, including Walmart and Best Buy, to get iPods into the hands of consumers. Accomplishing this task without incurring excessive transportation costs, excessive inventories, or shortages is quite a challenge. This is especially true when you consider that demand can be highly seasonal and the life cycle for earlier iPod generations was around one year. (Who wanted last year's model once the new one came out?)

Vicki Beaver/Alamy Stock Photo

- Finally, in addition to managing the physical flow of iPods to consumers, Apple established an *information* supply chain that allows users to download music and videos for a fee. In some ways, this is arguably the most important element behind the iPod's success. The iPod replaced the old physical supply chain of burning, packaging, and shipping CDs to warehouses or stores with a virtual one that allows the user to buy and instantly receive only the music and videos he or she wants.

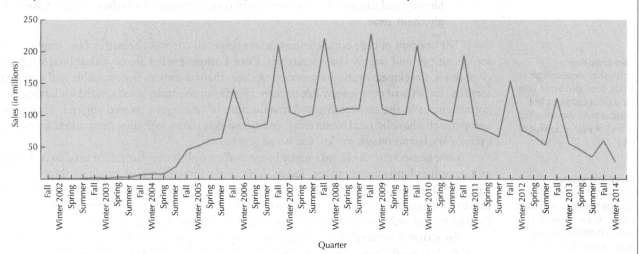

FIGURE 2.2 iPod Sales History

[10]Apple Inc. quarterly results, 2002–2014.

The model in Figure 2.1 shows how the mission statement, business strategy, and functional strategies are related to one another. Managers should be able to pick any specific strategic action at the functional level (e.g., "Develop a European source for raw material X") and trace it back to the business strategy ("Increase our European business presence") and, ultimately, to the firm's mission statement ("Become a world-class competitor in our industry"). When the different levels of the strategic planning process fit together well, an organization is said to have good strategic alignment.

A firm's strategies should also be aligned *across* the functional areas. Continuing with the above example, operations and supply chain efforts aimed at developing a European supply base should be matched by marketing, finance, and human resource efforts aimed at expanding the firm's global presence. Indeed, many so-called functional-level strategies—such as new product development and information technology—are really better described as *cross*-functional, as the responsibility, authority, and resources for these activities often reside in multiple areas.

2.3 OPERATIONS AND SUPPLY CHAIN STRATEGIES

Operations and supply chain strategy
A functional strategy that indicates how structural and infrastructural elements within the operations and supply chain areas will be acquired and developed to support the overall business strategy.

Now that we have some understanding of the relationship between business strategies and functional strategies, let's turn our attention to operations and supply chain strategies in particular. The **operations and supply chain strategy** is a functional strategy that indicates how structural and infrastructural elements within the operations and supply chain areas will be acquired and developed to support the overall business strategy. Table 2.1 lists some of the major structural and infrastructural decisions that must be addressed by an operations and supply chain strategy, as well as where they are discussed in this book. From this table, you can easily see how pervasive infrastructural decisions are in the operations and supply chain strategy. This list of decisions is by no means exhaustive, and it would be much longer and more detailed for an actual business. However, the point is this: Executing successful operations and supply chain strategies means choosing and implementing the right mix of structural and infrastructural elements.

TABLE 2.1
Operations and Supply Chain Decision Categories

STRUCTURAL DECISION CATEGORIES	INFRASTRUCTURAL DECISION CATEGORIES
Capacity (Chapter 6) • Amount of capacity • Type of capacity • Timing of capacity changes (lead, lag, or match market demands)	*Organization* • Structure—centralization/decentralization • Control/reward systems • Workforce decisions
Facilities (Chapters 3, 6, and 8) • Service facilities • Manufacturing plants • Warehouses • Distribution hubs • Size, location, degree of specialization	*Sourcing decisions and purchasing process (Chapter 7)* • Sourcing strategies • Supplier selection • Supplier performance measurement
Technology (Chapters 3, 8, and 12) • Manufacturing processes • Services processes • Material handling equipment • Transportation equipment • Information systems	*Planning and control (Chapters 9–13)* • Forecasting • Tactical planning • Inventory management • Production planning and control
	Business processes and quality management (Chapters 4 and 5) • Six Sigma • Continuous improvement • Statistical quality control
	Product and service development (Chapter 15) • The development process • Organizational and supplier roles

Source: Based on R. Hayes and S. Wheelwright, *Restoring Our Competitive Edge* (New York: John Wiley, 1984).

What constitutes the best mix of structural and infrastructural elements is a subject of ongoing debate among business and academic experts. Nevertheless, we can identify three primary objectives of an operations and supply chain strategy:

1. Help management choose the right mix of structural and infrastructural elements, based on a clear understanding of the performance dimensions valued by customers and the trade-offs involved.
2. Ensure that the firm's structural and infrastructural choices are strategically aligned with the firm's business strategy.
3. Support the development of core competencies in the firm's operations and supply chains.

These three objectives bring up a whole list of concepts: performance dimensions and customer value, trade-offs, strategic alignment, and core competencies in the operations and supply chain areas. In the remainder of this chapter, we describe these concepts more fully.

Customer Value

As we noted in Chapter 1, operations and supply chains help firms provide products or services that someone values. But how should we define *value*? To begin, most customers evaluate products and services based on multiple performance dimensions, such as performance quality, delivery speed, after-sales support, and cost. The organization that provides the best mix of these dimensions will be seen as providing the highest value. Example 2.1 shows how one might assess the value of a product or service.

EXAMPLE 2.1
Calculating a Value Index for Two Competing Products

John wants to buy a tablet PC to use for his school assignments. John decides to evaluate the choices on four dimensions:

1. **Performance quality.** How many programs come loaded on the tablet? How fast is the processor? What is the screen resolution and graphics capability of the tablet?
2. **Delivery speed.** How quickly can John receive the tablet?
3. **After-sales support.** Will the provider help John resolve any technical problems? Will John be able to get help 24 hours a day or just at certain times?
4. **Cost.** What is the total cost to own the tablet?

John rates the importance of each of these dimensions on a scale from 1 ("completely unimportant") to 5 ("critical") and comes up with the following values:

DIMENSION	IMPORTANCE
Performance quality	3
Delivery speed	1
After-sales support	2
Cost	4

The campus store carries two different tablet PCs: one made by WolfByte Computers and the other by Dole Microsystems. WolfByte's tablet has a relatively fast processor and a high-resolution screen, can be delivered in a week, includes around-the-clock technical support for a full year, and costs $800. The Dole Microsystems tablet is a little slower and has lower screen resolution. However, it is available immediately, comes with a month of technical support, and costs $500. John uses this information to rate the performance of each offering with regard to the four dimensions on a scale from 1 ("poor") to 5 ("excellent"):

DIMENSION	IMPORTANCE	WOLFBYTE PERFORMANCE	DOLE MICROSYSTEMS PERFORMANCE
Performance quality	3	4	3
Delivery speed	1	3	5
After-sales support	2	4	2
Cost	4	2	4

Value index
A measure that uses the performance and importance scores for various dimensions of performance for an item or a service to calculate a score that indicates the overall value of an item or a service to a customer.

To find which tablet provides the greater value, John calculates a value index for each. A **value index** is a measure that uses the performance and importance scores for various dimensions of performance for an item or a service to calculate a score that indicates the overall value of an item or a service to a customer. The formula for the value index is:

$$V = \sum_{i=1}^{n} I_n P_n \qquad (2.1)$$

where:

V = Value index for product or service

I_n = Importance of dimension n

P_n = Performance with regard to dimension n

For WolfByte, the value index equals ($3 \times 4 + 1 \times 3 + 2 \times 4 + 4 \times 2 = 31$); for Dole Microsystems, it is ($3 \times 3 + 1 \times 5 + 2 \times 2 + 4 \times 4 = 34$). So even though the Dole tablet has less performance quality and after-sales support, its lower cost makes it a better value for John.

Four Performance Dimensions

Operations and supply chains can have an enormous impact on business performance. Experience suggests that four generic performance dimensions are particularly relevant to operations and supply chain activities:

1. Quality
2. Time
3. Flexibility
4. Cost

Let's look at each of these performance dimensions in depth.

Quality
The characteristics of a product or service that bear on its ability to satisfy stated or implied needs.

Performance quality
A subdimension of quality that addresses the basic operating characteristics of a product or service.

Conformance quality
A subdimension of quality that addresses whether a product was made or a service performed to specifications.

Reliability quality
A subdimension of quality that addresses whether a product will work for a long time without failing or requiring maintenance.

Delivery speed
A performance dimension that refers to how quickly the operations or supply chain function can fulfill a need once it has been identified.

Quality. **Quality** is defined as the characteristics of a product or service that bear on its ability to satisfy stated or implied needs.[11] The concept of quality is broad, with a number of subdimensions, including **performance quality** (What are the basic operating characteristics of the product or service?), **conformance quality** (Was the product made or the service performed to specifications?), and **reliability quality** (Will a product work for a long time without failing or requiring maintenance? Does a service operation perform its tasks consistently over time?). Chapter 5 provides a comprehensive list of the various quality dimensions and discusses them in detail. The relative importance of these quality dimensions will differ from one customer to the next. One buyer may be more interested in performance, another in reliability. To compete on the basis of quality, a firm's operations and supply chain must consistently meet or exceed customer expectations or requirements on the most critical quality dimensions.

Time. Time has two basic characteristics: speed and reliability. **Delivery speed** generally refers to how quickly the operations or supply chain function can fulfill a need once it has been identified.

---

[11] American Society for Quality, **http://asq.org/glossary/q.html**.

Delivery reliability and delivery speed are critical performance dimensions for perishable goods such as fruits and vegetables.

Delivery reliability
A performance dimension that refers to the ability to deliver products or services when promised.

Delivery reliability refers to the ability to deliver products or services when promised. Note that a firm can have long lead times yet still maintain a high degree of delivery reliability. Typical measures of delivery reliability include the percentage of orders that are delivered by the promised time and the average tardiness of late orders.

Delivery reliability is especially important to companies that are linked together in a supply chain. Consider the relationship between a fish wholesaler and its major customer, a fish processing facility. If the fish arrive too late, the processing facility may be forced to shut down. On the other hand, fish that arrive too early may go bad before they can be processed. Obviously, these two supply chain partners must coordinate their efforts so that the fish will arrive within a specific **delivery window,** which is defined as the acceptable time range in which deliveries can be made. One automobile manufacturer charges suppliers a penalty fee of $10,000 for every minute a delivery is late. That practice may seem extreme until one considers that late deliveries may shut down an entire production line.

Delivery window
The acceptable time range in which deliveries can be made.

Another measure of delivery reliability is the accuracy of the quantity shipped. For example, Sam's Club demands 95% accuracy in stock deliveries from suppliers. If suppliers ship more than the quantity ordered, they are still considered to be in error. Some firms will consider a partial shipment to be on time if it arrives by the promised date, but others will accept only complete shipments, delivered within the scheduled window.

Flexibility
A performance dimension that considers how quickly operations and supply chains can respond to the unique needs of customers.

Flexibility. Many operations and supply chains compete by responding to the unique needs of different customers. Both manufacturing and service firms can demonstrate **flexibility.** A full-service law firm, for instance, will handle any legal issue a client faces. (Some law firms specialize in only real estate transactions or divorce settlements.) A full-service hotel will go to great lengths to fulfill a guest's every need. For example, a staff member at the Ritz-Carlton in Dearborn, Michigan, once noticed a guest standing outside the gift shop, waiting for it to open. The employee found out what the guest wanted, picked it up when the shop opened, and waited outside a conference hall to deliver it to the guest. Many firms distinguish among several types of flexibility, including **mix flexibility** (the ability to produce a wide range of products or services), **changeover flexibility** (the ability to provide a new product with minimal delay), and **volume flexibility** (the ability to produce whatever volume the customer needs).

Mix flexibility
The ability to produce a wide range of products or services.

Changeover flexibility
The ability to provide a new product with minimal delay.

Consider the case of Flex Ltd., a company that buys components and manufactures goods for many original equipment manufacturers (OEMs) in the electronics industry.[12] Because the

Volume flexibility
The ability to produce whatever volume the customer needs.

---

[12]Flex Ltd., *Wall Street Journal,* **http://quotes.wsj.com/FLEX/company-people.**

electronics industry is notorious for short product life cycles and unpredictable demand, Flex must be able to quickly adjust the mix and volume of the products it produces. Flex's supply chain partners must be equally flexible. For instance, Flex might order 10,000 units of Part A on Friday for delivery on Monday and then call back on Monday and ask the supplier to take back the 10,000 units and deliver 8,000 units of Part B instead.

Flexibility has become particularly valuable in new product development. Some firms compete by developing new products or services faster than their competitors, a competitive posture that requires operations and supply chain partners who are both flexible and willing to work closely with designers, engineers, and marketing personnel. Chapter 15 includes a detailed discussion of how operations and supply chains can support new product development.

Cost. Cost is always a concern, even for companies that compete primarily on some other dimension. However, "cost" covers such a wide range of activities that companies commonly categorize costs in order to focus their cost management efforts. Some typical cost categories include:

* Labor costs
* Material costs
* Engineering costs
* Quality-related costs (including failure costs, appraisal costs, and prevention costs)

This is just the tip of the iceberg: Firms have developed literally thousands of different cost categories, many of which are specific to the issues facing a particular firm. The point is that operations and supply chain activities are natural targets for cost management efforts because they typically account for much of an organization's costs. In fact, cost is such an important performance dimension we will return to it frequently throughout this book.

Trade-Offs among Performance Dimensions

Take a moment to think about the differences between a world-class sprinter and a marathon runner. The sprinter has trained for explosive speed off the line, while the marathon runner has trained for paced distance running. Both athletes are in peak condition, yet neither would dream of competing in both events.

The same is true in business. In a competitive marketplace, no firm can sustain an advantage on *all* performance dimensions indefinitely. Excellence in some dimensions might conflict with excellence in others, preventing any one firm from becoming the best in all. In such cases, firms must make **trade-offs,** or decisions to emphasize some dimensions at the expense of others. Nearly all operations and supply chain decisions require such trade-offs. To make logical and consistent decisions, operations and supply chain managers must understand which performance dimensions are most valued by the firm's targeted customers and act accordingly.

Consider some of the trade-offs Delta Air Lines might face in scheduling flights between Raleigh and Orlando. More flights mean greater flexibility for customers but higher costs. Similarly, larger, more comfortable seats improve the quality of the service but also raise costs and reduce the number of passengers a plane can carry. Delta managers know that business flyers will pay a premium for flexibility and comfortable seats, but casual flyers (such as families on their way to Disney World) will be more price-sensitive.

Now suppose a competitor of Delta's decides to offer flights between Raleigh and Orlando. Given this move, Delta's flight schedule and seat design take on added importance. If managers choose frequent flights and larger seats, costs may climb higher than the competitor's; if they choose fewer flights and smaller seats, flexibility and quality may suffer. Delta's managers must decide whose needs—those of business flyers or those of casual flyers—will guide their operational decisions.

Order Winners and Order Qualifiers

Some managers use the concepts of order winners and order qualifiers to highlight the relative importance of different performance dimensions.[13] **Order winners** are performance

Trade-off
A decision by a firm to emphasize one performance dimension over another, based on the recognition that excellence on some dimensions may conflict with excellence on others.

Order winner
A performance dimension that differentiates a company's products and services from its competitors. Firms win a customer's business by providing superior levels of performance on order winners.

---

[13]T. Hill, *Manufacturing Strategy: Text and Cases* (Boston: Irwin McGraw-Hill, 2000).

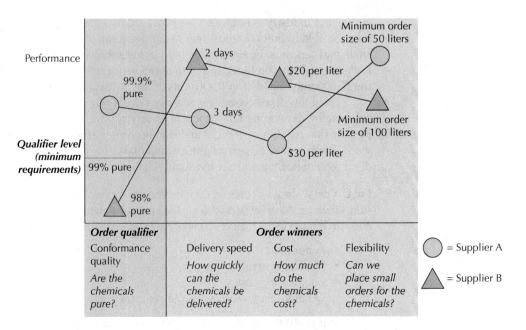

FIGURE 2.3
Performance of Two Chemical Suppliers vis-à-vis Customers' Order Winners and Qualifiers

Order qualifier
A performance dimension on which customers expect a minimum level of performance. Superior performance on an order qualifier will not, by itself, give a company a competitive advantage.

dimensions that differentiate a company's products and services from those of its competitors. A firm wins a customer's business by providing superior levels of performance on order winners. **Order qualifiers** are performance dimensions on which customers expect a minimum level of performance. Superior performance on an order qualifier will not, by itself, give a company a competitive advantage.

The industrial chemical market offers an example to illustrate the difference between order winners and order qualifiers. Buyers of industrial chemicals expect a certain level of purity (i.e., conformance quality) before they will even consider purchasing a chemical from a particular source. Because all potential sources must meet this minimum requirement, purity is incredibly important. Once the purity requirement has been satisfied, however, other performance dimensions—such as cost, delivery speed, and flexibility—will be used to determine the best source. From the supplier's perspective, product quality is the order qualifier; cost, delivery speed, and flexibility are order winners.

Now suppose we have two suppliers, A and B, who are competing head-to-head in this industry. Figure 2.3 illustrates how the order winner/qualifier logic can be used to evaluate the two suppliers. Supplier A meets the minimum requirements on quality but falls below Supplier B on all but one of the remaining dimensions (volume flexibility). Supplier B, however, has purity levels below the minimum requirement. So even though Supplier B is superior to A on two performance dimensions, Supplier B will be dropped from consideration because it fails to qualify on one of the dimensions.

Understanding what the relevant order qualifiers and order winners are helps operations and supply chain managers formulate strategy in three ways. First, it helps identify potential problem areas, as well as strengths. Second, it clarifies the issues surrounding decisions on trade-offs. Finally, it helps managers prioritize their efforts.

Take a look again at Supplier B. Supplier B must immediately address its quality problems if it wants to compete at all. After that, the company might look for ways to protect or even increase its delivery and cost advantages. Furthermore, if improving purity involves increasing costs (e.g., buying new equipment), Supplier B should understand what the appropriate trade-off is.

Stages of Alignment with the Business Strategy

The ultimate goal of any firm is to develop an operations and supply chain strategy that supports its business strategy. Management should be able to state how each operations and supply chain structural or infrastructural choice supports the customers' order winners and qualifiers and what trade-offs had to be considered when making these choices. However, as Bob Hayes and Steven Wheelwright recognized years ago,[14] at any point in time some organizations are further along toward achieving this than are others. They described four stages of alignment, and although the stages originally referred to manufacturing, their descriptions apply equally well to the operations and supply chain areas today. The four stages are as follows:

> **Stage 1—Internally neutral.** In this stage, management seeks only to minimize any negative potential in the operations and supply chain areas. There is no effort made to link these areas with the business strategy.
>
> **Stage 2—Externally neutral.** Here industry practice is followed, based on the assumption that what works for competitors will work for the company. Still, there is no effort made to link the operations and supply chain areas with the overall business strategy.
>
> **Stage 3—Internally supportive.** At this stage, the operations and supply chain areas participate in the strategic debate. Management recognizes that the operations and supply chain structural and infrastructural elements must be aligned with the business strategy.
>
> **Stage 4—Externally supportive.** At this stage, the operations and supply areas do more than just support the business strategy: The business strategy actively seeks to exploit the core competencies found within these areas.

To illustrate how a firm's operations and supply chain strategies might achieve Stage 3 alignment, let's revisit Dole Microsystems and WolfByte Computers. Suppose that as part of its business strategy, Dole decides to target price-sensitive buyers who need adequate, but not exceptional, performance, delivery, and after-sales support. In contrast, WolfByte decides to focus on buyers who want excellent performance, delivery, and after-sales support. Table 2.2 shows how managers might begin to align their operations and supply chain strategies with the business strategies of these two distinctive companies.

Notice how the operations and supply chain decisions outlined in Table 2.2 seem to naturally flow from the different business strategies. Table 2.2 vividly illustrates how operations and supply chain decisions that are appropriate in one case may be inappropriate in another. Purchasing low-cost components, for example, would make sense for Dole, given its business strategy, but would run counter to WolfByte's emphasis on performance.

TABLE 2.2 **Aligning Business and Operations and Supply Chain Strategies**		DOLE MICROSYSTEMS	WOLFBYTE COMPUTERS
	Business strategy	Assemble, sell, and support tablet PCs targeted at price-sensitive buyers who require adequate, but not exceptional, performance, delivery, and support.	Assemble, sell, and support tablet PCs targeted at buyers who are willing to pay extra for exceptional performance, delivery, and customer service.
	Operations and supply chain strategy	• Buy components from the *lowest-cost* suppliers who meet minimum quality and delivery requirements. • Keep minimum levels of inventory in factories to *hold down inventory costs.* • Hire and train support staff to provide *acceptable* customer service. • Use three-day ground shipment to *keep costs low.*	• Buy components from *state-of-the-art* suppliers. Price is important but not the critical factor. • Keep enough inventory in factories to *meet rush orders* and *shorten lead times.* • Hire and train support staff to provide *superior* customer service. • Use overnight air freight to *minimize lead time* to the customer.

---

[14]R. Hayes and S. Wheelwright, *Restoring Our Competitive Edge* (New York: John Wiley, 1984).

Many companies use cross-docking systems to simultaneously lower transportation and inventory costs. Such systems illustrate how supply chain management can provide a competitive advantage.

Core Competencies in Operations and Supply Chains

Before firms can think about progressing to the fourth stage of alignment (externally supportive), they must develop core competencies within the operations and supply chain areas. Consider the example of Lowe's, a national hardware retailer headquartered in North Carolina. Lowe's uses large regional distribution centers (RDCs) to coordinate shipments between suppliers and retail stores. The RDCs receive large truckload shipments from suppliers, a strategy that allows Lowe's to save on item costs as well as transportation costs. Employees at the RDCs then remix the incoming goods and deliver them to individual stores, as often as twice a day. To give you an appreciation of the scale of these operations, the typical RDC covers about *one million* square feet of space and serves up to *200* Lowe's stores.

But that isn't all. The RDCs use computer-based information systems to closely coordinate incoming shipments from suppliers with outgoing shipments to individual stores. In fact, more than half the goods that come off suppliers' trucks are immediately put onto other trucks bound for individual stores, a method known as *cross-docking*. The result is that both the RDCs and the retail stores hold minimal amounts of inventory, yet Lowe's receives the cost breaks associated with large shipments from suppliers (see Figure 2.4).

FIGURE 2.4
Building Core Competencies at the Operations and Supply Chain Level: Lowe's Distribution System

FIGURE 2.5
Closing the Loop
between Business
Strategy and
Functional Area
Strategies

Why did Lowe's spend millions of dollars and many years developing this distribution system? One reason is that it helps keep costs low and the availability of goods high—performance dimensions that its targeted customers value highly. Just as importantly, the Lowe's distribution system has emerged as a core competency that will serve the company well even as the marketplace changes.

Finally, we mentioned earlier in the chapter that core competencies at the functional level can feed back into the business strategy. This is exactly what Hayes and Wheelwright meant by the fourth stage of alignment. Some experts also refer to this as *closing the loop*. Figure 2.5 illustrates the idea. Firms such as Amazon, Honda, Lowe's, and others have developed significant core competencies at the functional level. It makes sense, then, for top managers to look for ways to exploit these strengths. More generally, by closing the loop, top managers ensure that the business strategy adequately considers the current capabilities—both positive and negative—within the functional areas.

CHAPTER SUMMARY

The operations and supply chain areas are important providers of value in any organization. To ensure that managers make sound operations and supply chain decisions, firms must develop strategies for these functions that are tied to the overall business strategy. This chapter has presented a top-down model of the strategic planning process, with particular attention to the concepts of value, competitive advantage, and core competency.

In the second half of the chapter, we defined the major operations and supply chain decision variables, outlined the four generic performance dimensions (quality, time, flexibility, and cost), and discussed the need to make trade-offs between these key dimensions. We showed how order winner and order qualifier information can help managers understand exactly what their customers demand, so they can make trade-offs in a logical fashion. We ended the chapter with a discussion of the four stages of alignment in operations and supply chain strategy, showing how firms can exploit core competencies in the operations and supply chain areas.

KEY FORMULA

Value index (page 27):

$$V = \sum_{i=1}^{n} I_n P_n \qquad \qquad \textbf{(2.1)}$$

where:

V = Value index for product or service

I_n = Importance of dimension n

P_n = Performance with regard to dimension n

KEY TERMS

Business strategy   23

Changeover flexibility   28

Conformance quality   27

Core competency   23

Delivery reliability   28

Delivery speed   27

Delivery window   28

Flexibility   28

Functional strategy   23

Infrastructural element   22

Mission statement   23

Mix flexibility   28

Operations and supply chain
   strategy   25

Order qualifier   30

Order winner   29

Performance quality   27

Quality   27

Reliability quality   27

Strategy   22

Structural element   22

Trade-off   29

Value index   27

Volume flexibility   28

SOLVED PROBLEM

PROBLEM   *Calculating Value Indices at WarsingWare*

WarsingWare produces specialized shipping containers for food products. The shipping containers help protect the food and keep it from spoiling. In addition, the shipping containers have security devices to ensure that the food is not tampered with. WarsingWare is not the fastest or the cheapest; however, the company prides itself on its ability to provide a wide range of styles to its customers, its strong conformance quality, and its ability to ship products on time. WarsingWare management has rated the firm's performance as shown in Table 2.3.

TABLE 2.3 Performance Dimension Ratings for WarsingWare

DIMENSION	PERFORMANCE (1 = "POOR" TO 5 = "EXCELLENT")
Performance quality	4
Conformance quality	5
Delivery speed	2
Delivery reliability	4
Mix flexibility	5
Cost	2
Volume flexibility	3

WarsingWare has two main customers, Sonco Foods and Gregg Groceries. The relative importance (1 = "completely unimportant" to 5 = "critical") each of these customers' places on the dimensions is shown in Table 2.4.

TABLE 2.4 Importance Ratings for Two Major Customers

DIMENSION	SONCO FOODS	GREGG GROCERIES
Performance quality	4	1
Conformance quality	5	4
Delivery speed	1	5
Delivery reliability	4	3
Mix flexibility	3	2
Cost	4	4
Volume flexibility	4	1

1. According to the value index, which customer—Sonco Foods or Gregg Groceries—currently gets more value out of WarsingWare's products?
2. Suppose WarsingWare decides to reduce its costs by offering fewer design variations. Cost performance will rise to 4, and mix flexibility will fall to 2. Will the customers be more satisfied? Explain.

Solution

Table 2.5 shows the value indices for Sonco Foods and Gregg. Sonco is currently receiving greater value from WarsingWare than Gregg is. This is due in part to the fact that Sonco places a fairly high degree of importance on the dimensions that WarsingWare is particularly good at—performance quality, conformance quality, delivery reliability, and mix flexibility. On the other hand, Gregg does not value any of these four dimensions as highly as Sonco.

TABLE 2.5 Value Indices for Two Major Customers

	IMPORTANCE			VALUE INDEX	
	PERFORMANCE	SONCO FOODS	GREGG	SONCO FOODS	GREGG
Performance quality	4	4	1	16	4
Conformance quality	5	5	4	25	20
Delivery speed	2	1	5	2	10
Delivery reliability	4	4	3	16	12
Mix flexibility	5	3	2	15	10
Cost	2	4	4	8	8
Volume flexibility	3	4	1	12	3
Totals:				**94**	**67**

Now suppose WarsingWare improves its costs but does this by reducing its mix flexibility. The *new* value indices are shown in Table 2.6.

TABLE 2.6 New Value Indices for Two Major Customers

	IMPORTANCE			VALUE INDEX	
	PERFORMANCE	SONCO FOODS	GREGG	SONCO FOODS	GREGG
Performance quality	4	4	1	16	4
Conformance quality	5	5	4	25	20
Delivery speed	2	1	5	2	10
Delivery reliability	4	4	3	16	12
Mix flexibility	**2**	3	2	6	4
Cost	**4**	4	4	16	16
Volume flexibility	3	4	1	12	3
Totals:				**93**	**69**

According to Table 2.6, the value index for Gregg rises to 69, but Sonco's value index actually falls to 93. Whether or not this is an acceptable trade-off will depend on the relative importance of these two customers to WarsingWare, and WarsingWare's position vis-à-vis competitors.

DISCUSSION QUESTIONS

1. Consider the sales history for the iPod, shown in Figure 2.2. In the early days of the iPod, Apple's business strategy was to introduce a new iPod generation around October, just in time for the holiday season. What were the advantages of doing this? From a supply chain perspective, what were the challenges? How might Apple's business strategy have affected the level of emphasis Apple placed on delivery speed and volume flexibility when choosing suppliers?

2. Go to the Web and see if you can find the mission statement for a business or school you are familiar with. Is it a useful mission statement? Why or why not? From what you can tell, are the operations and supply chain strategies consistent with the mission statement?

3. We have talked about how operations and supply chain strategies should be based on the business strategy. But can strategy flow the other way? That is, can operations and supply chain capabilities drive the business strategy? Can you think of any examples in industry?

4. Is it enough to just write down the business strategy of a firm? Why or why not? Conversely, what are the limitations of not writing down the strategy but rather depending on the firm's actions to define the strategy?

5. Chances are you are a college student taking a course in operations or supply chain management. What were the order winners and qualifiers you used in choosing a school? A degree program?

6. Different customers can perceive the value of the same product or service very differently. Explain how this can occur. What are the implications for developing successful operations and supply chain strategies?

7. Go back and look at Hayes and Wheelwright's four stages of alignment. Do firms actually have to develop and then exploit core competencies in the operations and supply chain areas in order to be successful? That is, do all firms need to reach Stage 4?

PROBLEMS

Additional homework problems are available at www.pearsonhighered.com/bozarth. These problems use Excel to generate customized problems for different class sections or even different students.

(* = easy; ** = moderate; *** = advanced)

Problems for Section 2.3: Operations and Supply Chain Strategies

1. (*) You have just graduated from college and are looking to buy your first car. Money is tight right now, so you are concerned with initial cost as well as ongoing expenses. At the same time, you don't want to drive a slow, outdated car like your parents do. You have narrowed your choices to two vehicles: a Honda Enigma and a Bizzarrini Booster. Based on the following numbers, calculate the value index for each car. Which car provides you with the greatest value?

DIMENSION	IMPORTANCE TO YOU	HONDA ENIGMA	BIZZARRINI BOOSTER
Fuel economy	3	5	2
Reliability	5	5	2
Speed and handling	4	2	5
Aesthetics	4	2	5
After-sales support	2	4	4
Purchase price	4	4	1

2. A Chicago-based manufacturer is looking for someone to handle its shipments to the West Coast. In order to evaluate potential transportation providers, the manufacturer has developed the following criteria.

At a minimum, a shipper must be able to:

a. Pick up shipments in less than eight hours from the time it is notified. (The manufacturer doesn't have enough space for shipments to sit around at the dock.)
b. Deliver shipments in 72 hours or less.

Beyond this, shippers will be evaluated according to cost and the percentage of shipments that arrive undamaged.

Three shippers—McAdoo, Klooless, and Big Al—have put in bids for the business. The relevant performance information for the shippers is shown in the following chart:

	McADOO	KLOOLESS	BIG AL
Pickup time	6 hours	8 hours	9 hours
Shipping time	48 hours	72 hours	36 hours
Cost per 100 lb. shipped	$20	$30	$15
% of shipments that arrive undamaged	98%	95%	99%

a. (**) Using Figure 2.3 as a guide, graph how well each of the shippers performs with regard to the order winners and order qualifiers.
b. (**) Who is most likely to win the business? Why?
c. (**) What's going on with Big Al? What does Big Al need to do in order to compete successfully for the business?
d. (**) Comment on Klooless's competitive position. Does it meet the minimum requirements? Is it very competitive? Why or why not?

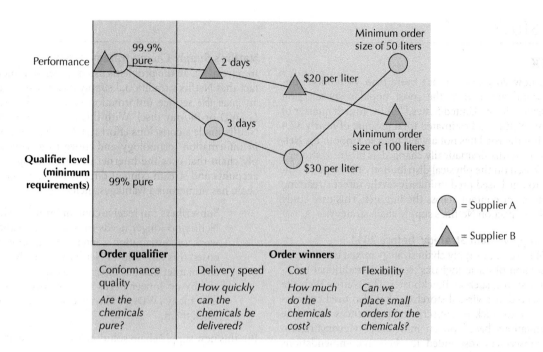

3. Reconsider Figure 2.3. Suppose Supplier B improves its conformance quality so that the chemicals it produces are now 99.9% pure. The chart at the top of this page shows the new competitive situation:

   a. (*) Will this be enough to make Supplier B competitive? Which supplier do you think will win the business?
   b. (**) Managers at Supplier A have determined that if they increase the minimum order size to 80 liters, they can decrease their costs to $18 per liter. Should they do it? Explain your logic. (*Hint:* There is no single right answer to this problem.)

4. (***) (*Microsoft Excel problem*) The following figure shows an Excel spreadsheet that calculates the value index for each of two alternative suppliers. Re-create this spreadsheet in Excel. You should develop the spreadsheet so that the results will be recalculated if any of the values in the high-lighted cells are changed. Your formatting does not have to be exactly the same, but the numbers should be. (As a test, see what happens if you change all of the importance scores to 3. Your new value indices for Supplier 1 and Supplier 2 should be 72 and 63, respectively.)

	A	B	C	D	E	F	G
1	Calculating the Value Index for Two Alternative Suppliers						
2							
3	Performance: 1 = "poor" to 5 = "excellent"						
4	Importance: 1 = "completely unimportant" to 5 = "critical"						
5							
6					Performance	Value Index	
7			Importance	Supplier 1	Supplier 2	Supplier 1	Supplier 2
8	Performance quality		5	4	3	20	15
9	Conformance quality		4	5	4	20	16
10	Delivery reliability		2	5	4	10	8
11	Delivery speed		3	1	3	3	9
12	Cost		2	3	5	6	10
13	Mix flexibility		2	2	1	4	2
14	Volume flexibility		3	4	1	12	3
15					Totals:	75	63

CASE STUDY

Netflix

NETFLIX, now 20 years old, has more than 94 million subscribers worldwide and is the most popular subscription media business in the United States.[15] In the fourth quarter of 2016 alone, Netflix had estimated total revenue of nearly $2.4 billion.[16] But the road has not always been so smooth for Netflix. In 2011, Netflix dramatically changed its business strategy from one based on the physical distribution of DVDs and Blu-ray discs, to one based predominantly on the direct streaming of entertainment content across the Internet. This case study looks at the impact on Netflix's supply chain strategy.

Netflix's Supply Chain Strategy, before 2011

Before 2011, Netflix's supply chain strategy mixed information technology and physical logistics to replace traditional brick-and-mortar stores, such as Blockbuster. The Netflix Web site not only served as a virtual storefront but also used customized software to track its subscribers' preferences and make recommendations based on an individual's viewing habits. Enough subscribers responded to these recommendations that Netflix could keep many of its older DVD titles circulating and continuing to earn revenue, while lowering demand somewhat for the "latest" releases.

The second major piece of Netflix's supply chain, its distribution system, was just as critical to the firm's success. By operating several distribution centers around the United States right from the start, the company was able to accept, inspect, and clean DVDs quickly and ship them out just as fast, so customers experienced very short wait times between placing their orders and receiving their DVDs. By 2011, Netflix had about 60 distribution centers in operation.

For the most part, Netflix's traditional supply chain, with its one-day delivery and same-day processing, was effective. Its inventory system not only automatically tracked incoming DVDs that customers had returned, it also emailed each customer a confirmation of receipt and alerted the appropriate shipping center to send the next title on that customer's list or queue. It also ensured that subscribers weren't sent more DVDs than they had paid for (customers were limited to a certain number of DVDs per month). However, a number of factors affected which DVDs a subscriber got and when they got them. If there weren't many copies in the system, the company would ship one from a center that was far from where a subscriber lived. Another was the popularity of the movies. Often there were fewer copies of a newly released film than there were people who wanted to see it. And the shipping process, which involved multiple handling steps, sometimes resulted in damage to the DVDs.

Netflix's Supply Chain Strategy, Today

In retrospect, all the problems listed earlier stemmed from the fact that Netflix's traditional supply chain tied the delivery of an *intangible* service (information content) to a *tangible* item (a DVD or Blu-ray disc). With this in mind, starting in 2007 Netflix made a conscious effort to take advantage of advances in information technology and move to a truly *virtual* supply chain that uses the Internet to both manage subscribers' accounts and stream content directly to them. Such a supply chain has numerous advantages, including:

- Subscribers can receive content immediately.
- Netflix no longer needs to manage an expensive network of distribution centers. In addition to cutting costs, this also allows Netflix to quickly expand into any market that has Internet access.
- Netflix no longer needs to make decisions regarding how many DVDs or Blu-ray discs to order or where to stock them.

But this new supply chain solution is not without its risks:

- **Upstream supplier risks.** Netflix depends on entertainment companies to provide the content subscribers want, yet many of these companies have concerns about having their content—particularly newer shows and movies—delivered in electronic format.[17] If entertainment companies refuse to license their products or provide only limited access to their "best" content, this could undermine the quality and range of Netflix's offerings.
- **Downstream distributor risks.** Instead of having the U.S. Postal Service deliver discs, Netflix's new supply chain strategy depends on Internet service providers (ISPs), such as cable companies and satellite network providers, to deliver the content. Many of these providers have been arguing that Netflix or its subscribers should pay higher fees due to the higher levels of traffic they generate. And even if these issues are resolved, higher traffic levels could result in overloaded networks and service interruptions.
- **Competitive risks.** Today, Netflix faces a new set of competitors, including Amazon, Google, and Hulu, and possibly new companies that have not yet entered the market.[18]

Nevertheless, Netflix provides an excellent example of how supply chain strategies can provide firms with a distinctive competitive advantage and how these strategies need to adapt to changes in technology and the marketplace.

---

[15]T. Team, "Netflix Subscriber Growth Continues Unabated, As Margins Improve," *Forbes*, January 19, 2017, **www.forbes.com/sites/ greatspeculations/2017/01/19/netflix-subscriber-growth-continues-unabated-as-margins-improve/#5579d8fc52dd.**

[16]Netflix letter to shareholders, January 18, 2017, **http://files.shareholder.com/downloads/NFLX/4178437955x0x924415/A5ACACF9-9C17- 44E6-B74A-628CE049C1B0/Q416ShareholderLetter.pdf.**

[17]B. Stelter, "In Setback for Netflix, Starz Won't Renew Distribution Deal," *The New York Times*, September 2, 2011, p. B2.

[18]Investopedia, "Analyzing Netflix's Degree of Rivalry among Competitors," **www.investopedia.com/. university/netflix-porters-5-forces-analysis/analyzing-netflixs-degree-rivalry-among-competitors.asp.**

Questions

1. What were some of the key structural and infrastructural elements that defined Netflix's supply chain strategy before 2011? Today?
2. How have the customers' order winners for Netflix's customers changed over time? Would today's customer be satisfied by the delivery performance or selection of Netflix's "old" supply chain?
3. As of early 2017, Netflix still supported customers who want to rent DVDs, although the number of subscribers has fallen to around 4.1 million (vs. 94 million online subscribers)[19]. Should Netflix abandon its physical distribution system altogether? Why or why not?

REFERENCES

Books and Articles

Hayes, R., and S. Wheelwright, *Restoring Our Competitive Edge* (New York: John Wiley, 1984).

Hill, T., *Manufacturing Strategy: Text and Cases* (Boston: Irwin McGraw-Hill, 2000).

Porter, M., "What Is Strategy?," *Harvard Business Review* 74, no. 6 (November–December 1996): 61–78.

Stelter, B., "In Setback for Netflix, Starz Won't Renew Distribution Deal," *The New York Times*, September 2, 2011, p. B2.

Internet

American Society for Quality, **http://asq.org/glossary/q.html**.

Apple Inc. quarterly results, 2002–2014.

Baker, D., "Hydrogen-Fueled Cars Face Uncertain Market in California," *SFGate*, June 1, 2014, **www.sfgate.com/news/article/Hydrogen-fueled-cars-face-uncertain-market-in-5519890.php**.

Chernova, Y., "Are Tesla's Plans for a Giant Battery Factory Realistic?," *Wall Street Journal*, May 18, 2014, **http://online.wsj.com/news/articles/SB10001424052702303647204579546060181430456**.

Flex Ltd., *Wall Street Journal*, **http://quotes.wsj.com/FLEX/company-people**.

"Gigfactory 1," **https://en.wikipedia.org/wiki/Gigafactory_1**.

Goreham, J., "J.D. Power Study Proves Why Tesla and the Model S Are So Popular," *Torque News*, January 16, 2014, **www.torquenews.com/1083/newest-jd-power-and-associates-study-proves-why-tesla-and-model-s-are-so-popular**.

Investopedia, "Analyzing Netflix's Degree of Rivalry among Competitors," **www.investopedia.com/university/netflix-porters-5-forces-analysis/analyzing-netflixs-degree-rivalry-among-competitors.asp**.

Lambert, F., "Tesla Gigafactory Reaches over $1 Billion in Construction Costs as Battery Production Ramps Up," *Electrek*, February 7, 2017, **https://electrek.co/2017/02/07/tesla-gigafactory-construction-costs-battery-production/**.

Netflix letter to shareholders, January 18, 2017, **http://files.shareholder.com/downloads/NFLX/4178437955x0x924415/A5ACACF9-9C17-44E6-B74A-628CE049C1B0/Q416ShareholderLetter.pdf**.

Pento, M., "Tesla Is a Hot Mess–There Is No Path to Profitability," CNBC, May 3, 2016, **www.investopedia.com/news/will-tesla-make-profit-2017-tsla/Tesla Motors**.

Team, T., "Netflix Subscriber Growth Continues Unabated, as Margins Improve," *Forbes*, January 19, 2017, **www.forbes.com/sites/greatspeculations/2017/01/19/netflix-subscriber-growth-continues-unabated-as-margins-improve/#5579d8fc52dd**.

Tesla Motors, **www.teslamotors.com/supercharger**.

Whener, M., "Here's How Many People Still Rent Netflix DVDs by Mail, and Why Netflix Loves It," January 20, 2017, **http://bgr.com/2017/01/20/netflix-dvd-rentals-subscribers/**.

---

[19]M. Whener, "Here's How Many People Still Rent Netflix DVDs by Mail, and Why Netflix Loves It," **January 20, 2017, http://bgr.com/2017/01/20/netflix-dvd-rentals-subscribers/**.

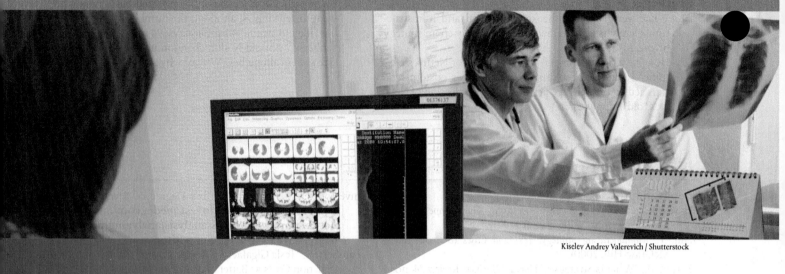

Kiselev Andrey Valerevich / Shutterstock

CHAPTER
three

Process Choice and Layout Decisions in Manufacturing and Services

CHAPTER OBJECTIVES

By the end of this chapter, you will be able to:

- Describe the characteristics of the five classic types of manufacturing processes.
- Discuss how different manufacturing process choices support different market requirements.
- Explain how different manufacturing processes can be linked together via the supply chain.
- Describe the critical role of customization in manufacturing, including the degree and point of customization, as well as upstream versus downstream activities.
- Discuss the three dimensions that differentiate services from one another— the service package, customization, and customer contact—and explain the different managerial challenges driven by these dimensions.
- Position a service on a conceptual model and explain the underlying managerial challenges.
- Explain how different service processes support different market requirements.
- Develop a product-based layout, using line balancing, and calculate basic performance measures for the line.
- Develop a functional layout based on total distance traveled.

SCHARFFEN BERGER CHOCOLATE

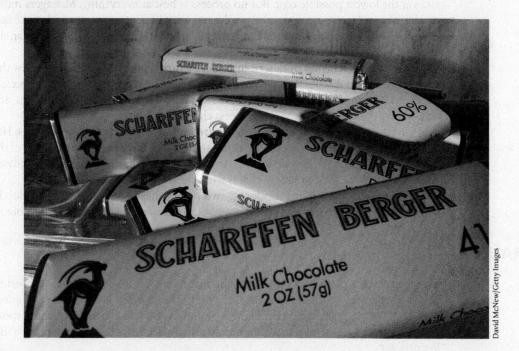

David McNew/Getty Images

FROM its start in a small Berkeley, California, plant in 1996, Scharffen Berger Chocolate has grown to become one of America's leading manufacturers of premium dark chocolate. In fact, chocolate connoisseurs view the company's products as more than candy—as chocolate meant to be savored.

Scharffen Berger's chocolate is produced using a *low-volume batch manufacturing process* carefully designed to ensure that the finished product continues to meet connoisseurs' expectations.[1] Scharffen Berger purchases premium beans months in advance and roasts the beans in 250-kg batches, using its own roasters. Once the company has removed the beans from their shells, it grinds them into a fine paste, using a melangeur (Scharffen Berger's first melangeur was built in Dresden, Germany, in the 1920s) and mixes them with other premium ingredients in specialized processes. The company then forms chocolate bars using tempering and molding

processes to ensure that the finished product has just the right look and feel, as well as the right "snap" when it is broken. At each step in the process, skilled operators use their eyes and taste buds—as well as other more high-tech measuring devices—to ensure that the product meets Scharffen Berger's high-quality standards.

In 2005, Hershey Company, one of the world's largest producers of confectionaries, purchased Scharffen Berger. Four years later, the original Scharffen Berger plant in Berkeley, California, was closed, and all manufacturing operations moved to Robinson, Illinois, where Hershey already produced Payday, Whoppers, and Milk Duds candies using *large-volume, continuous flow processes*. But Scharffen Berger fans need not worry: Hershey management clearly understands that Scharffen Berger products are different and has maintained a separate manufacturing process for its premium product line.

---

[1]D. Snow, S. Wheelwright, and A. Wagonfeld, "Scharffen Berger Chocolate Maker," Case 6-606-043, Harvard Business School, 2007.

INTRODUCTION

Manufacturing and service process decisions are very important to firms for at least two reasons. First, they tend to be expensive and far reaching. The decision to put in a production line, for example, dictates the types of workers and equipment that are needed, the types of products that can be made, and the kinds of information systems that are required to run the business. Because of the financial commitment, it is not a decision that can be easily reversed.

Second, process decisions deserve extra attention because different processes have different strengths and weaknesses. Some processes are particularly good at supporting a wide variety of goods or services, while others are better at providing standardized products or services at the lowest possible cost. But no process is best at everything. Managers must therefore carefully consider the strengths and weaknesses of different processes and make sure that the process they choose best supports their overall business strategy and, in particular, the needs of their targeted customers.

We start this chapter by describing manufacturing processes. We first review the five classic types and then discuss the concepts of hybrid and linked manufacturing processes. We pay particular attention to the roles that product standardization, production volumes, and customization play in determining the best process choice.

In the second half of the chapter, we turn our attention to service processes. How do they differ from one another? What are the key managerial challenges and capabilities of the different service process types? How can service firms position themselves for strategic advantage? The special role services play in supply chains will also be discussed.

We end the chapter by introducing two approaches that firms use to develop layouts. As you will see, the approach used differs dramatically, depending on the type of layout involved.

3.1 MANUFACTURING PROCESSES

Managers face a plethora of choices when deciding on a specific manufacturing process. Scharffen Berger Chocolate is a case in point: The choices it made were aligned with the company's business strategy of making a premium chocolate in relatively low volumes. Here are a few general principles to keep in mind when selecting and implementing a manufacturing process:

1. Selecting an effective manufacturing process means much more than just choosing the right equipment. Manufacturing processes also include people, facilities and physical layouts, and information systems. These pieces must work together for the manufacturing process to be effective.
2. Different manufacturing processes have different strengths and weaknesses. Some are best suited to making small numbers of customized products, while others excel at producing large volumes of standard items. Companies must make sure that their manufacturing processes support the overall business strategy.
3. The manufacture of a particular item might require many different types of manufacturing processes, spread over multiple sites and organizations in the supply chain. Effective operations and supply chain managers understand how important it is for these processes to work well together.

Much has changed in manufacturing over the past 20 years. High quality is no longer a way for manufacturers to differentiate themselves from competitors but rather a basic requirement of doing business. At the same time, many customers are demanding smaller quantities, more frequent shipments, and shorter lead times—not to mention lower prices. Add to this list of challenges the increasingly important role of information technologies (Chapter 12), and you can see that the hallmark of manufacturing in the twenty-first century will be *change*.

Despite the many changes in manufacturing, there is a basic truth that will not change: *No manufacturing process can be best at everything.* The choice of one manufacturing process over another will always bring trade-offs. **Flexible manufacturing systems (FMSs),** for instance, are highly automated batch processes (discussed later) that can reduce the cost of making groups of similar products. But as efficient as FMSs are, a production line dedicated to a smaller set of standard products will still be cheaper, if not as flexible. Similarly, today's high-volume line processes might be more flexible than their counterparts of just a few years ago, but they are still not as flexible as skilled laborers with general-purpose tools and equipment.

Obviously, the selection of a manufacturing system is a complex process. However, experienced managers find that several questions crop up regularly in the selection process:

- What are the physical requirements of the company's product?
- How similar to one another are the products the company makes?
- What are the company's production volumes?
- Where in the value chain does customization take place (if at all)?

Flexible manufacturing systems (FMSs) Highly automated batch processes that can reduce the cost of making groups of similar products.

FIGURE 3.1
Production Line and
Continuous Flow
Processes

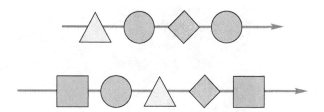

- Product-based layout: Equipment and people are highly specialized and arranged sequentially according to the steps required to make a product or product family.
- Production is often "paced."
- Best suited to high-volume production of standardized products.

We will use these criteria to describe five classic manufacturing processes: production lines, continuous flow processes, job shops, batch manufacturing, and fixed-position layout.

Production Lines and Continuous Flow Manufacturing

Production line
A type of manufacturing process used to produce a narrow range of standard items with identical or highly similar designs.

When most people think about manufacturing, they think about production lines. A **production line** is a type of manufacturing process used to produce a narrow range of standard items with identical or highly similar designs.[2] Production lines have several distinct characteristics. First, they follow a **product-based layout** (Figure 3.1), where resources are arranged sequentially according to the steps required to make a product. The various steps are usually linked by some system that moves the items from one step to the next, such as a conveyor belt. A production line for battery-powered hand tools might divide the assembly into three steps—mounting the motor inside the right half of the casing, putting the left and right halves together, and putting a safety warning sticker on the outside of the casing. All three steps are done continuously, so as one hand tool is having its motor mounted, another is having its safety warning sticker put on.

Product-based layout
A type of layout where resources are arranged sequentially, according to the steps required to make a product.

Second, items typically move through the production line at a predetermined pace. A line might, for example, complete 60 units an hour, or 1 every minute. The time between completions of successive units is known as the **cycle time** of the line. At each step in the process, equipment or people have a set amount of time to finish each task. By dividing the manufacturing process into a series of discrete, carefully timed steps, production lines achieve high degrees of equipment and worker specialization, as well as consistent quality and high efficiency.

Cycle time
For a line process, the actual time between completions of successive units on a production line.

Production lines are ideally suited to the high-volume production of a single product or of products characterized by similar design attributes, such as size, material, or manufacturing steps. An auto assembly line can handle the same model car with different transmissions, different engines, and even different interiors, one right after the other, because the line was designed to fit all possible options of the car model it produces.

Production lines have two drawbacks, however. First, high volumes are required to justify the required investment in specialized equipment and labor. Second, lines are inflexible with regard to products that do not fit the design characteristics of the production line. When production volumes are low or product variety is high, other solutions are needed.

Continuous flow process
A type of manufacturing process that closely resembles a production line process. The main difference is the form of the product, which usually *cannot* be broken into discrete units. Examples include yarns and fabric, food products, and chemical products such as oil or gas.

Continuous flow processes closely resemble production line processes in that they produce highly standardized products using a tightly linked, paced sequence of steps. The main difference is the *form* of the product, which usually *cannot* be broken into discrete units until the very end of the process. Examples include food processing, chemicals, and fiber formation processes. In many ways, a continuous flow process is even less flexible than a production line. The nature of the product tends to make shutdowns and start-ups expensive, which discourages flexibility and encourages product standardization. And the highly technical nature of many continuous flow processes means that specialists are needed to control operations. The only responsibilities of direct laborers might be to load and unload materials and monitor the process. Continuous flow processes also tend to be highly capital-intensive and very inflexible with respect to changes in output levels.

---

[2]J. H. Blackstone, ed., *APICS Dictionary*, 15th ed. (Chicago, IL: APICS, 2016).

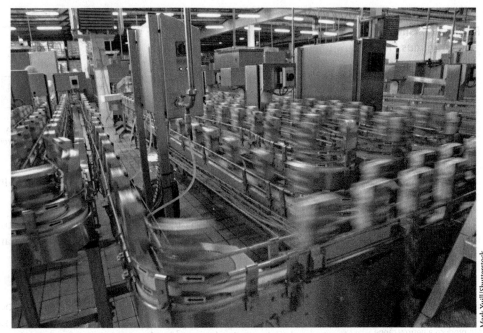

Products moving rapidly through an automated production line at a modern dairy factory.

Job Shops

Job shop
A type of manufacturing process used to make a wide variety of highly customized products in quantities as small as one. Job shops are characterized by general-purpose equipment and workers who are broadly skilled.

In contrast to production line and continuous flow processes, a **job shop** is a type of manufacturing process used to make a wide variety of highly customized products in quantities as small as one. Job shops are characterized by general-purpose equipment and broadly skilled workers. The main emphasis in a job shop is meeting a customer's unique requirements, whatever they may be. Products made in job shops include custom furniture, specialized machine tools used by manufacturers, and restoration and refurbishing work. In a job shop, the product design is *not* standardized. In fact, the shop may need to work closely with the customer to identify just what the product's characteristics should be, and these characteristics may even change once manufacturing starts. Obviously, estimating the time, cost, and specific production requirements for such products is not easy!

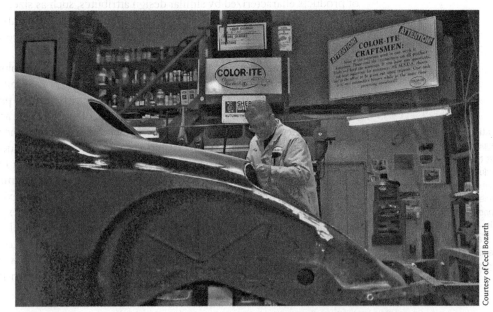

Even though this 1937 Lincoln-Zephyr was originally produced on an assembly line, its restoration took place in a job shop characterized by broadly skilled workers and general-purpose tools.

FIGURE 3.2
Job Shop Processes

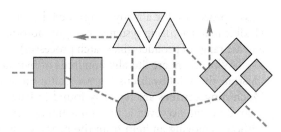

- General-purpose equipment and broadly skilled people.
- Functional layout: Work areas are arranged by function.
- Requirements can change dramatically from one job to the next.
- Best suited to low-volume production of one-of-a-kind products.
- Highly flexible, but not very efficient.

Functional layout
A type of layout where resources are physically grouped by function.

Job shops depend on highly flexible equipment and personnel to accomplish their tasks. Personnel in job shops commonly handle several stages of production. Job shops typically follow a **functional layout,** where resources are physically grouped by function (molding, welding, painting, etc.). This makes sense because the process steps required can change dramatically from one job to the next (Figure 3.2). Finally, job shops must be very flexible in their planning. While the manager of a paced assembly line might have clear expectations of what the output level should be (e.g., 200 ovens an hour), the manager of a job shop does not have that luxury. Manufacturing requirements can change dramatically from one job to the next. And the lack of a clear, predictable product flow means that some areas of a job shop can be idle while other areas are backed up.

Batch Manufacturing

Batch manufacturing
A type of manufacturing process where items are moved through the different manufacturing steps in groups, or batches.

Batch manufacturing gets its name from the fact that items are moved through the different manufacturing steps in groups, or batches. This process fits somewhere between job shops and lines in terms of production volumes and flexibility. Batch manufacturing covers a wide range of environments and is probably the most common type of manufacturing process.

As an example of a typical batch process, consider a manufacturer of golf and turf mowers, such as John Deere. Management might decide to make a batch of 50 engines of a particular model. Workers might then run the engines through one machine, stacking the semifinished engines on a pallet. After all 50 engines have completed this step, the entire batch will be moved to the next machine, where the 50 engines will wait their turn to be processed. This sequence of processing, moving, and waiting will continue throughout the production process.

While production volumes are higher in a batch process than in a job shop, the sequence of steps is not so tightly linked that units are automatically passed, one at a time, from one process step to the next, as they are on a production line. Thus, batch manufacturing strikes a *balance* between the flexibility of a job shop and the efficiency of a line.

Fixed-Position Layout

Fixed-position layout
A type of manufacturing process in which the position of the product is fixed. Materials, equipment, and workers are transported to and from the product.

The final classic manufacturing process type is known as **fixed-position layout.** The distinguishing characteristic here is that the position of the product, due to size or other constraints, is fixed. Materials, equipment, and workers are transported to and from the product. Fixed-position layouts are used in industries where the products are very bulky, massive, or heavy and movement is problematic.[3] Examples include shipbuilding, construction projects, and traditional home building.

Hybrid manufacturing process
A general term referring to a manufacturing process that seeks to combine the characteristics, and hence advantages, of more than one of the classic processes. Examples include flexible manufacturing systems, machining centers, and group technology.

Hybrid Manufacturing Processes

Not all manufacturing processes fall cleanly into the above categories. **Hybrid manufacturing processes** seek to combine the characteristics, and hence advantages, of more than one of the

---

[3]Ibid.

Machining center
A type of manufacturing process that completes several manufacturing steps without removing an item from the process.

Group technology
A type of manufacturing process that seeks to achieve the efficiencies of a line process in a batch environment by dedicating equipment and personnel to the manufacture of products with similar manufacturing characteristics.

Cellular layout
A type of layout typically used in group technology settings in which resources are physically arranged according to the dominant flow of activities for the product family.

Product family
In group technology, a set of products with very similar manufacturing requirements.

3D printing
An additive manufacturing process that creates a physical object from a digital design.

classic processes. We already mentioned flexible manufacturing systems earlier in the chapter. Flexible manufacturing systems are highly automated (like line processes) but are able to handle a wider range of products (like batch processes).

While there are literally hundreds of hybrid manufacturing processes out there, we will illustrate the point by discussing two common types: machining centers and group technology. **Machining centers** are typically found in batch manufacturing environments. What makes them different, however, is that a machining center will complete several manufacturing steps without removing an item from the process. By combining steps, a machining center tries to achieve some of the efficiencies of a production line while still maintaining the flexibility of a batch process.

Similarly, **group technology** is a type of manufacturing process that seeks to achieve the efficiencies of a line process in a batch environment by dedicating equipment and personnel to the manufacture of products with very similar manufacturing characteristics. Group technology cells typically follow a **cellular layout,** in which the resources are physically arranged according to the dominant flow of activities for the product family. To illustrate, a batch manufacturer might find that, while it makes 3,000 different items, 25% of them are products with very similar manufacturing requirements. These products might, therefore, be grouped together into a **product family.** Because of the relatively high percentage of production accounted for by the product family, management might find it worthwhile to dedicate specific equipment and personnel to just these products. The resulting group technology work cell should be able to improve its efficiencies, but at the expense of lower flexibility (Figure 3.3).

3D Printing

One of the most interesting developments in manufacturing in recent years is **3D printing,** also known as additive manufacturing. As 3D Hubs explains it:

> 3D printing is an additive manufacturing process that creates a physical object from a digital design. There are different 3D printing technologies and materials you can print with, but all are based on the same principle: a digital model is turned into a solid three-dimensional physical object by adding material layer by layer.[4]

While 3D printing is still limited with regard to the types of materials it uses and the products it can make, there are situations in which it has advantages over traditional manufacturing. Specifically, 3D printing allows manufacturing to occur *when* and *where* the item is needed. This can be a real advantage when time is of the essence or when shipping an item from a plant to its final destination is difficult. For instance, the U.S. Navy is considering putting 3D printers on its warships so that critical spare parts can be created when needed—"In many cases, the waiting time for [a replacement] order could be reduced from months or weeks to days or hours."[5]

FIGURE 3.3
Group Technology
Work Cell

- Equipment and personnel are dedicated to the production of a product family.
- Cellular layout: Resources are physically arranged according to the dominant flow of activities for the product family.

---

[4]3D Hubs, "What Is 3D Printing?: The Definitive Guide to 3D Manufacturing," **www.3dhubs.com/what-is-3d-printing.**

[5]J. Joyce, "Navy Officials: 3-D Printing to Impact Future Fleet with 'On Demand' Manufacturing Capability," *America's Navy,* May 19, 2016, **www.navy.mil/submit/display.asp?story_id=94769/.**

FIGURE 3.4
Linking Processes
Together to Make
a Sweater

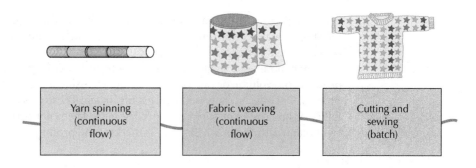

| Yarn spinning (continuous flow) | Fabric weaving (continuous flow) | Cutting and sewing (batch) |

Linking Manufacturing Processes across the Supply Chain

A manufacturing system may actually consist of several different types of processes linked across multiple supply chain partners. Consider the sequence of manufacturing processes needed to produce a sweater. Yarn production has all the characteristics of a continuous flow process: It is capital intensive, turns out a standardized product at a predetermined pace, and requires little or no user interaction. The finished yarn is then fed into a loom that weaves the yarn into fabric, also a continuous flow process. At this point, the rolls of woven fabric might be sent to another facility, where the fabric is cut into patterns and sewn into sweaters. The final sewing operation is highly labor intensive, requiring a classic batch process, in which individual workers are responsible for completing a lot of 50 or more garments. When the garments are finished, they might move on to another station for additional processing, followed by a packing operation. Figure 3.4 illustrates this idea.

Selecting a Manufacturing Process

With the exception of fixed-position layouts and continuous flow manufacturing (which are essentially dictated by the physical characteristics of the product), managers face several choices when selecting a manufacturing process. Job shops have a clear advantage when production volumes are low, customization levels are high, and the manufacturer is not competing on the basis of cost. Production lines excel when production volumes are high, products are standard rather than customized, and cost is important. Batch systems tend to fall somewhere between these extremes.

The Product-Process Matrix

The product-process matrix (Figure 3.5) makes the preceding points graphically. When the characteristics of a company's manufacturing processes line up with the products' characteristics, as shown by the points on the diagonal line, there is a strategic match. But consider the two shaded areas labeled as mismatches. The area in the top-right corner occurs when a job shop

FIGURE 3.5
The Product-Process
Matrix
Source: Based on R. Hayes and S. Wheelwright, *Restoring Our Competitive Edge: Competing through Manufacturing* (New York: Wiley, 1984), p. 209.

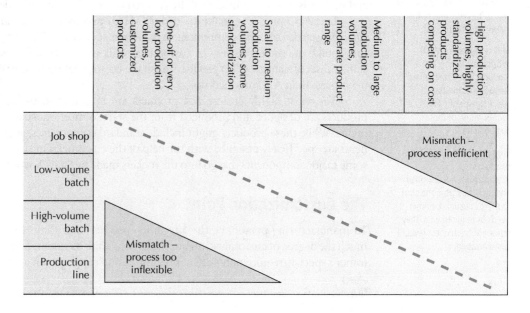

tries to support high-volume, standardized products. Although such products *could* be built in a job shop, it would be an unwise use of resources, and the job shop could never hope to compete on a cost basis with production lines.

In contrast, the shaded area in the bottom-left corner suggests an organization trying to produce low-volume or one-of-a-kind products using a high-volume batch or production line process. Once again, there is a strategic mismatch: These processes can't possibly meet the flexibility or broad skill requirements needed here. The point is that a company must choose the right manufacturing process, given its markets and product requirements.

3.2 PRODUCT CUSTOMIZATION WITHIN THE SUPPLY CHAIN

A word commonly heard in discussions of manufacturing is *customization*. But what does this term mean? True customization requires *customer-specific* input at some point in the supply chain. For instance, manufacturers of specialized industrial equipment often start with an *individual customer's* specifications, which drive subsequent design, purchasing, and manufacturing efforts. And hardware stores mix ready-made paints to match a customer's particular color sample. In both cases, the product is customized. However, the *degree* and *point* of customization differ radically between the two.

Four Levels of Customization

Manufacturers typically talk about four levels of product customization. From least to greatest customization, these are:

- Make-to-stock (MTS) products
- Assemble-to-order (ATO) or finish-to-order products
- Make-to-order (MTO) products
- Engineer-to-order (ETO) products

Make-to-stock (MTS) products
Products that require no customization. They are typically generic products and are produced in large enough volumes to justify keeping a finished goods inventory.

Make-to-stock (MTS) products involve no customization. They are typically generic products and are produced in large enough volumes to justify keeping a finished goods inventory. Customers typically buy these products "off the shelf." Examples include basic tools (e.g., hammers, screwdrivers), consumer products sold in retail stores, and many raw materials.

Assemble-to-order (ATO) or finish-to-order products
Products that are customized only at the very end of the manufacturing process.

Assemble-to-order (ATO) or finish-to-order products are products that are customized only at the very end of the manufacturing process. Even then, the customization is typically limited in nature. A T-shirt with a customer's name airbrushed on it is a simple example. The T-shirt itself is generic until the very last step. Many automobiles are also ATO products because the final set of options—deluxe or standard interior, navigation systems, and so on—is not determined until the very last stage, based on the dealer's or customer's order.

Make-to-order (MTO) products
Products that use standard components but have customer-specific final *configuration* of those components.

Like ATO products, **make-to-order (MTO) products** use standard components, but the final *configuration* of those components is customer specific. To illustrate, Balley Engineered Structures builds an endless variety of customized walk-in industrial coolers or refrigerators from a standard set of panels.[6] MTO products push the customization further back into the manufacturing process than ATO products do.

Engineer-to-order (ETO) products
Products that are designed and produced from the start to meet unusual customer needs or requirements. They represent the highest level of customization.

The most highly customized products are **engineer-to-order (ETO) products.** These products are designed and produced from the start to meet unusual customer needs or requirements. While these products might include standard components, at least some of these components are specifically designed with the help of the customer. One can imagine, for example, that some major components that go into the rockets made by SpaceX would fit into this category.

The Customization Point

To manufacturing personnel, the key difference between these four product types is not so much the degree of customization but the *point at which* it occurs. That is, *when and where* do a customer's specific requirements affect operations and supply chain activities? Consider Figure 3.6.

---

[6]B. J. Pine II, *Mass Customization: The New Frontier in Business Competition* (Boston: Harvard Business School Press, 1993).

FIGURE 3.6
Where Does Customization Occur in the Supply Chain?

Upstream activities
In the context of manufacturing customization, activities that occur prior to the point of customization.

Downstream activities
In the context of manufacturing customization, activities that occur at or after the point of customization.

Law of variability
According to Roger Schmenner and Morgan Swink, "The greater the random variability either demanded of the process or inherent in the process itself or in the items processed, the less productive the process is." This law is relevant to customization because completing upstream activities offline helps isolate these activities from the variability caused by either the timing or the unique requirements of individual customers.

For ETO products, the customer's needs become apparent at the design stage (at the far left in Figure 3.6). The exact content and timing of all subsequent activities, from design through distribution, are determined only after the customer's order arrives. Not surprisingly, ETO products are often found in job shop environments. In contrast, MTS products (at the far right in Figure 3.6) move along from the design stage to finished goods inventory, the warehouse, or even the retail outlet, without direct input from the final customer. The timing and volume of production activities for MTS products are more likely to be driven by internal efficiency or capacity utilization goals. As a result, production lines or even high-volume batch processes are usually the best choice for MTS products.

Drawing attention to the point at which customization occurs allows us to make crucial distinctions between manufacturing activities that occur on either side of the customization point. We refer to activities that take place prior to the customization point as **upstream activities,** while those that occur at or after the customization point are called **downstream activities.**

By definition, upstream activities are not affected by the particular nuances of an individual customer order. Thus, they can be completed offline, or prior to the arrival of a customer order. Completing activities offline has two advantages. First, it reduces lead time to the customer, as only the downstream activities remain to be completed. This can be particularly important in competitive situations where delivery speed is critical. At Dell Computer, all value chain activities in the manufacturing system except final assembly and shipping, which are downstream activities, take place before the customer order arrives. Upstream activities include the ordering, manufacturing, shipping, and stocking of standardized components. The result is two- to three-day lead times for the customer.[7]

A second advantage has to do with the **law of variability,** described by Roger Schmenner and Morgan Swink (1998). According to the authors, "the greater the random variability either demanded of the process or inherent in the process itself or in the items processed, the less productive the process is."[8] Completing upstream activities offline helps isolate these activities from the variability caused by either the timing or the unique requirements of individual customers.

But in ETO, MTO, and ATO environments, some activities *must* be completed on-line, once the customer's needs are known. This tends to increase lead times to the customer. The *Supply Chain Connections* feature describes how TimberEdge Cabinets changed from an MTO manufacturer to an ATO manufacturer. The change had dramatic implications for the efficiency of its manufacturing processes and TimberEdge's ability to meet customer needs in a timely manner.

To summarize, when customization occurs *early* in the supply chain:

• Flexibility in response to unique customer needs will be greater.
• Lead times to the customer will tend to be longer.
• Products will tend to be more costly.

When customization occurs *late* in the supply chain:

• Flexibility in response to unique customer needs will be limited.
• Lead times to the customer will tend to be shorter.
• Products will tend to be less costly.

[7]J. Magretta, "The Power of Virtual Integration: An Interview with Dell Computer's Michael Dell," *Harvard Business Review* 76, no. 2 (March–April 1998): 73–84.
[8]R. Schmenner and M. Swink, "On Theory in Operations Management," *Journal of Operations Management* 17, no. 1 (1998): 101.

SUPPLY CHAIN CONNECTIONS

FIGURE 3.7 TimberEdge Cabinets Before: Make-to-Order Manufacturing

TIMBEREDGE CABINETS

TimberEdge Cabinets[9] illustrates what can happen when a manufacturing organization changes its customization point. Originally, TimberEdge manufactured custom-fit cabinets for home kitchens and bathrooms. Manufacturing was make-to-order (MTO). Specifically, the customization point occurred in TimberEdge's fabrication area, where the cabinet sides and back and front panels were actually cut to a customer's exact specifications (Figure 3.7).

While the make-to-order system provided considerable flexibility, it also created several problems. First, lead times to the customer often ran several weeks or more because cabinet panels could not be fabricated in advance. The long lead times also made it more difficult to coordinate the completion of cabinets with the construction schedules of new homes. In addition, the slight dimensional differences from one job to the next forced TimberEdge to use highly flexible, albeit less efficient, equipment and labor in the fabrication area.

Management concluded that a selection of standard-sized panels (sized in two-inch increments) would provide enough product range to satisfy customers' needs. As a result, management transformed the product into an assemble-to-order (ATO) one (Figure 3.8). Under this arrangement, the fabrication area now became an *upstream* activity. New manufacturing equipment was used in the fabrication area to produce large batches of standard-sized panels *before* the customer orders arrived. Customization now took place in the assembly and finishing steps, which were organized around a job shop style of manufacturing process.

The results were impressive. The switch from MTO to ATO allowed greater efficiency in the fabrication area. Because fabrication—the longest and most labor-intensive value chain activity—was now offline, lead times to the customer shrank from weeks to days. Inventory levels were cut in half, and the workforce was decreased by 25%. Quality actually increased due to the focus on standard-sized panels.

FIGURE 3.8 TimberEdge Cabinets After: Assemble-to-Order Manufacturing

[9] The company name has been changed to protect the company's confidentiality.

SUPPLY CHAIN CONNECTIONS

CUSTOMER-INTRODUCED VARIABILITY IN SERVICES

In her article "Breaking the Trade-off between Efficiency and Service," Professor Frances Frei of the Harvard Business School poses an interesting question:

> What if a manufacturer had to deal with customers waltzing around its shop floor? What if they showed up, intermittently and unannounced, and proceeded to muck up the manufacturer's carefully designed processes left and right? For most service businesses, that's business as usual. In a restaurant or a rental car agency or most of the other service companies that make up the bulk of mature economies today, customers aren't simply the open wallets at the end of an efficient supply chain. They're directly involved in ongoing operations. The fact that they introduce tremendous variability—but complain about any lack of consistency—is an everyday reality.[10]

In fact, Professor Frei suggests that there are five distinct forms of customer-introduced variability:

1. **Arrival variability.** Customers arrive when they desire service. In some cases, this can be controlled (e.g., a hotel reservation system). In other cases, it cannot (e.g., emergency medical services).
2. **Request variability.** Customers demand and expect different services outcomes, even from the same service provider. One customer might want a restaurant to make a menu substitution, while another might want the restaurant to serve her after closing time.
3. **Capability variability.** Some customers are capable of performing many service tasks themselves, while others require substantial hand-holding.
4. **Effort variability.** Even if they are capable of performing certain tasks, customers can differ from one another with regard to the amount of effort they are willing to apply to these tasks. For example, some customers at a grocery checkout will bag their own groceries; others will wait for the cashier or someone else to do it.
5. **Subjective preference.** Different customers can perceive the same service outcome differently. What one customer might interpret as a "quick and efficient" answer to a question might strike another customer as a "cold, unsympathetic" response.

Professor Frei goes on to identify different strategies service organizations can use to manage these different forms of variability. For example, services can use targeted marketing to attract customers with very similar needs and capabilities, thereby reducing request and capability variability. In addition, services can use well-designed automation systems and low-cost labor to take over some of the "hand-holding" that might otherwise be done by more expensive skilled labor.

[10]F. Frei, "Breaking the Trade-off between Efficiency and Service," *Harvard Business Review* 84, no. 11 (November 2006): 92–101.

3.3 SERVICE PROCESSES

Business textbooks have traditionally differentiated between manufacturing and service operations. The reason for this distinction was that manufacturers produce tangible, physical products, while service operations provide intangible value. Unfortunately, this distinction has led some readers to assume that service operations are somehow "softer," or more difficult to pin down, than manufacturing operations.

In reality, service operations are more diverse than manufacturing operations. Some service operations even have more in common with manufacturing than they do with other services. Consider package sorting at a UPS center. Packages are sorted using highly specialized sorting and reading equipment. This activity occurs "behind the scenes," out of the customer's view. Furthermore, the equipment is arranged sequentially, following a product-based layout. One can readily see that package sorting has more in common with batch manufacturing than it does with other services, such as consulting or teaching. On the other hand, services frequently have to deal directly with customers, who introduce considerable variability into the service process (see the *Supply Chain Connections* feature).

To begin our discussion of services, then, let's consider three dimensions on which services can *differ*: the nature of the service package, the degree of customization, and the level of customer contact.[11] These dimensions have a great deal to do with how different services are organized and managed.

[11]Our discussion and model of service processes is derived from the work of Roger Schmenner and, in particular, from R. Schmenner, "How Can Service Businesses Survive and Prosper?," *Sloan Management Review* 27, no. 3 (Spring 1986): 21–32.

TABLE 3.1
Sample Activities in
Two Distinct Service
Packages

SERVICE	INTANGIBLE ACTIVITIES	PHYSICAL ACTIVITIES
University	Teaching Conducting research Performing service and outreach	Supporting the "physical plant" Providing transportation services Providing dining services
Logistics services provider	Finding the best transportation solution for the customer Handling government customs issues	Moving goods Storing goods

Service Packages

Service package
A package that includes all the value-added *physical* and *intangible* activities that a service organization provides to the customer.

A **service package** includes all the value-added *physical* and *intangible* activities that a service organization provides to the customer. For some service operations, the primary sources of value are physical activities, such as the storage, display, or transportation of goods or people. Airlines move passengers from one city to another; hotels provide travelers with rooms and meeting facilities. Retailers add value by providing customers with convenient access to a wide range of products at a fair price. Many of the same rules and techniques that are used to manage physical goods in a manufacturing setting apply equally well to these services, even though airlines, hotels, and retail stores do not actually "make" products.

For other services, the service package consists primarily of intangible activities. A lawyer or an editor, for example, creates value primarily through the knowledge he or she provides. The fact that this knowledge might be captured on paper or electronically is secondary.

Most service packages include a mix of physical and intangible value-adding activities. Table 3.1 lists some of the activities in the service packages offered by a university and a logistics services provider.

While the primary source of value that logistics companies provide might be the movement and storage of goods, such companies also routinely determine the best transportation options for customers and handle customs paperwork. Airlines are another example of a mix of physical and intangible services. In addition to providing physical transportation, airlines help travelers plan their itineraries and track their frequent flier miles.

The greater the emphasis on physical activities, the more management's attention will be directed to capital expenditures (buildings, planes, and trucks), material costs, and other tangible assets. Retailers, for instance, frequently spend more than 60 cents of every sales dollar on products. These products must be moved, stored, displayed, and in some cases returned. Hotel and airline executives also spend a great deal of time managing expensive tangible assets.

The greater the emphasis on intangible activities, the more critical are the training and retention of skilled employees and the development and maintenance of the firm's knowledge assets. Labor cost tends to be quite a high percentage of total cost in such environments. In some intellectually intensive services, such as consulting, labor costs may far outstrip expenditures on buildings and other physical assets.

Knowledge assets generally refer to the intellectual capital of the firm, which may be embedded in the people, the information systems, or the copyrights and patents owned by a firm. For example, Oracle spends an enormous amount of time developing, refining, and protecting its software offerings. Oracle's market intelligence about competitors' products and customer needs can also be viewed as a key knowledge asset.

Service Customization

Customization has an enormous impact on how services are designed and managed. *As the degree of customization decreases,* the service package becomes more standardized. To deliver a standardized service, managers can hire workers with more narrow skills and employ special-purpose technology. Within the same business sector, for instance, one law firm might specialize in divorce or traffic cases, while another might offer a full range of legal services, depending on the customer's needs. Law firms that specialize in divorces can use special software packages designed to help clients reach a quick and equitable settlement.

Controlling the degree of customization also allows better measurement and closer control over the service process. In some cases, managers might draw up a precise, step-by-step process map of the service and establish standard times for performing each step. Many fast-food restaurants follow such an approach.

Not surprisingly, businesses that offer less-customized services have more opportunity to focus on cost and productivity. A classic example is an automotive shop dedicated only to oil changes. Employees in this type of business do not need to be master mechanics or skilled electricians, nor do they need a broad range of expensive equipment and tools. Furthermore, customers can be handled at a predictable and relatively fast rate. The standardized nature of the service allows many such shops to guarantee that a customer's car will be serviced within some precise period, usually an hour or less.

As the degree of customization increases, the service package becomes less predictable and more variable. Efficiency and productivity, while they are important, become much more difficult to measure and control, as each customer may have unique needs. Organizations that offer customized services tend to compete less on cost and more on their ability to provide customers with exactly what they need.

Consider, for example, a general hospital that offers a full range of health care services, from pediatrics to surgery. On any given day, the mix of patients and ailments the hospital must treat is only partially predictable. The breadth and depth of skills required to deal with any and every eventuality are high, and labor costs are, therefore, high as well. Such a hospital also needs to invest in a wide range of technologies, some of which might be quite expensive.

Customer Contact

A third consideration in managing service processes is the level of customer contact. Contact is *not* the same as customization. A fast-food restaurant provides a high degree of customer contact but little customization. On the other hand, a health clinic provides a high degree of contact *and* customization: Physicians may need to see patients frequently to make diagnoses, prescribe treatments, and monitor the effectiveness of treatments.

The degree of customer contact determines the relative importance of front-room and back-room operations in a service process. The **front room** in a service organization is the point (either physical or virtual) where the customer interfaces directly with the service organization. It may be the sales floor in a retail store, the help desk for a software provider, or the Web page for a company. The front-room operations of an airline include the reservation desk, baggage check-in, and terminal gate, as well as the planes themselves. As a rule, *as the degree of customer contact increases*, more of the service package is provided by front-room operations.

In designing front-room operations, managers must consider how the customer interfaces with the service. Layout, location, and convenience become key. The physical layout must be comfortable, safe, and attractive, and the location must be convenient. In addition, front-room service must be available when the customer needs it. FedEx Kinko's is an example of a high-contact service: Its copying services are available 24 hours a day at locations convenient to colleges and universities.

As the degree of customer contact decreases, more of the service package is provided by back-room operations. The **back room** refers to the part of a service operation that is completed without direct customer contact. The back room is often hidden from the customer's view. Package sorting at FedEx or UPS is a classic example of a back-room operation, as is the testing of medical samples. Such services can be located to reduce transportation costs and laid out to improve productivity. Because back-room personnel do not deal directly with customers, the hours of operation are not as crucial as they are in front-room operations, and employees do not have to be skilled in dealing with customers. FedEx and UPS personnel sort packages in the middle of the night, while customers are sleeping. As you might expect, back-room service operations are usually easier to manage than front-room operations.

Table 3.2 summarizes the different managerial challenges faced by services, depending on the nature of the service package, the degree of customization, and the degree of customer contact.

Service blueprinting is a specialized form of business process mapping (Chapter 4) that allows the user to better visualize the degree of customer contact.[12] The service blueprint does

Front room
The physical or virtual point where the customer interfaces directly with the service organization.

Back room
The part of a service operation that is completed without direct customer contact.

---

[12]M. J. Bitner, "Managing the Evidence of Service," in E. E. Scheuing and W. F. Christopher, eds., *The Service Quarterly Handbook* (New York: AMACOM, 1993).

TABLE 3.2
Managerial Challenges in Service Environments

Nature of the service package	**Primarily physical activities -->** Greater emphasis on managing physical assets (airline, trucking firm).	**Primarily intangible activities -->** Greater emphasis on managing people and knowledge assets (law firm, software developer).
Degree of customization	**Lower customization -->** Greater emphasis on closely controlling the process and improving productivity (quick-change oil shop).	**Higher customization -->** Greater emphasis on being flexible and responsive to customers' needs (full-service car repair shop).
Degree of customer contact	**Lower contact -->** More of the service package can be performed in the back room. Service layout, location, and hours will be based more on cost and productivity concerns (mail sorting).	**Higher contact -->** More of the service package must be performed in the front room. Service layout, location, and hours must be designed with customer convenience in mind (physical therapist).

this in two ways. First, it lays out the service process from the viewpoint of the customer. It then parses out the organization's service actions based on (1) the extent to which an action involves direct interaction with the customer and (2) whether an action takes place as a direct response to a customer's needs.

Figure 3.9 provides a template for the service blueprint. The blueprint has four layers. The first layer represents specific *customer actions*, such as placing an order, calling up a service support hotline, or entering a service facility, such as a doctor's office or a retail store. The second layer represents *onstage actions* carried out by the service provider. Onstage actions provide a point of direct interaction with the customer. Some proponents of service blueprinting reserve this layer for activities that involve direct *face-to-face* interaction with the customer. Others argue that any form of direct interaction, whether it is a phone call or a visit to a Web site, would appear here. In this sense, onstage activities are synonymous with front-room operations. Because onstage actions involve direct interaction with the customer, they cross the *line of interaction* and occur above the *line of visibility*.

The third layer of the service blueprint consists of *backstage actions*. These actions take place in direct response to a customer action, but the customer does not "see" these activities carried out. They therefore take place below the line of visibility and are analogous to back-room operations. An example would be the activities required to pick, pack, and ship books and videos you order from Amazon.com. You don't see these activities take place, but nevertheless they occur as a direct result of your placing an order.

The fourth layer of the service blueprint contains *support processes*. Unlike onstage and backstage actions, these processes do not occur as a result of any particular customer's actions.

FIGURE 3.9
Service Blueprinting Template

Customer Actions

- - - - - - - - - - - - - - - - - - *Line of Interaction* - - - - - - - - - - - - - - - -

Onstage Activities   Service activities that involve direct interaction with the customer

- - - - - - - - - - - - - - - - - - *Line of Visibility* - - - - - - - - - - - - - - - -

Backstage Activities   Service activities that *do not* involve direct interaction with the customer, but nevertheless occur as a direct result of specific customer actions

- - - - - - - - - - - - - - - - - *Line of Internal Interaction* - - - - - - - - - - - - - - -

Support Processes   Service processes that facilitate the execution of onstage and backstage activities, but are not carried out due to any specific customer's actions; these processes are typically in place before the customer enters the system

Most of a personal trainer's activities occur onstage—that is, in direct interaction with the customer. Other activities, such as scheduling and billing, occur backstage or even as support activities.

Rather, these processes facilitate the execution of onstage and backstage actions. In the language of service blueprinting, they do this by crossing the *line of internal interaction*. Continuing with our example, Amazon's Web site development and inventory management processes ensure that there is a Web site that can take your order (and credit card information!) and that the products you want are in stock.

EXAMPLE 3.1	
Service Blueprinting at the Bluebird Café	Katie Favre, owner of the Bluebird Café, has developed a simple process map of all the steps that occur when a customer visits her café. This process map is shown in Figure 3.10.

FIGURE 3.10 Process Map for the Bluebird Café

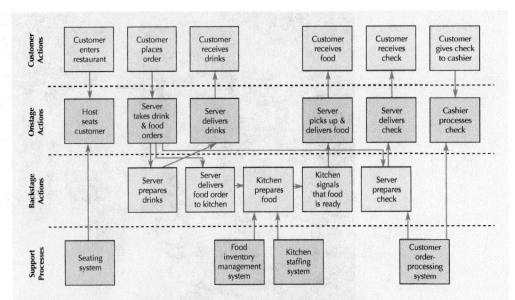

FIGURE 3.11 Service Blueprint for the Bluebird Café

Katie feels that it would be valuable to remap this process using service blueprinting so that she can better see how the customer interacts with her staff. Furthermore, Katie would like to understand what support processes are critical to carrying out the onstage and backstage actions. Figure 3.11 presents the resulting service blueprint.

Looking at the service blueprint provides Katie with new insights into her business. First, Katie notes that there are six points at which the customer directly interacts with her staff. Furthermore, four of these six interactions occur between the server and the customer. Katie has usually had her friendliest and most efficient people serve as hosts or cashiers, but the service blueprint makes her wonder about the wisdom of this policy.

Katie also observes that the ability of the kitchen to prepare food (a backstage activity) depends in part on two support processes: the food management inventory system, which makes sure that the right quantities of food are on hand and properly stored; and the kitchen staffing system, which makes sure the proper number and mix of personnel are available.

Katie has heard grumblings in the past about the kitchen staffing system (really just an informal sign-up sheet). She had dismissed this as a problem for the kitchen management staff to resolve, but now she begins to think about how this "invisible," indirect support process might potentially undermine key backstage and onstage actions.

Service Positioning

Service operations compete and position themselves in the marketplace based on the three dimensions—nature of the service package, degree of customization, and degree of customer contact—that were just discussed. Figure 3.12 shows a conceptual model of service processes containing these three dimensions. The three dimensions of the cube represent the nature of the service package, the degree of customization, and the level of contact with the customer.

To illustrate how positioning works, consider the case of public hospitals. Such community-sponsored hospitals are typically chartered to provide a wide selection of health services to the local population. These hospitals are characterized by:

- High levels of service customization.
- High levels of customer contact.
- A mix of physical and intangible service activities.

These characteristics make community hospitals very expensive to run and very challenging to manage. The position of such service operations is shown graphically in Figure 3.13.

FIGURE 3.12
A Conceptual Model
of Service Process

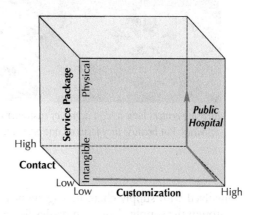

FIGURE 3.13
Positioning a Typical
Community Hospital

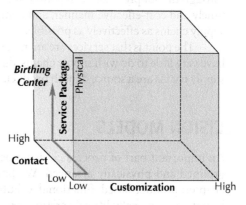

FIGURE 3.14
Positioning a Birthing
Center

Now compare this to a birthing center that specializes in low-risk births (Figure 3.14). All the center's personnel and equipment are focused on a single activity. While customer contact is high, customization of the service package is relatively low.

A birthing center competes by staking out a position quite different from that of the traditional public hospital. As a result, the birthing center and the hospital face different managerial challenges and meet different customer needs. While the typical birthing center competes by offering greater efficiency and a more "family-friendly" atmosphere than the typical public hospital, it cannot meet the broad range of health care needs found in a community hospital. A birthing center may "steal" some business from the local hospital, but it cannot replace it.

Services within the Supply Chain

Many people view supply chains as being dominated by manufacturers. However, take a moment to look back at the beginning of Chapter 1, which starts with descriptions of four companies: Walmart, FedEx, Flex Ltd., and SAP. Note that two of these companies, Walmart and FedEx, are service firms that provide both physical and intangible activities. SAP is a service firm that provides software for the management of supply chains. All three companies, in fact, are deeply

Birthing centers have a high degree of customer contact and represent a mix of physical and intangible activities. But because they focus on one particular health care need, the degree of customization is low.

involved with supply chain management issues. Large retailers like Walmart "pull" products through the supply chain, companies like FedEx make sure products and materials arrive in a timely and cost-effective manner, and companies like SAP provide the "smarts" needed to run supply chains as effectively as possible.

The point is that services are an integral part of any supply chain. Of course, some services have very little to do with supply chains, due to the nature of the service package. But for others, supply chains are a source of both products and business opportunities.

3.4 LAYOUT DECISION MODELS

An important part of process choice is deciding how the various resources will be logically grouped and physically arranged. We have already described four types of layouts in this chapter: product-based, functional, cellular, and fixed-position layouts. For a fixed-position layout, there is really little discretion regarding how the process is laid out because the productive resources have to be moved to where the product is being made or the service is being provided.

For the remaining three, however, managers face choices regarding how the processes are laid out. A product-based layout arranges resources sequentially, according to the steps required to make a product or provide a service. The security check-in at an airport is an example of a service process that follows a product-based layout (where the "product" is the passenger). Such an arrangement makes sense when the sequence of activities does not change from one period to the next. In contrast, a functional layout physically groups resources by function. A functional layout is better suited to environments where the process steps can change dramatically from one job or customer to the next. An example of this would be a full-service auto repair facility, with inspections done in one area, alignments in another, and major repairs in a third area. Finally, a cellular layout is similar in many ways to a product-based layout. The primary difference is that the cellular layout is used in a group technology cell, where the production resources have been dedicated to a subset of products with similar requirements, known as a product family.

In the remainder of this section, we introduce two approaches that managers use to develop effective product-based and functional layouts: line balancing and assigning department locations in functional layouts.

Line Balancing

Line balancing is a technique used in developing product-based layouts, as would be found in a production line or group technology work cell. The technique works by assigning tasks to a series of linked workstations in a manner that minimizes the number of workstations and minimizes the total amount of idle time at all stations for a given output level.[13] When the amount of work assigned to each workstation is identical, we say the line is perfectly balanced. In reality, most lines are unbalanced, as the actual amount of work varies from one workstation to the next. The six basic steps of line balancing are as follows:

1. Identify all the process steps required, including the time for each task, the immediate predecessor for each task, and the total time for all tasks.
2. Draw a precedence diagram based on the information gathered in step 1. This diagram is used when assigning individual tasks to workstations.
3. Determine the takt time for the line. **Takt time** is computed as the available production time divided by the required output rate:

$$\text{Takt time} = \frac{\text{available production time}}{\text{required output rate}} \tag{3.1}$$

Takt time
In a production line setting, the available production time divided by the required output rate. Takt time sets the maximum allowable cycle time for a line.

Simply put, takt time tells us the maximum allowable time between completions of successive units on the line. As we noted earlier, the actual time between completions is referred to as the *cycle time* of a line.

4. Compute the theoretical minimum number of workstations needed. The theoretical minimum number of workstations is defined as:

$$W_{Min} = \frac{\sum_{i=1}^{I} T_i}{\text{takt time}} \tag{3.2}$$

where:

T_i = time required for the *i*th task

$\sum_{i=1}^{I} T_i$ = total time for all *I* tasks

As you can see, the shorter the required takt time is, the more workstations we will require. This is because the tasks will need to be divided across more workstations to ensure that cycle time, which is determined by the total amount of work time in the largest workstation, remains below the takt time.

5. Working on one workstation at a time, use a decision rule to assign tasks to the workstation. Start with the first workstation and add tasks until you reach the point at which no more tasks can be assigned without exceeding the takt time. If you reach this point and all the tasks have not been assigned yet, close the workstation to any more tasks and open up a new workstation. Repeat the process until all tasks have been assigned.

   Be sure not to assign a task to a workstation unless all direct predecessors (if any) have been assigned. Common decision rules for determining which task to assign next are to (1) assign the largest eligible task that will still fit within the workstation without exceeding the takt time, (2) assign the eligible task with the most tasks directly dependent on it, or (3) assign based on some combination of the two.

6. Evaluate the performance of the proposed line by calculating some basic performance measures, including:

$$\text{Cycle time} = CT = \text{maximum amount of time spent in any one workstation} \tag{3.3}$$

$$\text{Idle time} = IT = W_{Actual}CT - \sum_{i=1}^{I} T_i \tag{3.4}$$

where:

W_{Actual} = actual number of workstations

---

[13]Blackstone, *APICS Dictionary*.

$$\text{Percent idle time} = PI = 100\%\left[\frac{IT}{W_{Actual}C}\right] \tag{3.5}$$

$$\text{Efficiency delay} = ED = 100\% - PI \tag{3.6}$$

In general, solutions with low idle times and high efficiency delay values are considered superior. It's important to realize that the decision rules mentioned above will not always generate the best solution; good decision makers, therefore, look for ways to improve the solution.

EXAMPLE 3.2
Line Balancing at Blackhurst Engineering

Blackhurst Engineering, a small contract manufacturer, has just signed a contract to assemble, test, and package products for another company. The contract states that Blackhurst must produce 500 units per eight-hour day. The list of tasks, including time requirements and immediate predecessors, is as follows:

TASK	TIME (IN SECONDS)	IMMEDIATE PREDECESSOR(S)
A	15	None
B	26	A
C	15	A
D	32	B, C
E	25	D
F	15	E
G	18	E
H	10	E
I	22	F, G, H
J	24	I
Total	**202**	

Now that Blackhurst has won the business, Griffin Blackhurst, founder of the company, has decided to set up a line process to make the units. He knows that he will have to staff each workstation with one of his employees. Therefore, Griffin does not want to have any more workstations than necessary, and he would like to keep their idle time down to a minimum. As a first step, Griffin draws out the precedence diagram for the various tasks (Figure 3.15). Each task is represented by a box, and precedence relationships are shown with arrows.

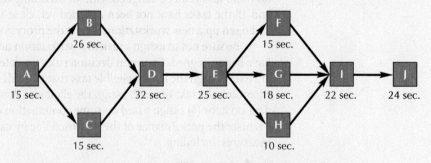

FIGURE 3.15 Precedence Diagram for Blackhurst Engineering

Next, Griffin calculates the maximum allowable cycle time, or takt time, for the proposed line. Because there are 28,800 seconds in an 8-hour shift:

$$\text{Takt time} = \frac{\text{available production time}}{\text{required output rate}} = \frac{28,800 \text{ seconds}}{500 \text{ units per day}} = 57.6 \text{ seconds}$$

With this information, Griffin calculates the theoretical minimum number of workstations:

$$W_{Min} = \frac{\sum_{i=1}^{I} T_i}{\text{takt time}} = \frac{202 \text{ seconds}}{57.6 \text{ seconds}} = 3.51, \text{ or 4 workstations}$$

Griffin rounds up when determining W_{Min} because there is no such thing as a fractional workstation, and anything less than the calculated value would not be enough. Now that Griffin knows the takt time and the theoretical minimum number of workstations that will be needed, he begins to assign tasks to the workstations. He has decided to use the following decision rules:

1. Assign the largest eligible task that can be added to the workstation without exceeding the takt time.
2. If there is a tie, assign the eligible task with the most tasks directly dependent on it.
3. If there is still a tie, randomly choose among any of the tasks that meet the above two criteria.

Following these rules, Griffin begins assigning tasks to the first workstation. He assigns task **A** first, followed by task **B** and task **C**. At this point, the first workstation has a total workload of 56 seconds:

WORKSTATION 1	
Task **A**	15 seconds
Task **B**	26 seconds
Task **C**	15 seconds
Total	56 seconds

Because there are no more tasks that can be added to workstation 1 without exceeding the takt time of 57.6 seconds, Griffin closes workstation 1 to any further assignments and starts assigning tasks to workstation 2. Ultimately, Griffin ends up with the following assignments to the four workstations:

WORKSTATION 1	
Task **A**	15 seconds
Task **B**	26 seconds
Task **C**	15 seconds
Total	56 seconds

WORKSTATION 2	
Task **D**	32 seconds
Task **E**	25 seconds
Total	57 seconds

WORKSTATION 3	
Task **G**	18 seconds
Task **F**	15 seconds
Task **H**	10 seconds
Total	43 seconds

WORKSTATION 4	
Task **I**	22 seconds
Task **J**	24 seconds
Total	46 seconds

Figure 3.16 shows the workstation assignments.

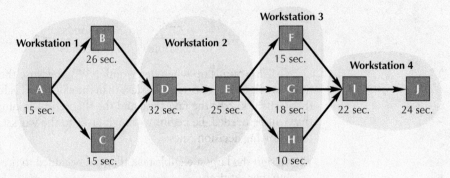

FIGURE 3.16 Workstation Assignments at Blackhurst Engineering

At 57 seconds, workstation 2 has the most task time of any workstation. Because units must be passed from one workstation to the next, units cannot move through the line any faster than the slowest workstation. Workstation 2 effectively dictates that the cycle time for the entire line will be 57 seconds.

The actual number of workstations (W_{Actual}) is the same as the theoretical minimum number (W_{Min}), which makes Griffin think he has developed a good solution. Nevertheless, he calculates the idle time, percent idle time, and efficiency delay for the proposed line:

$$\text{Idle time} = IT = W_{Actual}CT - \sum_{i=1}^{I} T_i = 4(57 \text{ seconds}) - 202 = 26 \text{ seconds}$$

$$\text{Percent idle time} = PI = 100\%\left[\frac{IT}{W_{Actual}CT}\right] = 100\%\left(\frac{26 \text{ seconds}}{228 \text{ seconds}}\right) = 11.4\%$$

$$\text{Efficiency delay} = ED = 100\% - PI = 88.6\%$$

Interpreting the numbers, the line has an idle time of 26 seconds because not all of the workstations have workloads equal to the cycle time of 57 seconds. In fact, the idle times for the four workstations are as follows:

WORKSTATION	CYCLE TIME – ACTUAL TIME = IDLE TIME
1	57 – 56 = 1 second
2	57 – 57 = 0 seconds
3	57 – 43 = 14 seconds
4	57 – 46 = 11 seconds
Total	26 seconds of idle time

Looking at the idle times for each workstation, Griffin realizes that the resulting line is not perfectly balanced. He will probably need to rotate his employees across the workstations to make sure no one feels slighted. The idle time and efficiency delay numbers tell us that a unit going through the process is idle 11.4% of the time. Conversely, the efficiency delay tells us that a unit going through the line is being worked on 88.6% of the time.

Assigning Department Locations in Functional Layouts

Because there is no clearly defined flow of tasks for functional layouts, a different approach to developing layouts is needed. In general, the objective here is to arrange the different functional areas, or *departments*, in such a way that departments that should be close to one another (such as packaging and shipping) are, while departments that don't need to be or shouldn't be near one another aren't.

While this may sound simple, developing functional layouts can actually be quite complex, especially when there is a large number of departments and the criteria for assigning locations are unclear. Experts have developed a variety of approaches to developing functional layouts. Under one approach, decision makers develop closeness ratings for each possible pairing of departments. These closeness ratings, which can be qualitative ("undesirable," "desirable," "critical," etc.) or quantitative (1, 2, 3, etc.), are then used to guide the layout decision.

Another approach, which we describe here, is to locate departments in such a way as to *minimize the total distance traveled*, given a certain number of interdepartmental trips per time period. The logic is that not only will this cut down on unproductive travel time, but also companies can gain natural synergies by locating highly interactive departments next to one another. As with line balancing, the process can be divided into several basic steps:

1. Identify the potential department locations and distances between the various locations.
2. For each department, identify the expected number of trips between the department and all other departments (interdepartmental trips).
3. Attempt to assign department locations in such a way as to minimize the total distance traveled. Several heuristics can be used when making these assignments:
    a. If a particular department can be assigned only to a certain location, do this first. For example, a firm may decide that the client waiting room must be located next to the building entrance. Making such assignments up front reduces the number of potential arrangements to consider.
    b. Rank order department pairings by number of interdepartmental trips and attempt to locate departments with the most interdepartmental trips next to one another.
    c. Centrally locate departments that have significant interactions with multiple departments. (This will help increase the likelihood that other departments can be located adjacent to it.)
    d. See if the solution can be improved by swapping pairs of departments.

In a practical sense, the only way to ensure that one has identified the optimal solution (i.e., the one that minimizes total distance traveled) is to evaluate all possible arrangements. However, this can be prohibitive, as there are N! ways of assigning N departments to N locations. This means that for just five departments, there are $5! = 5 \times 4 \times 3 \times 2 \times 1 = 120$ possible combinations to consider. If there are 10 departments that must be assigned, the possible number of arrangements is a staggering $10! = 3,628,800$. Therefore, most decision makers seek to identify a viable, if not optimal, solution.

EXAMPLE 3.3
Assigning Departments at Blackhurst Engineering

Blackhurst Engineering has been so successful that its founder, Griffin Blackhurst, has decided to relocate the company to a new facility. Griffin has five departments that must be located within the facility: Accounting, Marketing, Engineering, Production, and Shipping & Receiving (S&R).

Figure 3.17 shows the layout of the new facility. The facility has five different areas, any of which is large enough to house the various departments. Because Shipping & Receiving needs access to the bay doors, Griffin has already assigned this department to area E. In addition, Griffin has determined that Production will need to be in either area C or area D due to the significant flow of materials between Production and Shipping & Receiving. Beyond this, however, Griffin has not decided where to place the four unassigned departments.

FIGURE 3.17 Layout of New Facility for Blackhurst Engineering

Because material flow will be addressed by locating Production next to Shipping & Receiving, Griffin has decided to base the final layout on the number of trips personnel make between departments. Specifically, he would like to minimize the total distance traveled per day.

In order to accomplish this, Griffin creates two tables. Table 3.3 shows the distance between the five areas shown in Figure 3.17. Table 3.4 shows the number of interdepartmental trips personnel make each day between the various departments.

TABLE 3.3 Distances (in meters) between Areas, Blackhurst Engineering

AREA	A	B	C	D	E
A	—				
B	30	—			
C	40	50	—		
D	50	40	30	—	
E	70	70	35	35	—

TABLE 3.4 Numbers of Daily Interdepartmental Trips, Blackhurst Engineering

DEPARTMENT	ACCOUNTING	MARKETING	PRODUCTION	ENGINEERING	SHIPPING
Accounting	—				
Marketing	80	—			
Production	35	110	—		
Engineering	60	40	55	—	
Shipping	10	25	90	5	—

After ranking the interdepartmental trip data in Table 3.4 from highest to lowest (Table 3.5), Griffin notes that the greatest number of interdepartmental trips are made between Production and Marketing (110 trips) and between Shipping and Production (90). In addition, the smallest number of trips are made between Shipping and Accounting (10) and between Shipping and Engineering (5). Based on this information, Griffin decides to locate Production and Marketing in areas C and D, respectively, and Accounting and Engineering in areas A and B, respectively (see Figure 3.18).

TABLE 3.5 Ranked Number of Daily Interdepartmental Trips, Blackhurst Engineering

DEPARTMENTS	AVERAGE TRIPS PER DAY
Production ⇔ Marketing	110
Shipping ⇔ Production	90
Marketing ⇔ Accounting	80
Engineering ⇔ Accounting	60
Engineering ⇔ Production	55
Engineering ⇔ Marketing	40
Production ⇔ Accounting	35
Shipping ⇔ Marketing	25
Shipping ⇔ Accounting	10
Shipping ⇔ Engineering	5

FIGURE 3.18 Initial Layout Assignments at Blackhurst Engineering

Griffin evaluates his proposed solution by multiplying the number of interdepartmental trips by the distances between departments. As Table 3.6 shows, the proposed solution results in total distance traveled per day of 19,925 meters.

TABLE 3.6 Total Distance Traveled per Day, Initial Solution

INTERDEPARTMENTAL TRAVEL	DISTANCE TRAVELED PER DAY (METERS)
Production ⇔ Marketing	110 trips * 30 = 3,300
Shipping ⇔ Production	90 * 35 = 3,150
Marketing ⇔ Accounting	80 * 50 = 4,000
Engineering ⇔ Accounting	60 * 30 = 1,800
Engineering ⇔ Production	55 * 50 = 2,750
Engineering ⇔ Marketing	40 * 40 = 1,600
Production ⇔ Accounting	35 * 40 = 1,400
Shipping ⇔ Marketing	25 * 35 = 875
Shipping ⇔ Accounting	10 * 70 = 700
Shipping ⇔ Engineering	5 * 70 = 350
Total distance traveled	19,925 meters

Looking at his solution, Griffin realizes that Production has more interactions with Engineering than Marketing does, while Marketing has more interactions with Accounting than Production does. Griffin wonders if he could improve his results by switching the locations of the Accounting and Engineering departments.

Figure 3.19 shows the revised layout. Recalculating the results (Table 3.7), Griffin realizes that this change cuts the total distance traveled by 600 meters (19,925 − 19,325 meters), or about 3%.

TABLE 3.7 Total Distance Traveled per Day, Revised Solution

INTERDEPARTMENTAL TRAVEL	DISTANCE TRAVELED PER DAY (METERS)
Production ⇔ Marketing	110 trips * 30 = 3,300
Production ⇔ Shipping	90 * 35 = 3,150
Marketing ⇔ Accounting	80 * 40 = 3,200
Engineering ⇔ Accounting	60 * 30 = 1,800
Engineering ⇔ Production	55 * 40 = 2,200
Engineering ⇔ Marketing	40 * 50 = 2,000
Production ⇔ Accounting	35 * 50 = 1,750
Shipping ⇔ Marketing	25 * 35 = 875
Shipping ⇔ Accounting	10 * 70 = 700
Shipping ⇔ Engineering	5 * 70 = 350
Total distance traveled	19,325 meters

FIGURE 3.19 Revised Layout Assignments at Blackhurst Engineering

CHAPTER SUMMARY

In this chapter, we looked at some of the important issues managers face when selecting a manufacturing or service process. We started with a discussion of manufacturing processes, emphasizing the strengths and weaknesses of different types, and we described the impact of customization on the manufacturing process and the supply chain. As our discussion made clear, managers must be careful in selecting both the manufacturing process and the degree and point of customization.

We then turned our attention to service processes. We looked at three defining dimensions of services: the service package (the mix of physical and intangible activities), service customization, and customer contact. We showed how services face different managerial challenges, depending on where they stand on these dimensions. We also discussed how organizations can use this knowledge to position their services vis-à-vis their competition. Finally, we ended the chapter by demonstrating two approaches to developing layouts in manufacturing and service environments.

KEY FORMULAS

Takt time (page 59):

$$\text{Takt time} = \frac{\text{available production time}}{\text{required output rate}} \tag{3.1}$$

Theoretical minimum number of workstations (page 59):

$$W_{Min} = \frac{\sum_{i=1}^{I} T_i}{\text{takt time}} \tag{3.2}$$

where:

T_i = time required for the ith task

$\sum_{i=1}^{I} T_i$ = total time for all I tasks

Cycle time for a production line (page 59):

$$CT = \text{maximum amount of time spent in any one workstation} \tag{3.3}$$

Idle time (page 59):

$$IT = W_{Actual}CT - \sum_{i=1}^{I} T_i \tag{3.4}$$

where:

W_{Actual} = actual number of workstations

Percent idle time (page 60):

$$PI = 100\% \left[\frac{IT}{W_{Actual}CT} \right] \tag{3.5}$$

Efficiency delay (page 60):

$$ED = 100\% - PI \tag{3.6}$$

KEY TERMS

Assemble-to-order (ATO) or
    finish-to-order products   48

Back room   53

Batch manufacturing   45

Cellular layout   46

Continuous flow process   43

Cycle time   43

Downstream activities   49

Engineer-to-order (ETO) products   48

Fixed-position layout   45

Flexible manufacturing systems
    (FMSs)   42

Front room   53

Functional layout   45

Group technology   46

Hybrid manufacturing process   45

Job shop   44

Law of variability   49

Machining center   46

Make-to-order (MTO) products   48

Make-to-stock (MTS) products   48

Product-based layout   43

Product family   46

Production line   43

Service package   52

Takt time   59

3D printing   46

Upstream activities   49

SOLVED PROBLEM

PROBLEM

Monster Bags

Every Halloween, the sisters of Alpha Delta Pi put together "Monster Bags" for children at the local hospital. Each Monster Bag consists of a paper bag stuffed with candy. Each bag has a character's face drawn on it, with yarn hair and paper arms and legs attached.

For the past three years, several sisters have worked individually, putting together bags on their own. But because some of the women are much better artists than others, the quality of the Monster Bags has varied greatly.

Erika Borders, a supply chain major, has been thinking about this problem. She realizes that making each bag really consists of several steps:

A Draw the face on the bag.
B Cut out the arms and legs.
C Attach the arms and legs.
D Cut the yarn for the hair.
E Attach the hair to the bag.
F Fill the bag with candy.
G Staple the bag closed.

Erika decides that the ideal solution would be to develop a production line to make the bags. This way, the most talented artists can focus on what they do best—drawing the characters' faces. She has developed the time estimates and predecessor data for the tasks:

TASK	TIME (SECONDS)	IMMEDIATE PREDECESSORS
A	45	None
B	60	None
C	30	B
D	15	None
E	25	A, D
F	10	C, E
G	10	F
Total	195	

Alpha Delta Pi needs to make 200 bags, and Erika feels she would have no problem getting volunteers to help if they could get all the bags done in four hours.

Solution

After a couple of tries, Erika draws out the precedence diagram for the tasks:

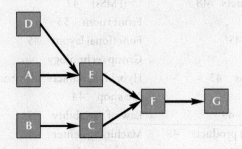

She then calculates the takt time for her production line:

$$\text{Takt time} = \frac{\text{available production time}}{\text{required output rate}} = \frac{14{,}400 \text{ seconds}}{200 \text{ bags}} = 72 \text{ seconds}$$

and the theoretical minimum number of workstations:

$$W_{Min} = \frac{\sum_{i=1}^{I} T_i}{\text{takt time}} = \frac{195 \text{ seconds}}{72 \text{ seconds}} = 2.7, \text{ or 3 workstations}$$

Next, Erika begins to assign tasks to the various workstations. The rule she uses is to assign the largest eligible task (i.e., the largest task that has all its predecessors assigned and that will still fit in the workstation without exceeding the takt time). In the case of a tie, she assigns the task with the most tasks depending directly on it. Working on one task at a time, Erika develops an initial solution:

WORKSTATION 1	
Task **B**	60 seconds
Total	60 seconds

WORKSTATION 2	
Task **A**	45 seconds
Task **D**	15 seconds
Total	60 seconds

WORKSTATION 3	
Task **C**	30 seconds
Task **E**	25 seconds
Task **F**	10 seconds
Total	65 seconds

WORKSTATION 4	
Task **G**	10 seconds
Total	10 seconds

Erika is not completely happy with her solution; workstation 4 has only 10 seconds of work, while every other workstation has 60 seconds or more. The current solution would generate a lot of idle time. To balance things out better, she decides to move task **D** into work-station 3 and tasks **E** and **F** into workstation 4:

WORKSTATION 1	
Task **B**	60 seconds
Total	60 seconds

WORKSTATION 2	
Task **A**	45 seconds
Total	45 seconds

WORKSTATION 3	
Task **D**	15 seconds
Task **C**	30 seconds
Total	45 seconds

WORKSTATION 4	
Task **E**	25 seconds
Task **F**	10 seconds
Task **G**	10 seconds
Total	45 seconds

Although Erika was not able to fit all the tasks into the theoretical minimum number of workstations, the new solution is much better balanced. Doing so also reduces the cycle time from 65 seconds to 60 seconds. Total idle time for the line is now:

$$\text{Idle time} = IT = W_{Actual}CT - \sum_{i=1}^{I} T_i$$

$$= 4(60 \text{ seconds}) - 195 \text{ seconds} = 45 \text{ seconds}$$

$$\text{Percent idle time} = PI = 100\%\left[\frac{IT}{W_{Actual}CT}\right] = 100\%\left(\frac{45 \text{ seconds}}{240 \text{ seconds}}\right) = 18.8\%$$

Efficiency delay = ED = 100% − PI = 81.2%

Now all Erika needs to do is to line up four volunteers, including a good artist to handle workstation 2. So where *are* the pledges?

DISCUSSION QUESTIONS

1. Suppose a firm invests in what turns out to be the "wrong" process, given the business strategy. What will happen? Can you think of an example?
2. In general, would you expect to see production lines upstream or downstream of the customization point in a supply chain? What about job shops? Explain.
3. At many college athletic events, you can find plastic drink cups with the school logo printed on them. Years ago, these cups came molded in a variety of colors. Now nearly all the cups are white with only the printed logos

containing any color. Use the concept of the customization point to explain what has happened and why.
4. Between 1964 and 1966, Ford made more than 1 million Mustangs. Today car collectors are spending tens of thousands of dollars to restore to "like new" vintage Mustangs that originally sold for around $3,000. What types of manufacturing processes do you think were originally used to produce Mustangs? What types of manufacturing processes do you think are used in the restoration of such cars? Why the difference?

5. How does a group technology process resemble a classic batch process? How does it resemble a classic production line? What are the advantages/disadvantages of such a hybrid manufacturing process?

6. Many universities now offer online courses in lieu of traditional classes. These courses often contain lecture notes, linkages to videos and other documents, and online testing capabilities. From a services perspective, how are online courses positioned vis-à-vis large lecture classes? What are the advantages and disadvantages of online courses? What are the managerial challenges?

PROBLEMS

(* = easy; ** = moderate; *** = advanced)

Problems for Section 3.4 Layout Decision Models

1. Burns Boats wants to assemble 50 boats per eight-hour day, using a production line. Total task time for each boat is 45 minutes.

   a. (*) What is the takt time? What is the theoretical minimum number of workstations needed?
   b. (**) Suppose the longest individual task takes four minutes. Will Burns be able to accomplish its goal? Justify your answer.

2. (*) A production line has four workstations and a 50-second cycle time. The total amount of actual task time across all four workstations is 170 seconds. What is the idle time? The percent idle time? The efficiency delay?

3. (**) Polar Containers makes high-end coolers for camping. The total task time needed to make a cooler is 360 seconds, with the longest individual task taking 50 seconds. Polar Containers would like to set up a line capable of producing 50 coolers per eight-hour day. What is the takt time? What is the maximum output per day? (*Hint:* Consider the longest individual task time.)

4. LightEdge Technologies would like to put in place an assembly line in its Mexican facility that puts together Internet servers. The tasks needed to accomplish this, including times and predecessor relationships, are as follows:

TASK	TIME (MINUTES)	IMMEDIATE PREDECESSOR
A	2.9	None
B	0.2	None
C	0.25	A, B
D	0.4	A, B
E	1.7	C
F	0.1	C, D
G	0.7	D
H	1.7	E, F, G
I	1.2	H
J	2.3	I
K	2.7	I
L	1.5	J, K

   a. (*) Draw a precedence diagram for the tasks. Suppose the takt time is 240 seconds (four minutes). What is the theoretical minimum number of workstations?

   b. (**) Develop workstation assignments using the "largest eligible task" rule (i.e., assign the largest task that will fit into the workstation without exceeding the takt time).
   c. (**) How many workstations does your solution require? What is the cycle time for the line? What is the idle time?

5. The state tax department wants to set up what would amount to a series of identical production lines (running eight hours a day) for processing state tax returns that are submitted on the state's "EZ" form. The various tasks, times, and precedence relationships for each line follow:

TASK	TIME (MINUTES)	DIRECT PREDECESSORS
A. Open return; verify filer's name, address, and taxpayer ID.	0.75	None
B. Make sure W2 and federal information match computer records.	1.25	A
C. Check key calculations on return for correctness.	2.50	B
D. Print report to go with return.	0.50	C
E. Route return to refund, payment, or special handling department, based on the results.	0.30	D
F. Update status of return on computer system.	3.0	D

The director has determined that each line needs to process 150 returns a day. The director has asked you to develop a proposed layout that would be shared across the lines.

   a. (*) What is the takt time for each line? What is the theoretical minimum number of workstations needed on each line?
   b. (**) Make workstation assignments using the "largest eligible task" rule. Calculate the cycle time, idle time, percent idle time, and efficiency delay for the resulting line.
   c. (***) Given the task times listed above, what is the minimum cycle time that can be achieved by a line? What is the maximum daily output that could be achieved by a single line?

6. Rayloc rebuilds automotive components. Its main facility has a work cell dedicated to rebuilding fuel pumps. The tasks, times, and predecessor relationships are as follows:

TASK	TIME (SECONDS)	IMMEDIATE PREDECESSOR
A	100	None
B	150	None
C	93	A
D	120	B
E	86	B
F	84	C
G	65	D, E
H	15	F, G

a. (**) Draw a precedence diagram for the tasks. Rayloc would like the cell to be able to handle 100 pumps a day. What is the takt time? What is the theoretical minimum number of workstations needed?
b. (**) Develop workstation assignments using the "largest eligible task" rule.
c. (**) How many workstations does your solution require? What is the cycle time for the line? What is the idle time? What is the percent idle time?
d. (***) Suppose Rayloc would like to double the output to 200 pumps a day. Is this possible, given the tasks listed above? Explain why or why not.

7. The local university has developed an eight-step process for screening the thousands of admissions applications it gets each year. The provost has decided that the best way to take a first cut at all these applications is by employing a line process. The following table shows the times and predecessors for the various tasks:

TASK	TIME (MINUTES)	IMMEDIATE PREDECESSOR
A	1.2	None
B	1	A
C	0.65	B
D	1.1	B
E	1.3	C
F	0.7	D
G	0.8	D
H	0.9	E, F, G

a. (**) Draw a precedence diagram for the tasks. Suppose the university needs to process 30 applications an hour during the peak season. What is the takt time? What is the theoretical minimum number of workstations?
b. (**) Develop workstation assignments by using the "largest eligible task" rule.
c. (**) How many workstations does your solution require? What is the cycle time for the line? What is the idle time? What are the percent idle time and the efficiency delay?
d. (***) In theory, what is the fastest cycle time possible, given the tasks listed above? How many applications per hour does this translate into?

8. (**) As the new facilities manager at Hardin Company, you have been asked to determine the layout for four departments on the fourth floor of the company's headquarters. Following is a map of the floor with distances between the areas:

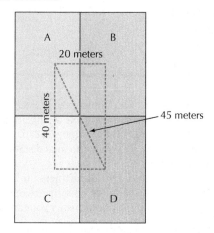

The number of interdepartmental trips made per day is as follows:

DEPARTMENT	1	2	3	4
1	—			
2	10	—		
3	5	60	—	
4	30	40	50	—

Generate at least *two* alternative layout solutions. What is the maximum possible number of arrangements? Which of your two alternatives is best? Why?

9. Dr. Mike Douvas is opening a new sports clinic and is wondering how to arrange the six different departments of the clinic:

1. Waiting
2. Reception
3. Records and staff lounge
4. Examination
5. Outpatient surgery
6. Physical therapy

A map of the clinic follows. The six marked areas are big enough to handle any of the departments, although Dr. Douvas wants to have Reception near the front door (for obvious reasons). Areas that share a side are approximately 15 feet apart, while those that share a corner are 25 feet apart. The distances between A and E and between B and F are 30 feet, while the distances between A and F and between B and E are approximately 40 feet.

Dr. Douvas also has estimates of the number of trips made by patients and staff between the various departments each day:

	WAITING	RECEPTION	RECORDS/ LOUNGE	EXAMINATION	OUTPATIENT SURGERY	PHYSICAL THERAPY
Waiting	—					
Reception	100	—				
Records/Lounge	0	150	—			
Examination	35	5	10	—		
Outpatient Surgery	15	5	10	5	—	
Physical Therapy	50	10	15	40	0	

a. (**) Given that Dr. Douvas wants Reception assigned to area A, how many possible arrangements are there?

b. (**) Generate the best solution you can, given the information below. Calculate the total distance traveled for your solution.

c. (***) Now select two departments to switch (except Reception). By carefully choosing two, can you come up with a better solution? Justify your answer.

10. (***) Omega Design is moving into an old Victorian building with a very unusual floor layout:

Distances, in meters, between the areas are as follows:

AREA	A	B	C	D	E
A	—				
B	14	—			
C	8	8	—		
D	14	20	8	—	
E	18	14	8	14	—

The numbers of daily interdepartmental trips are as follows:

DEPARTMENT	1	2	3	4	5	6
1	—					
2	23	—				
3	24	52	—			
4	13	5	17	—		
5	21	56	28	25	—	
6	60	15	57	3	42	—

Use the "minimal distance traveled" logic to develop a potential layout for Omega. What other information—including qualitative factors—might you want to know when developing your solution?

CASE STUDY

Manufacturing and Service Processes: Loganville Window Treatments

Introduction

For nearly 50 years, Loganville Window Treatments (LWT) of Loganville, Georgia, has made interior shutters that are sold through decorating centers. Figure 3.20 shows some of the various styles of shutters LWT makes.

Past Manufacturing and Service Operations: 2017

Traditionally, LWT supported a limited mix of standard products. At any particular point in time, the mix of products might consist of six different styles offered in five predetermined sizes, resulting in 30 possible end products. LWT would produce each of these end products in batches of 500 to 1,000 (depending on the popularity of each style/size combination) and hold the finished products in the plant warehouse. When a decorating center called in with an order, LWT would either meet the order from the finished goods inventory or hold the order to be shipped when the next batch was finished.

LWT's products were sold through independent decorating centers located across the United States and Canada. LWT would send each of these decorating centers a copy of its catalog, and the decorating centers would use these catalogs to market LWT's products to potential customers. It was the responsibility of the decorating centers to work with customers to price out the shutters, make sure the correct size and style were ordered from LWT, and resolve any problems. As a result, LWT almost never dealt directly with the final customers.

Manufacturing and Service Operations: 2018

By 2017, the influx of low-cost shutters made in China had forced LWT to reconsider its business model. Specifically, because of the low labor costs in China (20% of LWT's labor costs), Chinese manufacturers could make exact copies of LWT's products for substantially less and hold them in warehouses across the United States and Canada. LWT's traditional

FIGURE 3.20
Sample Products
Made by LWT

customers—the decorating centers—were turning more and more to these alternative sources.

LWT decided to fight back. As Chuck Keown, president of LWT, put it:

The only permanent advantage that we have over our competitors is that we are located here in the United States, closer to the final customer. So from now on, we will be a make-to-order manufacturer. We will deal directly with customers and make shutters to whatever specific measurements and finish they need. This means we can no longer count on producing batches of 500 to 1,000 shutters at a time and holding them in inventory. Rather, we will need to be able to make a few at a time in one-off sizes, if that's what the customer needs.

On the service and marketing side of the house, we will now take orders directly from the customer. We will reach them through the Internet and through catalogs. We will work with them to determine what style best suits their needs, and to take the measurements needed to make the shutters. When there is a problem, we will work directly with the customer to resolve them.

Yes, this will require dramatic changes to our business. But it also means we will be able to charge a premium for our products

and create a relationship with the customers that our Chinese rivals will find difficult to emulate. As I see it, this is the only way we can survive.

Questions

1. As of 2017, what type of manufacturing process did LWT appear to be using? What level of customization was it offering? *Where* was the point of customization?
2. Using Table 3.2 and Figure 3.12 as guides, how would you describe the service side of LWT's business prior to 2018? What were the managerial challenges?
3. What type of manufacturing process is needed to support the changes proposed by Chuck Keown? What level of customization will LWT be offering? *Where* will the point of customization be?
4. Using Table 3.2 and Figure 3.12 as guides, how will the service side of the house change in 2018? What will the *new* managerial challenges be?
5. Develop a list of 8 to 10 things that must happen in order to accomplish the changes Chuck Keown envisions. Will the new business model be more or less difficult to manage than the old one? Justify your answer.

REFERENCES

Books and Articles

Bitner, M. J., "Managing the Evidence of Service," in E. E. Scheuing and W. F. Christopher, eds., *The Service Quarterly Handbook* (New York: AMACOM, 1993).

Blackstone, J. H., ed., *APICS Dictionary*, 14th ed. (Chicago, IL: APICS, 2013).

Frei, F., "Breaking the Trade-off between Efficiency and Service," *Harvard Business Review* 84, no. 11 (November 2006): 92–101.

Hayes, R., and S. Wheelwright, *Restoring Our Competitive Edge* (New York: John Wiley, 1984).

Magretta, J., "The Power of Virtual Integration: An Interview with Dell Computer's Michael Dell," *Harvard Business Review* 76, no. 2 (March–April 1998): 73–84.

Pine II, B. J., *Mass Customization: The New Frontier in Business Competition* (Boston: Harvard Business School Press, 1993).

Schmenner, R., "How Can Service Businesses Survive and Prosper?," *Sloan Management Review* 27, no. 3 (Spring 1986): 21–32.

Schmenner, R., and M. Swink, "On Theory in Operations Management," *Journal of Operations Management* 17, no. 1 (1998): 97–113.

Snow, D., S. Wheelwright, and A. Wagonfeld, "Scharffen Berger Chocolate Maker," Case 6-606-043, Harvard Business School, 2007.

Internet

3D Hubs, "What Is 3D Printing?: The Definitive Guide to 3-D Manufacturing," **www.3dhubs.com/what-is-3d-printing.**

Joyce, J., "Navy Officials: 3-D Printing to Impact Future Fleet with 'On Demand' Manufacturing Capability," *America's Navy*, May 19, 2016, **www.navy.mil/submit/display.asp?story_id=94769/.**

Kiselev Andrey Valerevich/Shutterstock

CHAPTER four

CHAPTER OUTLINE

Business Processes

CHAPTER OBJECTIVES

By the end of this chapter, you will be able to:

- Explain what a business process is and how the business process perspective differs from a traditional, functional perspective.

- Create process maps for a business process and use them to understand and diagnose a process.

- Calculate and interpret some common measures of process performance.

- Discuss the importance of benchmarking and distinguish between competitive benchmarking and process benchmarking.

- Describe the Six Sigma methodology, including the steps of the DMAIC process.

- Use and interpret some common continuous improvement tools.

- Explain what the Supply Chain Operations Reference (SCOR) model is and why it is important to businesses.

INTERMOUNTAIN HEALTHCARE

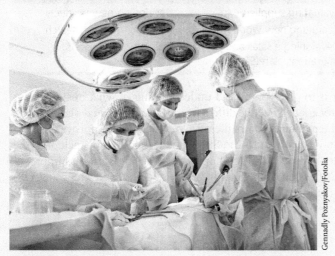

In the United States, the rising cost of health care has been a topic of concern for many years. One would expect, then, that health care providers would quickly move to incorporate any new practices that would improve both the quality and cost-effectiveness of their services. Yet this has not always been the case. In "Fixing Healthcare on the Frontlines,"[1] Richard Bohmer, a physician and professor of management practice at the Harvard Business School, notes two remarkable statistics:

1. It takes 10 to 20 years for new medical practices to move from the development stage to widespread adoption by health care providers.
2. "The chance of receiving healthcare that meets generally accepted standards is about 55%."

But how can this be? One reason noted by Bohmer and others is that health care providers have historically done a poor job putting in place business processes that standardize treatment steps for well-understood conditions, such as diabetes or hypertension. Clearly, standardizing the steps

followed by caregivers has the potential to improve patient outcomes in such situations while simultaneously driving down variability and costs.

Here's how one health care provider, Intermountain Healthcare, went about tackling the problem:

- For common and well-understood conditions, teams of specialist at Intermountain developed standardized processes, called "protocols," which define in a step-by-step manner how each condition should be diagnosed and treated.
- The protocols are then computerized and shared with caregivers in Intermountain's network of hospitals and clinics, who then follow the protocols when treating patients.
- To ensure that the protocols are both up-to-date and workable, Intermountain regularly updates the protocols based on the latest scientific evidence as well as actual caregivers' experiences. Furthermore, while the protocols are meant to capture "best practices" at any point in time, caregivers can override the protocols when they feel conditions warrant.

Because there is a great deal of overlap in patient needs, Intermountain found that over 90% of its case load could be addressed through just 70 protocols. The other 10% of cases include patients with complex or unique needs that doctors must handle on a case-by-case basis. Both Intermountain and its patients have benefited from the use of protocols. One example reported by James and Savitz illustrates the types of benefits that can be achieved: "a new [infant] delivery protocol helped reduce rates of elective induced labor, unplanned cesarean sections, and admissions to newborn intensive care units. That one protocol saves an estimated $50 million in Utah each year. If applied nationally, it would save about $3.5 billion."[2]

[1]R. Bohmer, "Fixing Health Care on the Front Lines," *Harvard Business Review*, April 2010, 62–69.
[2]B. James and L. Savitz, "How Intermountain Trimmed Health Care Costs through Robust Quality Improvement Efforts," *Health Affairs*, May 2011, **http://content.healthaffairs.org/content/30/6/1185.full.**

INTRODUCTION

In recent years, corporate executives and management theorists have recognized the importance of putting in place business processes that effectively manage the flow of information, products, and money across the supply chain. One reason is the dollars involved: Experts estimate that total supply chain costs represent the majority of the total operating budget for most organizations; in some cases, they may be as high as 75%.[3]

Another reason is the increased emphasis on providing value to the customer. Look again at Intermountain's experience with its infant delivery protocol: While Intermountain saves over $50 million per year, mothers (and babies!) benefit directly from fewer unplanned surgical procedures or visits to the ICU.

[3]F. Quinn, "What's the Buzz? Supply Chain Management: Part 1," *Logistics Management* 36, no. 2 (February 1997): 43.

TABLE 4.1
Examples of
Business Processes

PRIMARY PROCESSES	SUPPORT PROCESSES	DEVELOPMENT PROCESSES
Providing a service	Evaluating suppliers	Developing new products
Educating customers	Recruiting new workers	Performing basic research
Manufacturing	Developing a sales and operations plan (S&OP)	Training new workers

TABLE 4.1
Examples of
Business Processes

The purpose of this chapter is to give you a solid understanding of what business processes are and how the business process perspective differs from more traditional perspectives. We will describe various tools and techniques companies use to manage and improve business processes. In particular, we will introduce you to the Six Sigma methodology, including the DMAIC (Define–Measure–Analyze–Improve–Control) approach to business process improvement. We end the chapter with a discussion of the Supply Chain Operations Reference (SCOR) model, which gives companies a common language and model for designing, implementing, and evaluating supply chain business processes.

4.1 BUSINESS PROCESSES

Process
According to APICS, "A set of logically related tasks or activities performed to achieve a defined business outcome."

Primary process
A process that addresses the main value-added activities of an organization.

Support process
A process that performs necessary, albeit not value-added, activities.

Development process
A process that seeks to improve the performance of primary and support processes.

So, just what do we mean by the term *business process*? APICS defines a **process** as "a set of logically related tasks or activities performed to achieve a defined business outcome."[4] For our purposes, these outcomes can be physical, informational, or even monetary in nature. Physical outcomes might include the manufacture and delivery of goods to a customer; an informational outcome might be registering for college courses; and a monetary outcome might include payment to a supply chain partner for services rendered. Of course, many business processes have elements of all three.

Primary processes address the main value-added activities of an organization. They include activities such as delivering a service and manufacturing a product. These processes are considered "value-added" because some customer is willing to pay for the resulting outputs. In contrast, **support processes** perform necessary, albeit not value-added, activities. An example is tuition billing. No student wants to pay tuition, and the university would rather not spend the overhead required to collect it, but the university would not be able to sustain itself for very long without monetary flows from the students. Finally, **development processes** are processes that improve the performance of primary and support processes.[5] Table 4.1 gives examples of primary, support, and development processes.

As with our discussion of supply chains in Chapter 1, you may be saying to yourself that "business processes aren't new," and, once again, you'd be right. What *is* new is the level of attention these processes have attracted in recent years. Prior to the 1990s, most managerial attention was on the activities within specific business *functions*, such as marketing, operations, logistics, and finance. The assumption was that if companies concentrated on how these functions were organized, how individuals were trained, and how the individual functional strategies lined up with the overall business strategy (Chapter 2), then everything would be fine.

The problem was, however, that managing functions is not the same as managing what a business *does*. Look again at the business processes listed in Table 4.1. Nearly every one of these processes spans multiple functional areas and even multiple supply chain partners.

Figure 4.1 shows three of the many business processes we will discuss in this book and how they cut across both functions and organizations. There are other processes that we have not shown here, but our point is this: For many business processes, no single function or supply chain partner has a complete view or complete control of the situation. Developing superior business processes, therefore, requires a cross-functional and cross-organizational perspective that actively looks at the logical flow of activities that make up a business process. We will expand on this idea below.

Improving Business Processes

Let's illustrate the idea of improving business processes with an example many college students are familiar with: enrolling in classes each semester. Not too long ago, students had to interact

---

[4]J. H. Blackstone, ed., *APICS Dictionary*, 15th ed. (Chicago, IL: APICS, 2016).
[5]B. Andersen, *Business Process Improvement Toolbox* (Milwaukee, WI: ASQ Quality Press, 1999).

FIGURE 4.1
Examples of Business Processes That Cut across Functions and Organizations

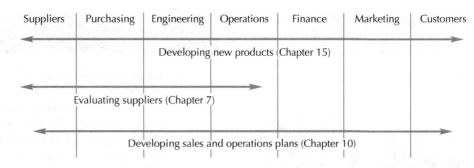

Suppliers	Purchasing	Engineering	Operations	Finance	Marketing	Customers

Developing new products (Chapter 15)

Evaluating suppliers (Chapter 7)

Developing sales and operations plans (Chapter 10)

with three distinct functional areas in order to register: the individual colleges or departments (which granted permission to take classes), the registrar's office (which managed the actual enrollment process), and the cashier's office (which handled tuition payments). A student would visit his home college or department to pick up the proper permission forms, schedule his or her classes, and finally pay tuition. Of course, any problem in the system could force the student to revisit one or more of these areas.

This process was convenient for everyone except the students. Now nearly all colleges and universities have reorganized these activities into a single process, with a focus on speed, accuracy, and convenience to the students. Students can now register and pay tuition all with one visit to a Web site. In some cases, students can even purchase their books and have them automatically delivered or downloaded to them. The key point is this: Improving the enrollment process required the different functional areas to look beyond their own activities and see the process through the *customers'* (i.e., students') eyes.

Improving business process is at the very core of operations and supply chain management. For one thing, the performance level of most processes tends to decrease over time unless forces are exerted to maintain it. In addition, even if an organization does not feel a need to improve its business processes, it may be forced to due to competitive pressures. Procter & Gamble's Streamlined Logistics initiative (see the *Supply Chain Connections* feature) forced competitors, such as Kraft Foods, to undertake similar process involvement efforts.[6] Finally, today's customers are becoming more and more demanding; what a customer might have considered quite satisfactory a few years ago might not meet his or her requirements today.

Most universities have already combined course registration with tuition payments into a single, integrated process. How long do you think it will be until all course and textbook information is integrated electronically into this process?

---

[6]S. Tibey, "How Kraft Built a 'One-Company' Supply Chain," *Supply Chain Management Review* 3, no. 3 (Fall 1999): 34–42.

SUPPLY CHAIN CONNECTIONS

PROCTER & GAMBLE[7]

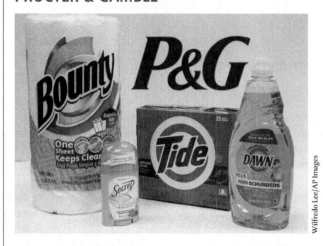

Wilfredo Lee/AP Images

PROCTER & GAMBLE (P&G) is one of the world's largest consumer goods firms, with such well-known brands as Tide detergent, Crest toothpaste, and Pampers disposable diapers. At one time, P&G was organized around five business sectors: laundry and cleaning, paper goods, beauty care, food and beverages, and health care. To the folks within P&G, this made a lot of sense. Dividing such a large organization along product lines allowed each business sector to develop product, pricing, and promotion policies, as well as supply chain strategies, independent of one another.

But to the distributors and retailers who were P&G's direct customers, the view was quite different. Each of these customers had to deal with five separate billing and logistics processes—one for each business sector (Figure 4.2).

As Ralph Drayer, vice president of Efficient Consumer Response for Procter & Gamble, noted, this created a wide range of problems:

> [P&G] did not allow customers to purchase all P&G brands together for delivery on the same truck. Some customers might go several days without receiving an order, only to have several trucks with P&G orders arrive at the receiving dock at the same time on the same morning. Different product categories were shipped on different trucks with different invoices. The trade promotions process was so complex that more than 27,000 orders a month required manual corrections.... The separate pricing and promotion policies, coupled with non-coordinated management of logistics activities across the five business sectors, resulted in as many as nine prices per item and order quantities of less-than-full truckload.

In response, P&G launched its Streamlined Logistics initiative. Among many other things, it drastically reduced the number of new products being introduced

- 5 different billing processes
  - Different terms and conditions
  - No volume price discounts based on total *business*

- 5 different sets of logistics processes
  - Small, uncoordinated shipments
  - Inflated transportation costs

FIGURE 4.2 Procter & Gamble before the Streamlined Logistics Initiative

---

[7]Adapted from R. Drayer, "Procter & Gamble's Streamlined Logistics Initiative," *Supply Chain Management Review* 3, no. 2 (Summer 1999): 32–43. Reprinted with permission of Supply Chain Management Review.

- *One integrated billing process*
  - *— Administrative cost savings passed on to customers*
  - *— Volume discounts applied across all purchases*
- *One set of logistics processes*
  - *— Full-truckload quantities shipped 98% of the time, resulting in substantial transportation cost savings*

FIGURE 4.3 **Procter & Gamble after the Streamlined Logistics Initiative**

(many of which only served to confuse consumers) and simplified the pricing and promotion structure. But, more importantly, P&G redesigned the information and physical flows across the business sectors so that customers had to deal with only *one* P&G billing process and *one* set of logistics processes (Figure 4.3).

The results were dramatic:

- Full truckloads were shipped 98% of the time, resulting in dramatically lower transportation costs.
- The number of invoices the typical P&G customer had to handle fell anywhere from 25% to 75%. At a

processing cost of $35 to $75 for each invoice, this represented substantial savings to P&G's customers.

- Customers were able to get volume discounts from P&G based on their *total* purchase volume. Under the previous system, this had been difficult, if not impossible, to do.

Procter & Gamble's Streamlined Logistics initiative not only improved profitability for P&G and its customers but also served as a model for other manufacturers in the industry who have made similar efforts to simplify and streamline their own business processes.

4.2 MAPPING BUSINESS PROCESSES

Mapping
The process of developing graphic representations of the organizational relationships and/or activities that make up a business process.

Before a firm can effectively manage and improve a business process, it must understand the process. One way to improve understanding is by developing graphic representations of the organizational relationships and/or activities that make up a business process. This is known as **mapping.** Done properly, mapping serves several purposes:

- It creates a common understanding of the content of the process: its activities, its results, and who performs the various steps.
- It defines the boundaries of the process.
- It provides a baseline against which to measure the impact of improvement efforts.

Process Maps

Process map
A detailed map that identifies the specific activities that make up the informational, physical, and/or monetary flow of a process.

A **process map** identifies the specific activities that make up the information, physical, or monetary flow of a process. Process maps often give managers their first complete picture of how a process works. Experts have developed a set of graphical symbols to represent different aspects of the process. Figure 4.4 shows some of the most common symbols used.

Because of the level of detail required, process flowcharts can quickly become overly complex or wander off the track unless a conscious effort is made to maintain focus. Some useful rules for maintaining this focus include:

1. **Identify the entity that will serve as the focal point.** This may be a customer, an order, a raw material, or the like. The mapping effort should focus on the activities and flows associated with the movement of that entity through the process.
2. **Identify clear boundaries and starting and ending points.** Consider a manufacturer who wants to better understand how it processes customer orders. To develop the process map, the manufacturer must decide on the starting and ending points. Will

FIGURE 4.4
Common Process
Mapping Symbols

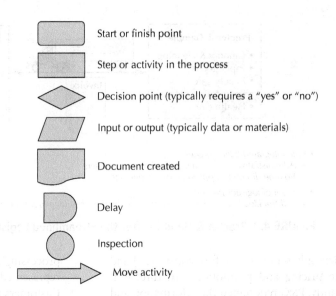

Start or finish point

Step or activity in the process

Decision point (typically requires a "yes" or "no")

Input or output (typically data or materials)

Document created

Delay

Inspection

Move activity

the starting point be when the customer places the order or when the manufacturer receives it? Similarly, will the flowchart end when the order is shipped out of the plant or when the order is actually delivered to the customer? The manufacturer might also decide to focus only on the physical and information flows associated with the order and not the monetary flows.

3. **Keep it simple.** Most people developing process maps for the first time tend to put in *too* much detail. They develop overly complex maps, often subdividing major activities into several smaller ones that don't provide any additional insight or include logical branches to deal with every conceivable occurrence, even ones that very rarely occur. There are no simple rules of thumb for avoiding this trap, other than to ask whether the additional detail is important to understanding the process and whether it is worth the added complexity.

Let's illustrate these ideas with an example we are all familiar with: a customer visiting a restaurant. The customer is greeted by a host, who then seats the customer. A server takes the customer's order, delivers the drinks and food, and writes up and delivers the check. Finally, a cashier takes the customer's money.

Figure 4.5 shows a simplified map of the Bluebird Café, which we first discussed in Chapter 3. In this example, the focal point is the customer: The process begins when the customer enters

FIGURE 4.5
Process Map for the
Bluebird Café

the Bluebird Café and ends when he or she leaves. Notice, too, that there are many activities that occur in the restaurant that are *not* included in this particular map—scheduling employee work hours, planning deliveries from suppliers, prepping food, etc. This is because our current focus is on the customer's interactions with the restaurant. Even so, our "simplified" map still has 11 distinct steps.

With the major customer interaction points laid out, we can start to see how important each of the steps is to the customer's overall satisfaction with his or her dining experience. We might also start to ask how the Bluebird Café can measure and perhaps improve its performance. Example 4.1 illustrates a somewhat more complex process map for a fictional distribution center. As you read through the example, ask yourself the following questions:

- What is the focal point of the process mapping effort?
- What are the boundaries and the starting and stopping points for the process map?
- What detail is not included in this example?

EXAMPLE 4.1

Process Mapping at a Distribution Center

A San Diego distribution center (DC) has responsibility for supplying products to dealers located within a 30-mile radius. Lately, the DC has been receiving a lot of complaints from dealers regarding lost orders and the time required to process orders for items that are already in stock at the DC. A process improvement team has decided to study the process in more detail by tracing the flow of a dealer order through the DC, starting from when the dealer emails in the order and ending with the order's delivery to the dealer. The team has collected the following information:

- The dealer emails an order to the DC, which is automatically printed out on the copier in the main office. Sometimes the paper gets jammed in the copier machine or an order gets thrown away accidentally. Employees estimate that about 1 in 25 orders is "lost" in this manner.
- The printed order sits in an inbox anywhere from 0 to 4 hours, with an average of 2 hours, before the order is picked up by the DC's internal mail service.
- It takes the internal mail service 1 hour, on average, to deliver the order to the picking area (where the desired items are picked off the shelves). In addition, 1 out of 100 orders is accidentally delivered to the wrong area of the DC, resulting in additional "lost" orders.
- Once an order is delivered to the picking area, it sits in the clerk's inbox until the clerk has time to process it. The order might wait in the inbox anywhere from 0 to 2 hours, with an average time of 1 hour.
- Once the clerk starts processing the order, it takes her about 5 minutes to determine whether the item is in stock.
- If the requested product is in stock, a worker picks the order and puts it into a box. Average picking time is 20 minutes, with a range of 10 minutes to 45 minutes.
- Next, an inspector takes about 2 minutes to check the order for correctness. Even with this inspection, 1 out of 200 orders shipped has the wrong items or quantities.
- A local transportation firm takes the completed order and delivers it to the dealer (average delivery time is 2 hours but can be anywhere from 1 to 3 hours). The transportation firm has an exemplary performance record: Over the past 5 years, the firm has never lost or damaged a shipment or delivered to the wrong dealer.
- If the item being ordered is out of stock, the clerk notifies the dealer and passes the order on to the plant, which will arrange a special shipment directly to the dealer, usually within a week.

Using the symbols from Figure 4.5, the process improvement team draws the process map for the order-filling process of in-stock items (Figure 4.6). The map includes detailed information on the times required at each step in the process, as well as various quality problems. Adding up the times at each process step, the team can see that the average time between ordering and delivery for an in-stock item is about 6.4 hours (387 minutes) and can be as long as 11.3 hours (682 minutes). If an item is not in stock, it will take even longer to be delivered.

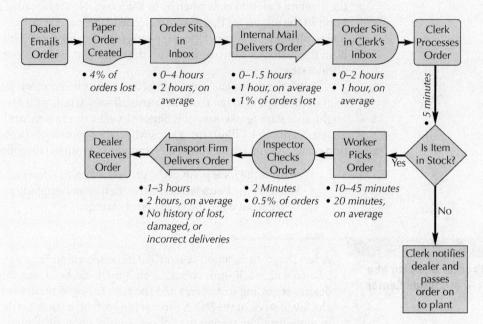

FIGURE 4.6 **Order-Filling Process for In-stock Items**

Of the 6.4 hours an order spends on average in the process, a full 3 hours is waiting time. Finally, 5% of the orders are "lost" before they even get to the picking area. For the orders that do survive to this point, 1 out of 200 will be shipped with the incorrect items or quantities. Clearly, there is room for improvement.

Once the process has been mapped, the team considers ways to improve the process. It is clear that the order-filling process is hampered by unnecessary delays, "lost" paperwork, and an inspection process that yields less-than-perfect results. One potential improvement is to have the dealers email their orders directly to the picking area. Not only would this cut down on the delays associated with moving a paper copy through the DC, but it would also cut down on the number of "lost" orders. Errors in the picking and inspection process will require additional changes.

Keep in mind that the idea is to document the process *as it is*—not the way people remember it. In some cases, employees might need to physically walk through a process, "stapling themselves" to a document or a product. Second, management needs to decide which parts of the process to look at. Areas that are beyond a manager's control or are not directly related to the problem at hand can be omitted from the process mapping effort. In Example 4.1, the focus was on *in-stock* items, so the flowchart did not go into detail regarding what happens if the product is out of stock.

Table 4.2 lists some guidelines to use in identifying opportunities to improve a process. In general, personnel should critically examine each step in the process. In many cases, steps can be improved dramatically or even eliminated.

Swim Lane Process Maps

Swim lane process map
A process map that graphically arranges the process steps so that the user can see who is responsible for each step.

Sometimes we are interested in understanding not only the steps in a process but *who* is involved and how these parties interact with one another. In the restaurant example, at least four people were involved in serving the customer—the host, the server, the cook, and the cashier. **Swim lane process maps** graphically arrange the process steps so that the user can see who is responsible for each step. This has two distinct benefits. First, swim lane maps allow the user to see where the process is handed off from one party to another, or where multiple parties are

TABLE 4.2
Guidelines for
Improving a Process

1. Examine each delay symbol ◗
   What causes the delay? How long is it?
   How could we reduce the delay or its impact?
2. Examine each activity symbol ▭
   Is this an unnecessary or redundant activity?
   What is the value of this activity relative to its cost?
   How can we prevent errors in this activity?
3. Examine each decision symbol ◆
   Does this step require an actual decision (e.g., "Do we want to accept this customer's order?"), or is it a simple checking activity (e.g., "Is the inventory in stock?")? If it is a checking activity, can it be automated or eliminated? Is it redundant?
4. Look for any loops (arrows that go back to a previous point in the process).
   Would we need to repeat these activities if we had no failures (e.g., cooking a new steak for a customer because the first one was cooked incorrectly)?
   What are the costs associated with this loop (additional time, resources consumed, etc.)? Can this loop be eliminated? If so, how?

involved in carrying out a process step. Too often, a lack of coordination or communication at these interface points leads to problems. Second, by visualizing the key parties involved in a process, swim lane maps often forces organizations to address the question, "Who is ultimately responsible for the success of the process?"

Figure 4.7 shows a swim lane process map for the San Diego DC order-filling process described in Example 4.1. In setting up a swim lane map, the first "lane" is usually reserved for the customer of the process. This customer can be an internal (i.e., within the company) or external customer. As Figure 4.7 shows, the order-filling process involves seven different parties, including the dealer who places the order. Furthermore, there are three parties—the sales office, internal mail, and picking clerk—that handle the order before it gets to the workers who actually do the picking. All these hand-offs and delays clearly add time and potential errors to the order-filling process.

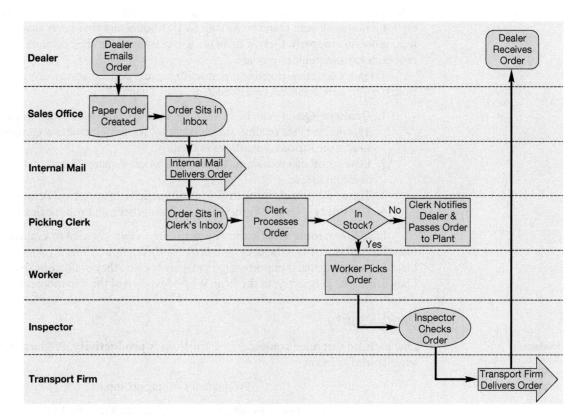

FIGURE 4.7 Swim Lane Process Map for Order-Filling Process

4.3 MANAGING AND IMPROVING BUSINESS PROCESSES

By now, you should appreciate how critical business processes are to the success of an organization. But you still might wonder how businesses should go about managing and improving these processes. For instance:

- How do we know if a business process is meeting customers' needs? Even if customers' needs are being met, how do we know whether the business process is being run efficiently and effectively?
- How should we organize for business process improvement? What steps should we follow? What roles should people play?
- What types of tools and analytical techniques can we use to rigorously evaluate business processes? How can we make sure we manage based on fact and not opinion?

Organizations have been asking these questions for years. As a result, experts have developed various measures, methodologies, and tools for managing business processes. In fact, the body of knowledge continues to evolve as more is learned about what works and what doesn't. In this section, we will introduce you to current thinking in the area.

Measuring Business Process Performance

Before we can answer the question "How is the process performing?" we must first understand what it is the customer wants and calculate objective performance information for the process. Let's reconsider the process mapping exercise in Example 4.1 for a moment. Suppose one of the San Diego DC's key customers has told DC management that:

1. All deliveries for in-stock items must be made within 8 hours from when the order was placed.
2. Order conformance quality must be 99% or higher. That is, 99% of the orders must be delivered with the right items in the right quantities.

Furthermore, the customer has told DC management that these are *order qualifiers*: If the DC cannot meet these minimum requirements, then the customer will take his business elsewhere. In Example 4.1, the DC managers determined that the time between ordering and delivery for an in-stock item could be as long as 11.3 hours and that fewer than 95% of the orders were processed properly. Clearly, there is a gap between what the customer needs and what the process is currently able to provide.

There are countless possible measures of process performance, many of which are derived from the four core measures described in detail in Chapter 2:

1. **Quality**—Quality can be further divided into dimensions such as performance quality, conformance quality, and reliability. Chapter 5 includes a comprehensive discussion of the various dimensions of quality.
2. **Cost**—Cost can include such categories as labor, material, and quality-related costs, to name just a few.
3. **Time**—Time includes such dimensions as delivery speed and delivery reliability.
4. **Flexibility**—Flexibility includes mix, changeover, and volume flexibility.

In addition, some specific measures that are frequently used to evaluate process performance are productivity, efficiency, and cycle (or throughput) time. Productivity and efficiency measures are particularly important to managers because they evaluate business process performance from the perspective of the firm. We discuss each of these in more detail.

Productivity

Productivity
A measure of process performance; the ratio of outputs to inputs.

One measure that often comes up in discussions is **productivity.** Productivity is a ratio measure, defined as follows:

$$\text{Productivity} = \text{outputs/inputs} \qquad (4.1)$$

Productivity measures are always expressed in terms of units of output per unit of input. The outputs and inputs can be expressed in monetary terms or in some other unit of measure.

In general, organizations seek to improve productivity by raising outputs, decreasing inputs, or both. Some examples of productivity measures include the following:

(Number of customer calls handled)/(support staff hours)

(Number of items produced)/(machine hours)

(Sales dollars generated)/(labor, material, and machine costs)

Single-factor productivity
A productivity score that measures output levels relative to single input.

Multifactor productivity
A productivity score that measures output levels relative to more than one input.

The first two examples represent single-factor productivity measures. **Single-factor productivity** measures output levels relative to a single input. In the first example, we are interested in the number of calls handled per support staff hour, while the second measure looks at the number of items produced per machine hour. The assumption is that there is a one-to-one relationship between the output and input of interest that can be managed. In contrast, when it's hard to separate out the effects of various inputs, **multifactor productivity** measures should be used. Look at the last example. "Sales dollars generated" is an output that depends on multiple factors, including labor, material, and machine costs. Considering just labor costs may be inappropriate, especially if labor costs could be driven down by driving up some other cost (e.g., machine costs). In situations like this, multifactor productivity measures may be preferable.

While there are some common productivity measures used by many firms, often organizations develop productivity measures that are tailored to their particular needs. Firms use productivity measures to compare their performance to that of other organizations, as well as to compare performance against historic levels or set targets.

EXAMPLE 4.2

Measuring Productivity at BMA Software

For the past 15 weeks, a project team at BMA Software has been working on developing a new software package. Table 4.3 shows the number of programmers assigned to the project each week, as well as the resulting total lines of computer code generated.

TABLE 4.3 Programming Results for the First 15 Weeks of the Project

WEEK	LINES OF CODE	NO. OF PROGRAMMERS
1	8,101	4
2	7,423	4
3	8,872	4
4	8,483	4
5	8,455	5
6	10,100	5
7	11,013	5
8	8,746	5
9	13,710	7
10	13,928	7
11	13,160	7
12	13,897	7
13	12,588	6
14	12,192	6
15	12,386	6

Susan Clarke, the project manager, has heard rumblings from other managers that her programmers aren't being as productive as they were a few weeks earlier. In order to determine whether this is true, Susan develops a measure of programmer productivity, defined as (lines of code)/(total number of programmers). Using this measure, Susan calculates the productivity numbers in Table 4.4 for the first 15 weeks of the project.

The results indicate that the programmers have actually been *more* productive over the past few weeks (weeks 13–15) than they were in the weeks just prior. In fact, the weekly productivity results for weeks 13–15 are higher than the average weekly productivity for all 15 weeks (1,992.70). Of course, Susan recognizes that there are other performance measures to consider, including the quality of the lines coded (whether they are bug-free) and the difficulty of the lines being coded (which would tend to hold down the number of lines generated).

TABLE 4.4 Productivity Results for the First 15 Weeks of the Project

WEEK	LINES OF CODE	NO. OF PROGRAMMERS	PRODUCTIVITY (LINES OF CODE PER PROGRAMMER)
1	8,101	4	2,025.25
2	7,423	4	1,855.75
3	8,872	4	2,218.00
4	8,483	4	2,120.75
5	8,455	5	1,691.00
6	10,100	5	2,020.00
7	11,013	5	2,202.60
8	8,746	5	1,749.20
9	13,710	7	1,958.57
10	13,928	7	1,989.71
11	13,160	7	1,880.00
12	13,897	7	1,985.29
13	12,588	6	2,098.00
14	12,192	6	2,032.00
15	12,386	6	2,064.33
		Average Productivity:	1,992.70

Efficiency

Efficiency
A measure of process performance; the ratio of actual outputs to standard outputs. Usually expressed in percentage terms.

While measures of productivity compare outputs to inputs, measures of **efficiency** compare *actual* outputs to some standard—specifically:

$$\text{Efficiency} = 100\% \text{ (actual outputs/standard outputs)} \qquad (4.2)$$

Standard output
An estimate of what should be produced, given a certain level of resources.

The **standard output** is an estimate of what should be produced, given a certain level of resources. This standard might be based on detailed studies or even historical results. The efficiency measure, then, indicates actual output as a percentage of the standard. An efficiency score of less than 100% suggests that a process is not producing up to its potential.

To illustrate, suppose each painter on an assembly line is expected to paint 30 units an hour. Bob actually paints 25 units an hour, while Casey paints 32. The efficiency of each painter is, therefore, calculated as follows:

$$\text{Efficiency}_{\text{Bob}} = 100\%\frac{25}{30} = 83\% \quad \text{Efficiency}_{\text{Casey}} = 100\%\frac{32}{30} = 107\%$$

Currently, Bob is performing below the standard. If his efficiency were to remain at this level, management might either intervene with additional training to raise his hourly output level or reassign Bob to another area.

EXAMPLE 4.3

Measuring Efficiency at BMA Analytics

Based on the results of her productivity study, Susan Clarke decides to set a standard for her software developers of 1,800 lines of code per developer per week. Susan consciously set the standard slightly below the average productivity figure shown in Table 4.4. Her reasoning is that she wants her developers to be able to meet the standard, even when they are dealing with particularly difficult code.

In week 16, Susan hires a new developer, Charles Turner. After five weeks on the job, Charles has recorded the results in Table 4.5.

TABLE 4.5 Programming Results for Charles Turner

WEEK	LINES OF CODE
16	1,322
17	1,605
18	1,770
19	1,760
20	1,820

Susan calculates Charles's efficiency by dividing the actual lines of code produced each week by the standard value of 1,800. Therefore, Charles's efficiency for week 16 is calculated as:

$$\text{Efficiency}_{\text{Week16}} = 100\%(1,332/1,800) = 73.4\%$$

Results for all five weeks are shown in Table 4.6.

TABLE 4.6 Efficiency Results for Charles Turner

WEEK	LINES OF CODE	EFFICIENCY
16	1,322	73.4%
17	1,605	89.2%
18	1,770	98.3%
19	1,760	97.8%
20	1,820	101.1%

Although Charles started off slowly, his efficiency has steadily improved over the five-week period. Susan is pleased with the results and recognizes that Charles needs some time to become familiar with the project. Nonetheless, she will continue to track Charles's efficiency performance.

Cycle Time

Cycle time
The total elapsed time needed to complete a business process. Also called throughput time.

The last measure of process performance we will discuss is cycle time. **Cycle time** (also called throughput time) is the total elapsed time needed to complete a business process. Many authors have noted that cycle time is a highly useful measure of process performance.[8] For one thing, in order to reduce cycle times, organizations and supply chains typically must perform well on other dimensions, such as quality, delivery, productivity, and efficiency.

Consider the order-filling process in Figures 4.6 and 4.7. In this case, cycle time is the time that elapses from when the dealer emails the order until she receives the product. Notice how the process suffers from delays due to waiting, lost orders, and incorrect orders. Therefore, in order to reduce cycle time, the San Diego DC must address these other problems as well. Notice, too, that reducing cycle times does not mean "fast and sloppy." The process cannot be considered "complete" until the dealer receives a *correctly filled* order.

A second advantage of cycle time is that it is a straightforward measure. In comparison to cost data, quality levels, or productivity measures—all of which may be calculated and interpreted differently by various process participants—the time it takes to complete a business process is unambiguous.

---

[8]J. Blackburn, *Time-Based Competition: The Next Battle Ground in American Manufacturing* (Homewood, IL: Irwin, 1991); G. Stalk and T. Hout, *Competing against Time: How Time-Based Competition Is Reshaping Global Markets* (New York: Free Press, 1990); C. Meyer, *Fast Cycle Time: How to Align Purpose, Strategy, and Structure for Speed* (New York: Free Press, 1993).

TABLE 4.7
Competitive Benchmarking Data for Selected U.S. Airline Carriers

AIRLINE CARRIER	PERCENTAGE OF FLIGHTS ARRIVING ON TIME, 12 MONTHS ENDING MARCH 2016	PERCENTAGE OF FLIGHTS CANCELLED, MARCH 2016	MISHANDLED BAGGAGE REPORTS PER 1,000 PASSENGERS, MARCH 2016
American	81.3%	0.5%	3.19
Delta	86.7%	0.1%	1.57
Frontier	77.5%	2.6%	2.62
Hawaiian	89.9%	0.1%	2.78
JetBlue	76.7%	0.5%	1.60
Southwest	81.0%	1.1%	2.65
United	79.9%	1.1%	2.58
Virgin America	79.4%	1.2%	0.82

Source: Based on U.S. Department of Transportation, "Air Travel Consumer Report," May 2016, **www.dot.gov/sites/dot.gov/files/docs/2016MayATCR.pdf.**

In addition to measuring cycle time in absolute terms, it is often useful to look at the **percent value-added time,** which is simply the percentage of total cycle time that is spent on activities that actually provide value:

Percent value-added time
A measure of process performance; the percentage of total cycle time that is spent on activities that actually provide value.

$$\text{Percent value-added time} = 100\% \text{ (value-added time)/(total cycle time)} \qquad \textbf{(4.3)}$$

For example, what is the percent value-added time for the typical "quick change" oil center? Even though the customer may spend an hour in the process, it usually takes only about 10 minutes to actually perform the work. According to Equation (4.3), then:

$$\text{Percent value-added time} = 100\% \text{ (10 minutes)/(60 minutes)} = 16.7\%$$

Of course, cycle time is not a perfect measure. Our discussion in Chapter 2 of trade-offs between performance measures applies here as well. It might not be cost-effective, for example, to drive down cycle times at the drivers' license bureau by quadrupling the number of officers (but don't you wish they would?). Therefore, organizations that use cycle time to measure process performance should also use other measures to make sure cycle time is not being reduced at the expense of some other key performance dimension.

Benchmarking

Organizations often find it helpful to compare their business processes against those of competitors or even other firms with similar processes. This activity is known as **benchmarking.** Sarah Cook defines benchmarking as "the process of identifying, understanding, and adapting outstanding practices from within the same organization or from other businesses to help improve performance."[9] Benchmarking involves comparing an organization's practices and procedures to those of the "best" in order to identify ways in which the organization or its supply chain can make improvements.

Benchmarking
According to Cook, "The process of identifying, understanding, and adapting outstanding practices from within the same organization or from other businesses to help improve performance."

Competitive benchmarking
The comparison of an organization's processes with those of competing organizations.

Process benchmarking
The comparison of an organization's processes with those of noncompetitors that have been identified as superior processes.

Some experts make a further distinction between competitive benchmarking and process benchmarking. **Competitive benchmarking** is the comparison of an organization's processes with those of competing organizations. In contrast, **process benchmarking** refers to the comparison of an organization's processes with those of noncompetitors that have been identified as having superior processes. As an example of the latter, many organizations have carefully studied Walmart's supply chain practices, even though Walmart might not be a direct competitor.

To give you an idea of the power of benchmarking, let's look at some competitive benchmarking results for the U.S. airline industry. The U.S. Department of Transportation (DOT) tracks and reports the performance of various U.S. carriers across several measures of interest to consumers, including the percentage of flights that arrive on time (within 15 minutes of schedule), the percentage of flights cancelled, and mishandled baggage reports filed per 1,000 passengers, and it reports these results at regular intervals. Table 4.7 shows March, 2016 results for a subset of U.S. carriers.

While some of these results might be due to conditions beyond the companies' control (e.g., weather), the hard-nosed nature of these data still gives carriers a clear idea of where they

---

[9]S. Cook, *Practical Benchmarking: A Manager's Guide to Creating a Competitive Advantage* (London: Kogan Page, 1995), p. 13.

TABLE 4.8
2008 Competitive Benchmarking Results for North American Automakers

MANUFACTURER	TOTAL ASSEMBLY HOURS PER VEHICLE	HOURS PER ENGINE	PRETAX PROFIT PER VEHICLE
Chrysler	21.31	3.35	−$142
Ford	22.65	4.32	−$1,467
GM	22.19	3.44	−$729
Honda	20.90	4.93	$1,641
Toyota	22.35	3.13	$922
Nissan	23.45	n/a	$1,641

Source: Based on *Harbour Report North America 2008*, Oliver Wyman, 2008.

stand relative to the competition. Whose management team do you think is happy with the results? Whose management team is not?

On the manufacturing side, Table 4.8 looks at some 2008 competitive benchmarking data that compare North American automotive plant performance across different manufacturers. The results suggest that while the productivity gap had closed between U.S. and Japanese-based manufacturers, the latter still enjoyed a significant per-vehicle profit advantage.

The Six Sigma Methodology

Of all the various approaches to organizing for business process improvement, the Six Sigma methodology arguably best represents current thinking. It certainly is popular, with many top companies, such as GE, Motorola, and Bank of America, citing it as a key element of their business strategy. Six Sigma has its roots in the quality management discipline. (Quality management is such an important topic to operations and supply chain managers that we have devoted Chapter 5 to the subject.)

The term *Six Sigma* refers to both a quality metric and a methodology. In *statistical terms*, a process that achieves Six Sigma quality will generate just 3.4 defects per 1 million opportunities (DPMO). As a *methodology* for process improvement, Six Sigma has a much broader meaning. Motorola[10] describes the **Six Sigma methodology** as:

A business improvement methodology that focuses an organization on:

- Understanding and managing customer requirements
- Aligning key business processes to achieve those requirements
- Utilizing rigorous data analysis to understand and ultimately minimize variation in those processes
- Driving rapid and sustainable improvement to business processes

Let's consider this definition for a moment. The first two points reinforce the idea that business process improvement efforts need to be driven by the needs of the customer. In this case, the "customer" can be someone inside the organization as well as someone from outside the organization. The third point emphasizes the use of rigorous data analysis tools to ensure that any diagnoses or recommendations are based on *fact* and not just opinion. Finally, there must an organizational mechanism in place for carrying out these efforts in a timely and efficient manner.

Six Sigma People. Six Sigma process improvement efforts are carried out by project teams consisting of people serving specialized roles. In the lexicon of Six Sigma, the teams consist of champions, master black belts, black belts, green belts, and team members. **Champions** are typically senior-level executives who "own" the projects and have the authority and resources needed to carry them out. This can be particularly important if a Six Sigma effort requires large investments of time or money, or if multiple functional areas or supply chain partners are affected. **Master black belts** are "fulltime Six Sigma experts who are responsible for Six Sigma strategy, training, mentoring, deployment and results."[11] These individuals often work across organizations and consult with projects on an as-needed basis, but are not permanently assigned to the projects.

Black belts are "fully-trained Six Sigma experts with up to 160 hours of training who perform much of the technical analyses required of Six Sigma projects, usually on a full-time

Six Sigma methodology According to Motorola, a business improvement methodology that focuses an organization on understanding and managing customer requirements, aligning key business processes to achieve those requirements, utilizing rigorous data analysis to understand and ultimately minimize variation in those processes, and driving rapid and sustainable improvement to business processes.

Champion A senior-level executive who "owns" a Six Sigma project and has the authority and resources needed to carry it out.

Master black belt A full-time Six Sigma expert who is "responsible for Six Sigma strategy, training, mentoring, deployment and results."

Black belt A fully trained Six Sigma expert "with up to 160 hours of training who perform[s] much of the technical analyses required of Six Sigma projects, usually on a full-time basis."

---

[10]Motorola University, **www.intrarts.com/Motorola/sigma.shtml.**
[11]J. Evans and W. Lindsay, *The Management and Control of Quality* (Mason, OH: Thomson South-Western, 2005).

PROFESSIONAL PROFILE

MILO JASSO, MERCK & CO., INC.

In his current role as interim director of supply chain at Merck's Wilson, North Carolina facility, Milo Jasso faces a number of challenges. Merck is one of the world's largest global health care companies, with products that include prescription medicines, vaccines, biologic therapies, and animal health products. The Wilson site where Milo works is a 500,000-square-foot facility that handles final packaging and distribution of solid dosage drugs for a number of other Merck plants. Because the Wilson site represents one of the last nodes in the supply chain, Milo and his team must effectively manage the business processes that "bridge the gap" between dozens of suppliers on the upstream side and Merck's fulfillment center and more than 90 different countries on the downstream side. As Milo notes, pharmaceutical distribution has some very unique challenges, some of which include:

Courtesy of Milo Jasso

- "Cold chain" distribution—Some pharmaceutical products require controlled refrigeration from the time they leave the Wilson facility until they arrive at their destination.
- Regulation—Because the Wilson facility distributes product worldwide, Milo and his team have to be on top of different regulatory requirements that may impact how products are packaged and delivered. For example, some countries require that the maximum price for a drug be included on the outside label; other countries require any artwork on the product packaging to be preapproved.
- Technology—In response to ever-increasing demands for higher product quality and safety, Merck now provides each package unit with a unique serial number.

This number will ultimately allow Merck to precisely track the location and distribution path for its products from the time they leave the plant until they arrive at their final destination. Such information will be particularly valuable in the fight against counterfeit drugs.

As with many supply chain management professionals, Milo has found his career building on skills he developed earlier. In fact, prior to his current assignment, Milo was an associate director for continuous improvement and learning. The skills he developed in this role have allowed Milo to bring a structured methodology to bear when improving processes and tackling problems. When asked what advice he would give to people entering the workforce, Milo had this to say, "If you are a new graduate, take the opportunity to gain full end-to-end knowledge of the business you are working in. The people who will be successful in the future are those who can span across the business and connect the dots."

Green belt
An individual who has some basic training in Six Sigma methodologies and tools and is assigned to a project on a part-time basis.

Team members
Individuals who are not trained in Six Sigma but are included on a Six Sigma project team due to their knowledge or direct interest in a process.

DMAIC (Define–Measure–Analyze–Improve–Control)
A Six Sigma process that outlines the steps that should be followed to improve an *existing* business process.

basis."[12] **Green belts** have some basic training in Six Sigma methodologies and tools and are assigned to projects on a part-time basis. Finally, **team members** are individuals with knowledge or direct interest in a process. While they may be included on a Six Sigma project team they are usually not trained in Six Sigma. This chapter's *Professional Profile* describes how Milo Jasso is building upon his expertise in Six Sigma to address some of the supply chain challenges facing Merck, a pharmaceutical company.

Six Sigma Processes. The Six Sigma methodology has its own specialized business processes that project teams follow. The first of these is the **DMAIC (Define–Measure–Analyze–Improve–Control)** process, which outlines the steps that should be followed to improve an *existing* business process. The steps are as follows:

Step 1: *Define* **the goals of the improvement activity.** The Six Sigma team must first clarify how improving the process will support the business, and establish performance targets. This ensures that the team doesn't waste time on efforts that will not see a pay-off to either the customer or the business.

---

[12]Ibid.

Step 2: *Measure* the existing process. The second step requires the team members to develop a basic understanding of how the process works. What are the process steps? Who are the parties who carry out or are otherwise touched by the process? How is the process currently performing? What data do we need to analyze the process and evaluate the impact of any changes?

Step 3: *Analyze* the process. Next, the Six Sigma team identifies the relationships and factors that cause the process to perform the way it does. In doing so, the team must make sure to identify the true underlying causes of the process's performance. We will talk later about two approaches for accomplishing this: cause-and-effect diagrams and the "Five Whys" approach.

Step 4: *Improve* the process. During this step, the team identifies ways to eliminate the gap between the current performance level and the performance targets established in step 1.

Step 5: *Control* the new process. The Six Sigma team must work with the individuals affected to maintain the process improvements. This may involve such activities as developing process control charts (described in Chapter 5), training workers in any new procedures, and updating information systems to monitor ongoing performance.

DMADV (Define–Measure–Analyze–Design–Verify)
A Six Sigma process that outlines the steps needed to create *completely new* business processes or products.

The second Six Sigma process **DMADV (Define–Measure–Analyze–Design–Verify),** outlines the steps needed to create *completely new* business processes or products. We review DMADV in Chapter 15.

Continuous Improvement Tools

Continuous improvement
The philosophy that small, incremental improvements can add up to significant performance improvements over time.

Organizations interested in process improvement have a broad collection of data analysis tools to help guide their efforts. Many of these tools, which first appeared in the engineering and quality management disciplines, were specifically designed to help users apply logical thinking and statistical concepts to process improvement efforts. The term **continuous improvement** refers to a managerial philosophy that small, incremental improvements can add up to significant performance improvements over time.

Already in this chapter we have talked about one continuous improvement tool: process mapping. This section highlights some additional tools: root cause analysis, cause-and-effect diagrams, scatter plots, check sheets, and Pareto charts. As the DMAIC steps suggest, firms need to follow a more formal process to make sure that they have indeed diagnosed problem(s) correctly. **Root cause analysis** is a process by which organizations brainstorm about possible causes of problems (referred to as "effects") and then, through structured analyses and data-gathering efforts, gradually narrow the focus to a few root causes. Root cause analysis fills the gap between the realization that a problem exists and the proposal and implementation of solutions to the problem.

Root cause analysis
A process by which organizations brainstorm about possible causes of problems (referred to as "effects") and then, through structured analyses and data-gathering efforts, gradually narrow the focus to a few root causes.

Organizations often divide root cause analysis into three distinct phases: open, narrow, and closed. The *open phase* is devoted to brainstorming. All team members should be free to make suggestions, no matter how far-fetched they might seem at the time. Teams often use a **cause-and-effect diagram** (also known as a *fishbone diagram* or *Ishikawa diagram*) to organize their thoughts at this stage. Figure 4.8 shows a generic format for a cause-and-effect diagram.

Cause-and-effect diagram
A graphical tool used to categorize the possible causes for a particular result.

To construct such a diagram, the team members must first describe the "effect" for which they are seeking a cause, such as late deliveries, high defect rates, or lost orders. This effect is

FIGURE 4.8
Cause-and-Effect Diagram

written on a large poster or chalkboard, at the end of a long arrow. Next, the team categorizes the possible causes and places them at the ends of branches drawn along the shaft of the arrow. These branches are often organized around five categories known as the **Five Ms:**

- **Manpower**—People who do not have the right skills, authority, or responsibility
- **Methods**—Poor business practices; poor process, product, or service designs
- **Materials**—Poor-quality inputs
- **Machines**—Equipment that is not capable of doing the job
- **Measurements**—Performance measurements that are not geared toward eliminating the problem

Five Ms
The five main branches of a typical cause-and-effect diagram: manpower, methods, materials, machines, and measurement.

EXAMPLE 4.4

Cause-and-Effect Diagram for a Pump Manufacturer

A Six Sigma team investigating variations in pump shaft dimensions at a pump manufacturer decided to develop a cause-and-effect diagram to identify the possible causes. The resulting diagram is shown in Figure 4.9. The team did not identify any potential causes along the "Measurements" branch; hence, it was left off. Notice that some of the branches are further subdivided in an effort to get to the true underlying causes. For example, "Low motivation" is listed as a possible cause under "Manpower." But why are employees unmotivated? One possible cause, "Low pay," is shown as a branch off of "Low motivation."

FIGURE 4.9 Cause-and-Effect Diagram for a Pump Manufacturer

The second phase of root cause analysis is known as the *narrow phase*. Here participants pare down the list of possible causes to a manageable number. Some teams formalize this process by using an approach called the **Five Whys.** With this approach, the team members brainstorm successive answers to the question "Why is this a cause of the original problem?" For each new answer, they repeat the question until they can think of no new answers. The last answer will probably be one root cause of the problem. The name comes from the general observation that the questioning process can require up to five rounds.

To illustrate, suppose a business is trying to understand why a major customer won't pay its bills on time. One possible explanation generated during the open phase is that, by delaying payment, the customer is getting a free loan at the business's expense ("Methods"). Using the Five Whys approach, the team members might ask the following series of questions:

Five Whys
An approach used during the narrow phase of root cause analysis, in which teams brainstorm successive answers to the question "Why is this a cause of the original problem?" The name comes from the general observation that the questioning process can require up to five rounds.

Q1: WHY does the customer use our credit as a free loan?
A1: Because there are no penalties for doing so.
Q2: WHY are there no penalties for late payment of our invoices?
A2: Because we charge no penalty fees.
Q3: WHY don't we charge penalty fees?
A3: Because we have never encountered this problem before.

Process improvement efforts must be based on facts, not opinions. Although team members may *think* they have discovered the root cause of a problem, they must verify it before moving on to a solution. In the *closed phase* of root cause analysis, the team validates the suspected root cause(s) through the analysis of available data. Three commonly used data analysis tools are scatter plots, check sheets, and Pareto charts. A **scatter plot** is a graphic representation of the relationship between two variables, typically the potential root cause and the effect of interest.

Scatter plot
A graphical representation of the relationship between two variables.

FIGURE 4.10
Example Scatter Plot Showing the Relationship between Overtime Hours (Cause) and Defect Rate (Effect)

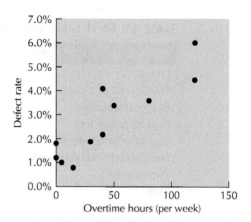

To illustrate, the scatter plot in Figure 4.10 shows how the defect rate at a manufacturer seems to increase as the amount of monthly overtime increases.

Figure 4.10 shows a strong relationship between the two variables of interest. But does the lack of a pattern in a scatter plot mean that a Six Sigma team has failed in its effort to identify a root cause? Not at all. In fact, a scatter plot that shows no relationship between a particular root cause and the effect of interest simply shortens the list of potential root causes that need to be investigated.

Check sheet
A sheet used to record how frequently a certain event occurs.

Pareto chart
A special form of bar chart that shows frequency counts from highest to lowest.

Whereas scatter plots highlight the relationship between two variables, check sheets and Pareto charts are used to assess the frequency of certain events. Specifically, **check sheets** are used to record how frequently certain events occur, and **Pareto charts** plot out the resulting frequency counts in bar graph form, from highest to lowest.

EXAMPLE 4.5

Check Sheets and Pareto Charts at Healthy Foods

Sasha Davas/Shutterstock

The Healthy Foods grocery store is attempting to isolate the root causes of unexpected delays at checkout counters. The open and narrow phases have resulted in a long list of possible causes, including the register being out of change, price checks, and customers going back to get items they forgot. In the closed phase, the quality team at Healthy Foods sets up check sheets at each checkout counter. Each time an unexpected delay occurs, the clerk records the reason for the delay. This process continues until the managers feel they have enough data to draw some conclusions. Table 4.9 shows summary results for 391 delays occurring over a one-week period.

To create the Pareto chart, the Six Sigma team ranks the causes in Table 4.9 from most frequent to least frequent and graphs the resulting data in bar graph form. The Pareto chart for Healthy Foods is shown in Figure 4.11.

TABLE 4.9 Check Sheet Results for Healthy Foods

CAUSE	FREQUENCY
Price check	142
Register out of money	14
Bagger unavailable	33
Register out of tape	44
Customer forgot item	12
Management override needed due to incorrect entry	86
Wrong item	52
Other	8
Total Delays	**391**

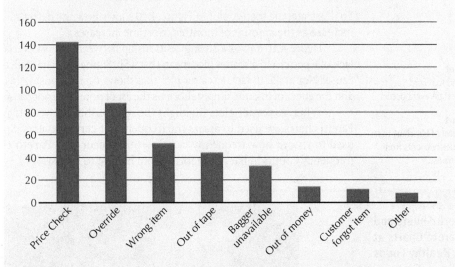

FIGURE 4.11 Pareto Chart Ranking Causes of Unexpected Delays at Checkout Counter

Run chart
A graphical representation that tracks changes in a key measure over time.

Bar graph
A graphical representation of data that places observations into specific categories.

Histogram
A special form of bar chart that tracks the number of observations that fall within a certain interval.

The check sheets and Pareto chart provide the process improvement team with some powerful information. Rather than complaining about customers who forget items (a small problem), the results suggest that Healthy Foods should instead concentrate on creating more comprehensive and accurate price lists and training clerks to properly use the cash registers. In fact, these two causes alone account for nearly 60% of the delays.

To complete our discussion of visual tools, Figure 4.12 contains examples and brief descriptions of **run charts, bar graphs,** and **histograms.**

In Example 4.6, we return to the Bluebird Café. The example demonstrates how the DMAIC process and continuous improvement tools can be used to address customer satisfaction problem.

FIGURE 4.12 Additional Data Analysis Tools

EXAMPLE 4.6

Applying DMAIC and Continuous Improvement Tools at the Bluebird Café

Katie Favre, owner of the Bluebird Café, is browsing a Web site that allows individuals to rate restaurants on a 1-to-5 scale, with 1 = "Highly Dissatisfied" and 5 = "Highly Satisfied." Katie is disappointed to learned that, based on several hundred responses, the average rating for the Bluebird Café is only 3.83 and that 12% of respondents actually rated their dining experience as a 1 or 2. Unfortunately, the Web site does not provide any specific information about *why* the customers rated the café as they did. Katie takes great pride in the reputation of the Bluebird Café, and she decides to use the DMAIC process and continuous improvement tools to tackle the customer satisfaction issue.

Step 1: *Define* the Goals of the Improvement Activity

At a meeting with the management team, Katie emphasizes the importance of customer satisfaction to the ongoing success of the business. The Bluebird Café is located in a college town and has plenty of competition; local customers can go elsewhere if they are dissatisfied, and out-of-town visitors often depend on Internet-based ratings to decide where they will dine. With this in mind, Katie and the management team set a target average rating of 4.5 or greater for any future Internet ratings, with no more than 2% of respondents giving a rating of 1 or 2.

Step 2: *Measure* the Existing Process

Katie already has a process map that identifies the major steps required to serve a customer (Figure 4.5). While this is a good start, the team feels that more data are needed. Katie spends a week measuring the time it takes to perform various activities, as well as the percentage of time certain process steps are completed correctly. Figure 4.13 shows the updated process map.

The management team also wants to know what process characteristics lead customers to rate the restaurant as satisfactory or unsatisfactory. To get this information, Katie puts together a survey card (see Figure 4.14) that is given out to a random sample

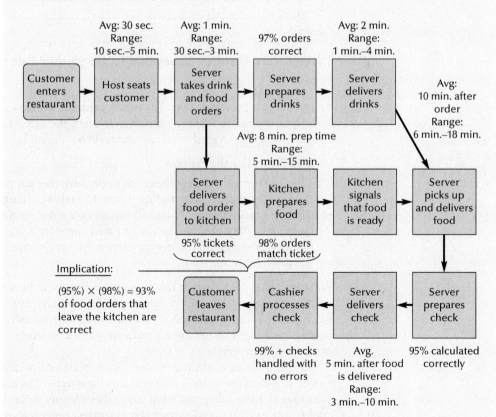

FIGURE 4.13 Process Map for Bluebird Café, Updated to Show Performance Results for Various Steps

GIVE US YOUR FEEDBACK, GET A FREE CUP OF JOE!

The Bluebird Café is always looking for ways to improve your dining experience. Please take a few moments to let us know how we are doing, and **your coffee (or tea or soda) will be on us!**

		Strongly Disagree				Strongly Agree
1.	I was seated quickly.	1	2	3	4	5
2.	My drink order was prepared correctly.	1	2	3	4	5
3.	My drink order was delivered promptly.	1	2	3	4	5
4.	My food order was prepared correctly.	1	2	3	4	5
5.	My food order was delivered promptly.	1	2	3	4	5
6.	The menu selection was excellent.	1	2	3	4	5
7.	The prices represent a good value.	1	2	3	4	5
8.	The café was clean and tidy.	1	2	3	4	5
9.	The café has a pleasant ambiance.	1	2	3	4	5

On a scale of 0–100, how would you rate your **overall satisfaction** with your dining experience?

_____

Are there any other ideas or comments you'd like to share with us?

_____

_____

_____

FIGURE 4.14 Customer Survey Card for the Bluebird Café

of customers over several weeks. The survey cards are similar to check sheets, in that they allow the customer to identify particular areas of the café's performance that they are uncomfortable with. A total of 50 customers fill out the cards.

Step 3: *Analyze* the Process

Katie and her team are now ready to begin analyzing the process in earnest. Among the tools they use are scatter plots. Figure 4.15 takes the data from the 50 survey cards and plots each customer's overall satisfaction score against his or her response to Question 4 ("My food order was prepared correctly"). Figure 4.16 is similar, except now overall satisfaction scores are plotted against Question 5 results ("My food order was delivered promptly").

Both scatter plots suggest that there is a relationship between customer satisfaction and how correctly and promptly the order is filled, but the results seem particularly strong with regard to order correctness. Put another way, whether or not the food order was prepared correctly appears to have a significant impact on whether the customer is satisfied with the dining experience.

Katie and the team now use the open phase of root cause analysis to brainstorm about possible causes of the orders being prepared incorrectly. The team documents their ideas on a cause-and-effect diagram, from which they identify some potential causes, including "cook not properly trained," "server takes incorrect order information," and "food doesn't match menu."

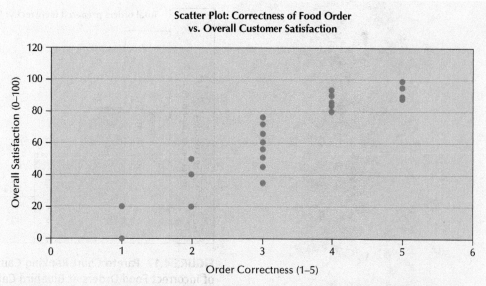

FIGURE 4.15 Scatter Plot Showing the Relationship between Survey Question 4 ("My food order was prepared correctly") and Customer's Overall Satisfaction Score

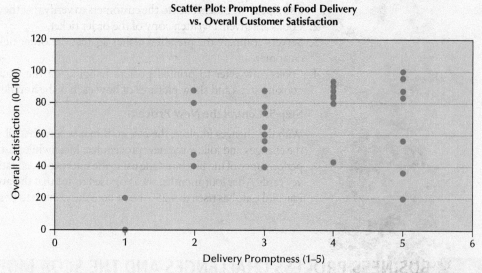

FIGURE 4.16 Scatter Plot Showing the Relationship between Survey Question 5 ("My food order was delivered promptly") and Customer's Overall Satisfaction Score

Entering the closed phase of root cause analysis, Katie develops a check sheet and, over the next few weeks, has the staff fill out these sheets each time a customer complains about an incorrect order. The check sheet data are then arranged into a Pareto chart, shown in Figure 4.17.

Step 4: *Improve* the Process

In looking at the Pareto chart, the team quickly realizes that the two highest-ranked items are really *communications* problems: The server gets the order wrong and the cook hears it incorrectly. Together, these problems account for roughly 60% of the incidences recorded. The third- and fourth-ranked items make up another 30% of the total and are tied to the failure of the kitchen staff to cook the food properly and match what's put on the plates to what's on the menu.

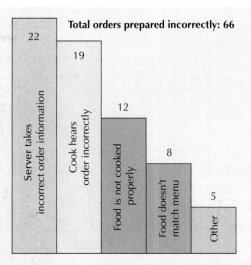

FIGURE 4.17 Pareto Chart Ranking Causes of Incorrect Food Orders at Bluebird Café

Armed with this information, the team makes some simple improvements aimed at bringing down the number of order prepared incorrectly:

1. Servers no longer take orders orally but write them down on an order ticket. The servers also repeat the orders back to the customers to verify that they have them right.
2. Cooks are given a written copy of the order ticket.
3. Servers compare the prepared dishes against the order ticket prior to taking it to the customer.
4. Cooks now refer to printed posters hanging on the wall that highlight important cooking steps and show pictures of how each dish should look.

Step 5: *Control* the New Process

With the changes in place, the café staff makes sure that all employees are familiar with the changes and follow the new procedures. Meanwhile, Katie continues to monitor the performance of the Bluebird Café using the Internet-based ratings as well as customer survey cards After four months, she is pleased to see that the average Internet rating for the Bluebird Café has risen to 4.25—not where she wants it to be, but it's on the right track.

4.4 BUSINESS PROCESS CHALLENGES AND THE SCOR MODEL

Most of the business process examples we have discussed to this point assume that we are working with a reasonably well-understood process that can be analyzed, improved, and controlled using the frameworks and tools described in Section 4.3. But this is not always true. Specifically:

- Some processes are artistic in nature. That is, they require flexibility in carrying out the various steps. Furthermore, customers actually *value* variability in the outcomes.
- Some processes may be so broken or so mismatched to the organization's strategy that only a total redesign of the process will do.
- Some processes cross organizational boundaries, which introduces additional challenges.

We talk about each of these challenges in turn.

How Standardized Should Processes Be?

According to some business experts, tools such as process mapping and the DMAIC cycle have become so popular that they have been *overused*—applied to process environments in which flexibility in the process and variability in outcomes are valued by the business and customers.

For example, while it certainly makes sense to standardize and control the process for administering intravenous drugs to a hospital patient, it makes less sense to control every step of a doctor's diagnosis process, especially when a patient has unique or unusual symptoms. To help managers understand when they should and shouldn't try to standardize processes, Joseph Hall and M. Eric Johnson developed a framework that divides processes into four main types based on (1) how much variability there is in the process and (2) whether customers actually value variability in outputs.[13]

Mass processes are perhaps the easiest to understand. Here, the goal of the process is to provide exactly the same output each time. The key to *mass customization* is *controlled* variation. For instance, when a customer orders a laptop computer from Dell, he or she can choose from a predetermined set of options. The goal is to provide some variability in output without undermining the stability of Dell's assembly operations.

At the other extreme from mass processes are *artistic processes* where *both* variability in the process and outputs are valued. A prime example would be a research and development (R&D) lab where employees are expected to use their creativity to identify new product or service opportunities. In fact, efforts to standardize R&D activities may actually interfere with the ability of a lab to generate breakthrough products or services.

The last type of process is what Hall and Johnson refer to as a *nascent, or broken process*. Unlike the other three types, processes that fall into this group have a fundamental mismatch between what the customer wants (standardized output) and what the process is currently capable of providing. Managers have two choices here: Reduce the variability of the process or switch to customers or markets that value output variability.

Business Process Reengineering (BPR)

An alternative approach to Six Sigma and the DMAIC process is **business process reengineering (BPR)**. As APICS notes, BPR is "a procedure that involves the fundamental rethinking and radical redesign of business processes to achieve dramatic organizational improvements in such critical measures of performance as cost, quality, service, and speed."[14] Proponents of BPR suggest that organizations start the BPR process with a "blank sheet" of paper rather than try to understand and modify processes that may be severely outdated or dysfunctional. Which approach a firm uses—Six Sigma or BPR—depends on several factors, including how severe the problems are with the current business process and the ability of process participants to make radical changes.

Coordinating Process Management Efforts across the Supply Chain

In Example 4.6, the Six Sigma process improvement effort was focused on the activities within a single organization, in this case a café. But many times, firms must extend their efforts to include external supply chain partners. Extending process management to include external partners is an important step, as significant opportunities for improvement often lie at the interfaces between various partners. But doing so adds greater complexity, given that multiple organizations and their representatives are now participating in the effort. The SCOR model, described next, provides one framework for understanding and managing cross-organizational supply chain processes.

The SCOR Model

We end this chapter with a discussion of the **Supply Chain Operations Reference (SCOR) model**.[15] The SCOR model is a comprehensive model of high-level business processes and detailed individual processes that together define the scope of supply chain management

---

[13]J. Hall and E. Johnson, "When Should a Process Be Art, Not Science?" *Harvard Business Review* (March 2009): 58–65.

[14]J. H. Blackstone, ed., *APICS Dictionary*, 15th ed. (Chicago, IL: APICS, 2016).

[15]SCOR Framework, **www.apics.org/apics-for-business/products-and-services/apics-scc-frameworks/scor.**

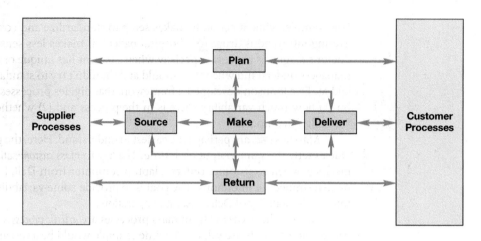

activity. The SCOR model is supported by the APICS Supply Chain Council, an industry group consisting of hundreds of companies and academics.

Why would companies spend time and money to develop a reference model such as SCOR? Actually, there are several good reasons. First, a reference model gives individuals a common language for discussing and comparing supply chain business processes. This can be especially important when benchmarking performance or coordinating with other firms to build a supply chain. Second, a reference model provides a template to guide the design and implementation of an organization's own supply chain processes. Third, seeing the processes laid out in a single, comprehensive model helps some managers better understand what supply chain management is all about.

The SCOR model looks at a firm's supply chain activities in three levels of increasing detail. Level 1 of the views SCM activities as being structured around five core management processes (Figure 4.18):

1. **Source**—Processes that procure goods and services to meet planned or actual demand.
2. **Make**—Processes that transform product to a finished state to meet planned or actual demand.
3. **Deliver**—Processes that provide finished goods and services to meet planned or actual demand. These processes include order management as well as logistics and distribution activities.
4. **Return**—Processes associated with returning or receiving returned products for any reason.
5. **Plan**—Processes that balance aggregate resources with requirements.

Level 2 processes break down level 1 activities into more detail. For example, SCOR differentiates between three types of "make" processes: make-to-stock, make-to-order, and engineer-to-order. As you might recall from our discussion in Chapter 3, make-to-stock, make-to-order, and engineer-to-order manufacturing processes differ with regard to the level of product customization and therefore require very different solutions.

Finally, SCOR level 3 processes describes in detail the actual *steps* required to execute level 2 processes. Companies can use these maps as a rough guide for developing their own unique processes or for identifying gaps. Consider the example in Figure 4.19, which shows the level 3 process map for one particular process type, "Make Engineer-to-Order Product."

The process map suggests that manufacturing an engineer-to-order product should consist of seven sequential process "elements," labeled in SCOR nomenclature as M3.1–M3.7. The map also shows the prescribed information inflows and outflows to these elements. For example, the second element, "Schedule Production Activities," should take place in response to information inflows, including the production plan, scheduled receipts, feedback from downstream "make" elements, and equipment and facilities schedules and plans. In turn, the information outflow of this element should be an updated production schedule used by the production, sourcing, and distribution areas. Note too that the entire "make engineer-to-order" process, as prescribed by the SCOR model, should contain information links to all five of the core management processes.

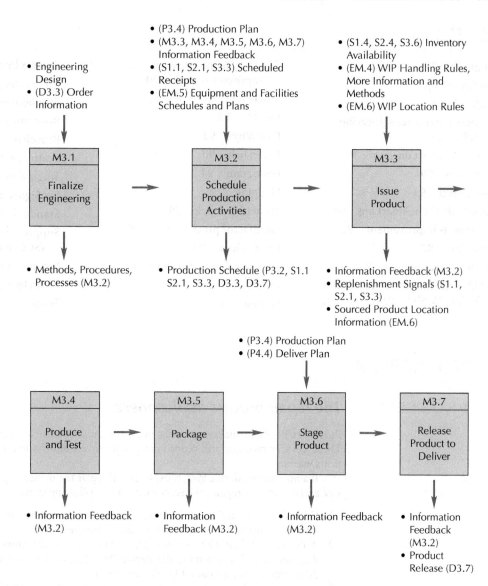

FIGURE 4.19
Detailed Process Map for SCOR's "Make Engineer-to-Order"
Source: "Phios Process Directory for SCOR," **http://repository .phios.com/SCOR/ Activity.asp?ID=5394 (Phios Corporation).**

CHAPTER SUMMARY

Although the term *business processes* has been in the management lexicon for years, not all organizations clearly understand the importance of business processes and their effects on operations and supply chain performance. In this chapter, we defined the concept of business processes and showed how the business process perspective is different from the traditional, functionally oriented view of business. Business processes change the focus from "How is the business organized?" to "What does the business do?"

Fortunately, practitioners and theorists continue to develop various tools and approaches for managing business processes.

In this chapter, we described two process mapping approaches and demonstrated how they can be used. We also spent considerable time talking about various approaches to managing and improving business processes, including performance measurement and benchmarking, the Six Sigma methodology, and continuous improvement tools. We concluded the chapter with a discussion of the SCOR model, which represents an attempt by industry partners to develop a comprehensive model of the various business processes that define supply chain management.

KEY FORMULAS

Productivity (page 84):

$$\text{Productivity} = \text{outputs}/\text{inputs} \tag{4.1}$$

Efficiency (page 86):

$$\text{Efficiency} = 100\% \,(\text{actual outputs}/\text{standard outputs}) \tag{4.2}$$

Percent value-added time (page 88):

$$\text{Percent value-added time} = 100\% \,(\text{value-added time})/(\text{total cycle time}) \tag{4.3}$$

KEY TERMS

Bar graph   94

Benchmarking   88

Black belt   89

Business process reengineering (BPR)   99

Cause-and-effect diagram   91

Champion   89

Check sheet   93

Competitive benchmarking   88

Continuous improvement   91

Cycle time   87

Development process   76

DMADV (Define–Measure–Analyze–Design–Verify)   91

DMAIC (Define–Measure–Analyze–Improve–Control)   90

Efficiency   86

Five Ms   92

Five Whys   92

Green belt   90

Histogram   94

Mapping   79

Master black belt   89

Multifactor productivity   85

Pareto chart   93

Percent value-added time   88

Primary process   76

Process   76

Process benchmarking   88

Process map   79

Productivity   84

Root cause analysis   91

Run chart   94

Scatter plot   92

Single-factor productivity   85

Six Sigma methodology   89

Standard output   86

Supply Chain Operations Reference (SCOR) model   99

Support process   76

Swim lane process map   82

Team members   90

SOLVED PROBLEM

PROBLEM

The repair process at Biosphere

Biosphere Products makes and sells environmental monitoring devices for use in industry. These devices monitor and record air quality levels and issue an alarm whenever conditions warrant.

If a monitoring device fails, Biosphere will repair the device as part of the customer's service agreement. The repair process consists of the following steps:

1. Once the device arrives at Biosphere's repair center, a work order is immediately entered into the computer system. This step takes 5 minutes.
2. A device will then wait, on average, 24 hours before a technician has a chance to run diagnostics and disassemble the device. The diagnostics procedure usually takes about 30 minutes, while disassembly takes around 1 hour.
3. Next the technician orders replacements for any broken/worn parts from the main plant. While it takes only 5 minutes to order the parts, it usually takes 48 hours for them to arrive from the main plant.
4. After the parts come in, the device will usually wait another 24 hours until a technician has time to reassemble and test the device. The reassembly and testing process takes, on average, 3 hours.
5. If the device still fails to work, the technician will repeat the process, starting with diagnostics and disassembly. The first time through, 10% of the devices aren't fixed; however, virtually all of them work by the time a second pass has been completed.
6. Once the device has been tested and passed, it is immediately boxed up (10 minutes) and a call is made to UPS, which picks up the package, usually within 1 hour.

Map Biosphere's current process. How long will it take, on average, to move a device through the system, assuming that everything "works" the first time? How long will it take if the device has to be repaired a second time? What is the percent value-added time under each scenario?

Solution

Figure 4.20 shows the process map, starting with the arrival of the device at the repair facility and ending when UPS picks it up. If the device has to be repaired only once, the total cycle time is 101 hours and 50 minutes. However, if the device has to be "repaired again," we must add another 76 hours and 35 minutes, resulting in a total cycle time of 178 hours and 25 minutes.

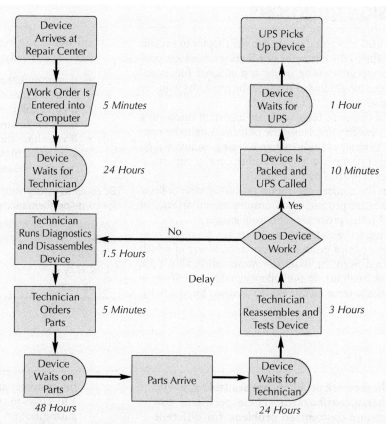

FIGURE 4.20 Process Map for Biosphere Products—Device Repair Process

It gets worse. One could argue that the only value-added activities are running the diagnostics, disassembling and reassembling the device, and testing. These activities total 4.5 hours. Therefore, if Biosphere correctly repairs the device the first time:

$$\text{Percent value-added time} = 100\% \, (4.5 \, \text{hours}/101.83 \, \text{hours}) = 4.4\%$$

If the device has to be repaired a second time:

$$\text{Percent value-added time} = 100\% \, (4.5 \, \text{hours}/178.42 \, \text{hours}) = 2.5\%$$

In other words, over 95% of the time is spent on non-value-added activities. A careful reader will notice that, in the second calculation, we didn't add in any more time for diagnostics, disassembling and reassembling the device, and testing. This was intentional: Our argument is that if these activities did not fix the device the first time, then the first pass through was *wasted* time, not value-added time.

So what should Biosphere do? Looking at the process map, it becomes clear that the vast majority of the time is spent waiting on a technician or on parts or looping through activities because a device wasn't fixed right the first time. If, for example, Biosphere could keep spare parts at the repair center, it could chop 48 hours off the cycle time. Management might also investigate why it takes technicians so long to get around to working on a device. Are they busy working on other devices, or are they involved in other activities that can wait? Management might even decide that more technicians are needed.

With regard to the relatively high failure rate of "repaired" devices, Biosphere might have to do some more detailed analysis: Are the technicians being trained properly? Are they making the same mistakes over and over again? If so, why? Clearly, Biosphere is an ideal candidate for DMAIC improvement efforts.

DISCUSSION QUESTIONS

1. Use the P&G example described in the chapter to explain the benefits to the customer of adopting a business processes perspective. Why might a traditional functional perspective have "blinded" P&G to the problems with the old system?

2. We noted that cycle time, while an important measure of process performance, is not the only measure to be considered. Give an example where focusing exclusively on reducing cycle times might hurt other, equally important, measures of process performance.

3. Consider the course registration process at your college. Is this a mass process, mass customization, artistic, or nascent/broken process? Justify your answer.

4. In the chapter, we stated that "there are countless possible measures of process performance, many of which are derived from the four core measures" quality, cost, time, and flexibility. In the following table, identify how you think the three measures we described (productivity,

efficiency, and cycle time) relate to the four core measures. Specifically:

- If you think the measure always has a positive impact on a core measure, mark the square with a "+".
- If you think the measure always has a negative impact, mark the square with "−".
- If you think the measure can have either a positive or a negative impact, depending on the circumstances, mark the square with "+/−".

Be ready to justify your answers. What are the implications for using performance measures to evaluate processes?

	QUALITY	COST	TIME	FLEXIBILITY
Productivity				
Efficiency				
Cycle time				

PROBLEMS

Additional homework problems are available at www.pearsonhighered.com/bozarth. These problems use Excel to generate customized problems for different class sections or even different students.

(* = easy; ** = moderate; *** = advanced)

Problems for Section 4.2: Mapping Business Processes

1. Billy's Hamburger Barn has a single drive-up window. Currently, there is one attendant at the window who takes the order (30–40 seconds), gathers up the food and bags it (30–120 seconds), and then takes the customer's money (30–40 seconds) before handing the food to the customer.

   a. (**) Map the current process. What is the minimum cycle time? The longest cycle time?

   b. (***) Suppose Billy's Hamburger Barn redesigns the process described in problem 11 so there are now two attendants. The first attendant takes the order. Once this step is finished, the first attendant then takes the money, and the second one gathers up and bags the food. If two of the process steps can now run in parallel (gathering the food and taking the money), what is the new minimum cycle time? What is the longest cycle time? What potential problems could arise by splitting the process across two individuals?

2. Faircloth Financial specializes in home equity loans, loans that customers can take out against the equity they have in their homes. ("Equity" represents the difference between the home's value and the amount a customer owns on any other loans.) The current process is as follows:

   - The customer downloads the loan application forms from the Web, fills them in, and mails them to Faircloth (3–5 days).
   - If there are any problems with the forms (and there usually are), a customer sales representative calls up

the customer and reviews these problems. It may take 1 to 2 days to contact the customer. After reaching the customer, resolving the problem can take anywhere from 5 minutes to 30 minutes. If the customer needs to initial or sign some new forms, it takes 5–7 days to mail the forms to the customer and have her send them back.

   - Every Monday morning, the customer sales representatives take a batch of completed, correct application forms to the loan officers. This means that if a correct loan application comes in on Tuesday, the soonest it can get to a loan officer is the following Monday. The loan officers then take 2 to 3 days to process the batch of loans, based on information on the forms and information available from credit rating bureaus. Customers are advised by email and regular mail regarding the final decision.

   a. (***) Map out the current process. Identify any rework loops and delays in the process. What causes these? What is the impact on cycle times? How might this affect customers' willingness to do business with Faircloth?

   b. (***) What changes might you recommend to redesign this process with the needs of the customer in mind? You might start by imagining how the "perfect" process would look to the customer and base your recommendations on that.

Problems for Section 4.3: Managing and Improving Business Processes

3. Marci spends 15 hours researching and writing a 20-page report for her philosophy class. Jack brags that he has a "streamlined process" for performing the researching and writing. Jack takes just 8 hours to research and write the paper, but his report is only 15 pages long.

a. (*) Calculate Marci's and Jack's productivity. What is the output? What is the input? Is this a single-factor or multifactor productivity measure?

b. (**) What are the limitations of using productivity measures to evaluate Marci's and Jack's performance? What other performance measures might the instructor use?

4. (**) Consider the output and labor hour figures shown in the following table. Calculate the labor productivity for each week, as well as the average labor productivity for all six weeks. Do any of the weeks seem unusual to you? Explain.

WEEK	OUTPUT (IN UNITS)	LABOR HOURS
1	1,850	200
2	1,361	150
3	2,122	150
4	2,638	250
5	2,599	250
6	2,867	300

5. Smarmy Sales, Inc. (SSI) sells herbal remedies through its Web site and through phone reps. Over the past six years, SSI has started to depend more and more on its Web site to generate sales. The figures below show total sales, phone rep costs, and Web site costs for the past six years:

YEAR	TOTAL SALES	PHONE REP COSTS	WEB SITE COSTS
2012	$4,790,000	$200,000	$50,000
2013	$5,750,000	$210,000	$65,000
2014	$6,900,000	$221,000	$85,000
2015	$8,280,000	$230,000	$110,000
2016	$9,930,000	$245,000	$145,000
2016	$11,920,000	$255,000	$190,000

a. (*) Calculate productivity for the phone reps for each of the past six years. Interpret the results.

b. (*) Calculate the productivity for the Web site for each of the past six years. Interpret the results.

c. (**) Compare your results in parts a and b. What are the limitations of these single-factor productivity measures?

d. (**) Now calculate a multifactor productivity score for each year, where the "input" is the total amount spent on both the phone reps and the Web site. Interpret the results. What can you conclude?

6. (*) A customer support job requires workers to complete a particular online form in 60 seconds. Les can finish the form in 70 seconds. What is his efficiency? What other performance measures might be important here?

7. (**) Precision Machinery has set standard times for its field representatives to perform certain jobs. The standard time allowed for routine maintenance is 2 hours (i.e., "standard output" = 0.5 jobs per hour). One of Precision's field representatives records the results below. Calculate the rep's efficiency for each customer and her average efficiency. Interpret the results.

CUSTOMER	ACTUAL TIME REQUIRED TO PERFORM ROUTINE MAINTENANCE
ABC Company	1.8 hours
Preztel	2.4 hours
SCR Industries	1.9 hours
BeetleBob	1.8 hours

8. Gibson's Bodywork does automotive collision work. An insurance agency has determined that the standard time to replace a fender is 2.5 hours (i.e., "standard output" = 0.4 fenders per hour) and is willing to pay Gibson $50 per hour for labor (parts and supplies are billed separately). Gibson pays its workers $35 per hour.

a. (**) Suppose Gibson's workers take 4 hours to replace a fender. What is Gibson's labor hour efficiency? Given Gibson's labor costs, will the company make money on the job?

b. (***) What does Gibson's labor hour efficiency have to be for Gibson to break even on the job? Show your work.

9. (**) When a driver enters the license bureau to have his license renewed, he spends, on average, 45 minutes in line, 2 minutes having his eyes tested, and 3 minutes to have his photograph taken. What is the percent value-added time? Explain any assumptions you made in coming up with your answer.

10. Average waiting times and ride times for two of Dizzy-World's rides are as follows:

RIDE	AVERAGE WAITING TIME	LENGTH OF RIDE	TOTAL PROCESS TIME
Magical Mushroom	30 minutes	10 minutes	40 minutes
Haunted Roller Coaster	40 minutes	5 minutes	45 minutes

a. (*) Calculate the percent value-added time for each ride.

b. (**) Now suppose DizzyWorld puts in place a reservation system for the Haunted Roller Coaster ride. Here's how it works: The customer receives a coupon that allows him to come back in 40 minutes and immediately go to the front of the line. In the meantime, the customer can wait in line and then ride the Magical Mushroom. Under this new system, what is the customer's total time waiting? Total time riding? What is the new percent-value added time?

11. Consider Example 4.1 and the accompanying Figure 4.6 from the book chapter.

a. (**) Calculate the percent value-added time for the current process. Which activities do you consider to be value added? Why?

b. (***) Suppose management actually *does* put a system in place that lets customers enter orders electronically, with this information sent directly to the picking area. Redraw the process map to illustrate the changes. What is the new cycle time for the process? What is the new percent value-added time? What do you think the impact would be on the number of lost orders? On customer satisfaction?

CASE STUDY

Swim Lane Process Map for a Medical Procedure

Figure 4.21 shows the swim lane process map for a patient undergoing a lumpectomy (the surgical removal of a small tumor from the breast). Nine parties, including the patient, were involved in the process. For many of the steps in Figure 4.21, a box has been drawn around multiple parties, indicating that two or more parties were involved in the step. For example, the "surgery" step involved three parties: the patient, the surgeon, and the hospital.

During the treatment process, the patient (who was a registered nurse) detected two errors. Error 1 occurred when the surgeon intended to employ a needle locator to identify the location of the tumor, but failed to forward an order to that effect to the hospital. The patient identified the omission prior to surgery. No harm occurred. Error 2 was a typographic error

on the pathology report indicating that the tumor was 1.6 *millimeters* diameter when in fact it was 1.6 *centimeters*. This could have been a more serious mistake, but a phone call to confirm the correction avoided any harm.

Questions

1. Who or what organization is responsible for this process from start to finish? What are the implications for managing and improving the treatment process?
2. Which process steps should be standardized? Which process steps should be more artistic? Explain.
3. Consider the errors that occurred during the treatment process. How might you use the Six Sigma methodology and continuous improvement tools to keep these errors from reoccurring? Looking ahead, what kinds of solutions might you see coming out of such an analysis?

FIGURE 4.21
Swim Lane Process Map for a Surgical Procedure
Source: John Grout, "Swim Lane," **http://facultyweb.berry.edu/jgrout/processmapping/Swim_Lane/swim_lane.html.**

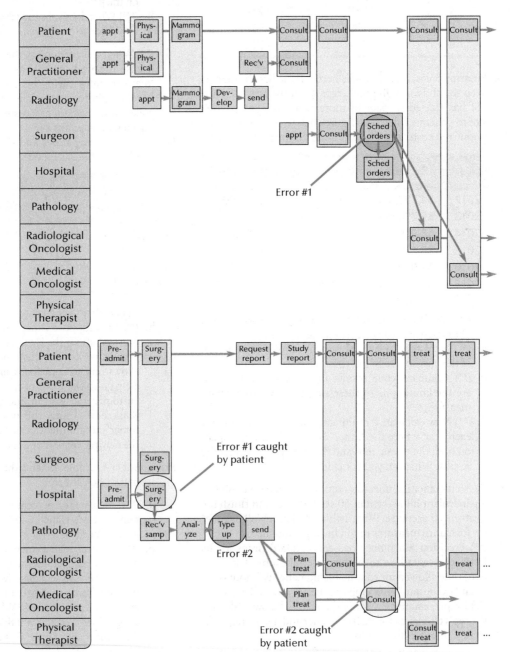

REFERENCES

Books and Articles

Andersen, B., *Business Process Improvement Toolbox* (Milwaukee, WI: ASQ Quality Press, 1999).

Blackburn, J., *Time-Based Competition: The Next Battle Ground in American Manufacturing* (Homewood, IL: Irwin, 1991).

Blackstone, J. H., ed., *APICS Dictionary*, 15th ed. (Chicago, IL: APICS, 2016).

Cook, S., *Practical Benchmarking: A Manager's Guide to Creating a Competitive Advantage* (London: Kogan Page, 1995).

Drayer, R., "Procter & Gamble's Streamlined Logistics Initiative," *Supply Chain Management Review* 3, no. 2 (Summer 1999): 32–43.

Evans, J., and W. Lindsay, *The Management and Control of Quality* (Mason, OH: Thomson South-Western, 2005).

Hall, J., and M. E. Johnson, "When Should a Process Be Art, Not Science?" *Harvard Business Review* (March 2009): 58–65.

Meyer, C., *Fast Cycle Time: How to Align Purpose, Strategy, and Structure for Speed* (New York: Free Press, 1993).

Quinn, F., "What's the Buzz? Supply Chain Management: Part 1," *Logistics Management* 36, no. 2 (February 1997): 43.

Stalk, G., and T. Hout, *Competing against Time: How Time-Based Competition Is Reshaping Global Markets* (New York: Free Press, 1990).

Tibey, S., "How Kraft Built a 'One-Company' Supply Chain," *Supply Chain Management Review* 3, no. 3 (Fall 1999): 34–42.

Internet

Grout, J., "Swim Lane," **http://facultyweb.berry.edu/jgrout/processmapping/Swim_Lane/swim_lane.html.**

Harbour Consulting, "Harbour Report North America 2006," **www.harbourinc.com.**

Motorola University, **www.motorolasolutions.com/US-EN/Home.**

Supply Chain Council, "Supply Chain Operations Reference (SCOR) Model Overview: Version 10.0," **http://supply-chain.org/f/Web-Scor-Overview.pdf.**

U.S. Department of Transportation, "Air Travel Consumer Report," May 2014, **www.dot.gov/sites/dot.gov/files/docs/2014MayATCR.pdf.**

Kiselev Andrey Valerevich / Shutterstock

CHAPTER
five

Managing Quality

CHAPTER OBJECTIVES

By the end of this chapter, you will be able to:

- Discuss the various definitions and dimensions of quality and why quality is important to operations and supply chains.

- Describe the different costs of quality, including internal and external failure, appraisal, and prevention costs.

- Describe what TQM is, along with its seven core principles.

- Calculate process capability ratios and indices and set up control charts for monitoring continuous variables and attributes.

- Describe the key issues associated with acceptance sampling, as well as the use of OC curves.

- Discuss some of the important issues associated with managing quality across the supply chain.

GETTING YOUR BAGS IS HALF THE FUN

The U.S. airline industry has experienced many changes in the past decade. Most carriers have reduced capacity in an effort to control costs, which means they're flying fewer and more crowded planes. And with many airlines tacking on extra fees to boost revenue, including charging for checked luggage, more passengers are trying to cram more of their belongings into overhead bins than ever before. In fact, some industry analysts believe nearly 60 million more bags are carried on board every year than the year before.

But plenty of bags are still being checked. How many are reaching their destinations? The U.S. Department of Transportation reported that in 2016, more than 1.7 million bags were lost or misplaced on domestic flights. That sounds like a lot, but it's actually 1.4 million *fewer* bags than were lost in 2008—just about the time most airlines adopted checked-baggage fees and inspired many passengers to start carrying their bags on board instead.

Other factors that might have helped reduce the number of lost bags are the more stringent airport security procedures being enforced by the federal government. Bags are more often scanned instead of being opened, streamlining the handling process and reducing errors. An increase in on-time arrivals has also helped, especially by reducing missed connections on multiple-leg flights. Bags checked through on connecting flights are usually the most likely to be misplaced, airlines report.

Airline executives also credit advances in technology that have helped replace labor-intensive processes with more efficient paperless ones. Bar-code scanners, long standard in the shipping industry, now help airlines track bags at several points in their journey and even let baggage workers know when they're loading something on the wrong plane. Delta Air Lines is taking it a step further, investing $50 million in radio-frequency identification (RFID) tags that will allow the airline to automatically track individual bags via 5,200 RFID readers located in 344 airports. The system will allow Delta to quickly pinpoint and resolve problems—ideally, before the customer even realizes anything is wrong.

RFID technology is just the latest investment made by Delta to improve its baggage-handling process. In 2006, Delta was near the bottom of the industry in terms of baggage-handling performance. In response, Delta made a $100 million investment in the baggage-handling systems at its largest hub, Atlanta's Hartsfield-Jackson International Airport. Conveyor belts and optical scanners, monitored from a central control room equipped with video screens, shortened the time it took bags to travel between five different terminals; what used to take 15 to 30 minutes was reduced to 10 minutes or less. A simple change to wider belts helped cut the number of conveyor jams in half, and four control-room employees were always on hand, prepared to tackle any trouble spots on the 14-mile system.

Figure 5.1 shows the impact of these changes on Delta's performance: The number of mishandled bags per 1,000 passengers fell from 9 in August 2006 to 2.11 in July 2016.

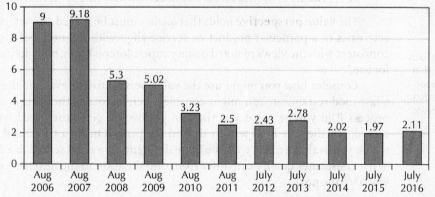

FIGURE 5.1 Decreasing the Number of Mishandled Bags at Delta Air Lines, 2006–2016

While Delta's performance is now better than the industry average of 2.72 bags, it still trails Virgin Airlines, which had the best performance at just 1.03 mishandled bags per 1,000 passengers. It's important to note that it is not just the customer who takes a hit if a bag is lost—according to the International Air Transport Association, the average lost bag generates an additional $100 in handling costs for the *airline.*

Sources: Based on "How Delta Is Trying to Fix the Problem of Lost and Delayed Luggage," *Los Angeles Times,* August 31, 2016, www.latimes.com/business/la-fi-lost-luggage-delta-20160831-snap-story.html.
Joe Sharkey, "Since Sept. 11, Years of Change for Airlines," *New York Times,* September 6, 2011, p. B6, www.nytimes.com.
"Keep Tabs on Your Bags on Delta's Website," August 28, 2011, *The Record,* NorthJersey.com.
Scott McCartney, "Better Odds of Getting Your Bags," *Wall Street Journal,* December 2, 2010, http://online.wsj.com.
U.S. Department of Transportation, Air Travel Consumer Reports, www.transportation.gov/airconsumer/air-travel-consumer-reports.

INTRODUCTION

Quality has been a mainstay of the operations and supply chain areas for nearly a century. Quality is a broad and complex topic, covering everything from companywide practices to the application of specific statistical tools. The purpose of this chapter is to give you an overview of the different perspectives on quality in today's business environment, as well as some of the tools and techniques companies use to improve and monitor quality levels.

Because the topic of quality is so broad, we have deliberately organized this chapter to flow from high-level descriptions of quality issues to more detailed tools and techniques for controlling quality. As you go through this chapter, pay attention to the flow from high-level perspectives to specific tools and techniques. Wherever you end up in an organization, you will be required to discuss and understand quality issues at *all* these levels. You may also notice that there are strong similarities between quality management and business process management, which was the focus of Chapter 4. This is no accident: Many of the perspectives, tools, and techniques used to manage business processes first appeared in the quality management area.

5.1 QUALITY DEFINED

When we talk about quality, it's important to realize that there are really two distinct, yet mutually dependent, perspectives on quality: the *value perspective* and the *conformance perspective.* The American Society for Quality recognizes this dichotomy in its two-part definition of **quality:**[1]

Quality
(a) The characteristics of a product or service that bear on its ability to satisfy stated or implied needs. (b) A product or service that is free of deficiencies.

1. The characteristics of a product or service that bear on its ability to satisfy stated or implied needs [the value perspective]
2. A product or service that is free of deficiencies [the conformance perspective]

Value perspective
A quality perspective that holds that quality must be judged, in part, by how well the characteristics of a particular product or service align with the needs of a specific user.

The **value perspective** holds that quality must be judged, in part, on how well the characteristics of a particular product or service align with the needs of a specific user. This is consistent with the views of noted quality expert Joseph Juran, who defined quality as "fitness for use."[2]

Consider how you might use the value perspective to evaluate the quality of a meal at a fast-food restaurant. You might consider such factors as the accuracy of the order-filling process (Did you get what you thought you would get?), the speed with which you were served, whether the food was fresh, and the price. On the other hand, the dimensions by which you evaluate quality will be quite different for a meal served in a four-star restaurant. What constitutes quality can differ from one situation to the next, as well as from one individual to the next.

[1] American Society for Quality, "Quality Glossary," **https://asq.org/quality-resources/quality-glossary/q.**
[2] J. DeFeo, and J. M. Juran, eds., *Juran's Quality Handbook,* 7th ed. (San Francisco: McGraw-Hill, 2016).

In an effort to provide some structure to the value perspective, David Garvin of the Harvard Business School identified eight dimensions on which users evaluate the quality of a product or service:[3]

1. *Performance.* What are the basic operating characteristics of the product or service?
2. *Features.* What extra characteristics does the product or service have, beyond the basic performance operating characteristics?
3. *Reliability.* How long can a product go between failures or the need for maintenance?
4. *Durability.* What is the useful life for a product? How will the product hold up under extended or extreme use?
5. *Conformance.* Was the product made or service performed to specifications?
6. *Aesthetics.* How well does the product or service appeal to the senses?
7. *Serviceability.* How easy is it to repair, maintain, or support the product or service?
8. *Perceived quality.* What is the reputation or image of the product or service?

Table 5.1 illustrates how these dimensions might be applied to both a manufactured good and a service.

As Table 5.1 indicates, not all of the dimensions will be relevant in all situations, and the relative importance will vary from one customer to the next. Furthermore, Garvin's list should really be viewed as a starting framework. There may be other dimensions of quality that would be unique to specific business situations.

While the value-based perspective on quality focuses on accurately capturing the end user's needs, the **conformance perspective** focuses on whether or not a product was made or a service was performed *as intended*. Conformance quality is typically evaluated by measuring the actual product or service against some preestablished standards.

Look again at Table 5.1. "Number of defects in the car" and "number of mistakes on the tax return" are two measures of conformance quality. A defect or mistake, by definition, means that the product or service failed to meet specifications. From these two perspectives on quality, we can start to see what an organization must do in order to provide high-quality products and services to users. Specifically, the organization must:

1. Understand what dimensions of quality are most important to users.
2. Develop products and services that will meet the users' requirements.
3. Put in place business processes capable of meeting the specifications driven by the users' requirements.
4. Verify that the business processes are indeed meeting the specifications.

Conformance perspective
A quality perspective that focuses on whether or not a product was made or a service was performed *as intended*.

TABLE 5.1
Dimensions of Quality for a Good and a Service

QUALITY DIMENSION	NEW CAR	TAX PREPARATION SERVICE
Performance	Tow capacity; maximum number of passengers	Cost and time to prepare taxes
Features	Accessories; extended warranty	Advance on refund check; automatic filing
Reliability	Miles between required major service visits	Not applicable
Durability	Expected useful life of the engine, transmission, body	Not applicable
Conformance	Number of defects in the car	Number of mistakes on the tax return
Aesthetics	Styling, interior appearance, look and feel of instrumentation	Neatness of the return; manner of presentation to the customer
Serviceability	Are there qualified mechanics in the area? What are the times and costs for typical maintenance procedures?	Will the tax preparation firm talk with the IRS in case of an audit?
Perceived quality	How do prices for used vehicles hold up?	What is the reputation of the firm?

[3]D. Garvin, "Competing on the Eight Dimensions of Quality," *Harvard Business Review* 65, no. 6 (November–December 1987): 101–109.

Consider Steve Walton's experiences with Decatur Trust Bank (see Example 5.1) in light of these four points. By keeping the bank open on Saturdays and offering a wide range of customer services, Decatur Trust seems to have done a fair job on the first two points—understanding the dimensions of quality important to users and developing services to meet them. However, on the other two points, Decatur Trust falls really short. No signs were in place to guide customers to the correct line or waiting area, and Decatur Trust failed to provide adequate training to the staff on hand. As a result, Steve Walton had to wait an excessively long time, and even then his IRA certificate was filled out incorrectly.

EXAMPLE 5.1
Decatur Trust Bank

Recently, the management at Decatur Trust Bank decided to keep its branch offices open on Saturday mornings. Only selected services would be offered, including withdrawals and deposits, the opening of new checking accounts, the purchase of certificates of deposit (CDs), and the establishment of individual retirement accounts (IRAs).

One Saturday morning, Steve Walton arrived at the bank. He wanted to (1) cash in a $2,000 CD that had matured; (2) withdraw $1,000 from his checking account; and (3) roll the combined $3,000 into an IRA, to be credited against his 2019 taxes. No signs were posted to indicate which employees could offer these specific services. After waiting in line for 10 minutes to see a teller, Steve learned that one of the two employees seated at desks would need to take care of his transactions. There was no formal waiting area for customers who wanted to see those employees. After two customers walked in front of Steve and obtained service, he finally spoke up and requested that he be served next.

After sitting down, Steve explained the three transactions he wanted to make to the employee, Nina Lau. Nina hesitated and then told Steve she had never opened an IRA before. When Steve suggested that someone else help him, Nina said there would not be a problem; if she made a mistake, the bank had up to seven days to correct it. Someone would call Steve about the matter.

Nina began to fill out various documents, repeatedly asking other employees for help. After she did 35 minutes of paperwork, including changes, additions, and deletions, Steve became visibly annoyed. Nina sensed his displeasure and became nervous. She apologized for the delay, explaining, "They told me to sit here today, but they never explained what I was supposed to do."

Nina finally finished the paperwork and handed it to Steve. Looking over the documents, he could not find any indication that his deposit was supposed to apply to his 2019 taxes. He asked Nina about the omission, but she didn't think it would make a difference. Steve then insisted that someone else review the document. When Jim Young, the bank manager, looked at it, he agreed that "IRA-2019" should be typed across the top of the form. As Steve got up to leave, over an hour after he had arrived, Nina assured him once again that he needn't worry about mistakes because they could be corrected within a week.

Pavel Losevsky/Fotolia

On Tuesday, Steve received an email from Nina, stating: "When you purchased the above-referenced IRA on Saturday, December 8, the certificate was inadvertently printed with both your name and your wife's. This, of course, is not permissible on an IRA. Please bring the original certificate in to the bank, and we will create a new one for you. This will not affect the account in any way."

5.2 TOTAL COST OF QUALITY

Internal failure costs
Costs caused by defects that occur prior to delivery to the customer, including money spent on repairing or reworking defective products, as well as time wasted on these activities.

External failure costs
Costs incurred by defects that are not detected until a product or service reaches the customer.

Appraisal costs
Costs a company incurs for assessing its quality levels.

Prevention costs
The costs an organization incurs to actually prevent defects from occurring to begin with.

Total cost of quality curve
A curve that suggests that there is some optimal quality level, Q^*. The curve is calculated by adding costs of internal and external failures, prevention costs, and appraisal costs.

Pioneers in the quality area attempted to quantify the benefits associated with improving quality levels. One such pioneer was Joseph Juran, who edited the widely recognized *Quality Handbook*.[4] Juran argued that there are four quality-related costs: internal failure costs, external failure costs, appraisal costs, and prevention costs.

Internal failure costs are costs caused by defects that occur prior to delivery to the customer, including money spent on repairing or reworking defective products (or scrapping them if they are completely ruined), as well as time wasted on these activities. As you might have guessed, this cost is not small. A *BusinessWeek* study[5] once found that the typical American factory spent 20% to 50% of its operating budget on finding and fixing mistakes. In fact, as many as one out of four factory employees didn't produce anything new that year because they were too busy reworking units not done right the first time.

If defects are not detected until a product or service reaches the customer, the organization incurs an **external failure cost.** These costs are difficult to estimate, but they are inevitably large, for they include not only the cost of fixing the problem, but also the costs of lost future business and, in some cases, costly litigation. Consider the opening case for this chapter, which estimated the cost of mishandling a *single* bag at $100.

Balanced against failure costs are appraisal and prevention costs. **Appraisal costs** are costs a company incurs for assessing its quality levels. Typical appraisal costs are the costs for inspections, the sampling of products or services, and customer surveys.

Note that appraising quality is *not* the same as preventing defects. For example, a manufacturer might inspect goods before they are shipped, but unless it takes steps to *improve* the production process, defect levels will not change. In contrast, **prevention costs** refer to the costs an organization incurs to actually prevent defects from occurring in the first place. Examples include the costs for employee training, supplier certification efforts, and investment in new processes, not to mention equipment maintenance expenditures. Figure 5.2 shows how these various costs behave as defect levels decrease.

According to Figure 5.2, as the level of defects is reduced from 100% to 0%, internal and external failure costs fall to zero, and prevention costs rise exponentially. The rationale behind the steeply rising prevention costs is as follows: As the defect level drops, it becomes even harder to find and resolve the remaining quality problems. You can see this effect in Figure 5.1; after making quick, significant reductions in the number of mishandled bags between 2007 and 2012, Delta Air Lines is having to spend millions of dollars more to get slight improvements in the numbers. Notice, too, that appraisal costs are flat across the various defect levels, as there is no direct relationship between appraising quality and defect levels. Therefore, while appraising quality levels may be necessary, appraisal by itself will not improve quality.

When we add internal and external failure, prevention, and appraisal costs together, we get a **total cost of quality curve.** This curve suggests that there is some optimal quality level, Q^*, that minimizes the total cost of quality. For defect levels higher than this level, exponentially increasing failure costs cause total quality costs to rise; for defect levels below Q^*, increases in prevention costs outstrip decreases in failure costs.

But as Juran continued his work, he began to notice something that contradicted the pattern shown in Figure 5.2. In particular, Juran noticed that as a business's processes improved

---

[4]Now in its seventh edition. See Note 2.
[5]D. Greising, "Quality: How to Make It Pay," *BusinessWeek* (August 8, 1994): 54–59.

FIGURE 5.2
Total Cost of Quality
(Traditional View)

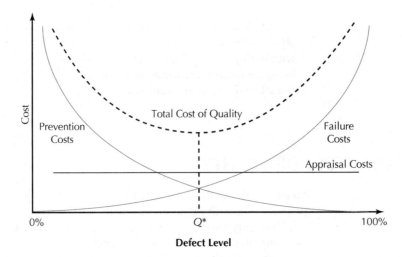

FIGURE 5.3
Total Cost of Quality
(Zero Defects View)

to the point where products and services were defect-free, the cost of appraisal fell. In effect, there was no need to inspect products or services for defects. Furthermore, prevention costs held steady (or even decreased) as managers and employees became more skillful at identifying and resolving problems. With the changing appraisal and prevention cost curves, the total cost of quality curve began to look more like the one in Figure 5.3. Note that in this graph, the lowest total cost of quality occurs at the 0% defects level.

But how could this be? Let's consider an example from industry. Many companies have supplier certification programs in which they work with key suppliers to improve the quality of purchased goods. As the suppliers become better at providing high-quality goods, the purchasing companies do not need to spend as much money on appraising the quality of incoming shipments. Furthermore, good-quality practices become embedded in the supplier's business processes, and prevention costs hold steady or even decrease as quality levels improve. Moving to the left on Figure 5.3 is not always easy, but as the total cost curve suggests, it can pay off in the long term.

5.3 TOTAL QUALITY MANAGEMENT

Of course, quality management involves more than just managing to the "optimum" defect level. As we noted earlier, to fully address both the value and the conformance perspectives on quality, organizations must:

1. Understand what dimensions of quality are most important to users.
2. Develop products and services that will meet the users' requirements.

3. Put in place business processes capable of meeting the specifications driven by the users' requirements.
4. Verify that the business processes are indeed meeting the specifications.

To accomplish this, all individuals within an organization must address quality within all of an organization's business processes. From design through purchasing, manufacturing, and distribution, an organization must have processes and people capable of delivering quality products and services.

This managerial approach is often referred to as total quality management. **Total quality management (TQM)** is the management of an entire organization so that it excels in all quality dimensions that are important to customers. TQM is such a broad concept that students often have a hard time understanding what it is. Indeed, one way to think about TQM is as a business philosophy centered around seven core ideas, or *principles*:

1. Customer focus
2. Leadership involvement
3. Continuous improvement
4. Employee empowerment
5. Quality assurance
6. Supplier partnerships
7. Strategic quality plan

Customer Focus. TQM starts with employees who are willing to place themselves in the customers' shoes. If employees do not understand how customers really feel about a product or service, they risk alienating customers. In some cases, an employee might not have direct contact with an *external* customer. But every employee has a "customer" whose expectations must be met, even if that customer is *internal* to the organization.

Total quality management (TQM)
A managerial approach in which an entire organization is managed so that it excels in all quality dimensions that are important to customers.

EXHIBIT 5.1

The Malcolm Baldrige National Quality Award

The Malcolm Baldrige National Quality Award is given annually by the president of the United States to business, education, and health care organizations that apply and are judged to be outstanding in five key areas:

* Product and process outcomes
* Customer outcomes
* Workforce outcomes
* Leadership and governance outcomes
* Financial and market outcomes

Congress established the award program in 1987 to recognize U.S. organizations for their achievements in quality and performance and to raise awareness about the importance of quality and performance excellence. The U.S. Commerce Department's National Institute of Standards and Technology (NIST) manages the Baldrige National Quality Program, in close cooperation with the private sector. The Baldrige performance excellence criteria are a framework that any organization can use to improve overall performance.

Source: Based on "Baldrige Performance Excellence Program: Malcolm Baldrige National Quality Award," **www.nist.gov/baldrige/baldrige-award.**

Leadership Involvement. If companies are serious about adopting a TQM mind-set, then change must begin at the top. Managers should carry the message that quality counts to everyone in the company. To inspire and guide managers, W. Edwards Deming presented "Fourteen Points for Management," a set of guidelines for managers to follow if they are serious about improving quality:[6]

1. Demonstrate consistency of purpose toward product improvement.
2. Adopt the new philosophy [of continuous improvement].

---
[6]W. E. Deming, *Quality, Productivity, and Competitive Position* (Boston: MIT Center for Engineering Study, 1982).

3. Cease dependence on mass inspection; use statistical methods instead.
4. End the practice of awarding business on the basis of price tag.
5. Find and work continually on problems.
6. Institute modern methods of training.
7. Institute modern methods of supervision.
8. Drive out fear—promote a company-oriented attitude.
9. Break down barriers between departments.
10. Eliminate numerical goals asking for new levels of productivity without providing methods.
11. Eliminate standards prescribing numerical quotas.
12. Remove barriers that stand between the hourly worker and his right to pride of workmanship.
13. Institute a program of education and retraining.
14. Create a corporate and management structure that will promote the above 13 points.

In promoting his ideas, Deming stressed that managers bear the ultimate responsibility for quality problems. To succeed, they must focus on the entire organization to excel in all dimensions that are important to the customer.

Continuous improvement
A principle of TQM that assumes there will always be room for improvement, no matter how well an organization is doing.

Continuous Improvement. **Continuous improvement** means never being content with the status quo but assuming that there will always be room for improvement, no matter how well an organization is doing. Think again about the opening case: While the number of mishandled bags on U.S. domestic flights has improved dramatically over the last 10 years, there were still 1.7 million bags lost or mishandled in 2016. With failure costs at $100 per bag, that's *$170 million* in lost value to the airlines.

Employee empowerment
Giving employees the responsibility, authority, training, and tools necessary to manage quality.

Employee Empowerment. Prior to TQM, the traditional business view has been that the executives at the top of a company do the thinking, the middle managers do the supervising, and the remaining employees are paid to work, not to think. However, in a TQM organization, quality is everybody's job, from the CEO to the entry-level employees. **Employee empowerment** means giving employees the responsibility, authority, training, and tools necessary to manage quality. An excellent example of this is training employees in the Six Sigma methodology and continuous improvement tools described in Chapter 4.

Quality assurance
The specific actions firms take to ensure that their products, services, and processes meet the quality requirements of their customers.

Quality function deployment (QFD)
A technique used to translate customer requirements into technical requirements for each stage of product development and production.

Quality Assurance. **Quality assurance** refers to the specific actions a firm takes to ensure that its products, services, and processes meet the quality requirements of its customers. Quality assurance activities take place throughout the organization. For example, during the product design phase, many companies use a technique called **quality function deployment (QFD)** to translate customer requirements into technical requirements for each stage of product development and production. (See Chapter 15 for a more detailed discussion of QFD.)

Another approach that falls under the quality assurance banner is **statistical quality control (SQC),** which we will describe in detail later in the chapter. SQC uses basic statistics to help organizations measure quality levels. Other quality assurance efforts can include "errorproofing," which is the deliberate design of a process to eliminate the possibility of an error, and quality auditing of suppliers by carefully trained teams.

Statistical quality control (SQC)
The application of statistical techniques to quality control.

Supplier Partnerships. As you would expect, companies must extend their TQM efforts to include supply chain partners. If members of the supply chain do not share the same commitment to TQM, quality will suffer because suppliers' materials and services ultimately become part of the company's product or service. To ensure that suppliers are willing to meet expectations, managers must monitor their performance carefully and take steps to ensure improvement, when necessary.

Strategic quality plan
An organizational plan that provides the vision, guidance, and measurements to drive the quality effort forward and shift the organization's course when necessary.

Strategic Quality Plan. TQM cannot be achieved without significant, sustained efforts over time. A well-developed **strategic quality plan** provides the vision, guidance, and measurements to drive the quality effort forward and shift the organization's course when necessary. Such a plan generally extends several years into the future and stipulates a broad set of objectives. However, it should also establish measurable quarterly (three-month) goals for the short term.

Every quarter, executives should review the company's quality performance against its goals and take action to sustain successes and remedy failures. Cross-functional teams consisting of process owners then implement their action plans. Process owners are held responsible for achieving specific goals by certain dates, and at every team meeting, members measure their progress against preestablished measures and deadlines.

TQM and the Six Sigma Methodology

As you read through the previous section, you might have noticed a lot of overlap between TQM and the Six Sigma methodology, which we introduced in Chapter 4. Some practitioners and researchers have even gone as far as to say that TQM is passé and has been replaced by Six Sigma. But this is misleading; the fundamental principles behind TQM took decades to develop and are still valid today. The main differences are:

- TQM is a managerial approach in which the entire organization is managed so that it excels in all quality dimensions that are important to customers. The "seven core principles" of TQM and Deming's 14 points illustrate the approach.
- The Six Sigma methodology builds on TQM and makes use of both the TQM philosophy and continuous improvement tools.
- Six Sigma includes *specific* processes for guiding process improvement and new process/product development efforts. The first of these, *DMAIC (Define–Measure–Analyze–Improve–Control)*, outlines the steps that should be followed to improve *existing* business processes. The second, *DMADV (Define–Measure–Analyze–Design–Verify)*, outlines the steps needed to create *completely new* business processes or products. DMAIC is described in Chapter 4; DMADV is discussed in Chapter 15.
- Six Sigma defines specific organizational roles and career paths. We discussed five of them in Chapter 4: champions, master black belts, black belts, green belts, and team members.
- Six Sigma has an expanded tool kit that includes computer simulation, optimization modeling, data mining, and other advanced analytical techniques. Typically, master black belts and black belts provide teams with the expertise required to use these tools.

Put another way, TQM encapsulates the managerial vision behind quality management; Six Sigma builds on this to provide organizations with the processes, people, and tools required to carry out this vision.

5.4 STATISTICAL QUALITY CONTROL

At the start of the chapter, we noted that organizations must:

1. Understand what dimensions of quality are most important to users.
2. Develop products and services that will meet the users' requirements.
3. Put in place business processes capable of meeting the specifications driven by the users' requirements.
4. Verify that the business processes are indeed meeting the specifications.

Statistical quality control (SQC) is directly aimed at the fourth issue—making sure that a business's current processes are meeting the specifications. Simply put, SQC is the application of statistical techniques to quality control. In this section, we describe some popular SQC applications and illustrate how basic statistical concepts can be applied to quality issues.

Process Capability

How does an organization know whether or not its business processes are capable of meeting certain quality standards? One-way organizations do this by comparing the requirements

Process capability ratio (C_p)
A mathematical determination of the capability of a process to meet certain quality standards. A $C_p \geq 1$ means the process is capable of meeting the standard being measured.

placed on a process to the actual outputs of the process. One simple measure of process capability is the **process capability ratio (C_p):**

$$C_p = \frac{UTL - LTL}{6\sigma} \qquad (5.1)$$

where:

UTL = upper tolerance limit

LTL = lower tolerance limit

σ = process standard deviation for the variable of interest

Upper tolerance limit (UTL)
The highest acceptable value for some measure of interest.

Lower tolerance limit (LTL)
The lowest acceptable value for some measure of interest.

The **upper tolerance limit (UTL)** and **lower tolerance limit (LTL)** (sometimes called the upper and lower specification limits) indicate the acceptable range of values for some measure of interest, such as weight, temperature, or time. Engineering, customers, or some other party typically sets UTL and LTL values. In contrast, σ is the standard deviation of the process with regard to the same measure. Because the true value of σ is rarely known, it is typically estimated from a sample of observations. This estimated value, $\hat{\sigma}$, is calculated as follows:

$$\hat{\sigma} = \sqrt{\frac{\sum_{i=1}^{n} (\overline{X} - X_i)^2}{n-1}} \qquad (5.2)$$

where:

$\overline{X}$ = sample mean

X_i = value for the ith observation

n = sample size

Wider tolerance limits and/or smaller values of σ will result in higher C_p values, while narrower tolerance limits and/or larger σ values will have the opposite result. Thus, higher C_p values indicate a more capable process.

To illustrate, suppose that the output values of a process are normally distributed. If this is the case, statistical theory says that individual observations should fall within $\pm 3\sigma$ of the process mean, μ, 99.7% of the time. The normal distribution given in Figure 5.4 illustrates this idea.

Now suppose that the difference between the upper and lower tolerance limits ($UTL - LTL$) just happens to equal 6σ. This suggests that the process is capable of producing within the tolerance limits 99.7% of the time and $C_p = 1$. However, if the tolerance limits are tighter than 6σ, $C_p < 1$ (Figure 5.5).

FIGURE 5.4
Normal Distribution

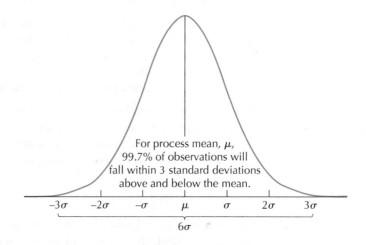

For process mean, μ, 99.7% of observations will fall within 3 standard deviations above and below the mean.

-3σ -2σ $-\sigma$ μ σ 2σ 3σ

6σ

FIGURE 5.5
C_p Values for Different Tolerance Limits

MyLab Operations Management
Animation

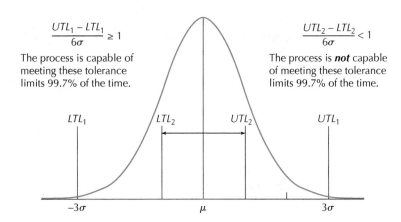

In some cases, the process mean, μ, is not exactly centered on the target value. In this case, we use the **process capability index (C_{pk})** to determine whether the process is capable of meeting the tolerance limits 99.7% of the time:

Process capability index (C_{pk})
A mathematical determination of the capability of a process to meet certain tolerance limits.

$$C_{pk} = \min\left[\frac{\mu - LTL}{3\sigma}, \frac{UTL - \mu}{3\sigma}\right] \tag{5.3}$$

where:

μ = process mean
UTL = upper tolerance limit
LTL = lower tolerance limit
σ = standard deviation

EXAMPLE 5.2

Calculating and Interpreting the Process Capability Ratio at Big Bob's Axles

Big Bob's Axles has a customer that requires axles with a diameter of 25 cm ± 0.02 cm. The customer has stated that Big Bob must be able to meet these requirements 99.7% of the time in order to keep the business. Currently, Big Bob is able to make axles with a process mean of exactly 25 cm and a standard deviation of 0.005 cm. Is Big Bob capable of meeting the customer's needs?

Notice that the UTL and LTL are 25.02 cm and 24.98 cm, respectively. Therefore, the process capability ratio is:

$$C_p = \frac{UTL - LTL}{6\sigma} = \frac{25.02 - 24.98}{6(0.005)} = \frac{0.04}{0.03} = 1.33$$

Because the process capability ratio is greater than 1, Big Bob's process is more than capable of providing 99.7% defect-free axles.

EXAMPLE 5.3

Calculating and Interpreting the Process Capability Index at Milburn Textiles

Engineers at Milburn Textiles have developed the following specifications for an important dyeing process:

Target value = 140 degrees
Upper tolerance limit (UTL) = 148 degrees
Lower tolerance limit (LTL) = 132 degrees

The UTL and LTL are based on the engineers' observations that results are acceptable as long as the temperature remains between 132 and 148 degrees. Currently, the dyeing process has a mean temperature of 139.8 degrees, with a standard deviation of 2.14 degrees. Because the process mean is slightly off from the target value of 140 degrees, the quality team uses the process capability index to evaluate the capability of the process:

$$C_{pk} = \min\left(\frac{\mu - LTL}{3\sigma}, \frac{UTL - \mu}{3\sigma}\right)$$

$$= \min\left(\frac{139.8 - 132}{3(2.14)}, \frac{148 - 139.8}{3(2.14)}\right)$$

$$= \min(1.21, 1.28) = 1.21$$

Even with the process mean being off-center, the process is still capable of meeting the tolerance limits more than 99.7% of the time.

Six Sigma Quality

Six Sigma quality
A level of quality that indicates that a process is well controlled. The term is usually associated with Motorola, which named one of its key operational initiatives Six Sigma Quality.

In this book, we have already talked about the Six Sigma methodology; now we turn our attention to the quality measure of the same name. The idea behind **Six Sigma quality** is to reduce the variability of a process to such a point that the process capability ratio is greater than or equal to 2:

$$\text{Six Sigma quality } C_p = \frac{UTL - LTL}{6\sigma} \geq 2$$

Notice that this is the same as squeezing 12 or more standard deviations between the tolerance limits. For a *perfectly* centered process with normally distributed output, this translates into around *2 defects per billion* (Figure 5.6).

In reality, most processes are not perfectly centered, resulting in a higher number of observations falling outside the tolerance limits. Practitioners, therefore, use a working definition of Six Sigma quality that allows for a possible shift in the process mean of ±1.5 standard deviations. The effect is to increase the allowable defect level to *3.4 defects per million*. Either way, you can begin to see why many firms like the term: Six Sigma quality levels serve as a quantifiable, if far-reaching, objective for many organizations.

EXAMPLE 5.4

Evaluating Six Sigma Quality at Milburn Textiles

Milburn Textiles has recalibrated its dyeing process so that the process mean is now exactly 140 degrees, with a new, lower standard deviation of 1.40 degrees. Given upper and lower tolerance limits of 148 and 132 degrees, does the dyeing process provide Six Sigma quality levels? Calculating the process capability ratio gives the following result:

$$C_p = \frac{UTL - LTL}{6\sigma} = \frac{148 - 132}{6(1.40)} = 1.90 < 2$$

Because $C_p < 2$, the process is still not capable of providing Six Sigma quality. To achieve Six Sigma quality, Milburn will have to reduce the standard deviation even further.

FIGURE 5.6
Six Sigma Quality

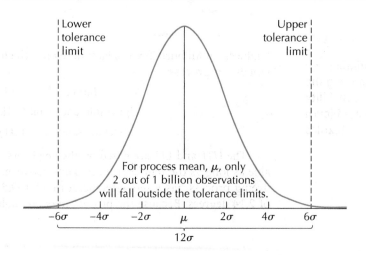

Lower tolerance limit — Upper tolerance limit

For process mean, μ, only 2 out of 1 billion observations will fall outside the tolerance limits.

$-6\sigma \quad -4\sigma \quad -2\sigma \quad \mu \quad 2\sigma \quad 4\sigma \quad 6\sigma$

12σ

Control Charts

Control chart
A specialized run chart that helps an organization track changes in key measures over time.

In contrast to the process capability ratio and index, **control charts** are specialized run charts that help organizations track changes in key measures over time. By using control charts, an organization can quickly determine whether a process is "in control" and take action if it is not. Before we describe the different types of control charts in more detail, however, we must first review the concepts of sampling and variable types.

Sampling. The idea behind sampling is that businesses do not have to examine *every* process outcome to assess how well a process is doing. Instead, they can use carefully selected samples to get a fairly good idea of how well a process is working. In fact, control charts are based on samples. In general, a good sample is one in which:

- Every outcome has an equal chance of being selected into the sample. This is typically accomplished by taking a random sample from the entire population.
- The sample size is large enough to not be unduly swayed by any single observation.

Continuous variable
A variable that can be measured along a continuous scale, such as weight, length, height, and temperature.

Attribute
A characteristic of an outcome or item that is accounted for by its presence or absence, such as "defective" versus "good" or "late" versus "on-time."

Variable Types. Most measures of interest fall into one of two types: continuous variables or attributes. **Continuous variables** are variables that can be measured along a continuous scale, such as weight, length, height, or temperature. **Attributes,** in contrast, refer to the presence or absence of a particular characteristic. To illustrate, suppose a pizza delivery chain promises to deliver a "hot, 16-inch, thick crust pizza in 30 minutes or less." The first three variables—temperature, diameter, and thickness—can all be measured on a continuous scale and are, therefore, continuous variables. However, on-time delivery is an attribute. The pizza is either delivered within the allotted time or it isn't.

Sample average ($\overline{X}$)
A key measure that represents the central tendency of a group of samples used in conjunction with range (R).

Range (R)
A key measure that represents the variation of a specific sample group, used in conjunction with sample average ($\overline{X}$).

When firms take samples of a continuous variable, two key measures of interest are the sample average and the range of values. The **sample average ($\overline{X}$)** and the **range (R)** for a continuous variable are defined as follows:

$$\text{Sample average for a continous variable} = \overline{X} = \frac{\sum_{i=1}^{n} X_i}{n} \tag{5.4}$$

where:

n = number of observations in the sample
X_i = value of the ith observation

$$\text{Range} = R = (\text{highest value in the sample}) - (\text{lowest value in the sample}) \tag{5.5}$$

The sample average tells us the central tendency for the measure of interest, while the range tells us something about the variation.

Proportion
A measure that refers to the presence or absence of a particular characteristic.

Because attributes refer to the presence or absence of a particular characteristic, the variable of interest is the proportion of the sample with the characteristic. The **proportion** for a sample is calculated as:

$$p = \frac{\sum_{i=1}^{n} a_i}{n} \tag{5.6}$$

where:

n = number of observations in the sample
a_i = 0 if the attribute is not present for the ith observation and 1 if it is

Control limits
The upper and lower limits of a control chart. They are calculated so that if a sample falls inside the control limits, the process is considered in control.

With this background, we can begin to describe control charts in more detail. As we said earlier, control charts are specialized run charts that help organizations track changes in key measures over time. A control chart has a center line showing the expected value for a sample measure, as well as upper and lower control limits. **Control limits** are derived using statistical techniques. They are calculated so that if a sample result falls inside the control limits, the process is considered "in control." If a sample result falls outside the control limits, the process is considered "out of control."

DanderNo Shampoo Company has taken a sample of 15 shampoo bottles and measured the number of ounces in each bottle (Table 5.2).

TABLE 5.2 Sample Results at DanderNo Shampoo Company

SAMPLE OBSERVATION	OUNCES
1	16.41
2	16.12
3	16.57
4	16.88
5	16.86
6	17.02
7	15.85
8	16.43
9	16.83
10	16.17
11	16.29
12	15.99
13	15.95
14	16.21
15	16.27
Sum:	**245.85**

The sample average, $\overline{X}$, is $245.85/15 = 16.39$ ounces. The range, R, is $17.02 - 15.85 = 1.17$.

The hotel manager at the Estonia Hotel has heard some rumblings that service is "not what it used to be." She would like to estimate the proportion of guests who are dissatisfied with the service they received. To accomplish this, the hotel manager asks a random sample of 100 guests if they were satisfied with their stay. Fourteen of the guests indicate that they were dissatisfied. The hotel manager then assigns a value of 1 to guests who said they were dissatisfied. Therefore, the estimated proportion of the entire population dissatisfied is:

$$p = \frac{14}{100} = 0.14, \text{ or } 14\%$$

In the following sections, we will discuss the development of three different control charts: $\overline{X}$ and R charts (for continuous variables) and p charts (for attributes). Regardless of the variable type, the process for setting up control charts is the same:

1. Take m samples of size n each while the process is in control.
2. Use the sample results to set up the control chart, using the tables or formulas provided.
3. Continue to take samples of size n and plot them against the control charts.
4. Interpret the results and take appropriate action.

We cannot overemphasize two points about control charts. First, control charts *should not* be employed until the process is capable of providing acceptable performance on a regular basis. Second, control charts, by themselves, *will not* result in improved quality levels. Rather, control charts are used to catch quality problems early, before they get out of hand. Therefore, the use of control charts falls under the appraisal activities of a firm's quality efforts (Figures 5.2 and 5.3).

$\overline{X}$ and R Charts. For continuous variables, we need two types of control charts. An **$\overline{X}$ chart** is used to track the average value for future samples (Equation [5.5]), while an **R chart** is used

$\overline{X}$ chart
A specific type of control chart for a continuous variable that is used to track the average value for future samples.

R chart
A specific type of control chart for a continuous variable that is used to track how much the individual observations within each sample vary.

TABLE 5.3
Calculations for $\overline{X}$ and R Charts

CHART TYPE	CENTER LINE		CONTROL LIMITS
$\overline{X}$ chart	$\overline{\overline{X}} = \dfrac{\sum_{j=1}^{m} \overline{X}_j}{m}$	**(5.7)**	(A2 values are given in Table 5.4)
	where:		
	$\overline{\overline{X}}$ = grand mean		Upper control limit = $UCL_{\overline{X}} = \overline{\overline{X}} + A2(\overline{R})$ **(5.9)**
	m = number of samples used to develop the $\overline{X}$ chart		Lower control limit = $LCL_{\overline{X}} = \overline{\overline{X}} - A2(\overline{R})$ **(5.10)**
	$\overline{X}_j$ average for the jth sample		
R chart	$\overline{R} = \dfrac{\sum_{j=1}^{m} R_j}{m}$	**(5.8)**	(D3 and D4 values are given in Table 5.4)
	where:		
	$\overline{R}$ = average range		
	m = number of samples used to develop the R chart		Upper control limit = $UCL_R = D4(\overline{R})$ **(5.11)**
	R_j = range for the jth sample		Lower control limit = $LCL_R = D3(\overline{R})$ **(5.12)**

TABLE 5.4
A_2, D_3, and D_4 Values for Developing $\overline{X}$ and R Charts

SAMPLE SIZE n	A2	D3	D4
2	1.88	0	3.27
3	1.02	0	2.57
4	0.73	0	2.28
5	0.58	0	2.11
6	0.48	0	2.00
7	0.42	0.08	1.92
8	0.37	0.14	1.86
9	0.34	0.18	1.82
10	0.31	0.22	1.78
11	0.29	0.26	1.74
12	0.27	0.28	1.72

to track how much the individual observations within each sample vary (Equation [5.6]). Table 5.3 summarizes the calculations required to set up these control charts, while Table 5.4 includes values needed to complete the control limit calculations.

EXAMPLE 5.7

Developing and Interpreting $\overline{X}$ and R Charts at Milburn Textiles

A quality team at Milburn Textiles has been charged with setting up control charts to monitor the dyeing process first described in Examples 5.3 and 5.4. Recall that the ideal temperature for the dyeing process is 140 degrees. If the temperature is too high, the fabric will be too dark; if the temperature is too low, streaks can develop. Either condition can ruin large rolls of expensive fabric.

Because temperature is a continuous variable, the quality team decides to set up $\overline{X}$ and R charts to monitor the temperature of the dyeing process. As a first step, the quality team measures the temperature five times a day during a 10-day period. Because these samples are going to be used to set up the control charts, the team makes sure that the process is behaving normally during the 10-day period.

The resulting 10 samples ($m = 10$) of 5 observations each ($n = 5$) are shown in Table 5.5.

TABLE 5.5 Sample Temperature Results for the Dyeing Process

DAY	OBSERVATION				
	1	2	3	4	5
1	136	137	144	141	138
2	143	138	140	140	139
3	140	141	144	137	135
4	139	140	141	139	141
5	137	138	143	140	138
6	142	141	140	139	138
7	143	141	143	140	140
8	139	139	141	140	136
9	140	138	143	141	139
10	139	141	142	140	136

The team calculates $\overline{X}$ and R values for each of the 10 samples and then takes the average values across all samples to calculate $\overline{\overline{X}}$ and $\overline{R}$ (Table 5.6):

TABLE 5.6 Calculating $\overline{X}$, R, $\overline{\overline{X}}$, and $\overline{R}$ Values for the Dyeing Process

DAY	OBSERVATION ($n = 5$)					X	R
	1	2	3	4	5		
1	136	137	144	141	138	139.2	8
2	143	138	140	140	139	140.0	5
3	140	141	144	137	135	139.4	9
4	139	140	141	139	141	140.0	2
5	137	138	143	140	138	139.2	6
6	142	141	140	139	138	140.0	4
7	143	141	143	140	140	141.4	3
8	139	139	141	140	136	139.0	5
9	140	138	143	141	139	140.2	5
10	139	141	142	140	136	139.6	6
					Sum	**1,398**	**53**

Note that the A2, D3, and D4 values have been specifically calibrated so that there is a 99.7% chance that future sample $\overline{X}$ and R values will plot within the control limits, *but only if the true mean and standard deviation have not changed.* Put another way, as long as the dyeing process temperature behaves as it has in the past, there is only a 0.3% probability that either the $\overline{X}$ or the R result for a future sample will fall outside these limits.

$$\overline{\overline{X}} = \frac{1,398}{10} = 139.8 \text{ degrees} \qquad \overline{R} = \frac{53}{10} = 5.3 \text{ degrees}$$

The team then calculates the upper and lower control limits for the $\overline{X}$ and R charts by selecting the A2, D3, and D4 values corresponding to samples of five observations each (Table 5.4). The resulting control charts are shown in Figure 5.7.

$$UCL_{\bar{X}} = 139.8 + 0.58 \times 5.3 = 142.9$$

$$\bar{\bar{X}} = 139.8$$

$$LCL_{\bar{X}} = 139.8 - 0.58 \times 5.3 = 136.7$$

$$UCL_R = 2.11 \times 5.3 = 11.2$$

$$\bar{R} = 5.3$$

$$LCL_R = 0 \times 5.3 = 0$$

FIGURE 5.7 Blank Control Charts for the Dyeing Process

Therefore, if an $\bar{X}$ or R value *does* fall outside the control limits, the quality team can assume one of two things:

1. The process has not changed, and the result is simply a random, albeit highly unlikely outcome.
2. The process has indeed shifted.

Either way, the team should investigate further. After setting up the control charts, the quality team continues to take samples, following the same routine as before. Sample results for the next six days are shown in Figure 5.8.

Sample Results (n = 5)		
Day	$\bar{X}$	R
11	141.2	8
12	142.0	9
13	144.0	12
14	140.0	5
15	139.6	4
16	140.8	5

FIGURE 5.8 Control Chart Results for Days 11 through 16

MyLab Operations Management
Animation

On day 13, both the $\bar{X}$ and R values fall outside the control limits. Because it is highly unlikely that this occurred due to random chance, the quality team immediately shuts down the process to determine the cause. After replacing a faulty thermostat, the process starts back up. The results for days 14 through 16 suggest that the dyeing process is again functioning normally. By catching the temperature problem early, the quality team is able to take corrective action before the problem gets out of hand.

p chart
A specific type of control chart for attributes that is used to track sample proportions.

***p* Charts.** When the measure of interest is an attribute, firms use **p charts** to track the sample proportions. As with $\bar{X}$ and R charts, a p chart has upper and lower control limits. If a sample p value falls outside these limits, management should immediately investigate to determine whether or not the underlying process has somehow changed. Table 5.7 describes the key calculations for developing a p chart.

TABLE 5.7 Calculations for p Charts

CENTER LINE	CONTROL LIMITS
Average p value across multiple samples: $$\bar{p} = \frac{\sum_{j=1}^{m} p_j}{m} \qquad (5.13)$$ Where p_j = p for the jth sample m = number of samples used to develop the control chart	Upper control limit = $UCL_p = \bar{p} + 3(S_p)$ **(5.14)** Lower control limit = $LCL_p = \bar{p} - 3(S_p)$ **(5.15)** where S_p = standard deviation for attribute samples and $$S_p = \sqrt{\frac{(\bar{p})(1 - \bar{p})}{n}} \qquad (5.16)$$ where: n = size of each sample

EXAMPLE 5.8

Developing and Interpreting p Charts at Gonzo's Pizzas

Since on-time delivery is a key order winner in the pizza business, the manager of Gonzo's Pizzas has decided to set up a control chart to track the proportion of deliveries that take longer than 30 minutes. The manager's first step is to take some samples of deliveries when things are working normally. As a general rule, when sampling by attribute, the sample size (n) should be large enough that:

$$\text{Min}\left[n(p), n(1 - p)\right] \geq 5 \qquad (5.17)$$

So if Gonzo's manager expects 10% of the pizzas to be late, he should choose a sample size of at least 50 observations (50*0.10 = 5), with an even larger sample size being preferable. Suppose then that the manager takes samples of 50 deliveries each (n = 50) over the next 15 days (m = 15). The manager is careful to select these deliveries at random in order to ensure that the sample data are representative of his business. The resulting p and $\bar{p}$ values for the 15 samples are:

Sample Results (n = 50)

DAY	p
1	0.16
2	0.20
3	0.00
4	0.14
5	0.10
6	0.20
7	0.10
8	0.06
9	0.14
10	0.16
11	0.00
12	0.04
13	0.00
14	0.10
15	0.10
Sum	**1.50**

$$\bar{p} = \frac{1.50}{15} = 0.10 \quad S_p = \sqrt{\frac{(\bar{p})(1 - \bar{p})}{n}} = 0.042$$

Based on the results of his first 15 samples, the Gonzo's manager sets up the control chart as follows:

$$UCL_p = 0.10 + 3 \times 0.042 = 0.226$$

$$\bar{p} = 0.10$$

$$LCL_p = 0.10 - 3 \times 0.042 = -0.026, \text{ or } 0$$

Like those for the $\overline{X}$ and R charts, the formulas for the p chart are set up so that sample p values should fall within the control limits 99.7% of the time, but *only if* the process itself has not changed. Note in this example that the *calculated* lower control limit calculation is actually negative. Because a negative p value is meaningless (Would this mean pizzas were delivered before they were ordered?), the lower control limit is effectively 0.

As long as the percentage of late deliveries in a sample stays below 22.6%, the Gonzo's manager can assume that the process is behaving normally. However, the Gonzo's manager might not be pleased with this definition of "normal." Indeed, he might decide to add more drivers or even shrink the store's delivery area in an effort to improve the proportion of on-time deliveries. If he takes any of these measures, the Gonzo's manager will need to recalculate the control charts based on the new p value.

p *charts are ideal for tracking the on-time performance of a pizza delivery service.*

As the preceding discussion suggests, results that fall outside the control limits might or might not signal trouble. Even so, it is highly unlikely that a sample $\overline{X}$, R, or p value will fall outside the control limits unless something about the process has indeed changed.

There are also patterns *within the control limits* that should be investigated. Two consecutive sample values near one of the control limits could indicate a process that is about to go out of control. Similarly, a run of five or more points on either side of the center line should be investigated, as should a definite upward or downward trend in the measures. The point is that managers do not have to wait until a sample point falls outside the control limits before taking action.

Acceptance Sampling

Even under the best circumstances, defects can occur and be sent on to the customer. Companies must, therefore, have some way to determine whether an incoming lot of material or products is of acceptable quality and to take action based on the results. One way to determine the quality levels is through 100% inspection (i.e., inspection of each and every item). While this may be necessary in some critical circumstances (e.g., donated blood), it has drawbacks.

First, 100% inspection can be extremely expensive and time-consuming, especially if there are hundreds or even thousands of items to inspect. Moreover, some quality inspection requires that goods be destroyed or otherwise used up in order to be tested. Wooden matches are a good example. When 100% inspection is not an option, companies depend on acceptance sampling to determine whether an incoming lot of items meets specifications. APICS defines **acceptance sampling** as "the process of sampling a portion of goods for inspection rather than examining the entire lot. The entire lot may be accepted or rejected based on the sample even though the specific units in the lot are better or worse than the sample."[7]

In the following example, we illustrate how acceptance sampling works and define OC curves, producer's risk, and consumer's risk.

Acceptance sampling
According to APICS, "The process of sampling a portion of goods for inspection rather than examining the entire lot."

---

[7]J. H. Blackstone, ed., *APICS Dictionary*, 15th ed. (Chicago, IL: APICS, 2016).

Acceptance Sampling at Chapman Industries

Acceptable quality level (AQL)
A term used in acceptance sampling to indicate a cut-off value that represents the maximum defect level at which a consumer would always accept a lot.

Lot tolerance percent defective (LTPD)
A term used in acceptance sampling to indicate the highest defect level a consumer is willing to "tolerate."

Consumer's risk (β)
A term used in acceptance sampling to indicate the probability of accepting a lot with quality worse than the LTPD level.

Producer's risk (α)
A term used in acceptance sampling to indicate the probability of rejecting a lot with quality better than the AQL level.

Operating characteristics (OC) curve
A curve used in acceptance sampling to show the probability of accepting a lot, given the actual fraction defective in the entire lot and the sampling plan being used. Different sampling plans will result in different OC curves.

Chapman Industries has received a shipment of 5,000 parts, each of which can be categorized as "good" or "defective." Rather than inspect all 5,000 parts, Chapman would like to make a decision based on a randomly selected sample of 10 parts ($n = 10$). If more than 1 part is found to be defective ($c = 1$), Chapman will reject the entire lot.

In addition, Chapman would like to accept all lots with a defect rate ≤5%. This is known as the **acceptable quality level (AQL)**. However, because Chapman will be making its decision based on a small sample of parts, there is always the possibility that the company will accidentally accept a lot with a much higher defect level. After much debate, management has agreed to risk accepting lots with defect levels as high as 30%. This upper limit is referred to as the **lot tolerance percent defective (LTPD)**.

Using random samples to make decisions about an entire lot has risks. On the one hand, Chapman may accept a lot that is even worse than the LTPD level. The probability of this occurring is called the **consumer's risk (β)**. On the other hand, Chapman may actually reject a lot that meets its AQL. The probability of this outcome is known as the **producer's risk (α)**.

Figures 5.9 and 5.10 illustrate these concepts. Under 100% inspection, the probability of accepting a "good" lot (defect level of 5% or less) is 100%, while the probability of accepting a bad lot is 0%. In contrast, the **operating characteristics (OC) curve** in Figure 5.9 shows the probability of accepting a lot, given the *actual* fraction defective in the entire lot and the sampling plan being used ($n = 10, c = 1$). It is important to note that different n and c values will result in differently shaped curves.[8]

According to the OC curve in Figure 5.9, there is an 80% chance that Chapman will accept a lot that is 90% defect-free but only a 5% chance that it will accept a lot that is around 40% defect-free. Figure 5.10 shows the actual producer's risks and consumer's risks faced by

FIGURE 5.9 OC Curve for Chapman Industries

FIGURE 5.10 Producer's and Consumer's Risk

[8]A. J. Duncan, *Quality Control and Industrial Statistics*, 5th ed. (Homewood, IL: Irwin, 1986), pp. 214–48.

Chapman under the current sampling plan. Specifically, for an AQL of 5%, the probability of rejecting a good lot (producer's risk) is around 8%. More importantly from Chapman's perspective, the probability of accepting a lot that doesn't meet Chapman's LTPD level (consumer's risk) is approximately 15%.

What can Chapman do to reduce these risks? In Figure 5.11, we show a new OC curve based on a sample plan that calls for a sample size of 20 ($n = 20$) and $c = 2$. Because the larger sample size is more representative of the entire lot and less likely to be overly influenced by a single observation, the result is a steeper OC curve, which lowers both the consumer's risk and the producer's risk. In fact, under the new OC curve, producer's risk drops to around 7%, and consumer's risk falls dramatically, to less than 5%. This highlights a general rule about acceptance sampling: The larger the sample size, the lower the producer's and consumer's risks. Of course, this greater accuracy must be balanced against the increased sampling costs.

FIGURE 5.11 New OC Curve Based on New Sampling Plan

Taguchi's Quality Loss Function

As you read through the previous sections, you may have thought to yourself, "Is a unit slightly within tolerances really of better quality than one just outside the tolerances?" After all, in Example 5.2, an axle with a diameter of 25.019 cm (within tolerances) is only slightly narrower than one with a diameter of 25.021 cm, and both are larger than the target value of 25 cm.

In fact, upper and lower tolerance limits are really just convenient fictions. If we were to take tolerance limits at face value, we would have to assume that there is no failure cost associated with units that fall within the tolerance limits, while units outside the tolerance limits immediately result in failure costs (Figure 5.12).

The reality is that the quality of any good or service starts to fall off as soon as the measure of interest drifts from the target value. Examples abound:

- The temperature of a cup of coffee
- The length of a pair of pants
- The amount of medicine in a capsule

Taguchi's quality loss function, shown in Figure 5.13, reflects the idea that any deviation from the target value results in some failure cost. The parabolic shape suggests that these costs

FIGURE 5.12
Implied Failure Costs Associated with Tolerance Limits

FIGURE 5.13
Taguchi's Quality
Loss Function

start to accrue as soon as there is any deviation from the target and that they grow exponentially as actual results drift even farther away.

Why do we mention Taguchi's quality loss function? First, it supports the continuous improvement philosophy we described earlier in the chapter. Figure 5.13 suggests that as long as there is *any* variability in the process, there is room for improvement. Taguchi's quality loss function is also consistent with our description of the total costs of quality: Failure costs do not disappear completely until the defect level is zero.

5.5 MANAGING QUALITY ACROSS THE SUPPLY CHAIN

So far, much of our attention has been devoted to managing and improving the quality of processes, products, and services within an organization. But the interdependent nature of supply chains suggests that quality management must extend beyond the four walls of an organization. In this section, we talk about two ways in which organizations manage quality across the supply chain. The first, ISO 9000, is a highly successful program that has helped spread quality management practices worldwide. Companies seek ISO 9000 certification both as a way to proactively address quality issues and as a way to signal to potential supply chain partners that they are serious about managing quality. Then we consider how companies deal with external failures in the supply chain.

ISO 9000 Family

ISO 9000
A family of standards, supported by the International Organization for Standardization, representing an international consensus on good quality management practices. ISO 9000 addresses business processes rather than specific outcomes.

Supported by the International Organization for Standardization (ISO), **ISO 9000** is a family of standards that represents an international consensus on good management practices. ISO 9000 seeks to help organizations deliver products or services that simultaneously:

- Meet the customer's quality requirements.
- Satisfy regulatory requirements, while aiming to
- Enhance customer satisfaction.
- Achieve continual improvement of the organization's performance in pursuit of these objectives.[9]

Unlike traditional standards, ISO 9000 focuses more on practices than outcomes. Companies following ISO 9000 standards will often have independent auditors "certify" that their business processes are ISO 9000 compliant. In some industries, certification is a requirement for doing business, and industry-specific standards may also apply. In others, ISO 9000 may simply signal potential supply chain partners that an organization has quality systems in place.

Since 1987, the ISO 9000 family of standards has been regularly updated to reflect developments in managerial thought. For example, ISO 9001:2015 is used by companies seeking to establish a quality management system that provides confidence in the conformance of their products and services to established or specified requirements. ISO 9004:2009 is used to extend the benefits obtained from ISO 9001 to all parties that are interested in or affected by a particular business's operations. The International Organization for Standardization has even used ISO 9001 as the basis for developing standards for specific industries, including petrochemical products, medical devices, and software engineering.

---

[9]International Organization for Standardization, **www.iso.org/iso-9001-quality-management.html.**

External Failures in the Supply Chain

Even with the best quality programs, companies still need to put in place processes to catch defective products once they have left the organization and entered the supply chain. How quickly and effectively companies handle this can have a great impact on the resulting external failure costs. Tracking systems, lot identification numbers, and explicit procedures for returning or destroying defective (and potentially harmful) goods are all examples of solutions that are used to deal with such problems. In *Supply Chain Connections*, we consider how one pharmaceutical firm dealt with the potential problems caused by mislabeled drugs.

SUPPLY CHAIN CONNECTIONS

REMOVING MISLABELED DRUGS FROM THE SUPPLY CHAIN

In May 2004, McNeil Consumer & Specialty Pharmaceuticals realized that it had made a serious mistake: It had accidentally put Adult-Strength Tylenol in bottles meant to hold Children's Motrin. What made this mistake especially worrisome is that the bottles had been released into the supply chain. In an effort to help retailers and consumers track down the defective bottles before anyone was seriously injured, McNeil released a notice that was listed on the Food and Drug Administration (FDA) Web site. The notice gave information regarding:

* The manufacturing lots affected (information readily found on the carton)

* The dates the bottles were distributed
* The visible differences between the two drugs (specifically, Children's Motrin Grape Chewable Tablets are round, purple-colored, scored tablets that have a grape smell, while the Tylenol 8-Hour Geltabs are hard, round, gelatin coated, and shiny)
* A contact number for anyone finding a bottle or having a question

Through its quick actions, McNeil hoped to minimize any injuries. Clearly, McNeil's job would have been much more difficult if it had not kept track of the manufacturing lot numbers or the shipping dates for the bottles in question.

CHAPTER SUMMARY

As an area of intense business interest, quality is here to stay. Operations and supply chain personnel in particular need to be familiar with the major quality topic areas, including the different philosophical perspectives on quality and the tools used to manage quality levels on a day-to-day basis. In this chapter, we gave you a solid introduction to quality topics, ranging from high-level discussions of quality issues to detailed descriptions of tools and techniques. We started by defining quality and describing a total cost of quality model. We then presented an overview of total quality management (TQM), as well as a section on statistical quality control

(SQC). We ended the chapter with a discussion of how organizations manage quality across the supply chain and some of the issues they face.

We encourage you not to let your quality education end here. The American Society for Quality (**www.asq.org**), the Juran Institute (**www.juran.com**), the W. Edwards Deming Institute (**www.deming.org**), and the ISO (**www.iso.org**) are four organizations that provide a wealth of information for those interested in quality. Regardless of what you do, you can be assured that you will deal with quality issues in your career.

KEY FORMULAS

Process capability ratio (page 118):

$$C_p = \frac{UTL - LTL}{6\sigma} \tag{5.1}$$

where:

UTL = upper tolerance limit

LTL = lower tolerance limit

σ = process standard deviation for the variable of interest

Estimated process standard deviation for the variable of interest (page 118):

$$\hat{\sigma} = \sqrt{\frac{\sum_{i=1}^{n}(\overline{X} - X_i)^2}{n - 1}}$$

(5.2)

where:

$\overline{X}$ = sample mean

X_i = value for the ith observation

n = sample size

Process capability index (page 119):

$$C_{pk} = \min\left[\frac{\mu - LTL}{3\sigma}, \frac{UTL - \mu}{3\sigma}\right]$$

(5.3)

where:

μ = process mean

UTL = upper tolerance limit

LTL = lower tolerance limit

σ = standard deviation

Sample average for a continuous variable (page 121):

$$\overline{X} = \frac{\sum_{i=1}^{n}X_i}{n}$$

(5.4)

where:

n = number of observations in the sample

X_i = value of the ith observation

Sample range (R) for a continuous variable (page 121):

$$R = \text{(highest value in the sample)} - \text{(lowest value in the sample)}$$

(5.5)

Sample proportion (page 121):

$$p = \frac{\sum_{i=1}^{n}a_i}{n}$$

(5.6)

where:

n = number of observations in the sample

a_i = 0 if the attribute is not present for the ith observation and 1 if it is

Average sample mean for a continuous variable (page 123):

$$\overline{\overline{X}} = \frac{\sum_{j=1}^{m}\overline{X}_j}{m}$$

(5.7)

where:

$\overline{\overline{X}}$ = grand mean

m = number of samples used to develop the $\overline{X}$ chart

$\overline{X}_j$ = Average for the jth sample

Average range value for samples of a continuous variable (page 123):

$$\overline{R} = \frac{\sum_{j=1}^{m}R_j}{m}$$

(5.8)

where:

m = number of samples used to develop the control charts

R_j = range for the jth sample

Upper control limit for p chart (page 123):

$$\text{Upper control limit} = UCL_{\bar{X}} = \bar{X} + A2(\bar{R}) \tag{5.9}$$

Lower control limit for p chart (page 123):

$$\text{Lower control limit} = LCL_{\bar{X}} = \bar{X} - A2(\bar{R}) \tag{5.10}$$

Upper control limit for R chart (page 123):

$$\text{Upper control limit} = UCL_R = D4(\bar{R}) \tag{5.11}$$

Lower control limit for R chart (page 123):

$$\text{Lower control limit} = LCL_R = D3(\bar{R}) \tag{5.12}$$

Average sample proportion for an attribute (page 126):

$$\bar{p} = \frac{\sum_{j=1}^{m} p_j}{m} \tag{5.13}$$

where:

p_j = p value for the jth sample

m = number of samples used to develop the control chart

Upper control limit for p chart (page 126):

$$\text{Upper control limit} = UCL_P = \bar{p} + 3(S_p) \tag{5.14}$$

Lower control limit for p chart (page 126):

$$\text{Lower control limit} = LCL_P = \bar{p} - 3(S_p) \tag{5.15}$$

where:

S_p = standard deviation for attribute samples

Standard deviation for attribute samples (page 126):

$$S_p = \sqrt{\frac{(\bar{p})(1 - \bar{p})}{n}} \tag{5.16}$$

where:

n = size of each sample

$$\text{Min}[n(p), n(1 - p)] \geq 5 \tag{5.17}$$

KEY TERMS

Acceptable quality level (AQL) 128
Acceptance sampling 127
Appraisal costs 113
Attribute 121
Conformance perspective 111
Consumer's risk (β) 128
Continuous improvement 116
Continuous variable 121
Control chart 121
Control limits 121
Employee empowerment 116
External failure costs 113
Internal failure costs 113

ISO 9000 130
Lot tolerance percent defective (LTPD) 128
Lower tolerance limit (LTL) 118
Operating characteristics (OC) curve 128
p chart 125
Prevention costs 113
Process capability ratio (C_p) 118
Process capability index (C_{pk}) 119
Producer's risk, (α) 128
Proportion 121
Quality 110
Quality assurance 116

Quality function deployment (QFD) 116
R chart 122
Range (R) 121
Sample average ($\bar{X}$) 121
Six Sigma quality 120
Statistical quality control (SQC) 116
Strategic quality plan 116
Total cost of quality curve 113
Total quality management (TQM) 115
Upper tolerance limit (UTL) 118
Value perspective 110
$\bar{X}$ chart 122

USING EXCEL IN QUALITY MANAGEMENT

Spreadsheet applications such as Microsoft Excel are ideally suited to performing the large numbers of calculations needed to support statistical quality control efforts. The following spreadsheet calculates the average sample proportion and standard deviation for 30 samples. (The sample results are arranged in two columns to save space.) The highlighted cells represent the input values. The calculated cells are as follows:

Cell D23

(average sample proportion):   = AVERAGE (*B7:C21*)/C4
Cell D24 (standard deviation):   = SQRT(D23*(1 − D23)/C4)

	A	B	C	D	E	F	G
1	Calculating the average sample proportion from 30 samples						
2	and standard deviation, S_p, from 30 samples						
3							
4	Sample size:		150				
5							
6	***No. of observations in each sample displaying the attribute***						
7		17	13				
8		10	10				
9		13	20				
10		12	6				
11		16	16				
12		17	21				
13		16	6				
14		13	10				
15		13	3				
16		12	10				
17		13	13				
18		12	7				
19		13	16				
20		10	16				
21		12	14				
22							
23	Average sample proportion:			0.08444			
24	Standard deviation, S_p:			0.0227			
25							

SOLVED PROBLEM

PROBLEM   ***Pulley Engineering***

Pulley Engineering manufactures needle bearings for use in high-tech machinery. The target diameter for one particular bearing is 0.125 inches. The quality control staff has taken 15 samples of five observations each with the manufacturing processes under control and has measured the diameter. The results are as follows:

SAMPLE	OBSERVATION				
	1	2	3	4	5
1	0.1253	0.1262	0.1254	0.1240	0.1230
2	0.1242	0.1247	0.1251	0.1238	0.1241
3	0.1225	0.1258	0.1229	0.1242	0.1255
4	0.1249	0.1259	0.1249	0.1240	0.1257
5	0.1245	0.1252	0.1261	0.1238	0.1225
6	0.1273	0.1234	0.1248	0.1241	0.1260
7	0.1226	0.1239	0.1227	0.1252	0.1259
8	0.1244	0.1238	0.1254	0.1261	0.1260
9	0.1236	0.1262	0.1250	0.1247	0.1250
10	0.1251	0.1264	0.1233	0.1233	0.1246
11	0.1253	0.1248	0.1237	0.1252	0.1226
12	0.1232	0.1251	0.1259	0.1263	0.1257
13	0.1231	0.1242	0.1256	0.1252	0.1257
14	0.1256	0.1240	0.1246	0.1250	0.1252
15	0.1243	0.1240	0.1239	0.1262	0.1246

Use these data to develop control limits for the $\overline{X}$ and R charts. In addition, suppose that engineering has established upper and lower tolerance limits of 0.129 inches and 0.121 inches, respectively. Calculate the process capability ratio and interpret the results.

Solution

The first step is to calculate the $\overline{X}$ and R values for each sample and then the $\overline{\overline{X}}$ and $\overline{R}$ values:

	OBSERVATION						
SAMPLE	1	2	3	4	5	X	R
1	0.1253	0.1262	0.1254	0.1240	0.1230	0.1248	0.0032
2	0.1242	0.1247	0.1251	0.1238	0.1241	0.1244	0.0013
3	0.1225	0.1258	0.1229	0.1242	0.1255	0.1242	0.0033
4	0.1249	0.1259	0.1249	0.1240	0.1257	0.1251	0.0018
5	0.1245	0.1252	0.1261	0.1238	0.1225	0.1244	0.0036
6	0.1273	0.1234	0.1248	0.1241	0.1260	0.1251	0.0039
7	0.1226	0.1239	0.1227	0.1252	0.1259	0.1241	0.0032
8	0.1244	0.1238	0.1254	0.1261	0.1260	0.1251	0.0024
9	0.1236	0.1262	0.1250	0.1247	0.1250	0.1249	0.0026
10	0.1251	0.1264	0.1233	0.1233	0.1246	0.1246	0.0031
11	0.1253	0.1248	0.1237	0.1252	0.1226	0.1243	0.0027
12	0.1232	0.1251	0.1259	0.1263	0.1257	0.1252	0.0031
13	0.1231	0.1242	0.1256	0.1252	0.1257	0.1248	0.0026
14	0.1256	0.1240	0.1246	0.1250	0.1252	0.1249	0.0016
15	0.1243	0.1240	0.1239	0.1262	0.1246	0.1246	0.0023
					Average:	**0.1247**	**0.0027**

Combining these results with the appropriate $A2$, $D3$, and $D4$ values from Table 5.4 yields the following control chart limits:

$$UCL_{\overline{X}} = 0.1247 + 0.58*0.0027 = 0.1263$$
$$LCL_{\overline{X}} = 0.1247 - 0.58*0.0027 = 0.1231$$

$$UCL_R = 2.11*0.0027 = 0.0057$$
$$LCL_R = 0*0.0027 = 0$$

To calculate the process capability ratio, we must first estimate the standard deviation of the individual observations, $\hat{\sigma}$. We can quickly do this by using the $= $ STDEV(number1, number2, …) function of Microsoft Excel, where the values in parentheses represent the raw diameter measurements. Doing so results in the following estimate:

$$\hat{\sigma} = 0.0011$$

Therefore, the process capability ratio is

$$C_p = \frac{0.129 - 0.121}{6(0.0011)} = \frac{0.008}{0.0066} = 1.21$$

The results suggest that the current process is capable of meeting the tolerance limits more than 99.7% of the time.

DISCUSSION QUESTIONS

1. What costs of quality were highlighted in the opening case study? How can Delta Air Lines justify spending $100 million to reengineer the baggage-handling process at just one airport?

2. Why can two people perceive the same product or service as having different quality levels? From a business perspective, why is it important, then, to "know your customer"?

3. Several years ago, a major automotive manufacturer was sued because the latch on a minivan's rear door failed after the vehicle was hit from the side at 30 miles per hour. The plaintiff argued that the latch was of poor quality

because it didn't hold up under the stress. The manufacturer disagreed, noting that the latch had met all government requirements and had been made to specifications. According to our definition of quality, can both sides be right?

4. Recall the DMAIC process described in Chapter 4. At what stage would statistical quality control tools be used?
5. Suppose that the actual range for a sample falls *below* the lower control limit for the R chart? Is this a good thing or a bad thing? Explain.

PROBLEMS

Additional homework problems are available at www .pearsonhighered.com/bozarth. These problems use Excel to generate customized problems for different class sections or even different students.

(* = easy; ** = moderate; *** = advanced)

Problems for Section 5.4: Statistical Quality Control

1. (*) Tyler Apiaries sells bees and beekeeping supplies. Bees (including a queen) are shipped in special packages according to weight. The target weight of a package is 1.4 kg. Historically, Tyler's shipments have weighed on average 1.4 kg, with a standard deviation of 0.15 kg.

   a. (*) Calculate the process capability ratio, assuming that the lower and upper tolerance limits are 1.1 kg and 1.7 kg, respectively. Is Tyler Apiaries currently able to meet the tolerance limits 99.7% of the time?
   b. (**) What would the standard deviation have to be for Tyler Apiaries to achieve Six Sigma quality levels with regard to the weight of the bee packages?
   c. (**) The average bee weighs 0.1 grams. Use this information to convert the target package weight and tolerance limits into number of bees for Tyler Apiaries. How might the company use this information to better control the package weights? Should Tyler Apiaries think about resetting the tolerance limits?

2. (*) Tyler Apiaries sells bees and beekeeping supplies. Bees (including a queen) are shipped in special packages according to weight. Suppose Tyler changes its processes so that the average package weight is now 1.5 kg, with a new standard deviation of 0.2 kg. Tyler markets the packages of bees as weighing 1.4 kg, and the tolerance limits remain as before. Calculate the process capability index for the weight of the bee packages. Is Tyler able to meet the tolerance limits?

3. (*) Leah's Toys produces molded plastic baby rattles. These rattles must be completely smooth. That is, there can be no rough edges where the molded halves fit together. Rattles are judged to be either acceptable or defective with regard to this requirement. Leah's has determined that the current process has an underlying p value of 0.01, meaning that, on average, 1 out of 100 rattles is currently judged to be defective. Calculate the standard deviation for the process and the resulting control limits for samples of 200 rattles each.

4. Leah's Toys makes rubber balls. The current process is capable of producing balls that weigh, on average, 3 ounces, with a standard deviation of 0.25 ounces.

a. (*) What is the process capability ratio, assuming upper and lower tolerance limits of 3.5 and 2.5 ounces? Is Leah's able to meet the tolerance limits 99.7% of the time? Explain.
b. (**) What would the standard deviation have to be to *exactly* meet the tolerance limits 99.7% of the time?
c. (**) Suppose Leah's Toys invests in process improvements that lower the standard deviation to just 0.10 ounces. Is this enough for Leah's to achieve Six Sigma quality levels with regard to the weight of the balls? Explain.

5. Leah's Toys guarantees to ship customer orders in 24 hours or less. The following chart contains results for five samples of nine customer orders each:

SAMPLE	SAMPLE CUSTOMER ORDERS (HOURS TO SHIP)								
1	3	5	21	4	15	9	7	3	6
2	22	16	8	16	11	38	11	25	15
3	9	2	5	17	2	19	4	2	4
4	6	7	18	9	16	18	7	10	1
5	11	10	20	18	1	6	3	18	9

a. (**) Based on these results, estimate the $\bar{p}$ and S_p values.
b. (**) A student comments, "Time is a continuous variable. We should really be looking at the $\bar{\bar{X}}$ and $\bar{R}$ values." Do you agree or disagree? Explain your rationale.

6. BlueBolt Bottlers has a bottle-filling process with a mean value of 64 ounces and a standard deviation of 8 ounces.

a. (**) Suppose that the upper and lower tolerance limits are 71 and 57 ounces, respectively. What is the process capability ratio? What would the standard deviation have to be in order for the process to meet the tolerance limits 99.7% of the time?
b. (***) Now suppose BlueBolt Bottlers makes some process improvements, thereby lowering the standard deviation of the process to 1.5 ounces, rather than 8 ounces. Using the data in problem 10 and the new standard deviation, calculate the process capability ratio. Is the filling process able to meet the tolerance limits 99.7% of the time? Does the process provide Six Sigma quality levels? Explain.

7. (*) The River Rock Company sells 200-pound bags of decorative rocks for landscaping use. The current bagging process yields samples with $\bar{X}$ and $\bar{R}$ values of 200 pounds and 12 pounds, respectively. Each sample consists of 12 observations. Develop the appropriate control charts.

8. (**) LaBoing produces springs, which are categorized as either acceptable or defective. During a period in which the manufacturing processes are under control, LaBoing takes multiple samples of 100 springs each, resulting in a calculated $\bar{p}$ value of 0.07. Develop the appropriate control chart for the springs.

9. AnderSet Laboratories produces rough lenses that will ultimately be ground into precision lenses for use in laboratory equipment. The company has developed the following thickness measures, based on 15 samples of four lenses that were taken when the process was under control:

MEAN (MICRONS) (n = 4)	MINIMUM	MAXIMUM
3.900	3.617	3.989
4.206	3.971	4.302
4.214	4.062	4.400
3.890	3.749	3.937
4.036	3.501	4.084
4.134	3.543	4.584
3.037	2.935	3.929
5.082	3.797	5.695
3.404	2.837	4.255
5.246	5.106	6.382
4.197	4.085	4.239
4.312	3.949	4.356
4.302	3.989	4.400
3.867	3.617	3.900
4.170	4.046	4.206

a. (**) Use these data to calculate $\overline{\overline{X}}$ and $\overline{R}$ and set up the appropriate control charts.

b. (**) Can the process be "under control" in statistical terms but still fail to meet the needs of AnderSet's customers? Explain, using a numerical example.

c. (**) Suppose AnderSet Laboratories takes some additional samples of the same size, yielding the following results. Plot these samples on the control charts and circle any observations that appear to be out of control.

MEAN (MICRONS) (n = 4)	MINIMUM	MAXIMUM
4.134	4.011	4.612
3.913	3.891	4.474
4.584	4.499	5.145
4.009	3.934	4.891
4.612	4.085	4.983
5.627	5.183	6.080

10. (**) Lazy B Ranch produces leather hides for use in the furniture and automotive upholstery industry. The company has taken 10 samples of nine observations each, measuring the square footage of each hide. Summary data are as follows:

MEAN (SQ FT) (n = 9)	MINIMUM	MAXIMUM
13.2	12.7	13.5
12.8	12.5	13.3
13.3	12.6	13.7
13.1	12.5	13.5
12.7	12.2	13.0
12.9	12.5	13.3
13.2	12.9	13.5
13.0	12.6	13.6
13.1	12.7	13.4
12.7	12.3	13.5

Use these data to set up control limits for the hides. Why would it be important for the Lazy B Ranch to track this information? Why might it be harder for the Lazy B Ranch to reduce process variability than it would be for a more typical "manufacturer"?

11. An insurance company has an online help service for its customers. Customer queries that take more than 5 minutes to resolve are categorized as "unsatisfactory" experiences. To evaluate the quality of its service, the company takes 10 samples of 100 calls each while the process is under control. The resulting p values are as follows:

p VALUES (n = 100)
0.08
0.11
0.12
0.06
0.13
0.09
0.16
0.09
0.18
0.15

a. (**) Calculate the $\bar{p}$ and S_p values and set up control limits so that future sample p values should fall within the control limits 99.7% of the time.

b. (**) Suppose the insurance company takes four additional samples, yielding the following p values: 0.9, 0.12, 0.25, and 0.10. Plot the results and circle all values that suggest that the process is "out of control." Is it possible that a sample result could fall outside the control limits due to pure chance? Explain.

c. (**) Now suppose that the sample size is actually 50, not 100. Recalculate the control limits for the p chart. What happened? Explain.

12. EK Chemical Company sells a specialty chemical in packages marked 100 g. In reality, EK has set the process mean at 100.5 g, and the process currently has a standard deviation of 0.50 g. Suppose the customer will accept anywhere from 98 to 102 g, as long as the average package has at least 100 g.

a. (**) Calculate the process capability index for the current manufacturing process. Is the process capable of meeting the tolerance limits more than 99.7% of the time? Explain.

b. (***) Now suppose EK recenters the manufacturing process so that the process mean is exactly 100 g, while the standard deviation remains the same. Calculate the process capability ratio. Is the process still capable of meeting the tolerance limits more than 99.7% of the time? Explain.

13. Crawford Pharmaceuticals has developed a new drug, Vaxidene. The target amount for a single dose of Vaxidene is 100 mg. Patients can receive as little as 98 mg or as much as 102 mg without experiencing any ill effects. Because of potential liability issues, Crawford has determined that it is imperative that manufacturing be able to provide Six Sigma quality levels. At present, the manufacturing process has a process mean of 100 mg and a standard deviation of 0.25 mg.

a. (*) What are the upper and lower tolerance limits for Vaxidene?

b. (**) Is Crawford's manufacturing process currently able to meet the dosage specifications at least 99.7% of the time? Show your work.

c. (**) What would the standard deviation for the process have to be in order for Crawford to achieve Six Sigma quality levels?

14. BHC produces bags of cement. The stated weight for a bag of cement is 100 pounds. Customers will accept an occasional bag weighing as little as 96 pounds, as long as the average weight is at least 100 pounds. At the same time, BHC doesn't want to give away cement, so it has set an upper tolerance limit of 104 pounds. The current filling process has an actual process mean of 101 pounds and a standard deviation of 0.65 pound.

a. (**) Calculate the process capability index for BHC. In this example, why should we use the process capability index rather than the process capability ratio to assess capability?

b. (**) Can you think of any reason BHC might want a process mean higher than the target value?

15. Central Airlines would like to set up a control chart to monitor its on-time arrival performance. Each day over a 10-day period, Central Airlines chose 30 flights at random and tracked the number of late arrivals in each sample. The results are as follows:

DAY	SAMPLE SIZE	NUMBER OF LATE-ARRIVING FLIGHTS
1	30	2
2	30	3
3	30	4
4	30	0
5	30	1
6	30	6
7	30	4
8	30	2
9	30	3
10	30	5

a. (*) Calculate $\bar{p}$.

b. (**) Set up a p chart to track the proportion of late arrivals. (*Note:* Each sample consists of 30 observations.)

c. (***) Airline travel is characterized by busy and slow seasons. As a result, what is "normal" during one time of the year wouldn't be "normal" at some other time. What difficulties might arise as a result of using a single control chart to track the proportion of late arrivals? What could Central Airlines do about this?

16. The Oceanside Apparel Company manufactures men's knit shirts. The production process requires material to be cut into large patterned squares, which are then sewn together. If the squares are not the correct length, the final shirt will be either too large or too small. The target length is 36 inches. In order to monitor the cutting process, Oceanside managers took 22 samples of four squares each and measured the lengths. For each sample, they then calculated the sample mean and range. Finally, they calculated the average sample mean (36.0 inches) and average range value (1.8 inches) for the 22 samples. Managers felt that these values were acceptable; that is, the process was in control.

a. (**) Develop the appropriate control chart(s) to monitor the fabric length.

b. (**) Using the control chart(s) you developed in part a, plot the following samples. Circle any that appear to be out of control.

SAMPLE ($n = 4$)	MEASUREMENTS (IN INCHES)			
1	37.3	36.5	38.2	36.2
2	33.4	35.8	37.9	36.2
3	32.1	34.8	39.1	35.3
4	36.1	37.2	36.7	34.2
5	32.1	34.0	35.6	36.1

17. (***) (*Microsoft Excel problem*) The following Excel spreadsheet calculates the upper and lower control limits for a continuous variable. **Re-create this spreadsheet in Excel.** You should develop the spreadsheet so that the results will be recalculated if any of the values in the highlighted cells are changed. Your formatting does not have to be exactly the same, but the numbers should be. (As a test, see what happens if all five observations in Sample 1 are 40. Your new upper and lower control limits for the sample means should be 36.05 and 34.28, respectively.)

	A	B	C	D	E	F	G	H	I	J	K
1	Calculating upper and lower control limits for a continuous variable (sample size = 5)										
2											
3			***Observations***								
4	Sample	1	2	3	4	5	$\bar{X}$	R			
5	1	34.26	34.66	35.53	34.62	35.87	34.99	1.61			
6	2	34.75	35.10	34.00	35.48	36.64	35.19	2.64			
7	3	34.11	35.17	34.54	35.25	34.97	34.81	1.14			
8	4	34.31	34.56	35.36	35.38	34.30	34.78	1.08			
9	5	34.65	35.39	34.87	34.90	35.70	35.10	1.05			
10	6	33.78	35.26	35.79	34.52	34.51	34.77	2.01			
11	7	35.13	35.42	34.73	36.27	34.67	35.24	1.60			
12	8	35.23	34.06	35.50	34.96	35.43	35.04	1.44			
13	9	34.80	34.60	34.69	32.94	33.87	34.18	1.86			
14	10	35.16	33.26	35.92	34.08	33.33	34.35	2.66			
15	11	33.81	34.81	34.27	34.54	35.17	34.52	1.36			
16	12	35.70	33.74	34.59	35.38	34.34	34.75	1.96			
17	13	33.97	34.81	34.93	34.27	35.47	34.69	1.50			
18	14	35.36	34.47	35.67	35.86	34.34	35.14	1.52			
19	15	35.39	35.41	35.06	34.52	34.27	34.93	1.14			
20						Average:	34.83	1.64			
21											
22		Upper control limit for sample means:				35.78					
23		Lower control limit for sample means:				33.88					
24											
25		Upper control limit for sample ranges:				3.46					
26		Lower control limit for sample ranges:				0.00					

18. (***) (*Microsoft Excel problem*) The following Excel spreadsheet calculates the upper and lower control limits for an attribute (in this case, the proportion of dissatisfied customers). **Re-create this spreadsheet in Excel.** You should develop the spreadsheet so that the results will be recalculated if any of the values in the highlighted cells are changed. Your formatting does not have to be exactly the same, but the numbers should be. (As a test, see what happens if you change the sample size to 200. The new *UCL* and *LCL* values should be 0.0909 and 0.0017, respectively.)

	A	B	C	D	E	F	G	H
1	Setting Up 99.7% Control Limits, Sampling by Attribute							
2								
3		No. of dissatisfied			Sample size =		100	
4	Sample	customers	*p*-value		$\bar{p}$ =		0.0927	
5	1	9	0.0900		S_p =		0.0290	
6	2	11	0.1100					
7	3	13	0.1300					
8	4	8	0.0800		UCL for sample p values:			0.1797
9	5	9	0.0900		LCL for sample p values:			0.0057
10	6	10	0.1000					
11	7	9	0.0900					
12	8	8	0.0800					
13	9	11	0.1100					
14	10	12	0.1200					
15	11	10	0.1000					
16	12	7	0.0700					
17	13	8	0.0800					
18	14	9	0.0900					
19	15	8	0.0800					
20	16	8	0.0800					
21	17	9	0.0900					
22	18	10	0.1000					
23	19	6	0.0600					
24	20	9	0.0900					
25	21	11	0.1100					
26	22	8	0.0800					
27	23	11	0.1100					
28	24	6	0.0600					
29	25	9	0.0900					
30	26	9	0.0900					
31	27	8	0.0800					
32	28	12	0.1200					
33	29	9	0.0900					
34	30	11	0.1100					

CASE STUDY

Dittenhoefer's Fine China

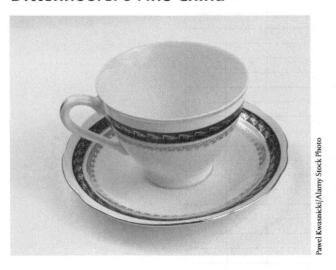

Pawel Kwasnicki/Alamy Stock Photo

Introduction

Overall, Steve Edwards, vice president of marketing at Dittenhoefer's Fine China, is very pleased with the success of his new line of *Gem-Surface* china plates. *Gem-Surface* plates are different from regular china in that the plates have a special polymer coating that makes them highly resistant to chipping and fading. Not only are the plates more durable, they are also completely dishwasher safe.

In order to manufacture the new plates, Dittenhoefer's has leased a special machine to apply the coating and has put in place a drying system to "cure" the coating on the plates. The research and development (R&D) lab has determined that in order to prevent defective plates, it is important that the machine apply the polymer coating at the proper temperature and in the proper thickness. Specifically, R&D has written up the following guidelines:

Coating thickness. The optimal polymer-coating thickness is 4 microns. If the coating is >5 microns, the plates will take too long to dry. If the coating is <3 microns, the plates will be inadequately protected.

Coating temperature. The polymer coating needs to be applied at a temperature between 160 degrees Fahrenheit and 170 degrees Fahrenheit, with the target temperature being 165 degrees Fahrenheit. If the temperature is lower than 160 degrees, the polymer will not adhere properly and will flake off. If the temperature is higher than 170 degrees, the polymer coating will fade the design on the plates.

Quality Problems

Traditionally, quality control at Dittenhoefer's has consisted of visually inspecting finished items for defects (chips, cracks, etc.) as they are being packed for shipment. This was acceptable in the past, when defects were few and far between. With the new polymer-coating technology, however, this has caused some serious problems.

For instance, on one Friday during the Christmas season, the packers noticed that nearly all of the plates they were getting ready to ship had faded designs, which suggested that the temperature of the polymer-coating machine might be too high. Sure enough, when a supervisor went back to check on the polymer-coating machine, he found that the thermostat was set at 190 degrees. Apparently, someone had set the temperature higher to clean the machine but had forgotten to reset it back to 165 degrees. The good news was that the problem was easily fixed. The bad news was that the machine had been running at 190 degrees since *Wednesday*. In the interim, 2,400 plates had been run through the coating machine. In the end, Dittenhoefer's had to destroy all 2,400 plates and was late making shipments to several important customers.

In another instance, a worker just happened to notice that the polymer-coating machine was not using as much raw material as expected. When the worker measured the thickness of the coating being applied to the plates, she found out why: The coating thickness was only 2.4 microns. A quick check of plates being dried and those being packed revealed that they, too, had a coating thickness of around 2.4 microns. While manufacturing was able to correct the problem and save *these* plates, no one knew how many plates had been shipped before the problem was discovered.

The Customer Service Department

The customer service office is responsible for pricing and entering customer orders, tracking the progress of orders, and making sure orders are shipped when promised. If an order is going to be late or there is some other problem, the customer service office is also responsible for notifying the customer. In addition, the customer service office handles customer complaints.

As would be expected, Steve Edwards often visits the larger dealers to find out how satisfied they are with the products and service they have received. During one of these trips, Steve realizes there might be problems with the customer service office. When visiting Nancy Sanders, owner of Lenoir Home Furnishings, Steve gets an earful:

> Steve, I understand that you have been busier ever since you introduced the new line of plates. However, I feel that the service quality has deteriorated and no one seems to care! Just last week, I found that an order I had expected in on Monday was not even ready to ship. No one called me—I just happened to find out when I was calling to place another order. Your information system also seems to be antiquated. The sales assistant apologized for the shipment delay and tried to be helpful, but she couldn't tell me the status of my order or even when I had placed it! It seemed that the previous sales assistant had changed jobs, and no one knew where her notes were. Notes!? Why isn't this stuff on a computer? It makes me have serious reservations about doing business with you.

Steve is caught flat-footed by the criticism. When he gets back to the office, he puts together a letter to his top 200 customers. In the letter, he gives customers a self-addressed stamped postcard and asks them to list any problems they have had dealing with the sales office. He gets responses from 93 of the customers. Their responses are summarized here:

PROBLEM	NUMBER OF RESPONDENTS CITING PROBLEMS
Incorrect pricing	23
Lost the order	8
Did not notify customer with regard to change in delivery date	54
Did not know status of customer's order	77
Order incorrect—wrong products shipped	4
Slow response to inquiries	80
Other problems, not listed above	11

Questions

1. On which dimensions of quality does Dittenhoefer's compete? How are these dimensions being threatened by the problems in the manufacturing and customer service areas?
2. What do you think are the problems with the current manufacturing process as a whole and with the polymer-coating machine in particular? How might you use process mapping and root cause analysis to get to the bottom of these problems?
3. Develop a Pareto chart based on the customer survey results for the customer service office. What seem to be the key problems? How might you use the PDCA cycle to go about resolving these problems?
4. Suppose the polymer-coating machine currently provides the following results:

VARIABLE	PROCESS MEAN	PROCESS STANDARD DEVIATION
Temperature	165 degrees	2.55 degrees
Thickness	4 microns	0.42 micron

Calculate the process capability ratio (C_p) for both the temperature and thickness variables. Is the polymer-coating process able to meet the engineering standards 99.7% of the time? Explain.

5. After making numerous process improvements, Steve Edwards decides to set up control charts to monitor the temperature and thickness results for the polymer-coating machine. Sample temperature and thickness data are shown in the following table. Set up the appropriate control charts.

Polymer-Coating Machine: Sample Temperature and Thickness Measurements (taken when the process was under control)

SAMPLE	TEMP/THICK	TEMP/THICK	TEMP/THICK	TEMP/THICK	TEMP/THICK
June 10	165/4.2	169/3.9	165/4.0	164/4.0	169/3.9
June 15	161/3.8	165/4.2	166/4.0	167/4.8	165/4.2
June 20	169/3.9	161/3.8	167/4.8	164/4.0	167/4.8
June 25	164/4.1	168/4.0	166/4.0	165/4.0	163/3.5
June 30	166/4.0	168/4.0	169/3.9	163/4.3	166/3.7
July 5	168/4.0	163/3.5	167/4.8	164/4.0	166/4.0
July 10	162/4.5	164/4.1	169/3.9	167/4.8	163/3.9
July 15	163/3.5	168/4.0	165/4.0	165/4.0	167/4.8
July 20	167/4.8	167/3.2	164/4.1	167/4.8	164/4.1
July 25	167/3.2	163/3.5	168/4.0	165/3.8	168/4.0
July 30	163/4.0	165/3.8	165/4.2	169/3.9	163/4.0
August 5	163/3.8	165/4.2	169/3.8	165/4.2	163/3.5

REFERENCES

Books and Articles

Blackstone, J. H., ed., *APICS Dictionary*, 15th ed. (Chicago, IL: APICS, 2016).

DeFeo, J., and J. M. Juran, eds., *Juran's Quality Handbook*, 7th ed. (San Francisco: McGraw-Hill, 2016).

Deming, W. E., *Quality, Productivity, and Competitive Position* (Boston: MIT Center for Engineering Study, 1982).

Duncan, A. J., *Quality Control and Industrial Statistics*, 5th ed. (Homewood, IL: Irwin, 1986), pp. 214–48.

Garvin, D., "Competing on the Eight Dimensions of Quality," *Harvard Business Review* 65, no. 6 (November–December 1987): 101–109.

Greising, D., "Quality, How to Make It Pay," *BusinessWeek* (August 8, 1994): 54–59.

Internet

American Society for Quality, "Quality Glossary," **https://asq .org/quality-resources/quality-glossary/q.**

"Frequently Asked Questions about the Malcolm Baldrige National Quality Award," **www.nist.gov/public_affairs/ factsheet/baldfaqs.cfm.**

"How Delta Is Trying to Fix the Problem of Lost and Delayed Luggage," *Los Angeles Times*, August 31, 2016, **www .latimes.com/business/la-fi-lost-luggage-delta-20160831-snap-story.html.**

International Organization for Standardization, "ISO 9000—Quality Management," **www.iso.org/iso/iso_catalogue/ management_and_leadership_standards/iso_9000.**

"Keep Tabs on Your Bags on Delta's Website," August 28, 2011, *The Record*, **NorthJersey.com.**

McCartney, S., "Better Odds of Getting Your Bags," *Wall Street Journal*, December 2, 2010, **http://online.wsj.com.**

Military Standard 105E Tables: Sampling by Attributes, **www.sqconline.com/military-standard-105e-tables-sampling-attributes.**

Sharkey, J., "Since Sept. 11, Years of Change for Airlines," *New York Times*, September 6, 2011, p. B6, **www.nytimes.com.**

Snyder, B., "No Bag? Then Airlines Should Refund Fee," CNN, August 15, 2011, **http://articles.cnn.com/2011-08-15/ travel/refund.bag.fees_1_bag-fees-first-bag-second-bag? _s=Pm:Travel.**

U.S. Department of Transportation, Air Travel Consumer Reports, **www.transportation.gov/airconsumer/air-travel-consumer-reports.**

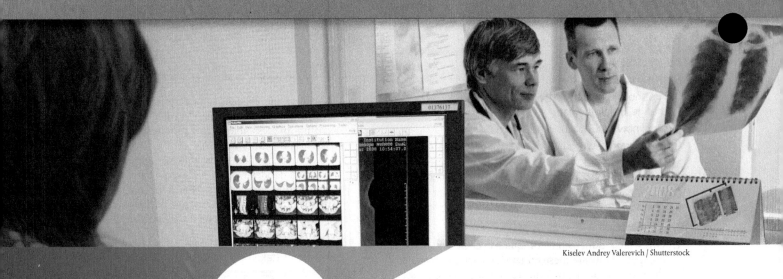

Kiselev Andrey Valerevich / Shutterstock

CHAPTER
SIX

Managing Capacity

CHAPTER OBJECTIVES

By the end of this chapter, you will be able to:

- Explain what capacity is, how firms measure capacity, and the difference between theoretical and rated capacity.

- Describe the pros and cons associated with three different capacity strategies: lead, lag, and match.

- Apply a wide variety of analytical tools for choosing between capacity alternatives, including expected value and break-even analysis, decision trees, and learning curves.

- Apply the Theory of Constraints, waiting line theory, and Little's Law to analyze and understand capacity issues in a business process environment.

THINKING OUTSIDE THE BOX: BUILDING THE NEXT-GENERATION PHARMACEUTICAL PLANT

Chip Chipman/Bloomberg/Getty Images

Many of today's breakthrough pharmaceutical drugs are produced via a process called biomanufacturing. Unlike traditional drug manufacturing, which is based on a chemical formulation, biomanufacturing uses biological systems to produce commercial volumes of important biomaterials and biomolecules. The key input to biomanufactured products are biological materials such as blood, animal cells and plant cells grown in special equipment. Some of these cells are naturally occurring, but others are created through genetic engineering.

Investing in a biomanufacturing facility is a long-term, strategic capacity decision. And as you can imagine, it is not for the faint-hearted. First, building a traditional plant can take three or more years and cost hundreds of millions of dollars. Even worse, construction often has to start years before the commercial success of the proposed drug is ensured. As a result, firms run the very real risk of spending several years and millions of dollars building a plant, only to learn that the drug does not perform as expected and the plant is not needed.

In response to these challenges, GE Healthcare Life Sciences has developed a new way to build biomanufacturing plants that cuts the time in half while reducing construction costs by 25% to 50%. Specifically, GE builds the plant in the form of prefabricated modules—literally, stand-alone rooms that represent the various steps in the biomanufacturing process. These modules are built in Germany and then shipped to the final site, where they are linked together into the final configuration. The modules "arrive 80 to 90% pre-equipped. The units include heating, ventilation and air-handling systems, the clean room, most of the utility equipment, and all of the piping needed to run the plant."[1]

Modular manufacturing has several benefits beyond lower construction costs. First, because modular construction reduces the overall time required to put a plant in place, firms can hold off building the plant until they have more information about whether the proposed drug is going to be a success or not. Even delaying the construction decision by one year can improve the odds of a successful outcome. Second, because the modules are built under controlled conditions at GE, conformance quality is enhanced while keeping costs under control.

---

[1]M. Egan, "Think Inside the Box: Pfizer Will Use GE's Mobile Biotech Factory to Make Next-Generation Drugs in China," *GE Reports*, June 30, 2016, **www.gereports.com/ pfizer-will-use-ges-modular-factory-to-make-next-generation-drugs-in-china/**.

INTRODUCTION

Some of the most important strategic decisions managers face revolve around capacity. *How much* capacity do we need? *When* do we need it? *What form* should the capacity take? This chapter starts with a discussion of capacity and introduces several tools that managers use to evaluate capacity choices, including break-even analysis, expected value analysis, and learning curves. The second half of the chapter deals with the unique challenge of understanding and analyzing capacity in a *business process* environment where work units (people or products) must travel through several different steps before they leave the process.

For now, as you go through this chapter, keep in mind the following points:

- Capacity can take many different forms, and capacity planning is an important activity in both service and manufacturing organizations.
- While there are many quantitative tools to help managers make informed capacity decisions, there is some degree of risk inherent in nearly all such decisions.

With that background, let's dive in.

TABLE 6.1
Examples of Capacity in Different Organizations

ORGANIZATION	CAPACITY MEASURE	FACTORS AFFECTING CAPACITY
Law firm	Billable hours available each month	Number of lawyers and paralegals; education and skill levels; supporting software
Textile-spinning plant	Spinning hours per shift; number of spindles produced per week	Number of machines running; quality of raw materials; maintenance
Automatic car wash	Cars per hour	Availability of water and chemicals; reliability of the car wash (Is it frequently down for repairs?)
Airline	(Seats) × (miles flown)	Number of jets, pilots, and terminals

6.1   CAPACITY

Capacity
The capability of a worker, a machine, a workcenter, a plant, or an organization to produce output in a time period.

Simply put, **capacity** is the capability of a worker, machine, workcenter, plant, or organization to produce output per time period.[2] As the definition suggests, there are many forms of capacity in an organization. Operations and supply chain managers must make decisions regarding how much capacity their organizations need and what types. In making these decisions, managers must consider several issues:

- How capacity is measured
- Which factors affect capacity
- The impact of the supply chain on the organization's effective capacity

Measures of Capacity

Managers are constantly evaluating whether their organizations' resources are adequate to meet current or future demands. To do so, they need measures of capacity. Such measurements vary widely. In general, though, companies measure capacity in terms of inputs, outputs, or some combination of the two. The manager of a textile plant that makes thread from raw cotton might express its capacity in terms of the number of spinning hours available each month or the number of square feet of available warehouse space (both of which are inputs) or in terms of the number of finished pounds it can produce in a single period (an output).

In organizations that provide standard products or services, capacity is likely to be expressed in terms of outputs because the output doesn't change radically from one period to the next. In organizations that provide customized services or products, capacity is more likely to be expressed in terms of inputs. That is why the managing partners in a consulting firm are more likely to think in terms of available consultant hours (an input) than of consulting projects completed over a certain period. Table 6.1 shows the capacity measures used in a variety of business settings. Note which measures express capacity in terms of inputs and which express it in terms of output. Note, too, that many of the measures have a time element—such as spinning hours *per shift* and units *per day*.

Theoretical capacity
The maximum output capability, allowing for no adjustments for preventive maintenance, unplanned downtime, or the like.

Rated capacity
The long-term, expected output capability of a resource or system.

Organizations also differentiate between theoretical capacity and rated capacity. **Theoretical capacity** is the maximum output capability, allowing no adjustments for preventive maintenance, unplanned downtime, or the like, while **rated capacity** represents the long-term, expected output capability of a resource or system.[3] Managers understand that work levels must sometimes exceed levels that are typical, or even desirable, over the long haul. High-tech manufacturers often experience a big surge in demand during the fourth quarter of the year, as customers seek to use up their budgets. A salmon-processing plant might run 24 hours a day during the peak season. And personnel at an accounting firm might work 18 hours a day the week before April 15. Peak periods such as these are usually short in duration and are often characterized by high levels of overtime and reactive "fire fighting" (instead of proactive planning). Yet running at or near the theoretical capacity for a short time is often a better option than increasing resource levels permanently. Good managers know the

[2]J. H. Blackstone, ed., *APICS Dictionary*, 15th ed. (Chicago, IL: APICS, 2016).
[3]Ibid.

difference between theoretical capacity and more sustainable rated capacity levels, and they use that knowledge when measuring and planning capacity.

Factors That Affect Capacity

Even in seemingly simple environments, many factors affect capacity, and many assumptions must be made. Take the following formula, which describes capacity for an assembly plant with three assembly lines and a maximum of two 8-hour shifts per day:

$$\text{Capacity} = (800 \text{ units per line per shift})(\text{number of lines})(\text{number of shifts})$$

What is the "capacity" of the plant? It could be as low as 800 units per day (1 line, 1 shift) or as high as 4,800 units per day (3 lines, 2 shifts). The number of shifts or lines active at any time is a controllable factor that managers can use to adjust capacity in response to market demands. Other examples of controllable factors include the number of jets an airline keeps on active status, the number of temporary workers, and the number of public storage facilities, which companies can add or drop as needed.

Product variations are another source of ambiguity in measuring capacity. Suppose our hypothetical factory can assemble several different models, so that 800 units represent an *average* rated capacity. The actual output can range from 700 to 900 units, depending on the complexity of the model being assembled. If that is the case, capacity can range from 700 to 5,400 units.

Another factor that affects capacity is conformance quality, which we discussed in Chapter 5. In general, poor conformance quality reduces available capacity because employees must spend valuable time and resources resolving quality problems or reworking "defective" products or service outcomes. In contrast, quality improvement can increase an organization's effective capacity by reducing the resources needed to provide a product or service.

Supply Chain Considerations

A firm's capacity concerns certainly aren't limited to just *its* activities. In many cases, a firm must also consider the capacities of key suppliers and distributors. Suppose Procter & Gamble (P&G) decides to launch a new line of children's shampoos. P&G will need to fill the downstream supply chain with product. Among other things, P&G managers must make sure that suppliers have adequate capacity to provide the necessary raw materials when they are needed. They must also arrange for adequate trucking, warehousing, and shelf space—all forms of capacity—in order to move the products and display the new line in retail stores. The point is this: A firm's ability to use its own capacity is often directly dependent on capacity up and down the supply chain. We will revisit this point in our discussion of the Theory of Constraints.

6.2 THREE COMMON CAPACITY STRATEGIES

Oftentimes capacity decisions are made to accommodate expected growth in demand or product lines. The question managers must deal with is how quickly to increase capacity. Three common strategies for timing capacity expansions are the lead, lag, and match strategies (see Figure 6.1).

FIGURE 6.1
When to Add Capacity: Lead, Lag, and Match Strategies

Lead capacity strategy
A capacity strategy in which capacity is added in anticipation of demand.

When using a **lead capacity strategy,** capacity is added in anticipation of demand. This strategy has several advantages. First, it ensures that the organization has adequate capacity to meet all demand, even during periods of high growth. This is especially important when the availability of a product or service is crucial, as in the case of emergency care or a hot new product. For many new products, being late to market can mean the difference between success and failure.

Another advantage of a lead capacity strategy is that it can be used to preempt competitors who might be planning to expand their own capacity. Being the first in an area to open a large grocery or home improvement store gives a retailer a definite edge. Finally, many businesses find that overbuilding in anticipation of increased usage is cheaper and less disruptive than constantly making small increases in capacity. Of course, a lead capacity strategy can be very risky, particularly if demand is unpredictable or technology is evolving rapidly.

Lag capacity strategy
A capacity strategy in which capacity is added only after demand has materialized.

The opposite of a lead capacity strategy is a **lag capacity strategy,** whereby organizations add capacity only *after* demand has materialized. Three clear advantages of this strategy are a reduced risk of overbuilding, greater productivity due to higher utilization levels, and the ability to put off large investments as long as possible. Organizations that follow this strategy often provide mature, cost-sensitive products or services. Many government agencies try to avoid adding extra capacity and their requisite costs until absolutely necessary. Yet one can easily imagine the drawbacks of a lag capacity strategy, the most evident being the reduced availability of products or services during periods of high demand.

Most organizations do not follow one strategy. For one thing, different products and services require different approaches. Consider a community hospital. If you are the chief executive officer, you will follow a lead capacity strategy for expanding critical emergency services, especially if yours is the only hospital in the region. You will not apply the same rationale to noncritical services.

Match capacity strategy
A capacity strategy that strikes a balance between the lead and lag capacity strategies by avoiding periods of high under- or overutilization.

A **match capacity strategy** strikes a balance between the lead and lag capacity strategies by avoiding periods of high under- or overutilization. A relatively new concept in capacity planning is the **virtual supply chain,** which is really a collection of firms, each of which does only one or two core activities—design, manufacturing, distribution, marketing, and so on. The firms coordinate their activities by using advanced information systems to share critical data.

Virtual supply chain
A collection of firms that typically exists for only a short period. Virtual supply chains are more flexible than traditional supply chains, but they are also less efficient.

Unlike a traditional supply chain, a virtual supply chain might exist for only a short period. The virtual supply chain might be pulled together during the holiday season to produce and market a new toy, after which it will disappear. The members of the virtual supply chain might even change from one week to the next. What virtual supply chains gain in short-term flexibility, however, they lose in long-term efficiency. As a result, traditional supply chains are more likely to prevail in markets in which long-term relationships or costs are critical.

6.3 METHODS OF EVALUATING CAPACITY ALTERNATIVES

An organization usually has many ways to meet its capacity needs. Manufacturers often have a choice between building their own facilities or leasing capacity from other firms. Airlines debate whether to purchase or lease jets. On the human side, organizations make choices between full-time and temporary employees and among different types of skills. An organization might even have to choose between using inventory ("stored" capacity) and using overtime to meet demand during peak seasons. Clearly, managers need some help in evaluating these alternatives.

In this section, we discuss several approaches that are useful in evaluating capacity alternatives. They include the concept of fixed versus variable costs, expected value, and break-even analysis. Keep in mind as we describe these approaches that they deal primarily with *financial* considerations—the costs and/or revenues associated with a particular capacity option. Nevertheless, they provide a good starting point.

Cost

Fixed costs
The expenses an organization incurs regardless of the level of business activity.

Many capacity alternatives have both fixed and variable cost components. **Fixed costs** are the expenses an organization incurs regardless of the level of business activity. Examples include lease payments on equipment, mortgage payments on buildings, and monthly maintenance

Variable costs
Expenses directly tied to the level of business activity.

charges for software. The company must pay these expenses regardless of the number of customers it serves or products it makes. **Variable costs,** on the other hand, are expenses that are directly tied to the level of business activity. Material costs are a good example. If the fabric cost per pair of jeans is $4.35, then we can calculate fabric cost as $4.35 \times$ (number of jeans produced). The general formula for describing the total cost of a capacity alternative is:

$$TC = FC + VC*X \tag{6.1}$$

where:

TC = total cost

FC = fixed cost

VC = variable cost per unit of business activity

X = amount of business activity (number of customers served, number of units produced, etc.)

The distinction between fixed and variable costs is important because it shows how the level of business activity affects costs. This kind of information can be critical in choosing between several capacity alternatives.

EXAMPLE 6.1

Analyzing the Cost of Capacity Alternatives at Ellison Seafood Company

Chuck Pefley/Alamy Stock Photo

Ellison Seafood Company ships fresh seafood to customers in a nearby city. The logistics manager has identified three shipping alternatives. The first is to call a common carrier (i.e., a trucking company) each time a shipment is ready to go. This alternative would have no fixed cost, but the variable cost per shipment would be about $750. At the other extreme, Ellison Seafood could lease its own refrigerated trucks. The logistics manager has determined that the yearly cost to lease three trucks would be $21,000, including insurance and prepaid maintenance. Because Ellison would have to pay the lease charge regardless of how many shipments were made, the $21,000 would be a fixed expense. On the other hand, the variable cost would drop dramatically to $50 per shipment—just enough to cover the cost of fuel and the driver's wages. Somewhere between these two extremes is the third option: a contractual arrangement with a local carrier. For a yearly fixed charge of $5,000, the local carrier would agree to make all of Ellison's deliveries at a variable cost of just $300 per delivery. Table 6.2 summarizes the three options.

TABLE 6.2 Capacity Alternatives and Costs for Ellison Seafood Company

	COMMON CARRIER	CONTRACT CARRIER	LEASING
Fixed cost	None	$5,000	$21,000
Variable cost	$750	$300	$50

Figure 6.2 shows the total cost (fixed cost + variable cost) of each alternative as the number of shipments increases. By looking at the graph, we can see that the cost of using a common carrier starts out the lowest, but it quickly becomes much more expensive than the other two options. As the number of shipments nears 11, using a contract carrier becomes cheaper. The contract carrier remains the cheapest option until the activity level approaches 64 shipments, at which point leasing becomes the cheapest option.

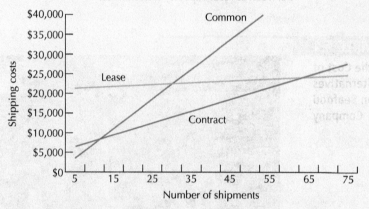

FIGURE 6.2 Total Cost of Three Capacity Alternatives, Ellison Seafood Company

Indifference point
The output level at which two capacity alternatives generate equal costs.

We can find the exact output level at which two capacity alternatives generate equal costs, called the **indifference point,** by setting their two cost functions equal to one another and solving for the number of shipments, X. For instance, the indifference point for the common carrier and contract carrier options would be calculated as follows:

Total cost of common carrier option = total cost of contract carrier option

$$\$0 + \$750X = \$5,000 + \$300X$$

$$X = (\$5,000 - \$0)/(\$750 - \$300) = 11.11, \text{ or about } 11 \text{ shipments}$$

We can use the same logic to find the indifference point for the contract carrier and leasing options:

Total cost of contract carrier option = total cost of leasing

$$\$5,000 + \$300X = \$21,000 + \$50X$$

$$X = (\$21,000 - \$5000)/(\$300 - \$50) = 64 \text{ shipments}$$

Figure 6.3 provides a different view of the same three options. In this case, we have plotted the cost *per shipment*, which is calculated by dividing total cost by the number of shipments. Not surprisingly, the cost per shipment for the common carrier option is flat. Notice, however, that as the number of shipments increases, the cost per shipment for the leasing option drops dramatically. This is because the total cost per shipment drops when the fixed cost of $21,000 is spread across more shipments. Finally, note that the cost curves in Figure 6.3 cross at the same levels shown in Figure 6.2—the two indifference points.

FIGURE 6.3 Total Cost per Shipment of Three Capacity Alternatives, Ellison Seafood Company

Demand Considerations

While understanding the cost structure of various capacity alternatives is important, it is not enough. Managers must also know something about the expected demand levels. Otherwise, how will they know which capacity alternative will provide the best financial result? Table 6.3 makes this point. If Ellison Seafood expects to make 40 shipments per year, the contract carrier option makes the most sense. However, if demand is expected to be as high as 75 shipments per year, leasing is cheaper.

Of course, predicting demand with certainty is rarely easy. In many business situations, it makes more sense to develop *multiple* estimates of demand that capture a range of possibilities, as in Table 6.3. Even so, how should we interpret Table 6.3? While leasing is the cheapest alternative for a yearly total of 75 shipments, how *likely* is demand to reach that level? Similarly, how likely is the number of shipments to fall in the range in which contracting is cheapest? To tackle this type of problem, managers turn to expected value analysis.

Expected Value

Expected value
A calculation that summarizes the expected costs, revenues, or profits of a capacity alternative, based on several demand levels, each of which has a different probability.

One way companies evaluate capacity alternatives when demand is uncertain is to use a decision tool called the expected value approach. In a nutshell, **expected value** is a calculation that summarizes the expected costs, revenues, or profits of a capacity alternative, based on several different demand levels, each of which has a different probability.

The major steps of the expected value approach are as follows:

1. Identify several different demand-level scenarios. These scenarios are not meant to identify all possible outcomes. Rather, the intent is to approximate the *range* of possible outcomes.
2. Assign a probability to each demand-level scenario.
3. Calculate the expected value of each alternative. This is done by multiplying the expected financial result (cost, revenue, or profit) at each demand level by the probability of each demand level and then summing across all levels. The equation is:

$$EV_j = \sum_{i=1}^{I} P_i C_i \tag{6.2}$$

where:

EV_j = expected value of capacity alternative j

P_i = probability of demand level i

C_i = financial result (cost, revenue, or profit) at demand level i

TABLE 6.3
Total Cost of Three Capacity Alternatives at Different Demand Levels, Ellison Seafood Company

TOTAL COST EQUATION	15 SHIPMENTS (LOW DEMAND)	40 SHIPMENTS (MEDIUM DEMAND)	75 SHIPMENTS (HIGH DEMAND)
Common carrier: $0 + $750X	$11,250	$30,000	$56,250
Contract carrier: $5,000 + $300X	**$9,500**	**$17,000**	$27,500
Leasing: $21,000 + $50X	$21,750	$23,000	**$24,750**

EXAMPLE 6.2

**Expected Value
Analysis at Ellison
Seafood Company**

Suppose Ellison Seafood wants to know the *expected cost* of one of the options, contracting. As a first step, management needs to identify some potential demand scenarios:

Low demand	→	30 shipments per year
Medium demand	→	50 shipments per year
High demand	→	80 shipments per year

Next, management must assign a probability to each. The only stipulation is that the probabilities must sum to 100%. This is what management finds:

Low demand	→	30 shipments per year	→	25%
Medium demand	→	50 shipments per year	→	60%
High demand	→	80 shipments per year	→	15%
		Total		100%

Based on the total cost equations in Table 6.3, the costs associated with contracting at each demand level are:

$$C(\text{low demand}) = \$5,000 + \$300(30) = \$14,000$$
$$C(\text{medium demand}) = \$5,000 + \$300(50) = \$20,000$$
$$C(\text{high demand}) = \$5,000 + \$300(80) = \$29,000$$

And the expected cost of contracting is:

$$EV_{Contract} = (\$14,000 * 25\%) + (\$20,000 * 60\%) + (\$29,000 * 15\%)$$
$$= \$3,500 + \$12,000 + \$4,350 = \$19,850$$

Using similar logic, we can calculate the expected costs of using a common carrier or of leasing:

$$EV_{Common} = (\$22,500 * 25\%) + (\$37,500 * 60\%) + (\$60,000 * 15\%)$$
$$= \$37,125$$
$$EV_{Lease} = (\$22,500 * 25\%) + (\$23,500 * 60\%) + (\$25,000 * 15\%)$$
$$= \$23,475$$

The analysis suggests that, on average, the contracting option has the lowest expected costs, at $19,850. Intuitively, this result seems consistent with Figures 6.2 and 6.3, which show that the contracting option is cheapest for a fairly wide range of shipping levels.

Decision Trees

Decision tree
A visual tool that decision makers use to evaluate capacity decisions. The main advantage of a decision tree is that it enables users to see the interrelationships between decisions and possible outcomes.

A **decision tree** is a visual tool that decision makers use to evaluate capacity decisions. The main advantage of a decision tree is that it enables users to see the interrelationships between decisions and possible outcomes. Decision trees are particularly good at helping users visualize complex *series* of decisions and outcomes.

The basic rules for using decision trees are as follows:

1. Draw a tree from left to right, starting with a decision point or an outcome point, and develop branches from there.
2. Represent each *decision point* with a square, with the different branches coming out of the square representing alternative choices.
3. Represent *outcome points* (which are beyond the control of the decision maker) with circles. Each possible outcome is represented by a branch off the circle. Assign each

branch a probability, indicating the possibility of that outcome, and ensure that the total probability for all branches coming out of an outcome equals 100%.

4. For expected value problems, calculate the financial result for each of the smaller branches and move backward by calculating weighted averages for the branches, based on their probabilities.

Figure 6.4 shows a decision tree for the transportation decision facing Ellison Seafood (Example 6.2). Reading from left to right, the tree starts with the selection of one of the three transportation options. Once the transportation decision is made, there are three possible demand outcomes: 30 shipments, 50 shipments, and 80 shipments, each with different probabilities. Because the actual demand is an outcome and not a decision, a circle is used to represent these branch points.

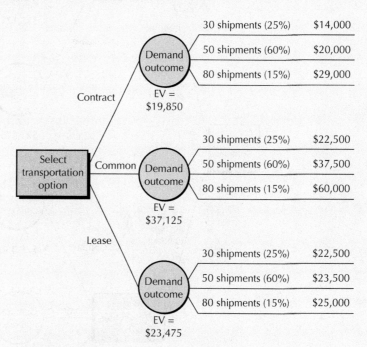

FIGURE 6.4 Decision Tree for Transportation Decision at Ellison Seafood Company

The combination of three different transportation options and three demand scenarios results in 3 × 3 = 9 branches, each of which has a resulting cost. Finally, the expected value of each decision branch is calculated as the weighted average of the possible demand outcome branches. Note that the numbers in Figure 6.4 match those in Example 6.2.

Now suppose that a potential new customer, Straley Grocers, has approached Ellison Seafood. Straley wants Ellison to sign a contract promising 30 deliveries a year. These deliveries would be *in addition to* Ellison's normal business. Ellison management would like to develop a decision tree to understand how the Straley contract might affect the transportation decision.

Figure 6.5 shows the updated decision tree. Ellison *first* has to make a decision about whether to accept the Straley contract, and, based on that decision, it has to select a transportation option. The added decision point effectively doubles the size of the tree.

Note how the demand levels and resulting costs for each demand outcome branch in the lower half have been updated to show the impact of the additional 30 shipments. Looking at the tree, it becomes clear that if Ellison decides *not* to accept the Straley contract, the lowest expected cost is to go with the contract carrier; this is the same result as in Example 6.2. But if Ellison *does* accept the contract, the lowest expected cost is to lease a truck.

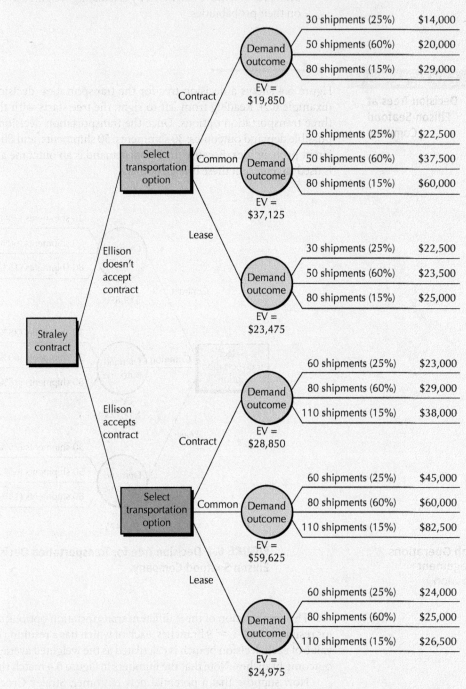

FIGURE 6.5 Updated Decision Tree for Transportation Decision at Ellison Seafood Company, Reflecting Straley Contract Decision

Break-Even Analysis

Break-even point
The volume level for a business at which total revenues cover total costs.

When the focus is on profitability, a key question managers often face is "At what volume level do total revenues cover total costs?" This volume level is referred to as the **break-even point.** Managers are very interested in knowing what the break-even point is because once business volume passes the break-even point, the company begins to make money.

The formula for the break-even point is:

$$BEP = \frac{FC}{R - VC}$$

(6.3)

where:

BEP = break-even point

FC = fixed cost

V = variable cost per unit of business activity

R = revenue per unit of business activity

EXAMPLE 6.4

Break-Even Analysis at Ellison Seafood Company

Ellison makes a $1,000 profit on each shipment *before* transportation costs are considered. What is the break-even point for each shipping option?

For the common carrier option:

$$BEP = \frac{FC}{R - VC}$$

BEP = $0/$250, or *0 shipments*

For the contracting option:

BEP = $5,000/$700 = 7.1, or, rounding up, *8 shipments*

And for the leasing option:

$$\$21,000 + \$50X = \$1,000X$$

BEP = $21,000/$950 = 22.1, or, rounding up, *23 shipments*

The common carrier option has the lowest break-even point, which arguably makes it the least risky option. However, Ellison Seafood will clear only ($1,000 − 750) = $250 on each shipment. On the other hand, the leasing option has a break-even point of 23 shipments, yet each additional shipment beyond 23 contributes ($1,000 − $50) = $950 to the bottom line. In choosing the appropriate shipping option, Ellison Seafood must carefully consider the risks as well as the expected demand levels.

Learning Curves

Here's a question to ponder: Can the effective capacity of operations or supply chains *increase* even though the level of resources remains the *same*? In many cases, the answer is "yes." Recall that in Chapter 4, we defined *productivity* as follows:

$$Productivity = outputs/inputs$$

(6.4)

Learning curve theory
A body of theory based on applied statistics which suggests that productivity levels can improve at a predictable rate as people and even systems "learn" to do tasks more efficiently. In formal terms, learning curve theory states that for every doubling of cumulative output, there is a set percentage reduction in the amount of inputs required.

If organizations can improve their productivity, they can get more output from the same amount of resources or, conversely, the same output from fewer resources. Either way, changes in productivity imply changes in effective capacity. **Learning curve theory** suggests that productivity levels can improve at a predictable rate as people and even systems "learn" to do tasks more efficiently. In formal terms, learning curve theory states that *for every doubling of cumulative output, there is a set percentage reduction in the amount of inputs required.* The learning curve is defined as follows:

$$T_n = T_1 n^b$$

(6.5)

where:

T_n = resources (usually labor) required for the *n*th unit

T_1 = resources required for the 1st unit

b = ln(Learning percentage)/ln2

The rate at which learning occurs is captured by the learning percentage, where 80% would be expressed as 0.80.

A video game producer has hired a new service technician to handle customer calls. The times it takes the new service technician to help the first, second, fourth, and eighth callers, as well as the resulting productivity figures, are shown below:

CALL	TIME FOR CALL	PRODUCTIVITY
1	5.00 minutes	0.20 calls per minute
2	4.00 minutes	0.25 calls per minute
4	3.20 minutes	0.31 calls per minute
8	2.56 minutes	0.39 calls per minute

Notice that the second call takes 80% of the time of the first ($4/5 = 80\%$). Similarly, the fourth call takes 80% of the time of the second, and the eighth call takes 80% of the time of the fourth. In effect, for every doubling of cumulative output, the service technician is experiencing a 20% reduction in the amount of time required. This represents an 80% learning curve.

For our service technician, then, we can use Equation (6.5) to estimate the time it will take her to handle her 25th call:

$$T_{25} = T_1 \left(25^{\frac{\ln(0.80)}{\ln(2)}} \right)$$
$$= (5 \text{ minutes})(25^{-0.32193})$$
$$= (5 \text{ minutes})(0.355)$$
$$= 1.78 \text{ minutes}$$

Figure 6.6 uses the learning curve equation to plot the expected service times for the first 50 calls, based on an 80% learning curve. As you can see, the learning curve is characterized by quick improvements in productivity early on, followed by more gradual improvements.

FIGURE 6.6 Eighty Percent Learning Curve for Service Technician

Table 6.4 contains calculated n^b values, as well as cumulative n^b values, for a wide range of n values and learning curve percentages.

To see how the table works, suppose the video game producer mentioned earlier hires a second service technician. The second service technician takes 5 minutes for his first call, followed by 4.5 minutes for the second call. Based on this information:

- Estimate the learning rate.
- Calculate the time it should take to handle the 25th call.
- Calculate the total time it should take to handle *the next 23 calls* (i.e., calls 3 through 25).

TABLE 6.4 Selected n^b and $\sum n^b$ Values for Different Learning Curves

UNIT NUMBER	70% LEARNING n^b	70% LEARNING $\sum n^b$	75% LEARNING n^b	75% LEARNING $\sum n^b$	80% LEARNING n^b	80% LEARNING $\sum n^b$	85% LEARNING n^b	85% LEARNING $\sum n^b$	90% LEARNING n^b	90% LEARNING $\sum n^b$
1	1.000	1.000	1.000	1.000	1.000	1.000	1.000	1.000	1.000	1.000
2	0.700	1.700	0.750	1.750	0.800	1.800	0.850	1.850	0.900	1.900
3	0.568	2.268	0.634	2.384	0.702	2.502	0.773	2.623	0.846	2.746
4	0.490	2.758	0.563	2.946	0.640	3.142	0.723	3.345	0.810	3.556
5	0.437	3.195	0.513	3.459	0.596	3.738	0.686	4.031	0.783	4.339
6	0.398	3.593	0.475	3.934	0.562	4.299	0.657	4.688	0.762	5.101
7	0.367	3.960	0.446	4.380	0.534	4.834	0.634	5.322	0.744	5.845
8	0.343	4.303	0.422	4.802	0.512	5.346	0.614	5.936	0.729	6.574
9	0.323	4.626	0.402	5.204	0.493	5.839	0.597	6.533	0.716	7.290
10	0.306	4.932	0.385	5.589	0.477	6.315	0.583	7.116	0.705	7.994
11	0.291	5.223	0.370	5.958	0.462	6.777	0.570	7.686	0.695	8.689
12	0.278	5.501	0.357	6.315	0.449	7.227	0.558	8.244	0.685	9.374
13	0.267	5.769	0.345	6.660	0.438	7.665	0.548	8.792	0.677	10.052
14	0.257	6.026	0.334	6.994	0.428	8.092	0.539	9.331	0.670	10.721
15	0.248	6.274	0.325	7.319	0.418	8.511	0.530	9.861	0.663	11.384
16	0.240	6.514	0.316	7.635	0.410	8.920	0.522	10.383	0.656	12.040
17	0.233	6.747	0.309	7.944	0.402	9.322	0.515	10.898	0.650	12.690
18	0.226	6.973	0.301	8.245	0.394	9.716	0.508	11.405	0.644	13.334
19	0.220	7.192	0.295	8.540	0.388	10.104	0.501	11.907	0.639	13.974
20	0.214	7.407	0.288	8.828	0.381	10.485	0.495	12.402	0.634	14.608
21	0.209	7.615	0.283	9.111	0.375	10.860	0.490	12.892	0.630	15.237
22	0.204	7.819	0.277	9.388	0.370	11.230	0.484	13.376	0.625	15.862
23	0.199	8.018	0.272	9.660	0.364	11.594	0.479	13.856	0.621	16.483
24	0.195	8.213	0.267	9.928	0.359	11.954	0.475	14.331	0.617	17.100
25	0.191	8.404	0.263	10.191	0.355	12.309	0.470	14.801	0.613	17.713
26	0.187	8.591	0.259	10.449	0.350	12.659	0.466	15.267	0.609	18.323
27	0.183	8.774	0.255	10.704	0.346	13.005	0.462	15.728	0.606	18.929
28	0.180	8.954	0.251	10.955	0.342	13.347	0.458	16.186	0.603	19.531
29	0.177	9.131	0.247	11.202	0.338	13.685	0.454	16.640	0.599	20.131
30	0.174	9.305	0.244	11.446	0.335	14.020	0.450	17.091	0.596	20.727
31	0.171	9.476	0.240	11.686	0.331	14.351	0.447	17.538	0.593	21.320
32	0.168	9.644	0.237	11.924	0.328	14.679	0.444	17.981	0.590	21.911
33	0.165	9.809	0.234	12.158	0.324	15.003	0.441	18.422	0.588	22.498
34	0.163	9.972	0.231	12.389	0.321	15.324	0.437	18.859	0.585	23.084
35	0.160	10.133	0.229	12.618	0.318	15.643	0.434	19.294	0.583	23.666
36	0.158	10.291	0.226	12.844	0.315	15.958	0.432	19.725	0.580	24.246
37	0.156	10.447	0.223	13.067	0.313	16.271	0.429	20.154	0.578	24.824
38	0.154	10.601	0.221	13.288	0.310	16.581	0.426	20.580	0.575	25.399
39	0.152	10.753	0.219	13.507	0.307	16.888	0.424	21.004	0.573	25.972
40	0.150	10.902	0.216	13.723	0.305	17.193	0.421	21.425	0.571	26.543
41	0.148	11.050	0.214	13.937	0.303	17.496	0.419	21.844	0.569	27.111
42	0.146	11.196	0.212	14.149	0.300	17.796	0.416	22.260	0.567	27.678
43	0.144	11.341	0.210	14.359	0.298	18.094	0.414	22.674	0.565	28.243
44	0.143	11.484	0.208	14.567	0.296	18.390	0.412	23.086	0.563	28.805
45	0.141	11.625	0.206	14.773	0.294	18.684	0.410	23.496	0.561	29.366
46	0.139	11.764	0.204	14.977	0.292	18.975	0.408	23.903	0.559	29.925
47	0.138	11.902	0.202	15.180	0.290	19.265	0.405	24.309	0.557	30.482
48	0.136	12.038	0.201	15.380	0.288	19.552	0.403	24.712	0.555	31.037
49	0.135	12.173	0.199	15.579	0.286	19.838	0.402	25.113	0.553	31.590
50	0.134	12.307	0.197	15.776	0.284	20.122	0.400	25.513	0.552	32.142

The estimated learning rate = 4.5 minutes/5 minutes = 90%. Looking at Table 6.4, we can see that we have an entire column of n^b values and cumulative n^b values $\left(\sum n^b\right)$ for a 90% learning curve. Looking down the table until we find the row for the 25th unit (in this case, a customer call), we find n^b for a 90% learning curve = 0.613. Therefore:

$$\text{Estimated time for the 25th call} = (5 \text{ minutes})(0.613) = 3.065 \text{ minutes}$$

To estimate the time for the next 23 calls, we calculate the expected time for the first 25 calls and subtract the time for the first 2. Working off the same row of Table 6.4:

$$
\begin{aligned}
\text{Estimated time for the next 23 calls} &= \text{Estimated time for the first 25 calls}\\
&\quad - \text{Time for the first 2 calls}\\
&= 5 \text{ minutes} \left(\sum n^b\right) - (5 + 4.5 \text{ minutes})\\
&= 5 \text{ minutes} (17.713) - 9.5 \text{ minutes}\\
&= 79 \text{ minutes}
\end{aligned}
$$

When learning occurs in an organization, productivity will improve over time, and the effective capacity of the organization will grow—even if the level of resources remains the same. This has important implications for capacity planning. If managers expect their employees or work systems to experience learning effects, then they must anticipate these effects when making capacity decisions. Otherwise, they may overestimate the capacity needed to meet future requirements.

Of course, in nearly every case there is a minimum amount of time or resource that will be required, regardless of how many times the task is repeated. This puts an effective limit on the learning curve effect. Also, it is normal for learning improvements to not follow a smooth trajectory of improvement, as suggested by Equation (6.5). Rather, organizations may be able to see the actual improvement only over large numbers of observations.

One final observation about learning curves: In many industrial buyer–supplier settings, buyers *expect* their suppliers to experience productivity improvements due to learning over time. Buyers might even build price reductions based on anticipated learning into long-term purchasing contracts. Walmart, for instance, may purchase a new item from a supplier, expecting overall costs to follow a 90% learning curve. This creates an incentive for the supplier to proactively look for ways to decrease costs through learning or other means.

Other Considerations

Not all capacity problems can be solved using the quantitative models just described. Other considerations that will affect a firm's choice include:

- The strategic importance of an activity to the firm
- The desired degree of managerial control
- The need for flexibility

These considerations are usually relevant to the choice between developing internal capacity and outsourcing, a topic we consider in more depth in Chapter 7.

The more strategically important an activity is to a firm, the more likely the firm is to develop the internal capacity to perform the activity. Strategic activities are often called *core activities* because they are a major source of competitive advantage. Product design at Cisco Systems, a provider of telecommunications equipment, is one example. Cisco spends millions of dollars each year on developing the internal capacity needed to design innovative products. Engineers, designers, equipment, and facilities are crucial to this strategic activity. But while Cisco does not want to depend on outside sources for new technologies or product ideas, the firm's managers will outsource nonstrategic manufacturing activities. For instance, Cisco depends on Flex Ltd., a contract manufacturer, to assemble many of its products.

Managerial control is another issue in the choice between internal and external capacity. Whenever a firm outsources an activity, it loses some control over it. Consider Cisco's relationship with Flex Ltd. No doubt Cisco and Flex Ltd. have a contract that establishes expected quality levels, volume levels, delivery times, and cost targets. However, Cisco's managers cannot just pick up the phone and tell Flex Ltd. to stop assembling another firm's products in order to make room for a new Cisco product. Cisco managers lose some control by outsourcing the company's assembly capacity.

The flip side of this is flexibility. A firm might favor the capacity alternative that requires the least commitment on its part, especially if long-term needs are uncertain. In the case of Ellison Seafood, while the common carrier option becomes quite expensive as the number of shipments increases, it is also the most flexible option. If it chooses this option, Ellison can decide to stop making shipments at any time and will not pay another dime for trucking.

6.4   UNDERSTANDING AND ANALYZING PROCESS CAPACITY

This section deals with the unique challenge of understanding and analyzing capacity in a *business process* environment. For example, think about a business process where work units (people or products) must travel through several different steps before they leave the process. How does the capacity at *each step* affect the capacity of the overall process? What impact does variability in arrival times and processing times have on the level of inventory and the length of time work units spend in the system? And what is the relationship between inventory levels, flow times, and process capacity? These are important and complex questions, and we use the Theory of Constraints, waiting line theory, and Little's Law to address them.

The Theory of Constraints

Theory of Constraints (TOC)
An approach to visualizing and managing capacity which recognizes that nearly all products and services are created through a series of linked processes, and in every case, there is at least one process step that limits throughput for the entire chain.

Constraint
The process step (or steps) that limits throughput for an entire process chain.

In recent years, a fundamentally different approach to visualizing and managing capacity has emerged. Developed by Eliyahu Goldratt,[4] the **Theory of Constraints (TOC)** is based on the recognition that many products and services proceed through a series of linked processes like the ones we described in Chapters 3 and 4. These process steps can be contained within a single organization or stretched across multiple organizations (i.e., a supply chain). Each process step has its own capacity level, and in every case there is at least one process step that limits throughput for the entire chain. This process step is referred to as the **constraint.** Consider Figure 6.7.

The movement of customers or products through a series of process steps is analogous to the movement of liquid through a pipeline. Each process step has a certain capacity, as represented by the diameter of the "pipe." In Figure 6.7, process E has the largest capacity, while process C has the smallest capacity. Because process C is the constraint, it will limit the amount of throughput for the entire process chain. Increasing the capacity at any other process step will not increase throughput for the entire process chain.

Figure 6.8 provides a numerical example. It should be clear from this simple illustration that process 3 limits total throughput for the chain to 40 units per hour. Pushing out more than 40 units an hour in processes 1 and 2 will simply create a glut of inventory in front of process 3. Furthermore, output from process 3 will limit process 4 to just 40 units per hour.

FIGURE 6.7
Throughput of a "Pipeline" Is Determined by the Smallest "Pipe"

FIGURE 6.8
Throughput Is Controlled by the Constraint, Process 3

---

[4]E. Goldratt, *The Goal*, 2nd ed. (Great Barrington, MA: North River Press, 1992).

TOC experts have suggested a five-step approach to managing the constraint, and hence throughput, for a process chain:

1. **Identify the constraint.** The constraint can be anywhere in the chain—including upstream or downstream supply chain partners. When the constraint occurs outside the company, it is often referred to as an *external constraint*. In contrast, if the constraint is within a company's set of activities, it is referred to as an *internal constraint*. Consider Figure 6.8. Suppose customers are buying products at the rate of only 30 per hour. In this case, demand, not process 3, is the constraint.
2. **Exploit the constraint.** An hour of throughput lost at the constraint is an hour of throughput lost for the entire chain. It is, therefore, imperative that organizations carefully manage the constraint to ensure an uninterrupted flow of customers or products through the constraint.
3. **Subordinate everything to the constraint.** If conflicts arise between exploiting the constraint and efforts to "improve" performance elsewhere (e.g., letting an upstream process decrease inventory in a way that "starves" the constraint for work), management needs to remember that it is the constraint that determines throughput and act accordingly.
4. **Elevate the constraint.** If the organization needs to increase throughput, find ways to increase the capacity of the constraint.
5. **Find the new constraint and repeat the steps.** As the effective capacity of the constraint is increased, it may cease to be a constraint. In that case, the emphasis should shift to finding and exploiting the new constraint.

In Example 6.6, we illustrate how the Theory of Constraints can be applied in a simple service environment.

EXAMPLE 6.6	
Constraint Management at Tracy's Hair Salon	Tracy's Hair Salon follows a three-step process in serving its customers. First, the customer's hair is shampooed. Next, a stylist cuts and styles the customer's hair. Finally, the customer pays $25 to the cashier.

At present, Tracy's Hair Salon has one shampooer, one stylist (Tracy), and one cashier (Tracy's son Larry). The average processing time for each worker, as well as his or her effective capacity and hourly wage, is shown in Table 6.5. Notice how the average processing time and effective capacity relate to one another. For example, it takes Tracy 15 minutes, on average, to cut and style a customer's hair. This implies that the effective capacity for a single stylist is (60 minutes)/(15 minutes per customer) = 4 customers per hour. Although Tracy has never performed a detailed market study, her experience tells her that approximately 10 customers an hour would use her service *if* she had the capacity to handle them all.

TABLE 6.5 Capacity and Cost Data for Workers at Tracy's Hair Salon

	SHAMPOO	CUT AND STYLE	COLLECT MONEY
Average processing time per customer	10 minutes	15 minutes	3 minutes
Effective capacity per worker	6 per hour	4 per hour	20 per hour
Labor cost per worker	$15 per hour	$20 per hour	$10 per hour

Figure 6.9 shows the potential hourly demand as well as hourly capacities for each process step. As the bar graph shows, styling is the current constraint, limiting throughput to four customers per hour. Financially, this translates into revenues of 4 customers* $25 = $100 an hour, for a profit of $55 after labor costs.

Constraint: Style step (Internal constraint)
Resulting process capacity: 4 customers per hour

Expected Hourly results:
Revenue: 4 customers *$25 = $100
Labor costs: (1 shampooer)*$15 + (1 stylist)*$20 + (1 cashier)$10 = $45
Profit = $100 − $45 = $55

FIGURE 6.9 Tracy's Hair Salon, Current Process

Tracy wonders if she can do better. She decides to hire a second stylist, thereby doubling capacity at this step to eight customers per hour. The result, shown in Figure 6.10, is that the *shampoo step* becomes the new constraint (6 customers per hour), and profit improves to $85 per hour.

Constraint: Shampoo step (Internal constraint)
Resulting process capacity: 6 customers per hour

Expected Hourly results:
Revenue: 6 customers *$25 = $150
Labor costs: (1 shampooer)*$15 + (2 stylists)*$20 + (1 cashier)$10 = $65
Profit = $150 − $65 = $85

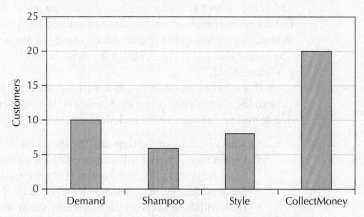

FIGURE 6.10 Tracy's Hair Salon, Adding a Second Stylist

Encouraged by the results, Tracy contemplates increasing her workforce to two shampooers, three stylists, and one cashier. Doing so would make *demand* the new constraint (Figure 6.11). But does hiring one additional shampooer and two additional stylists make financial sense? The results suggest yes: Revenues would increase to 10 customers * $25 = $250 per hour, while labor costs would increase to $100 per hour, resulting in an hourly profit of $150.

Even with all this expansion, Tracy notices that her cashier is not even close to being fully utilized. Maybe there are some other tasks she can have Larry do.

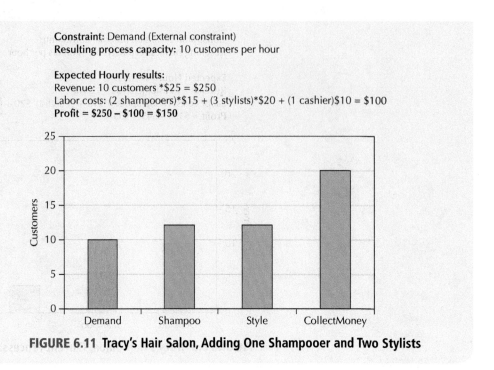

Constraint: Demand (External constraint)
Resulting process capacity: 10 customers per hour

Expected Hourly results:
Revenue: 10 customers *$25 = $250
Labor costs: (2 shampooers)*$15 + (3 stylists)*$20 + (1 cashier)$10 = $100
Profit = $250 – $100 = $150

FIGURE 6.11 Tracy's Hair Salon, Adding One Shampooer and Two Stylists

Waiting Line Theory

If you have ever sat in an emergency room, waiting for a doctor, you have experienced firsthand the relationship between capacity and waiting lines. Waiting lines are a concern for manufacturers as well. When materials and components must wait to be worked on, they tie up capital and push back the time manufacturers get paid by the customer.

The purpose here is twofold. First, we want to highlight the relationship between capacity and waiting lines. Second, we want to introduce you to some common tools that can be used to analyze waiting line performance. To illustrate the relationship between waiting lines and capacity, let's consider an environment we are all familiar with: the drive-up window at a fast-food restaurant. In the language of waiting lines, the drive-up window represents a *single-channel, single-phase system* (Figure 6.12). There is a single channel, or path, through the system. The single phase is at the drive-up window, where the employee takes your money and gives you your food.

If you have ever sat in line at a drive-up window, you may have thought about (or maybe cursed) the system's performance. Managers have the very same concerns. Some of the specific questions that managers have include the following:

- *What percentage* of the time will the server be busy?
- On average, *how long* will a customer have to wait in line? How long will the customer be in the system (i.e., waiting and being served)?
- On average, *how many* customers will be in line?
- How will these averages be affected by the arrival rate of customers and the service rate of the drive-up window personnel?

FIGURE 6.12
Single-Channel,
Single-Phase System

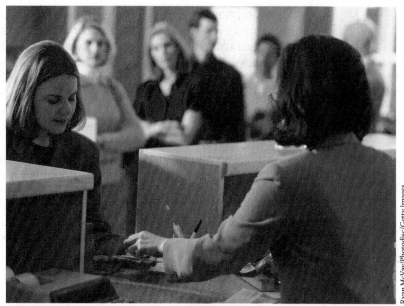

Ryan McVay/Photodisc/Getty Images

Long wait times can dramatically affect customers' perceptions of service performance. As a result, many service firms use waiting line theory to understand how capacity decisions affect waiting times.

Waiting line theory
A body of theory based on applied statistics that helps managers evaluate the relationship between capacity decisions and important performance issues such as waiting times and line lengths.

Fortunately, researchers have developed a body of theory based on applied statistics to address these types of questions. **Waiting line theory** helps managers evaluate the relationship between capacity decisions and such important performance issues as waiting times and line lengths.

Following are some of the key assumptions and terminology of waiting line theory and some basic formulas for determining waiting line performance for a single-channel, single-phase system. We should point out that there are many different waiting line environments, most of which are much more complex than the example we will present. In some cases, no formulas exist for estimating waiting line performance. When this occurs, more sophisticated simulation modeling techniques are needed to analyze the systems. The supplement at the end of this chapter discusses simulation modeling in more detail.

Arrivals. In most waiting line models, customers are assumed to arrive at *random* intervals, based on a Poisson distribution. The probability of *n* arrivals in *T* time periods is calculated as follows:

$$P_n = \frac{(\lambda T)^n}{n!}e^{-\lambda T} \tag{6.6}$$

where:

P_n = probability of *n* arrivals in *T* time periods

λ = arrival rate

T = number of time periods

EXAMPLE 6.7

Arrivals at a Drive-Up Window

Customers arrive at a drive-up window at a rate of three per minute ($\lambda = 3$). If the number of arrivals follows a Poisson distribution, what is the probability that two or fewer customers would arrive in 1 minute?

The probability of two or fewer customers is actually the probability of no arrivals *plus* the probability of one arrival *plus* the probability of two arrivals, or:

$$P(\leq 2) = P(0) + P(1) + P(2)$$
$$= 0.050 + 0.149 + 0.224 = 0.423, \text{ or } 42.3\%$$

Service Times. As with arrivals, waiting line models assume that service times will either be constant (a rare occurrence) or vary. In the latter case, modelers often use the exponential distribution to model service times, using the symbol μ to refer to the service rate.

Other Assumptions. Finally, we need to make some assumptions about the order in which customers are served, the size of the customer population, and whether customers can balk or renege. We will assume that customers are served on a first-come, first-served (FCFS) basis. Other **priority rules** might consider the urgency of the customers' needs (as in an emergency room), the speed with which customers can be served, or even the desirability of different customer types. In addition, we will assume that the population of customers is effectively infinite; that is, we are not likely to run through all the possible customers any time soon. This assumption seems reasonable for a fast-food restaurant next to a busy highway. On the other hand, different formulas are needed if the population is substantially restricted.

> **Priority rules**
> Rules for determining which customer, job, or product is processed next in a waiting line environment.

We will also assume that customers enter the system and remain there until they are served, regardless of the length of the line or the time spent waiting. They neither balk (i.e., decide against entering the system to begin with) nor renege (i.e., leave the line after entering).

With that background, we can now apply some basic formulas. Suppose that customers arrive at a rate of four per minute ($\lambda = 4$) and that the worker at the drive-up window is able to handle, on average, five customers a minute ($\mu = 5$). The average utilization of the system is:

$$\rho = \frac{\lambda}{\mu} \tag{6.7}$$

where:

ρ = average utilization of the system

λ = arrival rate

μ = service rate

For the drive-up example, $\rho = \dfrac{\lambda}{\mu} = 4/5$, or 80%.

"Great!" you say. "It looks like we have plenty of capacity. After all, the drive-up window is not being fully utilized." But there is a catch. Because the actual number of arrivals per minute and the service rate *both vary*, there can be periods of time where there is no one in line, but other times when significant queues develop. For instance, the drive-up window may go for 2 minutes without a customer, only to have four SUVs filled with screaming kids pull up at the same time.

In fact, according to waiting line theory, the *average number of customers waiting* (C_W) at the drive-up window can be calculated using the following formula:

$$C_W = \frac{\lambda^2}{\mu(\mu - \lambda)} \tag{6.8}$$

And the *average number of customers in the system* (C_S) is:

$$C_S = \frac{\lambda}{\mu - \lambda} \tag{6.9}$$

EXAMPLE 6.8
Average Number of Customers Waiting and in the System at a Drive-Up Window

Given an arrival rate of four customers per minute and a service rate of five customers per minute, the average number of customers waiting is:

$$C_W = \frac{\lambda^2}{\mu(\mu - \lambda)} = \frac{16}{5(1)} = 3.2 \text{ customers}$$

And the average number in the system is:

$$C_S = \frac{\lambda}{\mu - \lambda} = \frac{4}{1} = 4 \text{ customers}$$

But what about the average amount of *time* customers spend waiting and in the system? There are formulas to estimate these values as well:

$$\text{Average time spent waiting} = T_W = \frac{\lambda}{\mu(\mu - \lambda)} \tag{6.10}$$

$$\text{Average time spent in the system} = T_S = \frac{1}{\mu - \lambda} \tag{6.11}$$

EXAMPLE 6.9	Returning to the drive-up example, the average time spent waiting is:

EXAMPLE 6.9

Average Time a Customer Spends Waiting and in the System at a Drive-Up Window

Returning to the drive-up example, the average time spent waiting is:

$$T_W = \frac{\lambda}{\mu(\mu - \lambda)} = \frac{4}{5(1)} = 0.80 \text{ minutes, or 48 seconds}$$

And the average time spent in the system (waiting and being served) is:

$$T_S = \frac{1}{\mu - \lambda} = \frac{1}{1} = 1 \text{ minute}$$

The results in Examples 6.7 through 6.9 may not surprise you, but look at what happens as the arrival rate approaches the service rate (Table 6.6). *Even though the utilization level never reaches 100%*, the lines and waiting times get longer and longer—in fact, they grow exponentially. Note that the formulas don't even work for arrival rates greater than the service rate. This is because, under such conditions, the systems can never reach a steady-state, "average" level.

All of this points to an important general truth:

In operations and supply chain environments that must deal with random demand and variable processing times, it is virtually impossible to achieve very high capacity utilization levels and still provide acceptable customer service.

Some organizations get around this by attempting to "de-randomize" demand. For example, doctors' offices make appointments, and manufacturers fit jobs into a preset schedule. But this is not always an option. If you are injured in a car wreck, you need an ambulance now, not three hours from now. Capacity decisions in such environments often come down to striking the best balance between costs and customer service.

Suppose that the fast-food restaurant in our example can have a second worker help out at the drive-up window for $15,000 a year. The second worker would allow the drive-up window to handle six customers per minute. As Table 6.7 shows, waiting line performance statistics would improve considerably. Whether or not the restaurant should expand capacity may ultimately depend on whether the additional revenue from shorter lines and happier customers offsets the cost of hiring the second worker.

TABLE 6.6
Waiting Line Performance (service rate = 5 customers per minute)

ARRIVAL RATE (CUSTOMERS PER MINUTE)	AVERAGE UTILIZATION OF THE SYSTEM (ρ)	AVERAGE NUMBER OF CUSTOMERS WAITING (C_W)	AVERAGE TIME SPENT WAITING (MINUTES) (T_W)
3.0	60.0%	0.90	0.30
3.1	62.0%	1.01	0.33
3.2	64.0%	1.14	0.36
3.3	66.0%	1.28	0.39
3.4	68.0%	1.45	0.43
3.5	70.0%	1.63	0.47
3.6	72.0%	1.85	0.51
3.7	74.0%	2.11	0.57
3.8	76.0%	2.41	0.63
3.9	78.0%	2.77	0.71
4.0	**80.0%**	**3.20**	**0.80**
4.1	82.0%	3.74	0.91
4.2	84.0%	4.41	1.05
4.3	86.0%	5.28	1.23
4.4	88.0%	6.45	1.47
4.5	90.0%	8.10	1.80
4.6	92.0%	10.58	2.30
4.7	94.0%	14.73	3.13
4.8	96.0%	23.04	4.80
4.9	98.0%	48.02	9.80
4.95	99.0%	98.01	19.80
4.995	99.9%	998.00	199.80

TABLE 6.7
Waiting Line
Performance (service
rate = 6 customers
per minute)

ARRIVAL RATE (CUSTOMERS PER MINUTE)	AVERAGE UTILIZATION OF THE SYSTEM (ρ)	AVERAGE NUMBER OF CUSTOMERS WAITING (C_W)	AVERAGE TIME SPENT WAITING (MINUTES) (T_W)
3.0	50.0%	0.50	0.17
3.1	51.7%	0.55	0.18
3.2	53.3%	0.61	0.19
3.3	55.0%	0.67	0.20
3.4	56.7%	0.74	0.22
3.5	58.3%	0.82	0.23
3.6	60.0%	0.90	0.25
3.7	61.7%	0.99	0.27
3.8	63.3%	1.09	0.29
3.9	65.0%	1.21	0.31
4.0	**66.7%**	**1.33**	**0.33**
4.1	68.3%	1.47	0.36
4.2	70.0%	1.63	0.39
4.3	71.7%	1.81	0.42
4.4	73.3%	2.02	0.46
4.5	75.0%	2.25	0.50
4.6	76.7%	2.52	0.55
4.7	78.3%	2.83	0.60
4.8	80.0%	3.20	0.67
4.9	81.7%	3.64	0.74
4.95	82.5%	3.89	0.79
4.995	83.3%	4.14	0.83

EXAMPLE 6.10

Waiting Line
Performance at a
Snappy Lube

Snappy Lube is a quick-change oil center with a single service bay. On average, Snappy Lube can change a car's oil in 10 minutes. Cars arrive, on average, every 15 minutes. From these numbers, we can estimate the average arrival rate and service rate:

$$\text{Arrival rate} = \lambda = 60 \text{ minutes}/15 \text{ minutes} = 4 \text{ per hour}$$
$$\text{Service rate} = \mu = 60 \text{ minutes}/10 \text{ minutes} = 6 \text{ per hour}$$

Therefore:

$$\text{Average utilization} = 4/6 = 67\%$$
$$\text{Average number of cars waiting} = 16/(6*2) = 1.33 \text{ cars}$$
$$\text{Average number of cars in the system} = 4/2 = 2 \text{ cars}$$
$$\text{Average time spent waiting} = 4/(6*2) = 0.33 \text{ hour}$$
$$\text{Average time spent in the system} = 1/2 = 0.50 \text{ hour}$$

Little's Law

As you might have realized in our discussion of waiting line theory, there is a relationship between the number of units in the system and time spent in the system. *Little's Law*[5] formalizes this relationship:

$$I = RT \tag{6.12}$$

where:

I = average number of units in the system (also called *inventory*)

R = average arrival rate (i.e., *throughput rate*)

T = average time a unit spends in the system (i.e., *throughput time*)

Little's Law holds for any system that has reached *steady state*. The steady state is the point where inventory has had time to build up in the system and the average number of arrivals per period of time equals the average number of units leaving the system.

---

[5]Named for John D. C. Little, who provided the first mathematical proof for it in 1961.

FIGURE 6.13
**Using Little's Law to
Analyze Snappy Lube**

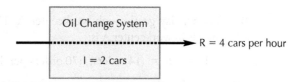

T = I/R = (2 cars)/(4 cars per hour) = 0.5 hours

To illustrate how we can use Little's Law, let's return to Snappy Lube from Example 6.10. Figure 6.13 shows what the system looks like.

Snappy Lube's throughput rate is four cars per hour. This is because, even though Snappy Lube is capable of handling up to six cars per hour, it cannot handle cars faster than the cars arrive. As we calculated in Example 6.10, the average number of cars in the Snappy Lube system is two. It stands to reason, then, that if Snappy Lube is processing four cars per hour, and the average inventory is two cars, each car will spend on average (2 cars/4 cars per hour) = 0.5 hours in the system.

While Little's Law may seem rather simple, it's actually very powerful. A major advantage of Little's Law is that the relationships expressed in Equation (6.12) are always true, regardless of how complex the system is, how much arrivals or service times vary, or what the flow units are (money, people, orders, etc.). Furthermore, we can apply Little's Law to a single activity, a multistep process, or even an entire supply chain. Example 6.11 illustrates how Little's Law can be applied in a more complex business situation.

EXAMPLE 6.11

**Applying Little's Law
in a Manufacturing
Plant**

A manufacturing plant has 100 orders arrive each day (Figure 6.14) All orders go through the order processing area, where, on average, there are 25 orders in the system. Of the incoming orders, 70% are "A" orders, which are routed through workcenter A, where the average inventory of orders is 14. The remaining 30% are "B" orders, which are routed through workcenter B, where the average inventory is 1.5 orders. Because the total number of orders that exit the system (70 + 30) equals the number coming in, the system is in steady state.

FIGURE 6.14 Order Flow in a Manufacturing Environment

The plant manager wants to know, on average:

1. How long does an order (A or B) stay in the order processing area?
2. How long does it take an A order to work its way through the plant?
3. How long does it take a B order to work its way through the plant?
4. How long does it take the average order (A or B) to work its way through the plant?

To answer the first question, note that the throughput rate for order processing is 100 orders per day. Since the average inventory level in the order processing area is 25, the average throughput time for just this step is calculated as:

T = I/R = (25 orders)/(100 orders per day) = 0.25 days in order processing

70 orders per day go through workcenter A. Therefore, the estimated average time an order spends in workcenter A is:

$$T = I/R = (14 \text{ orders})/(70 \text{ orders per day}) = 0.2 \text{ days in workcenter A}$$

Putting together these two pieces of information, we find that the amount of time the average A order spends in the plant is:

$$\text{Order processing time} + \text{workcenter A time}$$
$$= 0.25 \text{ days} + 0.2 \text{ days} = 0.45 \text{ days}$$

By analogy, the amount of time the average B order spends in the plant is:

$$\text{Order processing time} + \text{workcenter B time}$$
$$= 0.25 \text{ days} + (1.5 \text{ orders}/30 \text{ orders per day})$$
$$= 0.25 \text{ days} + 0.05 \text{ days} = 0.30 \text{ days}$$

Now for the last question: How much time does the *average* order stay in the plant? One way to determine this is to take a weighted average of the times for the A orders and the B orders:

$$70\%*0.45 \text{ days} + 30\%*0.30 \text{ days} = 0.405 \text{ days for the average order}$$

But a more clever way is to recognize that for the *entire* system, throughput rate $R = 100$ and average inventory $I = 25 + 14 + 1.5 = 40.5$. The estimated average throughput time for the entire system can then be calculated as:

$$T = I/R = (40.5 \text{ orders})/(100 \text{ orders per day}) = 0.405 \text{ days for the average order}$$

This result reinforces the idea that Little's Law can be used to analyze the process or system at multiple levels.

CHAPTER SUMMARY

Capacity decisions are among the most important strategic decisions operations and supply chain managers make. As the opening case study on adding pharmaceutical manufacturing capacity suggests, such decisions can have far-reaching effects for a business, its customers, and even society. Even though capacity decisions are inherently risky, this chapter showed how managers can think about and analyze these decisions in a logical manner.

Specifically, we talked about three common capacity strategies and also demonstrated various methods for evaluating the financial pros and cons of capacity alternatives. We devoted the last section of the chapter to analyzing *process* capacity using the Theory of Constraints (TOC), waiting line theory, and Little's Law. These advanced perspectives help us understand how capacity behaves across a supply chain, how higher resource levels drive down waiting times, and the relationship between inventory, throughput times, and throughput rates.

KEY FORMULAS

Total cost of a capacity alternative (page 147):

$$TC = FC + VC*X \tag{6.1}$$

where:

TC = total cost

FC = fixed cost

VC = variable cost per unit of business activity

X = amount of business activity (number of customers served, number of units produced, etc.)

Expected value of a capacity alternative (page 149):

$$EV_j = \sum_{i=1}^{I} P_i C_i \tag{6.2}$$

where:

EV_j = expected value of capacity alternative j

P_i = probability of demand level i

C_i = financial result (cost, revenue, or profit) at demand level i

Break-even point (page 153):

$$BEP = \frac{FC}{R - VC}$$

(6.3)

where:

BEP = break-even point

FC = fixed cost

V = variable cost per unit of business activity

R = revenue per unit of business activity

Productivity (page 153):

$$\text{Productivity} = \text{outputs/inputs}$$

(6.4)

Learning curve theory estimate of resources (usually labor) required to complete the nth unit (page 153):

$$T_n = T_1 n^b$$

(6.5)

where:

T_n = resources (usually labor) required for the nth unit

T_1 = resources required for the 1st unit

b = ln(Learning percentage)/ln2

Probability of n arrivals in T time periods (page 161):

$$P_n = \frac{(\lambda T)^n}{n!} e^{-\lambda T}$$

(6.6)

where:

P_n = probability of n arrivals in T time periods

λ = arrival rate

T = number of time periods

Average utilization of a waiting line system (page 162):

$$\rho = \frac{\lambda}{\mu}$$

(6.7)

where:

λ = arrival rate

μ = service rate

Average number of customers waiting in a waiting line (page 162):

$$C_W = \frac{\lambda^2}{\mu(\mu - \lambda)}$$

(6.8)

Average number of customers in the waiting line system (page 162):

$$C_S = \frac{\lambda}{\mu - \lambda}$$

(6.9)

Average time spent waiting in a waiting line (page 162):

$$T_W = \frac{\lambda}{\mu(\mu - \lambda)}$$

(6.10)

Average time spent in the waiting line system (page 162):

$$T_S = \frac{1}{\mu - \lambda}$$

(6.11)

Little's Law (page 164):

$$I = RT \tag{6.12}$$

where:

I = average number of units in the system (also called *inventory*)

R = average arrival rate (i.e., *throughput rate*)

T = average time a unit spends in the system (i.e., *throughput time*)

KEY TERMS

USING EXCEL IN CAPACITY MANAGEMENT

Many of the capacity decision models we have shown in this chapter can easily be incorporated into a spreadsheet application, such as Microsoft Excel. The following spreadsheet calculates the break-even points and indifference points for three capacity alternatives.

For instance, the break-even point for option B (cell C14) is calculated as follows:

BEP = fixed cost/(revenue per unit − variable cost per unit)

$\quad$ = C8/(D4 − D8) = 14.71

Likewise, the indifference point for options B and C (cell E15) is:

$$= \frac{\text{(option C fixed cost − option B fixed cost)}}{\text{(option B variable cost − option C variable cost)}}$$

$\quad$ = (C9 − C8)/(D8 − D9)

$\quad$ = 366.67

Of course, the key advantage of using the spreadsheet is that we can quickly evaluate new scenarios simply by changing the input values.

	A	B	C	D	E	F
1	**Evaluating Alternative Capacity Options**					
2	**(Enter inputs in shaded cells)**					
3						
4			Revenue per unit of output:	$100.00		
5						
6		Capacity Option	Fixed cost	Variable cost per unit of output	Max. output	
7		Option A	$0.00	$30.00	200	
8		Option B	$1,250.00	$15.00	300	
9		Option C	$4,000.00	$7.50	400	
10						
11				*** Indifference Points ***		
12			*** Break-even point ***	Option A	Option B	Option C
13		Option A	0.00	---		
14		Option B	14.71	83.33	---	
15		Option C	43.24	177.78	366.67	---

SOLVED PROBLEM

PROBLEM

Auvia Cruise Lines

With the market for luxury cruises burgeoning, Auvia Cruise Lines is debating whether to invest in a large cruise ship to serve what would be a new market for the company—cruises around Alaska. This is no small investment: Auvia management figures that the new 86,000-gross-registered-tons vessel will cost approximately $375 million. Spread over 25 years (the useful life of the ship), this amounts to a fixed cost of $375 million/25 = $15 million per year. The new ship can carry 2,000 passengers at a time, or up to 40,000 per year.

Management has determined that the average passenger will generate revenues of $2,400 and variable costs of $1,300. Furthermore, marketing has put together the following demand estimates for the new cruise:

ANNUAL DEMAND (PASSENGERS)	PROBABILITY
10,000	30%
30,000	50%
38,000	20%

Calculate the yearly break-even point for the new cruise ship. Determine the expected value of the new cruise ship and draw out the decision tree for Auvia Cruise Lines.

Solution

The break-even point for the new cruise ship is:

$$FC + VC(X) = R(X)$$
$$\$15,000,000 + \$1,300X = \$2,400X$$
$$X = \$15,000,000/\$1,100, \text{ or about 13,636 passengers per year}$$

And the expected financial results under the three demand scenarios are as follows:

$$(R - VC) * X - FC$$

10,000 passenger: ($2,400 − $1,300) * 10,000 − $15,000,000 = −$4,000,000
30,000 passenger: ($2,400 − $1,300) * 30,000 − $15,000,000 = $18,000,000
38,000 passenger: ($2,400 − $1,300) * 38,000 − $15,000,000 = $26,800,000

The expected value is simply the average of these three results, weighted by the respective probabilities:

Expected value for the new cruise ship =
30% * (−$4,000,000) + 50% * ($18,000,000) + 20% * ($26,800,000) = $13,160,000

The decision tree follows. Note that the expected value of not investing in the new ship is $0. This reflects the fact that if Auvia does not invest in the new ship, it will incur neither the expenses nor the revenues associated with cruises around Alaska. If Auvia is willing to take the risk of losing up to $4 million a year, the new cruise line looks very promising.

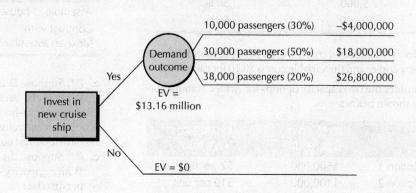

DISCUSSION QUESTIONS

1. Which type of operations and supply chain environment do you think would have a more difficult time managing capacity—an environment supporting standardized products/services or one supporting customized products/services? Why?
2. What kind of capacity strategy—lead, lag, or match—would you expect a fire station to follow? What about a driver's license testing center? Why?
3. Who do you think would benefit more from a "virtual supply chain" capacity strategy—a small start-up firm with few resources or an older, more established company? Why? What are the risks associated with such a strategy?
4. The manager at a grocery store says to you, "I want my checkout clerks to be busy 100% of the time. I can't afford to have them sit around." How would you use waiting line theory to explain the problems with this thinking? Is there some way to have checkout clerks do productive work even when they aren't dealing with customers?
5. What are the relationships among learning, productivity, and effective capacity? What are the pros and cons of using learning curves to estimate future resource requirements?
6. A manufacturer takes raw material from a supplier, processes it using a single manufacturing step, and then sells it to its customers. Suppose the manufacturer decides to double the capacity of the manufacturing step. Under what conditions will throughput for the system double? What other factors might be constraining the throughput of the system?

PROBLEMS

(* = easy; ** = moderate; *** = advanced)

Problems for Section 6.3: Methods of Evaluating Capacity Strategies

1. (*) The Shelly Group has leased a new copier that costs $700 per month plus $0.10 for each copy. What is the total cost if Shelly makes 5,000 copies a month? If it makes 10,000 copies a month? What is the per-copy cost at 5,000 copies? At 10,000 copies?
2. Arktec Manufacturing must choose between the following two capacity options:

	FIXED COST (PER YEAR)	VARIABLE COST (PER UNIT)
Option 1	$500,000	$2 per unit
Option 2	$100,000	$10 per unit

   a. (*) What would the cost be for each option if the demand level is 25,000 units per year? If it is 75,000 units per year?
   b. (**) In general, which option do you think would be better as volume levels increase? As they decrease? Why?
   c. (*) What is the indifference point?

3. (*) Suppose the Shelly Group has identified two possible demand levels for copies per month:

COPIES (PER MONTH)	PROBABILITY
5,000	50%
10,000	50%

   What is the expected cost if it costs $700 per month to lease a new copier and the variable cost is $0.10 for each copy?

4. Consider the two capacity options for Arktec Manufacturing shown below:

	FIXED COST (PER YEAR)	VARIABLE COST (PER UNIT)
Option 1	$500,000	$2 per unit
Option 2	$100,000	$10 per unit

   Suppose the company has identified the following three possible demand scenarios:

DEMAND (UNITS PER YEAR)	PROBABILITY
25,000	30%
60,000	40%
100,000	30%

   a. (**) What is the expected value of each option? Which option would you choose, based on this information?
   b. (**) Suppose the lowest and highest demand levels are updated to 40,000 and 110,000, respectively. Recalculate the expected values. What happened?
   c. (**) Draw the decision tree for Arktec Manufacturing. When drawing your tree, assume that managers must select a capacity option *before* they know what the demand level will actually be.
   d. (**) Calculate the expected value for each decision branch. Which option would you prefer? Why?

5. You are the new CEO of DualJet, a U.S. company that makes premium kitchen stoves for home use. You must decide whether to assemble the stoves in-house or to have a Mexican company do it. The fixed and variable costs for each option are as follows:

	FIXED COST	VARIABLE COST
Assemble in-house	$55,000	$620
Contract with Mexican assembler	$0	$880

   a. (**) Suppose DualJet's premium stoves sell for $2,500. What is the break-even volume point for assembling the stoves in-house?
   b. (*) At what volume level do the two capacity options have identical costs?
   c. (**) Suppose the expected demand for stoves is 3,000. Which capacity option would you prefer, from a cost perspective?

6. Emily Watkins, a recent college graduate, faces some tough choices. Emily must decide whether to accept an offer for a job that pays $35,000 or hold out for another job that pays $45,000 a year. Emily thinks there is a 75% chance that she will get an offer for the higher-paying job. The problem is that Emily has to make a decision on the lower-paying job within the next few days, and she will not know about the higher-paying job for two weeks.

   a. (**) Draw out the decision tree for Emily Watkins.
   b. (**) What is the key decision Emily faces? What is the expected value of each decision branch?
   c. (**) What other factors might Emily consider, aside from expected value?

7. Philip Neilson owns a fireworks store. Philip's fixed costs are $12,000 a month, and each fireworks assortment he sells costs, on average, $8. The average selling price for an assortment is $25.

   a. (*) What is the break-even point for Philip's fireworks store?

   Suppose Philip decides to expand his business. His new fixed expenses will be $20,000, but the average cost for a fireworks assortment will fall to just $5 due to Philip's higher purchase volumes.

   b. (*) What is the new break-even point?
   c. (**) At what volume level is Philip indifferent to the two capacity alternatives outlined above?

8. Merck is considering launching a new drug called Laffolin. Merck has identified two possible demand scenarios:

DEMAND LEVEL	PROBABILITY
1 million patients	30%
2 million patients	70%

   Merck also has the following information:

Revenue	$140 per patient
Fixed costs to manufacture and sell Laffolin	$70 million
Variable costs to manufacture and sell Laffolin	$80 per patient
Maximum number of patients that Merck can handle	3 million

   a. (*) How many patients must Merck have in order to break even?
   b. (**) How much money will Merck make if demand for Laffolin is 1 million patients? If demand is 2 million patients?
   c. (**) What is the expected value of making Laffolin?
   d. (**) Draw the decision tree for the Laffolin decision, showing the profits for each branch (Total revenues − total variable costs − total fixed costs) and all expected values.

9. Clay runs a small hotdog stand in downtown Chapel Hill. Clay can serve about 30 customers an hour. During lunchtime, customers randomly arrive at a rate of 20 per hour.

   a. (*) What percentage of the time is Clay busy?
   b. (*) On average, how many customers are waiting to be served? How many are in the system (i.e., waiting and being served)?

   c. (*) On average, how long will a customer wait to be served? How long will a customer be in the system?

10. Peri Thompson is the sole dispatcher for Thompson Termite Control. Peri's job is to take customer calls, schedule appointments, and in some cases resolve any service or billing questions while the customer is on the phone. Peri can handle about 15 calls an hour.

    a. (*) Typically, Peri gets about 10 calls an hour. Under these conditions, what is the average number of customers waiting, and what is the average waiting time?
    b. (**) Monday mornings are unusually busy. During these peak times, Peri receives around 13 calls an hour, on average. Recalculate the average number of customers waiting and the average waiting time. What can you conclude?

11. Benson Racing is training a new pit crew for its racing team. For its first practice run, the pit crew is able to complete all the tasks in exactly 30 seconds—not exactly world-class. The second time around, the crew shaves 4.5 seconds off its time.

    a. (*) Estimate the learning rate for the pit crew, based on the times for the first two practice runs.
    b. (**) Mark Benson, owner of Benson Racing, says that the pit crew must be able to complete all the tasks in less than 15 seconds in order to be competitive. Based on your answer to part a, how many times will the pit crew need to practice before it breaks the 15-second barrier?
    c. (**) Is it realistic to expect the pit crew to experience learning improvements indefinitely? Explain.

12. Wake County has a special emergency rescue team. The team is practicing rescuing dummies from a smoke-filled building. The first time, the team took 240 seconds (4 minutes). The second time, it took 180 seconds (3 minutes).

    a. (*) What is the estimated learning rate for the rescue team, based on the information provided?
    b. (**) Suppose that the team's learning rate for the rescue exercise is 80%. How many times will the team need to repeat the exercise until its time is *less than 120 seconds* (50% of the original time)?
    c. (**) How long will it take the emergency team to perform its 20th rescue if the learning rate is 80%?

13. After graduating from college, your friends and you start an Internet job search site called TriangCom. Business has been fantastic, with 10 million customer hits to the site in the past year. You have several capacity decisions to consider. One key decision involves the number of computer servers needed. You are considering putting in 10, 20, or 30 servers. Costs and capacity limits are as follows:

NUMBER OF SERVERS	FIXED COST PER YEAR	VARIABLE COST PER HIT	MAXIMUM HITS PER YEAR
10	$50,000	$.005	20 million
20	$90,000	$.003	40 million
30	$120,000	$.002	60 million

In addition, marketing has developed the following demand scenarios:

YEARLY DEMAND	PROBABILITY
15 million hits	30%
30 million hits	60%
45 million hits	10%

Finally, TriangCom generated $5 million last year, based on 10 million hits. Put another way, each hit generated, on average, $0.50 in revenue.

a. (**) Calculate the break-even point for each capacity alternative.

b. (**) At what demand level will you be indifferent to having either 10 or 20 servers?

c. (***) Calculate the expected value for each capacity alternative. (*Hint:* Don't forget about capacity constraints that can limit the number of hits each capacity alternative can handle.) Which alternative will you prefer if you want to maximize the expected value?

TriangCom has hired Donna Olway to add new features to the Web site. Donna completes her first job in five weeks and her second job in four weeks. Assume that (1) Donna continues to learn at this rate and (2) her time improvements will follow a learning curve.

d. (**) How long will you expect Donna to take to complete her sixth job?

e. (**) How long will you expect Donna to take to complete the next five jobs (jobs 3 through 7)?

With thousands of customers, TriangCom has established a hotline to take customer calls. The hotline is staffed by one person 24 hours a day. You have the following statistics:

Service rate for calls	15 per hour, on average
Arrival rate for calls	11 per hour, on average

As part of your customer service policy, you have decided that the average waiting time should not exceed 2.5 minutes.

f. (*) What is the average number of callers being served?

g. (*) On average, how many callers are waiting to be served?

h. (**) What is the average waiting time for a customer? Is this time acceptable, given the customer service policy?

14. Rich Sawyer runs a landscaping firm. Each year Rich contracts for labor and equipment hours from a local construction company. The construction company has given Rich three different capacity options:

CAPACITY OPTION	LABOR HOURS	EQUIPMENT HOURS
High capacity	9,000	6,000
Medium capacity	6,750	4,500
Low capacity	4,500	3,000

Cost per labor hour:	$10 per hour
Cost per equipment hour:	$20 per hour

Once Rich has chosen a capacity option, he cannot change it later. In addition, the cost for each capacity option is fixed. That is, Rich must pay for all labor and equipment hours he contracts for, even if he doesn't need them all. Therefore, there are essentially no variable costs. Rich also has information concerning the amount of revenue and the labor and equipment hours needed for the "typical" landscaping job:

Job revenue	$2,000 per job
Labor hours per job	30 hours
Equipment hours per job	20 hours

Finally, Rich has identified three possible demand levels. These demand levels, with their associated probabilities, are as follows:

DEMAND LEVEL	NUMBER OF JOBS	PROBABILITY
High demand	300	30%
Medium demand	200	40%
Low demand	120	30%

a. (***) Determine the total fixed costs and the break-even point for each capacity option. What is the maximum number of jobs that can be handled under each capacity option?

b. (***) Draw a decision tree for Rich's firm. What are the nine possible outcomes Rich is facing? (*Hint:* One is "Rich subcontracts for low capacity and demand turns out to be low.") What is the profit (Revenue − fixed costs) associated with each of the nine outcomes? Be sure to consider the capacity limits of each alternative when calculating revenues.

c. (***) Using the information from part b, calculate the expected profit of each capacity alternative. Which option will Rich prefer if he wants to maximize expected profit?

15. (***) (*Microsoft Excel problem*) The following figure shows an expanded version of the Excel spreadsheet described in *Using Excel in Capacity Management*. In addition to the break-even and indifference points, the expanded spreadsheet calculates financial results for three capacity options under three different demand scenarios. **Re-create this spreadsheet in Excel.** You should develop the spreadsheet so that the results will be recalculated if any of the values in the highlighted cells are changed. Your formatting does not have to be exactly the same, but the numbers should be. (As a test, see what happens if you change the "Max. output" and "Variable cost" for Capacity Option A to 250 units and $35, respectively. Your new expected value for Capacity Option A should be $14,218.75.)

	A	B	C	D	E	F
1	**Evaluating Alternative Capacity Options**					
2	**(Enter inputs in shaded cells)**					
3						
4			Revenue per unit of output:	$100.00		
5						
6		Capacity Option	Fixed cost	Variable cost per unit of output	Max. output	
7		Option A	$0.00	$30.00	200	
8		Option B	$1,250.00	$15.00	300	
9		Option C	$4,000.00	$7.50	400	
10						
11		Demand Scenario	Demand level	Probability		
12		Low	125	25%		
13		Medium	275	55%		
14		High	425	20%		
15			Total:	100%		
16						
17				*** Indifference Points ***		
18			*** Break-even point ***	Option A	Option B	Option C
19		Option A	0.00	---		
20		Option B	14.71	83.33	---	
21		Option C	43.24	177.78	366.67	---
22						
23				*** Results for different capacity/demand combinations ***		
24						
25			Low	Medium	High	*** Expected value ***
26		Option A	$8,750.00	$14,000.00	$14,000.00	$12,687.50
27		Option B	$9,375.00	$22,125.00	$24,250.00	$19,362.50
28		Option C	$7,562.50	$21,437.50	$33,000.00	$20,281.25

Problems from Section 6.4: Understanding and Analyzing Process Capacity

16. The Lenovo Refurbishing Center repairs used laptops that are returned under warranty.

- The center receives and processes, on average, 200 laptops per day.
- All laptops are tested upon receipt: 30% are immediately rejected, and the remaining 70% are sent to the refurbishing area.
- On average, there are 21 laptops in the testing area waiting or being worked on.
- On average, there are 16 laptops in the refurbishing area waiting or being worked on.

a. (*) What is the average throughput time for *all* laptops entering the system?

b. (**) What is the average throughput time for a laptop that goes through both testing and refurbishing? Suppose Lenovo wants this time to be less than one day.

Is the current system meeting this performance goal? Justify your answer.

17. ABS sells construction materials to commercial and home builders. One of ABS's key processes is the order fulfillment process shown below and described as follows:

- **All orders are assessed on arrival.** Of the orders, 30% are immediately declined for various reasons. The typical order spends 0.25 days in this order assessment step before moving on.
- **20% of all orders are large orders.** Average total time in this large orders processing step, including waiting and actual process time, is 2 days.

- **50% of all orders are small orders.** Average time in this small orders processing step, including waiting and processing, is 0.5 days.
- **ABS receives an average of 20 order requests a day.** The system is currently in steady state.

a. (**) What is the estimated total inventory for the entire order fulfillment process?

b. (**) Based on the information given above and your answer to part a, what is the estimated total flow time for the average order entering the process?

CASE STUDY

Forster's Market

Introduction

Forster's Market is a retailer of specialty food items, including premium coffees, imported crackers and cheeses, and the like. Last year, Forster's sold 14,400 pounds of coffee. Forster's pays a local supplier $3 per pound and then sells the coffees for $7 a pound.

The Roaster Decision

While Forster's makes a handsome profit on the coffee business, owner Robbie Forster thinks he can do better. Specifically, Robbie is considering investing in a large industrial-sized coffee roaster that can roast up to 40,000 pounds per year. By roasting the coffee himself, Robbie will be able to cut his coffee costs to $1.60 a pound. The drawback is that the roaster will be quite expensive; fixed costs (including the lease, power, training, and additional labor) will run about $35,000 every year.

The roaster capacity will also be significantly more than the 14,400 pounds that Forster's needs. However, Robbie thinks he will be able to sell coffee to area restaurants and coffee shops for $2.90 a pound. Robbie has outlined three possible demand scenarios:

Low demand	18,000 pounds per year
Medium demand	25,000 pounds per year
High demand	35,000 pounds per year

These numbers include the 14,400 pounds sold at Forster's Market. In addition, Robbie thinks all three scenarios are equally likely.

Questions

1. What are the two capacity options that Robbie needs to consider? What are their fixed and variable costs? What is the indifference point for the two options? What are the implications of the indifference point?
2. Draw the decision tree for the roaster decision. If Forster's does not invest in the roaster, does Robbie need to worry about the different demand scenarios outlined above? Why or why not?
3. Calculate the expected value for the two capacity options. Keep in mind that, for the roaster option, any demand above 14,400 pounds will generate revenues of only $2.90 a pound. Update the decision tree to show your results.
4. What is the worst possible financial outcome for Forster's? The best possible financial outcome? What other factors—core competency, strategic flexibility, etc.—should Robbie consider when making this decision?

REFERENCES

Books and Articles

Blackstone, J. H., ed., *APICS Dictionary*, 15th ed. (Chicago, IL: APICS, 2016).

Goldratt, E., *The Goal*, 2nd ed. (Great Barrington, MA: North River Press, 1992).

Internet

Egan, M., "Think Inside the Box: Pfizer Will Use GE's Mobile Biotech Factory to Make Next-Generation Drugs in China," *GE Reports*, June 30, 2016, **www.gereports.com/pfizer-will-use-ges-modular-factory-to-make-next-generation-drugs-in-china/https://en.wikipedia.org/wiki/Biomanufacturing.**

Kiselev Andrey Valerevich/Shutterstock

CHAPTER
six

Advanced Waiting Line Theory and Simulation Modeling

SUPPLEMENT OBJECTIVES

By the end of this supplement, you will be able to:

● Use statistics-based formulas to estimate waiting line lengths and waiting times for three different types of waiting line systems.

● Develop a simple Monte Carlo simulation using Microsoft Excel, and develop and analyze a system using SimQuick.

INTRODUCTION

Chapter 6 introduced waiting line theory and provided some formulas for calculating waiting times and line lengths for a simple waiting line situation. In this supplement, we describe two additional waiting line environments and demonstrate how statistically derived formulas can be used to assess the performance of these systems as well.

The second half of this supplement introduces simulation modeling. Simulation is often described in conjunction with waiting lines because many complex waiting line systems cannot be analyzed using neatly derived formulas. That said, simulation can be used in any environment where actual occurrences of interest—arrivals, quality problems, work times, etc.—can be modeled mathematically. We show how Monte Carlo simulation can be used to develop a very simple simulation using Excel. We then use one particular simulation package, SimQuick, to illustrate simulation model building and analysis.

6S.1 ALTERNATIVE WAITING LINES

In Chapter 6, we illustrated how waiting line theory works, using the example of a waiting line environment with a single path through one process step. In that example, both the arrival rate and service rate were probabilistic. In the language of waiting line theory, this is known as a *single channel, single phase system* (see Figure 6S.1).

We then illustrated how statistics-based formulas could be used to answer questions such as:

- What percentage of the time will the process be busy?
- On average, *how long* will a unit have to wait in line? How long will it be in the system (i.e., waiting and being served)?
- On average, *how many* units will be in line?
- How will these averages be affected by the arrival rate of units and the service rate at the process step?

Of course, there are many waiting line environments that do not fit this mold. An automatic car wash, for example, may have one line and one process step, but the service time is *constant*. Or we may be interested in a multiple-channel, single-phase system, such as a bank. Here, there is only a one-process step, but there can be multiple paths through the system, depending on how many tellers are working (see Figure 6S.2).

Or we may be interested in a single-channel, multiple-phase system. Examples include a hospital emergency room, where you wait to check in (phase 1) and then you wait to see a doctor or nurse (phase 2). Figure 6S.3 illustrates such a system. We can even have multiple-channel, multiple-phase systems. In general, the more complex the environment, the less likely we are to be able to analyze it using preestablished formulas.

In the remainder of this supplement, we review some of the key assumptions and terminology that make up waiting line theory and introduce some formulas for determining waiting line performance for two additional waiting line environments: the single-channel, single-phase system with constant service times and the multiple-channel, single-phase system. In the second half of the supplement, we introduce simulation modeling, which can be used to model more complex environments.

FIGURE 6S.1
Single-Channel,
Single-Phase System

FIGURE 6S.2
Multiple-Channel,
Single-Phase System

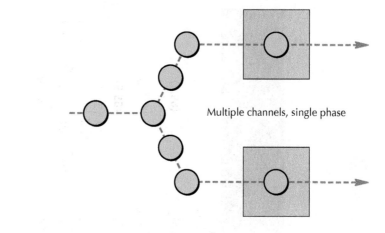

Multiple channels, single phase

FIGURE 6S.3
Single-Channel,
Multiple-Phase System

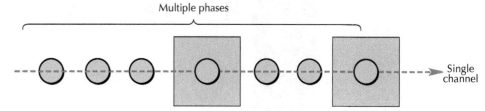

Multiple phases

Single channel

Assumptions behind Waiting Line Theory

Arrivals. In most waiting line models, customers are assumed to arrive at random intervals, based on a Poisson distribution. The probability of n arrivals in T time periods is calculated as follows:

$$P_n = \frac{(\lambda T)^n}{n!} e^{-\lambda T} \qquad\qquad (6S.1)$$

where:

  P_n = probability of n arrivals in T time periods
  λ = arrival rate
  T = number of time periods

Service Times. Waiting line models assume that service times will either be constant or vary. In the latter case, modelers often use the exponential distribution to model service times, using the symbol μ to refer to the service rate.

Other Assumptions. Finally, we need to make some assumptions about the order in which customers are served, the size of the customer population, and whether customers can balk or renege. All waiting line formulas assume that customers are served on a first-come, first-served (FCFS) basis. Other priority rules might consider the urgency of the customers' needs (as in an emergency room), the speed with which customers can be served, or the desirability of different customer types. In addition, we will assume that the population of customers is effectively infinite; that is, we are not likely to run through all the possible customers anytime soon.

  Finally, we will assume that customers enter the system and remain there until they are served, regardless of the length of the line or time spent waiting. They neither balk (decide against entering the system to begin with) nor renege (leave the line after entering).

Waiting Line Formulas for Three Different Environments

Table 6S.1 contains formulas for estimating performance in three different waiting line environments. In all three cases, the formulas require that we know:

  • The average number of arrivals per period of time, λ
  • The average time each server takes to service a unit, μ

TABLE 6S.1 Waiting Line Formulas for Three Different Environments

WAITING LINE ENVIRONMENT:
λ = average number of arrivals per period of time
μ = average time each server takes to service a unit
M = number of channels

WAITING LINE ENVIRONMENT	AVERAGE NUMBER OF UNITS WAITING, C_W	AVERAGE NUMBER OF UNITS IN SYSTEM, C_S	AVERAGE TIME SPENT WAITING, T_W	AVERAGE TIME SPENT IN SYSTEM, T_S
Single-channel, single-phase system with Poisson arrivals and exponential service times	$\dfrac{\lambda^2}{\mu(\mu-\lambda)}$ (6S.2)	$C_W + \dfrac{\lambda}{\mu}$ (6S.3)	$\dfrac{\lambda}{\mu(\mu-\lambda)}$ (6S.4)	$T_W + \dfrac{1}{\mu}$ (6S.5)
Single-channel, single-phase system with Poisson arrivals and constant service times	$\dfrac{\lambda^2}{2\mu(\mu-\lambda)}$ (6S.6)	$C_W + \dfrac{\lambda}{\mu}$ (6S.7)	$\dfrac{\lambda}{2\mu(\mu-\lambda)}$ (6S.8)	$T_W + \dfrac{1}{\mu}$ (6S.9)
Multiple-channel, single-phase system with Poisson arrivals and exponential service times ("multi-server model")	$C_S - \dfrac{\lambda}{\mu}$ (6S.11)	$\dfrac{\lambda\mu\left(\dfrac{\lambda}{\mu}\right)^M}{(M-1)!(M\mu-\lambda)^2}P_0 + \left(\dfrac{\lambda}{\mu}\right)$ (6S.12)	$T_S - \dfrac{1}{\mu}$ (6S.13)	$\dfrac{\mu\left(\dfrac{\lambda}{\mu}\right)^M}{(M-1)!(M\mu-\lambda)^2}P_0 + \left(\dfrac{1}{\mu}\right)$ (6S.14)

where:
P_0 = probability of 0 units in the system

$$P_0 = \frac{1}{\left[\displaystyle\sum_{n=0}^{M-1}\frac{1}{n!}\left(\frac{\lambda}{\mu}\right)^n\right] + \frac{1}{M!}\left(\frac{\lambda}{\mu}\right)^M\left(\frac{M\mu}{M\mu-\lambda}\right)}$$

(6S.10)

The first row of formulas is for a single-channel, single-phase system with probabilistic arrivals and service times. These are the same formulas we used in Chapter 6 to introduce waiting line theory. The second row is for a single-channel, single-phase system where service times are constant. The third row described a multiple-channel, single-phase system (Figure 6S.2). We illustrate how these formulas can be used in Examples 6S.1 through 6S.3.

EXAMPLE 6S.1

Luc's Deluxe Car Wash, Part 1: Probabilistic Arrivals and Service Times

Luc Shields, an enterprising high school student, runs a car wash where he has a single crew of workers wash cars by hand (i.e., a single-channel, single-phase system). Cars arrive about every 8 minutes, on average. Luc's crew can wash, on average, one car every 6 minutes. Arrivals follow a Poisson distribution, and the service times are exponentially distributed.

Luc would like to estimate (1) the average number of cars waiting and in the system and (2) the average time a car spends waiting and in the system. From the information provided, we know that:

$$\text{Arrival rate} = \lambda = \frac{60 \text{ minutes}}{8 \text{ minutes}} = 7.5 \text{ cars per hour}$$

$$\text{Service rate} = \mu = \frac{60 \text{ minutes}}{6 \text{ minutes}} = 10 \text{ cars per hour}$$

Therefore, applying Equations (6S.2) through (6S.5):

$$\text{Average number of cars waiting } (C_w) = \frac{\lambda^2}{\mu(\mu - \lambda)} = \frac{7.5^2}{10(10 - 7.5)} = 2.25 \text{ cars}$$

$$\text{Average number of cars in the system } (C_s) = C_w + \frac{\lambda}{\mu} = 2.25 + 0.75 = 3 \text{ cars}$$

$$\text{Average time a car spends waiting } (T_w) = \frac{\lambda}{\mu(\mu - \lambda)} = \frac{7.5}{10(10 - 7.5)}$$

$$= 0.3 \text{ hours, or about 18 minutes}$$

$$\text{Average time a car spends in the system } (T_s) = T_w + \frac{1}{\mu} = 0.3 + 0.1$$

$$= 0.4 \text{ hours, or about 24 minutes}$$

EXAMPLE 6S.2

Luc's Deluxe Car Wash, Part 2: Probabilistic Arrivals and Constant Service Times

Luc is contemplating replacing his work crew with an automated car wash system. Although the automated system is no faster than the current work crew, it can handle cars at a *constant* rate of one car every 6 minutes. Luc is not sure if this would make any difference with regard to the waiting line performance at his car wash, so he decides to use the equations in Table 6S.1 to find out.

Jose AS Reyes/Shutterstock

Notice that the arrival rate and service rate are still 7.5 cars and 10 cars per hour, respectively. The difference is that the service rate no longer follows an exponential distribution but is constant. Applying Equations (6S.6) through (6S.9), Luc gets the following estimates:

$$\text{Average number of cars waiting } (C_w) = \frac{\lambda^2}{2\mu(\mu - \lambda)} = \frac{7.5^2}{20(10 - 7.5)} = 1.125 \text{ cars}$$

$$\text{Average number of cars in the system } (C_s) = C_w + \frac{\lambda}{\mu} = 1.125 + 0.75 = 1.875 \text{ cars}$$

$$\text{Average time a car spends waiting } (T_w) = \frac{\lambda}{2\mu(\mu - \lambda)} = \frac{7.5}{20(10 - 7.5)}$$

$$= 0.15 \text{ hours, or about 9 minutes}$$

$$\text{Average time a car spends in the system } (T_s) = T_w + \frac{1}{\mu} = 0.15 + 0.10$$

$$= 0.25 \text{ hours, or about 15 minutes}$$

Looking at the results, Luc is surprised to see that average number of cars waiting and average time waiting are cut in half. The results impress upon Luc the negative impact of variability on process performance and capacity requirements.

EXAMPLE 6S.3

Luc's Deluxe Car Wash, Part 3: Adding a Second Crew

Even though Luc likes the fact that an automated car wash system with constant service time would decrease waiting times and line lengths, he doesn't feel that he can afford the investment at this point. Rather, Luc is thinking about adding a second crew. This would effectively make his car wash a multiple-channel, single-phase system, where $M = 2$. Assuming that the second crew has the same service rate numbers as the first ($\mu = 10$; service times are exponentially distributed), Luc can estimate the performance of the system by using Equations (6S.10) through (6S.14). To use these equations, we must first calculate the probability of zero cars in the system:

$$P_0 = \frac{1}{\left[\sum_{n=0}^{M-1} \frac{1}{n!}\left(\frac{\lambda}{\mu}\right)^n\right] + \frac{1}{M!}\left(\frac{\lambda}{\mu}\right)^M \left(\frac{M\mu}{M\mu - \lambda}\right)}$$

$$= \frac{1}{\left[1 + \frac{7.5}{10}\right] + \frac{1}{2!}\left(\frac{7.5}{10}\right)^2 \left(\frac{2*10}{2*10 - 7.5}\right)}$$

$$= \frac{1}{1.75 + \frac{1}{2}(0.5625)(1.6)} = \frac{1}{1.75 + 0.45} = 0.4545$$

Plugging the resulting P_0 value into the formula for C_s:

$$C_s = \frac{\lambda\mu\left(\frac{\lambda}{\mu}\right)^M}{(M-1)!(M\mu - \lambda)^2}P_0 + \left(\frac{\lambda}{\mu}\right) = \frac{7.5 \times 10\left(\frac{7.5}{10}\right)^2}{(2 \times 10 - 7.5)^2} \times (0.4545) + (7.5/10)$$

$$= \left(\frac{42.1875}{156.25}\right) \times (0.4545) + (7.5/10) = 0.873 \text{ cars in the system, on average}$$

The average number of cars waiting:

$$C_w = C_s - \frac{\lambda}{\mu} = 0.873 - 0.75 = 0.123 \text{ cars}$$

The average time a car spends in the system:

$$T_s = \frac{\mu\left(\frac{\lambda}{\mu}\right)^M}{(M-1)!(M\mu - \lambda)^2}P_0 + \left(\frac{1}{\mu}\right) = \frac{10\left(\frac{7.5}{10}\right)^2}{(20-7.5)^2}0.4545 + 0.10$$

$$= \left(\frac{5.625}{156.25}\right)0.4545 + 0.10 = 0.12 \text{ hours, or about 7 minutes}$$

Finally, we can calculate the average time a car spends waiting:

$$T_w = T_s - \frac{1}{\mu} = 0.12 - 0.10 = 0.02 \text{ hours, or roughly 1 minute}.$$

6S.2 SIMULATION MODELING

APICS defines simulation as "the technique of using representative or artificial data to reproduce in a model various conditions that are likely to occur in the actual performance of a system."[1] Although simulations can include physical re-creations of an actual system, most business simulations are computer based and use mathematical formulas to represent actual systems or policies. Simulation models have a number of advantages:

1. **Offline evaluation of new processes or process changes.** Simulation models allow the user to experiment with processes or operating procedures without endangering the performance of real-world systems. For example, the user can test new systems or evaluate the impact of changes to processes or procedures prior to implementing them.
2. **Time compression.** Simulation models allow the user to compress time. Many days, months, or even years of activity can be simulated in a short period of time.
3. **"What-if" analyses.** This type of analysis can be particularly valuable in understanding how processes or procedures would perform under extreme conditions. What if the demand rate were to double? What if one of our key support centers went down? With simulation models, managers can get an idea of the impact prior to an actual occurrence.

Of course, simulations also have disadvantages:

1. **They are, at best, only approximations of reality.** Most simulation models—like the waiting line formulas we reviewed in the first half of the supplement—make simplifying assumptions about how the real world works. While these assumptions make the model easier to develop and understand, they also make it less realistic.
2. **The more realistic a simulation model, the more costly it will be to develop and the more difficult it will be to interpret.** This is related to the first point. Model developers must strike a balance between cost, ease of use, and realism.
3. **Simulation models do not provide an "optimal" solution.** Simulation models reflect only the conditions and rules of the environments they are set up to model, not an optimal solution. This is in contrast to optimization models, discussed in Chapter 7, which do attempt to provide the user with a solution that optimizes some objective such as cost minimization or profit maximization.

---

[1]Definition of *simulation* in J. H. Blackstone, ed., *APICS Dictionary*, 15th ed. (Chicago, IL: APICS, 2016). Reprinted by permission.

Monte Carlo Simulation

By far, the most common form of simulation modeling is mathematical simulation, where mathematical formulas and statistical processes are used to simulate activities, decisions, and the like. One particularly well-known approach is *Monte Carlo simulation*, a technique in which statistical sampling is used to generate outcomes for a large number of trials. The results of these trials are then used to gain insight into the system of interest.

Monte Carlo simulation is used to simulate all types of systems and many types of statistical distributions. To illustrate the basic principles of the technique, we will examine a very simple system everyone is familiar with: flipping a coin. You probably understand that for a fair coin toss, each outcome—heads or tails—has a 50% chance of occurring. And you probably also understand that the outcome for any particular flip is *memoryless*; that is, the probability of coming up heads or tails is unaffected by what happened previously. Still, you may wonder how the pattern of outcomes might play out over, say, 50 flips.

Figure 6S.4 shows an Excel-based Monte Carlo simulation model for 50 coin flips, or trials. The random numbers for the 50 trials were generated using the following Excel formula:

$$=\text{RAND}()*100$$

This Excel formula generates a random number between 0 and 100, with all numbers having an equal probability of being generated. The adjacent column in the spreadsheet then translates these results into heads or tails. For example:

$$\text{Formula for cell C6: } = \text{IF}(\text{B6} < 50, \text{"Tails"}, \text{"Heads"})$$

FIGURE 6S.4
Excel-Based Monte Carlo Simulation of 50 Coin Tosses

	A	B	C	D	E	F	G
1	Monte Carlo simulation of 50 coin tosses						
2	Excel-generated random numbers generated between 0 and 100						
3	"Tails" if random number <50, "Heads" otherwise						
4							
5	Trial	Random Number	Simulated Outcome		Trial	Random Number	Simulated Outcome
6	1	75.79	Heads		26	41.23	Tails
7	2	54.88	Heads		27	28.41	Tails
8	3	3.20	Tails		28	80.16	Heads
9	4	89.32	Heads		29	79.27	Heads
10	5	64.62	Heads		30	6.34	Tails
11	6	25.56	Tails		31	89.72	Heads
12	7	60.99	Heads		32	14.85	Tails
13	8	77.68	Heads		33	15.76	Tails
14	9	77.14	Heads		34	99.29	Heads
15	10	51.42	Heads		35	40.66	Tails
16	11	14.43	Tails		36	19.91	Tails
17	12	27.02	Tails		37	55.73	Heads
18	13	25.73	Tails		38	83.07	Heads
19	14	43.28	Tails		39	69.75	Heads
20	15	36.91	Tails		40	14.89	Tails
21	16	49.08	Tails		41	45.60	Tails
22	17	88.84	Heads		42	0.40	Tails
23	18	45.94	Tails		43	80.11	Heads
24	19	97.69	Heads		44	16.58	Tails
25	20	27.94	Tails		45	19.35	Tails
26	21	78.90	Heads		46	15.19	Tails
27	22	90.03	Heads		47	32.78	Tails
28	23	64.11	Heads		48	25.08	Tails
29	24	60.71	Heads		49	95.15	Heads
30	25	2.02	Tails		50	45.36	Tails

Translated, if the random number in cell B6 is less than 50, write "Tails" in the cell; otherwise, write "Heads." Looking at the results, we can see that "Tails" came up 27 times and "Heads" came up 23 times—not exactly a 50/50 balance, but close. In addition, we can see that the simulated results do not alternate back and forth between heads and tails. In fact, there are several runs of four or more heads or tails.

Monte Carlo simulation can be used to simulate other statistical distributions as well. Figure 6S.5 shows another Excel-based Monte Carlo simulation model. In this case, we are trying to simulate arrivals, based on a Poisson distribution and an average arrival rate per time period of 3.

First, the spreadsheet calculates the probability of 0 through 8 arrivals per time period using Equation (6S.1). Notice that the total of these probabilities is essentially 100%. Next, we assigned random numbers between 0 and 100 to each possible arrival quantity. For example, there is a 5% chance of 0 arrivals. Therefore, we assigned all numbers r that meet the condition ($0 \leq r < 5$) to represent 0 arrivals. Since the probability of drawing such a number using the =RAND()*100 equation is also 5%, we can use this method to accurately simulate Poisson-distributed arrivals. Arrivals of 1 through 8 units per time period were simulated in a similar fashion.

FIGURE 6S.5
Excel-Based Monte Carlo Simulation of Poisson-Distributed Arrivals

Monte Carlo simulation of Poisson-distributed arrivals			
Arrival rate (λ) = 3			
Arrivals	Probability of n Arrivals	Cumulative Probability	Assigned Random Numbers (r) (0 to 100)
0	5%	5%	$0 \leq r < 5$
1	15%	20%	$5 \leq r < 20$
2	22%	42%	$20 \leq r < 42$
3	22%	64%	$42 \leq r < 65$
4	17%	82%	$65 \leq r < 82$
5	10%	92%	$82 \leq r < 92$
6	5%	97%	$92 \leq r < 97$
7	2%	99%	$97 \leq r < 99$
8	1%	100%	99 or greater
Time Period	Random no.	Simulated Arrivals	
1	75.60	4	
2	74.03	4	
3	80.70	4	
4	22.18	2	
5	88.12	5	
6	75.95	4	
7	47.38	3	
8	10.63	1	
9	34.96	2	
10	42.99	3	
11	83.14	5	
12	2.68	0	
13	8.21	1	
14	73.41	4	
15	39.71	2	
16	73.79	4	
17	99.70	8	
18	22.89	2	
19	19.32	1	
20	64.51	3	
	Average:	3.1	

The bottom half of Figure 6S.5 presents results for 20 simulated time periods. Notice how the simulated arrivals range anywhere from 0 to 8. For this particular simulation, the average arrival rate is 3.1, close to the expected arrival rate of 3 per time period.

Building and Evaluating Simulation Models with SimQuick

Developing a useful simulation model can require a great deal of creativity and practice, but the basic process can be divided into four steps:

1. Develop a picture of the system to be modeled. The process mapping material in Chapter 4 can be particularly helpful in this regard.
2. Identify the objects, elements, and probability distributions that define the system. *Objects* are the people or products that move through the system, while *elements* are pieces of the system itself, such as lines, workstations, and entrance and exit points.
3. Determine the experimental conditions and required output information. Many simulation packages provide the user with options regarding the output reports that are generated.
4. Build and test the simulation model for your system and capture and evaluate the relevant data.

When the process to be modeled is fairly complex, it usually makes sense to use a specialized simulation software package. These packages can range from very sophisticated applications that provide graphics and sophisticated what-if analyses and make use of existing company databases to simple stand-alone packages. In the following example, we build and test a simulation model of Luc's Deluxe Car Wash, using SimQuick,[2] a highly intuitive, easy-to-learn simulation package that runs under Microsoft Excel.

EXAMPLE 6S.4

Simulating Operations at Luc's Deluxe Car Wash

While Luc is generally happy with the statistics he was able to generate using the waiting line formulas (Examples 6S.1–6S.3), one thing troubles him: All of these statistics describe *averages*—average wait time, average number of cars in the system, and so on. They don't tell Luc how long the lines can actually get or what the maximum time might look like.

Luc's car wash is pictured in Figure 6S.6. For simulation modeling purposes, Luc's car wash has four elements: the car entrance, the driveway (where cars wait for an available crew), the crew, and washed cars. Two of these elements—cars arriving and the crews washing cars—are controlled by probability distributions.

Figure 6S.7 shows how the same system is defined in SimQuick. The first box is labeled "Simulation Controls." Luc has set the simulation to cover five iterations of 3,600 minutes each. In effect, *each* iteration represents a workweek consisting of five 12-hour days, or 3,600 minutes. The fact that Luc can run the simulation in a matter of seconds illustrates the time compression advantages of simulation.

FIGURE 6S.6 Luc's Car Wash

---

[2]D. Hartvigsen, *SimQuick: Process Simulation in Excel*, Third Edition, 2016.

	A	B	C	D	E	F
1	**Model View**					
2	(Note: Cannot edit model here)					
3						
4		**Simulation Controls:**				
5						
6		Time units per simulation ⟶	3,600			
7		Number of simulations ⟶	5			
8						
9						
10		**Entrances:**				
11						
12						
13		**Name** ⟶	Cars			
14		Time between arrivals ⟶	Exp(8)			
15		Num. objects per arrivals ⟶	1			
16		Output				
17		destination(s) ↓				
18		Driveway				
19						
20						
21						
22		**Work Stations:**				
23						
24						
25			**Name** ⟶	Crew 1		
26			Working time ⟶	Exp(6)		
27		Output	# of output	Resource	Resource	
28		destination(s) ↓	objects ↓	name(s) ↓	#units needed ↓	
29		Washed Cars				
30						
31						
32						
33		Buffers:				
34						
35		1			2	
36		**Name** ⟶	Driveway		**Name** ⟶	Washed Cars
37		Capacity ⟶	10,000		Capacity ⟶	10,000
38		Initial # objects ⟶	0		Initial # objects ⟶	0
39		Output	Output		Output	Output
40		destination(s) ↓	group size ↓		destination(s) ↓	group size ↓
41		Crew 1	1			
42						

FIGURE 6S.7 SimQuick Model Specification for Single-Channel, Single-Phase System, Luc's Deluxe Car Wash

The simulation model has one entrance point, "Cars." Cars arrive based on an exponential distribution, with an average of 8 minutes between arrivals. Note that this is the *same* as saying that the arrivals are Poisson-distributed with an average of $\frac{60 \text{ minutes}}{8 \text{ minutes}} = 7.5$ arrivals per hour.

Once a car arrives, it goes to the driveway, which is the first buffer point in the model. For now, Luc assumes that there is unlimited room for cars to wait here ("Capacity ⟶ 10,000"). If the washing crew is not busy, the car will immediately proceed to the workstation "Crew 1." Otherwise, it will wait in the driveway.

The earlier examples stated that a crew can wash, on average, 10 cars per hour. This is the same as saying that the time it takes to wash a car is 6 minutes, on average ("Exp(6)"). Once a car is finished, it proceeds to the "Washed Cars" buffer. By modeling the system this way, Luc can track how many cars are completed by the end of each iteration.

Figure 6S.8 shows the overall simulation results for five iterations of 3,600 minutes each (five workweeks, each consisting of five 12-hour days).

	A	B	C	D	E	F	G	H
1	**Results**							
2								
3	**Element**	**Statistics**	**Overall**	**Simulation Numbers**				
4	**names**		**means**	**1**	**2**	**3**	**4**	**5**
5								
6	Cars	Objects entering process	447.40	460	471	460	424	422
7		Objects unable to enter	0.00	0	0	0	0	0
8		Service level	1.00	1.00	1.00	1.00	1.00	1.00
9								
10	Crew 1	Final status	NA	Working	Working	Working	Working	Working
11		Final inventory (int. buff.)	0.00	0	0	0	0	0
12		Mean inventory (int. buff.)	0.00	0.00	0.00	0.00	0.00	0.00
13		Mean cycle time (int. buff.)	0.00	0.00	0.00	0.00	0.00	0.00
14		Work cycles started	444.20	459	466	453	421	422
15		Fraction time working	0.77	0.77	0.81	0.79	0.75	0.73
16		Fraction time blocked	0.00	0.00	0.00	0.00	0.00	0.00
17								
18	Driveway	Objects leaving	444.20	459	466	453	421	422
19		Final inventory	3.20	1	5	7	3	0
20		Minimum inventory	0.00	0	0	0	0	0
21		Maximum inventory	15.80	13	21	22	13	10
22		Mean inventory	2.58	2.07	3.74	3.84	1.75	1.47
23		Mean cycle time	20.64	16.22	28.89	30.55	15.01	12.54
24								
25	Washed Cars	Objects leaving	0.00	0	0	0	0	0
26		Final inventory	443.20	458	465	452	420	421
27		Minimum inventory	0.00	0	0	0	0	0
28		Maximum inventory	443.20	458	465	452	420	421
29		Mean inventory	219.71	233.76	228.58	223.11	196.72	216.40
30		Mean cycle time	Infinite	Infinite	Infinite	Infinite	Infinite	Infinite

FIGURE 6S.8 Simulation Results for Single-Channel, Single-Phase System, Luc's Deluxe Car Wash

Statistics regarding waiting times and waiting line lengths can be found by looking at the "Driveway" results. In this case, "inventory" represents cars waiting to be washed. The average inventory is 2.58 cars, and the mean cycle (i.e., waiting) time is 20.64 minutes. It's interesting to compare the simulation results to the formula-derived results in Example 6S.1:

Formula-derived estimate of average number of cars waiting (C_w) = 2.25 cars

Simulation estimate of average number of cars waiting = 2.58 cars

Formula-derived estimate of average waiting time (T_w) = 0.3 hours, or about 18 minutes

Simulation estimate of average number of cars waiting = 20.64 minutes

Figure 6S.8 also shows that the average maximum number of cars in line across all five simulations was 15.8, and the fraction of time the washing crew was busy was 0.77, or 77%.

EXAMPLE 6S.5

Simulating the Impact of Limited Waiting Space at Luc's Deluxe Car Wash

Satisfied that the simulation model adequately reflects his business, Luc decides to modify the model to capture one key characteristic that has not yet been considered: *There is only enough room in the driveway for two cars to be waiting.* This means that if the crew is busy washing a car and two cars are already waiting, any other car that drives up will have to go elsewhere. Luc wonders how this would affect the results.

The modified simulation model is identical to the one shown in Figure 6S.7, *except now the capacity for the driveway buffer is set at 2.* Simulation results for this new model are shown in Figure 6S.9.

	A	B	C	D	E	F	G	H
1	**Results**							
2								
3	**Elements**	**Statistics**	**Overall**	**Simulation Numbers**				
4	**names**		**means**	**1**	**2**	**3**	**4**	**5**
5								
6	Cars	Objects entering process	378.20	386	376	373	−396	360
7		Objects unable to enter	61.40	65	49	62	68	63
8		Service level	0.86	0.86	0.88	0.86	0.85	0.85
9								
10	Crew 1	Final status	NA	Working	Working	Not Working	Working	Not Working
11		Final inventory (int.buff.)	0	0	0	0	0	0
12		Mean inventory (int.buff.)	0.00	0.00	0.00	0.00	0.00	0.00
13		Mean cycle time (int.buff.)	0.00	0.00	0.00	0.00	0.00	0
14		Work cycle started	377.60	384	376	373	395	360
15		Fraction time working	0.64	0.65	0.60	0.61	0.69	0.63
16		Fraction time blocked	0.00	0.00	0.00	0.00	0.00	0.00
17								
18	Driveway	Objects leaving	377.60	384	376	373	395	360
19		Final inventory	0.60	2	0	0	1	0
20		Minimum inventory	0.00	0	0	0	0	0
21		Maximum inventory	2.00	2	2	2	2	2
22		Mean inventory	0.49	0.53	0.40	0.43	0.59	0.51
23		Mean cycle time	4.68	4.93	3.85	4.12	5.41	5.10
24								
25	Washed Cars	Objects leaving	0.00	0	0	0	0	0
26		Final inventory	377.00	383	375	373	394	360
27		Minimum inventory	0.00	0	0	0	0	0
28		Maximum inventory	377.00	383	375	373	394	360
29		Mean inventory	187.57	194.89	188.37	188.99	195.84	169.77
30		Mean cycle time	Infinite	Infinite	Infinite	Infinite	Infinite	Infinite

FIGURE 6S.9 Simulation Results for Single-Channel, Single-Phase System, with Driveway Capacity Limited to Two Cars

Looking at the results, Luc can clearly see the impact the small driveway is having on his business. According to the simulation results, on average, 61.4 cars per week are unable to enter the process. Because fewer cars enter the system, the fraction of time the washing crew is busy also suffers. In fact, it drops down to 64%. Finally, the mean time and mean number of cars in the driveway decrease dramatically, but this is only because a large number of cars are *turned away*. In Theory of Constraints terms (Chapter 6), the driveway is clearly a constraint that limits throughput for the entire system. If Luc can somehow find more space to queue up the cars (and assuming that the drivers are willing to wait), he could expect to achieve results closer to those in Figure 6S.8.

SUPPLEMENT SUMMARY

In this supplement, we described different types of waiting line systems. We also provided formulas for evaluating the steady-state performance of three different systems. The second half of the supplement introduced simulation modeling, including a discussion and examples of Monte Carlo simulation, as well as the development and analysis of a simulation model using SimQuick.

Simulation modeling is a particularly important tool that managers can use to model and gain insight into complex business processes. Simulation is often the only way managers can understand what impact changes in capacity, process flows, or other elements of the business will have on customer performance.

We encourage you not to let your education end here, however. There is much more to both of these topics, and especially simulation modeling, than can be covered in this supplement. In fact, there are books devoted to simulation modeling,[3] and many colleges offer courses or even series of courses on the topic.

---

[3]See, for example, J. Banks, J. Carson, B. Nelson, and D. Nicol, *Discrete-Event System Simulation* (Upper Saddle River, NJ: Prentice Hall, 2004).

DISCUSSION QUESTIONS

1. All things being equal, why do you think waiting line environments with constant service times have shorter waiting times and lines than environments with variable service times? Can you think of an example to illustrate your intuition?
2. Consider a supply chain where multiple manufacturers take turns processing a particular product. Which of the waiting line systems shown in Figures 6S.1 through 6S.3 best represent this environment? Explain.
3. We stated earlier that simulation modeling does not provide the user with an optimal solution. What did we mean by this? Explain, using one or more of the simulation examples given in the supplement.

PROBLEMS

(* = easy; ** = moderate; *** = advanced)

Problems for Section 6S.1: Alternative Waiting Lines

1. Horton Williams Airport is a small municipal airport with two runways. One of these runways is devoted to planes taking off. During peak time periods, about 8.5 planes per hour radio to the tower that they want to take off. The tower handles these requests in the order in which they arrive. Once the tower has given the go-ahead, it takes a plane, on average, 5 minutes to position itself on the runway and take off.

   a. (*) On average, how many planes will be waiting during peak time periods? How many will be in the system (i.e., waiting and on the runway)?
   b. (*) How long, on average, will a plane have to wait before it is allowed to take off?

   To deal with greater demand, Horton Williams Airport has opened a second runway devoted just to planes taking off. Peak demand has now been bumped up to 15 planes per hour. Furthermore, each plane still takes about 5 minutes to position itself and take off once it has been given the go-ahead.

   c. (***) On average, how many planes will be waiting during peak time periods? How many will be in the system (i.e., waiting and on the runway)?
   d. (***) How long, on average, will a plane have to wait before it is allowed to take off?

2. The women's department at Hector's Department Store has a single checkout register. Customers arrive at the register at the rate of 11 per hour. It takes the clerk, on average, 4 minutes to check out a customer.

   a. (**) On average, how many customers will be waiting to be checked out? Do you think this number is reasonable? Why or why not?
   b. (**) How long, on average, will a customer have to wait before the clerk starts serving him or her? Again, is this a reasonable time? If Hector's decides to open another register, what are the trade-offs to consider?

   Hector's Department Store has decided to add a second checkout register. This second register works at the same average speed as the first. Customer arrivals are the same as before.

   c. (***) On average, how many customers will be waiting to be checked out? From a business perspective, is this reasonable?
   d. (***) How long, on average, will a customer have to wait before the clerk starts serving him or her? Again, is this a reasonable time?

3. Parts arrive at an automated machining center at a rate of 100 per hour, based on a Poisson distribution. The machining center is able to process these parts at a fixed rate of 150 per hour. That is, each part will take exactly $150/6 = 0.4$ minutes to process.

   a. (*) How many parts, on average, will be waiting to be processed? How many will be in the system (i.e., waiting and being processed)?
   b. (*) How long, on average, will a part have to wait before it is processed?

Problems for Section 6S.2: Simulation Modeling

4. Consider the Monte Carlo simulation shown in Figure 6S.5.

   a. (***) Recalculate the values in the "Probability of n arrivals" and "Cumulative probability" columns for an arrival rate of 4. You may need to add some additional rows beyond just 8 arrivals.
   b. (***) Based on the results to part a, redo the "Assigned random numbers" column.
   c. (***) Using the same random numbers shown in Figure 6S.5, take the results from parts a and b and redo the column labeled "Simulated Arrivals." What is the new average number of arrivals per time period?

5. (***) Consider the SimQuick simulation model for Luc's Car Wash, shown in Figure 6S.6. Suppose Luc decides to put in place a second crew. Redraw Figure 6S.6 to reflect this change. What changes to the model specification (Figure 6S.7) would you need to make? (*Hint:* You will need to make changes not only to the workstations but to the "Driveway" buffer as well).

REFERENCES

Books and Articles
Banks, J., Carson, J., Nelson, B., and Nicol, D., *Discrete-Event System Simulation*, 3rd ed. (Upper Saddle River, NJ: Prentice Hall, 2004).

Blackstone, J. H., ed., *APICS Dictionary*, 15th ed. (Chicago, IL: APICS, 2016).

Hartvigsen, D., *SimQuick: Process Simulation in Excel*, Third Edition, 2016.

Gilles Lougassi/Shutterstock

CHAPTER
seven

CHAPTER OUTLINE

Supply Management

CHAPTER OBJECTIVES

By the end of this chapter, you will be able to:

- Identify and describe the various steps of the strategic sourcing process.
- Perform and interpret the results of a simple spend analysis.
- Use portfolio analysis to identify the appropriate sourcing strategy for a particular good or service.
- Describe the rationale for outsourcing and discuss when it is appropriate.
- Perform a simple total cost analysis.
- Show how multicriteria decision models can be used to evaluate suppliers and interpret the results.
- Understand when negotiations should be used and the purpose of contracts.
- Describe the major steps of the procure-to-pay cycle.
- Discuss some of the longer-term trends in supply management and why they are important.

SUPPLY CHAIN CONNECTIONS

RECYCLED MATERIALS IN SHORT SUPPLY

Picsfive/Shutterstock

"Reduce, reuse, recycle." This popular slogan suggests that if consumers learn to recycle metal, glass, and plastic, industry will find a way to reuse them. But so far the flow of recycled materials into new products has been less than smooth. One reason is that some recycled substances are in surprisingly short supply.

Electric car batteries, for instance, are rich sources of lithium, nickel, cobalt, and other metals and weigh up to 550 pounds each. But because they can still produce dangerous shocks and are fire hazards even when discharged, and because some of their components, such as lithium, remain cheaper to mine than to recycle, car makers are divided about whether or not to recycle batteries.

Car makers are often legally responsible for proper disposal or reuse of batteries, even if they didn't manufacture them. That's one reason that Honda and Toyota, for instance, are looking into global recycling partnerships, while General Motors and Nissan are working with energy companies to try remaking discharged car batteries into storage devices for wind or solar power. But the percentage of minerals returning to manufacturing assembly lines may remain low.

Meanwhile, in the soft-drink industry, the United States lags Europe in recycling plastic bottles (the U.S. rate is 31% compared to Europe's 50%). Recycled bottle-ready plastic, called PET after its main ingredient, is so scarce that it costs about 10% more than virgin plastic, and the recycled content of Coca-Cola bottles has dropped to less than 5% from 10% ten years ago. Coca-Cola Company, which wants to eventually recycle all its plastic bottles, has been running its $60 million recycling plant in Spartanburg, North Carolina, at only one-third of capacity because of the shortage, and after a recent retooling, it plans to reopen the plant at half its planned capacity.

Some feel PET recycling would increase if the soft-drink industry dropped its opposition to bottle deposits. The 10 U.S. states that mandate deposits have PET recycling rates about twice the national average.

Sources: Based on J. Kanter, "No Consensus on Reuse of Electric Car Batteries," *New York Times*, September 6, 2011, pp. B1, B7, **http://query.nytimes.com/gst/fullpage.html?res=9900E0DA133AF935A3575AC0A9679D8B63&ref=jameskanter;**

D. Pearson, "Car-Battery Shakeout Ahead," *Wall Street Journal*, August 31, 2011, p. B5, **http://online.wsj.com/article/SB10001424053111904199404576540170506631268.html;**

M. Verspej, "Recyclers Expansion-Minded Despite Short Supply," *Plastic News*, May 22, 2012, **www.plasticsnews.com/article/20120522/NEWS/305229967/recyclers-expansion-minded-despite-short-supply;**

J. Carroll, "US PET Recycling Rate Tops 30 Percent," *Plastic News*, October 9, 2013, **www.plasticsnews.com/article/20131009/NEWS/131009912/us-pet-recycling-rate-tops-30-percent.**

INTRODUCTION

In Chapter 1, we noted that a supply chain is a network of manufacturers and service providers that work together to create products or services needed by end users. These manufacturers and service providers are linked together through physical flows, information flows, and monetary flows. But how does a particular firm know *when* it needs to team up with an outside manufacturer or service provider or with *whom* it should partner? And even if a buying firm has identified a potential partner, what steps are required to formally establish and then manage the relationship?

These questions and others like them are the focus of supply management. **Supply management** refers to the broad set of activities carried out by organizations to analyze sourcing opportunities, develop sourcing strategies, select suppliers, and carry out all the activities required to procure goods and services. The purpose of this chapter is to introduce you to the activities and challenges that make up supply management and to give you an appreciation for why supply management is so critical to the success of many firms.

Supply management
The broad set of activities carried out by organizations to analyze sourcing opportunities, develop sourcing strategies, select suppliers, and carry out all the activities required to procure goods and services.

7.1 WHY SUPPLY MANAGEMENT IS CRITICAL

Supply management, sometimes referred to as *sourcing* or *purchasing*, has always been an important, if underappreciated, function in many businesses. Several factors have worked together to push supply management activities into the limelight. These include increased levels of global sourcing, the financial impact of sourcing, and the impact sourced goods and services have on other performance metrics, including quality and delivery performance.

Global Sourcing

Firms compete not only against global competitors but against their competitors' supply chains. Companies that were once content to purchase services and goods from local suppliers now seek to build relationships with world-class suppliers, regardless of their location. Managers have come to realize that to compete globally, companies need to source globally.

The automotive industry is a prime example of how globalization has affected sourcing. Original equipment manufacturers (OEMs) such as Toyota, Volkswagen, and GM are looking to partner with the best suppliers, regardless of location. Furthermore, the OEMs are requiring these suppliers to take on more design and manufacturing responsibility. The result has been the rise of large, multinational first-tier suppliers (Table 7.1). While these suppliers may be headquartered in Europe, Asia, or North America, their products can be found in all makes of cars assembled throughout the world.

To keep up with global competition and tap into the abilities of world-class suppliers, many companies have put in place global sourcing systems. GM is a case in point. Every Friday at 6:30 A.M., the vice president in charge of worldwide purchasing presides over a global videoconference in which dozens of purchasing executives share information and coordinate strategy. A few years back, a GM purchasing team went on a 12-day mission to Thailand, Taiwan, South Korea, and Japan. The primary purpose of the trip was to evaluate a dozen toolmakers as potential sources of stamping dies, but GM also used the opportunity to develop valuable new sources.[1]

TABLE 7.1
Top 10 First-Tier Suppliers in Global Automotive Industry

COMPANY	HOME COUNTRY	2015 SALES ($ BILLIONS)	PRODUCTS
Bosch	Germany	$45	Gasoline & diesel systems, chassis system controls
Denso	Japan	36	Powertrain control, electronic & electric systems
Magneti Marelli	Canada	32	Body, chassis, exterior, seating, powertrain, electronic, vision,
Continental	Germany	31	Driver assistance systems, electronic brakes, stability systems
ZF Friedrichshafen AG	Germany	39	Transmissions, chassis components and systems, steering
Hyundai Mobis	Korea	26	Chassis, cockpit & front-end modules; stability control steering
Aisin Seiki Co.	Japan	26	Body, brake & chassis systems, electronics, drivetrain,
Faurecia	France	23	Seating, emissions control technologies, interior systems
Johnson Controls Inc.	USA	20	Complete automotive seats & seat components
Lear Corp.	USA	18	Seating & electrical distribution systems
Toyota	*Japan*	*248*	
Volkswagen	*Germany*	*213*	
GM	*USA*	*152*	

Source: Based on *Automotive News,* "Top Suppliers," June 20, 2016, **www.autonews.com/assets/PDF/CA105764617.PDF.**

---

[1]R. L. Simison, "Buyer's Market: General Motors Drives Some Hard Bargains with Asian Suppliers," *Wall Street Journal,* April 2, 1999, p. A1.

TABLE 7.2
Material Cost Ratios for Different Manufacturing Industries, 2011

INDUSTRY	COST OF MATERIAL / VALUE OF SHIPMENTS
Food	63.1%
Chemicals	52.5%
Plastics and rubber	55.8%
Computers and electronics	38.8%
Transportation equipment	62.8%
All manufacturers	*59.1%*

Source: Based on *2011 Annual Survey of Manufactures*, U.S. Census Bureau, June 2014.

Advances in information systems have served as a catalyst for global sourcing efforts. For example, engineers and suppliers around the world can share electronic "blueprints" instantaneously. Similarly, an organization can maximize buying power by consolidating purchasing requirements for dozens of sites and suppliers around the world into one large order. Companies can share anticipated requirements with key suppliers around the clock, allowing suppliers to plan their activities accordingly.

Global sourcing applies to services and business processes, as well as manufactured goods. Many firms now outsource routine business processes such as invoice processing, routine financial analysis, call centers, and IT processing to lower-cost centers around the world. In a recent study of business process outsourcing trends, researchers found that 50% of companies have outsourced at least some of their back-office activities. About 40% have developed consolidated and technology-enabled service centers, especially for functions such as IT, voice services, accounting, human resources, and legal services.[2]

Financial Impact

If you were to look at the financial statements of an average organization, how much would you guess the company spends on purchased goods and services? In manufacturing, the figure is astonishingly high; for the average manufacturer, just over 59% of the value of shipments comes from materials (Table 7.2). For some services, such as retailing or wholesaling, the figure can be even higher.

When much of a firm's revenue is spent on materials and services, supply management represents a major opportunity to increase profitability through what is known as the *profit leverage effect* (Example 7.1).

EXAMPLE 7.1

Profit Leverage at Target Corporation

Consider the following financial information for Target Corporation, a leading U.S. retailer. Table 7.3 shows earnings for the company for 2010, as well as key balance statement figures from January 2011.

TABLE 7.3 Selected Financial Data for Target Corporation (all figures in $ millions)

EARNINGS AND EXPENSES, 2010	
Sales	$65,786
Cost of goods sold (COGS)	$45,725
Pretax earnings	$4,629
SELECTED BALANCE SHEET ITEMS (AS OF JANUARY 29, 2011)	
Merchandise inventory	$7,596
Total assets	$17,213

Cost of goods sold (COGS)
The purchased cost of goods from outside suppliers.

Merchandise inventory
A balance sheet item that shows the amount a company paid for the inventory it has on hand at a particular point in time.

Profit margin
The ratio of earnings to sales for a given time period.

Cost of goods sold (COGS) is the purchased cost of goods from outside suppliers. It tells us how much a company has paid for the goods that it sold to its customers. **Merchandise inventory** shows us how much the company paid for the inventory it had on hand at the time of the report.

With the preceding financial data, we can calculate some basic financial performance measurements for Target Corporation. **Profit margin** is defined as the ratio of earnings to sales for a given time period:

$$\text{Profit margin} = 100\% \times \frac{\text{Earnings}}{\text{Sales}} \qquad (7.1)$$

The pretax profit margin for the company is:

$$100\% \times \frac{\$4,629}{\$65,786} = 7.0\%$$

Return on assets (ROA)
A measure of financial performance, generally defined as earnings/total assets. Higher ROA values are preferred because they indicate that the firm is able to generate higher earnings from the same asset base.

The pretax profit margin means that every dollar of sales generates about 7 cents in pretax earnings. Another commonly used financial measure is **return on assets (ROA)**. ROA is a measure of financial performance, generally defined as earnings/total assets. Higher ROA values are preferred because they indicate that the firm is able to generate higher earnings from the same asset base:

$$\text{Return on assets (ROA)} = 100\% \times \frac{\text{Earnings}}{\text{Assets}} \qquad (7.2)$$

For this company, the pretax ROA for the fiscal year is:

$$100\% \times \frac{\$4,629}{\$17,213} = 26.9\%$$

What can this company do to improve these figures? There are two things to note:

Profit leverage effect
A term used to describe the effect of $1 in cost savings increasing pretax profits by $1 and a $1 increase in sales increasing pretax profits only by $1 multiplied by the pretax profit margin.

1. **Every dollar saved in purchasing lowers COGS by $1 and increases pretax profit by $1.** In contrast, because the current pretax profit margin is 7.0%, to have the same impact on pretax profit, Target would have to generate:

   $$\$1.00 / 7.0\% = \$14.29 \text{ in new sales}$$

   This is known as the profit leverage effect. The **profit leverage effect** holds that $1 in cost savings increases pretax profits by $1, while a $1 increase in sales increases pretax profits by only $1 multiplied by the pretax profit margin. This effect is particularly important for lower-margin businesses, such as retailing.

2. **Every dollar saved in purchasing also lowers the merchandise inventory figure—and as a result, total assets—by $1.** The result is a higher ROA for the same level of sales.

To illustrate these points, let's see what would happen if Target Corporation were able to cut its COGS by 3%. Notice that COGS and merchandise inventory each decrease by 3%:

$$\text{New COGS} = \text{old COGS} \times (100\% - 3\%)$$
$$= \$45,725 \times (0.97)$$
$$= \$44,353$$

$$\text{Reduction in COGS} = \text{old COGS} - \text{new COGS}$$
$$= \$45,725 - 44,353$$
$$= \$1,372$$

$$\text{Reduction in merchandise inventory} = \text{old merchandise inventory} \times (3\%)$$
$$= \$7,596 \times (0.03) = \$228$$

$$\text{New total assets} = \text{old total assets}$$
$$- \text{reduction in merchandise inventory}$$
$$= \$17,213 - \$228 = \$16,985$$

The updated financial results are shown below:

UPDATED EARNINGS AND EXPENSES	
Sales	$65,786
New cost of goods sold (COGS)	**$44,353**
Old pretax earnings	$4,629
+3% reduction in COGS:	+$1,372
New pretax earnings	**$6,001**
UPDATED BALANCE SHEET ITEMS	
New merchandise inventory	**$7,368**
Old total assets	$17,213
−3% reduction in merchandise inv.	−$228
Net total assets	**$16,985**

The result is that pretax earnings increase by nearly 30%, from $4,629 million to $6,001 million. Under the *old* pretax profit margin, sales would have to increase by ($6,001 − $4,629)/(7.0%) = $19,600 million to have the same impact.

Finally, the *new* pretax profit margin and ROA values are

$$\text{New pretax profit margin} = 100\% \times \frac{\$6,001}{\$65,786} = 9.1\%$$

$$\text{New ROA} = 100\% \times \frac{\$6,001}{\$16,985} = 35.3\%$$

Performance Impact

Cost is not the only consideration. Purchased goods and services can have a major effect on other performance dimensions, including quality and delivery performance. The following example illustrates how these metrics can come into play.

EXAMPLE 7.2

Purchasing Valves at Springfield Hospital

Springfield Hospital has two dialysis machines, each with a special valve that is normally replaced every two weeks when the machines are idle. As a result, Springfield uses about 50 valves per year. The hospital has two alternative sources for the valves. The purchase price and quality for these two suppliers are as follows:

	SUPPLIER A	SUPPLIER B
Price per valve	$10	$2
% Good	99.8%	95%

The fact that a valve is defective becomes apparent only once treatment starts. When this occurs, it can cause an interruption in the treatment of patients, which can lead to rescheduling nightmares, a reduction in the effective capacity of the dialysis machines, and possibly even a medical emergency. The quality of the medical service will clearly fall if Springfield goes with Supplier B.

Now suppose that Springfield Hospital management has estimated that the cost of a failed valve is about $1,000 per incident. Even before we calculate all of the costs associated with each supplier, we can see that using Supplier B has the potential to seriously disrupt Springfield's operations. These concerns are reflected in the following cost estimates:

YEARLY COSTS	SUPPLIER A	SUPPLIER B
Valves	50 × $10 = $500	50 × $2 = $100
Failure costs	0.2% of all valves fail: 0.2% × 50 valves × $1,000 = $100	5% of all valves fail: 5% × 50 valves × $1,000 = $2,500
Total cost:	$600	$2,600

7.2 THE STRATEGIC SOURCING PROCESS

In this section, we describe the strategic sourcing process. In contrast to more tactical day-to-day purchasing activities, which we describe later in the chapter, strategic sourcing is concerned with identifying ways to improve long-term business performance by better understanding sourcing needs, developing long-term sourcing strategies, selecting suppliers, and managing the supply base.

To illustrate the difference between strategic sourcing and tactical purchasing activities, commodity managers at a manufacturer might follow a *strategic* sourcing process to identify and negotiate three-year agreements with two major steel suppliers. Purchasing and materials managers at the manufacturer's three plants would then follow *tactical* procure-to-pay procedures to coordinate orders and shipments with these suppliers.

The six steps of the strategic sourcing process are shown in Figure 7.1. There are two things to keep in mind as we describe the strategic sourcing process. First, how much effort a company spends on each step will differ greatly from one situation to the next. The strategic sourcing process for a $30 billion contract for military jets will be much more complex and detailed than the strategic sourcing process for office supplies. Second, as we discuss the different steps in the strategic sourcing process, keep in mind that companies can often gain a competitive advantage by performing these steps *better* than their competitors do.

Step 1: Assess Opportunities

Spend analysis
The application of quantitative techniques to purchasing data in an effort to better understand spending patterns and identify opportunities for improvement.

While the strategic sourcing process is sometimes kicked off in response to an entirely new need within an organization, in the vast majority of cases, the strategic sourcing process is conducted to improve the performance of a firm's *existing* sourcing activities.

One of the most popular tools firms use to assess sourcing performance is spend analysis. **Spend analysis** is the application of quantitative techniques to purchasing data in an effort to better understand spending patterns and identify opportunities for improvement. Spend

FIGURE 7.1 The Strategic Sourcing Process

analysis can be used to answer a wide variety of questions. For example, management might want to know:

- What categories of products or services make up the bulk of company spending?
- How much are we spending with various suppliers?
- What are our spending patterns like across different locations?

Because the questions can vary so widely, there is no single correct approach to spend analysis. Rather, the approach used will depend on the questions at hand. This means that personnel responsible for spend analysis must have the flexibility and skills needed to analyze large quantities of data. The types of tools used can range from relatively sophisticated statistical techniques, such as regression analysis (Chapter 9), to simple graphing techniques, such as Pareto charts (Chapter 4). Furthermore, some organizations have sophisticated spend analysis applications that draw data from the company's financial and accounting applications, while others depend on simpler Excel spreadsheets or Access databases.

Example 7.3 illustrates how spend analysis might be used to assess the opportunity for a major spend category (office supplies) at El-Way Consultants.

EXAMPLE 7.3

Assessing Sourcing Opportunities at El-Way Consultants

Fred Franklin, a recent graduate in operations and supply chain management, has just been hired as a commodity manager at El-Way Consultants, a consulting firm with offices located in six major cities. The vice president of sourcing tells Fred that no one has ever paid attention to how money is spent on office supplies, and she thinks there may be an opportunity to save the company some money. She asks Fred to assess the opportunity and make recommendations.

To better understand the size of the opportunity, Fred decides to perform some simple spend analysis. First, Fred uses El-Way's available purchasing records to estimate office supply expenditures across El-Way's six locations for the previous year. The results are shown in Table 7.4. Figure 7.2 shows the results Pareto chart form, sorted by location.

TABLE 7.4 Office Supply Spend Analysis for El-Way Consultants, by Location

LOCATION	DOLLARS (000s)	PERCENTAGE
London, UK	$3,105	31%
New York, NY	$2,971	30%
Paris, France	$2,275	23%
San Francisco, CA	$618	6%
Chicago, IL	$545	5%
Atlanta, GA	$486	5%
Totals:	$10,000	100%

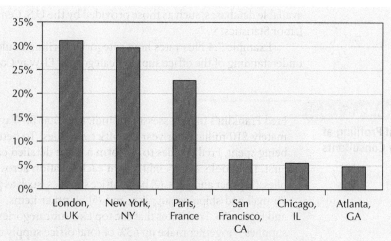

FIGURE 7.2 Office Supply Expenditures for El-Way Consultants, by Location

The spend analysis provides Fred with some useful insights. First, total office supply expenditures for last year were approximately $10 million. If Fred can cut these expenditures by 10% to 20%, he can save El-Way $1,000,000 to $2,000,000 per year. Second, three of El-Way's six locations—London, New York, and Paris—account for 84% of all office supply expenditures. To have a significant financial impact on office supply expenditures, any new sourcing strategy for office supplies will likely need to start with these three locations.

Step 2: Profile Internally and Externally

In the second step of the strategic sourcing process, decision makers often need to develop a more detailed picture, or profile, of the *internal* needs of the organization, as well as the characteristics of the *external* supply base. Two approaches that sourcing managers use to create these profiles are category profiles and industry analysis.

The main objective of a category profile is to understand all aspects of a particular sourcing category that could ultimately have an impact on the sourcing strategy. This might include a breakdown of the total category spend by subcategories, suppliers, and locations. It could also involve understanding how the purchased components or services are used and how demand levels in the organization will change over time. For example, a manufacturer looking at the spend category "purchased components" might break this down into electrical, mechanical, and molded components; components purchased for plants in Asia, the United States, and Canada; components used in production versus those used as spare parts; and components provided from the company's internal sources versus those purchased from external suppliers. Furthermore, discussions with other stakeholders in the firm might indicate that internal demand for molded components is expected to grow at a much higher rate than the other two subcategories. All these factors would affect the manufacturer's sourcing strategy for sourced components.

Industry analysis
Profiles the major forces and trends that are impacting an industry, including pricing, competition, regulatory forces, substitution, technology changes, and supply/demand trends.

While category profiling seeks to provide a better picture of internal needs, **industry analysis** profiles the major forces and trends that are impacting an industry, including pricing, competition, regulatory forces, substitution, technology changes, and supply/demand trends. For example, how many potential suppliers are there? Who are the major suppliers? Is the supply base growing or shrinking? What are the technological trends facing the industry? Where does negotiating power lie—with the suppliers or with the customers?

As you can imagine, industry analysis can require highly specialized knowledge. As a result, buying firms might choose to meet with a key supplier that is an industry expert or hire an external consultant who specializes in studying certain markets (e.g., chemicals, resins, IT providers). Secondary data sources include databases, reports, and Web sites. Examples might be "state of the industry" reports purchased from consulting companies, such as the Harbour Report (**www.theharbourreport.com**), which examines the automotive industry, or publicly available databases, such as those provided by the U.S. Census Bureau or the U.S. Department of Labor Statistics.

Example 7.4 illustrates how category profiling could be used to develop a more detailed understanding of the office supplies category at El-Way Consultants.

EXAMPLE 7.4

Internal Profiling at El-Way Consultants

Fred Franklin's initial assessment indicated that El-Way Consultants is spending approximately $10 million per year on office supplies. To better understand how this money is being spent, Fred decides to perform a more detailed category profile for office supplies. First, Fred looks at expenditures at each location across five subcategories of office supplies: (1) paper and pads, (2) basic office supplies (such as pens and staplers), (3) ink and toner, (4) mail and shipping supplies, and (5) all other items. The results are shown in Table 7.5 and Figure 7.3. Fred notes that the top two subcategories—paper and pads and basic office supplies—together make up 63% of total office supply expenditures.

TABLE 7.5 Office Supply Category Profile for El-Way Consultants, by Location and Subcategory

	Office Supply Subcategories						
LOCATION	PAPERS & PADS	BASIC OFFICE SUPPLIES	INK & TONER	MAIL & SHIPPING SUPPLIES	OTHER	TOTAL	
London, UK	$1,280	$840	$320	$200	$465	$3,105	31%
New York, NY	$1,010	$750	$450	$320	$441	$2,971	30%
Paris, France	$740	$600	$350	$130	$455	$2,275	23%
San Francisco, CA	$200	$180	$80	$40	$118	$618	6%
Chicago, IL	$200	$160	$60	$30	$95	$545	5%
Atlanta, GA	$160	$170	$70	$20	$66	$486	5%
Totals:	$3,590	$2,700	$1,330	$740	$1,640	$10,000	
	36%	27%	13%	7%	16%		

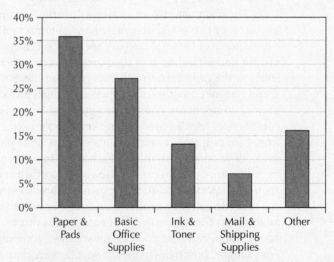

FIGURE 7.3 Office Supply Expenditures for El-Way Consultants, by Subcategory

Next, Fred decides to see which suppliers the various locations are spending their office supply dollars with. In looking through El-Way's purchasing records, Fred learns that in the previous year, El-Way bought office supplies from 150 different vendors; however, the top 7 accounted for 73% of all purchases. The summary results are shown in Table 7.6 and Figure 7.4.

TABLE 7.6 Office Supply Category Profile for El-Way Consultants, by Location and Supplier

	Supplier									
LOCATION	WORLD OFFICE	CLIPS	OPTI-OFFICE	PRINT-MAX	BOUNDARIES	TENDEX	PROTEUS	ALL OTHERS (*n* = 143)		
London, UK	$710	$610	$380	$160	$180	$140	–	$925	$3,105	31%
New York, NY	$580	$740	$640	$440	–	–	–	$571	$2,971	30%
Paris, France	$640	$560	$240	$100	–	–	$60	$665	$2,265	23%
San Francisco, CA	$140	$100	$80	$30	–	–	–	$268	$618	6%
Chicago, IL	$200	$120	$50	$20	–	–	–	$155	$545	5%
Atlanta, GA	$80	$60	$160	$60	–	–	–	$136	$496	5%
Totals:	$2,350	$2,190	$1,550	$810	$810	$140	$60	$2,720	$10,000	
	24%	22%	16%	8%	2%	1%	1%	27%		

FIGURE 7.4 Office Supply Expenditures for El-Way Consultants, by Supplier

Analyzing office supply expenditures by supplier provides Fred with additional insights. First, 62% of El-Way's expenditures are concentrated in three suppliers. In general, Fred considers this a positive result since office supplies are commodity items and spending large amounts with a particular supplier gives El-Way leverage in seeking favorable price discounts and delivery terms. However, 27% of El-Way's office supply expenditures are spread over the bottom 143 suppliers. These purchases provide little opportunity for price discounts, and they also create additional administrative burdens for El-Way, since each supplier represents a new relationship that must be tracked and managed. Furthermore, Fred suspects that many of these smaller purchases result from **maverick spending**—that is, spending that occurs when internal customers purchase directly from nonqualified suppliers and bypass established purchasing procedures.

Maverick spending
Spending that occurs when internal customers purchase directly from nonqualified suppliers and bypass established purchasing procedures.

Step 3: Develop the Sourcing Strategy

The first two steps of the strategic sourcing process—assessing opportunities and profiling internally and externally—provide motivation and information that feed into the third step, developing the sourcing strategy. We divide our discussion of this crucial step into three parts: (1) the make-or-buy decision, (2) total cost analysis, and (3) portfolio analysis.

The Make-or-Buy Decision. When developing a sourcing strategy, businesses sometimes face the question of whether to produce some product or service internally (i.e., **insource**) or to source it from an outside supply chain partner (i.e., **outsource**). This is called the **make-or-buy decision.** While nearly every organization depends on sourcing to some extent, the decision to outsource goods or services raises a host of strategic questions, including the following:

- What are the pros and cons of outsourcing?
- Are there suppliers capable of meeting our needs? Which supplier is the "best"?
- How many suppliers should be used to ensure supply continuity, maintain competition, yet achieve the benefits of a solid supply relationship?

Advantages and Disadvantages of Insourcing and Outsourcing. Insourcing gives a company a high degree of control over its operations. This is particularly desirable if the company owns proprietary designs or processes. Insourcing can also lower costs but *only* if a company enjoys the business volume necessary to achieve economies of scale. So when a company such as Nike decides to outsource the manufacturing of its running shoes, it also makes a conscious decision to retain the design and marketing of these shoes. Why? Because Nike excels at product innovation and marketing. This example points out an important concept: Companies should try to insource processes that are **core competencies**—organizational strengths or abilities, developed over a long period, that customers find valuable and competitors find difficult or even impossible to copy. Products or processes that could evolve into core competencies are prime candidates for insourcing.

On the downside, insourcing can be risky because it decreases a firm's strategic flexibility. Making a product or providing a service internally often requires a company to make long-term capacity commitments that cannot be easily reversed. Finally, if suppliers can provide a product or service more effectively, managers must decide whether to commit scarce resources to upgrading their processes or to outsource the product or service. Attempting to catch up to suppliers technologically can be an expensive proposition that could restrict a firm's ability to invest in other projects or even threaten its financial viability.

Outsourcing typically increases a firm's flexibility and access to state-of-the-art products and processes. As markets or technologies change, many firms find changing supply chain partners easier than changing internal processes. With outsourcing, less investment is required up front in the resources needed to provide a product or service. The benefits of outsourcing can be significant. For instance, many firms today are outsourcing their logistics capabilities to companies such as FedEx and UPS. Mike Eskew, CEO of UPS, described his organization as an "enabler of global commerce," coordinating the movement of goods from its customers' suppliers to their final destinations and sometimes becoming involved with assembly along the way.[3]

Of course, outsourcing has risks. Suppliers might misstate their capabilities: Their process technology might be obsolete, or their performance might not meet the buyer's expectations. In other cases, the supplier might not have the capability to produce the product to the quality level required.

Control and coordination are also issues in outsourcing. Buying firms may need to create costly safeguards to regulate the quality, availability, confidentiality, or performance of outsourced goods or services. Coordinating the flow of materials across separate organizations can be a major challenge, especially when time zone differences, language barriers, and even differences in information systems come into play.

Companies that outsource also risk losing key skills and technologies that are part of their core competencies. To counteract such threats, many companies oversee key design, operations,

---

Insourcing
The use of resources within the firm to provide products or services.

Outsourcing
The use of supply chain partners to provide products or services.

Make-or-buy decision
A high-level, often strategic, decision regarding which products or services will be provided internally and which will be provided by external supply chain partners.

Core competencies
Organizational strengths or abilities, developed over a long period, that customers find valuable and competitors find difficult or even impossible to copy.

---

[3]R. Kapadia, "The Brown Revolution," *Smart Money*, November 10, 2005, **www.smartmoney.com/invest/stocks/ The-Brown-Revolution-18573/**.

TABLE 7.7
Advantages and Disadvantages of Insourcing and Outsourcing

Insourcing	
ADVANTAGES	**DISADVANTAGES**
High degree of control	Reduced strategic flexibility
Ability to oversee the entire process	Required high investment
Economies of scale and/or scope	Potential suppliers may offer superior products and services

Outsourcing	
ADVANTAGES	**DISADVANTAGES**
High strategic flexibility	Possibility of choosing a bad supplier
Low investment risk	Loss of control over the process and core technologies
Improved cash flow	Communication/coordination challenges
Access to state-of-the-art	Increased risk of supply chain disruption
products and services	Customer social responsibility (CSR) risks

TABLE 7.8
Factors That Affect the Decision to Insource or Outsource

	FAVORS INSOURCING	FAVORS OUTSOURCING
Environmental uncertainty	Low	High
Competition in the supplier market	Low	High
Ability to monitor supplier's performance	Low	High
Relationship of product/service to buying firm's core competencies	High	Low

and supply chain activities and keep current on what customers want and how their products or services meet those demands.

Finally, there is the concept of **corporate social responsibility (CSR),** which Carroll defines as "the economic, legal, ethical, and discretionary expectations that society has of organizations at a given point in time."[4] Companies must bear in mind that in today's world, these expectations also extend to their supply chain partners. Various stakeholders, including the government, consumer groups, and individual customers, will hold companies responsible, not just for their own actions, but for the actions of their supply chain partners as well. The *Supply Chain Connections* box ("Outsourcing in the Apparel Industry and Corporate Social Responsibility") dramatically illustrates some of the challenges faced by the apparel industry in this regard. Table 7.7 summarizes the advantages and disadvantages of insourcing and outsourcing.

Table 7.8 looks at the debate from another angle: What factors will influence the decision to insource or outsource? As the table suggests, insourcing will generally be more favorable in situations where environmental uncertainty is low (thereby reducing the risk of investing in capacity), supplier markets are not well developed, and the product or service being considered is directly related to the buying firm's core competencies. In contrast, outsourcing becomes more attractive as competition in supplier markets increases, the product or service is not seen as strategically critical, and environmental uncertainty makes internal investment a risky prospect. Given this, it makes sense that a lot of high-tech companies, facing short product life cycles and uncertain market conditions, outsource more often than do firms in more stable industries.

Total Cost Analysis. Managers must understand the cost issues associated with the make-or-buy decision. Determining the actual cost of a product or service is a complicated task requiring both good judgment and the application of sound quantitative techniques. In this section we will first examine the different costs managers must consider in making such decisions.

Corporate social responsibility
The economic, legal, ethical, and discretionary expectations that society has of organizations at a given point in time.

---

[4]A. Carroll, "A Three-Dimensional Conceptual Model of Corporate Performance," *Academy of Management Review* 4, no. 4 (1979): 497–505.

SUPPLY CHAIN CONNECTIONS

OUTSOURCING IN THE APPAREL INDUSTRY AND CORPORATE SOCIAL RESPONSIBILITY

As companies have expanded their supply chains globally, many have outsourced activities that can be done more efficiently by suppliers in other parts of the world. The apparel industry was one of the first to broadly adopt the outsourced supply chain concept. By deploying the "fast fashion" business model, global brands such as Nike, H&M, and Abercrombie & Fitch were able to create extremely responsive supply chains and bring lower-priced apparel to store shelves. They accomplished this in part by outsourcing garment manufacturing to suppliers and subcontractors in low-cost countries, such as China, Vietnam, Malaysia, and Bangladesh. Furthermore, the time to design and deliver new garments to the market was reduced from more than one year in some cases to just a few weeks. More efficient processes, cheaper products, and faster delivery appeared to make for a winning supply chain model.

But in too many cases these supply chains had serious weaknesses that supply chain executives failed to recognize. By chasing cheap labor, Western retailers had put tremendous cost pressure on suppliers who, in turn, minimized capital investments and adopted questionable safety and labor practices. For example, in Bangladesh, many garment workers, including children, are exposed to hazardous conditions that would not be allowed in other parts of the world.

On April 24, 2013, one of the deadliest garment-factory incidents in history occurred in Bangladesh when an eight-story manufacturing plant, Rana Plaza, collapsed near Dhaka, taking the lives of more than 1,100 people.[5] This incident came just a few months after a fire at the Tazreen Fashions factory in Ashulia, Bangladesh, which killed more than 100 people. The Tazreen factory produced sweater jackets for C&A, shorts for Walmart, and lingerie for Sears.[6] These retailers were seen by many as sharing responsibility for these accidents.[7] These cases demonstrate that best practice supply chain thinking must also address the social aspects of running a global supply chain, and that companies who outsource can be held responsible in part for the actions of their supply chain partners.

Source: Adapted from A. Wieland and R. Handfield, "The Socially Responsible Supply Chain: An Imperative for Global Corporations," *Supply Chain Management Review*, September 2013. Used with permission from Bob Treibilock, Editor in Chief, *Supply Chain Management Review*.
[5]2013 Savar Building Collapse, **http://en.wikipedia.org/wiki/2013_Savar_building_collapse.**
[6]J. Yardley, "Horrific Fire Revealed a Gap in Safety for Global Brands," *New York Times*, December 6, 2012.
[7]S. Al-Mahmood, "Bangladesh Fire: What Wal-Mart's Supplier Network Missed," *Wall Street Journal*, December 1, 2012, **http://online.wsj.com/news/articles/SB10001424127887324024004578169400995615618.**

Total cost analysis
A process by which a firm seeks to identify and quantify all of the major costs associated with various sourcing options.

Direct costs
Costs tied directly to the level of operations or supply chain activities, such as the production of a good or service, or transportation.

Indirect costs
Costs that are not tied directly to the level of operations or supply chain activity.

Total cost analysis is a process by which a firm seeks to identify and quantify all of the major costs associated with various sourcing options. Table 7.9 lists some typical costs. As the table shows, these costs are often divided into direct and indirect costs. **Direct costs** are costs that are tied directly to the level of operations or supply chain activities, such as the production of a good or service, or transportation. If, for example, a product requires 1.3 square feet of sheet metal, and the cost of sheet metal is $0.90 per square foot, the direct cost of the sheet metal is:

$$\$0.90 \times (1.3 \text{ feet}) = \$1.17$$

Indirect costs, as the name implies, are not tied directly to the level of operations or supply chain activity. Building lease payments and staff salaries are classic examples of indirect costs, which in essence represent costs of doing business. To understand the true total cost of insourcing or outsourcing, managers must allocate indirect costs to individual units of production. That task is not as easy as it may sound, however. Suppose managers are trying to decide whether to make a product in-house or outsource it. They estimate that they will need to spend $600,000 just to design the new product. If they plan to produce 200,000 units, they might assign the design cost as follows:

$$\$600,000 / 200,000 \text{ units} = \$3.00 \text{ per unit}$$

But what if the results of the design effort could be applied to *future* products? Should part of the design cost be assigned to those future products, and if so, how? Because of problems such as this, outsourcing costs are usually easier to determine than insourcing costs. With

TABLE 7.9
Insourcing and Outsourcing Costs

	INSOURCING	OUTSOURCING
Direct Costs	Direct material	Price (from invoice)
	Direct labor	Freight costs
	Freight costs	
	Variable overhead	
Indirect Costs	Supervision	Purchasing
	Administrative support	
	Supplies	Receiving
	Maintenance costs	Quality control
	Equipment depreciation	
	Utilities	
	Building lease	
	Fixed overhead	

outsourcing, the indirect costs are included in the direct purchase price shown on the supplier's invoice. Generally, the only additional costs that need to be considered in the outsourcing decision are inbound freight (a direct cost) and administrative costs associated with managing the buyer–supplier relationship (such as purchasing and quality control). In contrast, the bulk of insourcing costs may fall into the indirect category, making the task of estimating the true total cost more difficult.

In determining total costs, managers must also consider the time frame of the make-or-buy decision. If an insourcing arrangement is expected to be of relatively short duration, as it might be for a product with a limited life cycle, then perhaps only direct costs and some portion of the indirect costs should be applied. In the short run, firms are better off recovering their direct costs and some portion of their indirect costs than risking a significant decline in their business. However, if managers expect an insourcing arrangement to become part of ongoing operations, they should consider all relevant costs that might reasonably be incurred over the long term, including all indirect costs.

EXAMPLE 7.5

Total Cost Analysis at the ABC Company

One of ABC's Taiwanese suppliers has bid on a new line of molded plastic parts that are currently being assembled at ABC's facility. The supplier has bid $0.10 per part, given a forecasted demand of 200,000 parts in year 1, 300,000 in year 2, and 500,000 in year 3. Shipping and handling of parts from the supplier's facility is estimated at $0.01 per unit. Additional inventory handling charges should amount to $0.005 per unit. Finally, administrative costs are estimated at $20 per month.

Although ABC's facility is capable of producing the part, the company would need to invest in another machine that would cost $10,000, depreciated over the life of the product. Direct materials can be purchased for $0.05 per unit. Direct labor is estimated at $0.03 per unit plus a 50% surcharge for benefits; indirect labor is estimated at $0.011 per unit plus 50% for benefits. Up-front engineering and design costs will amount to $30,000. Finally, ABC management has insisted that overhead (an indirect cost) be allocated to the parts at a rate of 100% of direct labor cost.

Table 7.10 shows one possible analysis of the total costs. Of course, different managers might come up with slightly different analyses. For instance, ABC's managers might want to experiment with different allocation rates for overhead and depreciation expense to see how a change in the rate might affect the decision. They might also want to consider the effect of exchange rates on the supplier's costs. Suppose that the outsourcing costs are based on an exchange rate of 30 Taiwanese dollars to 1 U.S. dollar. If the exchange rate were to fall to 25 to 1, ABC's outsourcing costs could rise by 20%. The point is that even a relatively simple cost analysis requires managerial judgment and interpretation. Total cost analyses are most useful when they are considered jointly with strategic factors.

TABLE 7.10 Total Cost Analysis for the Sourcing Decision at ABC

INSOURCING OPTION	
Operating Expenses	
Direct labor	$0.0300
Benefits (50%)	$0.0150
Direct material	$0.0500
Indirect labor	$0.0110
Benefits (50%)	$0.0055
Equipment depreciation	$0.0100 ($10,000 absorbed over 1 million units)
Overhead	$0.0300
Engineering/design costs	$0.0300 ($30,000 absorbed over 1 million units)
Total cost per unit	**$0.1815**
OUTSOURCING OPTION	
Purchase price	$0.1000
Shipping and handling	$0.0100
Inventory charges	$0.0050
Administrative costs	$0.0007 [($20 per month) * (36 months)] / 1 million units
Total cost per unit	**$0.1157**
Savings per unit	**$0.0658**
Total savings (1 million units)	**$65,800**

Portfolio analysis
A structured approach used by decision makers to develop a sourcing strategy for a product or service, based on the value potential and the relative complexity or risk represented by a sourcing opportunity.

Portfolio Analysis. Sourcing professionals have developed a wide range of approaches to help them in identifying the correct sourcing strategy. Figure 7.5 shows one such approach, called portfolio analysis.[8] In **portfolio analysis,** the products or services to be sourced are assigned to one of four strategic quadrants, based on their relative complexity and/or risk impact to the firm and their value potential. In general, the more money a company spends on a particular good or service, the higher its value potential. Depending on what quadrant a product or service is assigned to, the buying firm can then identify the most appropriate sourcing strategy, tactics, and actions.

To illustrate, a standardized product available from many sources represents a relatively low level of complexity and sourcing risk to the firm; the product characteristics are well understood, and if one supplier fails to meet the needs of the company, another one will be ready to pick up the business. On the other hand, a highly customized product or service, available from one or a handful of suppliers, introduces greater levels of complexity and risk. Likewise, a service that represents $30 million of annual spending has a greater value potential—and, hence, deserves more attention from the firm—than one with an annual spend of just $10,000.

The "Routine" Quadrant. Products or services in the routine quadrant are readily available and represent a relatively small portion of a firm's purchasing expenditures. Typical examples include office supplies, cleaning services, and the like. The sourcing strategy therefore becomes one of simplifying the acquisition process, thereby lowering the costs associated with purchasing items in this quadrant. Specific actions can include automating the purchasing process, reducing the number of suppliers used, and using **electronic data interchange (EDI)** or purchase cards to streamline payment.

Electronic data interchange (EDI)
An information technology that allows supply chain partners to transfer data electronically between their information systems.

The "Leverage" Quadrant. Products or services in the leverage quadrant tend to be standardized and readily available, and they represent a significant portion of spend. The sourcing strategy therefore focuses on leveraging the firm's spending levels to get the most favorable terms

---

[8]Adapted from R. Monczka, R. B. Handfield, L. C. Giunipero, and J. L. Patterson, *Purchasing and Supply Chain Management,* 5th ed. (Mason, OH: South-Western, 2011).

FIGURE 7.5
Sourcing Portfolio Analysis

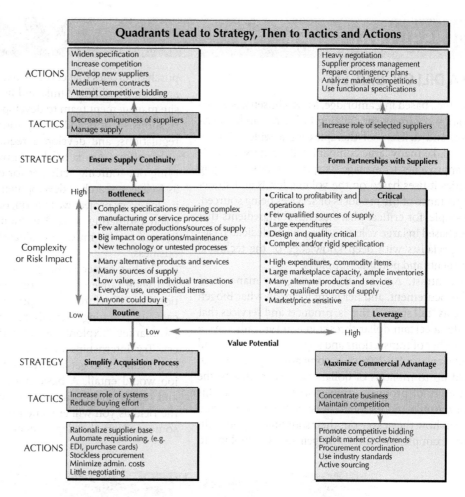

Preferred supplier
A supplier that has demonstrated its performance capabilities through previous purchase contracts and therefore receives preference during the supplier selection process.

possible. A **preferred supplier** is a supplier that has demonstrated its performance capabilities through previous purchase contracts and therefore receives preference during the supplier selection process. Preferred suppliers are frequently awarded business, with the understanding that they will reduce the cost of supplying these items in return for significant order volumes and multiple-year contracts. A high level of service is also expected, which may include such services as on-site inventory management by the supplier and e-purchasing.

The "Bottleneck" Quadrant. "Bottleneck" products or services have unique or complex requirements that can be met only by a few potential suppliers. In this case, the primary goal of the sourcing strategy is to not run out; in effect, the goal is to ensure supply continuity. This might involve carrying extra inventory to protect against interruptions in supply or contracting with multiple vendors to reduce supply chain risks.

The "Critical" Quadrant. Like bottleneck items, products or services in the critical quadrant have complex or unique requirements coupled with a limited supply base. The primary difference is that these items can represent a substantial level of expenditure for the sourcing firm. In cases such as this, the sourcing firm will spend considerable time negotiating favorable deals and building partnerships with suppliers, as well as preparing contingency plans in case of an interruption in supply.

This chapter's *Professional Profile* focuses on Amila Dillon of Biogen. As you are reading Amila's profile, ask yourself what quadrant of the sourcing portfolio matrix in Figure 7.5 best describes the "tail spend" she helps manage.

PROFESSIONAL PROFILE

AMILA DILLON, BIOGEN

Biogen, Inc., based in Cambridge, Massachusetts, is a biotechnology company specializing in the research, development, and delivery of therapies for a wide range of diseases. Like many large companies, Biogen uses a variety of approaches to manage its spend dollars, changing the tactics it uses based on the volume levels and strategic importance of the products or services being sourced. For example, for critical pharmaceutical ingredients that are purchased in large volumes, Biogen has dedicated category specialists with deep knowledge of the technical requirements and potential suppliers.

In contrast, Amila Dillon, a program manager in global procurement, and her team focus on what Biogen refers to as "tail spend"; that is, products and services that are under a certain dollar threshold and typically have a high number of transactions and suppliers. The tail spend is equivalent to 10–20% of a company's spend, which can add up to millions of dollars each year. Due to the wide variety of products and services that fall into this category, Amila and her team must be both creative and flexible in how they carry out their sourcing responsibilities. For example, one time a Biogen site was looking to

purchase drones that could be used to inspect hard-to-see areas on a building. Amila and her team worked with the site management team to develop detailed product specifications, identify and qualify sources, understand federal regulations, and develop a request for proposal (RFP). Other efforts Amila has been involved with include carrying out sourcing activities for engineering, marketing, as well as research & development (R&D). As Amila puts it, "for every project we take on, our analysis goes beyond solely estimating costs. The suppliers' capabilities, quality, and service must be evaluated prior to awarding the business."

In her career at Biogen, Amila has been involved in a wide range of operations and supply chain activities, including forecasting, process selection efforts, and capacity planning. Her advice for students entering the job market: "Explore careers within your field of interest. Try internships or co-op assignments as learning opportunities to get a better understanding of what that job would entail. A basic understanding of operations and supply chain is important even if you don't go into the field as you will at some point end up working with someone from that department."

Photo courtesy of Ron Carrea, Biogen

Single sourcing
A sourcing strategy in which the buying firm depends on a single company for all or nearly all of a particular item or service.

Multiple sourcing
A sourcing strategy in which the buying firm shares its business across multiple suppliers.

Single and Multiple Sourcing, Cross Sourcing, and Dual Sourcing. An important part of any sourcing strategy is determining how many suppliers to use when sourcing a good or service. In **single sourcing**, the buying firm depends on a single company for all or nearly all of a particular item. In **multiple sourcing**, the buying firm shares its business across multiple suppliers. The advantages and disadvantages of each are shown in Table 7.11.

One way that companies can overcome the dilemma of the single sourcing versus multiple sourcing decision is through a compromise known as **cross sourcing.** In this strategy, a company uses a single supplier for one product or service, and another supplier with the same capabilities for another, similar product or service. Each supplier is then awarded new business

TABLE 7.11
Advantages and
Disadvantages of
Multiple/Single
Sourcing

Multiple Sourcing		Single Sourcing	
ADVANTAGES	**DISADVANTAGES**	**ADVANTAGES**	**DISADVANTAGES**
Creates competition	Reduces supplier loyalty—suppliers may not be willing to "go the extra mile" for the purchaser	Volume leveraging as volumes go up, cost per unit decreases as supplier spreads fixed costs over larger volume	Knowing they have the business, suppliers can actually increase prices in the short term
Spreads risk (in event of a fire, strike, etc. at one supplier)	Can increase risk in the event of a shortage—supplier may supply only preferred customers	Transportation economics—fewer shipments and lower per-unit transportation costs	Increased supply risk—if a disaster occurs, the buyer can be left without a source of supply
Required if the purchased volume is too great for one supplier	May result in different product attributes with varying quality	Reduces quality variability; standardized products	Buyer can become "captive" to a supplier's technology—while other suppliers are surging ahead with newer technology that has better performance
Desired if firm wishes to meet obligations to support minority suppliers	Can actually result in increased prices over time, as suppliers are reluctant to provide cost-saving ideas	Builds stronger relationship with supplier, and gains access to design and engineering capabilities	Do not know if you have the "best" supplier available
Can ensure that suppliers do not become "complacent"	Suppliers can let performance slide if volume is not high enough to merit their attention	Required when supplier has a proprietary product	Dangerous strategy if the supplier has limited capacity or quality issues
Can help keep inventory levels down	In a global network, having multiple suppliers can also help reduce inbound freight cost and lower lead times	Required when volume is too small to split between two suppliers	

Cross sourcing
A sourcing strategy in which a company uses a single supplier for one particular part or service and another supplier with the same capabilities for a different part or service, with the understanding that each supplier can act as a backup for the other supplier.

Dual sourcing
A sourcing strategy in which two suppliers are used for the same purchased product or service.

based on its performance, creating an incentive for both to improve. This also provides for a backup supplier in case the primary supplier cannot meet a company's needs.

A similar purchasing strategy is **dual sourcing.** This strategy is exactly what it sounds like: Two suppliers are used for the same purchased product or service. Typically, the split of the business is 70% to Supplier A and 30% to Supplier B. In this case, Supplier A knows that if performance suffers, it will lose business to Supplier B. Dual sourcing combines the volume benefits of single sourcing with the added protection of multiple or cross sourcing.

Step 4: Screen Suppliers and Create Selection Criteria

While portfolio analysis can help identify the appropriate sourcing strategy for a product or service, the buying firm still needs some way to evaluate potential and current suppliers. Identifying the "best" supplier for a new product or service or evaluating past supplier performance is a difficult task. This is especially true when the criteria include not just quantitative measures (such as costs, on-time delivery rates, etc.) but other, more qualitative factors, such as management stability or trustworthiness. Some of the qualitative criteria that a company might use to evaluate suppliers include:[9]

- **Process and design capabilities.** Since different manufacturing and service processes have inherent strengths and weaknesses (Chapter 3), the buying firm must be aware of these characteristics up front. When the buyer expects suppliers to perform component design and production, it should also assess the supplier's design capability. One way to reduce the time required to develop new products is to use qualified suppliers who are able to perform product design activities.
- **Management capability.** Different aspects of management capability include management's commitment to continuous process and quality improvement, overall professional ability and experience, ability to maintain positive relationships with the workforce, and willingness to develop a closer working relationship with the buyer.
- **Financial condition and cost structure.** Selecting a supplier that is in poor financial condition presents a number of risks. First, there is the risk that the organization will go out of business, disrupting the flow of goods or services. Second, suppliers who are in poor financial condition may not have the resources to invest in required personnel, equipment, or improvement efforts.
- **Longer-term relationship potential.** In some cases, a buying firm may be looking to develop a long-term relationship with a potential supplier. Perhaps the supplier has a proprietary technology or foreign market presence that the sourcing firm wants to tap into.

Request for information (RFI)
An inquiry to a potential supplier about that supplier's products or services for potential use in the business. The inquiry can provide certain business requirements or be of a more exploratory nature.

Organizations often use a **request for information (RFI)** to gather data about potential suppliers. An RFI is an inquiry to a potential supplier about that supplier's products or services for potential use in the business. The inquiry can provide certain business requirements or be of a more exploratory nature.[10] Not only can an RFI provide useful quantitative and qualitative information about a supplier, a completed RFI serves as a signal that a supplier might be interested in entering into a business relationship with the buying firm. Buying firms typically use their own purchasing records and RFI results to develop a supplier long list that will be shortened during the supplier selection process.

Step 5: Conduct Supplier Selection

The objective of the supplier selection step is to identify a short list of suppliers with whom the buying firm will engage in competitive bidding or negotiations. **Multicriteria decision models,** as the name suggests, are models that allow decision makers to evaluate various alternatives across multiple decision criteria. Multicriteria decision models are especially helpful when there is a mix of quantitative and qualitative decision criteria, when there are numerous decision alternatives to be considered, and when there is no clear "best" choice. They are therefore well suited to supplier selection efforts. Multicriteria decision models can help formalize what would otherwise be an ill-structured, poorly understood process.

Multicriteria decision models
Models that allow decision makers to evaluate various alternatives across multiple decision criteria.

The Weighted-Point Evaluation System. A common multicriteria decision model is the weighted-point evaluation system. In this model, the user is asked up front to assign weights to the performance measures (W_Y), and rate the performance of each supplier with regard to each dimension ($Performance_{XY}$). The total score for each supplier is then calculated as follows:

$$Score_X = \sum_{Y=1}^{n} Performance_{XY} \times W_Y \qquad (7.3)$$

where:

$$X = \text{Supplier X}$$
$$Y = \text{performance dimension Y}$$
$$Perfomance_{XY} = \text{rated performance of Supplier X with regard to performance dimension Y}$$
$$W_Y = \text{assigned weight for performance dimension Y, where } \sum_{Y=1}^{n} W_Y = 1$$

---

[9] Ibid.
[10] Adapted from J. H. Blackstone, ed., *APICS Dictionary*, 15th ed. (Chicago, IL: APICS, 2016).

EXAMPLE 7.6

**Using the Weighted-
Point Evaluation
System to Support
Supplier Evaluation at
Electra Company**

Electra Company is looking to award a new contract for 500,000 integrated circuit boards (ICBs). Table 7.12 summarizes the expected performance of three possible suppliers with regard to price, quality, and delivery.

TABLE 7.12 Summary Data for Three Possible Suppliers

PERFORMANCE DIMENSION	AARDVARK ELECTRONICS	BEVERLY HILLS	CONAN THE ELECTRICIAN
Price	$4/unit	$5/unit	$2/unit
Quality	5% defects	1% defects	10% defects
Delivery Reliability	95% on-time	80% on-time	60% on-time

The process begins by developing a weight for each of the criteria used. The sum of the weights must equal one. In this case, the sourcing team assigned to evaluating suppliers for the new contract has decided that quality is the most important criterion, followed closely by delivery and price. The resulting weights are:

$$W_{Price} = 0.3$$
$$W_{Quality} = 0.4$$
$$W_{Delivery\ Reliability} = 0.3$$
$$Total = 1.0$$

Next, the sourcing team evaluates each supplier's performance on each of the criteria, using the scales in Table 7.13.

TABLE 7.13 Scoring Scheme for Weighted-Point Evaluation System

5 = Excellent
4 = Good
3 = Average
2 = Fair
1 = Poor

Based on the product design team's specifications, the Electra sourcing team has assigned performance scores for each criterion, as shown in Table 7.14.

TABLE 7.14 Values for the Three Suppliers

PERFORMANCE DIMENSION	AARDVARK ELECTRONICS	BEVERLY HILLS	CONAN THE ELECTRICIAN
Price	4	3	5
Quality	3	5	1
Delivery Reliability	4	2	1

The total score for each supplier is then calculated by multiplying the respective performance ratings by the weight assigned to each performance dimension and summing the results across all dimensions. For Aardvark Electronics:

$$Score_{Aardvark} = Performance_{Aardvark,\ Price} \times W_{Price}$$
$$+ Performance_{Aardvark,\ Quality} \times W_{Quality}$$
$$+ Performance_{Aardvark,\ Delivery\ Reliability} \times W_{Delivery\ Reliability}$$
$$= 4 \times 0.3 + 3 \times 0.4 + 4 \times 0.3 = 3.6$$

The scores for Beverly Hills and Conan the Electrician are calculated in a similar manner, and are 3.5 and 2.2, respectively. Based on the results, the Electra team must now decide which suppliers to negotiate with. Conan the Electrician is clearly out of the running. While this supplier has the lowest price by far, its delivery and quality record is abysmal. This leaves Aardvark and Beverly Hills. Aardvark has a lower price but needs to improve its quality. Beverly Hills has excellent quality, but it has a problem delivering on time and must also find a way to reduce prices. Because the final scores for the two suppliers are so close, Electra has several options:

1. Award the contract to Aardvark, after a detailed negotiation in which it asks Aardvark to provide details on how it will improve its quality.
2. Award the contract to Beverly Hills, after a detailed negotiation in which it asks Beverly Hills to reduce its price and explain how it will improve delivery performance.
3. Award a dual source contract, in which the volumes are split between two suppliers. The contract might state that future volumes will be assigned according to which supplier improves its performance more quickly.

Clearly, supplier evaluation requires a significant amount of judgment in awarding points and assigning weights. However, the process of identifying key criteria and assigning numerical scores to performance allows users to be more objective and comprehensive in their decision making. Furthermore, conscientious managers will make every effort to back up their ratings with hard data.

Step 6: Negotiate and Implement Agreements

The strategic sourcing process does not end until the buying firm has reached a formal agreement with one or more suppliers regarding terms and conditions such as the price to be paid, volume levels, quality levels, and delivery performance. In some cases, firms may maintain a list of preferred suppliers that receive the first opportunity for new business. A preferred supplier has demonstrated its performance capabilities through previous purchase contracts and therefore receives preference during the supplier selection process. By maintaining a preferred supplier list, purchasing personnel can quickly identify suppliers that have proven performance capabilities.

When there is not a preferred supplier, competitive bidding and negotiation are two methods commonly used to select a supplier. *Competitive bidding* entails a request for bids from suppliers with whom a buyer is willing to do business. The process is typically initiated when the buying firm sends a **request for quotation (RFQ)** to qualified suppliers. The RFQ is a formal request for the suppliers to prepare bids based on the terms and conditions set by the buyer.

In contrast to an RFI, an RFQ often includes a detailed description of the products or services to be purchased. **Description by market grade** or **industry standard** might be the best choice for standard items, where the requirements are well understood and there is common agreement between supply chain partners about what certain terms mean. **Description by brand** is used when a product or service is proprietary or when there is a perceived advantage to using a particular supplier's products or services. A builder of residential communities, for example, might want to purchase R21 insulation (an industry standard) for the walls and finish-grade lumber (a market grade) for the trim and fireplace mantles. In addition, he might specify brands such as Georgia-Pacific's Catawba hardboard siding, Kohler faucets, and TruGreen-Chemlawn lawn treatment for all the homes.

More detailed and expensive methods of description are needed when the items or services to be purchased are more complex, when "standards" do not exist, or when the user's needs are more difficult to communicate. In some cases, the buyer might need to provide potential suppliers very detailed descriptions of the characteristics of an item or a service. We refer to such efforts as **description by specification.** Specifications can cover such characteristics as the materials used, the manufacturing or service steps required, or even the physical dimensions of the product. In contrast, **description by performance characteristics** focuses attention on the *outcomes* the buyer wants, not on the precise configuration of the product or service. The assumption is that the supplier will know the best way to meet the buyer's needs. A company purchasing thousands of laptops from Hewlett-Packard

Request for quotation (RFQ)
A formal request for the suppliers to prepare bids, based on the terms and conditions set by the buyer.

Description by market grade/industry standard
A description method that is used when the requirements are well understood and there is common agreement between supply chain partners about what certain terms mean.

Description by brand
A description method that is used when a product or service is proprietary or when there is a perceived advantage to using a particular supplier's products or services.

Description by specification
A description method that is used when an organization needs to provide very detailed descriptions of the characteristics of an item or a service.

Description by performance characteristics
A description method that focuses attention on the outcomes the customer wants rather than on the precise configuration of the product or service.

might demand (1) 24-hour support available by computer or phone and (2) a 48-hour turn-around time on defective units. How HP chooses to meet these performance characteristics is its choice.

Competitive bidding is most effective when:[11]

- The buying firm can provide qualified suppliers with clear descriptions of the items or services to be purchased.
- Volume is high enough to justify the cost and effort.
- The buying firm does not have a preferred supplier.

Buying firms use competitive bidding when price is a dominant criterion and the required items or services have straightforward specifications. In addition, government agencies often require competitive bidding. If major nonprice variables exist, then the buyer and seller usually enter into direct negotiation. Competitive bidding can also be used to identify a short list of suppliers with whom the firm will begin detailed purchase contract negotiation.

In recent years, firms have also begun to use electronic competitive bidding tools such as *reverse auctions* and *e-auctions*. These mechanisms work like a regular auction but in reverse: The buyer identifies potential qualified suppliers, who go to a specific Web site at a designated time and bid to get the business. In such cases, the lowest bid often occurs as suppliers see what other suppliers are bidding for the business and submit lower bids in an effort to win the contract.

Negotiation is a more costly, interactive approach to final supplier selection. Negotiation is best when:

- The item is a new and/or technically complex item with only vague specifications.
- The purchase requires agreement about a wide range of performance factors.
- The buyer requires the supplier to participate in the development effort.
- The supplier cannot determine risks and costs without additional input from the buyer.

Contracting. Often, a detailed purchasing contact is required to formalize the buyer–supplier relationship. A contract can be required if the size of the purchase exceeds a predetermined monetary value (e.g., $10,000) or if there are specific business requirements that need to be put in writing. Purchasing contracts can be classified into different categories, based on their characteristics and purpose. Almost all purchasing contracts are based on some form of pricing mechanism and can be categorized as a variation on two basic types: fixed-price and cost-based contracts.

Fixed-price contract
A type of purchasing contract in which the stated price does not change, regardless of fluctuations in general overall economic conditions, industry competition, levels of supply, market prices, or other environmental changes.

The most basic contract is a **fixed-price contract.** In this type of purchase contract, the stated price does not change, regardless of fluctuations in general overall economic conditions, industry competition, levels of supply, market prices, or other environmental changes.

With a fixed-price contract, if market prices for a purchased good or service rise above the stated contract price, the seller bears the brunt of the financial loss. However, if the market price falls below the stated contract price due to outside factors such as competition, changes in technology, or raw material prices, the buyer assumes the risk of financial loss. If there is a high level of uncertainty from the supplier's point of view regarding its ability to make a reasonable profit under competitive fixed-price conditions, then the supplier might add to its price to cover potential increases in component, raw materials, or labor prices. If the supplier increases its contract price in anticipation of rising costs and the anticipated conditions do not occur, then the buyer has paid too high a price for the good or service. For this reason, it is very important for the buying firm to adequately understand existing market conditions prior to signing a fixed-price contract.

Cost-based contract
A type of purchasing contract in which the price of a good or service is tied to the cost of some key input(s) or other economic factors, such as interest rates.

In contrast, a **cost-based contract** ties the price of a good or service to the cost of some key input(s) or other economic factor(s), such as interest rates. Cost-based contracts are often used when the goods or services procured are expensive or complex or when there is a high degree of uncertainty regarding labor and material costs. Cost-based contracts typically represent a lower risk level of economic loss for suppliers, but they can also result in lower overall costs to the buyer through careful contract management. It is important for the buyer to include contractual terms and conditions that require the supplier to carefully monitor and control costs. The two parties must also stipulate how costs are to be included in the calculation of the price of the goods or services procured.

---

[11]D. Dobler, L. Lee, and D. Burt, *Purchasing and Materials Management* (Homewood, IL: Irwin, 1990).

From the moment of signing, it is the purchasing manager's responsibility to ensure that all of the terms and conditions of the agreement are fulfilled. If the terms and conditions of a contract are breached, purchasing is also responsible for resolving the conflict.

7.3 THE PROCURE-TO-PAY CYCLE

Procure-to-pay cycle
The set of activities required to first identify a need, assign a supplier to meet that need, approve the specification or scope, acknowledge receipt, and submit payment to the supplier.

Once the buyer and supplier have agreed to enter into a relationship and a contract has been signed, the buyer will signal to the supplier that delivery of the product or service is required. This begins what is known as the **procure-to-pay cycle,** which is defined as the set of activities required to first identify a need, assign a supplier to meet that need, approve the specification or scope, acknowledge receipt, and submit payment to the supplier. In contrast to the strategic sourcing process, the procure-to-pay cycle is decidedly *tactical* in nature: It involves day-to-day communications and transactions between the buyer and supplier, and it is completed once the goods or services have been received, the supplier has been paid, and the information has been recorded into the database.

The five main steps of the procure-to-pay cycle are described next:

1. Ordering
2. Follow-up and expediting
3. Receipt and inspection
4. Settlement and payment
5. Records maintenance

Ordering

Purchase order PO
A document that authorizes a supplier to deliver a product or service and often includes key terms and conditions, such as price, delivery, and quality requirements.

The most common way the ordering step begins is through the release of a purchase order. A **purchase order (PO)** is simply a document that authorizes a supplier to deliver a product or service and often includes terms and conditions, such as price, delivery, and quality requirements. Increasingly, POs are released through EDI, which is a technology that allows supply chain partners to transfer data electronically between their information systems. By eliminating the time associated with the flow of physical documents between supply chain partners, EDI can reduce the time it takes suppliers to respond to customers' needs. This, in turn, leads to shorter order lead times, lower inventory, and better coordination between supply chain partners.

Follow-Up and Expediting

Someone (typically purchasing or materials personnel) must monitor the status of open purchase orders. There may be times when the buying firm has to expedite an order or work with a supplier to avoid shipment delays. The buying firm can minimize order follow-up by selecting only the best suppliers and developing internally stable forecasting and ordering systems.

Receipt and Inspection

When the order for a physical good arrives at the buyer's location, it is received and inspected to ensure that the right quantity was shipped and that it was not damaged in transit. If the product or service was provided on time, it will be entered into the company's purchasing transaction system. Physical products delivered by suppliers then become part of the company's working inventory.

Statement of work, or scope of work (SOW)
Terms and conditions for a purchased service that indicate, among other things, what services will be performed and how the service provider will be evaluated.

In the case of services, the buyer must ensure that the service is being performed according to the terms and conditions stated in the purchase order. For services, the user will typically sign off on a supplier time sheet or another document to signal to purchasing that the supplier satisfied the conditions stated in the **statement of work,** or **scope of work (SOW).** An SOW documents the type of service required, the qualifications of the individual(s) performing the work, and the outcome or deliverables expected at the conclusion of the work, among other things. Deviations from the SOW must be noted and passed on to the supplier and in some cases might require modifications to the original agreement.

SUPPLY CHAIN CONNECTIONS

PROCURE-TO-PAY SOURCING EFFORTS AT DEUTSCHE BANK

Just like manufacturers, banks also have supply chains that involve sourcing from third-party suppliers. Much of the external spend at a bank involves buying services that directly impact the bank's ability to service its own customers. Examples include travel, human resources, information technology, servicing of ATMs, market data services, and many others.

Ken Litton joined Deutsche Bank (DB) AG in June 2004, and serves as managing director, chief procurement officer. Litton's first task was to develop a detailed cross-enterprise spend analysis to provide a detailed view of where dollars were going across all divisions at DB. Not surprisingly, many areas of opportunity were uncovered, including payments for services that weren't being used by anyone yet but were still being billed by suppliers, supplier proliferation in certain spend categories, and the lack of standard contracts in many areas. What was particularly surprising was that only 50% of DB's total spend was managed and monitored through formal contracts with suppliers. The first two years of Litton's time was spent establishing a rigorous procure-to-pay process, which culminated in the adoption of information technology to support a broad array of sourcing relationships across DB's lines of business.

Litton's second task was to ensure that suppliers and DB's managers were complying with existing contracts. Today, for example, almost all sourcing relationships are captured in a contracts database that is readily accessible by sourcing managers. A third effort was directed at driving category management. Category managers were assigned to major spend categories. All spending in a category, such as travel or IT, now goes through an assigned manager. Strict compliance is required to establish a single source of contact for all purchase orders and to capture all payments and transactional data. Aligned with this effort, beginning in 2010, all suppliers were required to submit invoices electronically via the DB's Ariba Supplier Network (ASN). This allowed suppliers not only to view invoice payment status, purchase orders, and exception handling but it also drove DB's ability to capture metrics and build the foundation for a risk management system. Today category management is a well-established way of working at Deutsche Bank.

Settlement and Payment

Electronic funds transfer (EFT)
The automatic transfer of payment from a buyer's bank account to a supplier's bank account.

Once an item or a service is delivered, the buying firm will issue an authorization for payment to the supplier. Payment is then made through the firm's accounts payable department. As with ordering, this is increasingly being accomplished through electronic means. Suppliers are often paid through **electronic funds transfer (EFT),** which is the automatic transfer of payment from the buyer's bank account to the supplier's bank account.

Records Maintenance

After a product or service has been delivered and the supplier paid, a record of critical events associated with the purchase is entered into a supplier performance database. The supplier performance database accumulates critical performance data over an extended period. These data are often used in future negotiations and dealings with the supplier in question. The data gathered here can also support spend analysis efforts, as described earlier in the chapter.

7.4 TRENDS IN SUPPLY MANAGEMENT

This chapter would not be complete without a look at two key trends affecting supply management: environmental sustainability and planning for supply chain disruptions.

Sustainable Supply

As more companies become conscious of the importance of being environmentally friendly, environmental performance is becoming an important criterion in selecting suppliers. Companies want to ensure that suppliers are in compliance with environmental regulations and that

As sustainability becomes more important, companies will look for suppliers who can provide environmentally friendly products and services, such as the packaging for these soups.

they are well positioned to deal with changes in the regulatory environment. Similarly, companies are looking for ways to reduce packaging, promote recycling, and use other strategies designed to reduce cost while being good for the environment.

Supply Chain Disruptions

As supply chains become more extended and firms depend even more on outside companies to provide critical goods and services, many firms are feeling the sting of disruptions to the supply chain.

The cause of these disruptions can take many forms, from natural disasters to economic or even political events. Some recent examples illustrate this phenomenon. A few years ago, Boeing experienced supplier delivery failure of two critical parts, with an estimated loss to the company of $2.6 billion. In 2002, striking dockworkers disrupted port operations on the U.S. West Coast. As a result, it took six months for some containers to be delivered and schedules to return to normal. In 2005, Hurricane Katrina caused billions of dollars of lost revenue to major retailers such as British Petroleum, Shell, Conoco Phillips, and Lyondell, as well as gasoline shortages in many parts of the United States. The 2010 BP oil spill was another incident that caused major havoc in the Gulf of Mexico and interrupted many supply chains.

In a recent survey of senior executives at Global 1000 companies, the respondents identified supply chain disruptions as the single biggest threat to their companies' revenue streams. Although senior executives now recognize that supply chain disruptions can be devastating to an enterprise's bottom line, strategies to mitigate supply chain disruptions are typically not well developed or even initiated. A concerning statistic is that only between 5% and 25% of Fortune 500 companies are estimated to be prepared to handle a major supply chain crisis or disruption.

One factor that is increasing the risk of supply chain disruptions is the propensity of companies to outsource processes to global suppliers. The complexity associated with multiple links in the supply chain increases the probability of disruptions. For example, as the number of "hand-offs" required to ship products through multiple carriers, multiple ports, and multiple government checkpoints increases, so does the likelihood of poor communication, human error, and missed shipments. An electronics executive we interviewed noted, "We have successfully outsourced production of our products to China. Unfortunately, we now recognize that we do not have the processes in place to manage risk associated with this supply chain effectively." As firms grapple with the risks associated with supply chain disruptions, we can expect to see more firms utilize the tactics and actions associated with bottlenecks and critical products (see Figure 7.5) and to develop comprehensive risk management strategies.

CHAPTER SUMMARY

In this chapter, we introduced you to some of the specific activities and challenges associated with supply management. We began by highlighting the importance of supply management, most notably the profit leverage effect. We then described in detail the strategic sourcing process (Figure 7.1) and demonstrated how spend analysis, total cost analysis, portfolio analysis, and weighted-point evaluation models can be used to support strategic sourcing efforts. We followed with a discussion of the procure-to-pay cycle, as well as some of the major challenges affecting supply management today.

We end this chapter with a brief discussion on the future of the purchasing profession. Every year, purchasing professionals perform fewer procure-to-pay activities and spend more time on strategic sourcing activities such as spend analysis, supplier evaluation and selection, and make-or-buy decisions. These activities require individuals with a solid mix of quantitative and interpersonal skills.

At the same time, information technology is reducing or even eliminating the clerical tasks that were traditionally carried out by purchasing professionals. By relying on information systems, end users can order directly what they require over the Internet. Also, production planning and control systems (Chapter 12) will generate orders automatically, based on production requirements. These systems will use online Web systems and portals to forward component requirements immediately to suppliers, reducing the need for direct purchasing intervention.

Another development that will reduce the clerical work assumed by purchasing is the use of suppliers to manage inventory at the customer's site. This is a classic example of an outsourced activity that was previously performed by purchasing or materials management professionals.

Organizations such as the Institute for Supply Management (ISM) help serve the needs of professionals in the purchasing area. The ISM's Web site, **www.ism.ws,** is an excellent place to learn about trends in purchasing and current research, as well ISM's professional certification programs.

KEY FORMULAS

Profit margin (page 193):

$$\text{Profit margin} = 100\% \times \frac{\text{Earnings}}{\text{Sales}} \tag{7.1}$$

Return on assets (ROA) (page 193):

$$\text{Return on assets (ROA)} = 100\% \times \frac{\text{Earnings}}{\text{Assets}} \tag{7.2}$$

Overall preference score for Supplier X, weighted-point evaluation system (page 208):

$$Score_X = \sum_{Y=1}^{n} Performance_{XY} \times W_Y \tag{7.3}$$

where:

$$X = \text{Supplier X}$$
$$Y = \text{performance dimension Y}$$
$$Performance_{XY} = \text{rated performance of Supplier X with regard to performance dimension Y}$$
$$W_Y = \text{assigned weight for performance dimension Y, where } \sum_{Y=1}^{n} W_Y = 1$$

KEY TERMS

SOLVED PROBLEM

PROBLEM

Aitken Engineering

Aitken Engineering (AE) is a Dallas engineering firm that produces customized instrumentation for the aerospace industry. AE is thinking about outsourcing the production of a particular component to a Fort Worth manufacturer. The Fort Worth manufacturer has offered to make the components for a price of $25 each, based on an annual volume of 32,000. However, there are additional costs associated with maintaining this supplier relationship. AE management has developed the following cost figures:

CURRENT MANUFACTURING OPERATIONS	FORT WORTH MANUFACTURER
Fixed Costs	**Price per Component**
Plant and overhead, $800,000 per year	$25
Variable Costs	**Other Costs**
Labor, $8.50 per unit	Administrative costs, $50,000 per year
Materials, $5.00 per unit	Inspection costs, $65,000 per year
	Shipping cost, $1.50 per unit

In addition to cost, AE management has identified two other dimensions to consider: quality (specifically, the percentage of defect-free items) and on-time delivery. AE management has established importance weights of 0.2, 0.5, and 0.3 for cost, quality, and on-time delivery, respectively. Finally, purchasing managers at AE have rated the performance of the current assembly operation and the Fort Worth manufacturer with regard to these three dimensions. Their ratings (1 = "poor" to 5 = "excellent") are as follows:

	Performance Ratings	
PERFORMANCE DIMENSION	CURRENT MFG. OPERATIONS	FORT WORTH CONTRACT MANUFACTURER
Cost	3	5
Quality	5	4
On-time delivery	3	3

Calculate the total cost of each option, as well as the overall preference score.

Solution

Total costs for the current manufacturing operations:

$800,000 + 32,000 units × ($8.50 + $5.00) = $800,000 + $432,000 = $1,232,000

Total cost for the Fort Worth contract manufacturer:

$50,000 + $65,000 + 32,000 units × ($25.00 + $1.50) = $115,000 + $848,000
= $963,000

The total cost analysis suggests that the Fort Worth manufacturer has a yearly cost advantage of ($1,232,000 − $963,000) = $269,000. This result would seem to strongly favor the Fort Worth option. However, the overall preference scores suggest that the choice is not so clear:

$$Score_{Current} = Performance_{Current,Cost} \times W_{Cost}$$
$$+ \ Performance_{Current,Quality} \times W_{Quality}$$
$$+ \ Performance_{Current,Delivery} \times W_{Delivery}$$
$$= 3 \times 0.2 + 5 \times 0.5 + 3 \times 0.3 = 4$$

and:

$$Score_{FtWorth} = Performance_{FtWorth,Cost} \times W_{Cost}$$
$$+ \ Performance_{FtWorth,Quality} \times W_{Quality}$$
$$+ \ Performance_{FtWorth,Delivery} \times W_{Delivery}$$
$$= 5 \times 0.2 + 4 \times 0.5 + 3 \times 0.3 = 3.9$$

What accounts for the discrepancy? Quite simply, the overall preference scores take into consideration more than just cost. This, plus the fact that AE management places higher importance on quality and on-time delivery, tilts the preference scores in favor of the current assembly operation. Given these results, AE might decide to stick with its current manufacturing operations or perhaps work with the Fort Worth contract manufacturer to improve its quality and delivery performance *prior* to outsourcing the business. MS Excel for calculating the weight average score would be a good idea. Excel Formula of SUMPRODUCT is very handy for this.

DISCUSSION QUESTIONS

1. Consider the cafeteria services available at a university. In many cases, these services are outsourced to a private firm. Use Tables 7.6 and 7.7 as guides to explain why this is the case. In what quadrant would such services be positioned when determining a sourcing strategy (Figure 7.5)?
2. Under what conditions might a company prefer to negotiate rather than use competitive bidding to select a supplier?
3. In the chapter, we suggested that advanced information systems will automate some of the more routine purchasing activities. What are the implications for purchasing professionals? Is this a good time to join the purchasing profession? Explain.
4. In Chapter 4, we discussed the Six Sigma methodology for process improvement, including the DMAIC (Define–Measure–Analyze–Improve–Control) process. Give an example of how this process could be used to structure a spend analysis effort.

PROBLEMS

(* = easy; ** = moderate; *** = advanced)

Problems for Section 7.1: Why Supply Management Is Critical

1. Dulaney's Stores has posted the following yearly earnings and expenses:

EARNINGS AND EXPENSES (YEAR ENDING JANUARY 2019)	
Sales	$50,000,000
Cost of goods sold (COGS)	$30,000,000
Pretax earnings	$5,000,000
SELECTED BALANCE SHEET ITEMS	
Merchandise Inventory	$2,500,000
Total assets	$8,000,000

  a. (*) What is Dulaney's current profit margin? What is its current yearly ROA?
  b. (**) Suppose COGS and merchandise inventory were each cut by 10%. What would be the new pretax profit margin and ROA?
  c. (**) Based on the *current* profit margin, how much additional sales would Dulaney have to generate in order to have the same effect on pretax earnings as a 10% decrease in merchandise costs?

Problems for Section 7.2: The Strategic Sourcing Process

2. (**) Looking back at Example 7.6, suppose Conan the Electrician has implemented a Six Sigma program and as a result has brought defect levels down to just 1%, the same as Beverly Hills. Recalculate the weighted performance score for Conan the Electrician, using the weights provided in Example 7.6. Should Electra change its preferred supplier, based on these results?
3. The ABC Company (Example 7.5) has identified another potential supplier for the molded plastic parts. The new supplier has bid $0.08 per part but also will impose a shipping and handling charge of $0.015 per unit. Additional inventory handling charges should amount to $0.007 per unit. Finally, purchasing costs are estimated at $25 per month for the length of the 36-month contract.

  a. (*) Calculate the total costs for the new supplier. Which is cheaper: insourcing or outsourcing with the new supplier?
  b. (**) Suppose the three-year volume is expected to rise to 1.5 million, rather than 1 million, molded plastic parts. Recalculate the total costs associated with insourcing. What explains the difference?

c. (**) What other factors, other than costs, should ABC consider when deciding whether to make the molded parts in-house?

4. Granville Community College is considering outsourcing the maintenance of its buildings and other facilities to an outside firm for $300,000 per year. The 2020 budget is as follows:

Granville Maintenance Budget—2020

Direct expenses (per worker)
- Wages—$2,500 per worker per month
- Benefits—35% of wages per worker per month
- Maintenance, repair, and operating supplies—$2,000 per worker per month

Indirect expenses
- Supervisor salary—$3,000 per month
- Benefits—40% of wages
- Other office expenses—$500 per month

a. (*) Calculate the total costs of insourcing versus outsourcing maintenance.
b. (**) What other reasons, other than costs, might Granville look at when deciding whether to outsource maintenance activities?

5. Lincoln Lights is considering hiring one of three software firms to implement a new IT system. Lincoln management has decided to evaluate the firms on three dimensions—reputation, skill level, and price. Weights for each dimension, as well as performance ratings for each of the firms (1 = "poor" to 5 = "excellent") are shown in the following table:

Software Firm				
DIMENSION	WEIGHT	ALTREX	TGI LTD.	PC ASSOCIATES
Reputation	0.2	3	4	5
Skill level	0.4	5	4	4
Price	0.4	5	3	2

a. (*) Use the weighted-point evaluation system to calculate weighted performance scores for each of the software firms. Would the results change if each dimension had a weight of one-third?
b. (**) In Chapter 2, we described order qualifiers as performance dimensions on which customers demand a *minimum* level of performance. Basically, if a supplier fails to meet the minimum requirements on any of the qualifiers, that supplier would be eliminated from contention. How would you incorporate the concept of order qualifiers into the weighted-point evaluation system?

6. Flynn Industries has outsourced the delivery of its products and now wants to develop a tool to help evaluate its transportation carriers. The table at the bottom of the page shows the rating values associated with different levels of price, quality, and delivery performance, as well as criteria weights that reflect the relative importance of these dimensions. To illustrate how the ratings work, suppose a carrier has a damage level of 0.82%. This would fall between 0.75% and 1.0%, thereby garnering a rating of 2. The second table shows actual average performance levels for three carriers.

a. (*) Use the weighted-point evaluation system to calculate the weighted average performance for each carrier. Which carrier is best under this system?
b. (**) How would the results change if the weights for price, quality, and delivery shifted to 0.6, 0.2, and 0.2, respectively?
c. (**) Based on the results, should Flynn Industries single source or not? What might stop Flynn from single sourcing?

Rating Values for Flynn Industries (Problem 6)					
SUPPLIERS ARE RATED ON A SCALE OF 1–5, DEPENDING ON THEIR SPECIFIC PERFORMANCE LEVELS					
CRITERION (WEIGHT)	1	2	3	4	5
Price (0.20)	>$2.50/lb.	$2.01–$2.50/lb.	$1.51–$2.00/lb.	$1.00–$1.50/lb.	<$1.00/lb.
Quality (0.20)	Damage > 1%	Damage 0.75–1.0%	Damage 0.5–0.74%	Damage 0.25–0.49%	Damage < 0.25%
Delivery (0.60)	<82% on-time	82–84% on-time	85–90% on-time	91–95% on-time	>95% on-time

Carrier Performance for Flynn Industries (Problem 6)			
	CARRIER A	CARRIER B	CARRIER C
Price	$1.98/lb.	Price $2.02/lb.	$98.00/100 lb.
Quality	0.35% damaged	Quality 0.26% damaged	0.86% damaged
Delivery	93% on-time	Delivery 98% on-time	83% on-time

7. (***) (*Microsoft Excel problem*) The following worksheet uses a weighted-point evaluation system to calculate weighted performance scores along four dimensions for up to four potential sources. **Re-create this spreadsheet in Microsoft Excel.** Code your spreadsheet so that any change in the highlighted cells will result in recalculated performance scores. Your formatting does not have to be exactly the same, but your numbers should be. (*Hint:* Changing all the importance weights to 0.25 should result in scores of 2.25 and 3.5 for sources X1 and X2, respectively.)

WEIGHTED-POINT EVALUATION SYSTEM

	A	B	C	D	E	F
1	Weighted-Point Evaluation System					
2						
3				Potential Sources		
4	Dimension	Importance	X1	X2	X3	X4
5	A	0.20	1	3	2	4
6	B	0.30	2	4	3	2
7	C	0.30	2	4	3	2
8	D	0.20	4	3	2	1
9	Total:	1.00				
10		Scores:	2.2	3.6	2.6	2.2

CASE STUDY

Pagoda.com

Introduction

Pagoda.com is an Internet service provider (ISP) that caters to individual consumers and small businesses who require a high level of service and are willing to pay a premium for it. Specifically, Pagoda.com offers state-of-the-art email applications and Web-building software, as well as plenty of storage space and the fastest access available. The marketing vice president, Jerry Hunter, puts it this way: "There are a lot of companies out there promising the cheapest Internet access. But what do you get for your money? Slow- or no-access and an endless stream of system crashes. And I won't even mention the lack of support if you have a technical question! For a few dollars more a month, we give our customers the environment they need to be productive. It's no surprise, then, that we have the highest customer satisfaction and retention rates in the industry."

The Online Help Desk

One of Pagoda's services is its online help desk. The online help desk works as follows: Customers who are experiencing technical problems, or who simply have questions about their account, enter a one-on-one chat room, where they can interact directly with an expert. Problems are usually resolved within 10 minutes, and customers have listed it as one of the top three reasons they stick with Pagoda.com. Presently, Pagoda has enough capacity to handle up to 900,000 requests per year, although management doesn't expect the number of requests to change much from the current level of 800,000 per year.

A firm located in New Delhi, India, has approached Pagoda about outsourcing the online help desk. The offer is attractive. The New Delhi firm's own personnel would handle the help desk function. These personnel all speak English fluently and have college degrees or appropriate technical backgrounds. And because they are located in India, labor costs would be a fraction of what they are in the United States. The savings would be passed on, in part, to Pagoda. And since the help desk chat room exists on the Internet, Pagoda's customers should be unaware of the switch.

Pagoda management has put together the following figures, outlining the yearly costs associated with the current system and the Indian proposal:

Current Online Help Desk

Personnel costs:
40 full-time-equivalent (FTE) technical experts @ $40,000 per year (salary and benefits); 3 supervisors @ $70,000 each per year (salary and benefits)

Equipment costs:
4 servers @ $2,000 per year
20 PCs @ $1,000 per year

Variable costs:
$1.50 per request (office supplies, fax paper, etc.)

New Delhi Proposal

Fixed cost:
$1,500,000 per contract year (to cover administrative and IT costs)

Charge:
$0.50 per request

Questions

1. Calculate the total cost of outsourcing the online help desk versus staying with the current solution. Which option is cheaper?
2. What other factors, other than costs, should Pagoda consider? How would you weight these factors? Given the above, how might you use a weighted-point evaluation system to evaluate the two options?
3. Should Pagoda.com outsource its online help desk? Why or why not? Be sure to consider Table 7.7 and 7.8 when framing your answer.

4. A statement of work typically specifies performance measurements that the buying firm can use to determine whether the service provider is meeting the terms of the contract. What performance measurements would you recommend be put in place? What should happen if the service provider fails to meet these requirements?

REFERENCES

Books and Articles

Blackstone, J. H., ed., *APICS Dictionary,* 15th ed. (Chicago, IL: APICS, 2016).

Carroll, A., "A Three-Dimensional Conceptual Model of Corporate Performance." *Academy of Management Review* 4, no. 4 (1979): 497–505.

Dobler. D., Lee, L., and Burt, D., *Purchasing and Materials Management* (Homewood, IL: Irwin, 1990).

Monczka, R., R. B. Handfield, L. C. Giunipero, and J. L. Patterson, *Purchasing and Supply Chain Management,* 5th ed. (Mason, OH: South-Western, 2011).

Simison, R. L., "Buyer's Market: General Motors Drives Some Hard Bargains with Asian Suppliers," *Wall Street Journal,* April 2, 1999, p. A1.

Wieland, A., and R. Handfield, "The Socially Responsible Supply Chain: An Imperative for Global Corporations," *Supply Chain Management Review,* September 2013.

Internet

Al-Mahmood, S. "Bangladesh Fire: What Wal-Mart's Supplier Network Missed," *Wall Street Journal,* December 1, 2012, **http://online.wsj.com/news/articles/SB1000142412 78873240240045781694000995615618.**

Automotive News, "Top Suppliers," June 20, 2016, **www.autonews .com/assets/PDF/CA105764617.PDF.**

Carroll, J., "USPET Recycling Rate Tops 30 Percent," *Plastic News,* October 9, 2013. **www.plasticsnews.com/article/ 20131009/NEWS/131009912/us-pet-recycling-rate-tops-30-percent.**

Flowers, L. F., "Walmart Sustainability Index, Packaging Scorecard Affect Pallet & Packaging Industries," *Pallet Enterprise,* May 1, 2010, **www.palletenterprise.com/ articledatabase/view.asp?articleID=3098.**

"The Green Supply Chain: Walmart Releases Packaging Scorecard Data, Plans for Electronics Suppliers," *Supply Chain Digest,* March 14, 2007, **www.scdigest.com/assets/ newsViews/07-03-14-3.cfm?cid=955&ctype =content.**

Handfield, R., "Are Companies Considering the Risks of BPO?" *Supply Chain View from the Field,* November 10, 2010, **http:// scm.ncsu.edu/blog/.**

Harrington, R., "Industry Hails First Global Measurement System for Packaging Sustainability," *Food Production Daily.com,* September 7, 2011, **www.foodproductiondaily.com/ Packaging/Industry-hails-first-global-measurement-system-for-packaging-sustainability.**

Kanter, J., "No Consensus on Reuse of Electric Car Batteries," *New York Times,* September 6, 2011, pp. B1, B7, **http://query .nytimes.com/gst/fullpage.html?res=9900E0DA133A F935A3575AC0A9679D8B63&ref=jameskanter.**

Kapadia, R., "The Brown Revolution," *Smart Money,* November 10, 2005, **www.smartmoney.com/invest/stocks/ The-Brown-Revolution-18573/.**

Pearson, D., "Car-Battery Shakeout Ahead," *Wall Street Journal,* August 31, 2011, p. B5, **http://online.wsj.com/article/SB10 0014240531119041994045765401705066631268.html.**

2011 Annual Survey of Manufactures, U.S. Census Bureau, June 2014, **http://factfinder2.census.gov/faces/tableservices/jsf/ pages/productview.xhtml?pid=ASM_2011_31GS201 &prodType=table.**

2013 Savar Building Collapse, **http://en.wikipedia.org/wiki/ 2013_Savar_building_collapse.**

Verspej, M., "Recyclers Expansion-Minded Despite Short Supply," *Plastic News,* May 22, 2012, **www.plasticsnews .com/article/20120522/NEWS/305229967/recyclers-expansion-minded-despite-short-supply.**

Walmart, *Packaging,* **http://walmartstores.com/ sustainability/9125.aspx.**

Yardley, J. "Horrific Fire Revealed a Gap in Safety for Global Brands," *New York Times,* December 6, 2012.

Gilles Lougassi/Shutterstock

CHAPTER
eight

Logistics

CHAPTER OBJECTIVES

By the end of this chapter, you will be able to:

- Describe why logistics is important and discuss the major decision areas that make up logistics.
- List the strengths and weaknesses of the various modes of transportation and discuss the role of multimodal solutions.
- Identify the major types of warehousing solutions and their benefits.
- Discuss the purpose of a logistics strategy and give examples of how logistics can support the overall business strategy.
- Calculate the percentage of perfect orders.
- Calculate landed costs.
- Explain what reverse logistics systems are and describe some of the unique challenges they create for firms.
- Use the weighted center of gravity method to identify a potential location for a business.
- Develop and then solve, using Microsoft Excel's Solver function, an assignment problem.

KRAFT FOODS[1]

Frank Polich/Reuters

Several years back, Kraft Foods set out to redesign the logistics system it used to deliver products to its various customers, such as major grocery store chains and food distributors. Kraft's efforts were centered on three major customer requirements:

1. Customers wanted to be able to order a wide variety of Kraft's products and receive the shipment the next day. This would give the customers greater flexibility and allow them to hold smaller inventories in their facilities.
2. Customers also wanted the option of being able to place large orders directly with Kraft's plants in return for significant price discounts. Under Kraft's old logistics system, this was not always possible.
3. Customers wanted a single order contact point and to receive volume discounts based on their entire purchase volume. Before, customers had to deal with three different divisions at Kraft, each with its own pricing and logistics system.

In response to these needs, Kraft set up a new logistics system. Figure 8.1 shows how the new system works. First, plant-based warehouses allow customers to place orders for direct plant shipments (DPSs) with any of the plants. At the same time, regional mixing centers hold the entire line of Kraft products. These mixing centers are strategically located to provide overnight shipments to the maximum number of customers. Kraft also consolidated all of its pricing, ordering, and invoicing systems into one single system to ease the administrative burden placed on customers and to ensure that customers received appropriate volume discounts. The ultimate result was that Kraft was able to meet its customers' key requirements, resulting in greater customer satisfaction and high profits for Kraft.

Kraft's efforts didn't end with the implementation of the new logistics system, however. Today, Kraft continues to make improvements with an eye on cutting costs, improving customer service, and reducing the environmental impact of its operations. For example, in Canada and the United States, Kraft is using software at its 20 largest plants and mixing centers to optimize outbound shipments and put more products on fewer trucks. This effort has had the effect of taking 1,500 trucks off the road and reducing highway usage by more than 1 million miles. In Brazil, the company eliminated 2.4 million pounds (1 million kg) of material by redesigning packaging and shipping materials for its *Tang*, *Lacta*, and *Club Social* brands.[2]

FIGURE 8.1   Redesigning the Logistics System at Kraft Foods to Satisfy Customer Needs

[1] S. Tibey, "How Kraft Built a 'One-Company' Supply Chain," *Supply Chain Management Review* 3, no. 3 (Fall 1999): 34–42.
[2] "Kraft Foods Sustainability Fact Sheet," April 2009, **www.kraftfoodscompany.com/assets/pdf/KFTFactSustainabilityProgress2009.04FINAL.pdf.**

INTRODUCTION

Logistics management
According to the Council of Supply Chain Management Professionals (CSCMP), "that part of supply chain management that plans, implements, and controls the efficient, effective forward and reverse flow and storage of goods, services, and related information between the point of origin and the point of consumption in order to meet customers' requirements."

According to the Council of Supply Chain Management Professionals (CSCMP), **logistics management** is "that part of supply chain management that plans, implements, and controls the efficient, effective forward and reverse flow and storage of goods, services, and related information between the point of origin and the point of consumption in order to meet customers' requirements."[3] Companies depend on their logistics systems to move goods and materials among supply chain partners and to manage the information flows necessary to carry out these tasks. Logistics incorporates a wide range of business activities, including:

* Transportation
* Warehousing
* Material handling
* Packaging
* Inventory management (Chapter 11)
* Logistics information systems (Chapter 12S)

As you can imagine, the interrelationships among these business activities are quite complex. At Kraft, inventory management tasks changed with the introduction of the mixing centers and direct plant shipments. Similarly, the decision to switch to more environmentally friendly packaging can directly affect how transportation and material handling are carried out.

The purpose of this chapter is to introduce you to the field of logistics. After describing its strategic importance, we survey the major decision areas that make up logistics: the choice of transportation modes, warehousing, logistics information systems, and material handling and packaging systems. We also pay particular attention to the interrelationship between inventory management and the other logistics decision areas. Then we turn to the concept of a logistics strategy and examine two measures of logistics performance: the perfect order and landed costs. We also highlight reverse logistics systems, which have become increasingly important as firms look to bring used products back into the supply chain to be repaired, refurbished, or recycled. We end the chapter with a detailed presentation of two commonly used logistics decision models: the weighted center of gravity method and the assignment problem.

8.1 WHY LOGISTICS IS CRITICAL

Sustainability
Performing activities in a manner that meet the needs of the present without compromising the ability of future generations to meet their needs.

As the interest in supply chain management continues to grow, more businesses are managing logistics in an effort to improve their cost, flexibility, and delivery performance. Today, advances in information systems, the globalization of markets, and the push toward **sustainability**—that is, performing activities in a manner that meets the needs of the present without compromising the ability of future generations to meet their own needs—continue to create challenges and opportunities that did not exist just a few years ago.

The performance effects of logistics are manifold. In 2012, the cost of logistics in the United States was $1.33 trillion, or 8.5% of gross domestic product (GDP).[4] Interestingly, this percentage has fallen dramatically since 1980, when logistics expenditures represented 17.9% of GDP. This improvement—despite more geographically extended supply chains—suggests that companies operating in the United States have made significant advances in managing their logistics systems. Recent studies show that in the United States, logistics costs account for between 5% and 35% of total sales costs, depending on the business, geographic area, and type of product being sold. These costs are expected to grow as businesses and consumers move toward

---

[3]CSCMP Supply Chain Management Definitions and Glossary, **http://cscmp.org/CSCMP/Educate/SCM_Definitions_and_Glossary_of_Terms/CSCMP/Educate/SCM_Definitions_and_Glossary_of_Terms.aspx?hkey=60879588-f65f-4ab5-8c4b-6878815ef921.**

[4]D. Gilmore, "State of the Logistics Union 2013," *Supply Chain Digest*, June 20, 2013, **www.scdigest.com/assets/FIRSTTHOUGHTS/13-06-20.php?cid=7172.**

PROFESSIONAL PROFILE

DWIGHT HENDRICKSON, CATERPILLAR

Throughout this book, we have made the point that supply chains cover everything from sourcing-to-producing-to-delivering the final product or service. Furthermore, supply chain *management* takes place at the strategic planning level, looking years into the future, down to the execution of day-to-day activities.

In over 20 years at Caterpillar, Dwight Hendrickson has experienced all of this firsthand. He has been a commercial purchasing analyst and a lead buyer; a general operations supervisor and certified Six Sigma black belt; and a logistics manager and product program manager. In fact, Dwight's experience is so comprehensive that outside professional organizations regularly look to him for his expertise and leadership. He currently serves on the North Carolina District Export Council (NCDEC), which is made up of professionals who act as consultants to small- and medium-sized businesses that want to export their products into markets outside of the United States. Dwight also served as the executive vice president and president for his local APICS chapter.

In his current role as a supply chain manager in Caterpillar's Building Construction Products (BCP) Division, Dwight is responsible for developing and putting in place distribution strategies for new BCP products, such as backhoe loaders and excavators.[5] Beyond the sheer size of these products (a typical backhoe can weigh around 10 tons), what makes Dwight's job particularly challenging are the "unknowns." For example, what kind of response time does the market require? Is it months, weeks, or days? Also, what will future business volumes

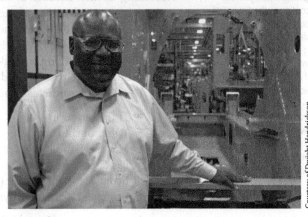

Courtesy of Dwight Hendrickson

be like? Since the demand for building construction products is tightly tied to the overall health of the world economy and other geopolitical factors, Dwight has to make sure Caterpillar is ready to increase volumes dramatically when the economy is strong and scale down activity when markets contract. Other considerations are more micro in nature—for instance, the required shipping configuration for a product (fully assembled or not) can depend on such factors as the actual shipping containers used and local regulations.

Even though his current responsibilities fall primarily in the logistics area, Dwight's experience as a Six Sigma black belt still shows through: "In business, defining the problem is often the most difficult thing to do." He also offers this advice to people entering the business world: "Be curious about whatever field you choose to be in. You can never stop learning."

---

[5]See **www.cat.com/en_US/products/new/equipment.html** for examples of the type of equipment manufactured by Caterpillar's BCP division.

---

smaller, more frequent shipments of goods and materials and as more companies depend on foreign sources. For many firms, logistics expenses now are second only to material costs in terms of their impact on cost of goods sold.

Logistics can also have a profound impact on other performance dimensions, such as delivery speed and reliability. Many companies have spent enormous amounts of money on decreasing the lead times within their organizations, only to discover that their customers never saw much benefit due to long shipping times once items left the organizations' facilities. These same companies are now concentrating intensively on the logistics systems that link them to their customers. Because logistics systems often interface directly with customers, they can have considerable impact on overall customer satisfaction. This chapter's *Professional Profile* features Dwight Hendrickson of Caterpillar. As you read Dwight's profile, consider the breadth of experience Dwight brings to his job as a supply chain planner and the importance of delivering his high-cost products to customers in a timely and cost-effective manner.

8.2 LOGISTICS DECISION AREAS

Logistics includes not just physical flows, such as the delivery of products to a customer, but also informational flows. Transportation and warehousing systems define the physical network of a logistics system and play a major role in determining its overall performance in terms of cost, delivery, and flexibility. Logistics information systems create and manage the informational flows in the network. Order management systems, warehouse storage and retrieval systems, transportation scheduling and package routing systems, and even tracking systems like the one UPS uses to track shipments are all part of the logistics information system. In the past 10 years, logistics information systems have seen explosive growth; in many supply chains, they represent the greatest opportunity for improvement in supply chain performance. Typically, a firm's material handling and packaging systems are tightly intertwined with both its transportation and information systems. While a full treatment of material handling and packaging is beyond the scope of this book, we will provide examples in this section to illustrate their importance.

Transportation

There are five widely recognized transportation modes: highway, water, air, rail, and pipeline.[6] Table 8.1 compares the total item value, tons, and ton-miles shipped via each mode in the United States.

Highway. Highway transportation dominates the U.S. logistics infrastructure. In 2012 alone, U.S. businesses and individuals moved over $10 *trillion* in goods via trucking—or 73% of the total value of goods moved. In the same year, trucking accounted for around 1.25 trillion ton-miles—or roughly 42% of the total ton-miles shipped. By whatever metric one uses (the value of goods shipped, tons moved, or ton-miles), highway transportation is dominant. Several factors account for this:

- **Geographic extension of supply chains.** As more companies developed supply chain relationships with nonlocal suppliers and customers, highway traffic increased.
- **Greater emphasis on delivery speed and flexibility.** Highway transportation has stolen market share from slower rail and water systems, which have experienced relatively significant increases in the value of shipments, but a decline in ton-miles shipped. In a world that places great emphasis on delivery speed and flexibility, highway transportation has a clear advantage over both rail and water.

Highway transportation in the United States continues to grow because it is one of the most flexible modes of transportation: If the source or destination point for goods can be reached by road, then the goods can be shipped by highway. In fact, very few goods are moved without highway transportation at some point in transit. Highway transportation has

TABLE 8.1
Modal Shares of U.S. Domestic Freight for 2012 (% change, 2002–2012)

TRANSPORTATION MODE	VALUE (BILLION $)	TONS (MILLIONS)	TON-MILES (BILLIONS)
Highway (trucking)	$10,132 (+63%)	8,060 (+3%)	1,248 (−1%)
Rail	$473 (+52%)	1,629 (−13%)	1,211 (−4%)
Water	$302 (+238%)	576 (−15%)	193 (−32%)
Air	$451 (+70%)	5 (29%)	6 (0%)
Pipeline	$543 (+264%)	636 (−7%)	Not available
Multimodal	$1,951 (+81%)	357 (+65%)	272 (+20%)

Source: U.S. Department of Transportation, *National Transportation Statistics, April 2017,* Washington, DC, Table 1-58, **www.rita.dot.gov/bts/sites/rita.dot.gov.bts/files/publications/national_transportation_statistics/html/table_01_58.html.**

[6]Unless otherwise stated, the figures given in this section are from U.S. Department of Transportation, *National Transportation Statistics 2010,* Washington, DC.

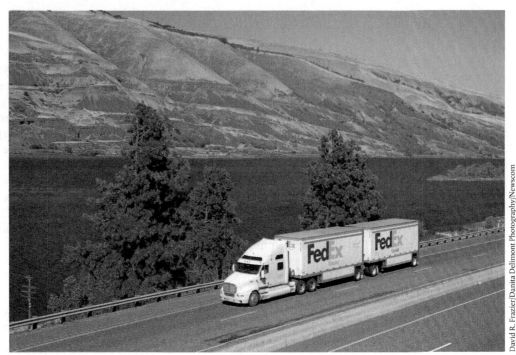

A truck pulling two pup trailers.

also become more cost-effective over time. Better scheduling and use of vehicle capacity, more efficient and reliable vehicles, and increased cost competition due to deregulation have all contributed to this trend.

Water. Water-based transportation accounts for around 9% of all ton-miles shipped in the United States and is ideal for materials with a high weight-to-value ratio, especially if delivery speed is not critical. Examples of such materials include farm produce, timber, and petroleum-based products. Because of the relatively high weight-to-value ratio of these commodities, shipping can significantly add to their costs. Water-based transportation, with one of the lowest ton-mile rates of any mode, helps to hold down those costs.

Air. At the opposite end of the scale from water transportation, air transportation is ideal for materials with a low weight-to-value ratio, especially if delivery speed or delivery reliability is critical. An example is a high-value electronic component, which might weigh only a few ounces yet be worth hundreds or even thousands of dollars. Spending $10 (or $2.50 per ounce) to guarantee next-day delivery of such a valuable product hardly seems outrageous. While air transportation is the least-used mode in terms of tons and ton-miles, it grew strongly between 2002 and 2012 in terms of the value of goods shipped.

Rail. Rail transportation has cost characteristics similar to those of water transportation, but it is somewhat more flexible. By 2012, rail's percentage of U.S. domestic ton-miles shipped had actually grown to 41%, up significantly from a 1997 estimate of 26.7%. The rail carriers' strategies for accomplishing this have included doubling the number of lines along busy corridors, changing the physical configuration of the trains themselves, and using multimodal solutions, which we describe in more detail in the following paragraphs.

Selecting a Transportation Mode

As Table 8.2 shows, the major transportation modes differ greatly in terms of their relative strengths and weaknesses. Firms must therefore carefully select a mode based on their particular competitive or operational requirements.

TABLE 8.2
Strengths and Weaknesses of the Major Transportation Modes

TRANSPORTATION MODE	STRENGTHS	WEAKNESSES
Highway	Flexibility to deliver where and when needed.	Neither the fastest nor the cheapest option.
	Often the best balance among cost, flexibility, and reliability/speed of delivery.	
Water	Highly cost-effective for bulky items.	Limited locations.
	Most effective when linked to a multimodal system.	Relatively poor delivery reliability/speed.
Rail	Highly cost-effective for bulky items.	Limited locations, although less so than with water.
	Can be most effective when linked to a multimodal system.	Not as fast as highway, but improving over time.
Air	Quickest mode of delivery.	Often the most expensive mode on a per-pound basis
	Flexible, especially when linked to the highway mode.	

EXAMPLE 8.1

Choosing a Transportation Mode at Seminole Glassworks[7]

Seminole Glassworks needs to ship 3,500 pounds of custom-built office windows from Miami, Florida, to Columbus, Ohio. Seminole has three transportation options:

MODE	DELIVERY SPEED	VEHICLES	EXTRA HANDLINGS	COST
Air	8.75 hours	3	2	$12,100
Direct truck	27.75 hours	1	0	$2,680
LTL truck	3 days	3	2	$445

Direct truck shipment
A shipment made directly, with no additional stops, changing of trucks, or loading of additional cargo.

Less than truckload (LTL) shipment
A smaller shipment, often combined with other loads to reduce costs and improve truck efficiencies.

With a **direct truck shipment,** Seminole would contract with a carrier to pick up the windows at its Miami plant and carry them *directly*—no stops, no changing of trucks or loading of additional cargo—to the customer's site in Columbus. With **LTL (less than truckload) shipping,** the carrier could combine Seminole's windows with other loads going to Columbus. Note that if LTL shipping is used, Seminole's windows are likely to switch trucks at a centralized sorting hub, which would result in additional handlings and delays.

Which option should Seminole choose? The answer depends on the firm's business requirements. While LTL shipping has a clear cost advantage, direct trucking is quicker and requires fewer handlings. Air transportation would get the windows to the customer about 19 hours earlier. That advantage might be critical if the glass is needed to replace broken windows in an occupied building or if leaving a new building without windows for just a day can risk damage to the interior.

Multimodal Solutions

Multimodal solution
A transportation solution that seeks to exploit the strengths of multiple transportation modes through physical, information, and monetary flows that are as seamless as possible.

Roadrailer
A specialized rail car the size of a standard truck trailer that can be quickly switched from rail to ground transportation by changing the wheels.

Few companies or supply chains use just one transportation mode. In fact, many depend on multimodal solutions to get goods from one end of the supply chain to the other. A garment manufacturer, for instance, might use ocean freight to move 40-foot containers from Vietnam to Long Beach, California; rail to move those same containers from Long Beach to Atlanta; and trucks to distribute the garments in the containers throughout the southeastern United States.

Multimodal solutions, as the name implies, are transportation solutions that seek to exploit the strengths of multiple transportation modes through physical, information, and monetary flows that are as seamless as possible. For instance, today's rail carriers regularly use standardized containers that can be quickly moved from flatcar to truck with no unloading and reloading of material. The result is significant time and cost savings. Some rail carriers even use **roadrailers,** which are railcars the size of standard truck trailers that can be quickly switched from rail to ground transportation by changing the wheels.

---

[7]Adapted from J. Childs, "Transportation and Logistics: Your Competitive Advantage or Your Downfall?" *APICS—The Performance Advantage* 6, no. 4 (April 1996): 44–48.

Airports and water ports are other major points of transfer from one mode to another. These ports, which serve as transfer points for global supply chains, have experienced significant growth over the past 15 years. For example, JFK International Airport in New York handled $89 billion worth of goods in 1997; by 2012, this figure had risen to nearly $200 billion.[8] The water port of Long Beach, California, saw similar increases, from $85 billion in 1997 to more than $285 billion in 2013.[9]

Just as important are recent improvements in information technology. Returning to the rail industry, the Union Pacific Railroad (**www.up.com**) has invested heavily in information technologies that allow it to plan and track customers' shipments across multiple transportation modes (rail, water, and highway), as well as multiple logistics firms. To its customers, Union Pacific offers one-stop logistics shopping.

As shipping containers have become more standardized across transportation modes and information systems for tracking and routing shipments have made such systems easier to manage, multimodal transportation has grown in importance. Look again at the data in Table 8.1. In both tons and ton-miles shipped, the use of multimodal solutions in the United States is growing at a faster rate than any single transportation mode. International freight saw similar rates of growth in multimodal shipments.

Warehousing

Transportation systems represent just one part of the physical flow of goods and materials. The other part is warehousing. Many companies have put an emphasis on minimizing inventory levels. As a result, many people now think of warehouses only as places where goods and materials sit idle, taking up space and tying up capital. This negative concept of warehousing is unwarranted, however.

In fact, warehousing plays a much broader role in a firm's operations and supply chain strategy. Formally defined, **warehousing** refers to any operation that stores, repackages, stages, sorts, or centralizes goods or materials. As we will see, warehousing can be used to reduce transportation costs, improve operational flexibility, shorten customer lead times, and lower inventory costs.

Reducing Transportation Costs. Anyone who thinks warehouses do nothing but store goods should consider consolidation, cross-docking, and hub-and-spoke systems. These systems have little or no long-term storage. Rather, all three are designed primarily to exploit economies of scale in transportation.

Consolidation warehousing pulls together shipments from a number of sources (often plants) in the same geographic area and combines them into larger—and hence more economical—shipping loads. Figure 8.2 shows an example of this.

There are several variations of this type of system. A single manufacturer may use a consolidation warehouse to pull together the output from several plants, combining it when possible into a single large shipment to a major customer. In another variation, a contract carrier may use its own consolidation warehouse to combine shipments from several local businesses.

Warehousing
Any operation that stores, repackages, stages, sorts, or centralizes goods or materials. Organizations use warehousing to reduce transportation costs, improve operational flexibility, shorten customer lead times, and lower inventory costs.

Consolidation warehousing
A form of warehousing that pulls together shipments from a number of sources (often plants) in the same geographic area and combines them into larger—and hence more economical—shipping loads.

FIGURE 8.2
Consolidation Warehousing

Small, flexible shipments in...

...large, economical shipments out

---

[8]The Port Authority of New York and New Jersey, "2012 Annual Traffic Report," **www.panynj.gov/airports/pdf-traffic/ATR2012.pdf.**
[9]"Port of Los Angeles Fact Sheet," June 2013, **www.portoflosangeles.org/about/facts.asp.**

EXAMPLE 8.2

Consolidation Warehousing at Bruin Logistics

Bruin Logistics handles hundreds of shipments from businesses in the Los Angeles area. At present, Bruin has three shipments to deliver to the Atlanta area:

CUSTOMER	SHIPMENT	WEIGHT
Venetian Artists Supply	100 boxes of drawing paper	3,000 lb.
Kaniko	100 PC printers	3,000 lb.
Ardent Furniture	10 dining room sets	4,000 lb.
	Total:	10,000 lb.

The cost to Bruin of sending a truck from Los Angeles to Atlanta is $2,000. The maximum load per truck is 20,000 pounds. If Bruin were to use a direct truck shipment for each customer, the shipping costs would be $2,000 per customer, or $6,000 total. The weight utilization across all three trucks would be 10,000 pounds/60,000 pounds, or just 17%—hardly an economic or environmentally wise use of resources.

But suppose Bruin has a consolidation warehouse where loads from multiple customers can be combined. Of course, there are costs associated with consolidation. Assume that the cost of running the warehouse is approximately $90 per 1,000 pounds, or in logistics lingo, $9 per hundred-weight. Furthermore, if Bruin decides to consolidate the three shipments, it must consider the additional cost of breaking them up for local delivery, which is not an issue in direct trucking. Suppose the cost of breaking up the shipments is $200 for each customer. Under these conditions, the costs of consolidating the three shipments to Atlanta would be:

Warehousing costs:	$9(10,000 lb./100 lb.) =	$900
Cost of one truck to Atlanta:		$2,000
Delivery to final customer:	3 customers × $200 =	$600
	Total:	$3,500

Note that the cost of consolidating the shipments is just over half the cost of the direct truck shipments. Furthermore, weight utilization increases to 10,000 pounds/20,000 pounds, or 50%.

Cross-docking
A form of warehousing in which large incoming shipments are received and then broken down into smaller outgoing shipments to demand points in a geographic area. Cross-docking combines the economies of large incoming shipments with the flexibility of smaller local shipments.

Break-bulk warehousing
A specialized form of cross-docking in which the incoming shipments are from a single source or manufacturer.

In **cross-docking,** another system that reduces transportation costs, the approach used in consolidation warehousing—large shipments in, small shipments out—is reversed. This type of system achieves essentially the same benefits, however, as is illustrated in Figure 8.3.

Like consolidation, cross-docking can be done in several ways. A manufacturer may use a cross-docking warehouse to break up large rail or truck shipments into smaller shipments to local customers. A cross-docking operation that receives goods from a single source or manufacturer is often referred to as **break-bulk warehousing.**

Retailers also use cross-docking to receive large shipments from multiple suppliers and re-sort the goods into customized shipments to individual stores. The regional distribution center

FIGURE 8.3
Cross-Docking

FIGURE 8.4
Cross-Docking at
Lowe's

Regional distribution center

Large shipments in... → ...some to inventory → ...and the rest immediately shipped ("cross-docked") to the stores

(DCs) network used by Lowe's to get goods to the retail stores is a classic example (Figure 8.4). The DCs receive large truckload shipments from suppliers. Employees then remix the incoming goods and deliver them to individual stores, often multiple times a day. Computer-based information systems closely coordinate *incoming* shipments from suppliers with *outgoing* shipments to individual stores so that more than half the goods that come off suppliers' trucks are immediately loaded onto trucks bound for individual stores. The result is that both the DCs and the retail stores hold minimal amounts of inventory, yet Lowe's receives the cost breaks associated with large shipments from suppliers.

Hub-and-spoke systems combine the benefits of consolidation and cross-docking warehouses, but they differ from them in two important ways. First, the warehouses, or "hubs," in these systems are purely sorting or transfer facilities. Hubs are designed to take advantage of transportation economies of scale; they do not hold inventory. Second, hubs are typically located at convenient, high-traffic locations, such as major airports, water ports, or the intersections of interstate highways. (In contrast, consolidation and cross-docking operations tend to be located close to the source of goods or to final customers.) One of the largest providers of transportation services in the United States, J. B. Hunt (**www.jbhunt.com**), has a comprehensive hub-and-spoke system consisting of 18 major hubs or terminals located throughout the United States, as well as 20 smaller satellite terminals.

Hub-and-spoke system
A form of warehousing in which strategically placed hubs are used as sorting or transfer facilities. The hubs are typically located at convenient, high-traffic locations. The "spokes" refer to the routes serving the destinations associated with the hubs.

EXAMPLE 8.3

Hub-and-Spoke System at Prakston Carriers

Pup trailer
A type of truck trailer that is half the size of a regular truck trailer.

Prakston Carriers is a trucking firm with 15 hubs throughout the United States. Prakston has two customers with shipments coming out of the Northeast. Each shipment is packed in a **pup trailer,** which is half the size of a regular trailer. One is bound for Los Angeles and the other for El Paso, Texas (Figure 8.5).

FIGURE 8.5 Hub-and-Spoke System at Prakston Carriers

Prakston might decide that the most economical way to ship the two pup trailers is to join them together at its hub in Syracuse, New York, and use a single truck to haul them to another hub in Phoenix, Arizona. In this case, Syracuse and Phoenix are the "hubs," while the routes to Los Angeles and El Paso are the "spokes." When the truck arrives in Phoenix, the two pup trailers will be separated and perhaps combined with different pup trailers for transport to their final destinations.

Postponement warehousing
A form of warehousing that combines classic warehouse operations with light manufacturing and packaging duties to allow firms to put off final assembly or packaging of goods until the last possible moment.

Improving Operational Flexibility. Warehouses not only help to lower transportation costs but can actually improve operational flexibility as well. **Postponement warehousing** combines classic warehouse operations with light manufacturing and packaging duties to allow firms to put off final assembly or packaging of goods until the last possible moment. This strategy adds flexibility because goods and materials can be maintained in their most generic (and therefore flexible) form as long as possible.

To illustrate, a Korean manufacturer might ship reinforced pallets carrying 1,440 light bulbs each to postponement warehouses throughout the world. At the warehouses, workers receive the pallets, break them down, and repackage the light bulbs in private-label boxes of three or six bulbs each. From the warehouses, the repackaged bulbs are shipped to local retailers. The manufacturer or distributor saves money on shipping costs (because reinforced pallets are less costly to ship than are cartons of smaller boxes) but can still provide customers with a wide variety of packaging options. Furthermore, the manufacturer or distributor can hold off on final packaging until customers' exact requirements are known.

Shortening Customer Lead Times. When the *total* transportation time to customers exceeds customers' requirements, firms can use warehousing to reduce the *realized* lead time to customers. They perform this service by breaking the total transportation time into two parts: (1) time to the warehouse and (2) time to the customer. In theory, goods arrive at the warehouse *prior* to the customer's order. As a result, transportation time to the warehouse is of no concern to the customer; it is "off-line." The only transportation time that is "on-line," or realized by the customer, is the time from the warehouse.

Assortment warehousing
A form of warehousing in which a wide array of goods is held close to the source of demand in order to ensure short customer lead times.

Assortment and spot stock warehousing are the two major approaches used to shorten customer lead times. **Assortment warehouses** tend to carry a wider array of goods than spot stock warehouses and for a longer period. **Spot stock warehouses** focus more on the positioning of seasonal goods such as lawn care products, fashion goods, and recreational equipment. Both are attractive options when distances between the originating source and the customers are long and when customers emphasize high availability or quick delivery.

Spot stock warehousing
A form of warehousing that attempts to position seasonal goods close to the marketplace. At the end of each season, the goods are either liquidated or moved back to a more centralized location.

Lowering Inventory-Related Costs. Used wisely, warehouses can dramatically lower overall inventory levels and related costs throughout the supply chain. To those who associate warehousing with increased inventory levels, this idea may seem counterintuitive. But consider the case of *inventory pooling* at Boyers', a fictional retailer with eight stores in the Seattle area. For its best-selling goods, Boyers' would like to keep extra inventory, called *safety stock*, to meet unexpected spurts in customer demand. However, management doesn't want to keep this safety stock in the stores, where floor space is expensive. And it seems wasteful to keep extra inventory in each store, as it is unlikely that *all* the stores will experience unusually high demand levels at the same time. Instead, Boyers' might consolidate the safety stock for all eight stores into one centralized location, which can provide same-day service to all the stores. Not only would this free up retail floor space, but also, as we will show in Chapter 11, it would actually reduce the amount of inventory needed to protect the stores against demand surges.

Logistics Information Systems

Now that we have discussed the physical infrastructure of a logistics system, we will turn our attention to the information systems piece. In the simplest terms, logistics information systems fall into three major categories: decision support tools, planning systems, and execution systems.

Decision Support Tools. Logistics managers often use decision support tools to design and fine-tune their logistics systems. Such tools help managers choose locations for their warehouses, determine the number of containers or vessels they need, and estimate costs and travel times. Some decision support tools even have simulation and optimization capabilities. For example, a simulation model might be used to simulate actual traffic conditions in order to evaluate the impact of traffic on a proposed warehousing system. An optimization model might be used to identify the warehousing network with the lowest overall cost or shortest average travel time. In the last section of this chapter, we show how optimization modeling can support logistics decisions.

Planning Systems. Planning systems help managers with specific activities, such as selecting a carrier for an outgoing shipment or developing a weekly schedule of deliveries. Of course, such activities have been going on for a long time. But with the aid of computer-based planning systems, today's logistics managers can more quickly analyze a wider range of options and identify the delivery schedule or carrier that best suits their needs.

Execution Systems. Execution systems are the most detailed level of a logistics information system. As the name implies, execution systems take care of the hundreds of small details associated with logistics activities, ensuring that planned activities take place as expected. They oversee order and shipment management, warehouse management, shipper/receiver management, satellite and bar code tracking, and automated payment and billing systems.

Execution systems can also help managers monitor the logistics system and identify problems before they get out of hand. Consider the online tracking system used by FedEx. Every time FedEx handles a package (picking it up, sorting it at a major hub, loading it onto a plane), a bar code is read into its execution system. Authorized users can then go online to track the package's progress. But this same information can also be used to identify potential problems automatically. Suppose the tracking system indicates that a package has not left the hub within a few hours, as expected. The tracking system may automatically generate an exception report, indicating that someone needs to check on the package's status.

One information technology that has garnered much attention recently is *radio-frequency identification (RFID)*. RFID systems use small electronic "tags" to track the position and movement of items. The *Supply Chain Connections* feature shows how businesses are using RFID to track the position and movement of everything from fashion goods to medical supplies.

SUPPLY CHAIN CONNECTIONS

USING RFID TO TRACK FASHION CLOTHING, RAIL CARS, MEDICAL SUPPLIES . . . YOU NAME IT

Radio-frequency identification (RFID) has grown to include applications in almost every industry imaginable, from high-fashion clothing to health care to rail transportation and more.

Brand-name fashion apparel at one Paris warehouse and shipping center that serves five corporate customers now moves out more quickly and more accurately, thanks to a newly installed RFID tracking system. The system improves the speed and accuracy of receiving, packing, storing, and distribution to fashion retail outlets of 5 to 10 million individual items a year. Once the installation of the RFID system at the warehouse is complete, every item will be tagged, and handheld tag readers will be available for warehouse workers looking for specific items to fill orders. Tunnel readers have already been installed at the warehouse docks. The new system

replaces a time-consuming bar code scanning operation and will also help warehouse workers verify orders by checking the contents before filled boxes are sealed and shipped. In addition to improving speed and accuracy, the RFID system will allow the logistics company that manages the warehouse to collect data for its customers so they can track the location and status of their goods.

The Finnish state-owned railroad company is now using RFID technology to better manage its rail yards by tracking inventory, maintenance, and the status of shipments for its shipping customers. With more than 10,000 locomotives, wagons, and passenger cars at 50 locations around Finland, the railroad needed an enormous number of RFID tags, two of which were placed on each side of each car, in compliance with regulations of the European Railway Agency. Now, instead of tracking each car with pencil and paper, as in the past, workers can simply walk alongside and read the car's identification information on their handheld tag readers, confirming that each one is in the right place, behind the right locomotive

Among its many applications, RFID can be used to track the movement and position of shipping containers at large ports such as this one.

and in the right order. The railroad's shipping customers benefit, too, since they can quickly and reliably find out where their orders are located on the train and which way the relevant car is facing (to ease loading and unloading). Rail workers can now also read maintenance orders on their RFID readers. In fact, maintenance planning and data entry have been so streamlined by RFID technology that only 14 sites are needed to cover the entire rail system's needs, instead of 50, as in the old manual method.

With medical supplies consuming up to 30% of their operating budgets, hospitals may well be next in line to adopt cost-saving RFID technology for stocking and inventory. Because such supplies are expensive, sometimes perishable, and often life-saving, hospitals must monitor their levels carefully to avoid both oversupply and stockout situations and to discourage costly hoarding. A recent study focused on how to improve resupply to nursing stations, the front line of many hospitals' supply distribution needs. The study combined RFID technology with a kanban system, using specially designed storage units and kanban-type cards. Two containers of each supply item were provided, and when the first was empty, a nurse scanned the kanban card into an RFID reader, which automatically logged a refill request for the appropriate item. While details such as how to set resupply levels will vary according to the item's consumption patterns, the hospital, and the department, the application holds much promise for saving costs as well as labor, and, most importantly, for improving patient care.

Sources: Based on Rhea Wessel, "Finnish Railroad Streamlines Operations," *RFID Journal*, July 14, 2011, **www.rfidjournal.com/article/view/8594/1;** Claire Swedberg, "Fashion Tracked by French Logistics Company," *RFID Journal*, July 11, 2011, **www.rfidjournal.com/article/view/8588;** Mary Catherine O'Connor, "Study Shows How to Optimize RFID-Enabled Resupply System for Nurse Stations," *RFID Journal*, June 22, 2011, **www.rfidjournal.com/article/view/8552/1.**

Material Handling and Packaging

Material handling system
A system that includes the equipment and procedures needed to move goods *within* a facility, *between* a facility and a transportation mode, and *between* different transportation modes (e.g., ship-to-truck transfers).

Material handling systems include the equipment and procedures needed to move goods *within* a facility, *between* a facility and a transportation mode, and *between* different transportation modes (e.g., ship-to-truck transfers). Forklifts, cranes, conveyor belts, and computer-controlled automated storage and retrieval systems (ASRS) are just a few examples of material handling equipment. From a logistics perspective, **packaging** refers to the way goods and materials are packed in order to facilitate physical, informational, and monetary flows through the supply chain.

Packaging
From a logistics perspective, the way goods and materials are packed in order to facilitate physical, informational, and monetary flows through the supply chain.

Next, we examine two examples that illustrate how intertwined material handling and packaging are with other aspects of logistics. The first example, Lowe's stores, shows how material handling can be integrated with logistics information systems and how a firm's material handling system can affect the performance characteristics of the overall logistics system. The second example, wine packaging, illustrates how a simple packaging decision can affect transportation costs and operational flexibility.

Material Handling at Lowe's DCs. Recall the discussion of the Lowe's cross-docking operation. In the DCs that perform the cross-docking, Lowe's uses a sophisticated conveyer system to move products to the trucks. Workers place the outgoing items into standardized trays, each of which bears a bar code indicating the item's final destination. The conveyor system "reads" these bar codes and automatically routes the trays to the appropriate trucks.

The Lowe's conveyer system is fast and accurate, and it minimizes labor costs. For the vast majority of goods Lowe's sells, the system is an effective material handling solution. But it does have one major limitation: It can handle only items that fit into the trays. Larger items, such as storage sheds, must be handled in separate warehousing facilities.

Packaging Wine. Many wine producers now ship wine in reinforced, vacuum-sealed plastic bags. While one could argue about the aesthetic appeal of the bags, they make good sense from a logistics perspective. First, plastic bags cost less to ship and handle than glass bottles (because they are lighter and less fragile). Plastic bags also keep the wine fresher, an important consideration for seasonal wines. Finally, the bags give the wine producers greater product flexibility. At postponement warehouses, wine that has been packaged in plastic bags can quickly be repackaged into bottles, wine boxes, or pseudo-"casks," as demand dictates.

Inventory Management

Inventory is such a critical resource in many organizations that we have devoted Chapter 11 to examining the tools and techniques firms used to manage it. However, it is worth taking some time here to consider how inventory decisions are intertwined with the physical network (transportation and warehousing).

In general, using slower and cheaper transportation modes will cause inventory levels within the supply chain to rise, while using faster and more expensive modes will enable firms to lower inventory levels. For example, transportation modes such as water and rail are economical only for high-volume shipments; therefore, the amount of inventory in the physical network will tend to rise when these transportation modes are favored. In contrast, air and truck allow goods to be delivered in a speedy fashion, thereby enabling firms to get by with less inventory in the network. Of course, the lower inventory levels (and associated costs) are offset by higher transportation costs.

With regard to warehousing, the relationship is more complex, and inventory managers have to work closely with warehouse managers to achieve the desired business outcome. For example, spot stock and assortment warehouses need inventory to shorten delivery lead times and provide better customer service. But unilateral efforts on the part of the material managers to cut inventory levels might "starve" such warehouses, reducing their usefulness. On the other hand, to make cross-docking economical, firms must be able to match the large incoming shipments from suppliers with the smaller outgoing shipments to customers or stores. If this doesn't happen, inventory levels can rapidly spin out of control.

8.3 LOGISTICS STRATEGY

Logistics strategy
A functional strategy which ensures that an organization's logistics choices—transportation, warehousing, information systems, and even form of ownership—are consistent with its overall business strategy and support the performance dimensions that targeted customers most value.

Rail or air? Consolidation warehousing or direct shipment? A **logistics strategy** ensures that an organization's logistics choices—transportation, warehousing, information systems, and even form of ownership—are consistent with its overall business strategy and support the performance dimensions that target customers most value. Like sourcing, a firm's logistics strategy is an extension of its overall operations and supply chain strategy.

We saw in Chapter 2 that operations and supply chain strategies address four key performance dimensions: quality, time, flexibility, and cost. Time can be further divided into delivery reliability and delivery speed, and flexibility can be subdivided into mix flexibility, design flexibility, and volume flexibility. Table 8.3 shows the transportation and warehousing choices that are consistent with these performance dimensions.

As Table 8.3 implies, a firm cannot select its transportation and warehousing options without first considering their strategic implications. A firm that is interested in keeping costs to a minimum is likely to favor different transportation and warehousing options from a company that is interested in maximizing flexibility.

TABLE 8.3
The Linkage between Key Performance Measures and Transportation and Warehousing Choices

PERFORMANCE DIMENSION	TRANSPORTATION MODE	WAREHOUSING SYSTEM
Delivery reliability—Deliver on time consistently	Highway Air	None (direct ship) Assortment Spot stock
Delivery speed—Minimal time from order to delivery	Air Highway	None (direct ship) Assortment Spot stock
Mix flexibility—Support a wide range of different products/delivery needs	Highway Air Rail	Assortment Spot stock
Design flexibility—Support design changes/unique customer needs	Highway Air	Postponement
Volume flexibility—Provide products/ delivery services in whatever volume the customer needs	Highway Air	None (direct ship) Assortment Spot stock
Cost—Minimize the cost of transportation	Rail Water Pipeline Highway	Consolidation Cross-docking Hub-and-spoke

Owning versus Outsourcing

One topic we have not discussed yet but that is critical to developing a firm's logistics strategy is ownership. Should a firm maintain its own trucks, warehouses, and information systems or outsource those services? As you might imagine, the best choice depends on many factors. Some of the major considerations are reflected in the following questions:

- **Does the firm have the volume needed to justify a private logistics system?** Firms with low volumes or sporadic shipping needs (e.g., transport of seasonal produce) are probably better off contracting for those services.
- **Would owning the logistics system limit the firm's ability to respond to changes in the marketplace or supply chain?** Investing in a private fleet of trucks or network of warehouses ties up capital and commits a firm to managing those systems. While that may be fine for firms with stable supply chains, it can present a problem for firms whose markets or supply chain partners are changing rapidly. A manufacturer that wants the flexibility to quickly change from domestic to foreign suppliers probably should not own the trucks and warehouses it uses.
- **Is logistics a core competency for the firm?** In Chapter 2, core competencies were defined as organizational strengths or abilities, developed over a long period, that customers find valuable and competitors find difficult or impossible to copy. Many firms have decided that logistics is not one of their core competencies. These firms generally outsource the logistics function to **common carriers** (also known as public carriers), which handle shipments on a case-by-case basis, or to **contract carriers,** which enter into long-term agreements with firms. Another choice is **third-party logistics providers (3PLs),** which are service firms that handle all of the logistics requirements for other companies. Using 3PLs allows companies to focus on their core competencies yet still enjoy access to state-of-the-art logistics capabilities.

The *Supply Chain Connections* feature highlights the logistics strategy employed by Kellogg Company. As you read through it, ask yourself the following questions:

- What product characteristics did managers consider in designing Kellogg's logistics system?
- What performance dimensions are most important to Kellogg?
- Who owns and manages Kellogg's transportation and warehousing systems? Why?
- What informational and physical flows must occur for an order to travel from Kellogg to a customer?

Common carrier
Also known as a public carrier, a transportation service provider that handles shipments on a case-by-case basis, without the need for long-term agreements or contracts.

Contract carrier
A transportation service provider that handles shipments for other firms based on long-term agreements or contracts.

Third-party logistics provider (3PL)
A service firm that handles all of the logistics requirements for other companies.

SUPPLY CHAIN CONNECTIONS

LOGISTICS STRATEGY AT THE KELLOGG COMPANY

The Kellogg Company of Battle Creek, Michigan, sells ready-to-eat cereal (RTEC), which accounts for 60% of the company's sales, as well as convenience foods, including Pop-tarts, Nutri-Grain Cereal Bars, Eggo Waffles, and Rice Krispies Treats. Kellogg's primary sales are made to grocery store chains in the United States. The company also has a manufacturing and distribution division in Canada (Kellogg's Canada) and another one in Europe. Competition in the food industry is fierce, and Kellogg is constantly under pressure to keep costs low.

For logistics purposes, Kellogg's products can be divided into two major types: frozen foods (e.g., bagels, waffles) and dry products (everything else). The two product types require different logistics solutions.

Dry Products

Kellogg produces dry products at 15 North American plants. To handle their distribution, the company depends on seven regional distribution centers (managed by outside firms) and multiple carriers. Managers recently went through a strategic sourcing exercise in which they attempted to lower warehousing and transportation costs. On the transportation side, they were able to reduce costs 15% by increasing the number of contract carriers from 25 to 30. But because the volume that the carriers handled decreased, Kellogg's business became less attractive to them. In the end, managers had to raise the prices paid to some key carriers.

Frozen Products

Kellogg's frozen products are more difficult to manage. To handle its frozen foods, Kellogg depends on 35 to 40 carriers with frozen-food capabilities. The company shares six distribution centers with other producers. Companies that specialize in frozen food operate these distribution centers for Kellogg and the other producers.

The Order Process

The order process begins when one of Kellogg's field representatives enters an order on behalf of the customer, typically a large grocery chain. Kellogg's customer service department receives the order and determines whether the quantity requested can be delivered by the desired delivery date. Customer service representatives may encourage customers to increase the size of their orders to take advantage of full truckload shipment rates.

Once an order has been confirmed, the customer service department must decide how to fulfill it. The department follows these general guidelines:

- If an order is for a full truckload and the lead time is long enough, the order will be filled and shipped directly from a plant. Kellogg personnel will take responsibility for arranging transportation.
- If an order is for a mix of products or if lead times are short, the order will be filled from one of Kellogg's distribution centers. In that case, the outside firm responsible for managing the distribution center will arrange for transportation.

Measuring Logistics Performance

To better understand the real impact of their logistics choices, many companies evaluate their logistics performance in terms of two measures: the perfect order and landed costs. The perfect order measure indicates how *effectively* logistics serves the customer. The second measure, landed costs, indicates how *efficiently* logistics provides that service.

Perfect order
A term used to refer to the timely, error-free provision of a product or service in good condition.

The Perfect Order. In theory, the **perfect order** represents the timely, error-free provision of a product or service in good condition. For example, a company might define the perfect order as one that is:

- Delivered on time, according to the buyer's requested delivery date
- Shipped complete
- Invoiced correctly
- Undamaged in transit

Under this concept, performance can be measured as the percentage of orders that meet these criteria. To find this percentage, managers must calculate the number of processed orders that did not meet all the company standards in a particular period:

$$\text{Percentage of perfect orders} = 100\%\left(\frac{\text{total orders} - \text{orders with} \geq 1 \text{ defect}}{\text{total orders}}\right) \quad (8.1)$$

Last year Bartley Company experienced the following results:

- 5.4 million orders processed
- 30,000 orders delivered late
- 25,000 orders incomplete
- 25,000 orders damaged
- 20,000 orders billed incorrectly

Furthermore, these 100,000 failures were spread across 90,000 orders, which meant that some orders had more than one problem. The percentage of perfect orders is therefore:

$$\text{Percentage of perfect orders} = 100\%\left(\frac{5,400,000 - 90,000}{5,400,000}\right) = 98.3\%$$

Landed Costs

Landed cost
The cost of a product plus all costs driven by logistics activities, such as transportation, warehousing, handling, customs fees, and the like.

Earlier we noted that U.S. logistics costs account for 5% to 35% of total sales costs. To make sure these costs aren't overlooked, particularly when making sourcing decisions, managers often estimate the landed cost of a product. **Landed cost** is the cost of a product plus all costs driven by logistics activities, such as transportation, warehousing, handling, customs fees, and the like.

Redwing Automotive has requested price quotations from two wiring harness manufacturers, Subassembly Builders Company (SBC) in Atlanta, Georgia, and Product Line Systems (PLS) of Nagoya, Japan. Redwing's estimated demand for the harnesses is 5,000 units a month. SBC's quote includes the following unit price, packing cost, and freight cost:

Unit price = $25.00
Packing cost = $0.75 per unit
Freight cost = $0.73 per unit

PLS quotes a lower unit price of $21.50. But each month PLS would also need to pack the harnesses in three containers, ship them overland to a Japanese port, transfer them to a container ship headed for Seattle, and then transport them overland again to Detroit. The costs associated with this movement—costs Redwing will have to pick up—are not reflected in PLS's unit price. The additional logistics-related costs Redwing would have to cover include:

- Packing cost = $1.00 per unit
- Inland transportation cost to the port of export = $200 per container (with three containers needed per month)
- Freight forwarder's fee = $100 per shipment (letter of credit, documentation for international shipments, etc.)
- Ocean transportation cost = $2,067 per container
- Marine insurance = $0.50 per $100 of shipment
- U.S. port handling charges = $640 per container
- Customs duty = 5% of unit price
- Customs broker's fee = $150 per year
- Transportation from Seattle to Detroit = $1.86 per unit
- Additional paperwork = $100 per year

Freight forwarder
An agent who serves as an intermediary between an organization shipping a product and the actual carrier, typically on international shipments.

Customs broker
An agent who handles customs requirements on behalf of another firm. In the United States, customs brokers must be licensed by the Customs Service.

A couple of these cost items deserve further explanation. A **freight forwarder** is an agent who serves as an intermediary between the organization shipping the product and the actual carrier, typically on international shipments. A **customs broker,** in contrast, is an agent who handles customs requirements on behalf of another firm. In the United States, customs brokers must be licensed by the Customs Service. To further complicate things, PLS has told Redwing that shipping lead times can be anywhere from six to eight weeks. To compensate for this uncertainty, Redwing would need to lease additional warehousing space to hold a safety stock of 1,000 harnesses, at a cost of $3.00 per harness per month. Redwing's personnel would also need to spend more time handling international shipments. Finally, each monthly PLS shipment is estimated to require four hours of additional administrative time, at a cost of $25 per hour.

Table 8.4 shows how these costs can add up. For SBC, logistics-related costs account for $1.48 per wiring harness, or approximately 5.6% ($1.48/$26.48) of the total cost of the wiring harnesses. For PLS, logistics-related costs amount to $6.43, or 23% ($6.43/$27.93) of the total cost of the wiring harnesses. In fact, PLS's logistics costs are so high that they eat up any advantage PLS might have with regard to unit price. This example shows why all costs—including logistics—must be considered in a sourcing decision. As more and more firms develop global supply chains, logistics costs will command more attention from managers.

TABLE 8.4 **Landed Costs Analysis at Redwing Automotive**

SBC QUOTE	PER UNIT	PER MONTH	PER YEAR
Acquisition	$25.00	$125,000.00	$1,500,000
Packing	0.75	3,750.00	45,000
Freight	0.73	3,650.00	43,800
Landed cost:	$26.48	$132,400.00	$1,588,800
PLS QUOTE	**PER UNIT**	**PER MONTH**	**PER YEAR**
Acquisition	$21.50	$107,500.00	$1,290,000
Packing	1.00	5,000.00	60,000
Inland transportation	0.12	600.00	7,200
Freight forwarder's fee	0.02	100.00	1,200
Ocean transportation	1.24	6,201.00	74,412
Marine insurance	0.11	537.50	6,450
U.S. port handling	0.38	1,920.00	23,040
Customs duty	1.08	5,375.00	64,500
Customs broker's fee	0.00	12.50	150
U.S. transportation	1.86	9,300.00	111,600
Warehousing	0.60	3,000.00	36,000
Administrative time	0.02	100.00	1,200
Paperwork	0.00	8.33	100
Landed cost:	$27.93	$139,654.33	$1,675,852

Reverse Logistics Systems

Reverse logistics system
According to APICS, "a complete supply chain dedicated to the reverse flow of products and materials for the purpose of returns, repair, remanufacture, and/or recycling."

So far we have spent most of our time talking about how logistics systems move products *from* upstream suppliers *to* downstream customers. In the past several years, however, interest has grown in reverse logistics systems. According to APICS, **reverse logistics system** is "a complete supply chain dedicated to the reverse flow of products and materials for the purpose of returns, repair, remanufacture, and/or recycling."[10] As the definition suggests, firms are interested in reverse logistics for a number of reasons. In the case of returns and repairs, reverse logistics can play a large role in determining overall customer satisfaction. In other cases, firms might find it more economical to harvest used products than to purchase new parts or materials. Also, many governments and consumer groups are putting pressure on firms to incorporate recycling into their operations, thereby reducing the amount of material that eventually gets thrown away.

[10]J. H. Blackstone, ed., *APICS Dictionary*, 15th ed. (Chicago, IL: APICS, 2016).

When incorporating a reverse logistics system into the overall logistics strategy, firms can face a number of challenges. Some of the key ones include:

- In general, firms have less control over the timing, transportation modes used, and packaging for goods flowing back up the supply chain. This often means reverse logistics systems have to be designed to be more flexible and less cost-efficient than forward-based systems.
- Goods can flow back up the supply chain for a variety of reasons. Some might do so for service and repair and others for remanufacturing or recycling, and others may simply represent excess goods that need to be deployed somewhere else. A reverse logistics system must be able to sort and handle these different flows.
- Forward logistics systems typically aren't set up to handle reverse logistics. For example, imagine a cross-docking facility, which usually deals with large inbound shipments, trying to incorporate low-volume return shipments into its operations. The information systems, material handling systems, and procedures simply aren't suited to the challenges of reverse logistics. In many cases, firms are better off setting up separate physical operations for their forward and reverse logistics.

8.4 LOGISTICS DECISION MODELS

Given the critical importance of logistics, it should be no surprise that experts have developed a wide range of tools to help make better decisions in this area. In this section, we look at two common models to demonstrate how modeling techniques can be applied to logistics decisions.

The weighted center of gravity method looks at the strategic location decision. This can be especially important when a firm is developing its logistics network and must decide where to place plants or warehouses. The second model, the assignment problem, is a specialized type of optimization model and looks at the tactical problem of deciding how to serve multiple demand points from various supply points at the least possible cost.

Weighted Center of Gravity Method

Weighted center of gravity method
A logistics decision modeling technique that attempts to identify the "best" location for a single warehouse, store, or plant, given multiple demand points that differ in location and importance.

The **weighted center of gravity method** attempts to identify the "best" location for a single warehouse, store, or plant, given multiple demand points that differ in location and importance. Location is typically expressed in (X, Y) coordinate terms, where the X and Y values represent relative positions on a map. Importance can be captured through weighting factors such as population, shipment quantities, sales dollars, or whatever best suits the situation. The weighted center of gravity works by calculating the weighted average (X, Y) values of the demand locations. Specifically:

$$\text{Weighted } X \text{ coordinate} = X^* = \frac{\sum_{i=1}^{I} W_i X_i}{\sum_{i=1}^{I} W_i} \tag{8.2}$$

$$\text{Weighted } Y \text{ coordinate} = Y^* = \frac{\sum_{i=1}^{I} W_i Y_i}{\sum_{i=1}^{I} W_i} \tag{8.3}$$

where:

(X_i, Y_i) = position of demand point i

W_i = weighting factor for demand point i

The resulting (X^*, Y^*) values represent the ideal location, given the relative weight (i.e., *importance*) placed on each demand point.

EXAMPLE 8.6

**Warehouse Location
Decision at CupAMoe's**

Robbie Roberts, owner of CupAMoe's Coffee, is trying to determine where to locate his newest distribution warehouse. Figure 8.6 shows the location and population of the three major towns to be served by the warehouse.

FIGURE 8.6 Coordinate Map of Demand Locations, CupAMoe's Coffee

Robbie would like to locate the warehouse to minimize transportation costs and provide the best overall delivery speed to his three markets. One way to do this is by using a weighted center of gravity method to identify a possible site.

Using the populations as weight, the weighted X and Y coordinates are:

$$X^* = (400{,}000*1 + 200{,}000*4.5 + 170{,}000*4)/770{,}000$$

$$= 1{,}980{,}000/770{,}000 = 2.57$$

$$Y^* = (400{,}000*5 + 200{,}000*3 + 170{,}000*1)/770{,}000$$

$$= 2{,}770{,}000/770{,}000 = 3.60$$

Figure 8.7 shows the suggested location of the new warehouse. Of course, a host of other factors, such as available space, zoning considerations, and labor availability, should be considered before Robbie makes a final decision. Nevertheless, the weighted center of gravity method provides a good first cut at the solution.

**FIGURE 8.7 Suggested Warehouse Location for CupAMoe's, Based on
Weighted Center of Gravity Method**

Optimization Models

Optimization models are a class of mathematical models used when the decision maker seeks to optimize some objective function subject to some constraints. An **objective function** is a quantitative function that we hope to optimize (i.e., maximize or minimize). **Constraints** are quantifiable conditions that place limitations on the set of possible solutions. A solution is acceptable only if it does not break any of the constraints. Some examples of business problems that can be addressed through optimization modeling are shown in Table 8.5.

In order for optimization modeling to work, the user must be able to state in mathematical terms both the objective function and the constraints, as well as the decision variables that will be manipulated to find the optimal solution. Once the user is able to do this, special modeling algorithms can be used to generate solutions.

The Assignment Problem

The **assignment problem** is a specialized form of an optimization model. Specifically, the assignment problem attempts to assign limited capacity (in this case, warehouse capacity) to various demand points in a way that minimizes costs. The generalized form of the assignment problem is as follows:

$$\text{Minimize} \sum_{i=1}^{I} \sum_{j=1}^{J} T_{ij} * S_{ij} \tag{8.4}$$

subject to the following constraints:

$$\sum_{j=1}^{J} S_{ij} \leq C_i \quad \text{for all warehouses } i \tag{8.5}$$

$$\sum_{i=1}^{I} S_{ij} \geq D_j \quad \text{for all demand points } j \tag{8.6}$$

$$S_{ij} \geq 0 \quad \begin{array}{l}\text{for all combinations of shipments from}\\ \text{warehouse } i \text{ to demand points } j\end{array} \tag{8.7}$$

where:

S_{ij} = number of units shipped from warehouse i to demand point j

T_{ij} = cost of shipping one unit from warehouse i to demand point j (these values are given)

C_i = capacity of warehouse i

D_j = demand at demand point j

The explanation behind these equations is actually quite simple. First, the only decision variables are the shipment quantities (S_{ij}). **Decision variables** are variables that will be manipulated to find the best solution. Shipping costs (T_{ij}), warehouse capacity (C_i), and demand values (D_j), in contrast, are not decision variables but known values.

The objective function (Equation [8.4]) reflects the total shipment costs from I warehouses to J demand points. Note that at this point we don't know which shipping routes will actually be used. Therefore, we include all possible S_{ij} values, multiplied by their associated per-unit shipping costs.

TABLE 8.5
Business Problems That Can Be Addressed through Optimization Modeling

OBJECTIVE FUNCTION	CONSTRAINTS
Maximize profits	Limited demand, materials, and processing capabilities
Minimize delivery costs	Need to meet all demand and not exceed warehouse capacities
Minimize health care costs	Need to meet all patient demand

The constraints are found in Equations (8.5) through (8.7). Equation (8.5) requires that the total number of shipments out of a warehouse not exceed the capacity of the warehouse. Similarly, Equation (8.6) requires that the total shipments into a demand point should at least cover the demand. Finally, Equation (8.7) ensures that the modeling algorithm we use to solve the problem doesn't recommend negative shipments.

This last constraint may seem like an odd requirement, but if you look at Equations (8.5) and (8.6), in mathematical terms, negative shipments could be used to bring down shipping costs or to "add" capacity to the warehouses. Equation (8.7) prevents this from happening. In Example 8.7, we illustrate how the assignment problem can be set up and then solved by using Microsoft Excel's Solver function.

<table>
<tr><td>**EXAMPLE 8.7**

The Assignment Problem at Flynn Boot Company</td><td>The Flynn Boot Company imports boots from all over the world and ships them to major retail customers in the United States. Flynn currently has three assortment warehouses in the cities of Atlanta, Fort Worth, and Tucson. On the demand side, Flynn has four major customers: BillyBob, DudeWear, Slickers, and CJ's. The weekly capacities for the warehouses and weekly demands for the customers are shown in the Excel spreadsheet in Figure 8.8. The spreadsheet also shows the cost to ship a pair of boots from each warehouse to each customer.</td></tr>
</table>

	A	B	C	D	E	F	G
1	The Assignment Problem: Flynn Boot Company						
2							
3			Weekly			Weekly	
4			Capacity			Demand	
5		Warehouse	(Ci)		Customer	(Dj)	
6							
7		Atlanta	20,000		BillyBob	27,800	
8		Fort Worth	40,000		DudeWear	8,000	
9		Tucson	30,000		Slickers	13,500	
10		TOTAL:	90,000		CJ's	33,000	
11					TOTAL:	82,300	
12							
13		Cost to ship one pair of boots from Warehouse i to Customer j (Tij)					
14							
15			BillyBob	DudeWear	Slickers	CJ's	
16		Atlanta	$2.00	$3.00	$3.50	$1.50	
17		Fort Worth	$5.00	$1.75	$2.25	$4.00	
18		Tucson	$1.00	$2.50	$1.00	$3.00	
19							

FIGURE 8.8 Spreadsheet for Flynn Boot Company

Total warehouse capacity (90,000 pairs per week) exceeds total demand (82,300), so Flynn has plenty of capacity. One question remains, however, given the different shipping costs: Which warehouse should serve which customer in order to minimize costs?

Following Equations (8.4) through (8.7) and using the first letter for each warehouse and customer as abbreviations, we can express the assignment problem as follows. Minimize total shipping costs (Equation [8.4]):

$$\$2.00*S_{AB} + \$3.00*S_{AD} + \$3.50*S_{AS} + \$1.50*S_{AC}$$
$$+ \$5.00*S_{FB} + \$1.75*S_{FD} + \$2.25*S_{FS} + \$4.00*S_{FC}$$
$$+ \$1.00*S_{TB} + \$2.50*S_{TD} + \$1.00*S_{TS} + \$3.00*S_{TC}$$

subject to the following constraints:

Total shipments out of each warehouse must be less than its capacity (Equation [8.5]):

$$S_{AB} + S_{AD} + S_{AS} + S_{AC} \leq 20,000$$
$$S_{FB} + S_{FD} + S_{FS} + S_{FC} \leq 40,000$$
$$S_{TB} + S_{TD} + S_{TS} + S_{TC} \leq 30,000$$

Total shipments to each customer must at least cover demand (Equation [8.6]):

$$S_{AB} + S_{FB} + S_{TB} \geq 27,800$$
$$S_{AD} + S_{FD} + S_{TD} \geq 8,000$$
$$S_{AS} + S_{FS} + S_{TS} \geq 13,500$$
$$S_{AC} + S_{FC} + S_{TC} \geq 33,000$$

All shipment quantities must be nonnegative (Equation [8.7]):

$$S_{AB}, S_{AD}, S_{AS}, S_{AC}, S_{FB}, S_{FD}, S_{FS}, S_{FC}, S_{TB}, S_{TD}, S_{TS}, S_{TC} \geq 0$$

So how do we solve this problem? Many software packages could be used to find the optimal answer. We use the Solver function of Microsoft Excel because it is readily available to most students. Solver is available as an add-on function for Excel.

The first step is to modify our spreadsheet so that we now have spaces to record the S_{ij} values and a cell that contains the formula for the objective function (in this case, total shipping costs). Figure 8.9 shows the expanded worksheet.

	A	B	C	D	E	F	G
1		The Assignment Problem: Flynn Boot Company					
2							
3			Weekly			Weekly	
4			Capacity			Demand	
5		Warehouse	(Ci)		Customer	(Dj)	
6							
7		Atlanta	20,000		BillyBob	27,800	
8		Fort Worth	40,000		DudeWear	8,000	
9		Tucson	30,000		Slickers	13,500	
10		TOTAL:	90,000		CJ's	33,000	
11					TOTAL:	82,300	
12							
13		Cost to ship one pair of boots from Warehouse i to Customer j (Tij)					
14							
15			BillyBob	DudeWear	Slickers	CJ's	
16		Atlanta	$2.00	$3.00	$3.50	$1.50	
17		Fort Worth	$5.00	$1.75	$2.25	$4.00	
18		Tucson	$1.00	$2.50	$1.00	$3.00	
19							
20							
21		Number of pairs of boots shipped from Warehouse i to Customer j					
22							
23			BillyBob	DudeWear	Slickers	CJ's	TOTALS:
24		Atlanta	0	0	0	0	0
25		Fort Worth	0	0	0	0	0
26		Tucson	0	0	0	0	0
27		TOTALS:	0	0	0	0	
28							
29		Objective Function: Minimum Total Shipping Costs:					$0.00
30							

FIGURE 8.9 Expanded Spreadsheet for Flynn Boot Company

The S_{ij} values are shown in the highlighted cells. For example, cell C24 contains the number of shipments from Atlanta to BillyBob's. These values are initially set to 0; we will let the Solver function determine the S_{ij} values that minimize total costs.

Some of the cells have formulas that calculate key values. In particular:

- **Cells C27 through F27:** Total shipments to each customer
- **Cells G24 through G26:** Total shipments out of each warehouse
- **Cell G29:** The objective function

To illustrate the formulas in these cells:

Formula in Cell C27 = $SUM(C24:C26)$ = total shipment to BillyBob's

Formula in Cell G24 = $SUM(C24:F24)$ = total shipment out of Atlanta

Formula in Cell G29 = $SUMPRODUCT(C16:F18, C24:F26)$ = total shipping costs

With all the relevant information now in the spreadsheet, we next code the assignment problem (Equations [8.4] through [8.7]) into Excel's Solver function. Figure 8.10 shows the Solver dialog box used to do this. The "Target Cell" is our objective function, cell G29. Just below, we have selected "Min" to indicate that we want a solution that minimizes the value in cell G29. Below that, there is a space labeled "By Changing Cells." Here we tell Solver where our decision variables are located.

FIGURE 8.10 Solver Dialog Box for Flynn Boot Company Example

At the bottom of the dialog box is a list of all the constraints that must be met. The first constraint, **$C$24:$F$26>=0,** ensures that none of our shipment quantities falls below zero (Equation [8.7]). The next four constraints are the demand constraints; shipments to a customer must at least meet customer demand (Equation [8.6]). Finally, **$G$24:$G$26 <=$C$7:$C$9** makes sure that total shipments from any warehouse do not exceed that warehouse's capacity (Equation [8.5]).

Once we have finished defining the objective function, target cells, and constraints, we click the "Solve" button at the top right of the Solver dialog box. The resulting solution is shown in Figure 8.11.

	A	B	C	D	E	F	G
1	The Assignment Problem: Flynn Boot Company						
2							
3			Weekly			Weekly	
4			Capacity			Demand	
5		Warehouse	(Ci)		Customer	(Dj)	
6							
7		Atlanta	15,000		BillyBob	27,800	
8		Fort Worth	40,000		DudeWear	8,000	
9		Tucson	30,000		Slickers	13,500	
10		TOTAL:	85,000		CJ's	33,000	
11					TOTAL:	82,300	
12							
13		Cost to ship one pair of boots from Warehouse i to Customer j (Tij)					
14							
15			BillyBob	DudeWear	Slickers	CJ's	
16		Atlanta	$2.00	$3.00	$3.50	$1.50	
17		Fort Worth	$5.00	$1.75	$2.25	$4.00	
18		Tucson	$1.00	$2.50	$1.00	$3.00	
19							
20							
21		Number of pair of boots shipped from Warehouse i to Customer j (Sij)					
22							
23			BillyBob	DudeWear	Slickers	CJ's	TOTALS:
24		Atlanta	0	0	0	20,000	20,000
25		Fort Worth	0	8,000	11,300	13,000	32,300
26		Tucson	27,800	0	2,200	0	30,000
27		TOTALS:	27,800	8,000	13,500	33,000	
28							
29		Objective Function: Minimum Total Shipping Costs:					$151,425.00

FIGURE 8.11 Lowest-Cost Solution for Flynn Boot Company

Does this answer make sense? First, none of the warehouse capacity limits are violated. Second, all the customer demand requirements are met. Two of the four customers (BillyBob and DudeWear) are completely served by the lowest-cost option, while the remaining two have at least part of their shipment handled from the cheapest warehouse.

But what if conditions change? That is, what if demand levels shift or shipping costs change over time? In that case, we go into the spreadsheet, modify the relevant data, and *re-solve* the problem using Solver.

Suppose, for example, that part of the Atlanta warehouse is shut down for repairs, cutting Atlanta's capacity to just 15,000. What should the new solution look like? Modifying the spreadsheet and using Solver to generate a new solution, we get the results shown in Figure 8.12.

With Atlanta's capacity reduced, Flynn is forced to ship 5,000 more pairs of boots from Fort Worth to CJ's. The resulting change in costs is:

$$5,000(T_{FC} - T_{AC}) = 5,000(\$4.00 - \$1.50) = \$12,500$$

which corresponds to the difference in total shipping costs between Figures 8.11 and 8.12:

$$\$163,925 - \$151,425 = \$12,500$$

	A	B	C	D	E	F	G
1	The Assignment Problem: Flynn Boot Company						
2							
3			Weekly			Weekly	
4			Capacity			Demand	
5		Warehouse	(Ci)		Customer	(Dj)	
6							
7		Atlanta	15,000		BillyBob	27,800	
8		Fort Worth	40,000		DudeWear	8,000	
9		Tucson	30,000		Slickers	13,500	
10		TOTAL:	85,000		CJ's	33,000	
11					TOTAL:	82,300	
12							
13		Cost to ship one pair of boots from Warehouse i to Customer j (Tij)					
14							
15			BillyBob	DudeWear	Slickers	CJ's	
16		Atlanta	$2.00	$3.00	$3.50	$1.50	
17		Fort Worth	$5.00	$1.75	$2.25	$4.00	
18		Tucson	$1.00	$2.50	$1.00	$3.00	
19							
20							
21		Number of pair of boots shipped from Warehouse i to Customer j (Sij)					
22							
23			BillyBob	DudeWear	Slickers	CJ's	TOTALS:
24		Atlanta	0.00	0.00	0.00	15,000.00	15,000
25		Fort Worth	0.00	8,000.00	11,300.00	18,000.00	37,300
26		Tucson	27,800.00	0.00	2,200.00	0.00	30,000
27		TOTALS:	27,800	8,000	13,500	33,000	
28							
29		Objective Function: Minimum Total Shipping Costs:					$163,925.00

FIGURE 8.12 Lowest-Cost Solution for Flynn Boot Company—Atlanta Capacity Reduced to 15,000

CHAPTER SUMMARY

As critical as logistics is today it will continue to grow in importance. In fact, several trends will keep logistics at the forefront of many firms' strategic efforts:

- Growth in the level of both domestic and international logistics
- Outsourcing opportunities
- Increased emphasis on sustainability at the company level

The last two points deserve special mention. As logistics becomes more globalized and information intensive, more firms are outsourcing the logistics function to specialists, most notably third-party logistics providers (3PLs). This trend is expected to continue. However, firms must carefully analyze the strategic benefits and risks of outsourcing. Firms must remember that outsourcing is *part* of a logistics strategy, not a substitute for one.

Second, logistics covers a wide range of business activities that are inherently resource intensive. It is therefore a natural focal point for many firm's sustainability efforts. Often, organizations have found solutions that improve sustainability as well as other important performance dimensions. For example, many manufacturers have switched to using reusable shipping containers that not only reduce the amount of material ending up in landfills but provide superior protection and are cheaper in the long run than one-time-use containers. In other cases, however, efforts to improve sustainability can hurt an individual firm's cost, quality, or delivery performance. When this occurs, government regulations are frequently used to rebalance business costs and societal costs and to "level the playing field" across competitors.

We started off this chapter by discussing why logistics is critical and by examining the major logistics decision areas, with particular emphasis on transportation modes and warehousing. We then discussed the concept of a logistics strategy and introduced some commonly used logistics decision models.

But we encourage you not to let your logistics education end here. The Council of Supply Chain Management Professionals (CSCMP; **www.cscmp.org**) is a valuable source of education materials, white papers on state-of-the-art research into logistics, and professional contacts.

KEY FORMULAS

Percentage of perfect orders (page 236):

$$\text{Percentage of perfect orders} = 100\%\left(\frac{\text{total orders} - \text{orders with} \geq 1 \text{ defect}}{\text{total orders}}\right) \quad (8.1)$$

Weighted center of gravity method (page 239):

$$\text{Weighted } X \text{ coordinate} = X^* = \frac{\sum_{i=1}^{I} W_i X_i}{\sum_{i=1}^{I} W_i} \quad (8.2)$$

$$\text{Weighted } Y \text{ coordinate} = Y^* = \frac{\sum_{i=1}^{I} W_i Y_i}{\sum_{i=1}^{I} W_i} \quad (8.3)$$

where:

(X_i, Y_i) = position of demand point i

W_i = weighting factor for demand point i

Assignment problem (page 241):

$$\text{Minimize } \sum_{i=1}^{I} \sum_{j=1}^{J} T_{ij} {}^* S_{ij} \quad (8.4)$$

subject to the following constraints:

$$\sum_{j=1}^{J} S_{ij} \leq C_i \quad \text{for all warehouses } i \quad (8.5)$$

$$\sum_{i=1}^{I} S_{ij} \geq D_j \quad \text{for all demand points } j \quad (8.6)$$

$$S_{ij} \geq 0 \quad \text{for all combinations of shipments from} \quad (8.7)$$
warehouse i to demand point j

where:

S_{ij} = number of units shipped from warehouse i to demand point j

T_{ij} = cost of shipping one unit from warehouse i to demand point j (these values are given)

C_i = capacity of warehouse i

D_j = demand at demand point j

KEY TERMS

SOLVED PROBLEM

PROBLEM

Vivette's Importers

Candace Button has just taken a job with Vivette's Importers in New York. Vivette's makes daily shipments to customers in the Boston area. However, the number of customers, shipment sizes, and associated transportation and warehousing costs can vary considerably from one day to the next.

Candace would like to put together a spreadsheet that would allow her to quickly determine whether or not she should consolidate shipments, based on changing demand and cost information. To test the new spreadsheet, Candace has the following information for the next week:

Number of customers: 15
Average shipment size: 1,400 pounds
Truck capacity: 20,000 pounds
Truck costs: $500 per truck going to Boston

For consolidated shipments:

Warehousing cost: $25 per hundred-weight
Delivery cost: $100 per customer

Solution

Figure 8.13 shows the resulting Microsoft Excel worksheet. The shaded cells represent the input variables; changes to these cells will result in changes to the number of trucks needed and the total costs of consolidation versus direct truck shipments.

	A	B	C	D
1	**Consolidation versus Direct Truck Shipments**			
2				
3	No. of customers:	15		
4	Ave. shipment size:	1,400	pounds	
5	Truck capacity:	20,000	pounds	
6	Truck cost:	$500.00	per shipment	
7	Consolidation costs			
8	Warehousing cost:	$25.00	per hundred-weight	
9	Delivery cost:	$100	per customer	
10				
11	**SOLUTION**			
12		Consolidation	Direct ship	
13	No. of trucks needed:	2	15	
14	Warehousing costs:	$5,250.00	$0.00	
15	Delivery cost:	$1,500.00	$0.00	
16	Trucking costs:	$1,000.00	$7,500.00	
17	Total:	$7,750.00	$7,500.00	

FIGURE 8.13 Consolidation versus Direct Truck Shipment Spreadsheet

Three of the spreadsheet cells deserve special mention. Specifically:

Cell B14 = warehousing cost under consolidation

$$= \frac{(\text{warehousing cost per hundred-weight}) \times (\text{number of customers}) \times (\text{average shipment size})}{100}$$

$$= \frac{\text{B8} \times \text{B3} \times \text{B4}}{100}$$

Cell B13 = number of trucks needed under consolidation

$$= \text{rounded up value of} \left[\frac{(\text{average shipment size}) \times (\text{number of customers})}{\text{truck capacity}} \right]$$

$$= \text{ROUNDUP}(B4*B3/B5,0)$$

Cell B14 = number of trucks needed under direct shipment

$$= (\text{number of customers}) \times \left(\text{rounded up value of} \left[\frac{\text{average shipment size}}{\text{truck capacity}} \right] \right)$$

$$= B3*\text{ROUNDUP}(B4/B5,0)$$

The last two formulas ensure that the number of trucks is correct, even if the average shipment size is greater than the load capacity for a single truck.

An added advantage of this spreadsheet is that Candace can use it to understand how the various costs affect the Ωfinal decision. For example, by playing around with the spreadsheet, Candace realizes that if she can lower the delivery cost to just $83 per customer, then the consolidation option looks less expensive (Figure 8.14).

	A	B	C	D
1	**Consolidation versus Direct Truck Shipments**			
2				
3	No. of customers:	15		
4	Ave. shipment size:	1,400	pounds	
5	Truck capacity:	20,000	pounds	
6	Truck cost:	$500.00	per shipment	
7	Consolidation cost:			
8	Warehousing cost:	$25.00	per hundred-weight	
9	Delivery cost:	$83	per customer	
10				
11	**SOLUTION**			
12		Consolidation	Direct ship	
13	No. of trucks needed:	2	15	
14	Warehousing costs:	$5,250.00	$0.00	
15	Delivery cost:	$1,245.00	$0.00	
16	Trucking costs:	$1,000.00	$7,500.00	
17	Total:	$7,495.00	$7,500.00	

FIGURE 8.14 Impact of Lower Delivery Cost per Customer

DISCUSSION QUESTIONS

1. Someone tells you that logistics is really just trucking and warehousing. Explain why this view is inadequate.
2. A colleague tells you that warehousing is inconsistent with efforts to minimize inventory levels throughout the supply chain. Is this true or false? Explain.
3. Can a firm actually be part of the logistics industry without physically touching a product? Explain.
4. Why will landed costs become a more important consideration as firms participate in more international logistics arrangements?
5. Why is it important for firms to have a logistics strategy? What could happen if a firm did not logically link its logistics decisions to the needs of its customers?
6. Can logistics be an area of core competency for a company? Can you think of an example?

PROBLEMS

Additional homework problems are available at www.
pearsonhighered.com/bozarth. These problems use
Excel to generate customized problems for different
class sections or even different students.

(* = easy; ** = moderate; *** = advanced)

Problems for Section 8.2: Logistics Decision Areas

1. Consider the consolidation warehousing decision facing
Bruin Logistics (Example 8.2). Recalculate the cost of the
consolidation option if all costs remain the same *except*:

   a. (*) The cost of running the warehouse doubles to $18
   per hundred-weight.
   b. (*) Delivery costs to each customer fall to $150.
   c. (**) The cost of sending a truck from Los Angeles to
   Atlanta falls to $1,800, but delivery costs rise to $250
   per customer.

2. Every week BosssMustang of Oakland, California, receives
shipments from 10 different suppliers in the Los Angeles
area. Each supplier's order weighs, on average, 500 pounds.
A direct truck shipment from Los Angeles to Oakland
costs $800.

   A Los Angeles 3PL provider has offered to run a consolidation warehousing operation for BosssMustang. The
3PL provider would pick up the shipments from each supplier, process them, and put them on a single truck bound
for Oakland. The pickup fee would be $100 per supplier,
and the warehousing cost would be $55 per hundred-
weight. The direct truck shipment cost would be the same
as before, $800.

   a. (*) How much would it cost BosssMustang per week
   to accept direct, single-order shipments from all of its
   suppliers? What would the utilization levels for the
   trucks look like, assuming that each truck was capable
   of carrying 10,000 pounds?
   b. (**) How much would it cost BosssMustang per week
   to use the consolidation warehousing option? What
   would the utilization level for the truck look like?
   c. (**) Suppose higher gasoline prices have caused the
   trucking cost to increase to $1,200. Which option
   looks best now?

3. Astro Industries of Minneapolis, Minnesota, makes weekly
shipments to 20 customers in the Dallas area. Each customer's order weighs, on average, 1,500 pounds. A direct
truck shipment from Minneapolis to Dallas costs $1,800.
The maximum load per truck is 40,000 pounds.

   a. (*) How much would it cost Astro to make direct, single-
   order shipments to all of its customers each week? What
   would the utilization levels for the trucks look like?
   b. (**) Suppose a Dallas-based warehousing firm has
   agreed to run a break-bulk warehousing operation for
   Astro at a cost of $75 per hundred-weight. Local deliv-
   eries to each customer would tack on another $100 per
   customer per week. How much money could Astro
   save by going with the break-bulk solution?
   c. (***) How high would the warehousing cost (currently
   $75 per hundred-weight) have to be before break-bulk
   warehousing is no more attractive than direct shipments? Round your answer to the nearest dollar.

Problems for Section 8.3: Logistics Strategy

4. Consider the perfect order calculation for Bartley Company (Example 8.4). Recalculate the percentage of perfect
orders if all performance results remained the same *except*:

   a. (*) 25,000 are delivered late, and total failures are now
   spread across 85,000 orders.
   b. (*) 25,000 are delivered late, but total failures are still
   spread across 90,000 orders.
   c. (**) According to the logic of the perfect order measure,
   does an incorrectly billed order have the same impact as
   a damaged order? Does this seem reasonable? What are
   the implications for interpreting this measure?

5. MountainMole Foods has decided to use the perfect order
measurement approach to track its logistics performance.
According to MountainMole, a perfect order is one that
(1) is delivered on time, (2) arrives in one complete shipment, (3) arrives undamaged, and (4) is correctly billed.
MountainMole has the following performance figures for
the past four years:

YEAR	2015	2016	2017	2018
Total shipments	100,000	150,000	175,000	190,000
On-time shipments	95,000	145,000	170,000	180,000
Complete shipments	99,000	142,500	157,500	161,500
Undamaged shipments	98,000	147,500	173,000	189,000
Correctly billed shipments	55,000	97,500	132,000	161,500

   a. (**) Calculate performance for each of the four years.
   What is the overall trend in the performance, if any?
   What factors explain the results?
   b. (**) If you were looking to improve MountainMole's
   logistics performance, what areas might you concentrate on, based on these results?

6. Northcutt manufactures high-end racing bikes and is
looking for a source of gear sprocket sets. Northcutt
would need 1,550 sets a month. Supplier A is a domestic
firm, and Suppliers B and C are located overseas. Cost
information for the suppliers is as follows:

   • **Supplier A**—Price of $100 per set, plus packing cost
   of $2 per set. Total inland freight costs for all 1,550
   units would be $800 per month.
   • **Supplier B**—Price of $96 per set, plus packing cost of
   $3.50 per set. International transportation costs would
   total $3,500 per month, while total inland freight costs
   would be $800 per month.
   • **Supplier C**—Price of $93 per set, plus packing cost of
   $3.00 per set. International transportation costs would
   total $5,000 per month, while total inland freight costs
   would be $1,000 per month.

   a. (**) Calculate total landed costs per unit and per month
   for the three potential suppliers. Who is the cheapest?
   Who is the most expensive?

b. (***) Suppose that international and inland freight costs are fixed for volumes up to 4,000 units a month. Under this assumption, which supplier would have the lowest landed cost if demand were cut in half? If demand doubled? Whose landed cost is most sensitive to volume changes?

c. (**) What factors other than landed costs might North-cutt consider when selecting the supplier? (*Hint:* Incorporate what you learned in Chapters 5 and 7.

7. Consider the Redwing Automotive total cost example summarized in Table 8.4.

a. (**) By how much would PLS have to cut its per-unit price in order to match SBC's landed costs? What percentage decrease does this translate into?

b. (**) If you were the president of PLS, where would you go about trying to lower your landed costs to better match those of SBC?

c. (**) What logistics performance dimensions other than landed costs might PLS emphasize in order to win Redwing's business?

Problems for Section 8.4: Logistics Decision Models

8. Consider the warehouse location decision facing CupAMoe's (Example 8.6).

a. (**) Suppose Robbie has learned that Capital City's population is expected to grow by just 5% over the next five years, while Springfield's population is expected to increase by 50,000 over the same time period. Recalculate the X and Y coordinates using this new information.

b. (**) Now suppose Robbie has also learned that Capital City generates $800,000 in sales per year, while Springfield and Shelbyville both generate only $150,000 in sales each. Using sales dollars as the weights, recalculate the X and Y coordinates.

c. (**) Which do you think is a better weighting factor to consider: population or sales dollars? Explain.

9. The city of Green Valley, Arizona, is trying to determine where to locate a new fire station. The fire station is expected to serve four neighborhoods. The locations and number of homes in the neighborhoods are as follows:

NEIGHBORHOOD	X COORDINATE	Y COORDINATE	NUMBER OF HOMES
Birchwood	5	4	163
Cactus Circle	7	1	45
De La Urraca	2	2	205
Kingston	3.5	1.5	30

a. (**) Calculate the weighted center of gravity for the new fire station, based on the information provided.

b. (**) What other factors (e.g., zoning laws, maximum response time) might come into play when making the final decision?

10. (***) (*Microsoft Excel problem*) The following figure shows an Excel spreadsheet that calculates weighted X and Y coordinates, based on values for up to five demand points. **Re-create this spreadsheet in Excel.** While your

formatting does not have to be exactly the same, your answers should be. Your spreadsheet should recalculate results whenever any changes are made to the shaded cells. To test your logic, change the weight on demand point D to 250. Your new weighted X and Y coordinates should be 3.04 and 2.96, respectively.

	A	B	C	D
1	Weighted Center of Gravity Model for Up to Five Demand Points			
2				
3	Demand point	X coordinate	Y coordinate	Weighting factor
4	A	1.00	5.00	300
5	B	2.00	4.00	200
6	C	3.00	3.00	100
7	D	4.00	2.00	300
8	E	5.00	1.00	300
9				
10		Weighted X coordinate:		3.08
11		Weighted Y coordinate:		2.92

11. (***) (*Microsoft Excel problem*) Re-create the assignment problem spreadsheet for Flynn Boot Company, described in Example 8.7 and Figures 8.9 through 8.11. While your formatting does not have to be exactly the same, your spreadsheet should work the same. Specifically, the user should be able to change the weekly capacity ( ), weekly demand ( ), or shipping cost ( ) values and generate a new solution using Excel's Solver function. Test your spreadsheet by seeing whether you get a new solution when Atlanta's warehouse capacity changes from 20,000 to 15,000. Make sure your answers match those in Example 8.7.

12. (***) (*Microsoft Excel problem*) Consider the following information:

PLANT	CAPACITY	STORE	DEMAND
A	400	X	200
B	500	Y	250
C	100	Z	300
Total:	1,000	Total:	750

Cost to shop from plant to store (per unit of demand)

PLANT	STORE		
	X	Y	Z
A	$2.00	$2.00	$3.50
B	$4.00	$5.00	$4.50
C	$3.00	$3.00	$3.00

a. Write out the assignment problem by hand, using Equations (8.4) through (8.7) and Example 8.7 as a guide.

b. Develop an Excel spreadsheet that uses the Solver function to find the optimal shipping patterns between the plants and the stores. (*Hint:* The objective function for the optimal solution is $2,200.) Interpret your answer. Is there any plant that is underutilized? If so, why do you think this is the case? How might you use this information in any future decision to expand plant capacities?

CASE STUDY

Green Reverse Logistics in the Electronics Industry[11]

The path to a greener supply chain is often paved with forward-looking ideas focused on environmentally friendly manufacturing, transportation, and distribution processes. For some companies, however, the key to jump-starting supply chain sustainability can be found in reverse. By embracing reverse logistics strategies—including returns management, product repair and refurbishment, recycling of goods and materials, and proper disposal of materials from unwanted goods—companies can move the sustainability while also cutting costs and reaping products with a longer shelf life.

One business sector that is championing these activities—and seeing the bottom-line benefits—is the electronics industry, largely because of skyrocketing growth in high-tech gadgets. Thanks to ever-changing technology, top sellers such as digital cameras, cell phones, video game systems, computers, televisions, and other electronic devices become obsolete in a few short years—leaving electronics manufacturers to deal with mountains of unwanted product.

Recycling

For electronics manufacturers, recycling unwanted components is one key aspect of green reverse logistics. In 2007, Samsung, a global leader in the electronics industry, began its Recycling Direct program—partnering with take-back and recycling companies that do not incinerate, send materials to solid waste landfills, or export toxic waste to developing countries—and has since recycled 14 million pounds of waste from its consumer goods and IT products. The company has established drop-off locations across all 50 states in more than 200 fixed locations, where consumers can take unwanted electronics (both Samsung and non-Samsung brands). "Our goal is to make it convenient for Samsung customers to recycle old TVs, phones, camcorders, printers, notebook computers, and other electronics at no charge," explains David Steel, senior vice president of marketing for Samsung North America.

The company has also teamed up with the U.S. Postal Service and third-party logistics company Newgistics to operate the Samsung Take Back & Recycling program, which enables consumers to recycle used printer cartridges. Using a prepaid Smart Label, customers can return old printer cartridges to Samsung by simply dropping them in any mailbox. Through this program, Samsung ensures that empty cartridges are safely reprocessed into their major usable component materials (including plastics, metals, and packaging materials), and then it makes those reprocessed materials available for reuse in new manufacturing for a range of products.

Refurbishing

When consumers return an electronics product because it is outdated or not functioning properly, they don't likely give much thought to what happens next. But what happens next is at the heart of business for companies such as ATC Logistics and Electronics (ATCLE), which performs asset recovery, repair, and refurbishing services. Brian Morris, director of engineering for this Texas-based 3PL, gave a detailed explanation of the process involved in giving a returned product a new life:

When we receive returns from customers, we do a test inspection to find out how many faults the product has. If there is nothing wrong with it, we can repackage it for sale. If it's a faulty product, we identify the failure and determine what it takes to repair or refurbish that product.

The next step is to weigh the economics of the repair: Given the cost of fixing a product, does it make sense to repair it? This goes back to the cost/benefit of conducting the testing and refurbishment processes. There must be an acceptable ratio to be profitable. The range is typically 70 to 80 percent of the product's original cost.

If a product is deemed worth fixing, we put it through our repair and refurbishment operation, and it emerges like new. If the product cannot be repaired, we look at its individual components. If the plastic housing is still in good shape, for instance, the plastic can be reclaimed and used to refurbish another product. Batteries are another key component. Most batteries are not exposed, so if they still hold a charge properly and are in good shape cosmetically, they are often put through reconditioning. After reconditioning, we use them as replacement batteries or sell them to other refurbishing operations. We also find uses for components such as keyboards and USB cables.

Products with components that don't make the grade are sorted into containers and sent to a recycling house. Recyclers crush and grind plastic components and send them to an injection mold facility, where that plastic is put back into production for new plastics manufacture. Circuit boards can be crushed and smelted, and the precious metals—such as titanium, copper, and small traces of gold—are removed and sold to another circuit board manufacturer or even a jewelry house.

We are working to help manufacturers utilize refurbished and reclaimed parts so they can cut down on purchasing new parts. This helps them reduce costs, and it allows us to keep waste from piling up in landfills.

Questions

1. Consider the examples of recycling and refurbishing described in the case. Who are the various stakeholders who benefit from these efforts? How do efforts to build sustainable supply chains differ from simple good business practice?

2. Would Samsung have put in place the Take Back & Recycling program in a business environment that did not emphasize sustainability? Why or why not? What about ATCLE's refurbishing services?

3. In your opinion, will sustainability become another core measure of operations and supply chain performance, in addition to cost, quality, delivery, and quality? Why or why not?

REFERENCES

Books and Articles

Blackstone, J. H., ed., *APICS Dictionary*, 15th ed. (Chicago, IL: APICS, 2016).

Childs, J., "Transportation and Logistics: Your Competitive Advantage or Your Downfall?" *APICS—The Performance Advantage* (April 1996): 44–48.

Partridge, A. R., "Green Reverse Logistics Brings Many Happy Returns," *Inbound Logistics*, January 2010.

Tibey, S., "How Kraft Built a 'One-Company' Supply Chain," *Supply Chain Management Review* 3 no. 3 (Fall 1999): 34–42.

U.S. Department of Transportation, *National Transportation Statistics 2010*, Washington, DC.

Internet

CSCMP Supply Chain Management Definitions and Glossary, **http://cscmp.org/CSCMP/Educate/SCM_Definitions_and_Glossary_of_Terms/CSCMP/Educate/SCM_Definitions_and_Glossary_of_Terms.aspx?hkey=60879588-f65f-4ab5-8c4b-6878815ef921g.**

Gilmore, D., "State of the Logistics Union 2013," *Supply Chain Digest*, June 20, 2013, **www.scdigest.com/assets/FIRSTTHOUGHTS/13-06-20.php?cid=7172.**

J.B. Hunt, **www.jbhunt.com.**

"Kraft Foods Sustainability Fact Sheet," April 2009, **www.kraftfoodscompany.com/assets/pdf/KFTFactSustainabilityProgress2009.04FINAL.pdf.**

O'Connor, M. C., "Study Shows How to Optimize RFID-Enabled Resupply System for Nurse Stations," *RFID Journal*, June 22, 2011, **www.rfidjournal.com/article/view/8552/1.**

The Port Authority of New York and New Jersey, "2012 Annual Traffic Report," **www.panynj.gov/airports/pdf-traffic/ATR2012.pdf.**

"Port of Los Angeles Fact Sheet," June 2013, **www.portoflosangeles.org/about/facts.asp.**

Swedberg, C., "Fashion Tracked by French Logistics Company," *RFID Journal*, July 11, 2011, **www.rfidjournal.com/article/view/8588.**

Union Pacific Railroad, **www.up.com.**

Wessel, R., "Finnish Railroad Streamlines Operations," *RFID Journal*, July 14, 2011, **www.rfidjournal.com/article/view/8594/1.**

Paul A. Souders/Corbis/VCG/Getty Images

CHAPTER
nine

Forecasting

CHAPTER OBJECTIVES

By the end of this chapter, you will be able to:

● Discuss the importance of forecasting and select the most appropriate type of forecasting approach, given different forecasting situations.

● Apply a variety of time series forecasting models, including moving average, exponential smoothing, and linear regression models.

● Develop causal forecasting models using linear regression and multiple regression.

● Calculate measures of forecasting accuracy and interpret the results.

CHEEZNAX SNACK FOODS, PART 1

GVictoria/Shutterstock

It's November 2019, and Jamie Favre, demand planner for Cheeznax Snack Foods, is working away at her desk. In just two days, Jamie will need to provide top management with a forecast of 2020 demand, broken down by month. Cheeznax makes three products: puffed cheese balls, cheese nachos, and cheese-flavored potato chips. Currently, Cheeznax's products are sold through 100 convenience stores owned by Gas N' Grub. Jamie knows how important an accurate demand forecast is to the supply chain:

- *On the downstream side of the supply chain*, Gas N' Grub expects Cheeznax to keep the store shelves stocked with fresh products. If Cheeznax fails to deliver, then Gas N' Grub will take its business elsewhere.
- Within Cheeznax, manufacturing needs the forecast to plan production. While manufacturing doesn't want to underproduce, it also doesn't want to overproduce and end up with excessive inventory levels and spoilage costs. Furthermore, the finance department needs the forecast to project revenues for the upcoming year.

- Finally, *on the upstream side of the supply chain*, Cheeznax's suppliers need the forecast to plan their overall production levels of raw ingredients and packaging material.

Jamie looks at the 2019 Cheeznax sales figures, shown in Table 9.1. She knows the 2019 numbers are a good starting point for developing the 2020 forecast, but she also knows that she needs more information. For instance, Gas N' Grub currently has 100 stores, but how many new stores will the company open in 2020? How will this affect demand? Also, in past years Gas N' Grub has launched advertising campaigns for its stores without informing Cheeznax first. Cheeznax was unable to meet the unplanned surges in demand, and Jamie and Gas N' Grub's purchasing manager ended up bickering. Ultimately, things would get smoothed over, but Jamie couldn't help but think about the lost sales opportunity. As Jamie contemplates all this information, she starts to formulate a plan for developing her forecast.

TABLE 9.1 2019 Monthly Sales Totals for Cheeznax

MONTH	SALES ($)
January	$230,000
February	$230,000
March	$240,000
April	$250,000
May	$240,000
June	$250,000
July	$270,000
August	$260,000
September	$260,000
October	$260,000
November*	$280,000
December*	$290,000
TOTAL:	**$3,060,000**

*Estimated demand

INTRODUCTION

Forecast
An estimate of the future level of some variable. Common variables that are forecasted include demand levels, supply levels, and prices.

A **forecast** is an estimate of the future level of some variable. The variable is most often demand, but it can also be something else, such as supply or price. As we shall see throughout this book, forecasting is often the very first step organizations must go through when determining long-term capacity needs, yearly business plans, and shorter-term operations and supply chain activities. For example, could you imagine being a hospital administrator and trying to decide on the physical size of a new hospital, the number of doctors and nurses needed, or even the amount of supplies needed *without* forecasting patient demand first?

In practice, most organizations use a number of different forecasting techniques, depending on the situation they face. Some forecasting approaches depend on informal human judgments; others depend primarily on statistical models and past data. Both types of forecasts are important in predicting the future.

In the first part of this chapter, we discuss the different types of forecasts firms use and the four laws of forecasting. We then differentiate between qualitative and quantitative forecasting techniques. Most of this chapter is devoted to illustrating some of the most common quantitative forecasting methods, as well as measures of model accuracy. Finally, we highlight the role of computer-based forecasting packages and the use of collaborative planning, forecasting, and replenishment (CPFR) programs by some supply chain partners to improve the accuracy of their forecasting efforts.

9.1 FORECAST TYPES

Organizations often need to forecast variables other than demand. In this section, we describe some of the most common forecast types: demand, supply, and price forecasts.

Demand Forecasts

When we talk about demand forecasts, we need to distinguish between overall market demand and firm-level demand. Both types of demand are of interest to businesses but for different reasons. For instance, suppose the worldwide demand for new hybrid vehicles is expected to reach 8 million by 2019. Working from this number, automotive manufacturers must decide what percentage of this overall demand they will capture. But the demand for new hybrid vehicles is not the only demand the automotive manufacturers face. It will combine with other sources of demand—including warranty repairs, spare parts, and the like—to determine firm-level demand for all assemblies and components that go into hybrid vehicles. Once firms have accurately forecasted this firm-level demand, they can begin to plan their business activities accordingly.

Supply Forecasts

Supply forecasts can be just as important as demand forecasts, as an interruption in supply can break the flow of goods and services to the final customer. A supply forecast might provide information on the number of current producers and suppliers, projected aggregate supply levels, and technological and political trends that might affect supply. To illustrate, one of the world's largest supplies of manganese is located in central Africa. Because political turmoil in this region has interrupted manganese shipments in the past, companies whose products depend on this mineral need to pay close attention to what is going on in this area of the world.

Price Forecasts

Many businesses need to forecast prices for key materials and services they purchase. When commodity prices are expected to increase, a good strategy is forward buying, in which companies buy larger quantities than usual, store them in inventory for future use, and save on the price they pay. Alternatively, companies can use futures contracts to protect themselves. A *futures contract* is a legal agreement to buy or sell a commodity at a future date at a price that is fixed at the time of the agreement. If prices are falling, a better strategy is to buy more frequently in smaller quantities than usual, with the expectation that prices will go down over time. But the point is this: In order to decide on a purchasing strategy, firms must first have the price forecasts. The *Supply Chain Connections* feature highlights how forecasts of jet fuel prices can affect a wide range of decisions for airlines.

SUPPLY CHAIN CONNECTIONS

FORECASTED PRICE OF JET FUEL TAKES OFF

April 2011. A recovering world economy combined with political upheaval in the Middle East threatened to send oil and fuel prices to near-record levels. At the end of the first quarter of 2011, the U.S. Energy Information Administration (EIA) published a report that included a price forecast for jet fuel for the remainder of 2011 and 2012. Figure 9.1 shows these forecasted values, as well as actual average jet fuel prices for 2010 and the first quarter of 2011.

Fuel costs can account for 25% to 35% of total operating expenses for an airline, rivaling (and sometimes even surpassing) labor costs. In the last quarter of 2010, for example, American Airlines spent $6.4 *billion* on jet fuel when the average price was around $2.14 per gallon. As one can imagine, then, with fuel prices forecasted to increase by more than 50%, airlines faced a number of critical decisions in early 2011:

- What type of purchasing strategy should be used? That is, should an airline enter into a futures contract with suppliers and "lock in" prices at the forecasted values, or should it hold off and hope that prices fall? What are the pros and cons of each approach?
- How should ticket prices for future flights be adjusted to account for the expected fuel price increases? What impact would raising ticket prices have on demand?
- Similarly, what impact would fuel prices have on the profitability of operations? Should an airline re-examine some of the less-profitable routes and consider eliminating them?

April 2014. Three years later, the same EIA report that forecasted prices of $3.26 in the latter half of 2011 now suggested that prices would stabilize at around $2.92 per gallon through 2014 and 2015. Several factors accounted for the change—improvements in supply, the deployment of more fuel-efficient jets, and greater political stability. While fuel prices were nowhere near as turbulent as they were just a few years earlier, one can be sure that the major airlines were still keeping a watchful eye on them.

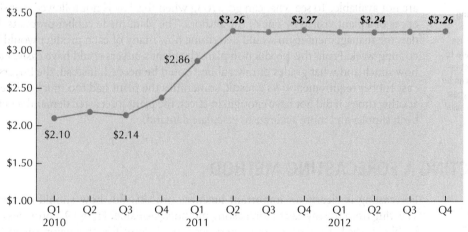

FIGURE 9.1 Actual and Forecasted Jet Fuel Prices, 2010–2012
Source: Data from Energy Information Administration, *Short-Term Energy Outlook—April 2011,* **www.eia.gov/emeu/steo/pub/2tab.pdf.**

9.2 LAWS OF FORECASTING

Now that we have discussed some of the major types of forecasts, let's review the basic laws of forecasting. By keeping these laws in mind, users can avoid the misapplication or misinterpretation of forecast results.

Law 1: Forecasts Are Almost Always Wrong (But They Are Still Useful)

Even under the best of conditions, no forecasting approach can predict the *exact* level of future demand, supply, or price. There are simply too many factors that can ultimately affect these numbers. Rather, businesses should use forecasting methods to get *close* estimates. The degree to which a forecast is *accurate* is a function of forecasting laws 2 and 3.

Law 2: Forecasts for the Near Term Tend to Be More Accurate

Law 2 recognizes that in the near term, the factors that affect the forecast variable are not likely to change greatly. Take, for instance, the price of gas. Given your understanding of current economic and political conditions, as well as the current price, you may feel reasonably comfortable predicting the price of gas for the next month or two. But what about 10 or 20 years from now? In addition to economic and political changes, other factors, such as technological breakthroughs and demographic changes, could radically affect the demand, and hence the price, of gas.

Law 3: Forecasts for Groups of Products or Services Tend to Be More Accurate

Many businesses have found that it is easier and more accurate to forecast for groups of products or services than it is to forecast for specific ones. The reason is simple: The demand, supply, or price of a *specific* item is usually affected by many more factors. Take, for example, the demand for dark green cars versus *all* cars. Color fashion may affect the precise demand for green cars. However, when we look at *overall* demand, the impact of color fashion disappears: Higher or lower demand for green cars is balanced out by demand for cars of other colors.

Law 4: Forecasts Are No Substitute for Calculated Values

Quantitative forecasting models
Forecasting models that use measurable, historical data to generate forecasts. Quantitative forecasting models can be divided into two major types: time series models and causal models.

Forecasts should be used only when better approaches to determining the variable of interest are not available. To see what can go wrong when this law is not followed, consider the experiences of a plant visited by one of the authors. The plant made rubber products. Every Wednesday, the management team would determine how many of each product would be made in the coming week. From this production plan, the plant's buyers could have easily calculated *exactly* how much and what grades of raw rubber would be needed. Instead, the buyers chose to forecast rubber requirements. As a result, sometimes the plant had too much rubber on hand, and at other times, it did not have enough. In effect, the plant forecasted demand when it would have been simpler and more accurate to calculate demand.

9.3 SELECTING A FORECASTING METHOD

Forecasting is clearly an important business process. But how should companies go about selecting from the myriad of forecasting methods available? Figure 9.2 provides a road map that highlights the key questions forecasters need to ask, as well as the major categories and types of forecasting models used in practice.

Qualitative forecasting techniques
Forecasting techniques based on intuition or informed opinion. These techniques are used when data are scarce, not available, or irrelevant.

The first set of issues concerns the availability of quantitative, historical data, and evidence that these data can be used to predict the future. When these conditions hold, forecasters can use quantitative forecasting models. **Quantitative forecasting models** are forecasting models that use measurable, historical data to generate forecasts. When these conditions don't hold, qualitative forecasting techniques must be used. **Qualitative forecasting techniques** are forecasting techniques based on intuition or informed opinion. These techniques are used when historical data are scarce, not available, or irrelevant.

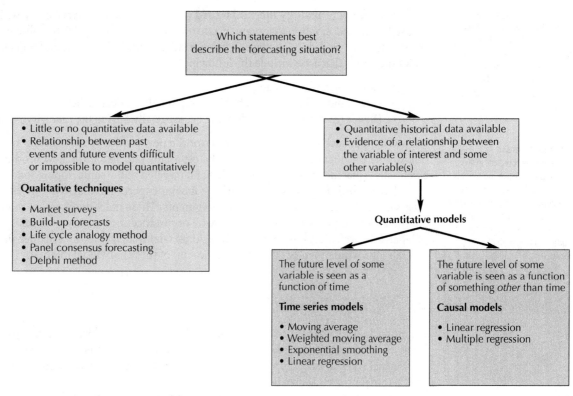

FIGURE 9.2 Selecting a Forecasting Method

To illustrate the distinction, consider two forecasting situations facing a large recording company:

- Total music sales, including downloads and CDs, for the year
- Music sales for a new recording artist

In the first case, last year's total sales may be a good predictor of total sales for this year (a classic example of time series modeling). The recording company may even be able to forecast total yearly sales based on the number of 18- to 25-year-olds or average personal disposable income figures (causal forecasting). Quantitative techniques are well suited to this situation.

But what about music sales for a new artist? The recording company might try to draw comparisons to similar artists or even test the new artist with focus groups, but ultimately the company's managers will have to depend more on their opinions than on any "hard" data.

Market survey
A structured questionnaire submitted to potential customers, often to gauge potential demand.

9.4 QUALITATIVE FORECASTING METHODS

Panel consensus forecasting
A qualitative forecasting technique that brings experts together to discuss and develop a forecast.

Delphi method
A qualitative forecasting technique in which experts work individually to develop forecasts. The individual forecasts are shared among the group, and then each participant is allowed to modify his or her forecast based on information from the other experts. This process is repeated until consensus is reached.

Even when qualitative forecasting must be used in situations where hard data does not exist, a forecast can still be developed in a rational manner. **Market surveys** are structured questionnaires submitted to potential customers. They solicit opinions about products or potential products and often attempt to estimate likely demand. If structured well and administered to a representative sample of the defined population, market surveys can be quite effective. A major drawback is that they are expensive and time-consuming to perform.

Both the Delphi method and the panel consensus forecasting method use panels of experts to develop a consensus forecast. The major difference between the two is the process used to collect the data. **Panel consensus forecasting** brings the experts together to discuss and develop forecasts. In contrast, the **Delphi method** has experts work individually to develop forecasts. The individual forecasts are shared among the group, and then each participant is allowed to modify his or her forecast based on information from the other experts. This process is repeated until consensus is reached. As you can imagine, these methods tend to be quite expensive, primarily due to the time requirements. The advantage is that when done correctly, they can be quite accurate.

Life cycle analogy method
A qualitative forecasting technique that attempts to identify the time frames and demand levels for the introduction, growth, maturity, and decline life cycle stages of a new product or service.

The **life cycle analogy method** is used when the product or service is new. The technique is based on the observation that many products and services have a fairly well-defined life cycle, consisting of an introduction stage, a growth stage, a maturity stage, and a decline stage. The major questions that arise include the following:

- How long will each stage last?
- How rapid will the growth be? How rapid will the decline be?
- How large will the overall demand be, especially during the maturity phase?

One approach is to base the forecast for the new product or service on the actual history of a similar product or service. This can be especially effective if the new product or service is essentially replacing another in the market and targeted to the same population.

Build-up forecast
A qualitative forecasting technique in which individuals familiar with specific market segments estimate the demand within these segments. These individual forecasts are then added up to get an overall forecast.

Finally, **build-up forecasts** work by having experts familiar with specific market segments estimate the demand within these segments. These individual market segment forecasts are then added up to get an overall forecast. For instance, a company with sales offices in each of Japan's 47 prefectures might ask each regional sales manager to estimate per-prefecture sales. Overall sales would then be calculated as the sum of these individual forecasts.

9.5 TIME SERIES FORECASTING MODELS

Quantitative forecasting models use statistical techniques and historical data to predict future levels. Such forecasting models are considered objective rather than subjective because they follow certain rules in calculating forecast values. The two main types of quantitative forecasting models are time series and causal models.

Time series
A series of observations arranged in chronological order.

A **time series** consists of observations arranged in chronological order. **Time series forecasting models,** then, are quantitative forecasting models that analyze time series to develop forecasts. With a time series model, the chronology of the observations, as well as their values, is important in developing forecasts.

Time series forecasting model
A quantitative forecasting model that uses a time series to develop forecasts. With a time series model, the chronology of the observations and their values are important in developing forecasts.

For example, suppose the director of an emergency care facility has recorded the number of patients who have arrived at the facility over the past 15 weeks. This demand time series is shown in Table 9.2.

Table 9.2 represents a time series because the values are arranged in chronological order. As Table 9.2 and Figure 9.3 show, this time series has two notable characteristics. First, the weekly values tend to hover around 100, although in some weeks the number of patients is higher, and in other weeks, the number is lower. Logic would suggest that, unless there are significant changes in either the population or the number of emergency care facilities in the area, future demand levels should be similar. Therefore, it would make sense to use the past demand numbers to forecast future demand levels. Second, the 15-week demand pattern shows

TABLE 9.2
Time Series Data for an Emergency Care Facility

WEEK	NUMBER OF PATIENTS
1	84
2	81
3	89
4	90
5	99
6	106
7	127
8	117
9	127
10	103
11	96
12	96
13	86
14	101
15	109
Average:	100.73

FIGURE 9.3
Time Series of
Weekly Demand
at an Emergency
Care Facility

FIGURE 9.4
Time Series Showing
Randomness, a
Downward Trend, and
Seasonality (Higher
Demand in the
Winter Months)

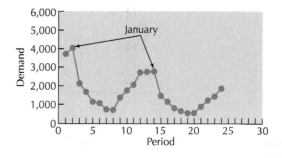

Randomness
In the context of forecasting, unpredictable movement from one time period to the next.

Trend
Long-term movement up or down in a time series.

Seasonality
A repeated pattern of spikes or drops in a time series associated with certain times of the year.

randomness, or unpredictable movement from one time period to the next. Even though the average number of patients is approximately 101, actual demand numbers range anywhere from 81 to 127. This randomness makes forecasting difficult.

In some cases, time series might also show trend and seasonality, as well as randomness. **Trend** represents a long-term movement up or down, while **seasonality** is a repeated pattern of spikes or drops in the variable of interest associated with certain times of the year. Figure 9.4 shows the time series for a product experiencing randomness, a downward trend, and seasonality in demand. By the end of this chapter, we will have presented methods for developing time series forecasts when all three of these characteristics are present.

Last Period

The simplest time series model is a last period model, which uses demand for the current period as a forecast for the next period. Stated formally:

$$F_{t+1} = D_t \tag{9.1}$$

where:

F_{t+1} = forecast for the next period, $t + 1$

D_t = demand for the current period, t

Consider the time series listed in Table 9.2 and graphed in Figure 9.3. Suppose the director of the emergency care facility decides to use a last period forecasting model to predict the number of patients each week. The demand in week 1 becomes the forecast for week 2, the demand in week 2 becomes the forecast for week 3, and so on, as can be seen in Table 9.3.

Figure 9.5 graphs the demand and forecast values from Table 9.3. As the results suggest, the main problem with a last period model is that it is based on only one observation. This makes it overly susceptible to unusually high or low values. Look at the week 10 forecast, which is based on week 9's demand of 127. The forecast turns out to be much higher than actual demand in week 10. In fact, week 10's demand is actually much closer to the average demand of 100.73.

TABLE 9.3
Last Period Forecasting for an Emergency Care Facility

WEEK	NUMBER OF PATIENTS	LAST PERIOD FORECAST
1	84	
2	81	84
3	89	81
4	90	89
5	99	90
6	106	99
7	127	106
8	117	127
9	127	117
10	103	127
11	96	103
12	96	96
13	86	96
14	101	86
15	109	101
16		109

FIGURE 9.5
Last Period Forecasting for an Emergency Care Facility

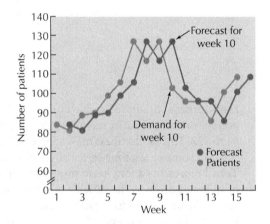

Moving Average

Moving average model
A time series forecasting model that derives a forecast by taking an average of recent demand values.

In response to the limitations of a last period forecasting model, a **moving average model** derives a forecast by taking an average of a set of recent demand values. By basing the forecast on more than one observed demand value, the moving average model is less susceptible to random swings in demand. The model is stated as follows:

$$F_{t+1} = \frac{\sum_{i=1}^{n} D_{t+1-i}}{n} \qquad (9.2)$$

where:

F_{t+1} = forecast for time period $t + 1$

D_{t+1-i} = actual demand for period $t + 1 - i$

n = number of most recent demand observations used to develop the forecast

For example, using the data in Table 9.2, the *three*-period moving average forecast for week 16 is derived from the demand figures for the previous three weeks (weeks 13–15):

$$F_{16} = \frac{\sum_{i=1}^{3} D_{16-i}}{3} = \frac{D_{15} + D_{14} + D_{13}}{3} = \frac{109 + 101 + 86}{3}$$

$$= 98.7$$

TABLE 9.4
Two-Period and Four-Period Moving Average Forecasts

WEEK	NUMBER OF PATIENTS	TWO-PERIOD MOVING AVERAGE FORECAST	FOUR-PERIOD MOVING AVERAGE FORECAST
1	84		
2	81		
3	89	82.5	
4	90	85.0	
5	99	89.5	86.0
6	106	94.5	89.8
7	127	102.5	96.0
8	117	116.5	105.5
9	127	122.0	112.3
10	103	122.0	119.3
11	96	115.0	118.5
12	96	99.5	110.8
13	86	96.0	105.5
14	101	91.0	95.3
15	109	93.5	94.8
16		105.0	98.0
Average:	100.7	101.0	102.6
Minimum:	81	82.5	86.0
Maximum:	127	122.0	119.3

FIGURE 9.6
Two-Period and Four-Period Moving Average Forecasts for an Emergency Care Facility

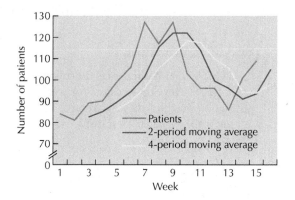

Smoothing model
Another name for a moving average model. The name refers to the fact that using averages to generate forecasts results in forecasts that are less susceptible to random fluctuations in demand.

By basing the forecast on multiple values, the moving average model generates "smoothed" forecasts that are less susceptible to random fluctuations in demand. It is because of this that moving average models are sometimes called **smoothing models.**

Table 9.4 shows two-period moving average and four-period moving average results for the emergency medical care center.

The smoothing effect is evident in the minimum and maximum values for the two forecasting models. The same effect can be seen graphically in Figure 9.6. Both the two-period and four-period models smooth out the peaks and valleys in the raw demand numbers. Because their forecasts are averages based on past data, the forecasts also echo the rises and falls in demand. These smoothing and delayed reaction characteristics are more pronounced in the four-period model than in the two-period one.

So which is better here: the two-period or four-period model? Generally speaking, the more randomness there is in the raw data, the more attractive the smoothing and delayed reaction characteristics are. The four-period model would be preferable in such a case. On the other hand, if rises or falls in demand are not random but really do indicate changes in the underlying demand pattern, we would prefer a more reactive model, such as the two-period model. Later in the chapter, we describe measurements that can be used to compare the relative performance of alternative forecasting models.

Weighted Moving Average

A variation of the moving average model is the **weighted moving average model.** In this case, the actual weights applied to past observations are allowed to differ:

$$F_{t+1} = \sum_{i=1}^{n} W_{t+1-i} D_{t+1-i} \qquad (9.3)$$

where:

$$W_{t+1-i} = \text{weight assigned to the demand in period } t + 1 - i$$

$$\sum_{i=1}^{n} W_{t+1-i} = 1$$

As the formulas suggest, the only real restriction is that the weights must add to 1. Allowing the weights to vary lets the user change the emphasis placed on the past observations. Suppose we want to use a three-period weighted moving average model with the following weights:

Weight given to the current time period $= W_t = 0.5$
Weight given to the last time period $= W_t - 1 = 0.3$
Weight given to the time period two periods earlier $= W_{t-2} = 0.2$

The different weights will place more emphasis on the most recent observations. Using the data in Table 9.2, the three-period weighted moving average forecast for week 16 would be:

$$F_{16} = \sum_{i=1}^{3} W_{16-i} D_{16-i} = W_{15} D_{15} + W_{14} D_{14} + W_{13} D_{13}$$

$$= 0.5*109 + 0.3*101 + 0.2*86 = 102$$

EXAMPLE 9.1

Flavio's Pizza

Flavio's Pizza has recorded the following demand history for each Friday night for the past 5 weeks. Develop forecasts for week 6 using a two-period moving average and a three-period weighted moving average. The weights for the three-period moving average model are 0.4, 0.35, and 0.25, starting with the most recent observation.

WEEK	DEMAND
1	62
2	45
3	55
4	73
5	60

The two-period moving average forecast would be:

$$F_6 = (60 + 73)/2 = 66.5 \text{ pizzas}$$

The three-period moving average forecast would be:

$$F_6 = 0.4*60 + 0.35*73 + 0.25*55 = 63.3 \text{ pizzas}$$

Exponential Smoothing

The **exponential smoothing model** is a special form of the moving average model in which the forecast for the next period is calculated as the weighted average of the current period's actual value and forecast. The formula for the exponential smoothing model is:

$$F_{t+1} = \alpha D_t + (1 - \alpha) F_t \qquad (9.4)$$

where:

F_{t+1} = forecast for time period $t + 1$ (i.e., the *new* forecast)

F_t = forecast for time period t (i.e., the *current* forecast)

D_t = actual value for time period t

α = smoothing constant used to weight D_t and F_t ($0 \leq \alpha \leq 1$)

There are a couple things to note about the exponential smoothing model. First, as Equation (9.4) shows, the exponential smoothing model works by "rolling up" the current period's actual and forecasted values into the next period's forecast. Because all forecasts are based on past actual values, all actual values back to the first period ultimately end up in the most recent forecast.

To show how it works, suppose the Emerald Pool Company has just started selling above-ground pools. In the first month, the company forecasted demand of 40 pools, while actual demand turned out to be 50. If we select an α value of 0.3, the exponential smoothing forecast for period 2 becomes:

$$F_2 = 0.3*D_1 + (1 - 0.3)F_1$$
$$= 0.3*50 + 0.7*40 = 15 + 28 = 43 \text{ pools}$$

Now suppose period 2 demand turns out to be 46 pools. The forecast for period 3 can now be calculated as:

$$F_3 = 0.3*D_2 + (1 - 0.3)F_2$$
$$= 0.3*46 + 0.7*43 = 13.8 + 13.0 = 43.9 \text{ pools}$$

Notice how period 3's forecast (F_3) is derived in part from the forecast in period 2 (F_2). Because F_2 is based in part on demand in period 1, so is the forecast for period 3. Table 9.5 shows this "rolling up" effect over the first six periods. By following the arrows, you can see how period 1's demand ultimately becomes part of the forecast for period 6. The same is true for periods 2 through 5.

Another critical feature of the exponential smoothing model is the smoothing constant, α. According to Equation (9.4), the forecast for the next period, F_{t+1}, is really just a weighted average, with α determining the relative weight put on the current period's actual and forecasted values, D_t and F_t. The closer α is to 1, the greater the weight put on the *most recent* actual demand value; the closer α is to 0, the more emphasis is put on *past* forecasts. Therefore, we can control how reactive the model is by controlling α.

The general rule for determining the α value is this: The greater the randomness in the time series data is, the lower the α value should be. Conversely, the less randomness in the time series data, the higher the α value should be.

Figure 9.7 shows a time series of demand data, as well as the resulting forecasts for an exponential smoothing model with a smoothing constant value of $\alpha = 0.2$. The time series contains a spike in demand in period 11 and a trough in period 18. After each of these periods, the actual demand numbers seem to return to the "normal" range of values between 8 and 12.

In a situation like this, we would not want the forecast model to overreact to the extreme demand levels in periods 11 and 18. And in fact, due to the low weight put on the most recent demand level, D_t, the exponential smoothing forecast values are only slightly affected by periods 11 and 18.

Now consider the demand numbers in Figure 9.8. Here, the demand spike in period 11 is followed by a shift up in the demand numbers. In other words, period 11 is *not* a random result

TABLE 9.5
Exponential Smoothing Forecasts for Periods 2–6, Emerald Pool Company

Period	Demand	Forecast
1	50	40
2	46	0.3 * 50 + (1 − 0.3) * 40 = 43
3	52	0.3 * 46 + (1 − 0.3) * 43 = 43.9
4	48	0.3 * 52 + (1 − 0.3) * 43.9 = 46.33
5	47	0.3 * 48 + (1 − 0.3) * 46.33 = 46.83
6		0.3 * 47 + (1 − 0.3) * 46.83 = 46.88

FIGURE 9.7
Exponential Smoothing Forecast ($\alpha = 0.2$) for Time Series A

$\alpha =$	0.2	EXPONENTIAL SMOOTHING
PERIOD	DEMAND	FORECAST
1	10	10*
2	11	10.00
3	9	10.20
4	11	9.96
5	10	10.17
6	8	10.14
7	12	9.71
8	9	10.17
9	10	9.94
10	11	9.95
11	20	10.16
12	11	12.13
13	9	11.90
14	11	11.32
15	10	11.26
16	9	11.01
17	11	10.61
18	4	10.68
19	10	9.34
20	11	9.48

*To start the process, the forecast for period 1 was set at 10.

FIGURE 9.8
Exponential Smoothing Forecast ($\alpha = 0.2$) for Time Series B

$\alpha =$	0.2	EXPONENTIAL SMOOTHING
PERIOD	DEMAND	FORECAST
1	10	10*
2	11	10.00
3	9	10.20
4	11	9.96
5	10	10.17
6	8	10.14
7	12	9.71
8	9	10.17
9	10	9.94
10	11	9.95
11	20	10.16
12	21	12.13
13	19	13.90
14	22	14.92
15	18	16.34
16	20	16.67
17	21	17.34
18	19	18.07
19	20	18.26
20	21	18.60

*To start the process, the forecast for period 1 was set at 10.

EXAMPLE 9.2

Exponential
Smoothing Forecast
with $\alpha = 0.8$

Using the time series data in Figure 9.8, calculate an exponential smoothing forecast for periods 2 through 20, using a smoothing constant value of 0.8. Graph the results.

The detailed calculations for F_2 through F_7 are as follows:

$$F_2 = 0.8*D_1 + 0.2*F_1 = 0.8*10 + 0.2*10 = 10$$
$$F_3 = 0.8*D_2 + 0.2*F_2 = 0.8*11 + 0.2*10 = 10.8$$
$$F_4 = 0.8*D_3 + 0.2*F_3 = 0.8*9 + 0.2*10.8 = 9.36$$
$$F_5 = 0.8*D_4 + 0.2*F_4 = 0.8*11 + 0.2*9.36 = 10.67$$
$$F_6 = 0.8*D_5 + 0.2*F_5 = 0.8*10 + 0.2*10.67 = 10.13$$
$$F_7 = 0.8*D_6 + 0.2*F_6 = 0.8*8 + 0.2*10.13 = 8.43$$

Forecasts for periods 8 through 20 are completed in a similar manner. Figure 9.9 shows the complete set of forecast values and graph. Because of the high α value, the exponential smoothing model now reacts quickly to the increase in demand levels.

$\alpha =$	0.8	EXPONENTIAL SMOOTHING
PERIOD	**DEMAND**	**FORECAST**
1	10	10.00*
2	11	10.00
3	9	10.80
4	11	9.36
5	10	10.67
6	8	10.13
7	12	8.43
8	9	11.29
9	10	9.46
10	11	9.89
11	20	10.78
12	21	18.16
13	19	20.43
14	22	19.29
15	18	21.46
16	20	18.69
17	21	19.74
18	19	20.75
19	20	19.35
20	21	19.87

*To start the process, the forecast for period 1 was set to 10.

FIGURE 9.9 Exponential Smoothing Forecast ($\alpha = 0.8$) for Time Series B

but an important indicator of a change in the underlying demand pattern. How does the exponential smoothing model perform in this case? Not as well as before. In fact, because of the low α value, the forecasting model still hasn't "caught up" by period 20.

Adjusted Exponential Smoothing

None of the models we have talked about so far will work when there is a pronounced upward or downward trend in the time series. This is because all of the previous models are just averages of past observations. If there is a strong upward or downward trend, the resulting forecasts will lag.

Adjusted exponential smoothing model
An expanded version of the exponential smoothing model that includes a trend adjustment factor.

In the next two sections, we describe two approaches to dealing with a trend in the time series. The first is the **adjusted exponential smoothing model,** which takes the simple exponential smoothing model and adds a trend adjustment factor to it. Specifically:

$$AF_{t+1} = F_{t+1} + T_{t+1} \tag{9.5}$$

where:

AF_{t+1} = adjusted forecast for the next period

F_{t+1} = unadjusted forecast for the next period = $\alpha D_t + (1 - \alpha)F_t$

T_{t+1} = trend factor for the next period = $\beta(F_{t+1} - F_t) + (1 - \beta)T_t$ (9.6)

T_t = trend factor for the current period

β = smoothing constant for the trend adjustment factor

To illustrate the adjusted exponential smoothing model, consider the demand time series shown in Table 9.6. Using an α value of 0.3, the unadjusted exponential smoothing forecast for period 2, F_2, is calculated as follows:

$$F_2 = 0.3*30 + 0.7*27 = 27.9$$

The trend adjustment factor for period 2, T_2, is then calculated as a weighted average of the difference between the last two unadjusted forecasts ($F_2 - F_1$) and the previous trend adjustment factor, T_1. Using a trend smoothing factor of $\beta = 0.6$:

$$T_2 = 0.6*(F_2 - F_1) + 0.4*T_1$$
$$= 0.6*(27.9 - 27) + 0.4*0 = 0.54$$

And adding F_2 and T_2 gives us the adjusted forecast for period 2:

$$AF_2 = 27.9 + 0.54 = 28.44$$

As can be seen from the results in Table 9.6 and Figure 9.10, the adjusted exponential smoothing model does a better job of picking up on the upward trend in the data than does the unadjusted model. The same would be true if there was a downward trend.

Linear regression
A statistical technique that expresses a forecast variable as a linear function of some independent variable. Linear regression can be used to develop both time series and causal forecasting models.

Linear Regression

An approach to forecasting when there is a trend in the data is linear regression. **Linear regression** is a statistical technique that expresses the forecast variable as a linear function of some independent variable. In the case of a time series model, the independent variable is the time period itself.

TABLE 9.6
Adjusted Exponential Smoothing Forecast for a Time Series
($\alpha = 0.3$, $\beta = 0.6$)

PERIOD	DEMAND	UNADJUSTED FORECAST F_t	TREND T_t	ADJUSTED FORECAST AF_t
1	30	27*	0	
2	34	27.90	0.54	28.44
3	37	29.73	1.31	31.04
4	40	31.91	1.83	33.75
5	44	34.34	2.19	36.53
6	48	37.24	2.62	39.85
7	51	40.47	2.98	43.45
8	55	43.63	3.09	46.72
9	58	47.04	3.28	50.32
10	62	50.33	3.29	53.61
11	65	53.83	3.42	57.24
12	66	57.18	3.38	60.56
13	67	59.83	2.94	62.76
14	66	61.98	2.47	64.44
15	67	63.18	1.71	64.90
16	65	64.33	1.37	65.70
17	66	64.53	0.67	65.20
18	67	64.97	0.53	65.50
19	67	65.58	0.58	66.16
20	66	66.01	0.49	66.50

*To start the process, F_1 was set equal to 27.

FIGURE 9.10
Comparing Exponential Smoothing (F_t) and Adjusted Exponential Smoothing (AF_t) Forecasts for a Time Series with a Trend

Linear regression works by using past data to estimate the intercept term and slope coefficient for the following line:

$$\hat{y} = \hat{a} + \hat{b}x \qquad (9.7)$$

where:

$\hat{y}$ = forecast for *dependent* variable y
x = *independent* variable x, used to forecast y
$\hat{a}$ = estimated intercept term for the line
$\hat{b}$ = estimated slope coefficient for the line

$\hat{a}$ and $\hat{b}$ are estimated using the raw time series data for variable y (the *dependent* variable) and variable x (the *independent* variable):

$$\hat{b} = \frac{\sum_{i=1}^{n} x_i y_i - \frac{\left[\sum_{i=1}^{n} x_i\right]\left[\sum_{i=1}^{n} y_i\right]}{n}}{\sum_{i=1}^{n} x_i^2 - \frac{\left[\sum_{i=1}^{n} x_i\right]^2}{n}} \qquad (9.8)$$

and:

$$\hat{a} = \bar{y} - \hat{b}\bar{x} \qquad (9.9)$$

where:

(x_i, y_i) = matched pairs of observed (x, y) values
$\bar{y}$ = average y value
$\bar{x}$ = average x value
n = number of paired observations

Once the line in Equation (9.7) has been estimated, the forecaster can then plug in values for x, the independent variable, to generate the forecast values, $\hat{y}$.

EXAMPLE 9.3

Clem's Competition Clutches

Mike Clem, owner of Clem's Competition Clutches, designs and manufactures heavy-duty car clutches for use in drag racing. In his first 10 months of business, Mike has experienced the demand shown in Table 9.7 and Figure 9.11.

TABLE 9.7 Ten-Month Time Series of Demand for Clem's Competition Clutches

MONTH (x)	DEMAND (y)
1	8
2	12
3	25
4	40
5	50
6	65
7	36
8	61
9	88
10	63

FIGURE 9.11 Ten-Month Time Series of Demand for Clem's Competition Clutches

Using the month as the independent variable (x) to forecast demand (y), Mike wants to develop a linear regression forecasting model and use the model to forecast demand for months 11, 12, and 13. Following Equations (9.8) and (9.9), the first step is to set up columns to calculate the average x and y values, as well as the sums of the x, y, x^2, and xy values for the first 10 months:

	MONTH x	DEMAND y	x^2	xy
	1	8	1	8
	2	12	4	24
	3	25	9	75
	4	40	16	160
	5	50	25	250
	6	65	36	390
	7	36	49	252
	8	61	64	488
	9	88	81	792
	10	63	100	630
Sum:	55	448	385	3,069
Average:	5.50	44.80		

Plugging these values into the equations gives the estimate of the slope coefficient, $\hat{b}$:

$$\hat{b} = \frac{3{,}069 - \dfrac{55*448}{10}}{385 - \dfrac{55^2}{10}} = \frac{3{,}069 - 2{,}464}{385 - 302.5} = 7.33$$

and the intercept term, $\hat{a}$:

$$\hat{a} = \bar{y} - \hat{b}\bar{x} = 44.80 - 7.33*5.50 = 4.49$$

The resulting regression line is:

$$\hat{y} = 4.49 + 7.33x$$

By plugging in 11, 12, and 13 for x, we can generate forecasts for months 11, 12, and 13:

Month 11 forecast: $4.49 + 7.33*11 = 85.12$ clutches
Month 12 forecast: $4.49 + 7.33*12 = 92.45$ clutches
Month 13 forecast: $4.49 + 7.33*13 = 99.78$ clutches

Figure 9.12 plots the regression line forecasts for months 1 through 13 and the first 10 months of demand. The graph shows how the regression line captures the upward trend in the data and projects it out into the future. Of course, these future forecasts are good only as long as the upward trend of around 7.33 additional sales each month continues.

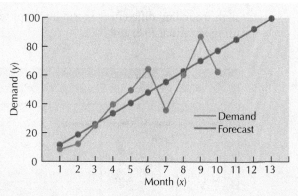

FIGURE 9.12 Regression Forecast for Clem's Competition Clutches

One of the data analysis tools available in Microsoft Excel is regression analysis. Figure 9.13 shows the demand data for Clem's Competition Clutches, as well as the dialog box for Excel's regression feature.

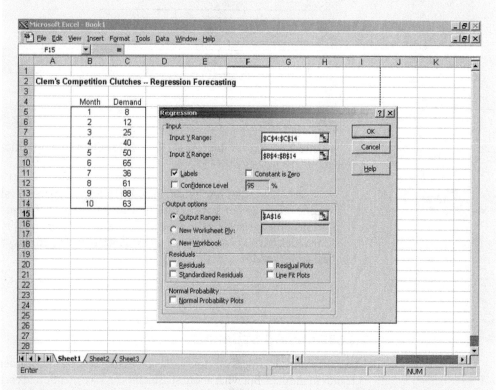

FIGURE 9.13 Using Excel's Regression Function for Clem's Competition Clutches
Microsoft Excel, Microsoft Corporation

The "Input $\underline{Y}$ Range" box shows where the y values for the model are located, and "Input $\underline{X}$ Range" identifies the location of the x values. Also note that we have selected the "Labels" box, indicating that the first cell in each range contains an identifying label. Finally, we have instructed Excel to print out the results of the regression starting in cell A16.

After filling out the appropriate boxes and clicking "OK" in the regression dialog box, we get the results shown in Figure 9.14. The "Coefficients" column contains the estimated value for the intercept term, as well as the slope coefficient associated with our independent variable, "Month." These values are 4.467 and 7.333, respectively. Except for some slight rounding differences in the intercept term, these are the same as those generated using Equations (9.8) and (9.9).

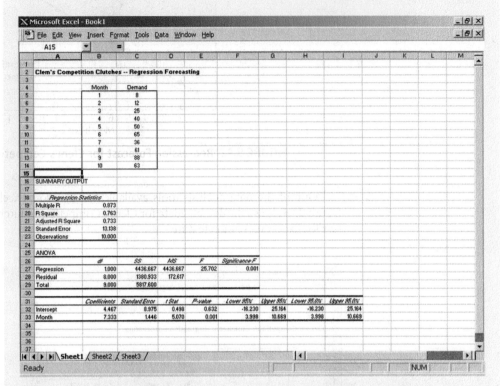

FIGURE 9.14 Excel's Regression Results for Clem's Competition Clutches
Microsoft Excel, Microsoft Corporation

Excel's regression results also include the R^2 ("R-squared") value for the model, as well as some other tests of statistical significance for the coefficients. R^2 indicates what proportion of the variance in the dependent y variable ("Demand") is explained by the regression model. In this case, 76.3% of the variance is explained, suggesting that the model fits the data very well.

Seasonal Adjustments

We have already described time series modeling approaches for dealing with randomness and trends in the data. But what about seasonality? As we mentioned earlier, seasonality is a repeated pattern of spikes or drops in a time series associated with certain times of the year. Many products and services have seasonal demand patterns (as well as seasonal supply and price patterns). Table 9.8 lists just a few examples of products or services that demonstrate seasonality.

TABLE 9.8
Examples of Products and Services That Experience Seasonality

PRODUCT OR SERVICE	PEAK SEASON(S)
Gasoline	Summer months, as more people are traveling
Caribbean cruises	Winter months
Cub Scout uniforms	Fall, as new scouts are joining up
Emergency medical care	Summer months, as more people are involved in outdoor activities
Fruitcake	November and December holiday season, after which *no one* buys it (or eats it)

When there is seasonality in the demand pattern, we have to have some way to adjust our forecast numbers to account for this effect. A simple four-step procedure for developing seasonal adjustments is as follows:

1. For each of the demand values in the time series, calculate the corresponding forecast, using the unadjusted forecast model.

2. For each demand value, calculate $\dfrac{\text{Demand}}{\text{Forecast}}$. If the ratio is less than 1, then the forecast model overforecasted; if it is greater than 1, then the model underforecasted.

3. If the time series covers multiple years, take the average $\dfrac{\text{Demand}}{\text{Forecast}}$ for corresponding months or quarters to derive the seasonal index. Otherwise, use $\dfrac{\text{Demand}}{\text{Forecast}}$ calculated in step 2 as the seasonal index.

4. Multiply the unadjusted forecast by the seasonal index to get the seasonally adjusted forecast value.

EXAMPLE 9.4
Linear Regression with Seasonal Adjustments

In this example, we develop a linear regression forecasting model using the following time series data. Based on the results of the regression model, we then develop a seasonal index for each month and reforecast months 1 through 24 (January 2019–December 2020), using the seasonal indices.

MONTH	DEMAND	MONTH	DEMAND
January 2019	51	January 2020	112
February	67	February	137
March	65	March	191
April	129	April	250
May	225	May	416
June	272	June	487
July	238	July	421
August	172	August	285
September	143	September	235
October	131	October	222
November	125	November	192
December	103	December	165

The time series and the corresponding regression forecasts for the first 24 months are shown in Figure 9.15.

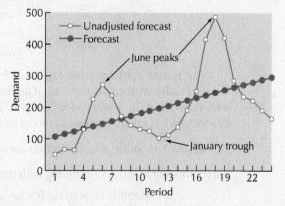

FIGURE 9.15 Plot of Unadjusted Regression Forecast against a Time Series with Seasonality

Notice that the forecast errors (actual demand − unadjusted regression forecast) are all over the place, ranging from −131 to 240.3. The magnitude of these forecast errors implies that the model is only marginally effective.

REGRESSION FORECAST MODEL

Forecasted demand $= 98.71 + 8.22 \times$ period

MONTH	PERIOD	DEMAND	UNADJUSTED REGRESSION FORECAST	FORECAST ERROR
January 2019	1	51	106.9	−55.9
February	2	67	115.2	−48.2
March	3	65	123.4	−58.4
April	4	129	131.6	−2.6
May	5	225	139.8	85.2
June	6	272	148.0	124.0
July	7	238	156.3	81.8
August	8	172	164.5	7.5
September	9	143	172.7	−29.7
October	10	131	180.9	−49.9
November	11	125	189.1	−64.1
December	12	103	197.4	−94.4
January 2020	13	112	205.6	−93.6
February	14	137	213.8	−76.8
March	15	191	222.0	−31.0
April	16	250	230.2	19.8
May	17	416	238.5	177.6
June	18	487	246.7	240.3
July	19	421	254.9	166.1
August	20	285	263.1	21.9
September	21	235	271.3	−36.3
October	22	222	279.6	−57.6
November	23	192	287.8	−95.8
December	24	165	296.0	−131.0

In fact, when the unadjusted regression forecasts are plotted against the actual demand values, it becomes clear that the regression model has picked up on the trend in the data but not the seasonality (Figure 9.15). The result is large positive forecast errors in the summer months and large negative forecast errors in the winter months.

In step 2, $\dfrac{\text{Demand}}{\text{Forecast}}$ is calculated for each of the time periods. For the two January observations, the calculations are:

$$\text{January 2019:} \frac{\text{Demand}}{\text{Forecast}} = \frac{51}{106.9} = 0.477$$

$$\text{January 2020:} \frac{\text{Demand}}{\text{Forecast}} = \frac{112}{205.6} = 0.545$$

The results confirm what Figure 9.15 suggests: The unadjusted regression model tends to badly *over*forecast demand in January. In fact, actual January demands were only 48% and 55% of the forecasts for 2019 and 2020, respectively. The effect is just the opposite for June, where the regression model badly *under*forecasts.

In step 3, monthly seasonal indices are calculated by averaging the $\dfrac{\text{Demand}}{\text{Forecast}}$ values for corresponding months. Continuing with the January example:

$$\text{Monthly seasonal index, January} = (0.477 + 0.545)/2 = 0.511$$

Finally, the seasonally adjusted forecasts are calculated as follows:

$$\text{Seasonally adjusted forecast} = \text{unadjusted forecast} \times \text{seasonal index}$$

$$\text{January 2019: } 106.9 \times 0.511 = 54.63$$

$$\text{January 2020: } 205.6 \times 0.511 = 105.06$$

Regression forecast model:

Forecasted demand = 98.71 + 8.22 × period

The adjusted forecast is calculated by multiplying the unadjusted forecast by the seasonal index. For January 2019: 106.9 × 0.511 = 54.6.

Month	Period	Demand	Unadjusted Regression Forecast	Demand/ Forecast		Monthly Seasonal Index	Adjusted Regression Forecast	New Forecast Error
January 2019	1	51	106.9	0.477		0.511	54.6	−3.6
February	2	67	115.2	0.582		0.611	70.4	−3.4
March	3	65	123.4	0.527		0.694	85.6	−20.6
April	4	129	131.6	0.980		1.033	135.9	−6.9
May	5	225	139.8	1.609		1.677	234.5	−9.5
June	6	272	148.0	1.837		1.906	282.1	−10.1
July	7	238	156.3	1.523	The percentages	1.587	248.0	−10.0
August	8	172	164.5	1.046	for January 2019	1.064	175.1	−3.1
September	9	143	172.7	0.828	and 2020 are	0.847	146.3	−3.3
October	10	131	180.9	0.724	averaged to	0.759	137.3	−6.3
November	11	125	189.1	0.661	develop the	0.664	125.6	−0.6
December	12	103	197.4	0.522	monthly seasonal	0.540	106.5	−3.5
January 2020	13	112	205.6	0.545	index for January.	0.511	105.0	7.0
February	14	137	213.8	0.641	The procedure	0.611	130.7	6.3
March	15	191	222.0	0.860	follows the same	0.694	154.0	37.0
April	16	250	230.2	1.086	pattern for other	1.033	237.8	12.2
May	17	416	238.5	1.745	months.	1.677	399.9	16.1
June	18	487	246.7	1.974		1.906	470.1	16.9
July	19	421	254.9	1.652		1.587	404.6	16.4
August	20	285	263.1	1.083		1.064	280.1	4.9
September	21	235	271.3	0.866		0.847	229.8	5.2
October	22	222	279.6	0.794		0.759	212.2	9.8
November	23	192	287.8	0.667		0.664	191.1	0.9
December	24	165	296.0	0.557		0.540	159.7	5.3

TABLE 9.9 Adjusted Regression Forecast for a Time Series with Seasonality

MyLab Operations Management
Animation

Table 9.9 shows the complete set of results for this problem. Note that the monthly seasonal indices in 2019 are repeated in 2020. In addition, notice how the new forecast errors (demand − adjusted regression forecast) are much smaller than before. In fact, if we plot actual demand against the adjusted forecast values, we can see how well the new forecast model fits the past data (Figure 9.16).

FIGURE 9.16 Plot of Seasonally Adjusted Regression Forecast against a Time Series Showing Seasonality

9.6 CAUSAL FORECASTING MODELS

Causal forecasting model
A class of quantitative forecasting models in which the forecast is modeled as a function of something other than time.

So far, the forecasting models we have dealt with treat the variable of interest as a function of time. In many cases, however, changes in the variable we want to forecast—demand, price, supply, etc.—are caused by something *other* than time. Under these conditions, **causal forecasting models** should be used. Consider the following examples:

VARIABLE	CAUSE OF CHANGE
Dollars spent on drought relief	Rainfall levels
Mortgage refinancing applications	Interest rates
Amount of food eaten at a party	Number and size of guests

Notice that in all three cases, what happened in the recent past is not necessarily a good predictor of what will happen in the future. If rainfall next year is unusually low, then dollars spent on drought relief will increase even if the past few years saw little money spent on drought relief. Similarly, a caterer would be unwise to bring only 10 pounds of barbecue to a party with 50 guests just because the same amount was plenty for yesterday's party of 17 people.

Linear Regression

Linear regression can be used to develop causal forecasting models as well as time series forecasting models. The only difference is that the independent variable, *x*, is no longer a time period but some other variable. Aside from that, the calculations are the same as before (Equations [9.7] through [9.9]).

EXAMPLE 9.5

SunRay Builders

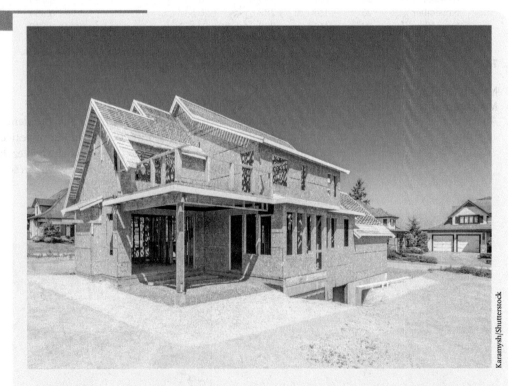

Karamysh/Shutterstock

SunRay Builders is a large, multistate home builder serving the southwestern United States. Table 9.10 shows the quarterly home sales and corresponding mortgage rates for the past four years. The president of SunRay Builders has asked you to develop a forecasting model that predicts the number of home sales based on the mortgage rate. He would then like you to forecast quarterly home sales when mortgage rates are 6% and 8%.

TABLE 9.10 Quarterly Home Sales and Mortgage Rate Values

QUARTER	30-YEAR MORTGAGE RATE	HOME SALES
1	7.5%	750
2	7.0%	790
3	6.0%	860
4	6.5%	870
5	7.0%	840
6	7.0%	830
7	8.0%	710
8	8.5%	650
9	9.0%	600
10	8.5%	640
11	8.0%	680
12	8.0%	690
13	6.0%	880
14	7.0%	800
15	6.5%	850
16	7.5%	750

Before applying a forecasting technique, let's look at why a causal forecasting model is well suited here. Figure 9.17 shows the time series for home sales. Note that there appears to be no clear relationship between the time period and home sales. We could try fitting one of the time series models to these data, but the apparent randomness in the data would probably result in a weak model.

FIGURE 9.17 Plot Showing Weak Relationship between Home Sales and Quarter

Now look at Figure 9.18, which plots mortgage rates against home sales. (Note that this is *not* a time series because the data are *not* arranged in chronological order.) Figure 9.18 shows a strong *negative* relationship between mortgage rates and home sales. Mortgage rates therefore look like an ideal variable for predicting home sales.

FIGURE 9.18 Plot Showing Strong Relationship between Home Sales and Mortgage Rates

To develop a regression forecasting model using mortgage rates as the independent variable, x, we follow the same procedures outlined earlier. Using Equations (9.8) and (9.9), we first set up columns to calculate the average x and y values, as well as the sums of the x, y, x^2, and xy values for the 16 pairs of observations:

30-YEAR MORTGAGE RATE, x	HOME SALES, y	x^2	xy
0.075	750	0.005625	56.25
0.070	790	0.004900	55.3
0.060	860	0.003600	51.6
0.065	870	0.004225	56.55
0.070	840	0.004900	58.8
0.070	830	0.004900	58.1
0.080	710	0.006400	56.8
0.085	650	0.007225	55.25
0.090	600	0.008100	54
0.085	640	0.007225	54.4
0.080	680	0.006400	54.4
0.080	690	0.006400	55.2
0.060	880	0.003600	52.8
0.070	800	0.004900	56
0.065	850	0.004225	55.25
0.075	750	0.005625	56.25
Sum: 1.180	12,190	0.088250	886.95
Average: 0.0738	761.875		

Plugging these values into Equation (9.8) gives the estimate of the slope coefficient, $\hat{b}$:

$$\hat{b} = \frac{886.95 - \dfrac{1.18*12{,}190}{16}}{0.08825 - \dfrac{1.18^2}{16}} = -9{,}846.94$$

and, from Equation (9.9), the intercept term, $\hat{a}$

$$\hat{a} = \bar{y} - \hat{b}\bar{x} = 761.875 + 9{,}846.94*.0738 = 1{,}488.58$$

The resulting regression model is:

Forecasted home sales $= 1{,}488.58 - 9{,}846.94(\text{mortgage rate}\%)$

Using the regression model to forecast home sales at 6% and 8% gives us the following results:

Forecasted home sales at 6% mortage rate: $1{,}488.58 - 9{,}846(6\%) = 898$ home sales
Forecasted home sales at 8% mortage rate: $1{,}488.58 - 9{,}846(8\%) = 701$ home sales

The results make intuitive sense: As mortgage rates rise, homes become less affordable, and the number of home sales should go down.

Multiple Regression

In some cases, there may be more than one causal variable. The amount of barbecue eaten at a party may be a function of not only the number of guests but also the average size of the guests. (After all, 20 football players will probably eat more than 20 normal-sized people.) In such cases, we can use a generalized form of linear regression that allows for more than one independent variable, called **multiple regression.** The multiple regression forecast model is defined as follows:

Multiple regression
A generalized form of linear regression that allows for more than one independent variable.

$$\hat{y} = \hat{a} + \sum_{i=1}^{k} \hat{b}_i x_i \qquad \textbf{(9.10)}$$

where:

$\hat{y} = $ forecast for *dependent* variable y
$k = $ number of independent variables
$x_i = $ ith *independent* variable, where $i = 1 \ldots k$
$\hat{a} = $ estimated intercept term for the line
$\hat{b}_i = $ estimated slope coefficient associated with variable x_i

The formulas for calculating $\hat{a}$ and $\hat{b}_i$ in a multiple regression setting are far too cumbersome to do by hand. Fortunately, many software packages, such as Excel's regression function, can easily handle multiple independent variables. Example 9.6 illustrates how Excel can be used to develop a multiple regression forecasting model.

EXAMPLE 9.6

Lance's BBQ Catering Service

Lance's BBQ Catering Service is a favorite of sports teams in the Raleigh, North Carolina, area. By counting and surreptitiously weighing each guest as he or she arrived at the party, Lance's BBQ Catering Service was able to capture the amount of barbecue eaten, the number of guests, and the average weight of each guest for 15 recent parties:

BARBECUE EATEN (LB.)	NUMBER OF GUESTS	AVERAGE WEIGHT (LB.)
46.00	50	150
40.00	20	175
60.00	30	250
45.00	25	200
44.00	40	150
42.50	15	200
58.50	25	250
43.00	30	175
43.50	15	200
36.00	10	150
49.00	80	250
63.00	70	200
39.00	20	175
46.00	60	150
65.00	40	250

Lance has a party coming up for members of the North Carolina State football team. He expects around 60 guests, with each having an average weight of around 240 pounds. Lance wants to use multiple regression to estimate how much barbecue these guests will eat, based on number of guests and average weight.

Figure 9.19 shows the Excel spreadsheet containing the historical demand data and independent variables, as well as the regression dialog box. In this example, the independent *x* variables are found in two columns, C and D ("$C$4:$D$19"), and we have chosen to print the regression results on this worksheet starting in cell A21.

The multiple regression results are shown in Figure 9.20. (We have scrolled down the spreadsheet to show the entire set of results.)

The R^2 value for the model is 0.63, indicating that the model explains 63% of the variance in the dependent variable. The model parameters are:

$$\text{Intercept term} = 12.52$$
$$\text{Slope coefficient for number of guests} = 0.15$$
$$\text{Slope coefficient for average weight} = 0.15$$

Therefore, Lance's forecasting model would be:

$$\text{Barbecue eaten(lb.)} = 12.52 + 0.15(\text{no. of guests}) + 0.15(\text{average weight})$$

According to the multiple regression model, then, Lance would expect 60 guests with an average weight of 240 pounds to consume:

$$12.52 + 0.15(60) + 0.15(240) = 57.52 \text{ lb. of barbecue}$$

How much barbecue should Lance bring to the party? If you said *more* than 57.52 pounds, your intuition is correct because 57.52 pounds represents Lance's best estimate

FIGURE 9.19 Multiple Regression Using Excel, Lance's BBQ Catering Service
Microsoft Excel, Microsoft Corporation

of what the guests will eat; the actual amount will probably be higher or lower. To ensure that he doesn't run out of barbecue (and anger an entire football team), Lance should plan on taking more than just 57.52 pounds.

FIGURE 9.20 Multiple Regression Results for Lance's BBQ Catering Service
Microsoft Excel, Microsoft Corporation

9.7 MEASURES OF FORECAST ACCURACY

In this section, we introduce five simple measures of forecast accuracy. These measures are commonly used to assess how well an individual model is performing or to compare multiple forecast models to one another. The five measures are:

$$\text{Forecast error for period } i \, (FE_i) = D_i - F_i \tag{9.11}$$

$$\text{Mean forecast error } (MFE) = \frac{\sum\limits_{i=1}^{n} FE_i}{n} \tag{9.12}$$

$$\text{Mean absolute deviation } (MAD) = \frac{\sum\limits_{i=1}^{n} |FE_i|}{n} \tag{9.13}$$

$$\text{Mean absolute percentage error } (MAPE) = \frac{\sum\limits_{i=1}^{n} 100\% \left| \dfrac{FE_i}{D_i} \right|}{n} \tag{9.14}$$

$$\text{Tracking signal} = \frac{\sum\limits_{i=1}^{n} FE_i}{MAD} \tag{9.15}$$

where:

D_i = Demand for time period i

F_i = Forecast for time period i

$\sum\limits_{i=1}^{n} FE_i$ = sum of the forecast errors for periods 1 through n

MFE measures the bias of a forecast model, or the propensity of a model to under- or over-forecast. A completely unbiased model would have an MFE of 0. A model with a negative MFE suggests that, on average, the model overforecasts, while a positive MFE suggests that the model underforecasts.

By taking the average of the absolute value of the forecast errors, MAD tracks the average *size* of the errors, regardless of direction. From the perspective of MAD, overforecasting or underforecasting by some value—say, 10—has the same impact. MAD will always be ≥ 0, with the ideal model having a MAD value of 0. We need to know MAD as well as MFE because a model could have, *on average*, forecast errors of 0 but still make large errors in over- and underforecasting.

MAPE is similar to MAD in that it considers the absolute value of the forecast errors. By dividing the absolute forecast error in each period by the actual period demand, MAPE also gives us an indication of the *magnitude* of the errors.

Finally, the tracking signal is used to flag a forecasting model that is getting out of control. In general, as long as the tracking signal value remains between −4 and 4, the forecasting model is considered to be performing normally. If, however, the tracking signal falls outside this range, the computer program or person responsible for the forecast will typically try to identify a better-fitting model or at least bring the poor performance of the model to the users' attention.

EXAMPLE 9.7	
Walk-In Advising at Wolf State University	Andi Irby, director of advising at Wolf State University, is trying to decide which of two forecasting models does a better job at predicting walk-in demand for student advising. Once she has selected a model, she would like to establish a tracking signal for it. Suppose Andi has demand and forecast information for the past 10 weeks, as shown in Table 9.11.

TABLE 9.11 Forecast Results for Walk-In Advising at Wolf State University

WEEK	ACTUAL WALK-IN DEMAND	FORECAST MODEL 1	FORECAST MODEL 2
1	**18**	20	21
2	**14**	18	21
3	**21**	19	21
4	**26**	21	25
5	**26**	23	25
6	**29**	24	25
7	**19**	25	19
8	**19**	22	19
9	**25**	23	19
10	**15**	24	19

For each model, Andi first calculates the forecast error for each week, as well as the absolute deviation of the forecast error (AD) and absolute percentage error (APE). Finally, she calculates the mean values for the relevant columns by summing up the values and dividing by the number of observations (10 weeks):

WEEK	ACTUAL WALK-IN DEMAND	FORECAST MODEL 1	FORECAST ERROR	ABSOLUTE DEVIATION	ABSOLUTE PERCENTAGE ERROR	FORECAST MODEL 2	FORECAST ERROR	ABSOLUTE DEVIATION	ABSOLUTE PERCENTAGE ERROR
1	**18**	20	−2	2	11.11%	21	−3	3	16.67%
2	**14**	18	−4	4	28.57%	21	−7	7	50.00%
3	**21**	19	2	2	9.52%	21	0	0	0.00%
4	**26**	21	5	5	19.23%	25	1	1	3.85%
5	**26**	23	3	3	11.54%	25	1	1	3.85%
6	**29**	24	5	5	17.24%	25	4	4	13.79%
7	**19**	25	−6	6	31.58%	19	0	0	0.00%
8	**19**	22	−3	3	15.79%	19	0	0	0.00%
9	**25**	23	2	2	8.00%	19	6	6	24.00%
10	**15**	24	−9	9	60.00%	19	−4	4	26.67%
		Mean values:	−0.70	4.10	21.26%		−0.20	2.60	13.88%

Because model 2 has the *MFE* value closest to 0, it appears to be the least biased. On average, model 2 overforecasted by 0.20 walk-ins, while model 1 overforecasted by 0.70. In addition, model 2 has the lowest *MAD* and *MAPE* values. Based on these results, model 2 appears to be the superior forecasting model.

Finally, for model 2, Andi develops a tracking signal for the first 10 weeks. For each week, she takes the most recent sum of forecast errors and divides it by the most recent estimate of MAD. The most recent sum of forecast errors is often called the *running sum of forecast errors* to emphasize the fact that it is updated each period. The results are as follows:

WEEK	ACTUAL WALK-IN DEMAND	FORECAST MODEL 2	FORECAST ERROR	ABSOLUTE DEVIATION	RUNNING SUM OF FORECAST ERRORS	MAD	TRACKING SIGNAL
1	18	21	−3	3	−3	3.00	−1.00
2	14	21	−7	7	−10	5.00	−2.00
3	21	21	0	0	−10	3.33	−3.00
				1			
4	26	25	1		−9	2.75	−3.27
5	26	25	1	1	−8	2.40	−3.33
6	29	25	4	4	−4	2.67	−1.50
7	19	19	0	0	−4	2.29	−1.75
8	19	19	0	0	−4	2.00	−2.00
9	25	19	6	6	2	2.44	0.82
10	15	19	−4	4	−2	2.60	0.77

Although the tracking signal for model 2 gets dangerously close to −4.0 in week 5, the model has since recovered, with a tracking signal after week 10 of −0.77. For future weeks, Andi will continue to update the tracking signal, making sure it doesn't get too high or low.

9.8 COMPUTER-BASED FORECASTING PACKAGES

While the logic behind the various quantitative forecasting models is straightforward, the amount of data that needs to be tracked, as well as the number of calculations, can grow quickly for realistic business situations. Imagine a large retailer that needs to forecast next month's demand for hundreds of thousands of different items, and you can see why developing forecasts by hand is not practical.

Companies use computer-based forecasting packages to develop, evaluate, and even change forecasting models as needed. With enough demand history (i.e., time series data), a computer-based forecasting package could quickly evaluate alternative forecasting methods for each item and select the model that best fits the past data. Furthermore, such packages can use MFE, MAD, MAPE, or tracking signal criteria to flag a poor forecasting model and *automatically* kick off a search for a better one. Many companies also use forecasting packages to develop *multiple* forecasts for a single item. These multiple forecasts can then be compared to one another or even combined to come up with a single forecast.

9.9 COLLABORATIVE PLANNING, FORECASTING, AND REPLENISHMENT (CPFR)

Throughout this book, we have made a point of highlighting ways in which practitioners implement the various concepts and tools. For example, in Chapter 4 we discussed the Six Sigma processes for improving existing processes. In Chapter 4, we also described the Supply Chain Operations Reference (SCOR) model, which outlines the core management processes and individual process types that, together, define the domain of supply chain management. In Chapter 14 , we point to the *Project Management Body of Knowledge* (PMBOK Guide). This guide, published by the Project Management Institute, serves as a basic reference source for project management.

Collaborative planning, forecasting, and replenishment (CPFR)

A set of business processes, backed up by information technology, in which supply chain partners agree to *mutual* business objectives and measures, develop *joint* sales and operational plans, and *collaborate* to generate and update sales forecasts and replenishment plans.

We have incorporated these discussions to emphasize a point: Operations and supply chain management is a *practice*, and companies really do use the concepts and tools presented here. It is in this spirit that we introduce **collaborative planning, forecasting, and replenishment (CPFR)**. CPFR is a set of business processes, backed up by information technology, in which supply chain partners agree to *mutual* business objectives and measures, develop *joint* sales and operational plans, and *collaborate* to generate and update sales forecasts and replenishment plans. What distinguishes CPFR from traditional planning and forecasting approaches is the emphasis on *collaboration*. Experience shows that supply chains are better at meeting demand and managing resources when the partners synchronize their plans and actions. The increased communication among partners means that when demand, promotions, or policies change, managers can adjust jointly managed forecasts and plans immediately, minimizing or even eliminating costly after-the-fact corrections. The *Supply Chain Connections* feature highlights how one division at Black & Decker used both organizational and information technology solutions to implement CPFR.

SUPPLY CHAIN CONNECTIONS

BLACK & DECKER HHI PUTS CPFR INTO ACTION

When your biggest customer comes calling with a new requirement, you must race to comply no matter your size or situation in order to maintain the much-coveted collaborative retail relationship. To better support its existing alliances with two superstore retailers—Home Depot and Lowe's—supply chain leaders at Black & Decker Hardware and Home Improvement (HHI) sought one synchronized view of demand throughout its supply chain. Upon project completion, a reformed collaborative planning, forecasting, and replenishment (CPFR) strategy backed by enabling technologies and an aligned business/information systems (IS) team allowed the manufacturer to realize benefits beyond improved collaboration at retail.

A Fixer Upper

Black & Decker HHI is one of three divisions under Black & Decker, the global manufacturer and marketer of quality power tools and accessories, hardware and home improvement products as well as technology-based fastening systems. Black & Decker HHI manufactures and markets architecturally inspired building products for the residential and commercial markets. With manufacturing and distribution facilities in the United States, Canada, Mexico, and Asia, Black & Decker HHI faced the challenge of managing both offshore and domestic supply chains where various products with complex product structures were produced. The complexities were compounded by the demands imparted by Black & Decker HHI's distribution model: "Two of our superstore retailers have high fill rate expectations—greater than 98 percent—and on-time delivery requirements. At the same time, homebuilders require made-to-order configured products within 14 days," explained Scott Strickland, vice

president of information systems, Black & Decker HHI. "Both of these customer group requirements must be balanced against internal inventory investments."

With a large amount of its sales tied to big-box corporations, Black & Decker HHI had dedicated demand forecasting teams in place working exclusively with personnel employed by Home Depot and Lowe's. These planners actually worked in the same cities where their clients were headquartered to enable close cooperation in efforts to maintain supply levels on par with consumer demand. However, with no central planning software in use, CPFR was a labor-intensive process; planners juggled massive amounts of product data downloaded in spreadsheets from retailers and eyeballed historical sales, projecting demand based on judgment analysis of trending and seasonality. Further compounding matters was a third set of planners who managed demand for the thousands of other distributors, retailers, and builders making up the remainder of sales. "In addition, the previous process and solution prevented us from analyzing the impact of a significant demand change in our manufacturing and distribution plan," said Strickland. As a result, the company was experiencing manufacturing overtime, expedited shipments, and flat inventory levels.

Solution Toolkit

In order to obtain full visibility of its supply chain, Black & Decker HHI developed essentially three software implementations, each customized to meet the requirements of the various planning groups yet all with a unified business purpose. Leveraging the process, system, and change management expertise from Plan4Demand, Black & Decker HHI embarked on a three-phased approach that targeted its worst pain point first: supply chain planning.

After holding a functionality and software review, the company chose to implement JDA Demand from JDA Software Group, starting with its manufacturing facilities in Mexico in 2006. The technology was rolled out to its Asian and U.S. facilities shortly thereafter.

The solution was configured to incorporate point-of-sale (POS) data from Home Depot and Lowe's, allowing one single process for its frequent line reviews, product promotions, and introductions as well as frequent price changes. The solution also helps determine the appropriate product mix and gauges the effectiveness of various promotions.

"We can compare forecasts, shipment history as well as POS and order history for any of our SKUs at any given time," said Strickland. "At the end of 2007, this resulted in a 10.4 percent improvement in forecast accuracy."

Next, Black & Decker HHI turned its attention to improving the demand signal by addressing the forecasting process. Implementing JDA Master Planning at the plant level helped to establish operational efficiency, create supply flexibility, and achieve fill rate commitments to customers.

Soon after, JDA Fulfillment was added into the technology mix to completely synchronize supply and demand. This tool leverages forecast and end-consumer demand signals to create an optimized, multi-level replenishment plan down to the store level.

Unlocking the Benefits

With full visibility into its supply chain operations, Black & Decker HHI had built truly collaborative relationships with its retail customers. But the benefits extended inside the organization as well. With process improvements, including transformed sales and operations planning as well as the realignment of the supply chain organization along category lines, Black & Decker HHI realized the following:

- 60 percent reduction in forecast creation cycle time
- 50 percent reduction in supply plan creation time
- 80 percent reduction in monthly production cycles

Source: A. Ackerman and A. Padilla, "Black and Decker HHI Puts CPFR into Action," *Consumer Goods Technology*, October 20, 2009, **https://consumergoods.com/black-decker-hhi-puts-cpfr-action.**

EXAMPLE 9.8

Cheeznax Snack Foods Revisited

We end this chapter by returning to Jamie Favre, the demand manager for Cheeznax Snack Foods. Cheeznax and its primary customer, Gas N' Grub, are interested in coordinating their supply chain activities so that Gas N' Grub stores can be stocked with fresh products at the lowest possible cost to both companies. With this in mind, the two supply chain partners enter into a CPFR arrangement. As part of the arrangement, Gas N' Grub agrees to share with Cheeznax its 2020 plans for promotions and new store openings:

1. Gas N' Grub plans to open 10 new convenience stores each month, starting in *June and ending in September*. This means that by the end of September, Gas N' Grub will have 140 stores.
2. Gas N' Grub will also launch an advertising campaign that is expected to raise sales in all stores by 5%. This advertising campaign will run from *July through September*, at which time store sales are expected to settle back down to previous levels.

Jamie now feels she is ready to start developing the monthly sales forecasts for 2020. As a first step, Jamie plots the 2019 sales data to see if there are discernable patterns. The results are shown in Figure 9.21.

FIGURE 9.21 2019 Sales Data for Cheeznax Snack Foods

Jamie notes that sales appear to show a slight upward trend over the year. Based on this information, Jamie uses Equations (9.8) and (9.9) to fit a regression model to the 2019 data. She chooses monthly total sales as her dependent variable, y, and month (January $= 1$, February $= 2$, etc.) as her independent variable, x. She then calculates the values she needs to plug into the formulas:

MONTH (x)	SALES (y)	x^2	xy
1	230,000	1	230,000
2	230,000	4	460,000
3	240,000	9	720,000
4	250,000	16	1,000,000
5	240,000	25	1,200,000
6	250,000	36	1,500,000
7	270,000	49	1,890,000
8	260,000	64	2,080,000
9	260,000	81	2,340,000
10	260,000	100	2,600,000
11	280,000	121	3,080,000
12	290,000	144	3,480,000
Sum: 78	3,060,000	650	20,580,000
Average: 6.5	255,000		

Next, Jamie uses these values to calculate the slope coefficient, $\hat{b}$:

$$\hat{b} = \frac{\sum_{i=1}^{n} x_i y_i - \frac{\left[\sum_{i=1}^{n} x_i\right]\left[\sum_{i=1}^{n} y_i\right]}{n}}{\sum_{i=1}^{n} x_i^2 - \frac{\left[\sum_{i=1}^{n} x_i\right]^2}{n}} = \frac{\$20,580,000 - \frac{78 \times \$3,060,000}{12}}{650 - \frac{78^2}{12}}$$

$$= \$4,825.17$$

And then the intercept term, $\hat{a}$:

$$\hat{a} = \bar{y} - \hat{b}\bar{x} = \$255,000 - \$4,825.17 \times 6.5 = \$223,636.36$$

These calculations result in the following regression forecasting model:

Forecasted total monthly sales $= \$223,636.36 + \$4,825.17 \times$ period

Jamie compares her model against actual 2019 demand. The results, including *MFE* and *MAPE*, are shown in Table 9.12. While the results seem promising, Jamie still remains cautious: She realizes that fitting a model to past data is *not* the same as forecasting future demand.

But Jamie is not finished. She still needs to do a 2020 forecast that takes into account the 10 stores being added each month from June through September, as well as the advertising campaign that is expected to increase demand by 5% from July through September.

TABLE 9.12 Comparison of Regression Forecast Model to Historical Demand

						ABSOLUTE
Forecasted Total Monthly Sales = $223,636.40 + $4,825.17 × Period						
MONTH	PERIOD	TOTAL SALES	REGRESSION FORECAST	FORECAST ERROR (*FE*)	ABSOLUTE DEVIATION (*AD*)	PERCENTAGE ERROR (*APE*)
January	1	$230,000	$228,462	$1,538	$1,538	0.67%
February	2	$230,000	$233,287	−$3,287	$3,287	1.43%
March	3	$240,000	$238,112	$1,888	$1,888	0.79%
April	4	$250,000	$242,937	$7,063	$7,063	2.83%
May	5	$240,000	$247,762	−$7,762	$7,762	3.23%
June	6	$250,000	$252,587	−$2,587	$2,587	1.03%
July	7	$270,000	$257,413	$12,587	$12,587	4.66%
August	8	$260,000	$262,238	−$2,238	$2,238	0.86%
September	9	$260,000	$267,063	−$7,063	$7,063	2.72%
October	10	$260,000	$271,888	$11,888	$11,888	4.57%
November	11	$280,000	$276,713	$3,287	$3,287	1.17%
December	12	$290,000	$281,538	$8,462	$8,462	2.92%

MFE = $0 *MAD* = $5,804

MAPE = 2.24%

Jamie uses a three-step approach to develop her 2020 forecast. These steps are outlined in Figure 9.22. First, Jamie uses the regression forecast model to develop an initial forecast for January through December 2020 (periods 13–24). Next, Jamie reasons that each new store should generate sales at a level similar to the existing stores. Therefore, if there are 100 stores to start with, adding 10 more stores in June will increase sales by 110/100 = 110% over what the sales would have been otherwise. By the end of the year, there will be 40% more stores than at the beginning of the year. Jamie uses this logic to develop lift factors to account for the new stores. These percentages are shown in the "Increase in Stores" column of Figure 9.22. Similarly, Jamie uses lift factors to reflect the impact of the July–September advertising campaign.

Month	Period	① Forecast, Total Monthly Sale	② Increase in Stores (Base = 100%)	Advertising Campaign Lift (Base = 100%)	③ Adjusted Forecast, Total Monthly Sale
January	13	$286,364	100%	100%	$286,364
February	14	$291,189	100%	100%	$291,189
March	15	$296,014	100%	100%	$296,014
April	16	$300,839	100%	100%	$300,839
May	17	$305,664	100%	100%	$305,664
June	18	$310,489	110%	100%	$341,538
July	19	$315,315	120%	105%	$397,297
August	20	$320,140	130%	105%	$436,991
September	21	$324,965	140%	105%	$477,699
October	22	$329,790	140%	100%	$461,706
November	23	$334,615	140%	100%	$468,461
December	24	$339,440	140%	100%	$475,216

$4,538,978

FIGURE 9.22 Adjusting Cheeznax Forecast to Take into Account Gas N' Grub's Store Openings and Advertising Campaign

In the third and final step, Jamie multiplies the initial monthly forecast by *both* the store and the advertising lift factors to get a final, adjusted forecast. To illustrate, the adjusted forecast for June 2020 is now:

$$(\$310{,}489) \times (110\%) \times (100\%) = \$341{,}538$$

Figure 9.23 plots the adjusted monthly forecasts for 2020. The dashed line shows what the forecasts would be if Jamie did *not* adjust for the store openings and advertising campaign. The impact of the store openings, as well as the advertising campaign, can clearly be seen. Looking at the graph, Jamie realizes that developing this forecast required not just the proper application of quantitative tools but also the sharing of critical information between Cheeznax and its major customer, Gas N' Grub.

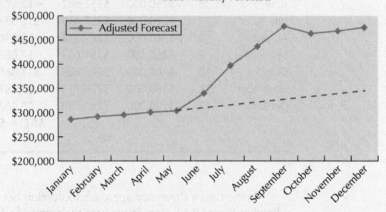

FIGURE 9.23 Cheeznax Adjusted Monthly Sales Forecasts for 2020

CHAPTER SUMMARY

Forecasting is a critical business process for nearly every organization. Whether the organization is forecasting demand, supply, prices, or some other variable, forecasting is often the first step an organization must take in planning future business activities. In this chapter, we described the different types of forecasts companies use and the four laws of forecasting. We also talked about when to use qualitative and quantitative forecasting techniques and explained several approaches to developing time series and causal forecasting models.

Of course, forecasting is not just about the "numbers." As the discussion and CPFR examples illustrate, organizations can collaborate with one another to improve the accuracy of their forecasting efforts or even reduce the need for forecasts.

KEY FORMULAS

Last period forecasting model (page 261):

$$F_{t+1} = D_t \tag{9.1}$$

where:

F_{t+1} = forecast for the next period, $t + 1$

D_t = demand for the current period, t

Moving average forecasting model (page 262):

$$F_{t+1} = \frac{\sum\limits_{i=1}^{n} D_{t+1-i}}{n} \tag{9.2}$$

where:

F_{t+1} = forecast for time period $t + 1$

D_{t+1-i} = actual demand for period $t + 1 - i$

n = number of most recent demand observations used to develop the forecast

Weighted moving average forecasting model (page 264):

$$F_{t+1} = \sum_{i=1}^{n} W_{t+1-i} D_{t+1-i}$$ (9.3)

where:

W_{t+1-i} = weight assigned to the demand in period $t + 1 - i$

$\sum_{i=1}^{n} W_{t+1-i} = 1$

Exponential smoothing forecasting model (page 264):

$$F_{t+1} = \alpha D_t + (1 - \alpha) F_t$$ (9.4)

where:

F_{t+1} = forecast for time period $t + 1$ (i.e., the *new* forecast)

F_t = forecast for time period t (i.e., the *current* forecast)

D_t = actual value for time period t

α = smoothing constant used to weight D_t and $F_t (0 \le \alpha \le 1)$

Adjusted exponential smoothing forecasting model (page 268):

$$AF_{t+1} = F_{t+1} + T_{t+1}$$ (9.5)

where:

AF_{t+1} = adjusted forecast for the next period

F_{t+1} = unadjusted forecast for the next period = $\alpha D_t + (1 - \alpha)F_t$

T_{t+1} = trend factor for the next period = $\beta(F_{t+1} - F_t) + (1 - \beta)T_t$

T_t = trend factor for the current period

β = smoothing constant for the trend adjustment factor (9.6)

Linear regression forecasting model (page 269):

$$\hat{y} = \hat{a} + \hat{b}x$$ (9.7)

where:

$\hat{y}$ = forecast for *dependent* variable y

x = *independent* variable x, used to forecast y

$\hat{a}$ = estimated intercept term for the line

$\hat{b}$ = estimated slope coefficient for the line

Slope coefficient $\hat{b}$ and intercept coefficient $\hat{a}$ for linear regression model (page 269):

$$\hat{b} = \frac{\sum_{i=1}^{n} x_i y_i - \dfrac{\left[\sum_{i=1}^{n} x_i\right]\left[\sum_{i=1}^{n} y_i\right]}{n}}{\sum_{i=1}^{n} x_i^2 - \dfrac{\left[\sum_{i=1}^{n} x_i\right]^2}{n}}$$ (9.8)

and:

$$\hat{a} = \bar{y} - \hat{b}\bar{x}$$ (9.9)

where:

(x_i, y_i) = matched pairs of observed (x, y) values

$\bar{y}$ = average y value

$\bar{x}$ = average x value

n = number of paired observations

Multiple regression forecasting model (page 278):

$$\hat{y} = \hat{a} + \sum_{i=1}^{k} \hat{b}_i x_i$$ (9.10)

where:

$\hat{y}$ = forecast for *dependent* variable y

k = number of independent variables

x_i = the ith *independent* variable, where $i = 1 \ldots k$

$\hat{a}$ = estimated intercept term for the line

$\hat{b}_i$ = estimated slope coefficient associated with variable x_i

Measures of forecast accuracy (page 281):

$$\text{Forecast error for period } i\ (FE_i) = D_i - F_i \tag{9.11}$$

$$\text{Mean forecast error (MFE)} = \frac{\sum_{i=1}^{n} FE_i}{n} \tag{9.12}$$

$$\text{Mean absolute deviation (MAD)} = \frac{\sum_{i=1}^{n} |FE_i|}{n} \tag{9.13}$$

$$\text{Mean absolute percentage error (MAPE)} = \frac{\sum_{i=1}^{n} 100\% \left|\frac{FE_i}{D_i}\right|}{n} \tag{9.14}$$

$$\text{Tracking signal} = \frac{\sum_{i=1}^{n} FE_i}{MAD} \tag{9.15}$$

where:

D_i = Demand for time period i

F_i = Forecast for time period i

$\sum_{i=1}^{n} FE_i$ = sum of the forecast errors for periods 1 through n

KEY TERMS

Adjusted exponential smoothing model   268

Build-up forecast   260

Causal forecasting model   276

Collaborative planning, forecasting, and replenishment (CPFR)   284

Delphi method   259

Exponential smoothing model   264

Forecast   255

Life cycle analogy method   260

Linear regression   268

Market survey   259

Moving average model   262

Multiple regression   278

Panel consensus forecasting   259

Qualitative forecasting techniques   258

Quantitative forecasting models   258

Randomness   261

Seasonality   261

Smoothing model   263

Time series   260

Time series forecasting model   260

Trend   261

Weighted moving average model   264

SOLVED PROBLEM

PROBLEM   *Chris Boote Industries*

Chris Boote Industries makes rebuild kits for old carbureted snowmobiles. (Newer snowmobiles have fuel-injected engines.) The demand values for the kits over the past two years are as follows:

PERIOD		DEMAND
January 2017	1	3,420
February	2	3,660
March	3	1,880
April	4	1,540
May	5	1,060

(Continued)

	PERIOD	DEMAND
June	6	900
July	7	660
August	8	680
September	9	1,250
October	10	1,600
November	11	1,920
December	12	2,400
January 2018	13	2,500
February	14	2,540
March	15	1,300
April	16	1,060
May	17	740
June	18	620
July	19	460
August	20	480
September	21	880
October	22	1,100
November	23	1,340
December	24	1,660

Chris would like to develop a model to forecast demand for the upcoming year.

Solution

As a first attempt, Chris develops a three-period moving average model to forecast periods 19 through 24 and evaluates the results by using *MAD*, *MFE*, and *MAPE*. The three-period moving average forecast for period 19 is calculated as follows:

$$F_{19} = (620 + 740 + 1060)/3 = 806.67 \text{ rebuild kits}$$

The rest of the forecasts are calculated in a similar manner. The results are shown in the following table:

	PERIOD	DEMAND	FORECAST	FORECAST ERROR	ABSOLUTE DEVIATION	ABSOLUTE PERCENTAGE ERROR
April	16	1,060				
May	17	740				
June	18	620				
July	19	460	806.67	−346.67	346.67	75.4%
August	20	480	606.67	−126.67	126.67	26.4%
September	21	880	520	360	360	40.9%
October	22	1,100	606.67	493.33	493.33	44.8%
November	23	1,340	820	520	520	38.8%
December	24	1,660	1,106.67	553.33	553.33	33.3%

Mean forecast error (*MFE*) = 242.22
Mean absolute deviation (*MAD*) = 400.00
Mean absolute percentage error (*MAPE*) = 43.3%

Because of the relatively large *MFE*, *MAD*, and *MAPE* values, Chris decides to try another model: a regression model with seasonal adjustments. To keep it simple, Chris wants to develop seasonal indices for the months of January and June and to forecast demand for January and June 2019.

First, Chris sets up the table to calculate the values that go into Equations (9.8) and (9.9):

PERIOD DEMAND				
	x	y	x^2	$x*y$
January 2017	1	3,420	1	3,420
February	2	3,660	4	7,320
March	3	1,880	9	5,640
April	4	1,540	16	6,160
May	5	1,060	25	5,300
June	6	900	36	5,400
July	7	660	49	4,620
August	8	680	64	5,440
September	9	1,260	81	11,340
October	10	1,600	100	16,000
November	11	1,920	121	21,120
December	12	2,400	144	28,800
January 2018	13	2,500	169	32,500
February	14	2,540	196	35,560
March	15	1,300	225	19,500
April	16	1,060	256	16,960
May	17	740	289	12,580
June	18	620	324	11,160
July	19	460	361	8,740
August	20	480	400	9,600
September	21	880	441	18,480
October	22	1,100	484	24,200
November	23	1,340	529	30,820
December	24	1,660	576	39,840
Sum:	300	35,660	4,900	380,500
Average:	12.50	1,485.83		

By plugging these terms into Equations (9.8) and (9.9), Chris gets:

$$\frac{380,500 - \dfrac{300 \times 35,660}{24}}{4,900 - \dfrac{300^2}{24}} = -56.74$$

$$\hat{a} = \bar{y} - \hat{b}\bar{x} = 1,485.83 + 56.74 \times 12.50 = 2,195.07$$

And Chris gets the resulting forecast model:

$$\text{Demand} = 2,195.07 - 56.74(\text{period})$$

Note that the negative slope coefficient suggests that there is a downward trend in demand. To calculate seasonal indices for January and June, Chris needs to generate the *unadjusted* forecasts for the past two years:

January 2017: $2,195.07 - 56.74(1) = 2,128.33$
January 2018: $2,195.07 - 56.74(13) = 1,457.46$

June 2017: $2,195.07 - 56.74(6) = 1,854.64$
June 2018: $2,195.07 - 56.74(18) = 1,173.77$

He then needs to calculate $\dfrac{\text{Demand}}{\text{Forecast}}$ values, using the unadjusted forecasts:

MONTH	PERIOD	DEMAND	UNADJUSTED FORECAST	DEMAND/ FORECAST
January 2017	1	3,420	2,138.33	1.60
June 2017	6	900	1,854.64	0.49
January 2018	13	2,500	1,457.46	1.72
June 2017	18	620	1,173.77	0.53

Next, Chris calculates the seasonal index for January by taking the average of the $\dfrac{\text{Demand}}{\text{Forecast}}$ ratio for 2017 and 2018:

$$(1.60 + 1.72)/2 = 1.66$$

He follows the same logic for June:

$$(0.49 + 0.53)/2 = 0.51$$

Finally, Chris can calculate the adjusted regression forecasts for January 2019 (period 25) and June 2019 (period 30):

January 2019: $[2,195.07 - 56.74(25)] * 1.66 = 1,289$ rebuild kits
June 2019: $[2,195.07 - 56.74(30)] * 0.51 = 251$ rebuild kits

An interesting thing to note is that eventually the forecast model will result in negative forecasts as the period count grows higher. In reality, demand will probably level off at some low level.

DISCUSSION QUESTIONS

1. Which forecasting techniques do you think should be used in calculating fuel prices? Time series models? Causal models? Qualitative models? In causal modeling, what types of independent variables might be used? Justify your answer.
2. Are time series forecast techniques such as moving average and exponential smoothing models well suited to developing forecasts for multiple periods into the future? Why or why not?
3. What are the advantages of having computer-based forecasting packages handle the forecasting effort for a business? What are the pitfalls?
4. Explain the differences in using linear regression to develop a time series forecasting model and a causal forecasting model.
5. If forecasting is so important, why do firms look to approaches such as CPFR as a way to reduce the need for forecasting?

PROBLEMS

Additional homework problems are available at www.pearsonhighered.com/bozarth. These problems use Excel to generate customized problems for different class sections or even different students.

(* = easy; ** = moderate; *** = advanced)

Problems for Section 9.5: Time Series Forecasting Models—Basic Problems

For problems 1 through 3, use the following time series data:

PERIOD	DEMAND
10	248
11	370
12	424
13	286
14	444

1. (*) Develop a three-period moving average forecast for *periods 13–15*.
2. (*) Develop a two-period weighted moving average forecast for *periods 12 through 15*. Use weights of 0.7 and 0.3, with the most recent observation weighted higher.
3. (*) Develop an exponential smoothing forecast ($\alpha = 0.25$) for *periods 11 through 15*. Assume that your forecast for period 10 was 252.

For problems 4 through 6, use the following time series data:

MONTH	DEMAND
January 2019	119
February	72
March	113
April	82
May	82
June	131
July	111
August	116
September	89
October	95
November	88
December	90

4. (**) Develop a three-period moving average forecast for *April 2019 through January 2020*. Calculate the *MFE, MAD*, and *MAPE* values for *April through December 2019*.

5. (**) Develop a two-period weighted moving average forecast for *March 2019 through January 2020*. Use weights of 0.6 and 0.4, with the most recent observation weighted higher. Calculate the *MFE, MAD*, and *MAPE* values for *March through December*.

6. (**) Develop an exponential smoothing forecast ($\alpha = 0.3$) for *February 2019 through January 2020*. Assume that your forecast for January 2019 was 100. Calculate the *MFE, MAD*, and *MAPE* values for *February through December 2020*.

For problems 7 through 9, use the following time series data:

PERIOD	DEMAND
1	221
2	247
3	228
4	233
5	240
6	152
7	163
8	155
9	167
10	158

7. (*) Develop a last period forecast for *periods 2 through 11*. Calculate the *MFE, MAD*, and *MAPE* values for *periods 2 through 10*. Is this a good model? Why?

8. (**) Develop a three-period weighted moving average forecast for *periods 4 through 11*. Use weights of 0.4, 0.35, and 0.3, with the most recent observation weighted the highest. Calculate the *MFE, MAD*, and *MAPE* values for *periods 4 through 10*. How do your results compare with those for problem 7?

9. (**) Develop *two* exponential smoothing forecasts for *periods 2 through 11*. For the first forecast, use $\alpha = 0.2$. For the second, use $\alpha = 0.7$. Assume that your forecast for period 1 was 250. Plot the results. Which model appears to work better? Why?

10. After graduating from college, you and your friends start selling birdhouses made from recycled plastic. The idea has caught on, as shown by the following sales figures:

MONTH	DEMAND
March	220
April	2,240
May	1,790
June	4,270
July	3,530
August	4,990

a. (*) Prepare forecasts for *June through September* by using a three-period moving average model.

b. (**) Prepare forecasts for *June through September* by using an exponential smoothing model with $\alpha = 0.5$. Assume that the forecast for May was 2,000.

c. (**) Prepare forecasts for *June through September* by using an adjusted exponential smoothing model with $\alpha = 0.5$ and $\beta = 0.3$. Assume that the unadjusted forecast (F_t) for May was 2,000 and the trend factor (T_t) for May was 700.

11. (***) Consider the time series data shown in Table 9.1. Use an adjusted exponential smoothing model to develop a forecast for the 12 months of 2019. (Assume that the unadjusted forecast and trend factor for January are 220,000 and 10,000, respectively.) How do your results compare to the regression model results shown in Table 9.12?

Cooper Toys sells a portable baby stroller called the Tot n' Trot. The past two years of demand for Tot n' Trots are shown in the following table. Use this information for problems 12 and 13.

	PERIOD	DEMAND
January 2018	1	1,200
February	2	1,400
March	3	1,450
April	4	1,580
May	5	1,796
June	6	2,102
July	7	2,152
August	8	2,022
September	9	1,888
October	10	1,938
November	11	1,988
December	12	1,839
January 2019	13	1,684
February	14	1,944
March	15	1,994
April	16	2,154
May	17	2,430
June	18	2,827
July	19	2,877
August	20	2,687
September	21	2,492
October	22	2,542
November	23	2,592
December	24	2,382

12. (***) (*Microsoft Excel problem*) Prepare forecasts for *February 2018 through 2020* for Cooper Toys, using an adjusted exponential smoothing model with $\alpha = 0.25$ and $\beta = 0.4$. Assume that the initial unadjusted forecast (F_1) for January 2018 was 1,100 and the trend factor (T_1) was 60.

13. (***) (*Microsoft Excel problem*) Using regression analysis, develop a forecasting model with monthly seasonal indices for Cooper Toys. Forecast demand for each of the months in the six-month period covering *January through June 2020*.

14. (***) (*Microsoft Excel problem*) The following figure shows an Excel spreadsheet that calculates a two-period weighted moving average and exponential smoothing model for a set of demand numbers, as well as the resulting *MFE* and *MAD* values. **Re-create this spreadsheet in Excel.** While your formatting does not have to be exactly the same, your answers should be. (*Hint:* Format the cells for the exponential smoothing model to show only two decimal places. Otherwise, the number of decimal places that shows will increase with each new forecast.)

Your spreadsheet should recalculate results whenever any changes are made to the shaded cells. If your logic is correct, changing the initial forecast for the exponential smoothing model to 50 will result in new *MFE* and *MAD* values of 0.76 and 5.62, respectively. Similarly, changing both weights for the two-period model to 0.5 should result in new *MFE* and *MAD* values of −0.077 and 7.692, respectively.

Problems for Section 9.6: Causal Forecasting Models

15. After graduation, you take a position at Top-Slice, a well-known manufacturer of golf balls. One of your duties is to forecast monthly demand for golf balls. Using the following data, you developed a regression model that expresses monthly sales as a function of average temperature for the month:

Monthly sales $= -767.7 + 98.5$ (average temperature)

	MONTHLY SALES	AVERAGE TEMPERATURE
March 2017	4,670	52
April	5,310	58
May	6,320	69
June	7,080	75
July	7,210	83
August	7,040	82
September	6,590	78
October	5,520	65
November	4,640	54
December	4,000	48
January 2018	2,840	41
February	3,170	42

	A	B	C	D	E	F	G	H	I
1	Comparing a Two-Period Moving Average and an Exponential Smoothing Model								
2									
3		Two-period moving average model					Exponential smoothing model		
4		Weight on Period t-2:		0.35			Initial forecast:		65
5		Weight on Period t-1:		0.65			Alpha (a):		0.3
6									
7	Period	Demand	Forecast	Forecast Error	Absolute Deviation		Forecast	Forecast Error	Absolute Deviation
8	1	60					65.00	−5.00	5.00
9	2	53					63.50	−10.50	10.50
10	3	65	55.45	9.55	9.55		60.35	4.65	4.65
11	4	72	60.8	11.2	11.2		61.75	10.26	10.26
12	5	72	66.55	2.45	2.45		64.82	7.18	7.18
13	6	74	72	2	2		66.98	7.02	7.02
14	7	50	73.3	−23.3	23.3		69.08	−19.08	19.08
15	8	60	58.4	1.6	1.6		63.36	−3.36	3.36
16	9	72	56.5	15.5	15.5		62.35	9.65	9.65
17	10	53	67.8	−14.8	14.8		65.25	−12.25	12.25
18	11	56	59.65	−3.65	3.65		61.57	−5.57	5.57
19	12	51	54.95	−3.95	3.95		59.90	−8.90	8.90
20	13	51	52.75	−1.75	1.75		57.23	−6.23	6.23
21	14	54	51	3	3		55.36	−1.36	1.36
22	15	55	52.95	2.05	2.05		54.95	0.05	0.05
23			MFE =	−0.008			MFE =	−1.380	
24			MAD =		7.292		MAD =		7.350

a. (**) Using Equations (9.8) and (9.9) from the text, show how the $\hat{a}$ and $\hat{b}$ values of -767.7 and 98.5 were calculated.
b. (*) Use the regression forecasting model to forecast total golf ball sales for *June and July 2018*. Average temperatures are expected to be 76 degrees in June and 82 degrees in July.
c. (*) Is this regression model a time series or a causal forecasting model? Explain.

16. (**) The following table lists the number of home improvement loans approved by a finance company, along with the loan interest rate:

MONTH	INTEREST RATE	NUMBER OF LOANS
1	7%	20
2	5%	30
3	4%	35
4	8%	18
5	10%	15
6	6%	22
7	11%	15
8	9%	20
9	5%	27
10	12%	10

a. Develop a regression forecast model using the interest rate as the predictor (i.e., independent) variable. Is this a time series or a causal forecasting model? Explain.
b. How many loans should the bank expect to make if the interest rate is 10%? 6.5%? Do these results make sense?

17. (**) While searching through your class notes, you stumble across the following forecasting model:

Demand = (35,000 + 4.8*period) seasonal index

SEASONAL INDICES	
Summer	1.25
Fall	0.90
Winter	0.75
Spring	0.90

Based *only* on this information, answer the following true/false questions. Justify your answers.

a. True or false? The forecast model is a time series model.
b. True or false? The forecast model suggests that the variable being forecasted is experiencing an upward trend in demand.
c. True or false? The variable being forecasted experiences a sharp increase during the summer months, followed by lower levels in the winter months.

18. (**) Suppose you are given the following demand and forecast data for the past four quarters:

QUARTER	DEMAND	FORECAST
Winter	285	250
Spring	315	300
Summer	300	350
Fall	400	400

Develop a seasonal index for each of the quarters. Does the fall quarter really need a seasonal adjustment index? Explain.

19. (***) After developing her 2020 forecast (Example 9.8), Jamie Favre gets a visit from Cheeznax's production manager, Mark Mobley. Mark says, "I think the forecast is fine, but I really need estimates of demand broken out by product type. In other words, how much of each month's demand do we think will consist of cheese balls, cheese nachos, and cheese potato chips?" Jamie goes back to the 2019 sales results and finds the following figures:

MONTH	CHEESE BALLS	CHEESE NACHOS	CHEESE POTATO CHIPS	TOTAL SALES
January	$126,500	$69,000	$34,500	$230,000
February	$119,600	$73,600	$36,800	$230,000
March	$115,200	$81,600	$43,200	$240,000
April	$125,000	$70,000	$55,000	$250,000
May	$112,800	$64,800	$62,400	$240,000
June	$115,000	$75,000	$60,000	$250,000
July	$126,900	$75,600	$67,500	$270,000
August	$124,800	$75,400	$59,800	$260,000
September	$135,200	$83,200	$41,600	$260,000
October	$135,200	$78,000	$46,800	$260,000
November	$151,200	$72,800	$56,000	$280,000
December	$142,100	$98,600	$49,300	$290,000
				$3,060,000

Using this information and the 2020 adjusted forecast results shown in Figure 9.22, develop a forecast for each product in each month of 2020. The sum of the individual product forecasts should equal the monthly total sales forecast. (*Hint:* Use the 2019 figures to estimate what percentage of demand is accounted for by each product type.)

20. (***) (*Microsoft Excel problem*) Wayne Banker is in charge of planning water usage for agriculturally intensive Burke County. August is the peak month of water usage for Burke County. Wayne has collected the following statistics from the past 15 years, showing the total March–June rainfall (in inches), average daily high temperature in July, and number of acre-feet of water used in August by farms in the area. Wayne wants to know if he can predict how much water will be needed in August, given the March–June rainfall and July temperature data.

YEAR	INCHES OF RAINFALL, MARCH–JUNE	AVERAGE PEAK DAILY TEMPERATURE, JULY	ACRE-FEET OF WATER USED, AUGUST
2005	12.5	78.4	39,800
2006	11.2	74.9	43,700
2007	12.2	84.1	45,100
2008	10.6	85.1	54,500
2009	9.3	70.6	32,900
2010	11.7	71.0	31,500
2011	10.0	87.4	35,500
2012	13.3	91.4	35,800
2013	8.4	98.3	69,700
2014	14.9	99.6	48,100
2015	10.0	91.7	53,700
2016	12.6	91.6	40,300
2017	10.6	81.5	32,600
2018	7.1	77.0	34,100
2019	11.3	83.9	36,800

Use Excel's regression function to develop a multiple regression forecast for Wayne. What is the R^2 for the model? Use the model to forecast water usage for 2005–2019. Calculate the MFE and MAPE for the model. In your opinion, how good is the model?

Problems for Section 9.7: Measures of Forecast Accuracy

21. (**) Your manager has come to you with the following data, showing actual demand for five periods and forecast results for two different models. He has asked you to tell him which forecast model is "best" and why. Using MFE, MAD, and MAPE, tell him which model is best and why.

PERIOD	ACTUAL DEMAND	FORECAST MODEL 1	FORECAST MODEL 2
8	248	364	486
9	357	280	341
10	423	349	295
11	286	416	364
12	444	354	380

22. (*) Consider the following forecast results. Calculate MFE, MAD, and MAPE, using the data for the months January through June. Does the forecast model under- or overforecast?

MONTH	ACTUAL DEMAND	FORECAST
January	1,040	1,055
February	990	1,052
March	980	900
April	1,060	1,025
May	1,080	1,100
June	1,000	1,050

CASE STUDY

Top-Slice Drivers

Introduction
Two years ago, Top-Slice Company moved from just making golf balls to also producing oversized drivers. Top-Slice makes three different models: the Bomber, the Hook King, and the Sir Slice-A-Lot. As the names suggest, the last two clubs help correct for golfers who either hook or slice the ball when driving.

While Top-Slice is pleased with the growing sales for all three models (see the following tables), the numbers present Jacob Lee, the production manager, with a dilemma. Jacob knows that the current manufacturing work cell is capable of producing only 2,700 drivers per month, and total sales seem to be rapidly approaching that number. Jacob's staff has told him it will take at least three months to plan for and implement an expanded work cell.

MONTH	BOMBER	HOOK KING	SIR SLICE-A-LOT
April 2017	1,410	377	343
May	1,417	381	344
June	1,434	387	346
July	1,452	391	349
August	1,466	396	350

MONTH	BOMBER	HOOK KING	SIR SLICE-A-LOT
September	1,483	400	352
October	1,490	403	354
November	1,505	409	357
December	1,521	412	359
January 2018	1,536	420	363
February	1,547	423	365
March	1,554	426	367
April	1,562	431	369
May	1,574	437	371
June	1,587	441	375
July	1,595	445	377
August	1,613	454	381
September	1,631	461	384
October	1,642	464	386
November	1,656	471	389
December	1,673	477	392
January 2019	1,685	480	394
February	1,703	485	396
March	1,720	490	399

(Continued)

Questions

1. Develop a quantitative forecast model for Jacob. Which modeling technique did you choose, and why? What are the assumptions behind your model?

2. According to your model, when will Top-Slice need to have the expanded work cell up and running? What are the implications for when Jacob should start the expansion effort?

3. Now suppose that over lunch the marketing vice president says to Jacob:

   We're feeling a lot of heat from Chinese manufacturers who are offering very similar clubs to ours, but at significantly lower prices.

The legal department is working on a patent infringement case, but if we can't block these clubs from entering the market, I expect to see our sales flatten, and maybe even fall, over the rest of the year.

What questions should Jacob ask? How would the answers to these questions affect the forecast? Does it still make sense to use quantitative forecasting under these circumstances? Why?

REFERENCES

Ackerman, A., and A. Padilla, "Black and Decker HHI puts CPFR into Action," *Consumer Goods Technology*, October 20, 2009, **https://consumergoods.com/black-decker-hhi-puts-cpfr-action.**

Collaborative Planning, Forecasting and Replenishment: An Overview, Voluntary Interindustry Commerce Standards, May 18, 2004, **www.gs1us.org/DesktopModules/Bring2mind/DMX/Download.aspx?command=core_download&entryid=492&language=en-US&PortalId=0&TabId=134.**

Energy Information Administration, *Short-Term Energy Outlook—April 2011*, April 15, 2011, **www.eia.gov/emeu/steo/pub/2tab.pdf.**

Paul A. Souders/Corbis/VCG/Getty Images

CHAPTER
ten

Sales and Operations Planning (Aggregate Planning)

CHAPTER OBJECTIVES

By the end of this chapter, you will be able to:

● Distinguish among strategic planning, tactical planning, and detailed planning and control.

● Describe why sales and operations planning (S&OP) is important to an organization and its supply chain partners.

● Generate multiple alternative sales and operations plans for a firm.

● Describe the differences between top-down and bottom-up S&OP and discuss the strengths and weaknesses of level, chase, and mixed production strategies.

● Discuss the organizational issues that arise when firms decide to incorporate S&OP into their efforts.

● Examine how S&OP can be used to coordinate activities up and down the supply chain.

● Apply optimization modeling techniques to the S&OP process.

COVOLO DIVING GEAR, PART 1

Khoroshunova Olga/Shutterstock

June 1, 2020—The senior staff members for Covolo Diving Gear were sitting down for their semiannual planning meeting. As it had been too often before, the mood was tense.

"This is nuts," complained David Griffin, the vice president of manufacturing. "Last January, marketing sat here and presented us with a sales forecast of 30,000 gauge sets each month, so that's what I planned on producing. But by March, they'd upped it to 33,000. How can I be expected to keep a smooth-running manufacturing organization under these conditions? I can't handle another six months like the last."

"We do the best we can, but it's hard to develop a dead-on forecast, especially for more than a few months in advance," countered Patricia Rodriguez, the vice president of marketing. "Besides, manufacturing was able to increase production to only 31,000, even though we both finally agreed on the higher number. Why is *that*?"

"I'll tell you why," said Jack Nelson, head of supply management. "Each gauge set we make requires special parts that come from Germany, and our German suppliers just can't increase their shipments to us without *some* notice. Next time you guys plan on changing production levels, why don't you include me in on the conversation?"

At this point, Gina Covolo, the CEO, spoke up: "OK, folks, settle down. We work for the same company, remember? I've been reading up on something called sales and operations planning. If I understand it right, it will help us coordinate our efforts better than we have in the past. We will have to meet more often, probably monthly, but if we do it right, we will all be working from the same sales forecast, and we will know exactly what each of our areas has to do to execute the plan. I think that's a whole lot better than getting angry at one another." And to the accompanying groans of everyone in the room, Gina added: "Who knows, we might even be able to keep our heads above water."

INTRODUCTION

Sales and operations planning (S&OP)
A process to develop tactical plans by integrating marketing plans for new and existing products with the management of the supply chain. The process brings together all the plans for the business into one integrated set of plans. Also called *aggregate planning*.

Aggregate planning
See sales and operations planning (S&OP).

Throughout this book, we have emphasized how critical it is to coordinate operations and supply chain decisions with other functional areas and the firm's supply chain partners. This theme appears in our discussions of strategy, new product development, capacity planning, and process choice, to name a few. This chapter takes the concept of cross-functional and interfirm coordination a step further, through a process known as **sales and operations planning (S&OP)** (sometimes called **aggregate planning**). Adapting from the APICS definition, we define sales and operations planning as a process to develop tactical plans by integrating marketing plans for new and existing products with the management of the supply chain. The process brings together all the plans for the business (sales, marketing, development, manufacturing, sourcing, and financial) into one integrated set of plans. It is performed at least once a month and is reviewed by management at an aggregate (product family) level.[1]

We start by describing how S&OP fits into an organization's planning scheme. We then present several methods for generating and selecting plans and for implementing the S&OP process in an organization.

10.1 S&OP IN THE PLANNING CYCLE

Strategic planning
Planning that takes place at the highest levels of the firm, addressing needs that might not arise for years into the future.

In most organizations, planning actually takes place at several levels, each covering a certain period of time into the future (Figure 10.1). **Strategic planning** takes place at the highest levels of the firm; it addresses needs that might not arise for years into the future. **Tactical planning**

---

[1] J. H. Blackstone, ed., *APICS Dictionary*, 15th ed. (Chicago, IL: APICS, 2016).

Detailed planning and control	Tactical planning	Strategic planning
• Limited ability to adjust capacity • Detailed planning (day to day, hour to hour) • Lowest risk	• Workforce, inventory, subcontracting, and logistics decisions • Planning numbers somewhat "aggregated" (month by month) • Moderate risk	• "Bricks and mortar" and major process choice decisions • Planning done at a very high level (quarterly or yearly) • High risk

Now ———→

Days/weeks out   *Months out*   *Years out*

FIGURE 10.1 Different Levels of Planning

Tactical planning
Planning that covers a shorter period, usually 12 to 24 months out, although the planning horizon may be longer in industries with very long lead times (e.g., engineer-to-order firms).

Detailed planning and control
Planning that covers time periods ranging from weeks down to just a few hours out.

covers a shorter period, usually 12 to 24 months out, although the planning horizon may be longer in industries with very long lead times (e.g., engineer-to-order firms). Tactical planning is typically more detailed, but it is constrained by the longer-term strategic decisions. For example, managers responsible for tactical planning might be able to adjust overall inventory or workforce levels, but only within the constraints imposed by strategic decisions such as the size of the facilities and types of processes used.

Detailed planning and control covers time periods ranging from weeks down to just a few hours out. Because the planning horizon is so short, managers who do detailed planning and control usually have few, if any, options for adjusting capacity levels. Rather, they must try to make the best use of available capacity in order to get as much work done as possible.

The three approaches differ in (1) the time frame covered, (2) the level of planning detail required, and (3) the degree of flexibility managers have to change capacity. See Figure 10.1. Strategic planning has the longest time horizon, has the least amount of specific information (after all, we are planning for years out), and affords managers the greatest degree of flexibility to change capacity. Detailed planning and control is just the opposite: Planning can cover daily or even hourly activity, and the relatively short time horizons leave managers with few, if any, options for changing capacity. Tactical planning fills the gap between these extremes.

S&OP is aimed squarely at helping businesses develop superior tactical plans. Specifically:

- **S&OP indicates how the organization will use its tactical capacity resources to meet expected customer demand.** Examples of tactical capacity resources include the size of the workforce, inventory, number of shifts, and even availability of subcontractors.
- **S&OP strikes a balance between the various needs and constraints of the supply chain partners.** For example, S&OP must consider not only customer demand but also the capabilities of all suppliers, production facilities, and logistics service providers that work together to provide the product or service. The result is a plan that is not only feasible but also balances costs, delivery, quality, and flexibility.
- **S&OP serves as a coordinating mechanism for the various supply chain partners.** At the end of the S&OP process, there should be a shared agreement about what each of the affected partners—marketing operations, and finance, as well as key suppliers and logistics providers—needs to do to make the plan a reality. Good S&OP makes it very clear what everyone should—and should not—do. This shared agreement allows the different parties to make more detailed decisions with the confidence that their efforts will be consistent with those of other partners.
- **S&OP expresses the business's plans in terms that everyone can understand.** Finance personnel typically think of business activity in terms of cash flows, financial ratios, and other measures of profitability. Marketing managers concentrate on sales levels and market segments, while operations and supply chain managers tend to focus more on the activities associated with the particular products or services being produced. As we shall see, S&OP makes a deliberate effort to express the resulting plans in a format that is easy for all partners to understand and incorporate into their detailed planning efforts.

FIGURE 10.2
Determining the
Appropriate Approach
to S&OP

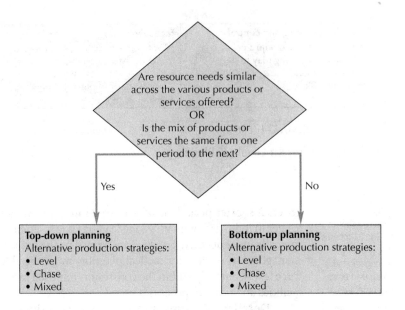

Top-down planning
An approach to S&OP in which a single, aggregated sales forecast drives the planning process. For top-down planning to work, the mix of products or services must be essentially the same from one time period to the next *or* the products or services to be provided must have very similar resource requirements.

10.2 MAJOR APPROACHES TO S&OP

There are two major approaches to S&OP: top-down planning and bottom-up planning. Figure 10.2 summarizes the criteria organizations must consider when choosing between the two.

The simplest approach is **top-down planning.** Here a single, aggregated sales forecast drives the planning process. For top-down planning to work, the mix of products or services must be essentially the same from one time period to the next *or* the various products or services must have very similar resource requirements to one another. The key assumption under top-down planning is that managers can make accurate tactical plans based on the *overall* forecast and then divide the resources across individual products or services later on, during the detailed planning and control stage.

Bottom-up planning
An approach to S&OP that is used when the product/service mix is unstable and resource requirements vary greatly across the offerings. Under such conditions, managers will need to estimate the requirements for each set of products or services separately and then add them up to get an overall picture of the resource requirements.

Bottom-up planning is used when the product/service mix is unstable and resource requirements vary greatly across the offerings. Under such conditions, a single forecast number is not very helpful in determining resource requirements. Instead, managers will need to estimate the requirements for each set of products or services separately and then add them up to get an overall picture of the resource requirements.

Planning values
Values that decision makers use to translate a sales forecast into resource requirements and to determine the feasibility and costs of alternative sales and operations plans.

Regardless of the approach used, managers will need planning values to carry out the analysis. **Planning values** are values, based on analysis or historical data, that decision makers use to translate a sales forecast into resource requirements and to determine the feasibility and costs of alternative sales and operations plans. Example 10.1 shows one method of developing planning values when the product mix is stable.

EXAMPLE 10.1

Calculating Planning Values for Ernie's Electrical

Ernie's Electrical performs three services: cable TV installations, satellite TV installations, and digital subscriber line (DSL) installations. Table 10.1 shows Ernie's service mix, as well as the labor hours and supply costs associated with each type of installation.

TABLE 10.1 Service Mix at Ernie's Electrical

SERVICE DESCRIPTION	SERVICE MIX	LABOR HOURS PER INSTALLATION	SUPPLY COSTS PER INSTALLATION
Cable TV installation	40%	2	$15
Satellite TV installation	40%	3	$90
DSL installation	20%	4	$155

Ernie's service mix is the same from one month to the next. As a result, the company can use a single set of planning values, based on the weighted averages of labor hours and supply costs:

Estimated labor hours per installation:

$$40\% * 2\,\text{hours} + 40\% * 3\,\text{hours} + 20\% * 4\,\text{hours} = 2.8\,\text{hours}$$

Estimated supply costs per installation:

$$40\% * \$15 + 40\% * \$90 + 20\% * \$155 = \$73$$

Ernie expects total installations for the next three months to be 150, 175, and 200, respectively. With this sales forecast and the planning values above, Ernie can quickly estimate labor hours and supply costs for each month (Table 10.2).

TABLE 10.2 Estimated Resource Requirements at Ernie's Electrical

MONTH	SALES FORECAST (INSTALLATIONS)	LABOR HOURS (2.8 PER INSTALLATION)	SUPPLY COSTS ($73 PER INSTALLATION)
Month 1	150	420	$10,950
Month 2	175	490	$12,775
Month 3	200	560	$14,600

Top-Down Planning

The process for generating a top-down plan consists of three steps:

1. **Develop the aggregate sales forecast and planning values.** Top-down planning starts with the aggregate sales forecast. The planning values are used in the next two steps to help management translate the sales forecast into resource requirements and determine the feasibility and costs of alternative S&OP strategies.
2. **Translate the sales forecast into resource requirements.** The goal of this second step is to move the analysis from "sales" numbers to the "operations and supply chain" numbers needed for tactical planning. Some typical resources include labor hours, equipment hours, and material dollars, to name a few.
3. **Generate alternative production plans.** In this step, management determines the feasibility and costs for various production plans. We will describe three particular approaches—level production, chase production, and mixed production—in more detail later.

We illustrate top-down planning through a series of examples for a fictional manufacturer, Pennington Cabinets.

EXAMPLE 10.2

Developing the Aggregate Sales Forecast and Planning Values for Pennington Cabinets

Pennington Cabinets is a manufacturer of several different lines of kitchen and bathroom cabinets that are sold through major home improvement retailers. Pennington's marketing vice president has come up with the following combined sales forecast for the next 12 months:

MONTH	SALES FORECAST (CABINET SETS)
January	750
February	760
March	800
April	800
May	820
June	840
July	910
August	910
September	910
October	880
November	860
December	840

Under top-down planning, managers base the planning process on *aggregated* sales figures, such as those shown here. For example, January's forecast value of 750 reflects total expected demand across Pennington's *entire* line of cabinets. The primary advantage of top-down planning is that it allows managers to see the relationships among *overall* demand, production, and inventory levels. There will be plenty of time to do detailed planning and control later on.

In addition to the sales forecast, Pennington has also developed the planning values shown in Table 10.3.

TABLE 10.3 Planning Values for Pennington Cabinets

CABINET SET PLANNING VALUES	
Regular production cost:	$2,000 per cabinet set
Overtime production cost:	$2,062 per cabinet set
Average monthly inventory holding cost:	$40 per cabinet set, per month
Average labor hours per cabinet set:	20 hours

PRODUCTION PLANNING VALUES	
Maximum regular production per month:	848 cabinet sets
Allowable overtime production per month:	1/10 of regular production

WORKFORCE PLANNING VALUES	
Hours worked per month per employee:	160 hours
Estimated cost to hire a worker:	$1,750
Estimated cost to lay off a worker:	$1,500

Planning values such as these are often developed from company records, detailed analysis, and managerial experience. "Average labor hours per cabinet set," for example, might be derived by looking at past production results, while "Maximum regular production per month" might be based on a detailed analysis of manufacturing capacity (see Chapter 6). In contrast, the human resources (HR) manager might use data on recruiting, interviewing, and training costs to develop estimates of hiring and layoff costs.

The sales forecast shows an expected peak from July through September. As stated in the planning values, Pennington can produce up to 848 cabinet sets a month, using regular production time. Figure 10.3 graphs the expected sales level against maximum regular production per month.

FIGURE 10.3 Graphing Expected Sales Levels versus Capacity

The implication of Figure 10.3 is clear: Pennington won't be able to meet expected demand in the peak months with just regular production.

<table>
<tr><td>**EXAMPLE 10.3**</td></tr>
</table>

Translating the Sales Forecast into Resource Requirements at Pennington Cabinets

The next step for Pennington is to translate the sales forecast into resource requirements. The key resource Pennington is concerned about is labor, although other resources could be examined, depending on the needs of the firm. Translating sales into labor hours and, ultimately, workers needed allows Pennington to see how demand drives resource requirements. Table 10.4 shows the start of this process.

TABLE 10.4 Translating Sales into Resource Requirements at Pennington Cabinets

MONTH	SALES FORECAST	SALES (IN LABOR HOURS)	SALES (IN WORKERS)
January	750	15,000	93.75
February	760	15,200	95.00
March	800	16,000	100.00
April	**800** ⟶	**16,000** ⟶	**100.00**
May	820	16,400	102.50
June	840	16,800	105.00
July	910	18,200	113.75
August	910	18,200	113.75
September	910	18,200	113.75
October	880	17,600	110.00
November	860	17,200	107.50
December	840	16,800	105.00

To illustrate, April's demand represents (20 hours per cabinet) × (800 cabinets) = 16,000 labor hours. If every worker works 160 hours a month, this is the equivalent of (16,000 labor hours)/(160 hours) = 100 workers.

Level, Chase, and Mixed Production Plans

Level production plan
A sales and operations plan in which production is held constant and inventory is used to absorb differences between production and the sales forecast.

Once a firm has translated the sales forecast into resource requirements, the next step is to generate alternative production plans. Three common approaches are level production, chase production, and mixed production plans. The fundamental difference among the three is how production and inventory levels are allowed to vary.

Under a **level production plan,** production is held constant, and inventory is used to absorb differences between production and the sales forecast. This approach is best suited to an

Chase production plan
A sales and operations plan in which production is changed in each time period to match the sales forecast.

Mixed production plan
A sales and operations plan that varies both production and inventory levels in an effort to develop the most effective plan.

environment in which changing the production level is very difficult or extremely costly (e.g., an oil refinery) and the cost of holding inventory is relatively low.

A **chase production plan** is just the opposite. Here production is changed in each time period to match the sales forecast in each time period. The result is that production "chases" demand. This approach is best suited to environments in which holding inventory is extremely expensive or impossible (as with services) or the costs of changing production levels are relatively low.

A mixed production plan falls between these two extremes. Specifically, a **mixed production plan** will vary both production and inventory levels, in an effort to develop the most effective plan.

EXAMPLE 10.4

Generating a Level Production Plan for Pennington Cabinets

After translating the sales forecast into resource requirements (Table 10.4), Pennington management decides to begin its analysis by generating a level production plan. Pennington starts off January with 100 workers and 100 cabinet sets in inventory, and it wants to end the planning cycle with these numbers. Table 10.5 shows a completed level production plan for Pennington Cabinets. Following is a discussion of the highlights of this plan.

TABLE 10.5 Level Production Plan for Pennington Cabinets

MONTH	SALES FORECAST	SALES (IN LABOR HOURS)	SALES (IN WORKERS)	ACTUAL WORKERS	REGULAR PRO-DUCTION	ALLOWABLE OVERTIME PRO-DUCTION	OVERTIME PRO-DUCTION	HIRINGS	LAYOFFS	INVENTORY/BACK ORDERS
				100.00						100.00
January	750	15,000	93.75	105.00	840.00	84.00	0	5.00	0.00	190.00
February	760	15,200	95.00	105.00	840.00	84.00	0	0.00	0.00	270.00
March	800	16,000	100.00	105.00	840.00	84.00	0	0.00	0.00	310.00
April	800	16,000	100.00	105.00	840.00	84.00	0	0.00	0.00	350.00
May	820	16,400	102.50	105.00	840.00	84.00	0	0.00	0.00	370.00
June	840	16,800	105.00	105.00	840.00	84.00	0	0.00	0.00	370.00
July	910	18,200	113.75	105.00	840.00	84.00	0	0.00	0.00	300.00
August	910	18,200	113.75	105.00	840.00	84.00	0	0.00	0.00	230.00
September	910	18,200	113.75	105.00	840.00	84.00	0	0.00	0.00	160.00
October	880	17,600	110.00	105.00	840.00	84.00	0	0.00	0.00	120.00
November	860	17,200	107.50	105.00	840.00	84.00	0	0.00	0.00	100.00
December	840	16,800	105.00	105.00	840.00	84.00	0	0.00	0.00	100.00
								0	5	
Totals:	10,080				10,080		0	5	5	2,870

Actual Workers and Regular Production

Under the level production plan, the actual workforce is held constant, at 105. Why 105? Because 105 represents the average workforce required over the 12-month planning horizon. By maintaining a workforce of 105 workers, Pennington produces:

$$105(160 \text{ hours per month}/20 \text{ hours per set}) = 840 \text{ sets per month}$$

or:

$$(840 \text{ sets per month}) (12 \text{ months}) = 10,080 \text{ cabinet sets for the year}$$

You may have noticed that this production total matches sales for the entire year. The difference, of course, is in the *timing* of the production and the sales: Inventory builds up when sales are less than the monthly production level and drains down when sales outstrip production. Finally, with 105 workers, Pennington comes close to reaching the regular production maximum of 848 cabinet sets per month but doesn't exceed it.

Hirings and Layoffs

Whenever the workforce level changes, Pennington must hire or release workers. This occurs at two different times in the level production plan. In January, Pennington hires 5 workers to bring the workforce up to 105 from the initial level of 100. To bring the workforce back down to its starting level, Pennington lays off 5 workers at the end of December. While this may seem unrealistic, doing so (at least for calculation purposes) ensures Pennington that it will be able to compare alternative plans under the same beginning and ending conditions.

Inventory Levels

The ending inventory level in any month is calculated as follows:

$$EI_t = EI_{t-1} + RP_t + OP_t - S_t \qquad (10.1)$$

where:

EI_t = ending inventory for time period t
RP_t = regular production in time period t
OP_t = overtime production in time period t
S_t = sales in time period t

For January, the ending inventory is:

$$EI_{\text{January}} = EI_{\text{December}} + RP_{\text{January}} + OP_{\text{January}} - S_{\text{January}}$$
$$= 100 + 840 + 0 - 750 = 190 \text{ cabinet sets}$$

Likewise, the ending inventory for February is:

$$EI_{\text{February}} = EI_{\text{January}} + RP_{\text{February}} + OP_{\text{February}} - S_{\text{February}}$$
$$= 190 + 840 + 0 - 760 = 270 \text{ cabinet sets}$$

As expected, the level production plan builds up inventory from January through May (when production exceeds sales) and then drains it down during the peak months of July through December. But look at the ending inventory levels for each month: They are all greater than zero, suggesting that Pennington is holding more cabinet sets than it needs to meet the forecast. This may seem wasteful at first glance. But remember that Pennington is developing a plan based on *forecasted* sales. The extra inventory protects Pennington if actual sales turn out to be higher than the forecast. Otherwise, Pennington might not be able to meet all the demand, resulting in back orders or even lost sales.

The Cost of the Plan

Of course, Pennington has no way of knowing at this point whether a level production plan is the best plan or not. To do so, management will need some way to compare competing plans. Management starts this process by calculating the costs of the level production plan, using the planning values in Table 10.3:

REGULAR PRODUCTION COSTS	
10,080 cabinet sets × ($2,000) =	$20,160,000
HIRING AND LAYOFF COSTS	
5 hirings × ($1,750) + 5 layoffs × ($1,500) =	$16,250
INVENTORY HOLDING COSTS	
2,870 cabinet sets × ($40) =	$114,800
Total:	$20,291,050

EXAMPLE 10.5

**Generating a Chase
Production Plan for
Pennington Cabinets**

Table 10.6 shows a chase production plan for Pennington Cabinets. Notice that the first four columns are identical to those for the level production plan (Table 10.5). However, results for the remaining columns are quite different:

- Actual workforce production and overtime production vary so that total production essentially matches sales for each month. Because total production "chases" sales, inventory never builds up, as it did under the level production plan. In fact, it never gets higher than 106 cabinet sets.
- From July through November, monthly sales are higher than the maximum regular production level of 848. Under the chase approach, Pennington will need to make up the difference through overtime production.
- While the chase production plan keeps inventory levels low, it results in more hirings and layoffs and in overtime production costs.
- Because Pennington can't hire fractional workers, the company can't always *exactly* match production to sales. In this example, Pennington ends up with slightly more cabinet sets in inventory at the end of the planning period (106 versus 100). Still, this is close enough to compare with other plans.

TABLE 10.6 Chase Production Plan for Pennington Cabinets

MONTH	SALES FORECAST	SALES (IN LABOR HOURS)	SALES (IN WORKERS)	ACTUAL WORKERS	REGULAR PRODUCTION	ALLOWABLE OVERTIME PRODUCTION	OVERTIME PRODUCTION	HIRINGS	LAYOFFS	INVENTORY/ BACK ORDERS
			100.00							100.00
January	750	15,000	93.75	94.00	752.00	75.20	0	0.00	6.00	102.00
February	760	15,200	95.00	95.00	760.00	76.00	0	1.00	0.00	102.00
March	800	16,000	100.00	100.00	800.00	80.00	0	5.00	0.00	102.00
April	800	16,000	100.00	100.00	800.00	80.00	0	0.00	0.00	102.00
May	820	16,400	102.50	103.00	824.00	82.40	0	3.00	0.00	106.00
June	840	16,800	105.00	105.00	840.00	84.00	0	2.00	0.00	106.00
July	910	18,200	113.75	106.00	848.00	84.80	62	1.00	0.00	106.00
August	910	18,200	113.75	106.00	848.00	84.80	62	0.00	0.00	106.00
September	910	18,200	113.75	106.00	848.00	84.80	62	0.00	0.00	106.00
October	880	17,600	110.00	106.00	848.00	84.80	32	0.00	0.00	106.00
November	860	17,200	107.50	106.00	848.00	84.80	12	0.00	0.00	106.00
December	840	16,800	105.00	105.00	840.00	84.00	0	0.00	1.00	106.00
								0	5	
Totals:	10,080				9,856		230	12	12	1,256

The cost calculations for the chase production plan follow. In this case, 9,856 cabinet sets were produced through regular production, and the remaining 230 were produced using overtime:

REGULAR PRODUCTION COSTS	
9,856 cabinet sets × ($2,000) =	$19,712,000
OVERTIME PRODUCTION COSTS	
230 cabinet sets × ($2,062) =	$474,260
HIRING AND LAYOFF COSTS	
12 hirings × ($1,750) + 12 layoffs × ($1,500) =	$39,000
INVENTORY HOLDING COSTS	
1,256 cabinet sets × ($40) =	$50,240
Total:	$20,275,500

EXAMPLE 10.6

Generating a Mixed Production Plan for Pennington Cabinets

In the real world, the best plan will probably be something other than a pure level or pure chase plan. A mixed production plan varies both production and inventory levels in an effort to develop the best plan. Because there are many different ways to do this, the number of potential mixed plans is essentially limitless.

Suppose Pennington's workers have strong reservations about working overtime during the summer months, a chief requirement under the chase plan. The mixed production plan shown in Table 10.7 limits overtime to just 12 cabinet sets per month in October and November. This is just one example of the type of qualitative issues a management team must consider when developing a sales and operations plan.

TABLE 10.7 Mixed Production Plan for Pennington Cabinets

MONTH	SALES FORECAST	SALES (IN LABOR HOURS)	SALES (IN WORKERS)	ACTUAL WORKERS	REGULAR PRODUCTION	ALLOWABLE OVERTIME PRODUCTION	OVERTIME PRODUCTION	HIRINGS	LAYOFFS	INVENTORY/ BACK ORDERS
				100.00						100.00
January	750	15,000	93.75	100.00	800.00	80.00	0	0.00	0.00	150.00
February	760	15,200	95.00	100.00	800.00	80.00	0	0.00	0.00	190.00
March	800	16,000	100.00	103.00	824.00	82.40	0	3.00	0.00	214.00
April	800	16,000	100.00	106.00	848.00	84.80	0	3.00	0.00	262.00
May	820	16,400	102.50	106.00	848.00	84.80	0	0.00	0.00	290.00
June	840	16,800	105.00	106.00	848.00	84.80	0	0.00	0.00	298.00
July	910	18,200	113.75	106.00	848.00	84.80	0	0.00	0.00	236.00
August	910	18,200	113.75	106.00	848.00	84.80	0	0.00	0.00	174.00
September	910	18,200	113.75	106.00	848.00	84.80	0	0.00	0.00	112.00
October	880	17,600	110.00	106.00	848.00	84.80	12	0.00	0.00	92.00
November	860	17,200	107.50	106.00	848.00	84.80	12	0.00	0.00	92.00
December	840	16,800	105.00	106.00	848.00	84.80	0	0.00	0.00	100.00
								0	6	
Totals:	10,080				10,056		24	6	6	2,210.00

The cost of the mixed production strategy is:

REGULAR PRODUCTION COSTS	
10,056 cabinet sets × ($2,000) =	$20,112,000

OVERTIME PRODUCTION COSTS	
24 cabinet sets × ($2,062) =	$49,488

HIRING AND LAYOFF COSTS	
6 hirings × ($1,750) + 6 layoffs × ($1,500) =	$19,500

INVENTORY HOLDING COSTS	
2,210 cabinet sets × ($40) =	$88,400

Total:	$20,269,388

Bottom-Up Planning

Top-down planning works well in situations where planners can use a single set of planning values to estimate resource requirements and costs. But what happens when this is not the case? As we noted earlier, bottom-up planning is used when the products or services have different resource requirements *and* the mix is unstable from one period to the next. The steps for generating a bottom-up plan are similar to those for creating a top-down plan. The main difference is that the resource requirements must be evaluated individually for each product or service and then added up across all products or services to get a picture of overall requirements.

EXAMPLE 10.7

**Bottom-up planning
at Philips Toys**

Philips Toys produces a summer toy line and a winter toy line. Machine and labor requirements for each product line are given in Table 10.8.

TABLE 10.8 Machine and Labor Requirements for Philips Toys

PRODUCT LINE	MACHINE HOURS/UNIT	LABOR HOURS/UNIT
Summer toys	0.75	0.25
Winter toys	0.85	2.00

Both product lines have fairly similar machine hour requirements. However, they differ greatly with regard to labor requirements; products in the winter line need, on average, eight times as much labor as products in the summer line.

The difference in labor requirements becomes important when the product mix changes. Look at the data in Table 10.9. Even though the *aggregate* forecast across both product lines is 700 units each month, the product mix changes as Philips moves into and then out of the summer season. The impact on resource requirements can be seen in the labor hours needed each month.

TABLE 10.9 Forecasted Demand and Resulting Resource Needs for Philips Toys

MONTH	Forecast SUMMER LINE	Forecast WINTER LINE	AGGREGATE FORECAST	MACHINE HOURS	LABOR HOURS
January	0	700	700	595	1,400
February	100	600	700	585	1,225
March	500	200	700	545	525
April	700	0	700	525	175
May	700	0	700	525	175
June	700	0	700	525	175
July	700	0	700	525	175
August	500	200	700	545	525
September	400	300	700	555	700
October	200	500	700	575	1,050
November	0	700	700	595	1,400
December	0	700	700	595	1,400

Figure 10.4 graphs the projected machine hours and labor hours shown in Table 10.9. Such graphs are often referred to as load profiles. A **load profile** is a display of future capacity requirements based on released and/or planned orders over a given span of time.[2] As the load profiles suggest, machine hour requirements are fairly constant throughout the year. This is because both product lines have similar machine time requirements. In contrast, the load profile for labor dips dramatically in the summer months, reflecting the lower labor requirements associated with the summer product line.

FIGURE 10.4 Load Profiles at Philips Toys

[2]Ibid.

To develop a sales and operations plan, Philips will need to maintain a separate set of planning values for each product line it produces and then total up the requirements. The rest of the planning process will be very similar to top-down planning. Philips will probably have to choose between adjusting the workforce to avoid excess labor costs in the summer months and finding some way to smooth the labor requirements, perhaps by making more winter toys in the summer months. This, however, will drive up inventory levels.

Cash Flow Analysis

Net cash flow
The net flow of dollars into or out of a business over some time period.

One of the key benefits of S&OP is that it expresses business plans in a common language that all partners can understand. Consider for instance the finance area. Among its many responsibilities, finance is charged with making sure that the business has the cash it needs to carry out the sales and operations plan and that any excess cash is put to good use. Finance personnel are therefore very interested in assessing the net cash flow for any production plan. **Net cash flow** is defined as the net flow of dollars into or out of a business over some time period:

$$\text{Net cash flow} = \text{cash inflows} - \text{cash outflows} \qquad (10.2)$$

EXAMPLE 10.8

Cash Flow Analysis at Pennington Cabinets

Pennington sells each cabinet set for $2,800, on average. Management has already determined that the regular production cost for a cabinet set is $2,000, the overtime production cost is $2,062, and the monthly holding cost per cabinet set is $40 (Table 10.3).

Now suppose that Pennington incurs these revenues and expenses in the month in which they occur. That is, each sale of a cabinet set generates a cash *inflow* of $2,800, and each cabinet set produced and each cabinet set held in inventory generate cash *outflows* of $2,000 ($2,062 if overtime is used) and $40, respectively. Table 10.10 shows a simplified cash flow analysis for the mixed production plan in Table 10.7.

TABLE 10.10 Cash Flow Analysis for Pennington Cabinets, Mixed Production Plan

MONTH	SALES FORECAST	REGULAR PRODUCTION	OVERTIME PRODUCTION	INVENTORY/ BACK ORDERS	CASH INFLOWS	CASH OUTFLOWS	NET FLOW	CUMULATIVE NET FLOW
January	750	800	0	150	2,100,000	1,606,000	494,000	494,000
February	760	800	0	190	2,128,000	1,607,600	520,400	1,014,400
March	800	824	0	214	2,240,000	1,656,560	583,440	1,597,840
April	800	848	0	262	2,240,000	1,706,480	533,520	2,131,360
May	820	848	0	290	2,296,000	1,707,600	588,400	2,719,760
June	840	848	0	298	2,352,000	1,707,920	644,080	3,363,840
July	910	848	0	236	2,548,000	1,705,440	842,560	4,206,400
August	910	848	0	174	2,548,000	1,702,960	845,040	5,051,440
September	910	848	0	112	2,548,000	1,700,480	847,520	5,898,960
October	880	848	12	92	2,464,000	1,724,424	739,576	6,638,536
November	860	848	12	92	2,408,000	1,724,424	683,576	7,322,112
December	840	848	0	100	2,352,000	1,700,000	652,000	7,974,112

To illustrate, the net cash flow calculation for January is:

$$
\begin{aligned}
\text{Net cash flow} &= \text{cash inflows} - \text{cash outflows} \\
&= \text{Sales revenues} - \text{regular production costs} - \text{overtime production costs} \\
&\quad - \text{inventory holding costs} \\
&= \$2,800(750 \text{ cabinet sets}) - \$2,000(800 \text{ cabinet sets}) \\
&\quad - \$2,062(0 \text{ cabinet sets}) - \$40(150 \text{ cabinet sets}) \\
&= \$2,100,000 - \$1,600,000 - \$0 - \$6,000 = \$494,000
\end{aligned}
$$

Applying the same logic, the net cash flow in February is $520,400. Finally, Pennington can calculate the cumulative net cash flow through February as $494,000 + $520,000 = $1,014,400. The cash flow analysis expresses the sales and operations plan in terms that are meaningful to financial managers. In this case, the cabinet set business is expected to generate anywhere from around $500,000 to $850,000 in positive cash flow each month and nearly $8 million over the course of the year. These additional funds can be used to cover other expenses, retire debt, or perhaps support additional business investments.

Now let's consider an alternative scenario, shown in Table 10.11. Everything, including total sales for the 12-month planning period, is the same as before, *except* now the *timing* of the sales has changed. Specifically, sales in the first half of the year are much lower than previously, while sales increase dramatically in the last half.

The new sales pattern results in *negative* net cash flows for the first three months of the year and a cumulative negative net cash flow that does not disappear until May. In this case, finance will need to find the funds necessary to support this particular plan, or the company will need to develop an alternative sales and operations plan that is not as burdensome. Finally, you may have noticed that the net cash flow at the end of the year is lower than before ($7,766,512 versus $7,974,112). This difference is due to the fact that the second plan results in higher inventory holding costs. Figure 10.5 compares the cash flow results for Tables 10.10 and 10.11.

TABLE 10.11 Cash Flow Analysis for Pennington Cabinets, *Different Sales Pattern*

MONTH	SALES FORECAST	REGULAR PRODUCTION	OVERTIME PRODUCTION	INVENTORY/ BACK ORDERS	CASH IN FLOWS	CASH OUTFLOWS	NET FLOW	CUMULATIVE NET FLOW
January	500	800	0	400	1,400,000	1,616,000	(216,000)	(216,000)
February	520	800	0	680	1,456,000	1,627,200	(171,200)	(387,200)
March	550	824	0	954	1,540,000	1,686,160	(146,160)	(533,360)
April	700	848	0	1,102	1,960,000	1,740,080	219,920	(313,440)
May	880	848	0	1,070	2,464,000	1,738,800	725,200	411,760
June	960	848	0	958	2,688,000	1,734,320	953,680	1,365,440
July	1,040	848	0	766	2,912,000	1,726,640	1,185,360	2,550,800
August	1,040	848	0	574	2,912,000	1,718,960	1,193,040	3,743,840
September	1,040	848	0	382	2,912,000	1,711,280	1,200,720	4,944,560
October	980	848	12	262	2,744,000	1,731,224	1,012,776	5,957,336
November	970	848	12	152	2,716,000	1,726,824	989,176	6,946,512
December	900	848	0	100	2,520,000	1,700,000	820,000	7,766,512

FIGURE 10.5 Cumulative Net Cash Flows under Two Different Sales Scenarios

10.3 ORGANIZING FOR AND IMPLEMENTING S&OP

We have spent a fair amount of time describing the basic calculations associated with S&OP. But S&OP is more than just "running the numbers." Richard Ling put it best when he stated, "S&OP is a people process supported by information."[3] In this section, we address some critical organizational questions associated with S&OP:

- How do we choose between alternative plans?
- How often should S&OP be done?
- How do we implement S&OP in our business environment?

Choosing between Alternative Plans

Coming up with a suitable sales and operations plan is an iterative process. An organization may have to change a plan several times before coming up with a plan that is acceptable to all parties. This fine-tuning often means that decision makers will need to make trade-offs. Figure 10.6 illustrates this idea.

A classic example is the trade-off between inventory and customer service. Suppose that after reviewing a plan, finance wants to reduce inventory levels further to bring down costs. Marketing might raise concerns that this could potentially hurt customer service. All parties would have to come to some agreement concerning the right balance between the two competing objectives—cost and customer service. As another example, operations might want marketing to use pricing and promotion to smooth out peaks and valleys in demand. S&OP could be used to see if the cost of these pricing and promotion efforts is more than offset by improvements in production and inventory costs.

In choosing a sales and operations plan, managers must consider all aspects of a plan, not just costs. For example:

- What impact will the plan have on supply chain partners such as key suppliers and transportation providers? This could be particularly important if production levels vary considerably from one period to the next.
- What are cash flows like? Some plans may be profitable at the end of the planning cycle but still include periods in which cash expenses exceed revenues. We discussed earlier how cash flow analysis can be used to evaluate such plans.
- Do the supply chain partners and the firm itself have the space needed to hold any planned inventories?
- Does the plan contain significant changes in the workforce? If so, what would be the impact on workforce satisfaction and productivity? Could the HR department handle the additional workload?
- How flexible is the plan? That is, how easy or difficult would it be to modify the plan as conditions warrant?

FIGURE 10.6
Fine-Tuning the Sales and Operations Plan

---

[3]R. Ling, "For True Enterprise Integration, Turn First to SOP," *APICS—The Performance Advantage* 10, no. 3 (March 2000): 40–45.

This is just a small sample of the kinds of questions that need to be addressed, but it raises a key point: *Sales and operations plans help managers make decisions. They do not make the decisions for managers.*

EXAMPLE 10.9

Selecting a Plan at Pennington Cabinets

Table 10.12 summarizes the costs, strengths, and weaknesses of the three alternative production strategies we developed for Pennington Cabinets in Examples 10.4 through 10.6. For practical purposes, the costs are too close for us to say that one plan is clearly cheapest. After all, these are plans based on *forecasts* and *planning* values that represent, at best, rough estimates of resource requirements and costs. We can almost guarantee that actual results will be different.

TABLE 10.12 Summary of Alternative Plans at Pennington Cabinet

	LEVEL PLAN	CHASE PLAN	MIXED PLAN
Regular production costs	$20,160,000	$19,712,000	$20,112,000
Overtime production costs	0	$474,260	$49,488
Hiring and layoff costs	$16,250	$39,000	$19,500
Inventory costs	$114,800	$50,240	$88,400
Total costs	$20,291,050	$20,275,500	$20,269,388
Key factors	Flat production level. Inventory levels grow as high as 370 cabinet sets.	Minimal inventory. Significant overtime required in peak months.	Reasonably stable production. Inventory levels grow, but not as high as under a pure level approach. Some overtime required.

To choose a plan, then, Pennington will need to consider other factors. The level plan has the advantage of consistency because the same amount is made each and every month. This eases production planning and allows for workforce stability for Pennington and its partners. Furthermore, it allows Pennington to avoid expensive overtime—but at the cost of holding additional inventory. The build-up of inventory under the level plan does pose a risk: What if actual demand takes a sharp downturn later in the year? If this happens, Pennington will have to cut production drastically or risk being stuck with expensive unwanted inventory.

The chase plan is just the opposite. Inventory levels never rise much above 100 (the starting level), but production levels vary anywhere from 752 in January to 910 in each month of the third quarter. Such instability in production and workforce levels may have unanticipated consequences.

The mixed plan strikes a balance between these extremes. Inventory levels increase over the slower months, but not as drastically as under the level approach. Similarly, the mixed plan uses overtime production, but not to the same extent as the chase plan. Based on these results, Pennington management might select a plan, or even develop another mixed plan in order to derive an even better solution.

Rolling Planning Horizons

Rolling planning horizon
A planning approach in which an organization updates its sales and operations plan regularly, such as on a monthly or quarterly basis.

Sales and operations plans *must* be updated on a regular basis to remain current. Most firms do this by establishing a **rolling planning horizon** which requires them to update the sales and operations plan regularly, usually on a monthly basis. For example, suppose that it is now the beginning of October, and Pennington has just completed the sales and operations plan for January through December of next year. (*Note:* October, November, and December are so close in time that they fall under detailed planning and control, discussed in Chapter 12.) One month later at the beginning of November, Pennington's planning team might come together and

FIGURE 10.7
Updating the Sales and Operations Plan

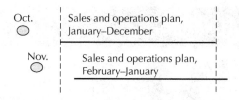

revisit the plan, rolling it forward one month and planning for February through January. Figure 10.7 illustrates the idea. By establishing a rolling planning horizon, a firm can fine-tune its sales and operations plan as new information becomes available.

Implementing S&OP in an Organization

We have already discussed the steps involved in generating a sales and operations plan. But before these steps can occur, managers have to commit themselves to the S&OP process. Furthermore, managers have to realize that excellent S&OP is an organizational skill that can take months, or even years, to develop. Ling describes the implementation of S&OP as a three-phase process:[4]

- Developing the foundation
- Integrating and streamlining the process
- Gaining a competitive advantage

Developing the Foundation. In the first phase of implementing S&OP, companies build the managerial support and infrastructure needed to make S&OP a success. Key steps include educating all participants about the benefits of S&OP, identifying the appropriate product or service families to plan around, and establishing the information systems needed to provide accurate planning values. Ling stresses the point that even though this phase typically takes six to nine months, many companies never progress further because "they expect the process to work immediately and don't establish the right quality and timing of information."[5]

Integrating and Streamlining the Process. In the second phase of implementing S&OP, S&OP becomes part of the organization's normal planning activities. Managers become accustomed to updating the plan on a regular basis, and more importantly, they use the planning results to guide key demand and resource decisions. The sales and operations plan becomes a focal point for cross-functional coordination. Managers also look for ways to improve the S&OP process further. As Ling puts it, "Because implementing a process like this may not yield the right structure and organization on the first attempt, some restructuring and streamlining usually occurs at this point."[6]

Gaining a Competitive Advantage. In the final phase of implementing S&OP, a few companies reach the point where their S&OP process actually becomes a source of competitive advantage—a core competency, if you will. Companies know they have reached this last phase when:[7]

- There is a well-integrated demand planning process, including the use of forecasting models.
- Continuous improvement is planned and monitored as an integral part of the S&OP process.
- Capital equipment planning can be triggered at any time.
- What-if analyses are a way of life, and the S&OP database is networked to provide ready access to S&OP data.

The last two points deserve further discussion. Capital equipment decisions typically fall under the auspices of strategic planning. Yet S&OP can give managers an "early warning" when changes in long-term capacity are needed. Pennington's sales and operations plans (Examples 10.4 through 10.6) all show that demand is bumping up against the company's capacity limits. Top management can use this information to start planning for additional investments in manufacturing capacity.

Finally, most organizations that perform S&OP for any length of time end up developing relatively sophisticated databases and decision tools to support their efforts. These tools, in turn,

---

[4]Ibid.
[5]Ibid.
[6]Ibid.
[7]Ibid.

PROFESSIONAL PROFILE

Courtesy of Joseph E. Perez Rosario

ESTEBAN PEREZ SUAREZ, PATHEON

As a leading contract development and manufacturing organization (CDMO) for the pharmaceutical industry, Patheon provides pharma and biotech companies with the resources and expertise needed to develop new drugs, as well as the capability to manufacture existing drugs on a commercial scale. With nearly 30 sites worldwide supporting everything from the development of biologics to high-volume tablet production and packaging, Patheon's management recognizes the importance of having an effective S&OP process in place at each of its manufacturing sites.

Enter Esteban Perez Suarez, the senior director of global S&OP at Patheon. In this role, Esteban and his team have developed a best-in-class S&OP process that can be adapted to the unique needs of each site. Sites that have implemented the new S&OP process are seeing improved operational performance, including improved on-time delivery and lower costs.

While Esteban's current role has him focused on S&OP, his operations and supply chain experience goes even deeper. Esteban joined Patheon in 2009 as a supply chain director, and then served as the interim site manager at the Manati, Puerto Rico plant. Before that, he was a manufacturing and materials manager in the pharmaceutical industry, and even served as an instructor for the Institute for Supply Management (ISM).

Given his background in education, it shouldn't be surprising that Esteban is a strong believer in continued learning: "To be successful, you should look for opportunities to learn on the job as well as in the classroom. It's a journey, and you start by adding pieces."

often give managers greater power to perform what-if analyses, in which the sales forecasts or even the planning values themselves can be varied to see how the plan reacts. The result is even more robust sales and operations plans.

The *Professional Profile* describes how Esteban Perez Suarez, senior director of global S&OP at Patheon, has helped implement sales and operations planning at his company, a worldwide manufacturer of pharmaceutical products.

10.4 SERVICES CONSIDERATIONS

In many ways, S&OP is even more critical in a service environment than it is in manufacturing. Service outputs cannot be built ahead of time and stored in inventory. An empty airline seat or an unused hour of a service technician's time is lost forever. For this reason, service capacity must be closely matched to demand in every period. The effect is to limit most services to following some form of a chase production plan.

That said, services have many options for aligning resources with demand. These options fall into two camps:

- Making sales match capacity
- Making capacity (typically the workforce) match sales

Making Sales Match Capacity

Yield management
An approach that services commonly use with highly perishable "products," in which prices are regularly adjusted to maximize total profit.

Firms have long used pricing and promotion to bring sales in line with production capacity. **Yield management** is an approach that services commonly use with *highly perishable* "products," such as airline seats and hotel rooms. These services have a real incentive to make sure every unit of capacity—whether it is an airline seat on the next flight or a hotel room for tonight—contributes to the firm's bottom line.

Services with highly perishable "products," such as a ski resort, often vary the price of their services to smooth out demand and maximize profits.

Put simply, the goal of yield management is to maximize total profit, where:

Total profit = (average profit per service unit sold) (number of service units sold)

Here's how it works. When demand levels are lower than expected, yield management systems boost demand by lowering the price, but *only if* the expected result is an increase in

By selling furniture unassembled, IKEA is able to offload part of the manufacturing task to the consumer, thereby holding down costs.

total profit. Conversely, when demand is higher than expected, prices are raised, but *only if* the expected result is higher total profit.

The idea seems pretty straightforward, but what makes yield management distinctive is the level of sophistication involved. The airline and hotel industries, in particular, have complex yield management systems that regularly and automatically adjust the price of their services for unbooked capacity in an effort to maximize total profit. If you have ever booked a hotel room or made a plane reservation, only to have the price for new reservations change two days later, you have seen yield management in action.

Making Capacity Match Sales

Tiered workforce
A strategy used to vary workforce levels, in which additional full-time or part-time employees are hired during peak demand periods, while a smaller permanent staff is maintained year-round.

We have already seen how overtime can be used to vary capacity. Another example is to use a **tiered workforce.** For example, some service organizations hire additional full-time or part-time employees during peak demand periods, while maintaining a smaller permanent staff year-round. This is common in the retailing, hospitality, and agricultural industries.

Offloading
A strategy for reducing and smoothing out workforce requirements that involves having customers perform part of the work themselves.

Other services use **offloading** to shift part of the work to the customer. Examples include companies that have customers deliver and assemble their own furniture (e.g., IKEA) and handle their own financial transactions online. This *reduces* overall workforce requirements for the service firm, and it also helps to *smooth out* workforce requirements. This is because the customer acts like a part-time employee, showing up just when the demand occurs.

EXAMPLE 10.10

Service Offloading at Adam's Carpet Cleaning Service

It takes Adam's Carpet Cleaning Service an average of four hours to clean the carpets in a home. This includes three hours of actual cleaning time plus one hour to move the furniture out of the way and then back into position. Adam's is considering modifying its service so that the customer takes responsibility for moving the furniture, in effect offloading 25% of the workload. The impact on Adam's labor hours can be seen in Table 10.13.

TABLE 10.13 Impact of Customer Offloading at Adam's Carpet Cleaning Service

		Labor Hours Needed	
MONTH	FORECAST	NO OFFLOAD TO CUSTOMER	25% OFFLOADED TO CUSTOMER
1	60	240	180
2	55	220	165
3	50	200	150
4	50	200	150
5	30	120	90
6	30	120	90
7	25	100	75
8	30	120	90
9	40	160	120
10	40	160	120
11	45	180	135
12	55	220	165
	Average:	170	127.5
	Lowest:	100	75
	Highest:	240	180
	Difference:	140	105

Average monthly labor requirements drop by 25%, and the absolute difference between the highest and lowest months drops by 25%. Of course, Adam's would need to balance the potential cost savings against the lowered revenues associated with the new service—after all, the customer can't be expected to work for free.

FIGURE 10.8
Linking S&OP Up and Down the Supply Chain

10.5 LINKING S&OP THROUGHOUT THE SUPPLY CHAIN

Earlier, we noted that the S&OP process should consider not only the impact on various parties *within* the firm but also the impact on *outside* parties—the firm's supply chain partners. It makes little sense, for example, to try to implement a plan that cannot be supported by key suppliers or service providers who move or store the goods. This represents the potential downside of *not* considering supply chain partners when developing a plan.

But there is an upside to linking the S&OP process with supply chain partners. For one thing, coordinating plans across the supply chain can help firms do a better job of improving overall supply chain performance, particularly in the area of cost. Pennington, for example, might discover that suppliers are willing to give the company substantial price discounts if Pennington stabilizes its orders for material—something easier to achieve under a level production plan.

Second, linking plans can help eliminate uncertainty, thereby improving synchronization between supply chain partners. For instance, once Pennington decides on a sales and operations plan, its supply chain partners can use the information to plan *their own* activities. By tying their plans to Pennington's, key suppliers can avoid "guessing" what demand will be. Even better, Pennington might try to establish linkages with its downstream partners—that is, its customers—in an effort to get even more accurate sales forecasts. If you've read Chapter 9, you might be saying to yourself, "That sounds a lot like what collaborative planning, forecasting, and replenishment (CPFR) hopes to accomplish," and you'd be right. In fact, the logical ties between CPFR and S&OP are so strong that a leading industry group has put together a road map that describes how businesses can integrate these efforts.[8]

Of course, the information can flow downstream as well as upstream. If, for example, a key supplier increases its capacity, such information would be useful for Pennington's S&OP effort. This linking of S&OP throughout the supply chain is shown in Figure 10.8. Sharing of plans already takes place in many industries, with the results being greater coordination, improved productivity, and fewer disruptions in the flow of goods and services through the supply chain.

Optimization model
A class of mathematical models used when the user seeks to optimize some objective function subject to some constraints.

Objective function
A quantitative function that an optimization model seeks to optimize (i.e., maximize or minimize).

10.6 APPLYING OPTIMIZATION MODELING TO S&OP

In Chapter 8, we introduced optimization models. As you will recall, **optimization models** are a class of mathematical models used when the user seeks to optimize some objective function subject to some constraints. An **objective function** is a quantitative function that we hope to optimize (for example, we might want to maximize profits or minimize costs). **Constraints** are quantifiable conditions that place limitations on the set of possible solutions (demand that must

Constraint
A quantifiable condition that places limitations on the set of possible solutions. The solution to an optimization model is acceptable only if it does not break any of the constraints.

[8]*Linking CPFR and S&OP: A Roadmap to Integrated Business Planning*, 2010, **www.gs1us.org/DesktopModules/ Bring2mind/DMX/Download.aspx?command=core_download&entryid=433&language=en-US&PortalId= 0&TabId=134.**

be met, limits on materials or equipment time, etc.). A solution is acceptable only if it does not break any of the constraints.

In order for optimization modeling to work, the user must be able to state in mathematical terms both the objective function and the constraints. Once the user is able to do this, special modeling algorithms can be used to generate solutions.

S&OP is ideally suited to such analyses. In particular, managers may be interested in understanding what pattern of resource decisions—labor, inventory, machine time, etc.—will result in the lowest total cost while still meeting the sales forecast. In Example 10.11, we show how Microsoft Excel's Solver function can be used to apply optimization modeling to S&OP.

EXAMPLE 10.11	
S&OP Optimization Modeling at Bob Irons Industries	Bob Irons Industries manufactures and sells DNA testing equipment for use in cancer clinics around the globe. Bob, the owner and CEO, has developed a spreadsheet (Figure 10.9) to help calculate the costs associated with various sales and operations plans.

It's worth taking a few minutes to see how Bob's spreadsheet works. The cells that contain the planning values are highlighted, as are the columns for the sales forecast, hirings, and layoffs, indicating that Bob can change these cells. The remaining numbers are all calculated values.

To illustrate, the calculations for January are as follows:

$$\text{Sales (in labor hours)} = B15 * D3 = 500 \text{ units} * 20 \text{ hours per unit}$$
$$= 10,000 \text{ labor hours}$$

$$\text{Sales (in worker hours)} = \frac{C15}{D4} = \frac{10,000 \text{ labor hours}}{160 \text{ hours per worker}} = 62.5 \text{ workers}$$

	A	B	C	D	E	F	G	H	I
1	**S&OP Spreadsheet**								
2									
3			Labor hrs. per unit:	20					
4			Worker hrs. per month:	160					
5			Beginning & ending workforce:	100					
6			Beginning & ending inventory:	100					
7						Total plan cost			
8			Production cost per unit:	$550.00		$6,600,000			
9			Hiring cost:	$300.00		$7,500			
10			Layoff cost:	$200.00		$5,000			
11			Holding cost per unit per month:	$4.00		$54,800			
12						$6,667,300	Grand total		
13	Month	Sales Forecast	Sales (in labor hrs.)	Sales (in workers)	Actual Workers	Actual Production	Hirings	Layoffs	Ending Inventory/ Back Orders
14					100				100
15	January	500	10,000	62.5	125.00	1,000.00	25.00	0.00	600.00
16	February	600	12,000	75	125.00	1,000.00	0.00	0.00	1,000.00
17	March	700	14,000	87.5	125.00	1,000.00	0.00	0.00	1,300.00
18	April	800	16,000	100	125.00	1,000.00	0.00	0.00	1,500.00
19	May	900	18,000	112.5	125.00	1,000.00	0.00	0.00	1,600.00
20	June	1,000	20,000	125	125.00	1,000.00	0.00	0.00	1,600.00
21	July	1,000	20,000	125	125.00	1,000.00	0.00	0.00	1,600.00
22	August	1,100	22,000	137.5	125.00	1,000.00	0.00	0.00	1,500.00
23	September	1,200	24,000	150	125.00	1,000.00	0.00	0.00	1,300.00
24	October	1,300	26,000	162.5	125.00	1,000.00	0.00	0.00	1,000.00
25	November	1,400	28,000	175	125.00	1,000.00	0.00	0.00	600.00
26	December	1,500	30,000	187.5	125.00	1,000.00	0.00	0.00	100.00
27							0.00	25.00	
28	**Totals:**	**12,000**				**12,000.00**	**25.00**	**25.00**	**13,700.00**
29			Average =	125					

FIGURE 10.9 S&OP Spreadsheet for Bob Irons Industries (Level Plan)

$$\text{Actual workers} = E14 + G15 - H15 = 100\text{ beginning workers} + 25\text{ hires} - 0\text{ layoffs}$$
$$= 125\text{ workers}$$

$$\text{Actual production} = \frac{E15*D4}{D3} = \frac{125\text{ workers}*160\text{ hours per month}}{20\text{ hours per unit}} = 1{,}000\text{ units}$$

$$\text{Ending inventory} = I14 + F15 - B15 = 100 + 1{,}000 - 500 = 600\text{ units}$$

The plan shown in Figure 10.9 is, in fact, a level production plan with a total cost of $6,667,300. Looking at the plan, Bob wonders if he can do better. As an alternative, Bob updates the spreadsheet to show a chase plan. The results are shown in Figure 10.10.

The results surprise Bob: The total cost for the chase plan is exactly the same as the cost for the level plan. He wonders if there is indeed a better solution that meets all of the constraints.

Bob decides to use the Solver function of Excel to find the lowest-cost solution. To start the process, Bob takes a few moments to identify the objective function, decision variables, and constraints for the optimization model and to match them up to his spreadsheet (Table 10.14).

As Table 10.14 indicates, Bob will need to set up the Solver function to minimize total costs (cell F12) by changing the hiring and layoff values (cells G15–H26). At the same time, the cells containing the ending inventory values must stay at or above 0 for the first 11 months (cells I15–I25), and at or above 100 in the last month (cell I26).

Furthermore, Bob wants to make sure that none of the hiring or layoff numbers (cells G15–H26) is negative. This may seem like a strange requirement, but unless Bob does this, the model will try to reduce costs forever by endlessly offsetting a negative hire with a negative layoff, each iteration of which would "save" $300 + $200 = $500.

	A	B	C	D	E	F	G	H	I
1	S&OP Spreadsheet								
2									
3			Labor hrs. per unit:	20					
4			Worker hrs. per month:	160					
5			Beginning & ending workforce:	100					
6			Beginning & ending inventory:	100					
7						Total plan cost			
8			Production cost per unit:	$550.00		$6,600,000			
9			Hiring cost:	$300.00		$37,500			
10			Layoff cost:	$200.00		$25,000			
11		Holding cost per unit per month:		$4.00		$4,800			
12						$6,667,300	Grand total		
13	Month	Sales Forecast	Sales (in labor hrs.)	Sales (in workers)	Actual Workers	Actual Production	Hirings	Layoffs	Ending Inventory/ Back Orders
14					100				100
15	January	500	10,000	62.5	62.50	500.00	0.00	37.50	100.00
16	February	600	12,000	75	75.00	600.00	12.50	0.00	100.00
17	March	700	14,000	87.5	87.50	700.00	12.50	0.00	100.00
18	April	800	16,000	100	100.00	800.00	12.50	0.00	100.00
19	May	900	18,000	112.5	112.50	900.00	12.50	0.00	100.00
20	June	1,000	20,000	125	125.00	1,000.00	12.50	0.00	100.00
21	July	1,000	20,000	125	125.00	1,000.00	0.00	0.00	100.00
22	August	1,100	22,000	137.5	137.50	1,100.00	12.50	0.00	100.00
23	September	1,200	24,000	150	150.00	1,200.00	12.50	0.00	100.00
24	October	1,300	26,000	162.5	162.50	1,300.00	12.50	0.00	100.00
25	November	1,400	28,000	175	175.00	1,400.00	12.50	0.00	100.00
26	December	1,500	30,000	187.5	187.50	1,500.00	12.50	0.00	100.00
27							0.00	87.50	
28	Totals:	12,000				12,000.00	125.00	125.00	1,200.00
29			Average =	125					

FIGURE 10.10 S&OP Spreadsheet for Bob Irons Industries (Chase Plan)

TABLE 10.14 Description of the Optimization Problem for Bob Irons Industries

DESCRIPTION	CELL REFERENCE
Objective function:	
Minimize total production, hiring, layoff, and inventory costs	F12
By changing the following decision variables:	
Hiring and layoffs	G15:H26
Subject to the following constraints:	
Inventory in the last period must be at least 100 units	I26 ≥ 100
Inventory cannot go below zero (i.e., the sales forecast must be met)	I15:I25 ≥ 0
Hiring and layoff values cannot be negative	G15:H26 ≥ 0

Figure 10.11 shows the lowest-cost solution, as identified by Solver. The open dialog box illustrates how the problem stated in Table 10.14 was encoded into Solver. The new plan is roughly $18,000 cheaper than either the level or the chase approach. The suggested solution is to keep the workforce at around 92 workers for the first six months and then bump it up to around 158 workers for the last six months. Under this plan, the inventory level falls to zero only once (at the end of June).

Before making a final decision, Bob has to consider other factors as well. The Solver solution contains fractional workers—will it still work for whole numbers? If so, will Bob be able to hire and train nearly 67 workers in July? Does the company have enough space to store up to 500 units? Is the savings worth the added complexity? Solver can help Bob identify ways to lower costs, but the final decision belongs to *Bob*, not the spreadsheet.

FIGURE 10.11 Solver-Generated Optimal Solution for Bob Irons Industries
Microsoft Excel, Microsoft Corporation

CHAPTER SUMMARY

S&OP fills the gap between long-term strategic planning and short-term planning and control. Through S&OP, firms can not only plan and coordinate efforts in their own functional areas—operations, marketing, finance, human resources, and so on—but also effectively communicate to other members of the supply chain what they expect to accomplish over the intermediate time horizon.

In this chapter, we described several approaches to S&OP and demonstrated the power of the technique. We discussed when and where top-down versus bottom-up planning can be used and showed three basic approaches to S&OP: level, chase, and mixed production.

We also touched on some of the qualitative issues surrounding S&OP: How do we select a plan? How can we use S&OP to foster agreement and cooperation among the various parties? How can we organize for S&OP?

We also argued for increased sharing of S&OP information across the supply chain. As organizations put more emphasis on building supply chain relationships, we can expect to see more and more sharing of S&OP information between supply chain partners. Finally, we ended the chapter with a discussion of how optimization modeling techniques can be applied to the S&OP process.

KEY FORMULAS

Ending inventory level (page 307):

$$EI_t = EI_{t-1} + RP_t + OP_t - S_t \qquad (10.1)$$

where:

EI_t = ending inventory for time period t
RP_t = regular production in time period t
OP_t = overtime production in time period t
S_t = sales in time period t

Net cash flow (page 311):

$$\text{Net cash flow} = \text{cash inflows} - \text{cash outflows} \qquad (10.2)$$

KEY TERMS

Aggregate planning 300
Bottom-up planning 302
Chase production plan 306
Constraint 319
Detailed planning and control 301
Level production plan 305
Load profile 310

Mixed production plan 306
Net cash flow 311
Objective function 319
Offloading 318
Optimization model 319
Planning values 302
Rolling planning horizon 314

Sales and operations planning (S&OP) 300
Strategic planning 300
Tactical planning 300
Tiered workforce 318
Top-down planning 302
Yield management 316

SOLVED PROBLEM

PROBLEM

Hua Ng Exporters

Hua Ng Exporters makes commercial exercise equipment that is sold primarily in Europe and the United States. Hua Ng's two major product lines are stair steppers and elliptical machines. Resource requirements for both product lines, as well as six-month forecasts, are as follows:

PRODUCT LINE	LABOR HOURS PER UNIT	FABRICATION HOURS PER UNIT	ASSEMBLY LINE HOURS PER UNIT
Stair steppers	2.5	0.8	0.15
Ellipticals	1.0	1.8	0.20

	Sales Forecast	
MONTH	**STAIR**	**ELLIPTICALS**
1	560	400
2	560	400
3	545	415
4	525	435
5	525	435
6	525	435

Assuming that Hua Ng follows a chase production plan, develop load profiles for the next six months for labor, fabrication, and assembly line hours. Interpret the results.

Solution

The first step is to translate the sales forecasts for the two product lines into resource requirements. This will require us to calculate and then combine the resource needs for both product lines. Table 10.15 shows the results.

To illustrate how we arrived at these results, we calculated the total labor hours for month 1 as follows:

$$(560 \text{ stair steppers})(2.5 \text{ hours}) + (400 \text{ ellipticals})(1 \text{ hour}) = 1{,}400 + 400 = 1{,}800 \text{ hours}$$

The remaining numbers are calculated in a similar fashion. Figure 10.12 shows the load profiles for the three resources.

Total labor hours are expected to fall somewhat over time, while fabrication hours are expected to increase slightly. The reason is the change in the mix of products. Specifically, the forecast for stair steppers is falling, while the forecast for ellipticals is rising.

TABLE 10.15 Resource Requirements at Hua Ng Exporters

	Sales Forecast		TOTAL LABOR	TOTAL	TOTAL
MONTH	**STAIR STEPPERS**	**ELLIPTICALS**	**HOURS**	**FABRICATION**	**ASSEMBLY**
1	560	400	1,800	1,168	164
2	560	400	1,800	1,168	164
3	545	415	1,777.5	1,183	164.75
4	525	435	1,747.5	1,203	165.75
5	525	435	1,747.5	1,203	165.75
6	525	435	1,747.5	1,203	165.75

FIGURE 10.12 Load Profiles for Hua Ng Exporters

DISCUSSION QUESTIONS

1. Some people have argued that the *process* of developing a sales and operations plan is as important as the final numbers. How could this be?
2. How does S&OP differ from strategic capacity planning? From detailed planning and control? What role does S&OP play in the overall planning activities of an organization?
3. In general, under what conditions might a firm favor a level production plan over a chase plan? A chase production plan over a level plan?
4. Services, in general, cannot put "products" in inventory to be consumed at some later time. How does this limit service firms' S&OP alternatives?

5. Why is it important to update a sales and operations plan on a regular basis, using a rolling time horizon approach?
6. Ling suggests that superior S&OP planning can provide a firm with a competitive advantage. Do you agree? Can you think of any organizations you know that might benefit from better sales and operations planning?
7. What are the advantages to a firm of coordinating its S&OP process with key supply chain partners? What are the potential drawbacks?

PROBLEMS

(* = easy; ** = moderate; *** = advanced)

Problems for Section 10.2: Major Approaches to S&OP

1. Consider the following information for Sandy's Cleaning Service:

SERVICE	SERVICE MIX	LABOR HOURS PER JOB
Light cleaning	20%	0.20
Medium cleaning	60%	0.25
Deep cleaning	20%	0.35

   a. (*) Calculate the weighted planning value for labor hours per job.
   b. (**) Recalculate the weighted planning value based on a new service mix of 10%, 65%, and 25% for light, medium, and deep cleaning, respectively. What happened?

2. Consider the following information for Covolo Diving Gear:

GAUGE SET	PRODUCT MIX	MACHINE HOURS PER UNIT	LABOR HOURS PER UNIT
A20	60%	0.20	0.15
B30	15%	0.35	0.10
C40	25%	0.25	0.12

   a. (*) Calculate weighted planning values for machine hours and labor hours per gauge set. Interpret these planning values.
   b. (**) Recalculate the weighted planning values based on a new product mix of 45%, 30%, and 25% for the A20, B30, and C40 sets, respectively. What happened?

3. The typical monthly production mix at Bangor Industries is as follows:

Deluxe models	45%
Regular models	30%
Economy models	25%

   Each deluxe model typically requires 5 hours of labor and 10 hours of machine time. Each regular model takes 4 hours of labor and 8 hours of machine time. Finally, the economy model needs, on average, 3.5 hours of labor and 6 hours of machine time.

   a. (**) What should the weighted per-unit planning values be for labor? For machine time? What assumptions must be made in order to use these values?
   b. (**) Suppose that for the next month the mix is expected to change to 30% deluxe, 30% regular, and 40% economy models. How would this affect the planning values?
   c. (**) When the product mix changes from month to month, should Bangor Industries use a top-down or a bottom-up approach to sales and operations planning? Explain.

4. (**) On average, each unit produced by the Kantor Company takes 0.90 worker hours and 0.02 hours of machine time. Furthermore, each worker and machine is available 160 hours a month. Use these planning values and the following sales forecast to estimate (1) the number of worker hours and machine hours needed each month and (2) the number of workers and machines needed each month. Round your estimates of the number of workers and machines needed to the nearest whole number.

MONTH	SALES FORECAST
October	44,000
November	52,000
December	68,000
January	69,000
February	58,000
March	46,000

5. Consider the following sales forecasts for products A and B:

	Sales Forecasts	
MONTH	**PRODUCT A**	**PRODUCT B**
January	3,500	700
February	3,300	1,000
March	3,200	1,200
April	3,000	1,500
May	2,700	1,900
June	2,600	2,100

Each unit of product A takes approximately 2.5 labor hours, while each unit of product B takes only 1.8 hours.

a. (**) What is the combined (aggregate) sales forecast for products A and B? If this were the *only* information you had, would you expect resource requirements to increase or decrease from January to June?

b. (**) Use the planning value information to calculate total labor hour requirements in each month. Compare your calculations to your answer to part a. Interpret the results.

c. (**) Would top-down planning or bottom-up planning be better suited to S&OP in this situation? Explain.

6. (**) Complete the *level production plan*, using the following information. The only costs you need to consider here are layoff, hiring, and inventory costs. If you complete the plan correctly, your hiring, layoff, and inventory costs should match those given here.

	LAYOFF	HIRING	INVENTORY
Totals:	25	25	32,224
Costs:	$50,000	$75,000	$193,344
Cost of plan:		$318,344	

Planning values

Starting inventory:	1,000
Starting and ending workforce:	227
Hours worked per month per worker:	160
Hours per unit:	20
Hiring cost per worker:	$3,000
Layoff cost per worker:	$2,000
Monthly per-unit holding cost:	$6

Second Table for Problem 6

MONTH	FORECASTED SALES	SALES IN WORKER HOURS	WORKERS NEEDED TO MEET SALES AVERAGE = 252	ACTUAL WORKERS	ACTUAL PRODUCTION	LAYOFFS	HIRINGS	ENDING INVENTORY
March	1,592							
April	1,400							
May	1,200							
June	1,000							
July	1,504							
August	1,992							
September	2,504							
October	2,504							
November	3,000							
December	3,000							
January	2,504							
February	1,992							

7. (**) Complete the *chase production plan*, using the following information. The only costs you need to consider here are layoff, hiring, and inventory costs. If you complete the plan correctly, your hiring, layoff, and inventory costs should match those given here.

	LAYOFF	HIRING	INVENTORY
Totals:	250	250	12,000
Costs:	$500,000	$750,000	$72,000
Cost of plan:		$1,322,000	

Planning values

Starting inventory:	1,000
Starting and ending workforce:	227
Hours worked per month per worker:	160
Hours per unit:	20
Hiring cost per worker:	$3,000
Layoff cost per worker:	$2,000
Monthly per-unit holding cost:	$6

Second Table for Problem 7

MONTH	FORECASTED SALES	SALES IN WORKER HOURS	WORKERS NEEDED TON MEET SALES AVERAGE = 252	ACTUAL EMPLOYEES	ACTUAL PRODUCTION	LAYOFFS	HIRINGS	ENDING INVENTORY
March	1,592							
April	1,400							
May	1,200							
June	1,000							
July	1,504							
August	1,992							
September	2,504							
October	2,504							
November	3,000							
December	3,000							
January	2,504							
February	1,992							

8. (**) Consider the following partially completed sales and operations plan. Using the planning values and filled-in values as a guide, complete the plan and calculate the layoff, hiring, and inventory costs. Does this sales and operations plan reflect a chase, level, or mixed strategy? Explain.

	LAYOFF	HIRING	INVENTORY
Totals:			
Costs:			
Cost of plan:			
Planning values			
Starting inventory:			500
Starting and ending workforce:			50
Hours worked per month per worker:			160
Hours per unit:			4
Hiring cost per worker:			$300
Layoff cost per worker:			$200
Monthly per-unit holding cost:			$4

Second Table for Problem 8

MONTH	FORECASTED SALES	SALES IN WORKER HOURS	WORKERS NEEDED TO MEET SALES AVERAGE = 252	ACTUAL WORKERS	ACTUAL PRODUCTION	LAYOFFS	HIRINGS	ENDING INVENTORY
March		8,000				3	0	380
April		7,680				0	0	
May		7,360				0	0	
June	1,800	7,200				0	0	
July	1,800					0	0	
August	1,800					0	0	
September	1,750					11	0	
October	1,640					0	0	
				50		0	14	

9. (***) (*Microsoft Excel problem*) Note that problems 6 through 8 could all be solved by using a *single* spreadsheet that allows the user to change the planning, "Forecasted Sales," and "Actual Workers" values. **Create this spreadsheet.** Your spreadsheet should calculate new results anytime the planning, "Forecasted Sales," or "Actual Workers" values change. Verify that your spreadsheet works by determining whether it generates the same costs for a level production plan and a chase production plan shown in problems 6 and 7.

10. Castergourd Home Products makes two types of butcher-block tables: the Beefeater and the Deutschlander. The two tables are made in the same facility and require the same amount of labor and equipment. In addition, we know the following:

   - Each table costs $300 to make, and each requires, on average, 3.2 hours of labor.
   - Each employee works 160 hours per month, and there is no effective limit on the number of employees.
   - The cost of hiring or laying off an employee is $300.
   - The monthly holding cost for a table is $15.
   - For planning purposes, Castergourd will begin and end with 20 employees and 0 tables in inventory.

   Forecasted sales for the tables are as follows:

MONTH	BEEFEATER	DEUTSCHLANDER
November 2019	650	3,048
December	676	2,899
January 2020	624	3,198
February	624	2,671
March	696	2,919
April	475	3,102
May	566	2,964
June	819	2,409
July	754	3,381
August	982	3,965

   a. (***) Develop a top-down *level production plan* for Castergourd for the 10-month planning period. Calculate the total production, hiring, layoff, and inventory costs for your plan.

   b. (***) Repeat part a, except in this case develop a *chase production plan.*

   c. (**) Suppose hiring and layoff costs increase dramatically. In general, will this make a level plan look better or worse than a chase plan? Explain.

11. (**) Consider the level production plan for Pennington Cabinets shown in Table 10.5. Perform a cash flow analysis for this production plan, using the cash flow analysis in Example 10.8 as a guide. Assume that each cabinet set sold generates a cash inflow of $2,800, while each unit produced using regular time generates a cash outflow of $2,000 and each cabinet set held in inventory at the end of the month generates a cash outflow of $40. How does this cash flow compare with the one for the mixed strategy (Table 10.10)? Which plan do you think finance would prefer?

12. Consider the following information:

MONTH	FORECASTED SALES	REGULAR PRODUCTION	OVERTIME PRODUCTION	ENDING INVENTORY
January	800 units	1,150 units	0 units	350 units
February	1,000	1,150	0	500
March	1,200	1,150	0	450
April	1,400	1,150	0	200
May	1,600	1,150	150	0
June	1,500	1,150	350	0

   Each unit sells for $500. Regular production and overtime production costs are $350 and $450 per unit, respectively. The cost to hold a unit in inventory for one month is $10.

   a. (**) Develop a cash flow analysis for this problem. Be sure to calculate net cash flow and cumulative net cash flow for each month.

   b. (**) Why do the net cash flows for April and May look so much better than those for the other months? What are the implications for building up and draining down inventories under a level production plan?

13. (***) (*Microsoft Excel problem*) Re-create the S&OP spreadsheet used in Table 10.10 and Example 10.11. (You do *not* have to build in the optimization model using the Solver function.) While your formatting may differ, your answers should be the same. Your spreadsheet should generate new results any time any of the planning, sales forecast, or hiring/layoff values are changed. To test your spreadsheet, change the planning values to match the following:

	A	B	C	D
3			Labor hrs. per unit:	24
4			Worker hrs. per month:	150
5			Beginning & ending workforce:	100
6			Beginning & ending inventory:	100
7				
8			Production cost per unit:	$475.00
9			Hiring cost:	$400.00
10			Layoff cost:	$300.00
11			Holding cost per unit per month:	$3.00

   If your spreadsheet works correctly, the new total cost for a *level production plan* should be $5,769,100, and for a *chase production plan*, it should be $5,755,600.

14. (***) (*Microsoft Excel problem*) Kumquats Unlimited makes large batches of kumquat paste for use in the food industry. These batches are made on automated production lines. Kumquats Unlimited has the capability to start up or shut down lines at the beginning of each month, but at a cost. If a line is up, management has determined that it's best to keep the line busy, even if the resulting batches must be put in inventory.

   Management has created the following Excel spreadsheet, which uses the Solver function to find the lowest-cost solution to the S&OP problem. **Re-create this spreadsheet, including the Solver optimization model** (using Example 10.11 as a guide). Your formatting does not have to be the same, but your answers should be. Your spreadsheet should allow the user to make changes *only* to the planning values, the sales forecast, and the number of production line start-ups and shutdowns. All other values should be calculated. Be sure that Solver does not let inventory drop below zero at the end of any month or end June

with less inventory than was available at the beginning of January. To test your spreadsheet, modify the spreadsheet so that each batch requires 32 hours of production line time. The new optimal cost should be $16,215,000.

	A	B	C	D	E	F	G	H	I
1	Sales & Operations Planning Spreadsheet for Kumquats Unlimited								
2	(with Solver optimization)								
3									
4		Production cost per batch:	$ 2,400				Production costs:	$	
5		Line hours per batch:	16				Line start-up costs:	$ 125,000	
6		Production line hours per month:	320	hours			Line shutdown costs:	$ 75,000	
7		Cost to start up a line:	$ 25,000				Inventory holding costs:	$ 165,000	
8		Cost to shut down a line:	$ 6,000						
9		Inventory holding cost:	$ 300	per batch, per month			Grand total:	$14,964,000	
10		Beginning and ending lines:	55	production lines					
11		Beginning and ending inventory:	100	batches					
12									
13	Month	Sales Forecast	Sales (in line hours)	Sales (in production lines)	Actual Production Lines	Actual Production	Production Line Start-ups	Production Line Shutdowns	Ending Inventory
14					55				100
15	January	1,000	16,000	50	55.00	1,100	0	0	200
16	February	1,200	19,200	60	55.00	1,100	0	0	100
17	March	1,200	19,200	60	55.00	1,100	0	0	0
18	April	1,000	16,000	50	50.00	1,000	0	5	0
19	May	800	12,800	40	43.00	860	0	7	60
20	June	800	12,800	40	43.00	860	0	0	120
21					55		5	0	
22	Total =	6000				6,020	5	12.5	480
23			Average =	50					

CASE STUDY

Covolo Diving Gear, Part 2

June 15, 2020—Two weeks have passed since Covolo Diving Gear's contentious semiannual planning meeting, and the senior staff members for Covolo Diving Gear are getting ready to start their first monthly S&OP meeting. Gina Covolo, CEO, gets the ball rolling:

I know it's been a busy two weeks for all of you, and I appreciate you working extra time to get ready for this meeting. Production is already set for the next two months, so we're going to start by planning for this September through the following August. I've had Patricia from marketing develop a sales forecast for these 12 months, and I've also had David from manufacturing estimate manufacturing costs and labor requirements, as well as capacity in the plant. Mary from HR was good enough to come up with some estimates of how much it costs to hire and train new workers, as well as the cost of laying off folks. Finally, Jack from supply management was able to get the accounting folks to estimate the cost of holding a gauge set in inventory for a month. So let's see what we've got.

Mary passes out the following information to all of the attendees:

MONTH	SALES FORECAST
September 2020	30,000 gauge sets
October	31,500
November	35,000

(Continued)

MONTH	SALES FORECAST
December	37,000
January 2021	22,000
February	18,000
March	17,500
April	27,000
May	38,000
June	40,000
July	42,000
August	40,000

- Manufacturing cost per gauge set: $74.50
- Holding cost: $8 per gauge set per month
- Average labor hours required per gauge set: 0.25 hours
- Labor hours available per employee per month: 160
- Plant capacity: 35,000 gauge sets per month
- Cost to hire and train a new employee: $1,250
- Cost to lay off an employee: $500
- Beginning and ending workforce: 50
- Beginning inventory: 10,000

Questions

1. Develop a *level production plan* for Covolo Diving Gear. What are the advantages and disadvantages of this plan? Could Covolo implement a pure chase plan, given the

current capacity? Why? If sales continue to grow, what are the implications for production capacity at Covolo?

2. Patricia Rodriguez, vice president of marketing, states, "I've got to tell you all that I'm pretty comfortable with the forecasts for September through November, but after that, a lot could change. It's just very hard to forecast for four or more months out in this kind of market." How will a monthly S&OP update with rolling planning horizons help alleviate Patricia's concerns? Are there still advantages to S&OP, even though the forecasts may change?

3. After looking over the level production plan, David Griffin, vice president of manufacturing, speaks up: "This looks OK, but you know what bugs me about it? The assumption that if a worker is available, that worker *has* to be making gauge sets, even if we don't need any more. It might make sense in some cases to just have the worker *not* produce rather than lay off a worker in one month and hire someone else back the next." Do you agree? What are the holding costs associated with having an extra worker produce gauge sets for one month? How do these compare to the layoff and hiring costs? How might a strategy of keeping extra workers idle affect the estimated manufacturing costs for the gauge sets? (*Hint:* Labor costs have to be accounted for *somewhere*.)

REFERENCES

Books and Articles

Blackstone, J. H., ed., *APICS Dictionary*, 15th ed. (Chicago, IL: APICS, 2016).

Ling, R., "For True Enterprise Integration, Turn First to SOP," *APICS—The Performance Advantage* 10, no. 3 (March 2000): 40–45.

Internet

Linking CPFR and S&OP: A Roadmap to Integrated Business Planning, 2010, **www.gs1us.org/DesktopModules/ Bring2mind/DMX/Download.aspx?command=core_ download&entryid=433&language=en-US&PortalI d=0&TabId=134.**

Paul A. Souders/Corbis/VCG/Getty Images

CHAPTER
eleven

Managing Inventory throughout the Supply Chain

CHAPTER OBJECTIVES

By the end of this chapter, you will be able to:

- Describe the various roles of inventory, including the different types of inventory and inventory drivers.

- Distinguish between independent demand and dependent demand inventory.

- Calculate the restocking level for a periodic review system.

- Calculate the economic order quantity (EOQ) and reorder point (ROP) for a continuous review system.

- Determine the best order quantity when volume discounts are available.

- Calculate the target service level and target stocking point for a single-period inventory system.

- Describe how inventory decisions affect other areas of the supply chain. In particular, describe the bullwhip effect, inventory positioning issues, and the impacts of transportation, packaging, and material handling considerations.

INVENTORY MANAGEMENT AT AMAZON.COM

Employees pick items off the shelves at an Amazon.com warehouse in Leipzig, Germany.

When they first started appearing in the late 1990s, Web-based "e-tailers" such as Amazon.com hoped to replace the "bricks" of traditional retailing with the "clicks" of online ordering. Rather than opening dozens or even hundreds of stores filled with expensive inventory, an e-tailer could run a single virtual store that served customers around the globe. Their business model suggested that inventory could be kept at a few key sites, chosen to minimize costs and facilitate quick delivery to customers. In theory, e-tailers were highly "scalable" businesses that could add new customers with little or no additional investment in inventory or facilities. (Traditional retailers usually need to add stores to gain significant increases in their customer base.)

But how has this actually played out for Amazon over the years? Table 11.1 contains sales and inventory figures, pulled from the company's annual reports, for Amazon for the years 1997 through 2015. The first column reports net sales for each calendar year, and the second column contains the amount of inventory on hand at the end of the year. The third column shows inventory turns, which is calculated as (net sales/ending inventory). Retailers generally want *higher* inventory turns, which indicate that they can support the same level of sales with less inventory. Inventory turns is often thought of as a key measure of asset productivity.

Looking at Amazon's performance over the years provides some interesting insights. Consider Figure 11.1. In late 1999, Amazon learned that managing inventory can be challenging even for e-tailers. That was the year the company expanded into new product lines, such as electronics and housewares, with which it had little experience.

TABLE 11.1 Amazon.com Financial Results, 1997–2015

YEAR	NET SALES ($MILLIONS)	INVENTORY ($MILLIONS) (DEC. 31)	INVENTORY TURNS
1997	$148	$9	16.4
1998	$610	$30	20.3
1999	$1,640	$221	7.4
2000	$2,762	$175	15.8
2001	$3,122	$143	21.8
2002	$3,933	$202	19.5
2003	$5,264	$294	17.9
2004	$6,921	$480	14.4
2005	$8,490	$566	15.0
2006	$10,711	$877	12.2
2007	$14,835	$1,200	12.4
2008	$19,166	$1,399	13.7
2009	$24,509	$2,171	11.3
2010	$34,204	$3,202	10.7
2011	$48,077	$4,992	9.6
2012	$61,093	$6,031	10.1
2013	$74,452	$7,411	10.0
2014	$88,988	$8,299	10.7
2015	$107,006	$10,243	10.4

Amazon's purchasing managers were faced with the question of how many of these items to hold in inventory. Too little, and they risked losing orders and alienating customers; too much, and they could lock up the company's resources in unsold products. Only later, when sales for the

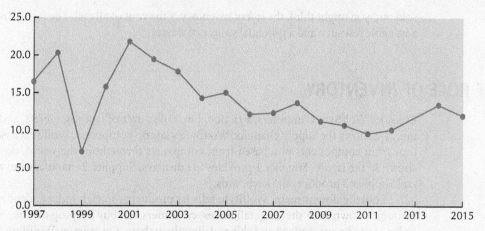

FIGURE 11.1 Inventory Turns at Amazon.com, 1997–2015

1999 holiday season fell flat and Amazon's inventory levels skyrocketed, did the purchasing managers realize they had overstocked. In fact, as the figures show, by the end of 1999, Amazon's inventory turnover ratio was 7.4—*worse* than that of the typical brick-and-mortar retailer at the time.

After 1999, Amazon seemed to learn its lesson. Inventory turns rose to nearly 22 in 2001, but have since fallen and stabilized at around 10 turns per year, even as Amazon's sales have risen sharply. But why? The decline in inventory turns over the past 15 years is due in large part to a shift in Amazon's business strategy. Instead of trying to build competitive advantage based on low-cost books

(Amazon's original business model), the company now seeks to provide customers with convenient shopping and fast delivery for a wide range of products. Such a strategy requires more inventory to support the same level of sales.

So today, how does Amazon compare to its brick-and-mortar competitors? Amazon handily beats traditional book retailer Barnes & Noble, whose inventory turns for 2016 were just 4.5. Yet Best Buy, which sells computers, phones, video games, and appliances, generated 7.8 inventory turns in 2016, a noticeable improvement over the 6.9 inventory turns in 2013—not bad, especially considering all the retail stores Best Buy must support.

INTRODUCTION

Inventory
According to APICS, "those stocks or items used to support production (raw materials and work-in-process items), supporting activities (maintenance, repair, and operating supplies) and customer service (finished goods and spare parts)."

APICS defines **inventory** as "those stocks or items used to support production (raw materials and work-in-process items), supporting activities (maintenance, repair, and operating supplies) and customer service (finished goods and spare parts)."[1] In this chapter, we discuss the critical role of inventory—why it is necessary, what purposes it serves, and how it is controlled.

As Amazon's experience suggests, inventory management is still an important function, even in the age of online retailing. In fact, many managers seem to have a love–hate relationship with inventory. Michael Dell once talked about inventory velocity—the speed at which components move through Dell Computer's operations—as a key measure of his company's performance.[2] In his mind, the less inventory the company has sitting in the warehouse, the better. Victor Fung of the Hong Kong–based trading firm Li & Fung goes so far as to say, "Inventory is the root of all evil."[3]

Yet look what happened to the price of gasoline in the southeastern United States during the fall of 2016. It skyrocketed due to an explosion in a major pipeline combined with inadequate reserves.[4] And if you have ever visited a store only to find that your favorite product is

---

[1]J. H. Blackstone, ed., *APICS Dictionary*, 15th ed. (Chicago, IL: APICS, 2016).

[2]J. Magretta, "The Power of Virtual Integration: An Interview with Dell Computer's Michael Dell," *Harvard Business Review* 76, no. 2 (March–April 1998): 72–84.

[3]J. Magretta, "Fast, Global, and Entrepreneurial: Supply Chain Management, Hong Kong Style," *Harvard Business Review* 76, no. 5 (September–October 1998): 102–109.

[4]C. Isodore, "Gas Price Spikes and Shortages Coming after Fatal Pipeline Blast," *CNN Money*, November 3, 2016, **http://money.cnn.com/2016/11/01/news/colonial-pipeline-explosion-gasoline-price-spike/.**

sold out, you might think the *lack* of inventory is the root of all evil. The fact is, inventory is both a valuable resource and a potential source of waste.

11.1 THE ROLE OF INVENTORY

Consider WolfByte Computers, a fictional manufacturer of laptops, tablets, and e-readers. Figure 11.2 shows the supply chain for WolfByte's laptop computers. WolfByte assembles the laptops from components purchased from companies throughout the world, three of which are shown in the figure. Supplier 1 provides the displays, Supplier 2 manufactures the hard drives, and Supplier 3 produces the keyboards.

Looking downstream, WolfByte sells its products through independent retail stores and through its own Web site. At retail stores, customers can buy a laptop off the shelf, or they can order one to be customized and shipped directly to them. On average, WolfByte takes about two days to ship a computer from its assembly plant to a retail store or a customer. Both WolfByte and the retail stores keep spare parts on hand to handle customers' warranty claims and other service requirements.

With this background, let's discuss the basic types of inventory and see how they fit into WolfByte's supply chain.

Inventory Types

Cycle stock
Components or products that are received in bulk by a downstream partner, gradually used up, and then replenished again in bulk by the upstream partner.

Two of the most common types of inventory are cycle stock and safety stock. **Cycle stock** refers to components or products that are received in bulk by a downstream partner, gradually used up, and then replenished again in bulk by the upstream partner. For example, suppose Supplier 3 ships 20,000 keyboards at a time to WolfByte. Of course, WolfByte can't use all those components at once. More likely, workers pull them out of inventory as needed. Eventually, the inventory runs down, and WolfByte places another order for keyboards. When the new order arrives, the inventory level rises and the cycle is repeated. Figure 11.3 shows the classic sawtooth pattern associated with cycle stock inventories.

Cycle stock exists at other points in WolfByte's supply chain. Almost certainly, Suppliers 1 through 3 have cycle stocks of raw materials that they use to make components. And retailers need to keep cycle stocks of both completed computers and spare parts in order to serve their customers.

Safety stock
Extra inventory that a company holds to protect itself against uncertainties in either demand or replenishment time.

Cycle stock is often thought of as active inventory because companies are constantly using it up, and their suppliers constantly replenishing it. **Safety stock,** on the other hand, is extra inventory that companies hold to protect themselves against uncertainties in either demand levels or replenishment time. Companies do not plan on using their safety stock any more than you plan on using a fire extinguisher; it is there *just in case.*

FIGURE 11.2
WolfByte Computers's Supply Chain

FIGURE 11.3
Cycle Stock at
WolfByte Computers

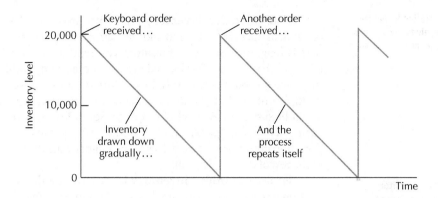

Let's return to the keyboard example in Figure 11.3. WolfByte has timed its orders so that a new batch of keyboards comes in just as the old batch is used up. But what if Supplier 3 is late in delivering the devices? What if demand makes inventory levels fall faster than expected? If either or both these conditions occur, WolfByte could run out of keyboards before the next order arrives.

Imagine the resulting chaos: Assembly lines would have to shut down, customers' orders couldn't be filled, and WolfByte would have to notify customers, retailers, and shippers about the delays.

One solution is to hold some extra inventory, or safety stock, of keyboards to protect against fluctuations in demand or replenishment time. Figure 11.4 shows what WolfByte's inventory levels would look like if the company decided to hold safety stock of 1,000 keyboards. As you can see, safety stock provides valuable protection, but at the cost of higher inventory levels. Later in the chapter, we discuss ways of calculating appropriate safety stock levels.

There are four other common types of inventory: anticipation, hedge, transportation, and smoothing. **Anticipation inventory,** as the name implies, is inventory that is held in anticipation of customer demand. Anticipation inventory allows instant availability of items when customers want them. **Hedge inventory,** according to APICS, is "a form of inventory buildup to buffer against some event that may not happen. Hedge inventory planning involves speculation related to potential labor strikes, price increases, unsettled governments, and events that could severely impair the company's strategic initiatives."[5] In this sense, hedge inventories can be thought of as a special form of safety stock. WolfByte has stockpiled a hedge inventory of two months' worth of hard drives because managers have heard that Supplier 2 may experience a temporary shutdown over the next two months.

Anticipation inventory
Inventory that is held in anticipation of customer demand.

Hedge inventory
According to APICS, a "form of inventory buildup to buffer against some event that may not happen. Hedge inventory planning involves speculation related to potential labor strikes, price increases, unsettled governments, and events that could severely impair the company's strategic initiatives."

FIGURE 11.4
Safety Stock at
WolfByte Computers

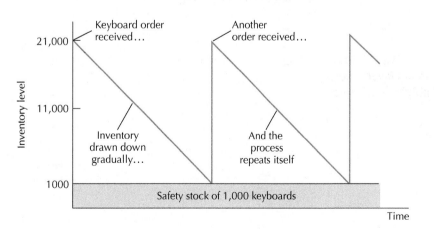

---

[5]Blackstone, *APICS Dictionary.*

Transportation inventory
Inventory that is moving from one link in the supply chain to another.

Smoothing inventory
Inventory that is used to smooth out differences between upstream production levels and downstream demand.

Transportation inventory represents inventory that is "in the pipeline," moving from one link in the supply chain to another. When the physical distance between supply chain partners is long, transportation inventory can represent a considerable investment. Suppose, for example, that Supplier 2 is located in South Korea, and WolfByte is located in Texas. Hard drives may take several weeks to travel the entire distance between the two companies. As a result, multiple orders could be in the pipeline on any particular day. One shipment of hard drives might be sitting on the docks in Kimhae, South Korea; two others might be halfway across the Pacific; a fourth might be found on Route I-10, just outside Phoenix, Arizona. In fact, the transportation inventory of hard drives alone might dwarf the total cycle and safety stock inventories in the rest of the supply chain.

Finally, **smoothing inventory** is used to smooth out differences between upstream production levels and downstream demand. Suppose management has determined that WolfByte's assembly plant is most productive when it produces 3,000 laptops a day. Unfortunately, demand from retailers and customers will almost certainly vary from day to day. As a result, WolfByte's managers may decide to produce a constant 3,000 laptops per day, building up finished goods inventory during periods of slow demand and drawing it down during periods of high demand. (Figure 11.5 illustrates this approach.) Smoothing inventories allow individual links in the supply chain to stabilize their production at the most efficient level and to avoid the costs and headaches associated with constantly changing workforce levels and/or production rates. If you think you may have heard of this idea before, you have: It's part of the rationale for following a level production strategy in developing a sales and operations plan (see Chapter 10).

Inventory Drivers

From this discussion, we can see that inventory is a useful resource. However, companies don't want to hold more inventory than necessary. Inventory ties up space and capital: A dollar invested in inventory is a dollar that cannot be used somewhere else. Likewise, the space used to store inventory can often be put to more productive use. Inventory also poses a significant risk of obsolescence, particularly in supply chains with short product life cycles. Consider what happens when Samsung announces its next generation of cell phones. Would you want to be stuck holding the old-generation cell phones when the new ones hit the market?

Finally, inventory is too often used to hide problems that management really should resolve. In this sense, inventory can serve as a kind of painkiller, treating the symptom without solving the underlying problem. Consider our discussion of safety stock. Suppose WolfByte's managers decide to hold additional safety stock of hard drives because of quality problems they have been experiencing with units received from Supplier 2. While the safety stock may buffer WolfByte from these quality problems, it does so at a cost. A better solution might be to improve the quality of incoming units, thereby reducing both quality-related costs and the need for additional safety stock.

FIGURE 11.5
Smoothing Inventories at WolfByte Computers

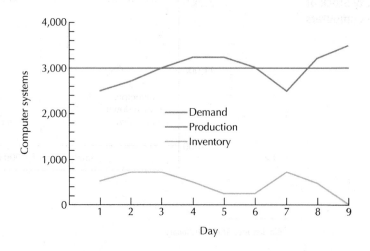

TABLE 11.2
Inventory Drivers and Their Impact

INVENTORY DRIVER	IMPACT
Uncertainty in supply or demand	Safety stock, hedge inventory
Mismatch between a downstream partner's demand and the most efficient production or shipment volumes for an upstream partner	Cycle stock
Mismatch between downstream demand levels and upstream production capacity	Smoothing inventory
Mismatch between timing of customer demand and supply chain lead times	Anticipation inventory, transportation inventory

Inventory drivers
Business conditions that force companies to hold inventory.

Supply uncertainty
The risk of interruptions in the flow of components from upstream suppliers.

Demand uncertainty
The risk of significant and unpredictable fluctuations in downstream demand.

With these concerns in mind, let's turn our attention to **inventory drivers**—business conditions that force companies to hold inventory. Table 11.2 summarizes the ways in which various inventory drivers affect different types of inventory. To the extent that organizations can manage and control the drivers of inventories, they can reduce the supply chain's need for inventory.

In managing inventory, organizations face uncertainty throughout the supply chain. On the upstream (supplier) end, they face **supply uncertainty,** or the risk of interruptions in the flow of components they need for their internal operations. In assessing supply uncertainty, managers need to answer questions such as these:

• How consistent is the quality of the goods being purchased?
• How reliable are the supplier's delivery estimates?
• Are the goods subject to unexpected price increases or shortages?

Problems in any of these areas can drive up supply uncertainty, forcing an organization to hold safety stock or hedging inventories.

On the downstream (customer) side, organizations face **demand uncertainty,** or the risk of significant and unpredictable fluctuations in the demand for their products. For example, many suppliers of automobile components complain that the big automobile manufacturers' forecasts are unreliable and that order sizes are always changing, often at the last minute. Under such conditions, suppliers are forced to hold extra safety stock to meet unexpected jumps in demand or changes in order size.

In dealing with uncertainty in supply and demand, the trick is to determine what types of uncertainty can be reduced and then to focus on reducing them. For example, poor quality is a source of supply uncertainty that can be substantially reduced or even eliminated through business process or quality improvement programs, such as those we discussed in Chapters 4 and 5. On the other hand, forecasting may help to reduce demand uncertainty, but it can never completely eliminate it.

Another common inventory driver is the mismatch between demand and the most efficient production or shipment volumes. Let's start with a simple example—facial tissue. When you blow your nose, how many tissues do you use? Most people would say 1, yet tissues typically come in boxes of 200 or more. Clearly, a mismatch exists between the number of tissues you need at any one time and the number you need to purchase. The reason, of course, is that packaging, shipping, and selling facial tissues one at a time would be highly inefficient, especially because the cost of holding a cycle stock of facial tissues is trivial. On an organizational scale, mismatches between demand and efficient production or shipment volumes are the main drivers of cycle stocks. As we will see later in this chapter, managers can often alter their business processes to reduce production or shipment volumes, thereby reducing the mismatch with demand and the resulting need for cycle stocks.

Likewise, mismatches between overall demand levels and production capacity can force companies to hold smoothing inventories (Figure 11.5). Of course, managers can reduce smoothing inventories by varying their capacity to better match demand or by smoothing demand to better match capacity. As we saw in Chapter 10, both strategies have pros and cons.

The last inventory driver we will discuss is a mismatch between the timing of the customer's demand and the supply chain's lead time. When you go to the grocery store, you expect to find fresh produce ready to buy; your expected waiting time is zero. But produce can come from almost anywhere in the world, depending on the season. To make sure that bananas and lettuce will be ready and waiting for you at your local store, someone has to initiate their movement through the supply chain days or even weeks ahead of time and determine how much anticipation inventory to hold. Whenever the customer's maximum waiting time is shorter than the supply chain's lead time, companies must have transportation and anticipation inventories to ensure that the product will be available when the customer wants it.

How can businesses reduce the need to hold anticipation inventory? Often they do so both by shrinking their own lead time and by persuading customers to wait longer. It's hard to believe now, but personal computers once took many weeks to work their way through the supply chain. As a result, manufacturers were forced to hold anticipation inventories to meet customer demand. Today manufacturers assemble and ship a *customized* laptop or tablet directly to the customer's front door in just a few days. Customers get fast and convenient delivery of a product that meets their exact needs. At the same time, the manufacturer can greatly reduce or even eliminate anticipation inventory.

In the remainder of this chapter, we examine the systems that are used in managing various types of inventory. Before beginning a detailed discussion of these tools and techniques of inventory management, however, we need to distinguish between two basic inventory categories: independent demand and dependent demand inventory. The distinction between the two is crucial because the tools and techniques needed to manage each are *very* different.

Independent versus Dependent Demand Inventory

Independent demand inventory
Inventory items whose demand levels are beyond a company's complete control.

Dependent demand inventory
Inventory items whose demand levels are tied directly to a company's planned production of another item.

In general, **independent demand inventory** refers to inventory items whose demand levels are beyond a company's complete control. **Dependent demand inventory,** on the other hand, refers to inventory items whose demand levels are tied directly to the company's planned production of another item. Because the required quantities and timing of dependent demand inventory items can be predicted with great accuracy, they are under a company's *complete* control.

A simple example of an independent demand inventory item is a kitchen table. While a furniture manufacturer may use forecasting models to predict the demand for kitchen tables and may try to use pricing and promotions to manipulate demand, the *exact* demand for kitchen tables is unpredictable. The fact is that *customers* determine the demand for these items, so finished tables clearly fit the definition of independent demand inventory.

But what about the components that are used to make the tables, such as legs? Suppose that a manufacturer has decided to produce 500 tables five weeks from now. With this information, a manager can quickly calculate exactly how many legs will be needed:

$$500 \times 4 \text{ legs per table} = 2{,}000 \text{ legs}$$

Furthermore, the manager can determine exactly when the legs will be needed, based on the company's production schedule. Because the timing and quantity of the demand for table legs are completely predictable and under the manager's total control, the legs fit the definition of dependent demand items. Dependent demand items require an entirely different approach to managing than do independent demand items. We discuss ways of managing dependent demand items in more depth in Chapter 12.

Three basic approaches are used to manage independent demand inventory items: periodic review systems, continuous review systems, and single-period inventory systems. We examine all three approaches in the following sections.

Periodic review system
An inventory system that is used to manage independent demand inventory. The inventory level for an item is checked at regular intervals and restocked to some predetermined level.

11.2 PERIODIC REVIEW SYSTEMS

One of the simplest approaches to managing independent demand inventory is based on a periodic review of inventory levels. In a **periodic review system,** a company checks the inventory level of an item at regular intervals and restocks to some predetermined level, R. The actual order quantity, Q, is the amount required to bring the inventory level back up to R. Stated more formally:

$$Q = R - I \tag{11.1}$$

FIGURE 11.6
Periodic Review
System

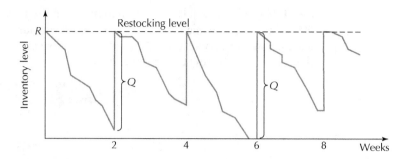

where:

Q = order quantity

R = restocking level

I = inventory level at the time of review

Figure 11.6 shows the fluctuations in the inventory levels of a single item under a two-week periodic review system. As the downward-sloping line shows, the inventory starts out full and then drains down as units are pulled from it. (Note that the line will be straight only if demand is constant.) After two weeks, the inventory is replenished, and the process begins again.

A periodic review system nicely illustrates the use of both cycle stock and safety stock. By replenishing inventory every two weeks, rather than daily or even hourly, the organization spreads the cyclical cost of restocking across more units. And the need to hold safety stock helps to determine the restocking level. Increasing the restocking level effectively increases safety stock: The higher the level, the less likely the organization is to run out of inventory before the next replenishment period. On the flip side, because inventory is checked only at regular intervals, the company could run out of an item before the inventory is replenished. In fact, that is exactly what happens just before week 6 in Figure 11.6. If you have ever visited your favorite vending machine, only to find that the item you wanted has been sold out, you have been the victim of a periodic review system stockout.

As you might imagine, a periodic review system is best suited to items for which periodic restocking is economical and the cost of a high restocking level (and hence a large safety stock) is not prohibitive. A classic example is a snack food display at a grocery store. Constantly monitoring inventory levels for low-value items such as pretzels or potato chips makes no economic sense. Rather, a vendor will stop by a store regularly and top off the supply of all the items, usually with more than enough to meet demand until the next replenishment date.

Restocking Levels

The key question in setting up a periodic review system is determining the restocking level, R. In general, R should be high enough to meet all but the most extreme demand levels during the reorder period (RP) and the time it takes for the order to come in (L). Specifically:

$$R = \mu_{RP+L} + z\sigma_{RP+L} \qquad \text{(11.2)}$$

where:

μ_{RP+L} = average demand during the reorder period and the order lead time

σ_{RP+L} = standard deviation of demand during the reorder period and the order lead time

z = number of standard deviations above the average demand (higher z values increase the restocking level, thereby lowering the probability of a stockout)

Service level
A term used to indicate the amount of demand to be met under conditions of demand and supply uncertainty.

Equation (11.2) assumes that the demand during the reorder period and the order lead time is normally distributed. By setting R a certain number of standard deviations above the average, a firm can establish a **service level,** which indicates what percentage of the time inventory levels will be high enough to meet demand during the reorder period. For example, setting

$z = 1.28$ would make R large enough to meet expected demand 90% of the time (i.e., provide a 90% service level), while setting $z = 2.33$ would provide a 99% service level. Different z values and the resulting service levels are listed in the following table. (More values can be derived from the normal curves area table in Appendix I.)

z VALUE	RESULTING SERVICE LEVEL
1.28	90%
1.65	95%
2.33	99%
3.08	99.9%

EXAMPLE 11.1

Establishing a Periodic Review System for McCreery's Chips

McCreery's Chips sells large tins of potato chips at a grocery superstore. Every 10 days, a McCreery's deliveryperson stops by and checks the inventory level. He then places an order, which is delivered 3 days later. Average demand during the reorder period and order lead time (13 days total) is 240 tins. The standard deviation of demand during this same time period is 40 tins. The grocery superstore wants enough inventory on hand to meet demand 95% of the time. In other words, the store is willing to take a 5% chance that it will run out of tins before the next order arrives.

Using this information, McCreery's establishes the following restocking level:

$$R = \mu_{RP+L} + z\sigma_{RP+L}$$
$$= 240 \text{ tins} + 1.65 * 40 \text{ tins} = 306 \text{ tins}$$

Suppose the next time the delivery person stops by, he counts 45 tins. Based on this information, he will order $Q = 306 - 45 = 261$ tins, which will be delivered in 3 days.

11.3 CONTINUOUS REVIEW SYSTEMS

While the periodic review system is straightforward, it is *not* well suited to managing critical and/or expensive inventory items. A more sophisticated approach is needed for these types of inventory. In a **continuous review system,** the inventory level for an item is constantly monitored, and when the reorder point is reached, an order is released.

A continuous review system has several key features:

Continuous review system
An inventory system used to manage independent demand inventory. The inventory level for an item is constantly monitored, and when the reorder point is reached, an order is released.

1. Inventory levels are monitored constantly, and a replenishment order is issued only when a preestablished reorder point has been reached.
2. The size of a replenishment order is typically based on the trade-off between holding costs and ordering costs.
3. The reorder point is based on both demand and supply considerations, as well as on how much safety stock managers want to hold.

To simplify our discussion of continuous review systems, we will begin by assuming that the variables that underlie the system are constant. Specifically:

1. The inventory item we are interested in has a constant demand per period, d. That is, there is no variability in demand from one period to the next. Demand for the year is D.
2. L is the lead time, or number of periods that must pass before a replenishment order arrives. L is also constant.
3. H is the cost of holding a single unit in inventory for a year. It includes the cost of the space needed to store the unit, the cost of potential obsolescence, and the opportunity cost of tying up the organization's funds in inventory. H is known and fixed.
4. S is the cost of placing an order, regardless of the order quantity. For example, the cost to place an order might be $100, whether the order is for 2 or 2,000 units. S is also known and fixed.
5. P, the price of each unit, is fixed.

FIGURE 11.7
Continuous Review
System (with Constant
Demand Rate *d*)

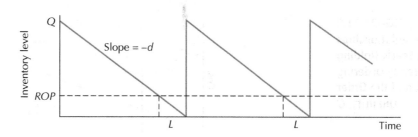

Under these assumptions, the fluctuations in the inventory levels for an item will look like those in Figure 11.7. Inventory levels start out at Q, the order quantity, and decrease at a constant rate, *d*. Because this is a continuous review system, the next order is issued when the reorder point, labeled ROP, is reached. What should the reorder point be? In this simple model, in which the demand rate and lead time are constant, we should reorder when the inventory level reaches the point where there are just enough units left to meet requirements until the next order arrives:

$$ROP = dL \tag{11.3}$$

For example, if the demand rate is 50 units a week and the lead time is 3 weeks, the manager should place an order when the inventory level drops to 150 units. If everything goes according to plan, the firm will run out of units just as the next order arrives. Finally, because the inventory level in this model goes from Q to 0 over and over again, the average inventory level is $\frac{Q}{2}$.

The Economic Order Quantity (*EOQ*)

How do managers of a continuous review system choose the order quantity (Q)? Is there a "best" order quantity, and if so, how do holding costs (H) and ordering costs (S) affect it? To understand the role of holding and ordering costs in a continuous review system, let's see what happens if the order quantity is sliced in half, to Q' as shown in Figure 11.8. The result: With quantity Q' the manager ends up ordering twice as often, which doubles the company's ordering costs. On the other hand, cutting the order quantity in half also halves the average inventory level, which lowers holding costs.

The relationship between holding costs and ordering costs can be seen in the following equation:

Total holding and ordering cost for the year = total yearly holding cost

+ total yearly ordering cost

$$= \left(\frac{Q}{2}\right)H + \left(\frac{D}{Q}\right)S \tag{11.4}$$

Yearly holding cost is calculated by taking the average inventory level (Q/2) and multiplying it by the per-unit holding cost. Yearly ordering cost is calculated by calculating the number of times we order per year (D/Q) and multiplying this by the fixed ordering cost.

As Equation (11.4) suggests, there is a trade-off between yearly holding costs and ordering costs. Reducing the order quantity, Q, will decrease holding costs, but force the organization to order more often. Conversely, increasing Q will reduce the number of times an order must be placed but result in higher average inventory levels.

FIGURE 11.8
The Effect of Halving
the Order Quantity

FIGURE 11.9
The Relationships among Yearly Holding Costs, Yearly Ordering Costs, and the Order Quantity, Q

Figure 11.9 shows graphically how yearly holding and ordering costs react as the order quantity, Q, varies. In addition to showing the cost curves for yearly holding costs and yearly ordering costs, Figure 11.9 includes a total cost curve that combines these two. If you look closely, you can see that the lowest point on the total cost curve also happens to be where yearly holding costs equal yearly ordering costs.

Economic order quantity (EOQ)
The order quantity that minimizes annual holding and ordering costs for an item.

Figure 11.9 illustrates the **economic order quantity (EOQ),** the particular order quantity (Q) that minimizes holding costs and ordering costs for an item. This special order quantity is found by setting yearly holding costs equal to yearly ordering costs and solving for Q:

$$\left(\frac{Q}{2}\right)H = \left(\frac{D}{Q}\right)S$$

$$Q^2 = \frac{2DS}{H} \tag{11.5}$$

$$Q = \sqrt{\frac{2DS}{H}} = EOQ$$

where:

Q = order quantity
H = annual holding cost per unit
D = annual demand
S = ordering cost

As Figure 11.9 shows, order quantities that are higher than the EOQ will result in annual holding costs that are higher than ordering costs. Conversely, order quantities that are lower than the EOQ will result in annual ordering costs that are higher than holding costs.

EXAMPLE 11.2

Calculating the EOQ at Boyer's Department Store

You are in charge of ordering items for Boyer's Department Store, located in Seattle. For one of the products Boyer's carries, the Hudson Valley Model Y ceiling fan, you have the following information:

$$\text{Annual demand } (D) = 4{,}000 \text{ fans a year}$$
$$\text{Annual holding cost } (H) = \$15 \text{ per fan}$$
$$\text{Ordering cost } (S) = \$50 \text{ per order}$$

Your predecessor ordered fans four times a year, in quantities (Q) of 1,000. The resulting annual holding and ordering costs were:

$$\text{Holding costs for the year } + \text{ ordering costs for the year}$$
$$= (1{,}000 / 2) + (4{,}000 / 1{,}000)\$50$$
$$= \$7{,}500 + \$200 = \$7{,}700$$

Because holding costs are much higher than ordering costs, we know that the EOQ must be much lower than 1,000 fans. In fact:

$$EOQ = \sqrt{\frac{2*4{,}000*\$50}{\$15}}, \text{ which rounds to 163 fans per order}$$

The number 163 seems strange, so let's check to see if it results in lower annual costs:

$$\text{Holding costs + ordering costs}$$
$$= (163/2)\$15 + (4{,}000/163)\$50$$
$$= \$1{,}222.50 + \$1{,}226.99 = \$2{,}449.49$$

Notice that holding costs and ordering costs are essentially equal, as we would expect. More important, *simply by ordering the right quantity*, you could reduce annual holding and ordering costs for this item by

$$\$7{,}700 - \$2{,}449 = \$5{,}251$$

Now suppose Boyer's carries 250 other products with cost and demand structures similar to that of the Hudson Valley Model Y ceiling fan. In that case, you might be able to save $250*\$5{,}251 = \$1{,}312{,}750$ per year in ordering and holding costs just by ordering the right quantities!

Of course, the EOQ has some limitations. Holding costs (*H*) and ordering costs (*S*) cannot always be estimated precisely, so managers may not always be able to calculate the true EOQ. However, as Figure 11.9 suggests, total holding and ordering costs are relatively flat over a wide range around the EOQ. So order quantities can be off a little and still yield total costs that are close to the minimum.

A more valid criticism of the EOQ is that it does not take into account volume discounts, which can be particularly important if suppliers offer steep discounts to encourage customers to order in large quantities. Later in the chapter, we examine how volume discounts affect the order quantity decision.

Other factors that limit the application of the EOQ model include ordering costs that are not always fixed and demand rates that vary throughout the year. However, the EOQ is a good starting point for understanding the impact of order quantities on inventory-related costs.

Reorder Points and Safety Stock

The EOQ tells managers *how much* to order but not *when* to order. We saw in Equation (11.3) that when the demand rate (*d*) and lead time (*L*) are constant, the reorder point is easily calculated as:

$$ROP = dL$$

But *d* and *L* are rarely fixed. Consider the data in Table 11.3, which lists 10 different combinations of demand rates and lead times. The average demand rate, $\bar{d}$, and average lead

TABLE 11.3
Sample Variations in Demand Rate and Lead Time

DEMAND RATE (*d*) IN UNITS PER WEEK	LEAD TIME (*L*), IN WEEKS	DEMAND DURING LEAD TIME (*dL*), IN UNITS
60	3	180*
40	4	160*
55	2	110
45	3	135
50	3	150
65	3	195*
35	3	105
55	3	165*
45	4	180*
50	2	100
Average = 50 units	Average = 3 weeks	Average = 148 units

*Demand greater than $\overline{dL}$

FIGURE 11.10
**The Impact of Varying
Demand Rates and
Lead Times**

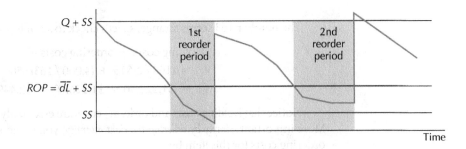

time, $\bar{L}$, are 50 units and 3 weeks, respectively. Our first inclination in this case might be to set the reorder point at $\bar{d}\bar{L} = 150$ units. Yet 5 out of 10 times, dL exceeds 150 units (see Table 11.3). A better solution—one that takes into account the variability in demand rate and lead time—is needed.

When either lead time or demand—or both—varies, a better solution is to set the reorder point higher than $ROP = dL$. Specifically:

$$ROP = \bar{d}\bar{L} + SS \qquad (11.6)$$

where:

$SS = $ safety stock

Recall that WolfByte Computers carried a safety stock of 1,000 keyboards (Figure 11.4). Again, safety stock (SS) is an extra amount beyond that needed to meet average demand during lead time. This is added to the reorder point to protect against variability in both demand and lead time. Safety stock raises the reorder point, forcing a company to reorder earlier than usual. In doing so, it helps to ensure that future orders will arrive before the existing inventory runs out.

Figure 11.10 shows how safety stock works when both the demand rate and the lead time vary. We start with an inventory level of Q plus the safety stock (Q + SS). When we reach the new reorder point of $\bar{d}\bar{L} + SS$, an order is released. But look what happens during the first reorder period: Demand exceeds $\bar{d}\bar{L}$, forcing workers to dip into the safety stock. If the safety stock had not been there, the inventory would have run out. In the second reorder period, even though the lead time is longer than before, demand flattens out so much that workers do not need the safety stock.

In general, the decision of how much safety stock to hold depends on five factors:

1. The variability of demand
2. The variability of lead time
3. The average length of lead time
4. The desired service level
5. The average demand

Let's talk about each of these factors. First, the more the demand level and the lead time vary, the more likely it is that inventory will run out. Therefore, higher variability in demand and lead time will tend to force a company to hold more safety stock. Furthermore, a longer average lead time exposes a firm to this variability for a longer period. When lead times are extremely short, as they are in just-in-time (JIT) environments (see Chapter 13), safety stocks can be very small.

The service level is a managerial decision. Service levels are usually expressed in statistical terms, such as "During the reorder period, we should have stock available 90% of the time." While the idea that management might agree to accept even a small percentage of stockouts may seem strange, in reality, whenever demand or lead time varies, the *possibility* exists that a firm will run out of an item, no matter how large the safety stock. The higher the desired service level, the less willing management is to tolerate a stockout, and the more safety stock is needed.

EXAMPLE 11.3

Calculating the Reorder Point and Safety Stock at Boyer's Department Store

Let's look at one approach to calculating the reorder point with safety stock. Like other approaches, this one is based on simple statistics. To demonstrate the math, we'll return to Boyer's Department Store and the Hudson Valley Model Y ceiling fan. Boyer's sells, on average, 16 Hudson Valley Model Y ceiling fans a day ($\bar{d} = 16$), with a standard deviation in daily demand of 3 fans ($\sigma_d = 3$). This demand information can be estimated easily from past sales history.

If the store reorders fans directly from the manufacturer, the fans will take, on average, 9 days to arrive ($\bar{L} = 9$), with a standard deviation in lead time of 2 days ($\sigma_L = 2$). The store manager has decided to maintain a 95% service level. In other words, the manager is willing to run out of fans only 5% of the time before the next order arrives.

From these numbers, we can see that:

$$\text{Average demand during the reorder period} = \bar{d}\bar{L} = 144 \text{ fans}$$

Taking the analysis a step further, we can show using basic statistics that:

$$\text{Standard deviation of demand during the reorder period}$$
$$= \sigma_{dL}$$
$$= \sqrt{\bar{L}\sigma_d^2 + \bar{d}^2\sigma_L^2} = \sqrt{9*9 + 256*4} \qquad \text{(11.7)}$$
$$= 33.24$$

To ensure that Boyer's meets its desired service level, we need to set the reorder point high enough to meet demand during the reorder period 95% of the time. Put another way, the reorder point (ROP) should be set at the 95th percentile of demand during the reorder period. Because demand during the reorder period is often normally distributed, basic statistics tells us that:

$$\text{Reorder point (ROP)} = \text{95th percentile of demand during the reorder period}$$
$$= \bar{d}\bar{L} + z\sigma_{dL}$$
$$= 144 + 1.65*33.24$$
$$= 198.8, \text{ or } 199$$

In this equation, 1.65 represents the number of standard deviations (z) above the mean that corresponds to the 95th percentile of a normally distributed variable. (Other z values and their respective service levels are shown in Table 11.4.) The more general formula for calculating the reorder point is, therefore:

$$\text{ROP} = \bar{d}\bar{L} + z\sqrt{\bar{L}\sigma_d^2 + \bar{d}^2\sigma_L^2} \qquad \text{(11.8)}$$

where:

$\bar{d}$ = average demand per time period

$\bar{L}$ = average lead time

σ_d^2 = variance of demand per time period

σ_L^2 = variance of lead time

z = number of standard deviations above the average demand during lead time (higher z values lower the probability of a stockout)

TABLE 11.4 z Values Used in Calculating Safety Stock

z VALUE	ASSOCIATED SERVICE LEVEL
0.84	80%
1.28	90
1.65	95
2.33	99

Notice that the first part of the equation, $\overline{d}\overline{L}$, covers only the average demand during the reorder period. The second part of the equation, $z\sqrt{\overline{L}\sigma_d^2 + \overline{d}^2\sigma_L^2}$, represents the safety stock. For Boyer's, then, the amount of safety stock needed is:

$$z\sqrt{\overline{L}\sigma_d^2 + \overline{d}^2\sigma_L^2} = 1.65 * 33.24 = 54.88, \text{ or } 55 \text{ fans}$$

Of course, there are other methods for determining safety stock. Some managers consider variations in both the lead time and the demand rate; others use a definition of service level that includes the frequency of reordering. (Firms that reorder less often than others are less susceptible to stockouts.) In practice, many firms take an unscientific approach to safety stock, such as setting the reorder point equal to 150% of expected demand. Whatever the method used, however, these observations will still hold: The amount of safety stock needed will be affected by the variability of demand and lead time, the length of the average lead time, and the desired service level.

Quantity Discounts

In describing the economic order quantity, one of our assumptions was that the price per unit, P, was fixed. This was a convenient assumption because it allowed us to focus on minimizing just the total holding and ordering costs for the year (Equation [11.3]). But what if a supplier offers a price discount for ordering larger quantities? How will this affect the EOQ?

When quantity discounts are in effect, we must modify our analysis to look at total ordering, holding, *and item costs* for the year:

$$\text{Total holding, ordering, and item costs for the year} = \left(\frac{Q}{2}\right)H + \left(\frac{D}{Q}\right)S + DP \quad \textbf{(11.9)}$$

where:

Q = order quantity
H = holding cost per unit
D = annual demand
P = price per unit (which can now vary)
S = ordering cost

Because the EOQ formula (Equation [11.5]) considers only holding and ordering costs, the EOQ may not result in lowest total costs when quantity discounts are in effect. To illustrate, suppose we have the following information:

D = 1,200 units per year
H = $10 per unit per year
S = $30 per order
P = $35 per unit for orders less than 90; $32.50 for orders of 90 or more

If we ignore the price discounts and calculate the EOQ, we get the following:

$$EOQ = \sqrt{\frac{2*1,200*\$30}{\$10}}, \text{ which rounds to 85 units}$$

Total annual holding, ordering, and item costs for an order quantity of 85 are:

$$\left(\frac{85}{2}\right)\$10 + \left(\frac{1,200}{85}\right)\$30 + \$35x1,200$$

$$= \$425 + \$423.53 + \$42,000$$

$$= \$42,848.53$$

But note that if we increase the order size by just 5 units, to 90, we can get a discount of $35 − $32.50 = $2.50 per unit. Selecting an order quantity of 90 would give us the following annual holding, ordering, and item costs:

$$\left(\frac{90}{2}\right)\$10 + \left(\frac{1,200}{90}\right)\$30 + \$32.50x1,200$$
$$= \$450 + \$400 + \$39,000$$
$$= \$39,850.00$$

When volume price discounts are in effect, we must follow a two-step process:

1. Calculate the *EOQ*. If the *EOQ* number represents a quantity that can be purchased for the lowest price, stop—we have found the lowest cost order quantity. Otherwise, we go to step 2.
2. Compare total holding, ordering, and item costs at the *EOQ* quantity with total costs at each price break *above* the EOQ. There is no reason to look at quantities below the *EOQ*, as these would result in higher holding and ordering costs, as well as higher item costs.

EXAMPLE 11.4

Volume Discounts at Hal's Magic Shop

Robert Landau/Alamy Stock Photo

Hal's Magic Shop purchases masks from a Taiwanese manufacturer. The manufacturer has quoted the following price breaks to Hal:

ORDER QUANTITY	PRICE PER MASK
1–100	$15
101–200	$12.50
201 or more	$10

Hal sells 1,000 masks a year. The cost to place an order is $20, and the holding cost per mask is about $3 per year. How many masks should Hal order at a time?

Solving for the *EOQ*, Hal gets the following:

$$EOQ = \sqrt{\frac{2*1,000*\$20}{\$3}} = 115 \text{ masks}$$

Unfortunately, Hal cannot order 115 masks and get the lowest price of $10 per mask. Therefore, he compares total holding, ordering, and item costs at Q = 115 masks to those at the next price break, which occurs at 201 masks:

Total annual holding, ordering, and item costs for an order quantity of 115 masks =

$$\left(\frac{115}{2}\right)\$3 + \left(\frac{1,000}{115}\right)\$20 + \$12.50\text{x}1,000$$

$$= \$172.50 + \$173.91 + \$12,500$$

$$= \$12,846.41$$

Total annual holding, ordering, and item costs for an order quantity of 201 masks =

$$\left(\frac{201}{2}\right)\$3 + \left(\frac{1,000}{201}\right)\$20 + \$10.00\text{x}1,000$$

$$= \$301.50 + \$99.50 + \$10,000$$

$$= \$10,401.00$$

So even though an order quantity of 115 would minimize holding and ordering costs, the price discount associated with ordering 201 masks more than offsets this. Hal should use an order quantity of 201 masks.

11.4 SINGLE-PERIOD INVENTORY SYSTEMS

So far, our discussions have assumed that any excess inventory we order can be held for future use. But this is not always true. In some situations, excess inventory has a very limited life and must be discarded, sold at a loss, or even hauled away at additional cost if not sold in the period intended. Examples include fresh fish, magazines and newspapers, and Christmas trees. In other cases, inventory might have such a specialized purpose (such as spare parts for a specialized machine) that any unused units cannot be used elsewhere. When such conditions apply, a company must weigh the cost of being short against the cost of having excess units, where:

$$\text{Shortage cost} = C_{\text{Shortage}} = \text{value of the item } if \text{ demanded} - \text{item cost} \qquad \textbf{(11.10)}$$

$$\text{Excess cost} = C_{\text{Excess}} = \text{item cost} + \text{disposal cost} - \text{salvage value} \qquad \textbf{(11.11)}$$

For example, say that an item that costs \$50 sells for \$200, but must be disposed of at a cost of \$5 if not sold. This item has the following shortage and excess costs:

$$C_{\text{Shortage}} = \$200 - \$50 = \$150$$

$$C_{\text{Excess}} = \$50 + \$5 = \$55$$

Single-period inventory system
A system used when demand occurs in only a single point in time.

Target service level (SL_T)
For a single-period inventory system, the service level at which the expected cost of a shortage equals the expected cost of having excess units.

Target stocking point (TS)
For a single-period inventory system, the stocking point at which the expected cost of a shortage equals the expected cost of having excess units.

The goal of a **single-period inventory system** is to establish a stocking level that strikes the *best balance* between expected shortage costs and expected excess costs. Developing a single-period system for an item is a two-step process:

1. Determine a **target service level (SL_T)** that strikes the best balance between shortage costs and excess costs.
2. Use the target service level to determine the **target stocking point (TS)** for the item.

We describe each of these steps in more detail in the following sections.

Target Service Level

For the single-period inventory system, service level is simply the probability that there are enough units to meet demand. Unlike a periodic and continuous review system, there is no reorder period to consider here—either there is enough inventory or there isn't. The target service level, then, is the service level at which the expected cost of a shortage equals the expected cost of having excess units:

$$\text{Expected shortage cost} = \text{expected excess cost}$$

or:

$$(1 - p)C_{\text{Shortage}} = pC_{\text{Excess}} \qquad \textbf{(11.12)}$$

where:

$$p = \text{probability that there are enough units to meet demand}$$
$$(1 - p) = \text{probability that there is a shortage}$$
$$C_{\text{Shortage}} = \text{shortage cost}$$
$$C_{\text{Excess}} = \text{excess cost}$$

The target service level (SL_T) is the p value at which Equation (11.12) holds true:

$$(1 - SL_T)C_{\text{Shortage}} = SL_T C_{\text{Excess}}$$

$$SL_T = \frac{C_{\text{Shortage}}}{C_{\text{Shortage}} + C_{\text{Excess}}} \qquad (11.13)$$

where:

$$C_{\text{Shortage}} = \text{shortage cost}$$
$$C_{\text{Excess}} = \text{excess cost}$$

Let's use Equation (11.13) to test our intuition. Suppose the shortage cost and the excess cost for an item are both $10. In this case, we would be indifferent to either outcome, and we would set the inventory level so that each outcome would be equally likely. Equation (11.13) confirms our logic:

$$SL_T = \frac{C_{\text{Shortage}}}{C_{\text{Shortage}} + C_{\text{Excess}}} = \frac{\$10}{\$10 + \$10} = 0.50, \text{ or } 50\%$$

But what if the cost associated with a shortage is much higher—say, $90? In this case, we would want a much higher target service level because shortage costs are so much more severe than excess costs. Again, Equation (11.13) supports our reasoning:

$$\frac{C_{\text{Shortage}}}{C_{\text{Shortage}} + C_{\text{Excess}}} = \frac{\$90}{\$90 + \$10} = 0.9, \text{ or } 90\%$$

EXAMPLE 11.5

Determining the Target Service Level at Don's Lemonade Stands

Don Washing is trying to determine how many gallons of lemonade to make each day. Don needs to consider a single-period system because whatever lemonade is left over at the end of the day must be thrown away due to health regulations. Every gallon he mixes costs him $2.50 but will generate $10 in revenue if sold.

In terms of the single-period inventory problem, Dan's shortage and excess costs are defined as follows:

$$C_{\text{Shortage}} = \text{revenue per gallon} - \text{cost per gallon} = \$10.00 - \$2.50 = \$7.50$$
$$C_{\text{Excess}} = \text{cost per gallon} = \$2.50$$

From this information, Don can calculate his target service level:

$$SL_T = \frac{C_{\text{Shortage}}}{C_{\text{Shortage}} + C_{\text{Excess}}} = \frac{\$7.50}{\$7.50 + \$2.50} = 0.75, \text{ or } 75\%$$

Interpreting the results, Don should make enough lemonade to meet all demand approximately 75% of the time.

EXAMPLE 11.6

Determining the Target Service Level at Fran's Flowers

Every day, Fran Chapman of Fran's Flowers makes floral arrangements for sale at the local hospital. The arrangements cost her approximately $12 to make, but they sell for $25. Any leftover arrangements can be sold at a heavily discounted price of $5 the following day. Fran wants to know what her target service level should be.

Fran's shortage and excess costs are as follows:

$$C_{Shortage} = \text{revenue per arrangement} - \text{cost per arrangement} = \$25 - \$12 = \$13$$
$$C_{Excess} = \text{cost per arrangement} - \text{salvage value} = \$12 - \$5 = \$7$$

Fran's target service level is, therefore:

$$SL_T = \frac{C_{Shortage}}{C_{Shortage} + C_{Excess}} = \frac{\$13}{\$13 + \$7} = 0.65, \text{ or } 65\%$$

Fran should make enough arrangements to meet all demand approximately 65% of the time.

Target Stocking Point

To complete the development of a single-period inventory system, we next have to translate the target service level (a probability) into a target stocking point. To do so, we have to know something about how demand is distributed. Depending on the situation, we can approximate the demand distribution from historical records, or we can use a theoretical distribution, such as the normal distribution or Poisson distribution. Furthermore, the distribution may be continuous (i.e., demand can take on fractional values) or discrete (i.e., demand can take on only integer values). Example 11.7 shows how the process works when we can model demand by using the normal distribution, while Example 11.8 demonstrates the process for a historically based discrete distribution.

EXAMPLE 11.7

Determining the Target Stocking Point for Normally Distributed Demand

In Example 11.5, Don Washing determined that the target service level for lemonade was:

$$\frac{C_{Shortage}}{C_{Shortage} + C_{Excess}} = \frac{\$7.50}{\$7.50 + \$2.50} = 0.75, \text{ or } 75\%$$

Don knows from past experience that the daily demand follows a normal distribution. Therefore, Don wants to set a target stocking point (TS) that is higher than approximately 75% of the area under the normal curve. Figure 11.11 illustrates the idea.

FIGURE 11.11 Target Stocking Point for Don's Lemonade Stands

The general formula for calculating the target stocking point when demand is normally distributed is:

$$\text{Target stocking point (normally distributed demand)} = \mu + z_{SLT}*\sigma \quad (11.14)$$

where:

μ = mean demand per time period
z_{SLT} = number of standard deviations above the mean required to meet the target service level
σ = standard deviation of demand per period

To further complicate things, Don also knows that the mean values and standard deviations for demand differ by day of the week (Table 11.5). Therefore, he will have to calculate different target stocking points for Monday through Friday, Saturday, and Sunday.

TABLE 11.5 Demand Values for Don's Lemonade Stands

DAY OF THE WEEK	MEAN DEMAND, μ	STANDARD DEVIATION OF DEMAND, σ
Monday–Friday	422 gallons	67 gallons
Saturday	719 gallons	113 gallons
Sunday	528 gallons	85 gallons

Using Equation (11.14) and the cumulative normal table (Table I.2 in Appendix I), Don quickly determines that a service level of 75% would require the target stocking point to be approximately 0.68 standard deviations above the mean. Therefore, the target stocking points are as follows:

$$\mu + z_{SLT}{}^*\sigma$$

Monday–Friday:	422 + 0.68*67 = 467.56 gallons
Saturday:	719 + 0.68*113 = 795.84 gallons
Sunday:	528 + 0.68*85 = 585.8 gallons

<table>
<tr><td>

EXAMPLE 11.8

Determining the
Target Stocking Point
for Discrete Demand

</td><td>

In Example 11.6, Fran Chapman calculated her target service level for floral arrangements:

$$\frac{C_{\text{Shortage}}}{C_{\text{Shortage}} + C_{\text{Excess}}} = \frac{\$13}{\$13 + \$7} = 0.65, \text{ or } 65\%$$

Fran has kept track of arrangement sales for the past 34 days and has recorded the demand numbers shown in Table 11.6.

</td></tr>
</table>

TABLE 11.6 Demand History for Fran's Flowers

DAILY DEMAND	NO. OF DAYS WITH THIS DEMAND LEVEL DURING THE PAST 34 DAYS	PERCENTAGE OF DAYS EXPERIENCING THIS DEMAND LEVEL	CUMULATIVE PERCENTAGE
10 or fewer	0	0/34 = 0%	0%
11	2	2/34 = 5.9%	5.9%
12	5	5/34 = 14.7%	20.6%
13	5	5/34 = 14.7%	35.3%
14	6	6/34 = 17.6%	52.9%
15	7	7/34 = 20.6%	73.5%
16	5	5/34 = 14.7%	88.2%
17	3	3/34 = 8.8%	97.0%
18	1	1/34 = 2.9%	100%
19 or more	0	0%	100%

Looking at Table 11.6, Fran realizes that if she wants to meet her target service level of 65%, she will need to stock 15 arrangements each day. This is because 15 arrangements is the first stocking point at which the probability of meeting expected demand (73.5%) is greater than the target service level of 65%. Conversely, if Fran stocked just 14 arrangements, according to Table 11.6, she would meet demand only 52.9% of the time.

11.5 INVENTORY IN THE SUPPLY CHAIN

So far, we have discussed the functions and drivers of inventory, and we have identified some basic techniques for managing independent demand inventory items. In this section, we broaden our scope to consider the ramifications of inventory decisions for the rest of the supply chain.

The Bullwhip Effect

A major limitation of the EOQ model is that it considers the impact on costs for only a single firm. No consideration is given to how order quantity decisions for one firm affect other members of the supply chain. Therefore, even though the EOQ minimizes costs for a particular firm, it can cause problems for other partners and may actually increase *overall* supply chain costs. An example of this is the bullwhip effect.[6] APICS defines the **bullwhip effect** as "an extreme change in the supply position upstream in a supply chain generated by a small change in demand downstream in the supply chain."[7]

Bullwhip effect
According to APICS, "an extreme change in the supply position upstream in a supply chain generated by a small change in demand downstream in the supply chain."

To illustrate, suppose the ABC plant makes pool cleaners that are sold through six distributors. The distributors have similar demand patterns and identical EOQ and ROP quantities:

Average weekly demand for each distributor = 500 pool cleaners (standard deviation = 100)

Reorder quantity for each distributor = 1,500

Reorder point for each distributor = 750

Figure 11.12 shows the results of a simulation covering 50 weeks of simulated demand across the six distributors. Even though total weekly *demand* across the six distributors ranged from 2,331 to 3,641, the quantities *ordered by the distributors to be shipped from the plant* ranged from 0 to 7,500 in any one week.

FIGURE 11.12
Total Demand across the Six Distributors

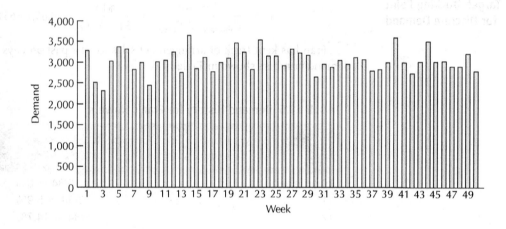

Resulting Total Quantities (Q = 1,500 for Each Distributor) Ordered from the ABC Plant

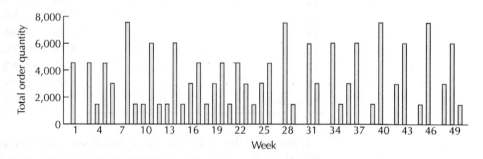

---

[6]Hau L. Lee, V. Padmanabhan, and S. Whang, "The Bullwhip Effect in Supply Chain," *Sloan Management Review* 38, no. 3 (Spring 1997): 70–77.
[7]Blackstone, *APICS Dictionary.*

FIGURE 11.13
Resulting Total Quantities ($Q = 750$ for Each Distributor) Ordered from the ABC Plant

What causes this? Quite simply, if a distributor reaches its reorder point, it places a large order. Otherwise, it does nothing. Therefore, a single-unit change in demand may determine whether or not a distributor places an order. So even though the distributors may be following good inventory practice by ordering in quantities of 1,500, the impact on the supply chain is to increase demand variability at the plant. Ultimately, this demand variability will drive up costs at the plant, which will then be forced to pass on at least some of these costs to the distributors.

In order to reduce the bullwhip effect, many supply chain partners are working together to reduce order quantities by removing volume discount incentives and reducing ordering costs. Figure 11.13 shows, for example, what the quantities ordered from the plant would look like if order quantities were cut in half, to 750. Now the orders range from 750 to 4,500; this is not perfect, but it's a big improvement over what the range was before.

Inventory Positioning

Managers must decide *where* in the supply chain to hold inventory. In general, the decision about where to position inventory is based on two general truths:

1. The cost and value of inventory increase as materials move down the supply chain.
2. The flexibility of inventory decreases as materials move down the supply chain.

That is, as materials work their way through the supply chain, they are transformed, packaged, and moved closer to their final destination. All these activities add both cost and value. Take breakfast cereal, for example. By the time it reaches the stores, cereal has gone through such a significant transformation and repackaging that it appears to have little in common with the basic materials that went into it. But the value added goes beyond transformation and packaging; it includes location as well. A product that is in stock and available immediately is always worth more to the customer than the same product available later.

What keeps organizations from pushing inventory as far down the supply chain as possible? Cost, for one thing. By delaying the transformation and movement of materials, organizations can postpone the related costs. Another reason for holding inventory back in the supply chain is flexibility. Once materials have been transformed, packaged, and transported down the chain, reversing the process becomes very difficult, if not impossible. Wheat that has been used to make a breakfast cereal cannot be changed into flour that is suitable for making a cake. Likewise, repackaging shampoo into a different-sized container is impractical once it has been bottled. The same goes for transportation: Repositioning goods from one location to another can be quite expensive, especially compared to the cost of delaying their movement until demand has become more certain. This loss of flexibility is a major reason materials are often held back in the supply chain. In short, supply chain managers are constantly trying to strike a balance between costs on the one hand and flexibility on the other in deciding where to position inventory.

Inventory pooling
Holding safety stock in a single location instead of multiple locations. Several locations then share safety stock inventories to lower overall holding costs by reducing overall safety stock levels.

EXAMPLE 11.9

Pooling Safety Stock at Boyer's Department Store

An especially good case for holding back inventory can be made if an organization can hold all of its safety stock in a single central location while still providing reasonably fast service to customers. This is one example of **inventory pooling,** in which several locations share safety stock inventories in order to lower overall holding costs. Suppose, for instance, that Boyer's has eight stores in the Chicago area. Each store sells, on average, 10 ceiling fans a day. Suppose that the standard deviation of daily demand at each store is 3 ($\sigma_d = 3$) and the average lead time from the fan manufacturer is 9 days, with a standard deviation of 2 days. We showed in Example 11.3 that to maintain a 95% service level ($z = 1.65$), a store would need to maintain a safety stock of 55 fans. The total safety stock across all eight stores would therefore be $8*55 = 440$ fans.

But what if Boyer's could pool the safety stock for all eight stores at a single store that could provide same-day service to the other seven stores? Because a single location would have a demand variance equal to n times that of n individual stores:

Standard deviation of demand during lead time, across n locations $= \sqrt{n}*\sigma_{dL}$

For Boyer's, this calculates out to:

$$= \sqrt{8}*\sqrt{\overline{L}*\sigma_d^2 + \overline{d}^2*\sigma_L^2}$$
$$= \sqrt{8}*33.24$$
$$= 94\,\text{fans}$$

And the pooled safety stock would be:

$$z*94 = 1.65*94 = 155.1, \text{or}\ 155\,\text{fans}$$

By pooling its safety stock, Boyer's could reduce the safety stock level by $(440 - 155) = 285$ fans, or 65%. Considering the *thousands* of items stocked in Boyer's eight stores, centralizing Boyer's safety stock could produce significant savings.

Transportation, Packaging, and Material Handling Considerations

We will wrap up our discussion of inventory in the supply chain by considering how inventory decisions—most notably, order quantities—are intertwined with transportation, packaging, and material handling issues. The point of this discussion is to recognize that, in the real world, there is more to determining order quantities than just holding, ordering, and item price.

SUPPLY CHAIN CONNECTIONS

INVENTORY MANAGEMENT AND POOLING GROUPS AT AUTOMOTIVE DEALERSHIPS

Greg Balfour Evans/Alamy Stock Photo

Automobile dealerships face a classic dilemma in deciding how to manage their inventories of service parts. On the one hand, customers expect their cars to be fixed promptly. On the other hand, dealerships typically do not have the space or financial resources to stock all the possible items a customer's car may need. If this wasn't difficult enough, most dealerships do not have the inventory expertise on site to deal with these issues.

To address these concerns, many automotive manufacturers have developed information systems in which the manufacturer makes inventory decisions for dealerships, based on calculated reorder points. Of course, the dealerships may override these recommendations if they like. And if a part placed in the dealership under the recommendation of the system sits at the dealership too long, the manufacturer will typically buy it back.

In addition, dealerships in the same geographic region typically establish "pooling groups." These dealerships agree to share safety stocks for expensive or slow-moving items. If one dealership runs out of the part, it can instantly check on the part's availability within the pooling group (via an information system) and arrange to have the item picked up. The result is lower overall inventories and better parts availability for customers.

Consider an example. Borfax Industries buys specialized chemicals from a key supplier. These chemicals can be purchased in one of two forms:

FORM	QUANTITY	WEIGHT	DIMENSIONALITY (WIDTH/DEPTH/HEIGHT)	PRICE PER BAG
Carton	144 bags	218 lb.	2' × 2' × 1'	$25
Pallet	12 cartons; 1,728 bags	2,626 lb.	4' × 4' × 3.5'	$18

First, notice that the chemicals can be purchased in multiples of 144 (cartons) or 1,728 (pallets). It is highly unlikely that any EOQ value calculated by Borfax will fit perfectly into either of these packaging alternatives.

If Borfax purchases a full pallet, it can get a substantial price discount. The supplier will also make a direct truck shipment if Borfax purchases five or more pallets at a time. This will reduce the lead time from 15 days to 5. However, pallets require material handling equipment capable of carrying nearly 3,000 pounds, as well as suitable storage space. On the other hand, the cartons are less bulky but will still require some specialized handling due to their weight. In choosing the best order quantity, Borfax must not only look at the per-bag price but also consider its material handling capabilities, transportation costs, and inventory holding costs.

CHAPTER SUMMARY

Inventory is an important resource in supply chains, serving many functions and taking many forms. But like any other resource, it must be managed well if an organization is to remain competitive. We started this chapter by examining the various types of inventory in a simple supply chain. We also discussed what drives inventory. To the extent that organizations can leverage inventory drivers, they can bring down the amount of inventory they need to hold in order to run their supply chains smoothly.

In the second part of this chapter, we introduced some basic tools for managing independent demand inventory. These tools provide managers with simple models for determining how much to order and when to order. We then examined the relationship between inventory decisions and the bullwhip effect, the decision about where to position inventory in the supply chain, and how transportation, packaging, and material handling considerations might impact inventory decisions.

KEY FORMULAS

Restocking level under a periodic review system (page 339):

$$R = \mu_{RP+L} + z\sigma_{RP+L} \tag{11.2}$$

where:

μ_{RP+L} = average demand during the reorder period and the order lead time

σ_{RP+L} = standard deviation of demand during the reorder period and the order lead time

z = number of standard deviations above the average demand (higher z values lower the probability of a stockout)

Total holding and ordering costs for the year (page 341):

$$\left(\frac{Q}{2}\right)H + \left(\frac{D}{Q}\right)S \tag{11.4}$$

where:

Q = order quantity

H = annual holding cost per unit

D = annual demand

S = ordering cost

Economic order quantity (EOQ) (page 342):

$$Q = \sqrt{\frac{2DS}{H}} = EOQ \tag{11.5}$$

where:

Q = order quantity

H = annual holding cost per unit

D = annual demand

S = ordering cost

Reorder point under a continuous review system (page 345):

$$ROP = \bar{d}\bar{L} + z\sqrt{\bar{L}\sigma_d^2 + \bar{d}^2\sigma_L^2}$$ (11.8)

where:

$\bar{d}$ = average demand per time period

$\bar{L}$ = average lead time

σ_d^2 = variance of demand per time period

σ_L^2 = variance of lead time

z = number of standard deviations above the average demand during lead time (higher z values lower the probability of a stockout)

Total holding, ordering, and item costs for the year (page 346):

$$\left(\frac{Q}{2}\right)H + \left(\frac{D}{Q}\right)S + DP$$ (11.9)

where:

Q = order quantity

H = holding cost per unit

D = annual demand

P = price per unit

S = ordering cost

Target service level under a single-period inventory system (page 349):

$$SL_T = \frac{C_{Shortage}}{C_{Shortage} + C_{Excess}}$$ (11.13)

where:

$C_{Shortage}$ = shortage cost

C_{Excess} = excess cost

KEY TERMS

Anticipation inventory 335
Bullwhip effect 352
Continuous review system 340
Cycle stock 334
Demand uncertainty 337
Dependent demand inventory 338

Hedge inventory 335
Independent demand inventory 338
Inventory 333
Inventory drivers 337
Inventory pooling 353
Periodic review system 338
Safety stock 334

Service level 339
Single-period inventory system 348
Smoothing inventory 336
Supply uncertainty 337
Target service level (SL_T) 348
Target stocking point (TS) 348
Transportation inventory 336

USING EXCEL IN INVENTORY MANAGEMENT

Several of the models described in this chapter depend on estimates of average demand and average lead time and on associated measures of variance (σ^2) or standard deviation (σ). The spreadsheet model in Figure 11.14 shows how such values can be quickly estimated from historical data, using Microsoft Excel's built-in functions. The spreadsheet contains historical demand data for 20 weeks, as well as lead time information for 15 prior orders. From this information, the spreadsheet calculates average values and variances and then uses these values to calculate average demand during lead time, safety stock, and the reorder point. The highlighted cells represent the input values. The calculated cells are as follows:

Cell C32 (average weekly demand):	= AVERAGE(C12:C31)
Cell C33 (variance of weekly demand):	= VAR(C12:C31)
Cell G27 (average order lead time):	= AVERAGE(G12:G26)
Cell G28 (variance of lead time):	= VAR(G12:G26)
Cell F5 (average demand during lead time):	= C32*G27
Cell F6 (safety stock):	= F3*SQRT (G27*C33 + C32^2*G28)
Cell F7 (reorder point):	= F5 + F6

	A	B	C	D	E	F	G	H	I
1		Calculating the Reorder Point from Demand and Order History							
2									
3			z value (for desired service level:)			1.65			
4									
5				Average demand during lead time:		280.72	units		
6					+ Safety stock:	125.47	units		
7					Reorder point:	406.19	units	(Equation 10-6)	
8									
9			*** Demand History ***				*** Order History ***		
10							Lead time		
11		Week	Demand			Order	(days)		
12		1	33			1	10		
13		2	14			2	6		
14		3	18			3	12		
15		4	37			4	9		
16		5	34			5	10		
17		6	53			6	8		
18		7	31			7	8		
19		8	21			8	8		
20		9	19			9	7		
21		10	44			10	3		
22		11	43			11	8		
23		12	37			12	9		
24		13	45			13	7		
25		14	43			14	8		
26		15	36			15	8		
27		16	40			Average:	8.07		
28		17	28			Variance:	4.07		
29		18	41						
30		19	36						
31		20	43						
32		Average:	34.80						
33		Variance:	106.27						

FIGURE 11.14 Excel Solution to the Reorder Point Problem

SOLVED PROBLEMS

PROBLEM 1

Jake Fleming sells graphic card update kits for computers. Jake purchases these kits for $20 and sells about 250 kits a year. Each time Jake places an order, it costs him $25 to cover shipping and paperwork. Jake figures that the cost of holding an update kit in inventory is about $3.50 per kit per year. What is the economic order quantity? How many times per year will Jake place an order? How much will it cost Jake to order and hold these kits each year?

Solution

The economic order quantity for the kits is:

$$\sqrt{\frac{2*250*\$25}{\$3.50}} = 59.76, \text{ or } 60 \text{ kits}$$

The number of orders placed per year is:

$$\frac{250}{60} = 4.17 \text{ orders per year}$$

The total holding and ordering costs for the year (not counting any safety stock Jake might hold) are:

$$\frac{60}{2}\$3.50 + \frac{250}{60}\$25 = \$105 + \$104.17 = \$209.17$$

PROBLEM 2

The manufacturer of the graphic card update kits has agreed to charge Jake just $15 per kit if Jake orders 250 kits at a time. Should Jake accept the manufacturer's offer?

Solution

For the *EOQ*, the total holding, ordering, and item costs for the year are:

$$\frac{60}{2}\$3.50 + \frac{250}{60}\$25 = 250*\$20 = \$105 + \$104.17 + \$5,000 = \$5,209.17$$

If Jake takes the volume discount, he will order 250 kits at a time (after all, ordering more than 250 would only move him further away from the *EOQ*, which minimizes holding and ordering costs):

$$\frac{250}{2}\$3.50 + \frac{250}{250}\$25 + 250*\$15 = \$437.50 + \$25 + \$3,750 = \$4,212.50$$

Therefore, Jake should take the volume discount and order just once a year.

DISCUSSION QUESTIONS

1. You hear someone comment that *any* inventory is a sign of waste. Do you agree or disagree? Can managers simultaneously justify holding inventories and still seek out ways to lower inventory levels?

2. In your own words, what is an inventory driver? What is the difference between a controllable inventory driver and an uncontrollable inventory driver? Give examples.

3. Which of the following are independent demand inventory items? Dependent demand inventory items?

   a. Bicycles in a toy store
   b. Bicycle wheels in a bicycle factory
   c. Blood at a blood bank
   d. Hamburgers at a fast-food restaurant
   e. Hamburger buns at a plant that produces frozen dinners

4. In a supply chain, what are the pros and cons of pushing inventory downstream, closer to the final customer? How might modular product designs (Chapter 15) make it more profitable for companies to postpone the movement of inventory down the supply chain?

5. (Use the *EOQ* and *ROP* formulas to answer this question.) Which variables could you change if you wanted to reduce inventory costs in your organization? Which ones would you prefer to change? Why?

6. The JIT/lean production movement has long argued that firms should:

   a. Maximize their process flexibility so that ordering costs are minimized;
   b. Stabilize demand levels;
   c. Shrink lead times as much as possible; and
   d. Assign much higher holding costs to inventory than has traditionally been the case.

   Using the *EOQ* and *ROP* formulas, explain how such efforts would be consistent with JIT's push for lower inventory levels.

PROBLEMS

Additional homework problems are available at www. pearsonhighered.com/bozarth. These problems use Excel to generate customized problems for different class sections or even different students.

(* = easy; ** = moderate; *** = advanced)

Problems for Section 11.2: Periodic Review Systems

1. Jimmy's Delicatessen sells large tins of Tom Tucker's Toffee. The deli uses a periodic review system, checking inventory levels every 10 days, at which time an order is placed for more tins. Order lead time is 3 days. Average daily demand is 7 tins, so average demand during the reorder period and order lead time (13 days) is 91 tins. The standard deviation of demand during this same 13-day period is 17 tins.

   a. (*) Calculate the restocking level. Assume that the desired service level is 90%.

   b. (**) Suppose that the standard deviation of demand during the 13-day period drops to 4 tins. What happens to the restocking level? Explain why.

   c. (***) Draw a sawtooth diagram similar to the one in Figure 11.3. Assume that the beginning inventory level is equal to the restocking level and that the demand rate is a *constant* 7 tins per day. What is the safety stock level? (*Hint:* Look at the formula for calculating restocking level.) What is the average inventory level?

2. Mountain Mouse makes freeze-dried meals for hikers. One of Mountain Mouse's biggest customers is a sporting goods superstore. Every 5 days, Mountain Mouse checks the inventory level at the superstore and places an order to restock the meals. These meals are delivered by UPS in 2 days. Average demand during the reorder period and order lead time is 100 meals, and the standard deviation of demand during this same time period is about 20 meals.

a. (**) Calculate the restocking level for Mountain Mouse. Assume that the superstore wants a 90% service level. What happens to the restocking level if the superstore wants a higher level of service—say, 95%?

b. (*) Suppose there are 20 meals in the superstore when Mountain Mouse checks inventory levels. How many meals should be ordered, assuming a 90% service level?

Problems for Section 11.3: Continuous Review Systems

3. Pam runs a mail-order business for gym equipment. Annual demand for TricoFlexers is 16,000. The annual holding cost per unit is $2.50, and the cost to place an order is $50.

a. (*) What is the economic order quantity?

b. (**) Suppose demand for TricoFlexers doubles, to 32,000. Does the EOQ also double? Explain what happens.

c. (**) The manufacturer of TricoFlexers has agreed to offer Pam a price discount of $5 per unit ($45 rather than $50) if she buys 1,500. Assuming that annual demand is still 16,000, how many units should Pam order at a time?

4. KraftyCity is a large retailer that sells power tools and other hardware supplies. One of its products is the Krafty-Man workbench. Information on the workbench is as follows:

$$\text{Annual demand} = 1{,}200$$
$$\text{Holding cost} = \$15 \text{ per year}$$
$$\text{Ordering cost} = \$200 \text{ per order}$$

a. (*) What is the economic order quantity for the workbench?

b. (**) Suppose that KraftyCity has to pay $50 per workbench for orders under 200 but only $42 per workbench for orders of 201 or more. Using the information provided in problem 3-4, what order quantity *should* KraftyCity use?

c. (*) The lead time for KraftyCity workbenches is 3 weeks, with a standard deviation of 1.2 weeks, and the average weekly demand is 24, with a standard deviation of 8 workbenches. What should the reorder point be if KraftyCity wants to provide a 95% service level?

d. (**) Now suppose the supplier of workbenches guarantees KraftyCity that the lead time will be a constant 3 weeks, with no variability (i.e., standard deviation of lead time = 0). Recalculate the reorder point, using the demand and service level information in problem 3-6. Is the reorder point higher or lower? Explain why.

5. Ollah's Organic Pet Shop sells about 4,000 bags of free-range dog biscuits every year. The fixed ordering cost is $15, and the cost of holding a bag in inventory for a year is $2.

a. (*) What is the economic order quantity for the biscuits?

b. (**) Suppose Ollah decides to order 200 bags at a time. What would the total ordering and holding costs for the year be? (For this problem, don't consider safety stock when calculating holding costs.)

c. (**) Average weekly demand for free-range dog biscuits is 80 bags per week, with a standard deviation of 16 bags. Ollah uses a continuous inventory review system to manage inventory of the biscuits. Ollah wants to set

the reorder point high enough that there is only a 5% chance of running out before the next order comes in. Assuming that the lead time is a constant 2 weeks, what should the reorder point be?

d. (**) Suppose Ollah decides to use a periodic review system to manage the free-range dog biscuits, with the vendor checking inventory levels every week. Under this scenario, what would the restocking level be, assuming the same demand and lead time characteristics listed in problem 13 and the same 95% service level? (Note that because the standard deviation of weekly demand is 16, basic statistics tells us the standard deviation of demand over 3 weeks will be $\sqrt{3} \times 16 \approx 28$.)

6. Ollah's Organic Pet Shop sells bags of cedar chips for pet bedding or snacking (buyer's choice). The supplier has offered Ollah the following terms:

Order 1–100 bags, and the price is $6.00 a bag.
Order 101 or more bags, and the price is $4.50 a bag.

Annual demand is 630, fixed ordering costs are $9 per order, and the per-bag holding cost is estimated to be around $2 per year.

a. (*) What is the economic order quantity for the bags?

b. (**) What order quantity should Ollah order, based on the volume discount? Is this different from the EOQ? If so, how could this be?

c. (**) Suppose the lead time for bags is a constant 2 weeks, and average weekly demand is 12.6 bags, with a standard deviation of 3.2 bags. If Ollah wants to maintain a 98% service level, what should her reorder point be?

Problems for Section 11.4: Single-Period Inventory Systems

7. (**) David Polston prints up T-shirts to be sold at local concerts. The T-shirts sell for $20 each but cost David only $6.50 each. However, because the T-shirts have concert-specific information on them, David can sell a leftover shirt for only $3. Suppose the demand for shirts can be approximated with a normal distribution and the mean demand is 120 shirts, with a standard deviation of 35. What is the target service level? How many shirts should David print up for a concert?

8. Sherry Clower is trying to figure out how many custom books to order for her class of 25 students. In the past, the number of students buying books has shown the following demand pattern:

NUMBER OF STUDENTS WHO BOUGHT A BOOK	PERCENTAGE OF OBSERVATIONS
16 or fewer	0%
17	4%
18	15%
19	17%
20	18%
21	26%
22	10%
23	6%
24	4%
25	0%

a. (**) Suppose each custom book costs Sherry $12 to print, and she sells the books to the students for $50 each. Excess books must be scrapped. What is the target service level? What is the target stocking point?

b. (**) Suppose printing costs increase to $22. Recalculate the new target service level and target stocking point. What happens?

9. One of the products sold by OfficeMax is a Hewlett-Packard LaserJet Z99 printer. As purchasing manager, you have the following information for the printer:

Average weekly demand (52 weeks per year):	60 printers
Standard deviation of weekly demand:	12 printers
Order lead time:	3 weeks
Standard deviation of order lead time:	0 (lead times are constant)
Item cost:	$120 per printer
Cost to place an order:	$2
Yearly holding cost per printer:	$48
Desired service level during reordering period:	99% ($z = 2.33$)

a. (*) What is the economic order quantity for the printer?

b. (**) Calculate annual ordering costs and holding costs (ignoring safety stock) for the EOQ. What do you notice about the two?

c. (**) Suppose OfficeMax currently orders 120 printers at a time. How much more or less would OfficeMax pay in holding and ordering costs per year if it ordered just 12 printers at a time? Show your work.

d. (**) What is the reorder point for the printer? How much of the reorder point consists of safety stock?

For parts e and f, use the following formula to consider the impact of safety stock (SS) on average inventory levels and annual holding costs:

$$\left(\frac{Q}{2} + SS\right)H$$

e. (***) What is the annual cost of holding inventory, including the safety stock? How much of this cost is due to the safety stock?

f. (***) Suppose OfficeMax is able to cut the lead time to a constant 1 week. What would the new safety stock level be? How much would this reduce annual holding costs?

10. (***) OfficeMax is considering using the Internet to order printers from Hewlett-Packard. The change is expected to make the cost of placing orders drop to almost nothing, although the lead time will remain the same. What effect will this have on the order quantity? On the holding and ordering costs for the year? Explain, using any formulas and examples you find helpful.

11. Through its online accessory store, Gateway sells its own products, as well as products made by other companies. One of these products is the WB150 WolfByte laptop computer:

Estimated *annual* demand:	15,376 laptops (50 weeks per year)
Cost:	$640 per laptop
Lead time:	2 weeks
Standard deviation of weekly demand:	16 laptops
Standard deviation of lead time:	0.3 weeks
Holding cost per unit per year:	40% of item cost
Ordering cost:	$25 per order
Desired service level:	95% ($z = 1.65$)

a. (*) What is the economic order quantity for the laptops? Calculate annual ordering costs and holding costs (ignoring safety stock) for the EOQ.

b. (**) What is the reorder point for the laptops? How much of the reorder point consists of safety stock?

c. (**) Suppose Gateway decides to order 64 laptops at a time. What would its yearly ordering and holding costs (ignoring safety stock) for the monitor be?

d. (**) Because computer technologies become obsolete so quickly, Gateway is thinking about raising holding costs from 40% of item cost to some higher percentage. What will be the impact on the economic order quantity for laptops? Explain why.

For parts e and f, use the following formula to consider the impact of safety stock (SS) on average inventory levels and annual holding costs:

$$\left(\frac{Q}{2} + SS\right)H$$

e. (***) What is the annual cost of holding inventory, including the safety stock? How much of this cost is due to the safety stock?

f. (***) Suppose Gateway is able to cut the lead time to a constant 1 week. What would the new safety stock level be? How much would this reduce annual holding costs?

12. One of the products stocked by a Sam's Club store is *Sams Cola*, which is sold in cases. The demand level for *Sams Cola* is highly seasonal:

- During the *slow season*, the demand rate is approximately 650 cases a month, which is the same as a yearly demand rate of 650*12 = 7,800 cases.
- During the *busy season*, the demand rate is approximately 1,300 cases a month, or 15,600 cases a year.
- The cost to place an order is $5, and the yearly holding cost for a case of *Sams Cola* is $12.

a. (**) According to the EOQ formula, how many cases of *Sams Cola* should be ordered at a time during the slow season? How many cases of *Sams Cola* should be ordered during the busy season?

b. (**) Suppose Sam's Club decides to use the same order quantity, $Q = 150$, throughout the year. Calculate total holding and ordering costs for the year. Do not consider safety stock in your calculations. (Annual demand can be calculated as an average of the slow and busy rates given above.)

13. (**) During the busy season, the store manager has decided that 98% of the time, she does not want to run out of *Sams Cola* before the next order arrives. Use the following data to calculate the reorder point for *Sams Cola*:

Weekly demand during the busy season:	325 cases per week
Lead time:	0.5 weeks
Standard deviation of weekly demand:	5.25
Standard deviation of lead time:	0 (lead time is constant)
Number of standard deviations above the mean needed to provide a 98% service level (z):	2.05

14. (**) Dave's Sporting Goods sells Mountain Mouse freeze-dried meals. Dave's uses a continuous review system to manage meal inventories. Suppose Mountain Mouse offers the following volume discounts to its customers:

1–500 meals: $7 per meal
501 or more meals: $6.50 per meal

Annual demand is 2,000 meals, and the cost to place an order is $15. Suppose the holding cost is $2 per meal per year. How many meals should Dave's order at a time? What are the total holding, ordering, and item costs associated with this quantity?

15. (***) (*Microsoft Excel problem*) The following figure shows an Excel spreadsheet that compares total ordering and holding costs for some current order quantity to the same costs for the EOQ and calculates how much could be saved by switching to the EOQ. **Re-create this spreadsheet in Excel.** You should develop the spreadsheet so that the results will be recalculated if any of the values in the highlighted cells are changed. Your formatting does not have to be exactly the same, but the numbers

should be. (As a test, see what happens if you just change the annual demand and cost per order to 5,000 and $25, respectively. Your new EOQ should be 91.29, and the total savings under the EOQ should be $5,011.39.)

	A	B	C	D	E	F
1	Calculating Savings under *EOQ*					
2						
3			Annual demand:	4,000		
4		Annual holding cost, per unit:		$30.00		
5			Cost per order:	$30.00		
6						
7			Current order quantity:	500		
8		Current annual holding cost:		$7,500.00		
9		Current annual ordering cost:		$240.00		
10			Total cost:	$7,740.00		
11						
12			Economic order quantity:	89.44		
13		EOQ annual holding cost:		$1,341.64		
14		EOQ annual ordering cost:		$1,341.64		
15			Total cost:	$2,683.28		
16						
17		Total savings under *EOQ*:		$5,056.72		
18						

16. (***) (*Microsoft Excel problem*) The following figure shows an Excel spreadsheet that calculates the benefit of pooling safety stock. Specifically, the sheet calculates how much could be saved in annual holding costs if the safety stocks for three locations were held in a single location. **Re-create this spreadsheet in Excel.** You should develop the spreadsheet so that the results will be recalculated if any of the values in the highlighted cells are changed. Your formatting does not have to be exactly the same, but the numbers should be. (As a test, see what happens if you change Location 1's average daily demand and variance of daily demand to 100 and 15, respectively. Your new pooled safety stock should be 30.34, and the total savings due to pooling safety stock should be $108.21.)

	A	B	C	D	E	F	G
1	Calculating Savings Due to Pooling Safety Stock						
2							
3	Annual holding cost per unit:			$5.00			
4	Lead time (fixed):			8	days		
5	z value (for desired service level):			2.33			
6							
7						Average demand	
8			Average	Variance of	Reorder	during	
9			daily demand	daily demand	point	lead time	Safety stock
10		Location 1	50	4.5	413.98	400.00	13.98
11		Location 2	40	6.2	336.41	320.00	16.41
12		Location 3	30	5	254.74	240.00	14.74
13						Total units:	45.13
14						Total annual holding cost:	$225.63
15							
16						Average demand	
17			Average	Variance of	Reorder	during	
18			daily demand	daily demand	point	lead time	Safety stock
19		Pooled SS	120	15.7	986.11	960.00	26.11
20						Total annual holding cost:	$130.56
21							
22						Savings due to pooling safety stock:	$95.07

CASE STUDY

Northcutt Bikes: The Service Department

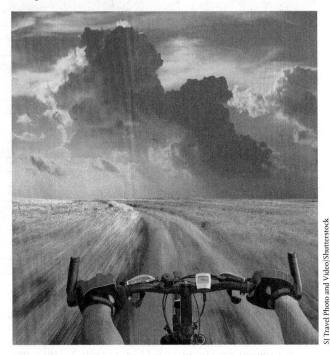

SJ Travel Photo and Video/Shutterstock

Introduction

Several years ago, Jan Northcutt, owner of Northcutt Bikes, recognized the need to organize a separate department to deal with service parts for the bikes her company makes. Because the competitive strength of her company was developed around customer responsiveness and flexibility, she felt that creating a separate department focused exclusively on after-market service was critical in meeting that mission.

When she established the department, she named Ann Hill, one of her best clerical workers at the time, to establish and manage the department. At first, the department occupied only a corner of the production warehouse, but now it has grown to occupy its own 100,000-square-foot warehouse. The service business has also grown significantly, and it now represents over 15% of the total revenue of Northcutt Bikes. The exclusive mission of the service department is to provide parts (tires, seats, chains, etc.) to the many retail businesses that sell and service Northcutt Bikes.

While Ann has turned out to be a very effective manager (and now holds the title of Director of Aftermarket Service), she still lacks a basic understanding of materials management. To help her develop a more effective materials management program, she hired Mike Alexander, a recent graduate of an outstanding business management program at North Carolina State University, to fill the newly created position of Materials Manager of Aftermarket Service.

The Current Situation

During the interview process, Mike got the impression that there was a lot of opportunity for improvement at Northcutt Bikes. It was only after he selected his starting date and requested some information that he started to see the full extent of the challenges that lay ahead. His first day on the job really opened his eyes. One of the first items he had requested was a status report on inventory history and shipped orders. In response, the following note was on his desk the first day from the warehouse supervisor, Art Demming:

> We could not compile the history you requested, as we keep no such records. There's just too much stuff in here to keep a close eye on it all. Rest assured, however, that we think the inventory positions on file are accurate, as we just completed our physical count of inventory last week. I was able to track down a demand history for a couple of our items, and that is attached to this memo. Welcome to the job!

Mike decided to investigate further. Although the records were indeed difficult to track down and compile, by the end of his second week he had obtained a fairly good picture of the situation, based on an investigation of 100 parts selected at random. He learned, for example, that although there was an average of over 70 days' worth of inventory (annual sales/average inventory), the fill rate for customer orders was less than 80%, meaning that only 80% of the items requested were in inventory; the remaining orders were backordered. Unfortunately, the majority of customers viewed service parts as generic and would take their business elsewhere when parts were not available from Northcutt Bikes.

What really hurt was when those businesses sometimes canceled their entire order for parts and placed it with another parts supplier. The obvious conclusion was that while there was plenty of inventory overall, the timing and quantities were misplaced. Increasing the inventory did not appear to be the answer, not only because a large amount was already being held but also because the space in the warehouse (built less than two years ago) had increased from being 45% utilized just after it moved in to its present utilization of over 95%.

Mike decided to start his analysis and development of solutions on the two items for which Art had already provided demand history. He felt that if he could analyze and correct any problems with those two parts, he could expand the analysis to most of the others. The two items on which he had history and concentrated his initial analysis were the FB378 Fender Bracket and the GS131 Gear Sprocket. Northcutt Bikes purchases the FB378 from a Brazilian source. The lead time has remained constant, at three weeks, and the estimated cost of a purchase order for these parts is given at $35 per order. Currently Northcutt Bikes uses an order lot size of 120 for the FB378 and buys the items for $5 apiece.

The GS131 part, on the other hand, is a newer product only recently being offered. A machine shop in Nashville, Tennessee, produces the part for Northcutt Bikes, and it gives Northcutt Bikes a fairly reliable six-week lead time. The cost of placing an order with the machine shop is only about $15, and currently Northcutt Bikes orders 850 parts at a time. Northcutt Bikes buys the item for $10.75.

Following is the demand information that Art gave to Mike on his first day for the FB378 and the GS131:

	FB378		GS131	
WEEK	FORECAST	ACTUAL DEMAND	FORECAST	ACTUAL DEMAND
1	30	34		
2	32	44		
3	35	33		
4	34	39		
5	35	48		
6	38	30		
7	36	26		
8	33	45		
9	37	33		
10	37	30		
11	36	47	10	16
12	37	40	18	27
13	38	31	30	35
14	36	38	42	52
15	36	32	55	51
16	35	49	54	44
17	37	24	52	57
18	35	41	53	59
19	37	34	53	46
20	36	24	52	62
21	34	52	53	51
22	36	41	53	60
23	37	30	54	46
24	36	37	53	58

	FB378		GS131	
WEEK	FORECAST	ACTUAL DEMAND	FORECAST	ACTUAL DEMAND
25	36	31	54	42
26	35	45	53	57
27	36		53	

Mike realized he also needed input from Ann about her perspective on the business. She indicated that she felt strongly that with better management, Northcutt Bikes should be able to use the existing warehouse for years to come, even with the anticipated growth in business. Currently, however, she views the situation as a crisis because "we're bursting at the seams with inventory. It's costing us a lot of profit, yet our service level is very poor, at less than 80%. I'd like to see us maintain a 95% or better service level without back orders, yet we need to be able to do that with a net reduction in total inventory. What do you think, Mike? Can we do better?"

Questions

1. Use the available data to develop inventory policies (order quantities and reorder points) for the FB378 and GS131. Assume that the holding cost is 20% of unit price.
2. Compare the inventory costs associated with your suggested order quantities with those of the current order quantities. What can you conclude?
3. Do you think the lost customer sales should be included as a cost of inventory? How would such an inclusion impact the ordering policies you established in question 1?

REFERENCES

Books and Articles

Blackstone, J. H., ed., *APICS Dictionary*, 15th ed. (Chicago, IL: APICS, 2016).

Isodore, C., "Gas Price Spikes and Shortages Coming after Fatal Pipeline Blast," *CNN Money*, November 3, 2016, **http://money.cnn.com/2016/11/01/news/colonial-pipeline-explosion-gasoline-price-spike/.**

Lee, H. L., V. Padmanabhan, and S. Whang, "The Bullwhip Effect in Supply Chain," *Sloan Management Review* 38, no. 3 (Spring 1997): 70–77.

Magretta, J., "Fast, Global, and Entrepreneurial: Supply Chain Management, Hong Kong Style," *Harvard Business Review* 76, no. 5 (September–October 1998): 102–109.

Magretta, J., "The Power of Virtual Integration: An Interview with Dell Computer's Michael Dell," *Harvard Business Review* 76, no. 2 (March–April 1998): 72–84.

Paul A. Souders/Corbis/VCG/Getty Images

CHAPTER
twelve

CHAPTER OUTLINE

Introduction

12.1 Master Scheduling

12.2 Material Requirements Planning

12.3 Production Activity Control and Vendor Order Management Systems

12.4 Synchronizing Planning and Control across the Supply Chain

Chapter Summary

Managing Production across the Supply Chain

CHAPTER OBJECTIVES

By the end of this chapter, you will be able to:

● Explain the activities that make up planning and control in a typical manufacturing environment.

● Explain the linkage between sales and operations planning (S&OP) and master scheduling.

● Complete the calculations for the master schedule record and interpret the results.

● Explain the linkage between master scheduling and material requirements planning (MRP).

● Complete the calculations for the MRP record and interpret the results.

● Discuss the role of production activity control and vendor order management and how these functions differ from higher-level planning activities.

● Explain how distribution requirements planning (DRP) helps synchronize the supply chain and complete the calculations for a simple example.

BIGDAWG CUSTOMS, PART 1

Supertrooper/Shutterstock

Steve Barr, owner of BigDawg Customs, still wasn't sure whether making the new KZ1 scooter seat was a good business move or a bad one. On the one hand, tapping into the scooter market had definitely boosted sales for BigDawg, which had traditionally made motorcycle accessories. The company was selling over 1,500 KZ1 seats each month and demand was growing. On the other hand, production planning and control for the KZ1 seat was a mess. Big-Dawg only produced the KZ1 scooter seat in large batches every few weeks, but there were parts inventories all over

the place, even in the weeks when BigDawg was not making seats. What was even more worrisome to Steve was that no one had a good handle on how many of the seats being made had already been sold to someone. More than once, a BigDawg salesperson had promised to ship seats to an important customer, only to find out that the inventory in the warehouse was spoken for. Steve worried that if this kept up, his customers would take their business elsewhere. Steve realized it was time to have a meeting with two of his key managers, Traci Griggs, vice president of marketing, and Brad Ashbaugh, vice president of production.

"Folks, as you know the KZ1 has been a big success in the marketplace, and I can see us offering more scooter seats over the next year. I appreciate your efforts to get us to this point, but we've got some issues to resolve. First, we need some way to match up production with the actual orders we have coming in. We just can't tell customers that we will ship them something in a couple of weeks— we have to *know* when seats are available and when we can ship them. Also, it seems to me that we can do a better job managing our parts inventories. We have stacks of saddles, hardware kits, and seat covers out on the plant floor, but we aren't going to be making another batch of seats for another week. There's got to be a way to do it. Let's meet again next week and you can show me what you've got."

INTRODUCTION

Planning and control
A set of tactical and execution-level business activities that includes master scheduling, material requirements planning, and some form of production activity control and vendor order management.

The purpose of this chapter is to introduce you to some of the systems manufacturers use to manage production and to coordinate these activities with their supply chain partners. While the focus here is on physical goods, bear in mind that many service firms also depend on the information generated by these efforts. For instance, distributors and transportation carriers all use information generated by manufacturers to plan their own activities.

Planning and control can be thought of as a set of tactical and execution-level business processes that include master scheduling, material requirements planning, and some form of production activity control and vendor order management. Planning and control begins where sales and operations planning (S&OP) ends, as Figure 12.1 shows. The first step in planning and control is master scheduling, in which the overall resource levels established by S&OP begin to be fleshed out with specifics. The master schedule states exactly when and in what quantities specific products will be made. It also links production with specific customer orders, allowing the firm to tell the customer exactly when an order will be filled. Finally, master scheduling informs the operations manager what inventory or resources are still available to meet new demand. As we shall see, the concept of *available to promise* is an important function of master scheduling.

Material requirements planning (MRP) takes the process one step further: It translates the master schedule for final products into detailed material requirements. For example, if the master schedule indicates that 500 chairs will be finished and ready to sell in week 5, MRP determines when the individual pieces—seats, legs, back spindles, and so on—need to be made or purchased.

At the lowest level in the hierarchy are two systems: production activity control (PAC) and vendor order management. At this point, all the plans have been made; the primary task remaining is to make sure they are executed properly. Because materials ultimately come either from in-house manufacturing or from outside suppliers, two distinct types of control systems have sprung up to handle those different environments.

Our description of planning and control seems to suggest a top-down process, with higher-level plans feeding into more detailed lower-level systems. Why, then, do the arrows in Figure 12.1 run in both directions? The reason is simple: Changes in the business environment or other conditions may become apparent at lower levels, requiring the organization to adjust its plans and actions in real time.

In the rest of this chapter, we describe planning and control tools in more detail, starting with master scheduling and ending with PAC and vendor order management systems. We also discuss distribution requirements planning (DRP), one tool for synchronizing planning and control across the supply chain. As thorough as this chapter is, it cannot begin to cover all the choices manufacturers face in designing their planning and control systems. Our intent, rather, is to give you an appreciation of both the advantages of and the effort needed to run these systems.

12.1   MASTER SCHEDULING

Master scheduling
A detailed planning process that tracks production output and matches this output to actual customer orders.

Master scheduling is a detailed planning process that tracks production output and matches this output to actual customer orders. We have already said that master scheduling picks up where S&OP leaves off. Figure 12.2 gives an example of this linkage. The top of the figure shows four months of a sales and operations plan for a fictional manufacturer of lawn equipment. Note that management has established *overall* targets for demand, production, and ending inventory. These targets will guide the firm's tactical decisions, including planned workforce levels, storage space requirements, and cash flow needs. The bottom half of the figure shows the monthly master schedules for the three products the company produces. For every week in March, it shows what the expected demand is, how many of each product will be produced, and what the projected ending inventory is.

If we add up the numbers for production and demand across the three master schedules, we see that they match the figures in the sales and operations plan. Similarly, if we add up the ending inventory figures in week 4 of the master schedules, we see that they, too, match the figures in the plan. As long as the sales and operations planning values (for instance, the number of

FIGURE 12.2
The Link between the Sales and Operations Plan and the Master Schedule

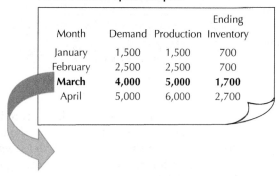

Partial sales and operations plan

Month	Demand	Production	Ending Inventory
January	1,500	1,500	700
February	2,500	2,500	700
March	**4,000**	**5,000**	**1,700**
April	5,000	6,000	2,700

Master schedules for March

			Week 1	Week 2	Week 3	Week 4
Push mowers	Demand		200	250	300	350
	Production		650	0	650	0
	Ending inventory	200	650	400	750	**400**
Power mowers	Demand		400	500	600	700
	Production		0	1,350	0	1350
	Ending inventory	400	0	850	250	**900**
Lawn tractors	Demand		100	150	200	250
	Production		250	250	250	250
	Ending inventory	100	250	350	400	**400**

Beginning inventory =	700
Total monthly production =	+5,000
Total monthly demand =	−4,000
Ending inventory =	**1,700**

labor hours required per unit) are correct, the company should have enough capacity to implement these master schedules. In reality, however, the demand and production numbers in the master schedule are unlikely to match the sales and operations plan exactly. Furthermore, the actual capacity requirements might not match the planning values. For example, the plan may state that the average product needs an estimated 4.5 hours of labor, but the actual figure may turn out to be 4.7 hours. In such cases, firms may need to dip into their safety stock, schedule overtime, or take other measures to make up the difference between the plan and reality. As long as the numbers in the sales and operations plan are *close* to those in the master schedule, firms will be able to manage the differences.

The Master Schedule Record

Now that we understand the linkage between the sales and operations plan and the master schedule, let's look at the master schedule record in more detail. Because firms tailor the master schedule record to their manufacturing environment and the characteristics of their product, generalizing about its precise form is difficult. Nevertheless, most master schedule records track several key pieces of information:

- Forecasted demand
- Booked orders
- Projected inventory levels
- Production quantities
- Units still available to meet customer needs (*available to promise*)

To illustrate how the master schedule works, let's look at the master schedule record for Sandy-Built, a company that makes snowblowers (Figure 12.3).

Forecasted Demand versus Booked Orders. At the beginning of November (week 45), Sandy-Built's management is reviewing the master schedule for the company's newest model,

FIGURE 12.3
**Partial Master
Schedule Record
for the MeltoMatic
Snowblower**

MeltoMatic snowblower								
Month	************November***********				************December***********			
Week	45	46	47	48	49	50	51	52
Forecasted demand	150	150	150	150	175	175	175	175
Booked orders	170	165	140	120	85	42	20	0
Master production schedule	300	0	300	0	350	0	350	0

Forecasted demand
In the context of master scheduling, a company's best estimate of the demand in any period.

Booked orders
In the context of master scheduling, confirmed demand for products.

Master production schedule (MPS)
The amount of product that will be finished and available for sale at the beginning of each week. The master production schedule drives more detailed planning activities, such as material requirements planning.

Projected ending inventory
A field in the master schedule record that indicates estimated inventory level at the end of each time period.

the MeltoMatic. The master schedule record in Figure 12.3 shows the **forecasted demand**—the company's best estimate of the demand in any period—for the months of November and December. It also shows **booked orders,** which represent confirmed demand for products. At this point, forecasted demand is running behind booked orders. In week 45, for instance, the forecasted demand for snowblowers is 150, yet Sandy-Built already has confirmed orders for 170.

Now look at the forecasts and booked orders for December. In that month, booked orders appear to be lagging behind forecasted demand. Perhaps more orders will materialize as December draws nearer. But if booked orders do not increase, managers may need to take action, either by cutting back production or by lowering the price of the MeltoMatic to move more units. One of the benefits of master scheduling is that it allows managers to see ahead and take corrective action when needed.

Another line on the master schedule record, called the **master production schedule (MPS),** shows how many products will be finished and available for sale at the beginning of each week. In our example, Sandy-Built seems to be producing enough snowblowers every other week to meet the forecasted demand.

Ending Inventory. With the basic numbers we have so far, we can start to get a picture of what overall inventory levels should look like and, more importantly, how many more snowblowers we can sell. Figure 12.4 contains a new row called **projected ending inventory,** which is simply our best estimate of what inventory levels will look like at the end of each week, based on current information.

Projected ending inventory is calculated as follows:

$$EI_t = EI_{t-1} + MPS_t - \text{maximum} (F_t, OB_t) \qquad (12.1)$$

where:

$$EI_t = \text{ending inventory in time period } t$$
$$MPS_t = \text{master production schedule quantity available in time period } t$$
$$F_t = \text{forecasted demand for time period } t$$
$$OB_t = \text{orders booked for time period } t$$

Note that projected ending inventory is a *conservative* estimate of the inventory position at the end of each week. In our example, the inventory at the end of week 44 is 100. Therefore, the projected inventory at the end of week 45 is $100 + 300 - 170 = 230$, and the same calculation for week 46 is $230 + 0 - 165 = 65$. In each case, we use booked orders because this number is higher than the forecasted demand. This makes sense because using the lower forecasted demand numbers would overestimate inventory levels.

But what about other weeks, such as week 47, in which the forecasted demand is *higher* than booked orders? In this case, the assumption is that the booked orders (140) probably do

FIGURE 12.4
**Partial Master
Schedule Record
for the MeltoMatic
Snowblower**

On-hand inventory at end of week 44	100							
MeltoMatic snowblower								
Month	************November***********				************December***********			
Week	45	46	47	48	49	50	51	52
Forecasted demand	150	150	150	150	175	175	175	175
Booked orders	170	165	140	120	85	42	20	0
Projected ending inventory	230	65	215	65	240	65	240	65
Master production schedule	300	0	300	0	350	0	350	0

FIGURE 12.5
Calculating Available
to Promise (*ATP*)
for Week 45

Available to promise (*ATP*)
A field in the master schedule record that indicates the number of units that are available for sale each week, given those that have already been promised to customers.

not reflect all the demand that will eventually occur in that week (150). To be conservative, we subtract the higher number in calculating ending inventory: 65 + 300 − 150 = 215.

Available to Promise. Now suppose you work for Sandy-Built's sales department and it is the beginning of week 45. You have the information shown in Figure 12.4 sitting in front of you. A customer calls and asks how many snowblowers you can sell to him at the beginning of week 45 and at the beginning of week 47. To answer this question, you need to know how many of the snowblowers in inventory have not been sold and are therefore available to promise. **Available to promise (*ATP*)** indicates the number of units that are available for sale each week, given those that have already been promised to customers.

To illustrate how *ATP* is calculated, consider Figure 12.5, which represents MeltoMatic's master schedule at the beginning of week 45. On the supply side, there are 100 snowblowers left over from the previous week. Another 300 snowblowers are scheduled to be finished in week 45. As a result, there will be a total supply of 400 snowblowers. On the demand side, Sandy-Built has already booked orders for 170 and 165 snowblowers in weeks 45 and 46, respectively. (We need to consider orders through week 46 because no more snowblowers are expected to be completed until week 47.) When we take the difference between the supply (400) and the demand (170 + 165 = 335) shown in Figure 12.5, we get a value of 65. This figure represents the number of additional units we can sell—that is, available to promise—until the next *MPS* quantity comes in.

Figure 12.5 tells us the available to promise quantity for the next two weeks, but what about for week 47, which corresponds with the next *MPS* quantity? Figure 12.6 shows the logic. Since week 47 is still two weeks away (remember, we're in the beginning of week 45), we can't be sure how many snowblowers will be left over from week 46. Therefore, the only supply we can count on is the 300 units being completed in week 47. On the demand side, whatever supply we have in week 47 must carry us through weeks 47 and 48. Total booked orders for these weeks equals (140 + 120) = 260. Therefore, the available to promise for week 47 is (300 − 260) = 40 snowblowers.

FIGURE 12.6
Calculating Available
to Promise (*ATP*)
for Week 47

Now that you understand the logic behind *ATP*, let's state it more formally. The formula for *ATP* for the *first week* of the master schedule record is:

$$ATP_t = EI_{t-1} + MPS_t - \sum_{i=t}^{z-1} OB_i \tag{12.2}$$

For any subsequent week in which *MPS* > 0, it is:

$$ATP_t = MPS_t - \sum_{i=t}^{z-1} OB_i \tag{12.3}$$

where:

ATP_t = available to promise in week t

EI_{t-1} = ending inventory in week $t-1$

MPS_t = master production schedule quantity in week t

$\sum_{i=t}^{z-1} OB_i$ = sum of all orders booked from week t until week z (when the next positive *MPS* quantity is due)

Because week 45 is the first week of the master schedule record, we use Equation (12.2) to calculate the available-to-promise numbers:

$$ATP_t = EI_{t-1} + MPS_t - \sum_{i=t}^{z-1} OB_i$$

$$ATP_{45} = EI_{44} + MPS_{45} - \sum_{i=45}^{46} OB_i$$

$$= 100 + 300 - (170 + 165) = 65 \text{ snowblowers}$$

Note that an *ATP* number must *always* be calculated for the first week in the record, regardless of whether any units are finished that week. Look at Figure 12.7. The *ATP* calculation for week 47 follows Equation (12.3), which assumes that there is no holdover inventory:

$$ATP_t = MPS_t - \sum_{i=t}^{z-1} OB_i$$

$$ATP_{47} = MPS_{47} - \sum_{i=47}^{48} OB_i$$

$$= 300 - (140 + 120) = 40 \text{ snowblowers}$$

Looking at it another way, total booked orders for November are 170 + 165 + 140 + 120 = 595 snowblowers, while the total units that we can sell are 100 + 300 + 300 = 700. The difference between these two totals is 700 − 595 = 105 snowblowers: 65 in the first two weeks of November and 40 in the last two weeks.

To summarize, Equation (12.2) is used to calculate the *ATP* for the first week of the master schedule record; Equation (12.3) is used for subsequent periods in which the *MPS* is positive. In calculating the *ATP*, managers must look ahead to see how many periods will go by before the next batch of finished products is ready.

FIGURE 12.7
Complete Master Schedule Record for the MeltoMatic Snowblower

On-hand inventory at end of week 44	100							
MeltoMatic snowblower								
Month	***********November***********				***********December***********			
Week	45	46	47	48	49	50	51	52
Forecasted demand	150	150	150	150	175	175	175	175
Booked orders	170	165	140	120	85	42	20	0
Projected ending inventory	**230**	**65**	**215**	**65**	**240**	**65**	**240**	**65**
Master production schedule	300	0	300	0	350	0	350	0
Available to promise	**65**		**40**		**223**		**330**	

EXAMPLE 12.1

Completing the Master Schedule Record for Karam's Alpine Hiking Gear

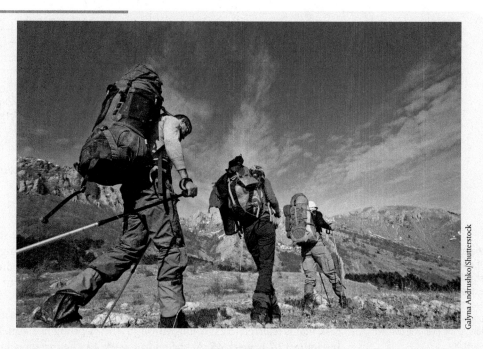

Lisa Karam is the owner of Karam's Alpine Hiking Gear. Lisa has set up the following master schedule record for one of her most popular products, the Eiger1 backpack. She needs to complete the projected ending inventory and available-to-promise calculations (Figure 12.8).

Using Equation (12.1), the projected ending inventory values for weeks 37 through 39 are calculated as follows:

$$EI_t = EI_{t-1} + MPS_t - \text{maximum}(F_t, OB_t)$$
$$EI_{37} = 2,000 + 0 - \text{maximum}(1500, 1422) = 500\text{ backpacks}$$
$$EI_{38} = 500 + 4,500 - \text{maximum}(1500, 1505) = 3,495\text{ backpacks}$$
$$EI_{39} = 3,495 + 0 - \text{maximum}(1500, 1471) = 1,995\text{ backpacks}$$

The remaining projected ending inventory values are calculated in a similar fashion. The master schedule record will also have *four* ATP calculations: one for the first week (week 37) and one for each week in which the MPS is positive (weeks 38, 41, and 44):

$$ATP_{37} = 2,000 + 0 - 1,422 = 578\text{ backpacks}$$
$$ATP_{38} = 4,500 - (1,500 + 1,471 + 1,260) = 264\text{ backpacks}$$
$$ATP_{41} = 4,000 - (980 + 853 + 534) = 1,633\text{ backpacks}$$
$$ATP_{44} = 3,700 - 209 = 3,491\text{ backpacks}$$

The completed master schedule record is shown in Figure 12.9. Interpreting the results, Lisa would expect the inventory to drop no lower than about 500 backpacks (week 37). In addition, Lisa has 578 backpacks left to sell in the current week. If she enters week 38 with no inventory, she will have only an additional 264 backpacks to sell over the following three weeks. Because of this, Lisa might try to get customers who aren't in a hurry to book orders in October, when the ATP quantities are much higher.

On-hand inventory at end of week 36	2,000							
Eiger1 backpack								
Month	***********September***********				************October*************			
Week	37	38	39	40	41	42	43	44
Forecasted demand	1,500	1,500	1,500	1,400	1,400	1,250	1,250	1,250
Booked orders	1,422	1,505	1,471	1,260	980	853	534	209
Projected ending inventory								
Master production schedule		4,500			4,000			3,700
Available to promise								

FIGURE 12.8 Incomplete Master Production Schedule Record for Eiger1 Backpack

On-hand inventory at end of week 36	2,000							
Eiger1 backpack								
Month	***********September***********				***********October***********			
Week	37	38	39	40	41	42	43	44
Forecasted demand	1,500	1,500	1,500	1,400	1,400	1,250	1,250	1,250
Booked orders	1,422	1,505	1,471	1,260	980	853	534	209
Projected ending inventory	**500**	**3,495**	**1,995**	**595**	**3,195**	**1,945**	**695**	**3,145**
Master production schedule		4,500			4,000			3,700
Available to promise	578	264			1,633			3,491

FIGURE 12.9 Completed Master Production Schedule Record for Eiger1 Backpack

The Planning Horizon. The master schedule records we have shown so far happen to extend eight weeks into the future. In reality, the appropriate **planning horizon** will depend on the lead time a firm needs to source parts and build a product. Products with very short lead times may have planning horizons that are just a few weeks long, but more complex products may need horizons of several months or more.

As the weeks go by, a firm will need to revise the numbers in the master schedule record, a task that is referred to as "rolling through" the planning horizon. For example, the current week in Figure 12.7 is week 45. At the end of week 45, the master schedule record will roll forward, and the new current week will be week 46.

Planning horizon
The amount of time the master schedule record or *MRP* record extends into the future. In general, the longer the production and supplier lead times, the longer the planning horizon must be.

Using the Master Schedule

We have shown how to calculate the master schedule numbers, but how do real firms use the results of these calculations? Look again at Figure 12.7. Imagine that Sandy-Built receives a call from a large retail chain that the company has never dealt with before. The buyer needs 150 snowblowers "as soon as possible." Sandy-Built would like to do business with this customer, but management had not anticipated such a huge order. When can Sandy-Built ship the snowblowers, and what will be the impact on production?

With a formal master schedule, managers can quickly answer these questions. According to the *ATP* figures in Figure 12.7, Sandy-Built can ship 65 snowblowers now, 40 more in week 47, and the remaining 45 in week 49 (65 + 40 + 45 = 150). If Sandy-Built decides to accept this order, however, managers will need to recalculate the ending inventory and *ATP* numbers. Figure 12.10 shows the updated master schedule record.

Booked orders in weeks 45, 47, and 49 are now 235, 180, and 130. Because the new order is so large, projected ending inventories drop dramatically. In fact, the calculations suggest that inventories will drop to zero on a regular basis *unless* management alters production levels to increase the safety stock. Finally, the retailer's large order will use up all the *ATP* for November. Unless another order is canceled, Sandy-Built cannot accept new orders until December—a change the sales force should be made aware of.

The master schedule calculations might seem complicated at first, but imagine what could go wrong if a business did not have this information available. Salespeople wouldn't be sure if and when they could fill customer orders. Production managers might not become aware of the impact of new demand on inventory levels in time to do something about it. Worse still, salespeople might continue to promise products to customers, unaware that all output has already

FIGURE 12.10 Updated Master Schedule Record for the MeltoMatic Snowblower

On-hand inventory at end of week 44	100							
MeltoMatic snowblower								
Month	***********November***********				***********December***********			
Week	45	46	47	48	49	50	51	52
Forecasted demand	150	150	150	150	175	175	175	175
Booked orders	**235**	165	**180**	120	**130**	42	20	0
Projected ending inventory	165	0	120	0	175	0	175	0
Master production schedule	300	0	300	0	350	0	350	0
Available to promise	**0**		**0**		**178**		**330**	

been spoken for. In short, chaos would result. When master scheduling works well, it allows organizations to avoid these problems by closely matching demand with supply, anticipating customers' needs, and adjusting the organization's plans accordingly.

EXAMPLE 12.2	
Booking More Orders at Karam's Alpine Hiking Gear	After completing the master schedule record in Figure 12.9, Lisa receives a call from a hiking outfitter in Montana. The customer would like Lisa to send 50 of the Eiger1 backpacks in the third week of September (week 39). Can Lisa do it? Lisa updates the master schedule record to reflect the change. The results are shown in Figure 12.11.

When Lisa compares the updated master schedule record to the old one in Figure 12.9, she sees that booking the new order increases orders booked in week 39 by 50 backpacks and reduces the *ATP* for week 38 by 50. The projected ending inventory for week 39 also falls but not by 50 backpacks, as one might expect. Rather, it falls by just 21 backpacks—the difference between new orders booked and forecasted demand (1,521 − 1,500).

On-hand inventory at end of week 36	2,000							
Eiger1 backpack								
Month	************September************				*************October************			
Week	37	38	39	40	41	42	43	44
Forecasted demand	1,500	1,500	1,500	1,400	1,400	1,250	1,250	1,250
Booked orders	1,422	1,505	**1,521**	1,260	980	853	534	209
Projected ending inventory	500	3,495	**1,974**	**574**	**3,174**	**1,924**	**674**	**3,124**
Master production schedule		4,500			4,000			3,700
Available to promise	578	**214**			1,633			3,491

FIGURE 12.11 Updated Master Production Schedule Record for Eiger1 Backpack

12.2 MATERIAL REQUIREMENTS PLANNING

With strategic capacity planning (Chapter 6), S&OP (Chapter 10), and master scheduling, we have a comprehensive set of high-level planning tools. Master scheduling, as we have seen, is particularly valuable because it allows managers to match production figures to actual customer demand. In addition, some firms use the master production schedule to monitor key resource requirements, an activity called **rough-cut capacity planning.** For instance, Sandy-Built's managers, seeing that 350 snowblowers are scheduled to be completed in week 49, might check to make sure the company has the capacity to meet that production goal. Rough-cut capacity planning verifies the feasibility of the master schedule.

Material requirements planning, more commonly known as **MRP,** takes planning one step further by translating the master production schedule into planned orders for the actual parts and components needed to produce the master schedule items. The logic of the MRP approach to inventory management is *completely different* from the independent inventory approaches described in Chapter 11. This is because MRP is used to manage **dependent demand inventory,** or inventory items whose demand levels are tied directly to the production of another item. Suppose, for instance, that each MeltoMatic snowblower Sandy-Built produces requires three wheels. Once managers know how many snowblowers they are going to make, they can calculate exactly how many wheels they will need and when they will need them. The demand for wheels is completely dependent on the number of snowblowers made. Unlike independent demand items, then, there is no mystery about how many dependent demand items a firm will need and when. MRP takes advantage of this fact to manage inventory quite differently—and more efficiently—than an *EOQ*-based system.

MRP is based on three related concepts:

1. The bill of material (BOM)
2. Backward scheduling
3. Explosion of the bill of material

We will illustrate these concepts using a simple example, the assembly of a furniture piece called the King Philip chair.

Rough-cut capacity planning
A capacity planning technique that uses the master production schedule to monitor key resource requirements.

Material requirements planning (MRP)
A planning process that translates the master production schedule into planned orders for the actual parts and components needed to produce the master schedule items.

Dependent demand inventory
Inventory items whose demand levels are tied directly to the production of another item.

Bill of material (BOM)
According to APICS, "a listing of all the subassemblies, intermediates, parts, and raw materials that go into a parent assembly showing the quantity of each required to make an assembly."

The **bill of material (BOM)** is "a listing of all the subassemblies, intermediates, parts, and raw materials that go into a parent assembly, showing the quantity of each required to make an assembly."[1] The bill of material for the King Philip chair has 10 different components, shown in Figure 12.12.

FIGURE 12.12 Bill of Material (BOM) for the King Philip Chair

Product structure tree
A record or graphical rendering that shows how the components in the BOM are put together to make the level 0 item.

The **product structure tree** in Figure 12.13 shows how the components in the BOM are put together to make the chair. The chair is assembled using a leg assembly, a back assembly, and a seat; the leg and back assemblies, in turn, are assembled from individual components such as legs, back slats, and crossbars. In MRP jargon, the complete chair is a level 0 item; the leg assembly, back assembly, and seat are level 1 items; and the remaining components are level 2 items. In practice, product assemblies can be dozens of levels deep.

FIGURE 12.13 Product Structure Tree for the King Philip Chair

Planning lead time
In the context of MRP, the time from when a component is ordered until it arrives and is ready to use.

The product structure tree also shows the planning lead time for each component. The **planning lead time** is the time from when a component or material is ordered until it arrives and is ready to use. For instance, the finished chair has a planning lead time of one week, the amount of time workers need to assemble a typical batch of chairs using the level 1 items. Seats have a planning lead time of two weeks, which may reflect the time an outside supplier takes to fill an order for seats. We will discuss planning lead times in more detail later in this chapter.

We can now show how backward scheduling (exploding the BOM) is used in MRP. The master schedule record in Figure 12.14 shows that 500 finished chairs should be ready to sell at the beginning of week 5. How do managers ensure that this commitment is met?

To complete the manufacture of 500 chairs by the beginning of week 5, workers must start assembling the chairs at the beginning of week 4. (Recall from Figure 12.13 that the planning lead time for the assembled chair is one week.) This deadline can be met only

---

[1] J. H. Blackstone, ed., *APICS Dictionary*, 15th ed. (Chicago, IL: APICS, 2016).

On-hand inventory at end of December	600							
King Philip chair								
Month	***********January***********				***********February***********			
Week	1	2	3	4	5	6	7	8
Forecasted demand	100	100	100	100	100	100	100	100
Booked orders	100	90	85	80	70	85	80	90
Projected ending inventory	500	400	300	200	600	500	400	300
Master production schedule	0	0	0	0	**500**	0	0	0
Available to promise	245				175			

FIGURE 12.14 Master Schedule Record for the King Philip Chair

if the back assemblies, leg assemblies, and seats are available at the beginning of week 4. Continuing to work backward in time, we see that workers must start the back and leg assemblies at the beginning of week 3 in order to have them ready by the beginning of week 4. Seats have a two-week lead time, so they must be ordered no later than the beginning of week 2. Back slats, crossbars, side rails, and legs must be ordered at the beginning of week 1—*right now!*—if managers want to have 500 chairs ready to go in week 5.

The time line in Figure 12.15 shows the logic behind backward scheduling. From a single order for 500 chairs in week 5, we worked backward, first through the level 1 items and then through the level 2 items. This process is called **exploding the BOM.**

Exploding the BOM
The process of working backward from the master production schedule for a level 0 item to determine the quantity and timing of orders for the various subassemblies and components. Exploding the BOM is the underlying logic used by MRP.

FIGURE 12.15 Exploding the BOM for the King Philip Chair

The MRP Record

The simple MRP record builds on the backward scheduling logic but provides some additional information. Like the master schedule record, the format of the MRP record may differ slightly from one firm to the next, but the basic principle—working backward from the planned completion date for the final item—is the same.

Figure 12.16 shows an example of how the MRP record is calculated. Looking at point A in the top row of Figure 12.16, we see that management has committed to having 500 chairs ready at the beginning of week 5. Given the planning lead time from Figure 12.13, workers need to start assembling the chairs in week 4 (point B). This assembly task triggers the need for level 1 components such as seats.

The bottom half of Figure 12.16 shows the MRP record for the seat. The top row shows *gross requirements*—that is, how many seats are needed each week. Because no chairs are being assembled in weeks 1 through 3, the gross requirement for seats in those weeks is zero (point C). In week 4, the gross requirement for seats is 500 (point D). This number is drawn directly from the "Start assembly" quantity at point B.

Gross requirements can be met by drawing from three sources: inventory carried over from the previous week, or the projected ending inventory; units already on order, referred to as

FIGURE 12.16
Calculating the MRP Record for Seats (King Philip Chair)

scheduled receipts; and new orders, termed *planned receipts*. To determine whether any new orders need to be placed, we must first calculate *net requirements*:

$$NR_t = \text{maximum } (0; GR_t - EI_{t-1} - SR_t) \tag{12.4}$$

where:

NR_t = net requirement in time period t

GR_t = gross requirement in time period t

EI_{t-1} = ending inventory from time period $t - 1$

SR_t = scheduled receipts in time period t

In lay terms, if enough seats can be obtained from inventory and scheduled receipts to cover the gross requirements, then managers don't need to order any more seats (i.e., the net requirement equals zero). Otherwise, they have a net requirement that must be met with new planned receipts.

In our chair example, the projected inventory at the end of week 3 is zero, and there are no scheduled receipts in week 4. Therefore, the net requirement for seats in week 4 is:

$$NR_4 = \text{maximum } (0; GR_4 - EI_3 - SR_4)$$
$$= \text{maximum } (0; 500 - 0 - 0) = 500$$

This result is shown in Figure 12.16 as point E. If you look in the lower-left corner of Figure 12.16, you will see that the minimum order size for seats is 1. In general, a business would not want to order more units than necessary as doing so would increase inventory levels and costs. Therefore, managers should plan on ordering just enough seats to meet the net requirement (point F). If they plan to receive 500 seats in week 4, they must release the order no later than week 2 (point G) because of the two-week planning lead time for seats. Finally, the ending inventory for week 4 (point H) is calculated using Equation (12.5):

$$EI_t = EI_{t-1} + SR_t + PR_t - GR_t \tag{12.5}$$

where:

EI_t = ending inventory from time period t

EI_{t-1} = ending inventory from time period $t - 1$

SR_t = scheduled receipts in time period t

PR_t = planned receipts in time period t

GR_t = gross requirements in time period t

$$EI_4 = EI_3 + SR_4 + PR_4 - GR_4$$
$$= 0 + 0 + 500 - 500 = 0 \text{ seats}$$

To test your understanding of the MRP record, try tracing the calculations through weeks 5 and 6. Figure 12.17 shows the complete MRP record for all the level 1 items, including the leg assembly and the back assembly. The logic behind the calculations is the same, but a couple of things should be noted. First, the factory begins week 1 with 25 leg assemblies in inventory (point I). Because there are no gross requirements in the first three weeks, these assemblies

FIGURE 12.17
MRP Records for the
Level 1 Components

King Philip chair
LT (weeks) = 1

		WEEK						
		1	2	3	4	5	6	7
MPS due date		0	0	0	0	500	400	300
Start assembly	0	0	0	0	500	400	300	0

Seat
LT (weeks) = 2

Min. order = 1

		WEEK						
		1	2	3	4	5	6	7
Gross requirements		0	0	0	500	400	300	0
Scheduled receipts		0	0	0	0	0	0	0
Projected ending inventory	0	0	0	0	0	0	0	0
Net requirements		0	0	0	500	400	300	0
Planned receipts		0	0	0	500	400	300	0
Planned orders		0	500	400	300	0	0	0

Leg asm
LT (weeks) = 1

Min. order = 1,000

		WEEK						
		1	2	3	4	5	6	7
Gross requirements		0	0	0	500	400	300	0
Scheduled receipts		0	0	0	0	0	0	0
Projected ending inventory	25	25	25	25	525	125	825	825
Net requirements		0	0	0	475	0	175	0
Planned receipts		0	0	0	1,000	0	1,000	0
Planned orders		0	0	1,000	0	1,000	0	0

Back asm
LT (weeks) = 1

Min. order = 250

		WEEK						
		1	2	3	4	5	6	7
Gross requirements		0	0	0	500	400	300	0
Scheduled receipts		250	0	0	0	0	0	0
Projected ending inventory	0	250	250	250	0	0	0	0
Net requirements		0	0	0	250	400	300	0
Planned receipts		0	0	0	250	400	300	0
Planned orders		0	0	250	400	300	0	0

gather dust until they are needed in week 4. Though the net requirement in week 4 is only 475, managers place an order for 1,000 (point J) because that is the minimum order size. The result is excess inventory at the end of week 4.

In week 5, the factory has more than enough leg assemblies (525) in beginning inventory to meet the gross requirement (400). As a result, managers do not place any additional orders (point K). Finally, for the back assemblies, the factory has a scheduled receipt of 250 units in week 1 (point L). These units will sit in inventory until week 4, when they are needed.

Just as the gross requirements for level 1 items are determined by the number of finished chairs (level 0) to be manufactured, the gross requirements for level 2 items depend on the *planned orders* for level 1 items.

Figure 12.18 shows the complete MRP calculations for all components in the King Philip chair. Notice that managers want to put together 1,000 leg assemblies in week 3 (planned orders = 1,000). Because each leg assembly requires two legs (Figure 12.13), the gross requirement for legs in week 3 is 2,000 (point M). Similarly, each back assembly requires two side rails. Therefore, a planned order for 300 back assemblies in week 5 results in a gross requirement of 600 side rails in the same week (point N).

Now for a *real* test. Where do the crossbar's gross requirements in Figure 12.18 come from? Because the crossbar is used in two different level 1 items, we must calculate gross requirements based on planned orders for *both* the leg assemblies and the back assemblies. Therefore:

Gross requirements for crossbars = leg assembly planned orders

+ back assembly planned orders

Week 3; 1,000 + 250 = 1,250

Week 4:   0 + 400 = 400

Week 5: 1,000 + 300 = 1,300

Once we have calculated the gross requirements, filling out the rest of the MRP records is a matter of following the rules outlined earlier.

FIGURE 12.18
Complete MRP Records for the King Philip Chair

MyLab Operations Management
Animation

Item		Week 1	Week 2	Week 3	Week 4	Week 5	Week 6	Week 7
Chair kit LT (weeks) = 1	MPS due date					500	400	300
	Start assembly				500	400	300	
Seat LT (weeks) = 2 Min. order = 1	Gross requirements				500	400	300	
	Scheduled receipts							
	Projected ending inventory 0	0	0	0	0	0	0	0
	Net requirements				500	400	300	
	Planned receipts				500	400	300	
	Planned orders		500	400	300			
Leg asm LT (weeks) = 1 Min. order = 1,000	Gross requirements				500	400	300	
	Scheduled receipts							
	Projected ending inventory 25	25	25	25	525	125	825	825
	Net requirements				475		175	
	Planned receipts				1,000		1,000	
	Planned orders			1,000		1,000		
Back asm LT (weeks) = 1 Min. order = 250	Gross requirements				500	400	300	
	Scheduled receipts	250						
	Projected ending inventory 0	250	250	250	0	0	0	0
	Net requirements				250	400	300	
	Planned receipts				250	400	300	
	Planned orders			250	400	300		
Legs LT (weeks) = 2 Min. order = 1	Gross requirements			2,000		2,000		
	Scheduled receipts							
	Projected ending inventory 25	25	25	0	0	0	0	0
	Net requirements			1,975		2,000		
	Planned receipts			1,975		2,000		
	Planned orders	1,975		2,000				
Side rails LT (weeks) = 2 Min. order = 500	Gross requirements			500	800	600		
	Scheduled receipts	500						
	Projected ending inventory 100	600	600	100	0	0	0	0
	Net requirements				700	600		
	Planned receipts				700	600		
	Planned orders		700	600				
Back slats LT (weeks) = 2 Min. order = 1	Gross requirements				750	1,200	900	
	Scheduled receipts				75			
	Projected ending inventory 0	0	0	0	0	0	0	0
	Net requirements				750	1,125	900	
	Planned receipts				750	1,125	900	
	Planned orders		750	1,125	900			
Crossbars LT (weeks) = 2 Min. order = 1,000	Gross requirements				1,250	400	1,300	
	Scheduled receipts							
	Projected ending inventory 0	0	0	0	600	300	300	300
	Net requirements				1,250	400	700	
	Planned receipts				1,250	1,000	1,000	
	Planned orders		1,250	1,000	1,000			

EXAMPLE 12.5

Using MRP at Karam's Alpine Hiking Gear

The BOM and associated planning lead times for the Eiger1 backpack are shown in Figure 12.19.

*To save on shipping and assembly costs, the Eiger1 backpack is sold unassembled. The dealer takes the level 1 components and puts them together at the shop.

FIGURE 12.19 BOM for the Eiger1 Backpack

Lisa Karam has asked you to set up the MRP records for all the components for the next six weeks. Lisa also tells you the following:

- According to the master production schedule, Karam is planning on having 850 new backpacks ready to sell at the beginning of each of weeks 4, 5, and 6.
- Currently, there is no component inventory of any kind in the plant.
- The soft bag, shoulder straps, and belt straps all have minimum order quantities of 1,500 units. All of the other components have no minimum order quantity.

			1	2	3	4	5	6
						WEEK		
Eiger1 packs	MPS due date					850	850	850
LT (weeks) = 0	Start assembly					850	850	850
** Soft bag **	Gross requirements		0	0	0	850	850	850
LT (weeks) = 2	Scheduled receipts							
	Projected ending inventory	0	0	0	0	650	1,300	450
	Net requirements					850	200	
Min. order = 1,500	Planned receipts					1,500	1,500	
	Planned orders			1,500	1,500			
** Frame **	Gross requirements		0	0	0	850	850	850
LT (weeks) = 1	Scheduled receipts							
	Projected ending inventory	0	0	0	0	0	0	0
	Net requirements					850	850	850
Min. order = 1	Planned receipts					850	850	850
	Planned orders				850	850	850	
** Shoulder straps **	Gross requirements		0	0	0	1,700	1,700	1,700
LT (weeks) = 1	Scheduled receipts							
	Projected ending inventory	0	0	0	0	0	0	0
	Net requirements					1,700	1,700	1,700
Min. order = 1,500	Planned receipts					1,700	1,700	1,700
	Planned orders				1,700	1,700	1,700	
** Belt **	Gross requirements		0	0	0	850	850	850
LT (weeks) = 1	Scheduled receipts							
	Projected ending inventory	0	0	0	0	0	0	0
	Net requirements					850	850	850
Min. order = 1	Planned receipts					850	850	850
	Planned orders				850	850	850	
** Left frame **	Gross requirements		0	0	850	850	850	0
LT (weeks) = 1	Scheduled receipts		50					
	Projected ending inventory	0	50	50	0	0	0	0
	Net requirements				800	850	850	
Min. order = 1	Planned receipts				800	850	850	
	Planned orders			800	850	850		
** Right frame **	Gross requirements		0	0	850	850	850	0
LT (weeks) = 1	Scheduled receipts							
	Projected ending inventory	0	0	0	0	0	0	0
	Net requirements				850	850	850	
Min. order = 1	Planned receipts				850	850	850	
	Planned orders			850	850	850		
** Buckle **	Gross requirements		0	0	850	850	850	0
LT (weeks) = 1	Scheduled receipts							
	Projected ending inventory	0	0	0	0	0	0	0
	Net requirements				850	850	850	
Min. order = 1	Planned receipts				850	850	850	
	Planned orders			850	850	850		
* Belt straps *	Gross requirements		0	0	1,700	1,700	1,700	0
LT (weeks) = 2	Scheduled receipts							
	Projected ending inventory	0	0	0	0	0	0	0
	Net requirements				1,700	1,700	1,700	
Min. order = 1,500	Planned receipts				1,700	1,700	1,700	
	Planned orders		1,700	1,700	1,700			

FIGURE 12.20 MRP Records for the Eiger1 Backpack

- At present, the only scheduled receipt is for 50 left frames in week 1 (the result of an earlier partial shipment on the part of a vendor).

The completed MRP records are shown in Figure 12.20. There are a couple of interesting points to note:

1. In the current week, the *only* action that needs to be taken is to release an order for 1,700 belt straps.
2. Because the Eiger1 backpacks do not have to be assembled, the final assembly planning lead time is zero.
3. The gross requirements for the shoulder straps are twice those of any other level 1 item. This is because each backpack requires two shoulder straps.
4. The MRP record for the left frame is nearly identical to that for the right frame. The difference is due to the 50 "extra" left frames arriving in week 1. These extra left frames reduce the planned order release in week 2 by 50 units.

The Advantages of MRP

Just as in master scheduling, getting lost in the calculations is easy to do with MRP. Figure 12.16 and Figure 12.18 showed all the MRP records for two *very* simple products. Imagine what the MRP records must look like in a firm that produces hundreds of products, with dozens of BOM levels and thousands of components!

So now is a good time to pull back and consider the benefits of MRP:

1. MRP is *directly tied* to the master production schedule and indicates the *exact* timing and quantity of orders for *all* components. By eliminating a lot of the guesswork associated with the management of dependent demand inventory, MRP simultaneously lowers inventory levels and helps firms meet their master schedule commitments.
2. MRP allows managers to trace every order for lower-level items through all the levels of the BOM, up to the master production schedule. This logical linkage between higher and lower levels in the BOM is sometimes called the **parent/child relationship.** If for some reason the supply of a lower-level item is interrupted, a manager can quickly check the BOM to see the impact of the shortage on production.
3. MRP tells a firm and its suppliers precisely what needs to be made when. This information can be invaluable in scheduling work or shipments, or even in planning budgets and cash flows. In fact, MRP logic is often called the "engine" of planning and control systems. MRP plays a big part in many enterprise resource planning (ERP) systems, described in the supplement.

Parent/child relationship
The logical linkage between higher- and lower-level items in the BOM.

Special Considerations in MRP

The complexity of MRP demands that these systems be computerized. But even with the help of computers, MRP requires *organizational discipline.* Like the calendar function on your smartphone, MRP provides little benefit to those who do not understand and exploit the system.

For an MRP system to work properly, it must have *accurate information.* Key data include the master production schedule, the BOM, inventory levels, and planning lead times. If any of this information is inaccurate, components will not be ordered at the right time or in the right quantities. In some cases, the correct components won't be ordered at all. As a result, most firms that want to implement MRP find that they must first ensure accurate planning information.

MRP systems must also accommodate *uncertainty* about a host of factors, including the possibility of variable lead times, shipment quantities and quality levels, and even changes to the quantities in the master production schedule. In general, firms deal with this uncertainty by lengthening the planning lead times or by holding additional units as safety stock. Of course, such buffers increase the amount of inventory in the system. As a result, many firms make a conscious effort to *eliminate* uncertainty. They do so by choosing suppliers and processes that offer reliable lead times and high quality levels and by keeping the quantities on the master

MRP nervousness
A term used to refer to the observation that any change, even a small one, in the requirements for items at the top of the bill of material can have drastic effects on items further down the bill of material.

production schedule firm. Reducing uncertainty requires a high degree of organizational discipline, but the rewards can be great.

A final consideration in implementing an MRP system is a phenomenon called **MRP nervousness.** Because higher-level items drive the requirements for lower-level items in an MRP system, any change, even a small one, in the requirements for upper-level items can have drastic effects on items listed further down the bill of material. Example 12.6 shows how such changes can affect the MRP records.

EXAMPLE 12.6

MRP Nervousness for the King Philip Chair

After completing the MRP records for the King Philip chair (Figure 12.18), management decides to change the number of chairs to be completed in week 7 from 300 to 125. Figure 12.21 shows the impact of this change on the MRP records. As you can see, no MRP record is left untouched.

		WEEK						
		1	2	3	4	5	6	7
** Chair kit**	MPS due date					500	400	**125**
LT (weeks) = 1	Start assembly				500	400	**125**	
** Seat **	Gross requirements				500	400	**125**	
LT (weeks) = 2	Scheduled receipts							
	Projected ending inventory 0	0	0	0	0	0	0	0
	Net requirements				500	400	**125**	
Min. order = 1	Planned receipts				500	400	**125**	
	Planned orders		500	400	**125**			
** Leg asm **	Gross requirements				500	400	**125**	
LT (weeks) = 1	Scheduled receipts							
	Projected ending inventory 25	25	25	25	525	**125**	0	0
	Net requirements				475			
Min. order = 1,000	Planned receipts				1,000			
	Planned orders			1,000				
** Back asm **	Gross requirements				500	400	**125**	
LT (weeks) = 1	Scheduled receipts	250	0					
	Projected ending inventory 0	250	250	250	0	0	0	0
	Net requirements				250	400	**125**	
Min. order = 250	Planned receipts				250	400	**125**	
	Planned orders			250	400	**125**		
** Legs **	Gross requirements			**2,000**				
LT (weeks) = 2	Scheduled receipts							
	Projected ending inventory 25	25	25	0	0	0	0	0
	Net requirements			1,975				
Min. order = 1	Planned receipts			1,975				
	Planned orders	1,975						
** Side rails **	Gross requirements				500	800	**250**	
LT (weeks) = 2	Scheduled receipts	500						
	Projected ending inventory 100	600	600	100	0	**250**	**250**	**250**
	Net requirements				700	**250**		
Min. order = 500	Planned receipts				700	**500**		
	Planned orders		700	**500**				
** Back slats **	Gross requirements				750	1,200	375	
LT (weeks) = 2	Scheduled receipts				75			
	Projected ending inventory 0	0	0	0	0	0	0	0
	Net requirements				750	1,125	**375**	
Min. order = 1	Planned receipts				750	1,125	**375**	
	Planned orders		750	1,125	**375**			
** Crossbars **	Gross requirements				1,250	400	125	
LT (weeks) = 2	Scheduled receipts							
	Projected ending inventory 0	0	0	0	600	**475**	**475**	**475**
	Net requirements				1,250	400		
Min. order = 1,000	Planned receipts				1,250	1,000		
	Planned orders		1,250	1,000				

FIGURE 12.21 MRP Nervousness for the King Philip Chair

Compared to Figure 12.18, the change eliminates the need for a second planned order of 1,000 leg assemblies in week 5. This, in turn, affects the gross requirements for legs and crossbars. The change in planned production also spills over to the records for seats, back assemblies, side rails, and back slats, although the impact is not quite as pronounced.

The point is that a minor change at the top can cause huge changes at lower levels. Planners must take MRP nervousness into consideration when making changes, especially with higher-level items. They must also choose their minimum order quantities with care. Notice the impact of the minimum order, or *lot size*, for leg assemblies: The firm went from ordering 1,000 leg assemblies in week 5 to ordering none at all that week. Because large lot sizes make MRP systems more nervous, firms that take this approach to inventory management usually try to keep their minimum order quantities as small as possible, especially for higher-level items that have the potential to disrupt lower-level requirements.

12.3 PRODUCTION ACTIVITY CONTROL AND VENDOR ORDER MANAGEMENT SYSTEMS

To this point, we have been discussing planning tools: S&OP for planning overall resource levels, master scheduling for planning the production and shipment of end items, and MRP for planning orders for manufacturing components. With production activity control (PAC) and vendor order management systems, the emphasis shifts from planning to *execution*. Besides their many other capabilities, these systems can:

1. Route and prioritize jobs going through the supply chain
2. Coordinate the flow of goods and materials between a facility and other supply chain partners
3. Provide supply chain partners with performance data on operations and supply chain activities

Job Sequencing

Job sequencing rules
Rules used to determine the order in which jobs should be processed when resources are limited and multiple jobs are waiting to be done.

The tools and techniques used to perform PAC and vendor order management are as varied as the operational environments in which they are used. They can be as simple as the rules for deciding which manufacturing job should be processed next or as complex as high-tech software or hardware solutions for tracking the flow of materials among supply chain partners. **Job sequencing rules** have been used for decades to determine the order in which jobs should be processed when resources are limited and multiple jobs are waiting to be done. And as Example 12.7 shows, job sequencing is just as valid in a services environment as it is in manufacturing.

EXAMPLE 12.7

Job Sequencing at Carlos's Restoration Services

Carlos's Restoration Services restores antique paintings. The process consists of three steps. Each of these steps must be completed prior to moving on to the next step. Furthermore, Carlos's can work on only one job at a time at each step.

Carlos's has four jobs waiting to be started. Information on these jobs, shown in the order in which they arrived, is contained in Table 12.1.

TABLE 12.1 Job Requirements for Carlos's Restoration Services

JOB	Estimated Days			TOTAL TASK TIME	DAYS UNTIL DUE	CRITICAL RATIO
	STEP 1	STEP 2	STEP 3			
Uptown Gallery	3	2	3.5	8.5	21	2.47
High Museum	5	2	1	8	20	2.50
Chester College	3	2	5	10	10	1.00
Smith	6	4	1	11	15	1.36

Total task times range from 8 to 11 days. Chester College has requested that its job be completed in 10 days, while Uptown Gallery is willing to wait 21 days. One way to determine the order in which jobs should be sequenced is based on the critical ratio. The *critical ratio* is calculated as follows:

$$\text{Critical ratio} = \frac{\text{days until due}}{\text{total task time remaining}} \qquad (12.6)$$

A critical ratio of 1 indicates that the amount of task time equals the amount of time left; hence, any time spent waiting will make the job late. A critical ratio less than 1 indicates that the job is going to be late unless something changes. When the critical ratio is used to sequence work, the jobs with the lowest critical ratio are scheduled to go first. Carlos's decides to test three common job sequencing rules—first come, first served (FCFS), earliest due date (EDD), and the critical ratio—to see which one performs best. The results are shown in Table 12.2.

TABLE 12.2 Testing Three Common Job Sequencing Rules at Carlos's Restoration Services

First come, first served	Step 1		Step 2		Step 3		
JOB	START	END	START	END	START	END	DAYS LATE
Uptown Gallery	0	3	3	5	5	8.5	0
High Museum	3	8	8	10	10	11	0
Chester College	8	11	11	13	13	18	8
Smith	11	17	17	21	21	22	7
						Average lateness:	**3.75** days

Earliest due date	Step 1		Step 2		Step 3		
JOB	START	END	START	END	START	END	DAYS LATE
Chester College	0	3	3	5	5	10	0
Smith	3	9	9	13	13	14	0
High Museum	9	14	14	16	16	17	0
Uptown Gallery	14	17	17	19	19	22.5	1.5
						Average lateness:	**0.375** days

Critical ratio	Step 1		Step 2		Step 3		
JOB	START	END	START	END	START	END	DAYS LATE
Chester College	0	3	3	5	5	10	0
Smith	3	9	9	13	13	14	0
Uptown Gallery	9	12	13	15	15	18.5	0
High Museum	12	17	17	19	19	20	0
						Average lateness:	**0** days

Processing the jobs on a first-come, first-served basis might seem the fairest, but in this case, the result is that two jobs are finished long before they're due, while two jobs are considerably late. Sequencing the jobs according to the earliest due date results in somewhat better results: Only the Uptown Gallery job is late (1.5 days), for an average lateness of 0.375 days.

Carlos's then sequences the jobs from highest to lowest critical ratio value. In this case, all the jobs are completed prior to the due date. Based on these results, Carlos's decides to use the critical ratio to set the sequence.

Monitoring and Tracking Technologies

Radio-frequency identification (RFID), bar coding, and online order tracking systems have been developed to trace the movement and location of materials in the supply chain and report on the progress of specific jobs. Such systems depend on computer hardware and software that can interpret the information gathered by the system. Herman Miller, a designer and manufacturer of high-end office furniture, incorporates PAC and vendor order management tools. Besides helping the company to control its operations and supply chain activities, these systems also alert managers to potential problems. For example, computer displays located throughout Herman Miller's plant provide users with real-time information about the status of manufacturing jobs and required materials. If a shortage of materials threatens to delay a job, the system flags the problem and indicates which jobs will be affected. Managers at Herman Miller or at supply chain partners' facilities can then take corrective action.[2]

12.4 SYNCHRONIZING PLANNING AND CONTROL ACROSS THE SUPPLY CHAIN

Throughout this book, we have emphasized the need to synchronize decisions across the supply chain. This need is especially critical in planning and control activities. In this section, we introduce one technique for synchronizing planning and control decisions: distribution requirements planning (DRP). In Chapter 13, we will talk about another technique, called *kanban*. DRP helps to synchronize supply chain partners at the *master schedule level*, while kanban systems help to synchronize them at the PAC and vendor order management levels (Figure 12.22).

Distribution Requirements Planning

Distribution requirements planning (DRP)
A time-phased planning approach similar to MRP that uses planned orders at the point of demand (customer, warehouse, etc.) to determine forecasted demand at the source level (often a plant).

Distribution requirements planning (DRP) is a time-phased planning approach similar to MRP that uses planned orders at the point of demand (customer, warehouse, etc.) to determine forecasted demand at the source level (often a plant). DRP is one of many ways in which supply chain partners can synchronize their planning efforts at the master schedule level. These forecasted demand numbers then become input to the master scheduling process.

To illustrate how DRP works, let's return to the example of Sandy-Built's MeltoMatic snowblower. When you first looked at the master schedule record shown in Figure 12.7, you may have wondered where the forecasted demand numbers came from. After all, much of the value of master scheduling hinges on the accuracy of forecasts. Managers typically base their forecasts on past history or educated guesses, but DRP forecasts are calculated directly from downstream supply partners' requirements. That is, DRP uses MRP-style logic to feed accurate demand information into the master schedule.

**FIGURE 12.22
Synchronized Planning
and Control**

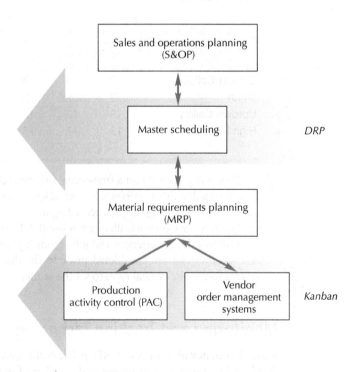

FIGURE 12.23
Downstream Supply Chain for MeltoMatic Snowblowers

Suppose the MeltoMatic is sold through two regional distribution centers, one in Minneapolis, Minnesota, and the other in Buffalo, New York. These distribution centers, in turn, sell directly to retailers. Figure 12.23 shows the structure of this downstream supply chain.

Each distribution center has its own weekly demand forecasts, inventory data, order lead times, and minimum order quantities. Both centers use this information to estimate when they will need to place orders with the main plant.

The two sections at the top of Figure 12.24 show the DRP records for the two distribution centers. Note that these records are almost identical to MRP records, with one exception: Instead of gross requirements, they show forecasted demand. Here, the term *forecasted demand* refers to the number of snowblowers each center expects to ship to retail customers each week. By substituting forecasted demand for gross requirements, managers at the distribution centers can calculate net requirements, planned receipts, and planned orders. Finally, activities at these two distribution centers are synchronized when their total weekly planned orders become forecasted demand in the factory's master schedule (see the third section of Figure 12.24). Master scheduling occurs as usual, except that the forecasted demand is tied explicitly to planned orders at the distribution centers.

Now look at what happens when forecasted demand changes at the distribution centers (Figure 12.25). Starting in week 49, the forecasted demand at the Minneapolis distribution center has increased dramatically. What is the impact of this change on the master schedule? Logic suggests that in order to meet the increased demand, Sandy-Built's managers will need to increase

Minneapolis distribution center

	Month	********November********				********December********				********January********			
	Week	45	46	47	48	49	50	51	52	1	2	3	4
Forecasted demand		60	60	60	60	75	75	75	75	90	90	120	120
Scheduled receipts			120										
Projected ending inventory	75	15	75	15	75	0	45	90	15	45	75	75	75
Net requirements		0	0	0	45	0	75	30	0	75	45	45	45
Planned receipts		0	0	0	120	0	120	120	0	120	120	120	120
Planned orders		0	120	0	120	120	0	120	120	120	120	0	0

LT (weeks) = 2
Min. order = 120

Buffalo distribution center

	Month	********November********				********December********				********January********			
	Week	45	46	47	48	49	50	51	52	1	2	3	4
Forecasted demand		80	80	85	85	90	90	95	95	100	100	105	105
Scheduled receipts		100											
Projected ending inventory	25	45	65	80	95	5	15	20	25	25	25	20	15
Net requirements		0	35	20	5	0	85	80	75	75	75	80	85
Planned receipts		0	100	100	100	0	100	100	100	100	100	100	100
Planned orders		100	100	100	0	100	100	100	100	100	100	100	0

LT (weeks) = 1
Min. order = 100

Master schedule, MeltoMatic snowblowers

	Month	********November********				********December********			
	Week	45	46	47	48	49	50	51	52
Forecasted demand		100	220	100	120	220	100	220	220
Booked orders		100	0	0	0	0	0	0	0
Projected ending inventory	37	257	37	157	37	137	37	257	37
Master production schedule		320		220		320		440	0
Available to promise		257		220		320		440	

FIGURE 12.24 DRP Records for the MeltoMatic Snowblower

Minneapolis distribution center	Month	********November********				********December********				********January********			
	Week	45	46	47	48	49	50	51	52	1	2	3	4
Forecasted demand		60	60	60	60	90	90	90	90	110	110	130	130
LT (weeks) = 2 Scheduled receipts			120			0							
Projected ending inventory	75	15	75	15	75	105	15	45	75	85	95	85	75
Net requirements		0	0	0	45	15	0	75	45	35	25	35	45
Min. order = 120 Planned receipts		0	0	0	120	120	0	120	120	120	120	120	120
Planned orders		**0**	**120**	**120**	**0**	**120**	**120**	**120**	**120**	**120**	**120**	**0**	**0**

Buffalo distribution center	Month	********November********				********December********				********January********			
	Week	45	46	47	48	49	50	51	52	1	2	3	4
Forecasted demand		80	80	85	85	90	90	95	95	100	100	105	105
LT (weeks) = 1 Scheduled receipts		100											
Projected ending inventory	25	45	65	80	95	5	15	20	25	25	25	20	15
Net requirements		0	35	20	5	0	85	80	75	75	75	80	85
Min. order = 100 Planned receipts		0	100	100	100	0	100	100	100	100	100	100	100
Planned orders		100	100	100	0	100	100	100	100	100	100	100	0

Master schedule, MeltoMatic snowblowers	Month	********November********				********December********			
	Week	45	46	47	48	49	50	51	52
Forecasted demand		**100**	**220**	**220**	**0**	**220**	**220**	**220**	**220**
Booked orders		100	0	0	0	**0**	0	0	0
Projected ending inventory	37	257	37	37	37	**257**	37	257	37
Master production schedule		320		220		**440**		440	
Available to promise		257		220		**440**		440	

FIGURE 12.25 The Impact of Forecast Changes on DRP Records

the master production schedule to 440 snowblowers in week 49. The point is that DRP quickly translates downstream demand into upstream production decisions.

Figure 12.26 provides a final, high-level view of how DRP helps synchronize Sandy-Built's supply chain. Retailer orders drive not only Sandy-Built's plans but also those of upstream suppliers who plan their activity based on Sandy-Built's material orders. In effect, every *MPS* quantity or MRP planned order can be traced back to demand from the retailers.

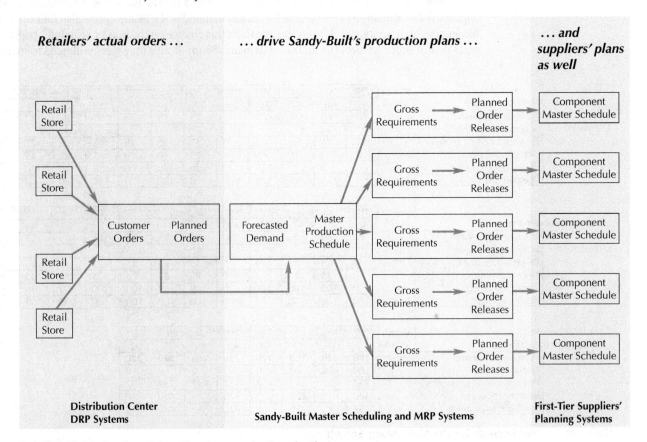

FIGURE 12.26 Synchronizing Plans across the Supply Chain

CHAPTER SUMMARY

This chapter has provided a comprehensive overview of the various tools companies use to manage production, starting with master scheduling, then MRP and job sequencing, and ending with DRP. Planning and control systems aid manufacturers and service firms alike by helping them to determine the quantities and timing of their activities. Put another way, production management should be of interest not only to manufacturing firms but to virtually all firms involved in the flow of physical products.

Today, advances in information technology are radically changing planning and control systems in two fundamental ways. First, faster computers and extensive communications

networks are expanding the depth and breadth of planning and control activities. Firms can replan and share new information with their supply chain partners almost instantaneously. Second, planning and control software tools are becoming more sophisticated. Some firms even have advanced decision support tools that allow them to quickly evaluate multiple plans or even to generate an optimal plan.

That said, the usefulness of planning and control systems still depends on people who understand how they work and how to use them correctly. This fundamental requirement will never change.

EXAMPLE 12.8
BigDawg Customs Revisited

"OK, so what should we do?" asked Steve Barr, owner of BigDawg Customs.

Traci Griggs, vice president of marketing, spoke up. "One of the problems you mentioned was that currently we really didn't have a way to match up production of KZ1 seats with actual customer orders. So I've worked with Brad in manufacturing to develop a master production schedule for the KZ1. Brad, show Steve how it works."

Brad Ashbaugh handed Steve a preliminary master schedule for the KZ1 (Figure 12.27). "The master schedule really does several things. First, it allows us to compare the weekly forecasts Traci has developed against our planned production levels. Second, it allows us to …"

KZ1 inventory at end of March =					252			
Month	************April***************				***************May**************			
Week	14	15	16	17	18	19	20	21
Forecast demand	300	300	400	450	500	500	500	500
Orders booked	240	295	170	150	90	0	0	0
Projected ending inventory	−48	852	452	2	1,002	502	2	1,002
Master production schedule	0	1,200	0	0	1,500	0	0	1,500
Available-to-promise	12	585			1,410			1,500

FIGURE 12.27 Master Schedule for KZ1 Scooter Seat

"Woah!" Steve Barr interjected. "What does that negative inventory number in week 14 mean? Have we overpromised again?"

Brad replied, "Good question. No, we haven't overpromised yet. In fact, the 'available-to-promise' line for week 14 tells us we still have another 12 seats that we can sell this week before we make more seats next week. The −48 means that, given what we've already promised and what we have available, we expect that we'll have to turn away orders for 48 seats this week. This is not great and we want to avoid this in the future, but not meeting demand is still better than promising something we can't deliver."

"OK, I think I get it. So how will this master schedule work as time goes on?" asked Steve. Traci answered, "Every week, Brad and I will get together and roll the schedule forward one week. We will update the forecast numbers and see what adjustments if any should be made to the master production schedule. Also—and this is key—every time a salesperson makes a sale, he or she will first need to check to see whether inventory is available, and then make sure the master schedule is updated every time there is a change to the orders booked. This way we can make sure we don't promise something we can't deliver."

Steve replied, "OK, that sounds good, but what about our parts inventory problem?" Brad spoke up, "The KZ1 seat is assembled from three components we order from vendors: the saddle, the cover, and a hardware kit. We can use material requirements planning to tell us when we need to order stuff so that we don't order too earlier and we don't order too much. Brad then handed Steve a preliminary copy of the MRP for the KZ1 seat (Figure 12.28).

KZ1 Seat		WEEK							
		14	15	16	17	18	19	20	21
LT (weeks) = 1	MPS due date	0	1,200	0	0	1,500	0	0	1,500
	Start assembly	1,200	0	0	1,500	0	0	1,500	0

Saddle			WEEK							
			14	15	16	17	18	19	20	21
	Gross requirements		1,200	0	0	1,500	0	0	1,500	0
LT (weeks) = 2	Scheduled receipts		0	0	0	0	0	0	0	0
	Projected ending inventory	1,650	450	450	450	0	0	0	0	0
$30	Net requirements		0	0	0	1,050	0	0	1,500	0
	Planned receipts		0	0	0	1,050	0	0	1,500	0
Min. order = 1	Planned orders	0	0	1,050	0	0	1,500	0	0	0

Hardware Kit			WEEK							
			14	15	16	17	18	19	20	21
	Gross requirements		1,200	0	0	1,500	0	0	1,500	0
LT (weeks) = 1	Scheduled receipts		0	0	0	0	0	0	0	0
$20	Projected ending inventory	2,200	1,000	1,000	1,000	500	500	500	0	0
	Net requirements		0	0	0	500	0	0	1,000	0
Min. order = 1,000	Planned receipts		0	0	0	1,000	0	0	1,000	0
	Planned orders	0	0	0	1,000	0	0	1,000	0	0

Cover			WEEK							
			14	15	16	17	18	19	20	21
	Gross requirements		1,200	0	0	1,500	0	0	1,500	0
LT (weeks) = 2	Scheduled receipts		0	250	0	0	0	0	0	0
$10	Projected ending inventory	1,200	0	250	250	0	0	0	0	0
	Net requirements		0	0	0	1,250	0	0	1,500	0
Min. order = 250	Planned receipts		0	0	0	1,250	0	0	1,500	0
	Planned orders	0	0	1,250	0	0	1,500	0	0	0

FIGURE 12.28 MRP Record for KZ1 Scooter Seat

Brad continued, "We are about to go into week 14 of the year, and we currently have 1,650 saddles, 2,200 hardware kits, and 1,200 covers sitting in inventory. At current costs, this inventory is worth:

$$1,650 \text{ saddles} * (\$30 \text{ each}) + 2,200 \text{ hardware kits} * (\$20 \text{ each})$$
$$+ \$1,200 * (\$10 \text{ each}) = \$105,500$$

"Ugh! And most of that stuff has been sitting around for a couple weeks," interjected Steve. "Exactly," Brad continues, "but if we use MRP to plan the timing and quantities of orders, we can reduce component inventories to zero by the end of week 21."

Steve, Traci, and Brad discuss the master schedule and MRP records for a while longer until Steve is satisfied and has a basic understanding of how the planning tools work. Finally he says:

"This looks like a really good start, and I'll be interested to see how this works in practice. I guess I have a couple of questions. First, what do we need to do to help make sure everyone follows the rules—that is, placing customer orders through the master schedule, and keeping accurate inventory records? Also, once we get this system working for the KZ1 seats, how might we apply it to other areas of our business?"

KEY FORMULAS

Projected ending inventory for the master schedule record (page 368):

$$EI_t = EI_{t-1} + MPS_t - \text{maximum}(F_t, OB_t) \tag{12.1}$$

where:

EI_t = ending inventory in time period t

MPS_t = master production schedule quantity available in time period t

F_t = forecasted demand for time period t

OB_t = orders booked for time period t

Available to promise for the master schedule record (page 370):

For the *first week* of the master schedule record:

$$ATP_t = EI_{t-1} + MPS_t - \sum_{i=t}^{z-1} OB_i \tag{12.2}$$

For any subsequent week in which $MPS > 0$:

$$ATP_t = MPS_t - \sum_{i=t}^{z-1} OB_i \tag{12.3}$$

where:

ATP_t = available to promise in week t

EI_{t-1} = ending inventory in week $t - 1$

MPS_t = master production schedule quantity in week t

$\sum_{i=t}^{z-1} OB_i$ = sum of all orders booked from week t until week z (when the next positive MPS quantity is due)

Net requirements for the MRP record (page 376):

$$NR_t = \text{maximum}(0; GR_t - EI_{t-1} - SR_t) \tag{12.4}$$

where:

NR_t = net requirement in time period t

GR_t = gross requirement in time period t

EI_{t-1} = ending inventory from time period $t - 1$

SR_t = scheduled receipts in time period t

Projected ending inventory for the MRP record (page 376):

$$EI_t = EI_{t-1} + SR_t + PR_t - GR_t \tag{12.5}$$

where:

EI_t = ending inventory from time period t

EI_{t-1} = ending inventory from time period $t - 1$

SR_t = scheduled receipts in time period t

PR_t = planned receipts in time period t

GR_t = gross requirements in time period t

Critical ratio (page 383):

$$\text{Critical ratio} = \frac{\text{days until due}}{\text{total task time remaining}} \tag{12.6}$$

KEY TERMS

SOLVED PROBLEM

PROBLEM

Completing a Master Schedule Record

Complete the projected ending inventory and available to promise calculations for the following master schedule record. Interpret the results.

On-hand inventory at end of week 15: 222								
Week	16	17	18	19	20	21	22	23
Forecasted demand	220	220	215	215	210	210	205	205
Booked orders	192	189	233	96	135	67	85	40
Projected ending inventory								
Master production schedule		450		430		415		400
Available to promise								

Solution

The projected ending inventory values can be found using Equation (12.1):

$$EI_t = EI_{t-1} + MPS_t - \text{maximum } (F_t, OB_t) \qquad\qquad \textbf{(12.1)}$$

For weeks 16 through 18, the projected ending inventories are:

$$EI_{16} = 222 + 0 - \text{maximum } (220, 192) = 2$$
$$EI_{17} = 2 + 450 - \text{maximum } (220, 189) = 232$$
$$EI_{18} = 232 + 0 - \text{maximum } (215, 233) = -1$$

Weeks 19 through 23 are calculated in a similar manner. In the projected ending inventory in week 18, the negative value suggests that there is not enough inventory to meet the forecasted demand. But has the company overpromised yet? To see, we need to calculate the ATP numbers:

$$ATP_{16} = 222 + 0 - 192 = 30$$
$$ATP_{17} = 450 - (189 + 233) = 28$$
$$ATP_{19} = 430 - (96 + 135) = 199$$
$$ATP_{21} = 415 - (67 + 85) = 263$$
$$ATP_{23} = 400 - 40 = 360$$

The completed master schedule record is as follows:

On-hand inventory at end of week 15: 222								
Week	16	17	18	19	20	21	22	23
Forecasted demand	220	220	215	215	210	210	205	205
Booked orders	192	189	233	96	135	67	85	40
Projected ending inventory	2	232	-1	214	4	209	4	199
Master production schedule		450		430		415		400
Available to promise	30	28		199		263		360

The master schedule record suggests that, as of right now, the company has not overpromised. However, if the company wants to meet all the forecasted demand (or keep some safety stock available, just in case), it should consider taking steps to bump up its master production schedule quantities.

DISCUSSION QUESTIONS

1. Someone says to you, "If a company is already using sales and operations planning to coordinate marketing and operations, then it doesn't need master scheduling as well." Is this true? How are S&OP and master scheduling similar? How are they different? What information does master scheduling provide that S&OP does not? How difficult would it be to develop successful master schedules without doing S&OP first?

2. Can a company complete its material requirements plans before it does master scheduling? Explain.

3. Discuss the importance of accurate forecasting to planning and control systems. What happens if an organization's planning efforts are strong, except for forecasting?

4. What is MRP nervousness? Can this condition affect DRP systems as well?

5. Master scheduling, MRP, and DRP have been around for a long time, but too many companies still do an inadequate job of using these tools. How can this be? In particular, what role do you think organizational discipline plays in making these tools work?

6. What are the benefits of having a formal master scheduling process? What could happen to firms that don't follow some of the basic rules of master scheduling?

7. Explain in your own words how tools such as master scheduling, MRP, and DRP can be used to coordinate activity up and down a supply chain. For example, what information might we share with our customers? Our suppliers? What information might we want from them to do master scheduling, MRP, and DRP effectively?

PROBLEMS

(* = easy; ** = moderate; *** = advanced)

Problems for Section 12.1: Master Scheduling

1. (*) Complete the following master schedule record:

On-hand inventory at end of week 1: 65								
Week	2	3	4	5	6	7	8	9
Forecasted demand	45	50	55	60	65	70	75	80
Booked orders	15	100	48	25	72	22	67	10
Projected ending inventory								
Master production schedule	150			200			150	
Available to promise							**73**	

2. (**) Consider the master schedule record shown in problem 1. Suppose marketing books an order for an additional 10 units in week 4. Recalculate the projected ending inventory and available-to-promise numbers. How low does the projected ending inventory get? What actions might the company take as a result?

3. (**) Complete the following master schedule record:

On-hand inventory at end of week 1: 100								
Week	2	3	4	5	6	7	8	9
Forecasted demand	250	250	300	300	350	350	250	250
Booked orders	265	255	270	245	260	235	180	100
Projected ending inventory								
Master production schedule	500		600		700		500	
Available to promise							**220**	

4. (**) Consider the master schedule record shown in problem 3. Suppose the production manager calls and says that only 600 units will be finished in week 6, not the 700 units originally called for. Recalculate the projected ending inventory and available-to-promise numbers. What does a negative projected ending inventory value mean? How does it differ from a negative available-to-promise number? As a manager, which would be easier to deal with—a negative projected inventory value or a negative ATP?

5. Consider the following partially completed master schedule record:

On-hand inventory at end of April: 40								
Month	***********May***********				***********June***********			
Week	19	20	21	22	23	24	25	26
Forecasted demand	200	200	200	225	225	225	200	200
Booked orders	205	203	201	195	193	190	182	178
Projected ending inventory								
Master production schedule	600	0	0	675	0	0	600	0
Available to promise							**240**	

a. (*) Complete the projected on-hand inventory calculations and the available-to-promise calculations.

b. (**) Suppose that a customer calls and cancels an order for 50 units in week 25. Which of the following statements are *true*?

- The *ATP* for week 25 will increase by 50 units.
- The projected ending inventory for week 25 will increase by 50 units.
- The *ATP* for weeks 19 and 22 will be unaffected.

Problems for Section 12.2: Material Requirements Planning

6. (*) Complete the following MRP record. All gross requirements, beginning inventory levels, and scheduled receipts are shown.

WEEK		1	2	3	4	5	6
A2	Gross requirements	200	200	200	300	300	300
LT (weeks) = 2	Scheduled receipts		200				
	Projected ending inventory: 260						
	Net requirements						
Min. order = 1	Planned receipts						
Planned orders							

7. (**) Now suppose the lead time for item A2, shown in problem 6, is three weeks rather than two weeks. Based on this information, can the company support the current gross requirements for the A2? Why? What are the implications of having reliable supplier and manufacturing lead times in an MRP environment?

8. (**) Complete the following MRP record. Note that the minimum order quantity is 900. What is the average ending inventory over the six weeks?

WEEK		1	2	3	4	5	6
B3	Gross requirements	0	400	400	400	0	400
LT (weeks) = 1	Scheduled receipts						
	Projected ending inventory: 0						
	Net requirements						
Min. order = 900	Planned receipts						
	Planned orders						

9. (**) Now suppose the minimum order quantity for item B3 in problem 8 is reduced to 300 units. Redo the MRP record. What is the new average ending inventory level over the six weeks? What are the implications for setting order quantities in an MRP environment?

10. (**) The following figure shows the bill of material (BOM) for the Acme PolyBob, a product that has proven unsuccessful in capturing roadrunners. Complete the MRP records. All the information you need is shown in the BOM and on the MRP records.

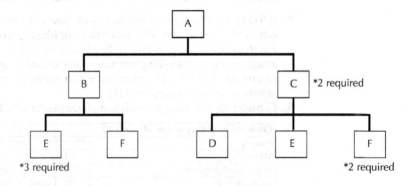

Item B: Lead time = 1 week; Minimum order quantity = 1

WEEK	1	2	3	4	5	6
Gross requirements		250	300	300	300	200
Scheduled receipts						
Projected ending inventory: 0						
Net requirements						
Planned receipts						
Planned orders						

Item C: Lead time = 3 weeks; Minimum order quantity = 500

WEEK	1	2	3	4	5	6
Gross requirements						
Scheduled receipts		500	600			
Projected ending inventory: 0						
Net requirements						
Planned receipts						
Planned orders						

Item E: Lead time = 4 weeks; Minimum order quantity = 5,000

WEEK	1	2	3	4	5	6
Gross requirements						
Scheduled receipts						
Projected ending inventory: 5,750						
Net requirements						
Planned receipts						
Planned orders						

Item F: Lead time = 5 weeks; Minimum order quantity = 750

WEEK	1	2	3	4	5	6
Gross requirements						
Scheduled receipts						
Projected ending inventory: 4,750						
Net requirements						
Planned receipts						
Planned orders						

11. (**) Republic Tool and Manufacturing Company of Carlsbad, California, makes a wide variety of lawn care products. One of Republic's products is the Model Number 540 Broadcast Spreader:

Complete the following MRP records. Note the following:

- Republic intends to start assembling 2,000 broadcast spreader kits in weeks 2, 4, and 6.
- The gross requirements for the gear and rotor plate assembly have already been given to you. For the remaining items, you will need to figure out the gross requirements.
- All scheduled receipts, lead times, and beginning inventory levels are shown.
- Note that cotter pins appear *twice* in the bill of material.

Gear and rotor plate assembly: Lead time = 1 week; Minimum order quantity = 2,500

WEEK	1	2	3	4	5	6
Gross requirements		2,000		2,000		2,000
Scheduled receipts						
Projected ending inventory: 1,000						
Net requirements						
Planned receipts						
Planned orders						

Wheels: Lead time = 1 week; Minimum order quantity = 1

WEEK		1	2	3	4	5	6
Gross requirements							
Scheduled receipts							
Projected ending inventory: 0							
Net requirements							
Planned receipts							
Planned orders							

Cotter pins: Lead time = 3 weeks; Minimum order quantity = 15,000

WEEK		1	2	3	4	5	6
Gross requirements							
Scheduled receipts							
Projected ending inventory: 11,000							
Net requirements							
Planned receipts							
Planned orders							

12. (**) Each Triam Deluxe gamer computer system consists of *two* speakers, a monitor, a system unit, a keyboard, and an installation kit. These pieces are packed together and shipped as a complete kit. In MRP terms, all of these items are level 1 items that make the level 0 kits. Complete the MRP records, using the following information:

- Production plans for complete kits are as follows:

  Start assembling 2,500 kits in week 2
  Start assembling 3,000 kits in weeks 3, 4, and 5
  Start assembling 2,000 kits in week 6

- The gross requirements for the system unit have already been given to you. For the remaining items, you will need to figure out the gross requirements.
- All scheduled receipts, lead times, and beginning inventory levels are shown.

System unit: Lead time = 1 week; Minimum order quantity = 1

WEEK	1	2	3	4	5	6
Gross requirements		2,500	3,000	3,000	3,000	2,000
Scheduled receipts						
Projected ending inventory: 0						
Net requirements						
Planned receipts						
Planned orders						

Speakers: Lead time = 1 week; Minimum order quantity = 5,000

WEEK	1	2	3	4	5	6
Gross requirements						
Scheduled receipts	5,000					
Projected ending inventory: 0						
Net requirements						
Planned receipts						
Planned orders						

CD-ROM drives: Lead time = 6 weeks; Minimum order quantity = 5,000

WEEK	1	2	3	4	5	6
Gross requirements						
Scheduled receipts						
Projected ending inventory: 13,500						
Net requirements						
Planned receipts						
Planned orders						

Vaxidene (Problems 13 and 14)

After graduating from college, you take a job with Baxter Pharmaceuticals. You are made the product manager for Vaxidene, a new vaccine used to fight bacterial meningitis. The bill of material (BOM) for a *single 4-milligram dose* of Vaxidene follows:

Each dose is actually a mixture of three proprietary compounds, called compounds X, Y, and Z. It takes one week to mix them together to make doses of Vaxidene. You also have the following information:

- Compound X is made up of two chemicals (A and B) and takes one week to synthesize (i.e., lead time = 1 week).
- Compound Y is made up of two chemicals (A and C) and takes one week to synthesize.
- Compound Z is made up of two chemicals (C and D) and takes one week to synthesize.
- The lead times for chemicals A through D are all one week.

13. Consider the following master schedule record for Vaxidene:

On-hand inventory at end of December: 916 doses								
Month	*********January**********				********February********			
Week	6	7	8	9	10	11	12	13
Forecast demand	1,000	1,000	1,250	1,250	1,500	1,500	1,750	1,750
Orders booked	1,095	950	1,100	963	1,125	1,095	1,243	1,208
Projected on-hand inventory								
Master schedule	3,250	0	0	4,250	0	0	3,500	0
Available-to-promise								

a. (*) Complete the master schedule record.
b. (**) Suppose a hospital in the Tucson area calls and says it is facing an epidemic of bacterial meningitis. It needs 2,000 doses as soon as possible. Assuming that Baxter can make no changes to the master production schedule quantities or orders booked, how quickly can it get the hospital the 2,000 doses? Be specific with regard to what quantities Baxter can ship and when.
c. (**) Suppose the hospital says it needs the doses now, not in three weeks. What steps could Baxter Pharmaceuticals take to deal with this emergency? Who would Baxter need to talk to? (*Hint:* Consider the current booked orders and their sources.)

14. (***) Complete the following MRP records for the Vaxidene drug. Note the following:

- Doses have been converted into milligrams to facilitate material planning (4,250 doses = 17,000 milligrams).
- Make sure that you calculate the correct requirements for each compound and drug. For instance, each 4-milligram dose requires 2 milligrams of compound X (2 to 1). Therefore, to start mixing 17,000 milligrams of Vaxidene, Baxter Pharmaceuticals will need 8,500 milligrams of compound X.

Vaxidene

		WEEK						
		1	2	3	4	5	6	7
LT (weeks) = 1 start mixing	MPS due date		0	0	17,000	0	0	14,000
				17,000			14,000	
Compound X	Gross requirements							
LT (weeks) =	Scheduled receipts							
	Projected ending inventory: 1,500							
	Net requirements							
Minimum order (mg) 20,000	Planned receipts							
	Planned orders							
Compound Y	Gross requirements							
LT (weeks) =	Scheduled receipts							
	Projected ending inventory: 1,000							
	Net requirements							
Minimum order (mg) 5,000	Planned receipts							
	Planned orders							
Compound Z	Gross requirements	200						
LT (weeks) =	Scheduled receipts							
	Projected ending inventory: 0							
	Net requirements							
Minimum order (mg) 1	Planned receipts							
	Planned orders							
Chemical A	Gross requirements							
LT (weeks) =	Scheduled receipts							
	Projected ending inventory: 500							
	Net requirements							
Minimum order (mg) 9,500	Planned receipts							
	Planned orders							
Chemical B	Gross requirements							
LT (weeks) =	Scheduled receipts							
	Projected ending inventory: 0							
	Net requirements							
Minimum order (mg) 4,000	Planned receipts							
	Planned orders							
Chemical C	Gross requirements							
LT (weeks) =	Scheduled receipts							
	Projected ending inventory: 0							
	Net requirements							
Minimum order (mg) 2,000	Planned receipts							
	Planned orders							
Chemical D	Gross requirements							
LT (weeks) =	Scheduled receipts							
	Projected ending inventory: 3,000							
	Net requirements							
Minimum order (mg) 1	Planned receipts							
	Planned orders							

Problems for Section 12.3: Production Activity Control and Vendor Order Management Systems

15. (**) Consider the following job information. Each job must proceed sequentially through the different work areas, and each area can work on only one job at a time. Sequence the jobs according to the (1) first-come, first-served rule, (2) earliest due date, and (3) critical ratio. Calculate the average lateness under each rule. Which rule performs best? Are any of the results completely satisfactory? What are the implications?

| JOB | Estimated Days | | | TOTAL TASK TIME | DAYS UNTIL DUE |
	PAINTING	ASSEMBLY	PACKING		
A	1.5	2	0.5	4	15
B	4	3	1	8	16
C	3	2	0.5	5.5	8
D	6	4	1	11	20

16. (**) Recall Example 12.7, where Carlos's Restoration Services wanted to determine the best sequence for four jobs. According to Table 12.2, the critical ratio was the only rule tested that resulted in an estimated average lateness value of 0 days.

Now suppose a representative of Chester College calls and says the college won't need the restored art piece for 14 days. At the same time, the High Museum leaves a message saying it would really like its job completed in 15 days.

How would these requests change the suggested sequence, based on the critical ratio rule? If Carlos's uses the critical ratio rule to sequence the jobs, will they all be done on time?

Problems for Section 12.4: Synchronizing Planning and Control across the Supply Chain

17. (***) Due to unusual weather conditions in Minneapolis and Buffalo, Sandy-Built has changed the forecasted demand numbers for MeltoMatic snowblowers at its two distribution centers. Using Figures 12.24 and 12.25 as guides, complete the following DRP records and master schedule record.

Minneapolis Distribution Center

| | Month | November | | | | December | | | | January | | | |
	WEEK	45	46	47	48	49	50	51	52	1	2	3	4
	Forecasted demand	80	80	80	80	90	90	100	100	120	120	140	140
LT (weeks) = 2	Scheduled receipts												
	Projected ending inventory: 160												
	Net requirements												
Minimum order =	Planned receipts												
120	Planned orders												

Buffalo Distribution Center

| | Month | November | | | | December | | | | January | | | |
	WEEK	45	46	47	48	49	50	51	52	1	2	3	4
	Forecasted demand	60	60	70	70	80	80	80	80	90	90	95	95
LT (weeks) = 1	Scheduled receipts	100											
	Projected ending inventory: 25												
	Net requirements												
Minimum order =	Planned receipts												
100	Planned orders												

Master Schedule

| | Month | November | | | | December | | | |
	WEEK	45	46	47	48	49	50	51	52
Total planned orders									
Booked orders		120	0	0	0	0	0	0	0
Projected ending inventory: 37									
Master production schedule		340		320		340		440	
Available to promise									

CASE STUDY

The Realco Breadmaster

Two years ago, Johnny Chang's company, Realco, introduced a new breadmaker, which, due to its competitive pricing and features, was a big success across the United States. While delighted to have the business, Johnny felt uneasy about the lack of formal planning surrounding the product. He found himself constantly wondering, "Do we have enough breadmakers to meet the orders we've already accepted? Even if we do, will we have enough to meet expected future demands? Should I be doing something *right now* to plan for all this?"

To get a handle on the situation, Johnny decided to talk to various folks in the organization. He started with his inventory manager and found out that inventory at the end of last week was 7,000 units. Johnny thought this was awfully high.

Johnny also knew that production had been completing 40,000 breadmakers every other week for the last year. In fact, another batch was due this week. The production numbers were based on the assumption that demand was roughly 20,000 breadmakers a week. In over a year, no one had questioned whether the forecast or production levels should be readjusted.

Johnny then paid a visit to his marketing manager to see what current orders looked like. "No problem," said Jack Jones, "I have the numbers right here."

WEEK	PROMISED SHIPMENTS
1	23,500
2	23,000
3	21,500
4	15,050
5	13,600
6	11,500
7	5,400
8	1,800

Johnny looked at the numbers for a moment and then asked, "When a customer calls, how do you know if you can meet the order?" "Easy," said Jack. "We've found from experience that nearly all orders can be filled within two weeks, so we promise them three weeks. That gives us a cushion, just in case. Now look at weeks 1 and 2. The numbers look a little high, but between inventory and the additional 40,000 units coming in this week, there shouldn't be a problem."

Questions

1. Develop a master production schedule for the breadmaker. What do the projected ending inventory and available-to-promise numbers look like? Has Realco overpromised? In your view, should Realco update either the forecast or the production numbers?

2. Comment on Jack's approach to order promising. What are the advantages? The disadvantages? How would formal master scheduling improve this process? What organizational changes would be required?

3. Following up on question 2, which do you think is worse: refusing a customer's order up front because you don't have the units available or accepting the order and then failing to deliver? What are the implications for master scheduling?

4. Suppose Realco produces 20,000 breadmakers every week rather than 40,000 every other week. According to the master schedule record, what impact would this have on average inventory levels?

REFERENCES

Books and Articles

Blackstone, J. H., ed., *APICS Dictionary*, 15th ed. (Chicago, IL: APICS, 2016).

Bundy, W. "Miller SQA: Leveraging Technology for Speed and Reliability," *Supply Chain Management Review* 3, no. 2 (Spring 1999): 62–69.

SUPPLEMENT

Paul A. Souders/Corbis/VCG/Getty Images

CHAPTER
twelve

Supply Chain Information Systems

SUPPLEMENT OBJECTIVES

By the end of this supplement, you will be able to:

● Explain why information flows are a necessary part of any supply chain.

● Describe in detail how supply chain information needs vary according to the organizational level and the direction of the linkages (upstream or downstream).

● Describe and differentiate among ERP, DSS, CRM, SRM, and logistics applications.

● Describe what business process management (BPM) tools and cloud computing are and how they might impact future operations and supply chain activities.

IBM'S WATSON SUPPLY CHAIN

Imagine that you are the supply chain manager for a new product being launched by your company. Marketing has promised eager customers that the product will start shipping in two weeks. Unfortunately, weather reports indicate that a major snowstorm is about to strike one of your key European suppliers. Some of the questions you might have:

- Will delivery from our European supplier be delayed due to the snowstorm? If so, for how long?
- What will the impact be, if any, on our ability to ship product on time? What will be the ultimate impact on revenues?
- Are there any alternative suppliers who can help us? Do they have the production capacity? What would be the impact on production schedules and costs?

Supply chain information systems, the topic of this supplement, support everything from day-to-day production activities to long-term strategic planning. And as the above example suggests, managers depend on supply chain information systems to help them quickly *replan* based on changing events.

This is where solutions like IBM's Watson Supply Chain come into play. Watson Supply Chain is one example of a technology platform known as cognitive comput-

ing. *Cognitive computing* "refers to systems that learn at scale, reason with purpose and interact with humans naturally. Rather than being explicitly programmed, they learn and reason from their interactions with us and from their experiences with their environment." As Alex Zhuong, senior marketing manager, IBM Watson Supply Chain, suggests: "Cognitive technology will shape the future, creating a more intelligent, predictive and agile supply chain." For instance, in response to your concerns about the European supplier, Watson Supply Chain might inform you that:

- There is an 80% chance that supplier deliveries will be delayed approximately 96 hours.
- If unresolved, your company will be three days late getting product, resulting in lost revenues of $3 million.
- Fortunately, there are three suppliers with the capacity to meet your short-term needs.

Alex goes on to note, "The focus of the cognitive supply chain is to compare and understand both structured data, such as traditional enterprise records, and unstructured data, including images, natural language, and social media, to provide real time and deep insights with the ultimate goal of allowing professionals to optimize decision making across the supply chain."

Source: J. Kelly, "Computing, Cognition and the Future of Knowing," *IBM Research: Cognitive Computing,* IBM Corporation, 2015, **www.research.ibm.com/software/IBMResearch/multimedia/Computing_Cognition_WhitePaper.pdf.**

INTRODUCTION

Whether we are talking about purchasing or forecasting, master scheduling or project planning, information is an essential part of managing operations and supply chains. Imagine, for example, trying to decide how much capacity your organization needs or how much of a product to make if you don't have a clear idea of what the demand will be or what the relevant costs are.

The importance of information is reflected in the APICS definition of a *supply chain:* "The global network used to deliver products and services from raw materials to end customers through an engineered flow of information, physical distribution, and cash."[1] In fact, one could argue that neither physical nor monetary flows could take place without information flows.

In this supplement, we look at supply chain information flows and the types of information systems firms use to carry them out. Laudon and Laudon define an **information system (IS)** as "a set of interrelated components that collect (or retrieve), process, store, and distribute information to support decision making, coordination, and control in an organization."[2] We should note that not all information systems are computer-based. Nevertheless, much of the growth and interest in supply chain information systems lies in computer-based applications.

Information system (IS)
According to Laudon and Laudon, "a set of interrelated components that collect (or retrieve), process, store, and distribute information to support decision making, coordination, and control in an organization."

---

[1] J. H. Blackstone, ed., *APICS Dictionary,* 15th ed. (Chicago IL: APICS, 2016).
[2] K. Laudon and J. Laudon, *Management Information Systems: Managing the Digital Firm,* 13th ed. (Upper Saddle River, NJ: Prentice Hall, 2013).

This chapter is divided into two parts. In the first part, we discuss the critical role information flows play in the supply chain. Our purpose here is to give you an understanding of the different ways in which information is used. The second section shifts the focus away from information *flows* to information *systems*. In particular, we discuss some of the major categories of supply chain information systems, including enterprise resource planning (ERP) systems.

12S.1 UNDERSTANDING SUPPLY CHAIN INFORMATION NEEDS

Companies use information to help do everything from handling customers' orders to developing new business strategies. It makes sense, then, to start our discussion of supply chain information flows by describing the different ways in which information supports supply chain activities. Common sense tells us that if we understand what the information needs are, we will be in a better position to identify possible solutions later on.

Differences across Organizational Levels

Some of the supply chain activities we have described in this book are particularly information intensive. These include:

1. Execution and transaction processing (e.g., vendor order management systems);
2. Routine decision making (e.g., master scheduling and supplier evaluation systems);
3. Tactical planning (e.g., S&OP); and
4. Strategic decision making (e.g., location modeling, qualitative forecasting, capacity decisions).

Table 12S.1 arranges these categories vertically, with longer-term strategic decision making at the top and day-to-day, routine activities at the bottom. By looking at supply chain activities in this way, we can begin to see how supply chain information needs differ at various levels of the organization.

At the lowest levels, supply chain information flows record and retrieve necessary data and execute and control physical and monetary flows. This is referred to as *execution and transaction processing*. Information flows at this level tend to be highly automated, with a great deal of emphasis on performing the activity the same way each time. The best execution and transaction processing flows require little or no user intervention and are very accurate and fast.

TABLE 12S.1 Supply Chain Information Needs

SUPPLY CHAIN ACTIVITY	PURPOSE	CHARACTERISTICS	KEY PERFORMANCE DIMENSIONS FOR INFORMATION FLOWS
Strategic decision making	Develop long-range strategic plans for meeting the organization's mission	• Focus is on long-term decisions, such as new products or markets and brick-and-mortar capacity decisions • Least structured of all; information needs can change dramatically from one effort to the next • Greatest user discretion	• Flexibility
Tactical planning	Develop plans that coordinate the actions of key supply chain areas, customers, and suppliers across the tactical time horizon	• Focus is on tactical decisions, such as inventory or workforce levels • Plans, but does not carry out, physical flows • Greater user discretion	• Form • Flexibility
Routine decision making/Replanning	Support rule-based decision making	• Fairly short time frames • User discretion	• Accuracy • Timeliness • Limited flexibility
Execution and transaction processing	Record and retrieve data and execute and control physical and monetary flows	• Very short time frames, very high volumes • Highly automated • Standardized business practices • Ideally no user intervention	• Accuracy • Timeliness

FIGURE 12S.1
Supply Chain
Information Flows

At a somewhat higher level, information flows are used to support routine decision making and replanning. Here, users often must have some flexibility to handle exceptions. For example, a retailer might use an inventory management system to forecast, calculate order quantities, establish reorder points, and release orders for the vast majority of items. But the retailer may still want the ability to override the software when the situation warrants. Our opening case study on IBM's Watson Supply Chain is a sophisticated state-of-the-art example of this capability.

The next level up is tactical planning. Here managers are responsible for developing plans that coordinate the actions of key supply chain areas, customers, and suppliers across some tactical time horizon, usually a few months to a year out. Information requirements at this level differ from those at lower levels in a number of ways. First, the information must support *planning* activities, *not* actual execution. Therefore, the time frames are somewhat longer and accuracy is important, but not to the same degree as at lower levels. Second, the information must be widely available and in a form that can be interpreted, manipulated, and used by parties with very different perspectives. A classic example is sales and operations planning (S&OP), which we described in Chapter 10.

Finally, information is needed to support strategic decision making. Here sophisticated analytical tools are often used to search for patterns or relationships in data. Examples include customer segment analysis, product life cycle forecasting, and what-if analyses regarding long-term product or capacity decisions. An excellent example of this is the simulation model we developed for Luc's Deluxe Car Wash in the Chapter 6 supplement. Information systems at the strategic level must be highly flexible in how they manipulate and present the data because the strategic question of interest may change from one situation to the next. Later in this chapter, we talk about decision support systems (DSS), which are specifically geared to support strategic decision making. Notice how the name emphasizes the fact that these systems *support*, but do not *make*, decisions for top managers.

Direction of Linkages

In addition to the organizational level, we need to consider the direction of the linkages. For example, there are planning and control activities that link a firm with its downstream customers, broadly referred to as **customer relationship management (CRM)** activities, and those that link a firm with its upstream suppliers, known as **supplier relationship management (SRM)** activities (Figure 12S.1). There are also flows that link higher-level planning and decision making with lower-level activities *within* the firm (dubbed **internal supply chain management** by Chopra and Meindl[3]).

12S.2 SUPPLY CHAIN INFORMATION SYSTEMS

In this section, we shift our focus from a general discussion of supply chain information flows to a description of the different *solutions* currently being offered. The basis of our map was first laid out more than a decade ago by Steven Kahl,[4] then a software industry analyst. Kahl's map

Customer relationship management (CRM)
A term that broadly refers to planning and control activities and information systems that link a firm with its downstream customers.

Supplier relationship management (SRM)
A term that broadly refers to planning and control activities and information systems that link a firm with its upstream suppliers.

Internal supply chain management
A term that refers to the information flows between higher and lower levels of planning and control systems within an organization.

[3]S. Chopra and P. Meindl, *Supply Chain Management: Strategy, Planning and Operation*, 5th ed. (Upper Saddle River, NJ: Prentice Hall, 2012).
[4]S. Kahl, "What's the 'Value' of Supply Chain Software?" *Supply Chain Management Review* 2, no. 4 (Winter 1999): 59–67.

FIGURE 12S.2
A Map of Supply Chain Management Information Systems

was later refined by Chopra and Meindl,[5] who applied the labels CRM, SRM, and internal supply chain management (ISCM) to various areas of the map.

Our map (Figure 12S.2) parallels Figure 12S.1 in that it distinguishes the various applications by organizational level and the direction of linkages. We add an additional column labeled "Logistics." Logistics applications deal with facilities and transportation issues, such as determining facility locations, optimizing transportation systems, and controlling the movement of materials between supply chain partners.

Enterprise resource planning (ERP) systems are large, integrated, computer-based business transaction processing and reporting systems. The primary advantage of ERP systems is that they pull together all of the classic business functions, such as accounting, finance, sales, and operations, into a single, tightly integrated package that uses a common database (Figure 12S.3).

To understand why this is such a big deal, imagine what the information systems for a typical company looked like before ERP. First, every functional area had its own set of software applications, often running on completely different systems. Sharing information (e.g., forecasts, customer information) between systems was a nightmare. To make matters worse, the same information often had to be entered multiple times in different ways. ERP pulled all of these disparate systems into a single integrated system. In practice, few companies use ERP systems to serve all of their information requirements. Rather, companies use ERP systems to meet the bulk of their needs and "plug in" preexisting legacy systems and best-in-class applications to tailor the system to their exact needs. Figure 12S.4 illustrates the idea. As you can imagine, making ERP systems integrate with other applications presents a significant technological challenge.

ERP's traditional strengths lie in routine decision making and in execution and transaction processing. To the extent that ERP systems support higher-level planning and decision making, the focus is on the internal supply chain. ERP systems also capture much of the raw data needed to support higher-level decision support systems. **Decision support systems (DSS)**

Enterprise resource planning (ERP) systems
Large, integrated, computer-based business transaction processing and reporting systems. ERP systems pull together all of the classic business functions such as accounting, finance, sales, and operations into a single, tightly integrated package that uses a common database.

Decision support systems (DSS)
Computer-based information systems that allow users to analyze, manipulate, and present data in a manner that aids higher-level decision making.

FIGURE 12S.3
ERP Systems

Applications with a common technological platform and built-in integration...

Finance | Accounting | Marketing | Sales | Operations | Purchasing | ...and others

Centralized database

...can share a common set of data

[5]Chopra and Meindl, *Supply Chain Management.*

FIGURE 12S.4
Integrating ERP Systems with Legacy and Best-in-Class Applications

are computer-based information systems that allow users to analyze, manipulate, and present data in a manner that aids higher-level decision making.

SRM and CRM applications, in contrast, are computer-based information systems specifically designed to help plan and manage the firm's external linkages with its suppliers and customers, respectively. Table 12S.2 gives examples of the types of functionality provided by SRM and CRM applications.

Vendors specializing in CRM and SRM applications tend to provide greater functionality in their chosen areas than do ERP vendors. As a result, many firms choose a standard ERP package for routine decision making and for execution and transaction processing and use best-in-class CRM and SRM applications to manage external relationships. However, this situation has changed in recent years, as ERP vendors, such as SAP and Oracle, increase the CRM and SRM functionality of their own systems.

The last set of supply chain IS applications we will discuss deals directly with logistics decisions. These applications can be divided into three main categories: network design applications, warehouse and transportation planning systems, and warehouse management and transportation execution systems. **Network design applications** address such long-term strategic questions as facility location and sizing, as well as transportation networks. These applications often make use of simulation and optimization modeling.

Warehouse and transportation planning systems support tactical planning efforts by allocating "fixed" logistics capacity in the best possible way, given business requirements. These IS applications can also use optimization modeling and simulation. The warehouse assignment problem in Chapter 8, where we had to decide how many units to ship from each warehouse to each demand point, is a classic example of a warehouse and transportation planning system. To find the optimal answer, we built an optimization model that used data on fixed warehouse capacities, demand levels, and shipping costs to generate the lowest-cost solution.

Finally, **warehouse management and transportation execution systems** initiate and control the movement of materials between supply chain partners. Within a warehouse, for example, sophisticated execution systems tell workers where to store items, where to go to pick them up, and how many to pick. Similarly, bar-code systems and global positioning systems (GPSs) have dramatically changed the ability of businesses to manage actual movements in the distribution system. Not too long ago, the only thing most transportation firms could tell you was that your shipment was "on the way" and "should be there in a day or two." Now carriers can tell their customers the exact location of a shipment and the arrival time within minutes.

Network design applications
Logistics information systems that address such long-term strategic questions as facility location and sizing, as well as transportation networks. These applications often make use of simulation and optimization modeling.

Warehouse and transportation planning systems
Logistics information systems that support tactical planning efforts by allocating "fixed" logistics capacity in the best possible way, given business requirements.

Warehouse management and transportation execution systems
Logistics information systems that initiate and control the movement of materials between supply chain partners.

TABLE 12S.2 Examples of SRM and CRM Applications

SRM APPLICATIONS	CRM APPLICATIONS
Design collaboration	Market analysis
Sourcing decisions	Sell process
Negotiations	Order management
Buy process	Call/service center management
Supply collaboration	

Source: Chopra, S., and Meindl, P., *Supply Chain Management: Strategy, Planning, and Operation,* 5th Edition, pp. 491–494. © 2012. Reprinted by permission of Pearson Education, Inc., Upper Saddle River, NJ.

12S.3 TRENDS TO WATCH

Of course, operations and supply chain information systems continue to evolve. Three trends of particular interest to operations and supply chain professionals are (1) the emergence of sophisticated business process management (BPM) tools, (2) cloud computing, and (3) the Internet of Things (IoT).

BPM Tools

As we noted earlier, there may be times when a prepackaged software solution does not meet an organization's needs. This is especially true when an organization wants to implement its own unique business processes. In his book, *Business Process Change: A Guide for Business Managers and Six Sigma Professionals*, Harmon describes a number of software tools aimed at business process analysis and design. He highlights two key tools:

> **Business process modeling tools**
> According to Harmon, "software tools that aid business teams in the analysis, modeling, and redesign of business processes."

> **Business process management systems (BPMS) products**
> According to Harmon, "software tools that allow analysts to model processes and . . . then automate the execution of the process at run time."

- **Business process modeling tools** are "software tools that aid business teams in the analysis, modeling, and redesign of business processes."[6] BP modeling tools do more than just chart work flows; they allow users to graphically define a process and simulate the performance of the new process to gain insights into how it might work in the real world. BP modeling tools can also help users develop cost estimates based on the sequence of activities in a process and save defined processes in a database so that they can be reused again in other parts of the business.
- **Business process management systems (BPMS) products** are state-of-the-art software tools for developing and implementing business processes. As Harmon puts it, BPMS products are "software tools that allow analysts to model processes and... then automate the execution of the process at run time."[7] Imagine how this would work: Experts use a BPMS product to develop a process map of how they want a process to work. They then define business rules to manage the flow of work through process (e.g., "If an order is scheduled to be finished late by X or more days, initiate the defined expedited shipping process"). When the users are satisfied that the new process works the way they want it to, the BPMS product can be used to automatically carry out future business activity, without requiring developers to write new software code.

Cloud Computing

Prior to the Internet, the vast majority of computer systems were isolated from one another, requiring their own hardware, software, and databases. Even when organizations put in place private networks to link these systems, sharing software applications and data was a relatively difficult task. The Internet has changed all that and has led to the advent of what is broadly called **cloud computing.** Peter Mell and Timothy Grance of the National Institute of Standards and Technology (NIST) define cloud computing as "a model for enabling ubiquitous, convenient, on-demand network access to a shared pool of configurable computing resources (e.g., networks, servers, storage, applications, and services) that can be rapidly provisioned and released with minimal management effort or service provider interaction."[8] According to Mell and Grance, the cloud model has five essential characteristics:

> **Cloud computing**
> According to a National Institute of Standards and Technology (NIST) report "a model for enabling ubiquitous, convenient, on-demand network access to a shared pool of configurable computing resources (e.g., networks, servers, storage, applications, and services) that can be rapidly provisioned and released with minimal management effort or service provider interaction."

1. **On-demand self-service.** Users can automatically access applications and storage space whenever they need them.
2. **Broad network access.** Capabilities are available over the network and accessed through standard mechanisms that promote use by a wide range of platforms, including mobile phones, laptops, and PDAs.
3. **Resource pooling.** The provider's computing resources are pooled to serve multiple consumers, with different physical and virtual resources dynamically assigned and reassigned according to consumer demand.

[6]P. Harmon, *Business Process Change: A Business Process Management Guide for Managers and Process Professionals*, 3rd ed. (Waltham, MA: Morgan Kaumann Publishers, 2014), p. 382.

[7]Ibid., p. 384.

[8]P. Mell and T. Grance, *The NIST Definition of Cloud Computing (Draft): Recommendations of the National Institute of Standards and Technology*, NIST Special Publication 800–145, **http://csrc.nist.gov/publications/nistpubs/800-145/SP800-145.pdf.**

4. **Rapid elasticity.** Capabilities can be rapidly and elastically provisioned, in some cases automatically, to quickly scale out, and they can be rapidly released to quickly scale in. To the consumer, the capabilities available for provisioning often appear to be unlimited and can be purchased in any quantity at any time.

5. **Measured service.** Resource usage can be monitored, controlled, and reported, providing transparency for both the provider and consumer of the utilized service.

So what does cloud computing mean for operations and supply chain management? Consider two quick examples. First, cloud computing makes it much easier for firms to outsource key portions of their business process information flows (e.g., credit checking, satellite tracking) to outside firms. Second, broad network access allows individual or computer systems to upload and retrieve information through a wide range of devices and virtually anywhere. In a nutshell, cloud computing will make supply chain information flows faster, more flexible, and cheaper than ever. How organizations take advantage of these breakthroughs to improve their existing operations or provide new products and services remains to be seen.

Internet of Things (IoT)

Internet of Things (IoT)
According to *Business Insider*, "a network of internet-connected objects able to collect and exchange data using embedded sensors."

Business Insider defines the **Internet of Things (IoT)** as "a network of internet-connected objects able to collect and exchange data using embedded sensors."[9] Unlike cloud computing, the IoT includes not only computer resources, but any physical device that can be monitored and controlled from a remote location via the Internet. A simple example you may be familiar with is using your smartphone to lock the doors or turn off the lights in your house. In an industrial setting, IoT devices tend to be more advanced in terms of functionality, security, and reliability.[10] With more than 2.4 billion IoT devices expected to be in place by 2020,[11] the implications of and challenges for operations and supply chain management are endless.

SUPPLEMENT SUMMARY

In this supplement, we discussed the critical role information flows play in the supply chain and laid out a map of supply chain information systems. To conclude, we will consider the various ways in which information adds value and how breakthroughs in technology will affect supply chain management activities over time. A number of years ago, Jeffrey Rayport and John Sviokla wrote an article in which they talked about three ways information adds value.[12] These ways were, in order of increasing value added:

1. Visibility;
2. Mirroring; and
3. Creation of new customer relationships.

Visibility represents the most basic function of information in the supply chain. Here information allows managers to "see" the physical and monetary flows in the supply chain and, as a result, better manage them. Classic examples include forecasts and point-of-sales data, as well as information regarding inventory levels and the status of jobs in the production system.

Mirroring takes visibility a step further and seeks to *replace* certain physical processes with virtual ones. For example, Rayport and Sviokla describe Boeing's efforts to design new engine housings. In the past, Boeing had to create physical mock-ups of the housings and test them in a wind tunnel in order to evaluate their performance. This was a time-consuming and expensive process. But with the advent of powerful computers, Boeing was able to replace this physical process altogether:

> Boeing engineers developed the prototype as a virtual product that incorporated relevant laws of physical and material sciences and enabled the company to test an evolving computer-simulated model in a virtual wind tunnel. As a result, engineers could test many more designs at dramatically lower costs and with much greater speed.[13]

The third stage, creation of new customer relationships, involves taking raw information and organizing, selecting, synthesizing, and distributing it in a manner that creates whole new sources of value. Creating virtual, customized textbooks with access to instructor-led videos and online quizzes is one example. Other examples include taking raw supply chain data and turning

---

[9]A. Meola, "What Is the Internet of Things (IoT)?," *Business Insider*, December 19, 2016, **www.businessinsider.com/what-is-the-internet-of-things-definition-2016-8.**

[10]J. Thatcher, "Leveraging the Internet of Things (IOT) and the Industrial Internet of Things (IIOT)," *APICS Blog*, March 13, 2017, **www.apics.org/sites/apics-blog/think-supply-chain-landing-page/thinking-supply-chain/2017/03/13/leveraging-the-internet-of-things.**

[11]Meola, A., "What Is the Internet of Things (IoT)?"

[12]J. Rayport and J. Sviokla, "Exploiting the Virtual Value Chain," *Harvard Business Review* 73, no. 6 (November–December 1995): 75–85.

[13]Ibid., p. 79.

them into graphical executive "dashboards" that allow managers to see, at a glance, how the overall business is performing.

So how has all this played out? Visibility systems continue to improve and provide more real-time data, especially as more organizations take advantage of cloud computing. In fact, many managers find themselves making decisions more often to take advantage of the increased availability of timely information. Second, more mirroring is occurring as many physical flows are replaced with virtual ones. Of course, mirroring will

be limited to those physical flows whose mission is to create or disseminate information. It is highly unlikely that physical goods will be transformed and moved over the electronic superhighway anytime soon!

Finally, we can expect to see more information-based products aimed at the creation of new customer relationships. Because raw data can be used repeatedly and the variable costs of rearranging and organizing information are so low, this area is limited only by the imagination and needs of businesses.

KEY TERMS

Business process management systems (BPMS) products   405

Business process modeling tools   405

Cloud computing   405

Customer relationship management (CRM)   402

Decision support systems (DSS)   403

Enterprise resource planning (ERP) systems   403

Information system (IS)   400

Internal supply chain management   402

Internet of Things (IoT)   406

Network design applications   404

Supplier relationship management (SRM)   402

Warehouse and transportation planning systems   404

Warehouse management and transportation execution systems   404

DISCUSSION QUESTIONS

1. What is the difference between an information *flow* and an information *system*? Do information systems always have to be computerized? Why?
2. Consider Figure 12S.1. Some people have argued that companies need to put in place information systems that address routine decision making and transactional requirements *prior to* tackling higher-level planning and decision making. Others strongly disagree, pointing out that the higher-level functions are a prerequi-

site to good tactical planning and execution. What do you think?
3. SAP, the world leader in ERP systems software, has developed tailored ERP systems for different industries. Go to **www.sap.com/solution.html** and examine the solutions for (1) a service industry and (2) a manufacturing industry of your choice. How are they similar? How are they different?

REFERENCES

Books and Articles

Blackstone, J. H., ed., *APICS Dictionary*, 15th ed. (Chicago IL: APICS, 2016).

Chopra, S., and P. Meindl, *Supply Chain Management: Strategy, Planning, and Operation*, 5th ed. (Upper Saddle River, NJ: Prentice Hall, 2012).

Harmon, P., *Business Process Change: A Business Process Management Guide for Managers and Process Professionals*, 3rd ed. (Waltham, MA: Morgan Kaufmann Publishers, 2014).

Kahl, S., "What's the 'Value' of Supply Chain Software?" *Supply Chain Management Review* 2, no. 4 (Winter 1999): 59–67.

Laudon, K., and Laudon, J., *Management Information Systems: Managing the Digital Firm*, 13th ed. (Upper Saddle River, NJ: Prentice Hall, 2013).

Rayport, J., and Sviokla, J., "Exploiting the Virtual Value Chain," *Harvard Business Review* 73, no. 6 (November–December 1995): 75–85.

Internet

Kelly, J., "Computing, Cognition and the Future of Knowing," *IBM Research: Cognitive Computing*, IBM Corporation, 2015, **www.research.ibm.com/software/IBMResearch/ multimedia/Computing_Cognition_WhitePaper.pdf.**

Mell, P., and Grance, T., *The NIST Definition of Cloud Computing (Draft): Recommendations of the National Institute of Standards and Technology*, NIST Special Publication 800-145. **http:// csrc.nist.gov/publications/nistpubs/800-145/SP800-145.pdf.**

Meola, A, "What Is the Internet of Things (IoT)?," *Business Insider*, December 19, 2016, **www.businessinsider.com/ what-is-the-internet-of-things-definition-2016-8.**

Thatcher, J., "Leveraging the Internet of Things (IOT) and the Industrial Internet of Things (IIOT)," *APICS Blog*, March 13, 2017, **www.apics.org/sites/apics-blog/ think-supply-chain-landing-page/thinking-supply-chain/2017/03/13/leveraging-the-internet-of-things.**

Paul A. Souders/Corbis/VCG/Getty Images

CHAPTER
thirteen

JIT/Lean Production

CHAPTER OBJECTIVES

By the end of this chapter, you will be able to:

- Describe JIT/Lean and differentiate between the Lean philosophy and kanban systems.

- Discuss the Lean perspective on waste and describe the eight major forms of waste, or *muda*, in an organization.

- Discuss the Lean perspective on inventory and describe how a kanban system helps control inventory levels and synchronize the flow of goods and material across a supply chain.

- Describe how the concepts of the Lean supply chain and Lean Six Sigma represent natural extensions of the Lean philosophy.

- Explain how a two-card kanban system works.

- Calculate the number of kanban cards needed in a simple production environment.

- Show how MRP and kanban can be linked together and illustrate the process using a numerical example.

CHAPTER OUTLINE

Introduction
13.1 The Lean Perspective on Waste
13.2 The Lean Perspective on Inventory
13.3 Recent Developments in Lean
13.4 Kanban Systems
Chapter Summary

PORSCHE'S "SHOCK THERAPY" PAYS OFF

Porsche Badge

Ben Smith/Shutterstock

If imitation is the sincerest form of flattery, Porsche—a perennial winner in the J.D. Power and Associates annual quality study and the firm whose profit margins are among the highest in the auto industry—is prepared to make the most of it with its thriving Lean consulting business.

The luxury carmaker is already well known to its European competitors as the manufacturer that carries the smallest material inventories. In fact, it keeps a current inventory level of only 0.8 workdays. Porsche has mastered the just-in-time (JIT) method, assembling only the parts it needs and only when it needs them. It smoothes progress every step of the way with sophisticated time- and labor-saving techniques. Working closely with its many suppliers and transportation providers, the company manages a components flow so precisely tuned to its assembly process that car and engine parts can be delivered right to the factory floor and can be installed moments later in the individual cars for which they were ordered. Porsche virtually eliminated warehousing in 2009, freeing up space and capital in the process of improving efficiency, scheduling, waste reduction, and the accuracy of its delivery dates.

These benefits have flowed to its suppliers as well, since only the most disciplined and committed can live up to Porsche's high standards. With lower inventories and minimal fallback levels, these suppliers enjoy increased efficiency and shorter response times. Customers benefit in several ways, too, from lower prices for Porsche's cars to precise product delivery schedules that ensure customer satisfaction at the dealership.

Where does the imitation come in? With such enviable and lucrative results from its well-planned JIT processes, Porsche soon realized it could also profit by selling advice about how to streamline operations and reduce waste. Thus, in 1994, the Porsche Consulting subsidiary was born, with offices in Italy and Brazil to begin with and, by 2014, additional sites in Atlanta, Georgia, and Shangai, China.

Customers of the consulting subsidiary include such manufacturing giants as Deutsche Lufthansa AG, Volkswagen AG, and Meyer Werft GmbH. They and about 150 other corporate clients stand to learn much from Porsche's run-in with near-insolvency in 1993. That watershed experience left the company battered by high inventory, excess factory space, weak sales, a legacy of inefficient and labor-intensive work processes, and a net loss of $162 million. The company had no alternative, says a former Porsche executive, but to resort to "shock therapy" to turn itself around.

So Porsche looked to Toyota, the pioneer in implementing JIT and Lean production techniques. Toyota already had a consulting wing, and from its trainers, Porsche learned how to fine-tune its manufacturing processes and develop new relationships with its suppliers that made JIT operations a feasible remedy. Its embrace of JIT and continuous improvement was soon complete, and every production step is now carefully defined and perfectly orchestrated to maximize resources and minimize waste. For example, Porsche uses small, standardized containers for shipments of its parts orders and loads the empty containers on the same trucks that deliver full ones so they can make a closed transportation circuit. The height of the tow trains in its manufacturing plants is calibrated to match that of the racks in its order-picking departments, so workers can simply slide containers full of parts onto the driverless transport system that takes them to the engine assembly line.

JIT has now been widely adopted in the auto industry, and thanks in part to Porsche Consulting, it is transforming many other industries, including not only auto parts suppliers but also airplane and furniture manufacturers, airlines, construction companies, and even hospitals. One of Porsche Consulting's recent clients was a German manufacturer of cruise ships that now employs a JIT system to reduce inventory from its 1,800 suppliers and has set up its own in-house training academy to ensure that the improvements take hold permanently. Porsche helped shorten service time for Lufthansa's Airbus 340 planes by 10 days, and the airline's catering division, which produces more than 400 million meals a year for other passenger airlines, is now working with Porsche to improve its own logistics. Shorter highway construction schedules and reduced costs for staff and equipment were the goals of another Porsche client, the biggest construction company in central Europe.

As if happy clients weren't enough, the enviable financial results of Porsche's car manufacturing unit are themselves an advertisement for Porsche Consulting. Its operating margin for one recent quarter was 19% versus 11% for Volkswagen's Audi and 9.5% for Mercedes-Benz.

Says the head of Porsche Consulting, "Many clients come to us and say, 'Please turn us into the Porsches of our industries.'"

Sources: Based on Noah Joseph, "Porsche Consulting Sets Up Shop in Atlanta," Autoblog, July 21, 2011, **www.autoblog.com/2011/07/21/porsche-consulting-sets-up-shop-in-atlanta/**; "Typical Porsche: No Superfluous Parts," *Porsche Consulting*, no. 10, January 2011, **www.porsche-consulting.com/it/stampa/porsche-consulting-the-magazine/detail/issue-10-january-2011-4/**; Andreas Cremar, "Porsche 'Shock Therapy' Spurs VW, Lufthansa Efficiency Drive," *Automotive News Europe*, December 13, 2010, **http://europe.autonews.com/article/20101213/ANE/101209816/porsche-%E2%80%98shock-therapy-spurs-vw-lufthansa-efficiency-drive.**

INTRODUCTION

Just-in-time (JIT)
A philosophy of manufacturing based on planned elimination of all waste and on continuous improvement of productivity. In a broad sense, it applies to all forms of manufacturing and to many service industries as well. Used synonymously with *Lean*.

Lean
A philosophy of production that emphasizes the minimization of the amount of all the resources (including time) used in the various activities of an enterprise. It involves identifying and eliminating non-value-adding activities in design, production, supply chain management, and dealing with customers. Used synonymously with *JIT*.

In Chapter 12, we presented a top-down model of production planning and control and offered detailed discussion of several of the most common techniques, including master scheduling, MRP, and DRP. The focus of this chapter is the **just-in-time (JIT)** or **Lean** philosophy and, in particular, kanban production techniques.

As the following APICS definition suggests, Lean touches on many of the areas we have dealt with throughout this book:

Lean is a philosophy of production that emphasizes the minimization of the amount of all the resources (including time) used in the various activities of the enterprise. It involves identifying and eliminating non-value-adding activities in design, production, supply chain management, and dealing with the customers. Lean producers employ teams of multiskilled workers at all levels of the organization and use highly flexible, increasingly automated machines to produce volumes of products in potentially enormous variety. It contains a set of principles and practices to reduce cost through the relentless removal of waste and through the simplification of all manufacturing and support processes.[1]

The Lean philosophy has extended beyond just manufacturing to include services and essentially all aspects of supply chain management. Firms following a Lean philosophy often experience remarkable improvements in their productivity (outputs/inputs), inventory levels, and quality.

To understand why Lean has made such an impact, consider some eye-opening statistics from 1986, which compared performance at Toyota's Takaoka facility with that at GM's Framingham plant (Figure 13.1). Numbers such as these kicked off what was then called the JIT/Lean production revolution in the U.S. automotive industry during the late 1980s and early 1990s.

Notice how the Toyota plant needed fewer hours and much less inventory to do its job. This ability to do more with less is what first led people to refer to JIT as *Lean production*. Similarly, the phrase *just-in-time* reflected the idea that the timing and level of inventory and production activities are closely matched to demand. With average inventory levels of only two hours, the Toyota plant was clearly receiving parts and materials "just" before they were needed.

Even though we cover Lean production and kanban in a separate chapter from the other production planning techniques, it would be erroneous to assume that companies using traditional planning and control techniques can't adopt a Lean philosophy. For one thing, the underlying emphasis of Lean—to eliminate all forms of waste—is relevant to all organizations, regardless of the specific planning and control tools used. Second, even though some techniques such as kanban are not suitable in all production and service environments, it is entirely possible that an organization can follow the Lean philosophy. To summarize:

- The Lean philosophy can be applied to a wide range of production and service environments. In fact, one could easily argue that there is no environment that wouldn't benefit from adopting its core principles.

FIGURE 13.1
The Performance Advantage of a JIT Plant, Circa 1986
Source: Based on J. Womack, D. Jones, and D. Daniel Roos, *The Machine That Changed the World: The Story of Lean Production* (New York: HarperCollins, 1991).

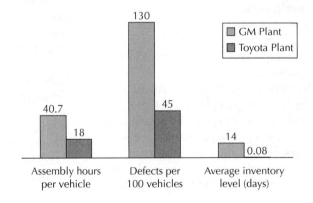

---

[1]J. H. Blackstone, ed., *APICS Dictionary*, 15th ed. (Chicago, IL: APICS, 2016).

- Companies following the Lean philosophy can and do use a wide range of planning and control techniques, not just kanban.
- The Lean philosophy is entirely consistent with business process improvement (Chapter 4), quality improvement (Chapter 5), and supplier management initiatives (Chapter 7). It's no surprise, then, that the business world has seen the advent of such approaches as *Lean Six Sigma* and *Lean supply chain management*, which we describe in Section 13.3.

With this background, let's look at the historical roots of JIT/Lean, the various forms of waste and uncertainty, the special role of inventory in a Lean environment, and kanban systems in particular.

13.1 THE LEAN PERSPECTIVE ON WASTE

Waste
According to APICS, in the JIT/Lean philosophy, "any activity that does not add value to the good or service in the eyes of the consumer."

Muda
A Japanese term meaning waste.

A key component of the Lean philosophy is a never-ending effort to eliminate **waste,** which is defined as "any activity that does not add value to the good or service in the eyes of the consumer."[2] Starting with Taiichi Ohno, a Toyota engineer, experts have sought to identify the major sources of waste (or **muda** in Japanese). The following are eight commonly recognized sources:[3]

1. **Overproduction.** Inflexible or unreliable processes may cause organizations to produce goods before they are required.
2. **Waiting.** Inefficient layouts or an inability to match demand with output levels may cause waiting.
3. **Unnecessary transportation.** Transporting goods always increases costs and the risk of damage, but it does not necessarily provide value to the final customer.
4. **Inappropriate process.** Companies sometimes use overly complex processes when simpler, more efficient ones would do.
5. **Unnecessary inventory.** Uncertainty with regard to quality levels, delivery lead times, and the like can lead to unnecessary inventory.
6. **Unnecessary/excess motion.** Poorly designed processes can lead to unnecessary motion.
7. **Defects.** Not only do defects create uncertainty in the process, they rob production capacity by creating products or services that require rework or must be scrapped.
8. **Underutilization of employees.** This is the newest form of waste added to the list, and it recognizes that too often companies do not fully utilize the skills and decision-making capabilities of their employees.

To put these forms of waste in context, suppose it takes an inspector at a manufacturing plant 15 minutes to inspect an incoming batch of material. The pre-Lean perspective would be that inspections like these are a necessary and prudent business expense. But according to Lean, this is a waste of *both* time and human resources caused by defects. Services examples abound as well. If you have to wait even *five minutes* at the doctor's office before being seen, then waste has occurred.

If this definition seems harsh, it is meant to be. The point is to get organizations to think critically about the business processes they use to provide products and services, as well as the outcomes of these processes. As far as Lean is concerned, if there is any waste at all, there is room for improvement.

EXAMPLE 13.1

Unnecessary Inventory Caused by Supplier Problems at Riggsbee Boating Supply

For several years, Riggsbee Boating Supply has purchased life vests from the same U.S. supplier. Jermaine Riggsbee, owner of the company, has collected the following information on the life vests:

Weekly demand:	50 vests, with a variance of 9.5 vests
Supplier lead time:	6 weeks, with a variance of 3.2 weeks

---
[2]Ibid.
[3]J. Womack and D. Jones, *Lean Thinking: Banish Waste and Create Wealth in Your Corporation, Revised and Updated* (New York: Free Press, 2003).

Using Equation (11.8) from Chapter 11, Jermaine calculates the reorder point for the life vests based on a 90% service level ($z = 1.28$):

$$ROP_{US} = \overline{d}L + z\sqrt{L\sigma_d^2 + \overline{d}^2\sigma_L^2}$$
$$= 50 \times 6 + 1.28\sqrt{6 \times 9.5 + 2{,}500 \times 3.2}$$
$$= 300 + 114.9$$
$$= 414.9, \text{ or } 415 \text{ life vests}$$

Looking at the results, Jermaine realizes that the second half of the equation, or about 115 vests, represents safety stock, or extra inventory *he* has to hold (and pay for!).

Jermaine had already been considering switching to a Mexican supplier with similar quality levels and prices but a *constant* lead time of two weeks. Plugging the new numbers into the equation, Jermaine generates the following results:

$$ROP_{Mexico} = \overline{d}L + z\sqrt{L\sigma_d^2 + \overline{d}^2\sigma_L^2}$$
$$= 50 \times 2 + 1.28\sqrt{2 \times 9.5 + 2{,}500 \times 0}$$
$$= 100 + 5.6$$
$$= 105.6, \text{ or } 106 \text{ life vests}$$

With the Mexican supplier, the reorder point drops to about 106 vests. More importantly, the safety stock level falls to just 5.6, or 6 vests. Put another way, supplier problems were causing Jermaine to hold a safety stock of $(115 - 6) = 109$ more vests than he needed, a clear example of unnecessary inventory.

13.2 THE LEAN PERSPECTIVE ON INVENTORY

One hallmark of a Lean environment is the strong emphasis placed on reducing raw material, work-in-process, and finished goods inventories throughout the system. This is not only because inventory is seen as a form of waste in and of itself but also because inventory can *cover up* wasteful business practices. Under the Lean philosophy, lowering inventory levels *forces* firms to address these poor practices.

To illustrate how inventory can hide problems, consider a simple facility consisting of three work centers (A, B, and C), shown in Figure 13.2. The triangles in the diagram represent inventory. In addition, between the work centers is plenty of room for inventory. Take one of the work centers—say, center B—and consider what happens if it has an equipment breakdown that reduces its output. The answer is that, *in the short run*, only center B is affected. Because there is plenty of space for inventory between centers A and B, center A can continue to work. And because inventory exists between centers B and C, center C can continue to work as long as the inventory lasts. Most importantly, the customer can continue to be served. The same result occurs regardless of the reason for any disruption in center B, including worker absenteeism, poor quality levels, and so forth. Whatever the problem, inventory hides it (but at a cost).

Now let's take the same facility after a successful Lean program has been put in place. The work centers have been moved closer together, eliminating wasted movement and space where inventory could pile up. Setup times have also been reduced, allowing the work centers to make only what is needed when it is needed. If we assume that the program has been in place for a while, we can also assume that the inventory levels have been reduced dramatically, giving us a revised picture of the facility (Figure 13.3).

Now inventory has been reduced to the point where it shows up only in the customer facility. Under these conditions, what happens in the short run if the equipment at center B breaks down? The answer this time is that *everything stops*, including shipments to the customer. Center A has to stop because there is no spot for it to put inventory and no demand for it. Center C has to stop because there is no inventory on which to work.

FIGURE 13.2
Inventory Positioned throughout a Supply Chain

FIGURE 13.3
Supply Chain after the Elimination of Excess Inventories

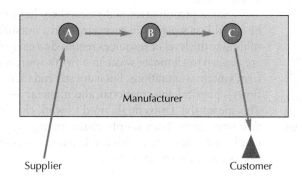

FIGURE 13.4
How Inventory Hides Problems

Inventory in the supply chain is often compared to water in a river. If the "water" is high enough, it will cover all the "rocks" (quality problems, absenteeism, equipment breakdowns, etc.), and everything will appear to be running smoothly.

Under Lean, the approach is to gradually remove the "water" until the first "rock" is exposed, thereby establishing a priority as to the most important obstacle to work on. After resolving this problem, inventory levels are reduced further, until another problem (and opportunity to eliminate waste) appears. This process continues indefinitely, or until all forms of waste and uncertainty have been eliminated (Figure 13.4).

This is not an easy approach to implement. The implication is that every time a process is working smoothly, there may be too much inventory, and more should be removed until the organization hits another "rock." This is certainly not a natural action for most people, and the performance evaluation system needs to be altered to reflect this type of activity.

13.3 RECENT DEVELOPMENTS IN LEAN THINKING

It shouldn't be surprising that businesses have looked for ways to combine the Lean philosophy with other management efforts. One such hybrid is Lean Six Sigma. In Chapter 4, we defined the Six Sigma methodology as "a business improvement methodology that focuses an organization on understanding and managing customer requirements, aligning key business processes to achieve those requirements, utilizing rigorous data analysis to understand and ultimately

Lean Six Sigma
A methodology that combines the organizational elements and tools of Six Sigma with Lean's focus on waste reduction.

minimize variation in those processes, and driving rapid and sustainable improvement to business processes."[4]

Lean Six Sigma combines the organizational elements and tools of Six Sigma, with Lean's focus on waste reduction. As Paul Mullenhour and Jamie Flinchbaugh put it, "Lean encourages action along a broad front by empowering people at all levels to contribute. This allows organizations to welcome challenges and implement improvement initiatives. . . . Six Sigma brings the discipline of define, measure, analyze, improve and control, as well as the rigor of statistical analysis, to identify a root cause, sustain improvement and provide the solid measurements that create a balanced scorecard."[5]

The *Supply Chain Connections* feature contains an extended example of how Lean Six Sigma was applied in a hospital setting. Notice how this example combines all the elements of the Six Sigma methodology—black belts and green belts, process mapping, careful use of statistics, and the DMAIC cycle—with Lean's focus on waste reduction—in this case, patient waiting time and unused beds.

Lean supply chain management
An extension of the Lean philosophy to supply chain efforts beyond production. Lean supply chain management seeks to minimize the level of resources required to carry out *all* supply chain activities.

Some practitioners and researchers have moved beyond Lean production to what can be called *Lean supply chain management*. In a nutshell, **Lean supply chain management** seeks to minimize the level of resources required to carry out *all* supply chain activities. Lean principles are applied to eliminate waste in a firm's sourcing and logistics activities, as well as within the firm's internal operations. But it doesn't end there. The Lean philosophy is applied to all relevant flows—physical, informational, and monetary—and, where possible, to supply chain partners. This means that firms might need to work closely with key partners to eliminate waste within *their* operations. Lean supply chain management is certainly consistent with what we have emphasized throughout this book; namely, it is not enough for a firm to manage the activities that occur within its four walls.

13.4 KANBAN SYSTEMS

The first part of this chapter dealt with the philosophical underpinnings of the Lean philosophy. In this section, we take a decidedly more *executional* view, focusing on one particular approach to production control in a Lean environment, known as kanban. But even as you are working through the logic of kanban systems, keep in mind that the focus is still on reducing waste.

Kanban system
A production control approach that uses containers, cards, or visual cues to control the production and movement of goods through the supply chain.

A **kanban system** is a production control approach that uses containers, cards, or visual cues to control the production and movement of goods through the supply chain. These systems have several key characteristics:

1. Kanban systems use simple signaling mechanisms, such as a card or even an empty space or container, to indicate when specific items should be produced or moved. Most kanban systems, in fact, do not require computerization.
2. Kanban systems can be used to synchronize activities either within a plant or between different supply chain partners. Therefore, a kanban system can be an important part of both production activity control (PAC) and vendor order management systems (Chapter 12).
3. Kanban systems are *not* planning tools. Rather, they are control mechanisms that are designed to pull parts or goods through the supply chain, based on downstream demand. As a result, many firms use techniques such as MRP (Chapter 12) to *anticipate* requirements but depend on their kanban systems to control the actual execution of production and movement activities.

Two-card kanban system
A special form of the kanban system that uses one card to control production and another card to control movement of materials.

To illustrate how a kanban system works, we will describe a **two-card kanban system** that links the production and movement of units at two work centers, A and B. Suppose that in

---

[4]Motorola University, **www.motorolasolutions.com/US-EN/Home.**
[5]P. Mullenhour and J. Flinchbaugh, "Bring Lean Systems Thinking to Six Sigma," *Quality Digest*, March 2005, **www.qualitydigest.com/mar05/articles/05_article.shtml.**

SUPPLY CHAIN CONNECTIONS

CREATING A LEAN SIX SIGMA HOSPITAL DISCHARGE PROCESS[6]

A lengthy, inefficient process for discharging inpatients is a common concern of hospitals. It not only causes frustration for patients and family members but also leads to delays for incoming patients from Admitting, the Post Anesthesia Care Unit, or the Emergency Department.

When Valley Baptist Medical Center in Harlingen, Texas, faced this issue, it decided to apply Lean Six Sigma and change management techniques within one pilot unit. A multidisciplinary project team led by a black belt included nursing staff, case managers, an information technology green belt, and the chief medical officer, also a green belt.

The project was to reduce the time between when a discharge order for a patient is entered into the computer and when the room is ready for the next patient. During the initial scoping of this project, the team divided the process into four components:

1. From discharge order entry to discharge instructions signed
2. From discharge instructions signed to patient leaving
3. From patient leaving to room cleaned
4. From room cleaned to discharge entered in the computer (thus indicating that the bed is ready for another patient)

Because of the hospital's commitment to customer service, the team was asked to concentrate on the first two components. The goal was for this first subprocess to be completed in less than **45** minutes. To minimize the time a bed was empty, the team realized it would also need to address the time between when a patient's room was cleaned and the time a discharge was entered into the computer, or the second subprocess. This would address the problem that arises when Admitting does not have the necessary information to assign a new patient to a clean and empty bed.

Mapping the Process

The team began with a process map to visually understand how the process was currently working. When several nurses were asked to help develop a detailed process map on the discharge process, they initially could not reach consensus since they each followed their own methods for discharging the patient. This lack of standard operating procedures had led to widespread process variation.

Michal Heron/Pearson Prentice Hall–College

The team developed a representative process map, printed a large copy, and placed it in the nurses' lounge. Each staff member was encouraged to review the map and add comments on the flow. After a week, the team retrieved the inputs and revised the "as is" process map accordingly. Elements of Lean thinking were combined with this map to help identify waste (or muda). To understand which steps were not contributing to timely discharge, aspects of the existing process were categorized as value-added, non-value-added, and value-enablers.

Baseline data revealed the "from discharge order entry to patient leaving" subprocess required 184 minutes, with a standard deviation of 128 minutes. The second subprocess, "from patient leaving to discharge in computer" required an average of 36 minutes, with a standard deviation of 36 minutes. When compared against an upper specification limit of 45 minutes, the first subprocess had a yield of 7% (i.e., 7% of the patients were able to leave in 45 minutes or less), and the second subprocess did only slightly better, with a yield of 25% compared to its upper specification of 5 minutes.

Behind the Waste and Variation

The most important tool for determining the critical drivers of waste and variation was the Lean process map. The staff segmented the process into key steps and used the value-added and non-valued-added times to understand the delays and rework involved.

The segments of the process were:

- Secretary processes discharge order entry
- Discharge order processed to nurse begins (delay)
- Nurse begins computer entry (to create discharge instructions)
- Computer entry to patient signature

The team found that three factors were critical drivers of waste and variation:

1. **Clarification.** In 21% of the cases, clarification from the physician was needed before the nurse could enter the information in the computer. The team confirmed that clarification processes added a significant amount of time. The median flow time of the process increased from 12 minutes to 45 minutes when clarification was required.
2. **Handoff.** The current process required a handoff as the charge nurse placed vital signs and other relevant information in the computer system, printed out the discharge instructions, and then placed them in a bin for the primary nurse to pick up. In many cases, the primary nurse would then review the information with the patient and obtain the patient's signature. In a small number of cases, however, the primary nurse completed all tasks without any handoff. The median time increased from 9 minutes

when one nurse completed all tasks to 73 minutes when a handoff between nurses was required. Without a signal for the handoff, the patient's paperwork often waited up to an hour before it was acted upon.
3. **Aftercare.** Finally, the team tested the hypothesis that when aftercare was required (for example, ordering equipment), there was an increase in median cycle time from 121 minutes in the current process to 160 minutes.

Improving the Process

Since variations in the "as is" process were contributing greatly to long cycle times and delays, a new six-step standard operating procedure (SOP) was developed:

1. Unit secretary enters discharge order.
2. Unit secretary tells primary nurse via spectra link phone that he or she is next in the process.
3. Primary nurse verifies order and provides assessment.
4. Primary nurse enters information into computer system.
5. Primary nurse prints instructions and information.
6. Primary nurse reviews instructions and obtains patient signature.

Having the primary nurse complete all discharge tasks eliminated the bottlenecks created by time-consuming handoffs, the need for signaling those handoffs, and the fact that the charge nurse, who has many responsibilities, was not always readily available.

With the first subprocess of the deliverable improved—from discharge order entry to patient leaving—the team focused on getting information into the computer so the bed could be filled. A session was conducted with transporters and unit secretaries to determine the best way to improve the computer entry process. It was immediately clear that the current process was not working. Unit secretaries were not always aware when a patient was transferred from the unit. No signal was provided when a transporter moved a patient. Since the secretaries performed numerous activities (not always at the nurses' station), they could easily forget that a patient had been discharged.

A small discharge slip was developed, containing the patient name, room number, and time of call. The transporter would pick up the patient and then go to the nurses' station and ask the secretary to provide the time on the computer. The transporter would write the time and hand the slip to the secretary. This served as a trigger and transferred the process from the transporter to the secretary.

Maintaining Improvement

Two tactics employed simultaneously helped to sustain the improvements. The first was the use of a change acceleration process (CAP) and the second was an ongoing tracking system. Four CAP sessions were guided by the black belt and process owner, increasing understanding about why the initiative was undertaken, providing baseline data, and establishing the rationale for improvements.

Each session also included an exercise to help participants better appreciate Lean and Six Sigma, with a catapult exercise as a learning tool. Participants split into groups and worked to meet customer needs. They then reviewed the process, made adjustments, and developed standard operating procedures. Upon execution, the new plan showed improved performance.

A tracking system included three components:

1. A daily report of the prior day's discharges, including discharge times, primary nurse, and unit secretary responsible for discharging the patient from the computer

2. A performance tracker to ensure individual accountability for primary nurses and unit secretaries in terms of mean, standard deviation, and yield

3. A control chart that tracked the means and standard deviations

Summary: Process in Control

With the process now in control, the components were remeasured (Table 13.1). The "from discharge order entry to patient leaving" subprocess showed a mean improvement of 74%, with a 70% decrease in the standard deviation. The second subprocess, "from patient leaving to discharge in computer," showed an improvement of 90% in the mean and 58% in the standard deviation. With success in this unit, a translation effort would be undertaken for the entire hospital. This will be an ongoing effort requiring change management for the entire hospital and training sessions on the new standard operating procedures.

TABLE 13.1 Results of Lean Six Sigma Effort at Valley Baptist Medical Center

	From Discharge Order Entry to Patient Leaving: Upper Specification Limit = 45 Minutes		From Patient Leaving to Discharge in Computer: Upper Specification Limit = 5 Minutes	
	BEFORE	AFTER	BEFORE	AFTER
Mean	184.8 min.	47.8 min.	36.6 min.	3.47 min.
St. Dev.	128.7 min.	37.2 min.	36.1 min.	16.9 min.
Yield	6.9% patients leave within 45 min.	61.7% patients leave within 45 min.	24.6% entered into computer within 5 min.	95.4% entered into computer within 5 min.

work center A, metal rectangles are bent to form a bracket. In work center B, two holes are then drilled into the brackets. Figure 13.5 shows a diagram of the system.

Note that each work center has boxes of raw material in front of the work center and finished material directly after. For work center A, the raw material is unbent metal; the finished material is undrilled brackets. For work center B, the raw material is undrilled brackets and the

Move card—signal to move material to the next step in the supply chain

Production card—signal to produce more material at the current step

FIGURE 13.5 Kanban System for Two Work Centers

Move card
A kanban card that is used to indicate when a container of parts should be moved to the next process step.

Production card
A kanban card that is used to indicate when another container of parts should be produced.

finished material is drilled brackets. Under kanban system rules, each box of raw material must have a **move card,** while each box of finished material must have a **production card.** These cards are used to precisely control the amount and movement of material in the supply chain. We will see in a moment how the system works.

Now suppose a downstream customer places an order. The effect is to "pull" a box of finished drilled brackets (box 1) out of work center B. Immediately, the production card is removed from the box and placed in a conspicuous location in work center B. The card signals to personnel in work center B that they need to drill more brackets (Figure 13.6).

To drill more brackets, employees in work center B must pull a box of undrilled brackets (box 2) into the production process. As they do so, they remove the move card from box 2 and replace it with the production card that was removed from box 1. The newly freed-up move card then signals to employees that they need to move, or "pull," more materials out of work center A (Figure 13.7).

When the freed-up move card arrives at work center A, it takes the place of a production card on a box of undrilled brackets (box 3), and that box is transferred to work center B (Figure 13.8). The freed-up production card then signals employees in work center A to produce more parts.

To summarize this system:

- A downstream station pulls finished material out of work center B (Figure 13.6).
- Work center B pulls raw material into production (Figure 13.7).
- Demand for more raw material in work center B pulls finished material out of work center A (Figure 13.8).

The beauty of this system is that all production and movement of materials is controlled by a set of cards. If workers see a freed-up production card, they produce more units; if they

FIGURE 13.6
Release of Finished Materials from Work Center B

MyLab Operations Management
Animation

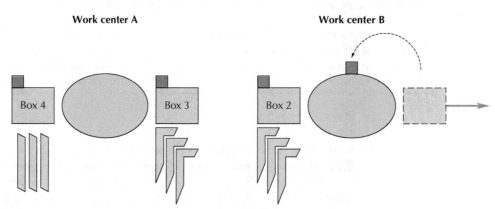

- Box of drilled brackets (Box 1) is "pulled" out of work center B
- Freed-up production card is signal to produce more

FIGURE 13.7
Pulling of Raw Materials into Production at Work Center B

MyLab Operations Management
Animation

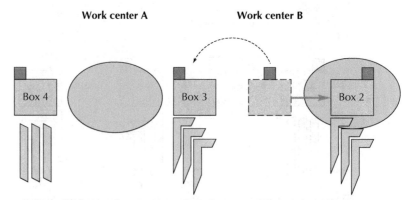

- Box of undrilled brackets (Box 2) is "pulled" into production at work center B
- Freed-up move card is signal to move more undrilled brackets (Box 3) from work center A into work center B

FIGURE 13.8
Removal of Finished Materials from Work Center A

MyLab Operations Management
Animation

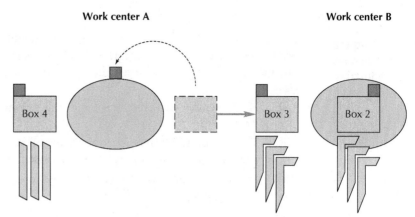

• Box of undrilled brackets from work center A (Box 3) is "pulled" into raw material area at work center B
• Freed-up production card is signal to produce more parts at work center A
• And the cycle continues with work center A . . .

don't, they stop producing units. Likewise, if they see a move card, they move materials; if not, they leave materials where they are. You can see now why a kanban system is also called a **pull system:** Actual downstream demand sets off a chain of events that pull materials through the various process steps.

As we noted before, cards aren't the only signaling method used in a kanban system. Some other methods include:

- Single-card systems, where the single card is the production card and the empty container serves as the move signal
- Color coding of containers
- Designated storage spaces
- Computerized bar-coding systems

Pull system
A production system in which actual downstream demand sets off a chain of events that pulls material through the various process steps.

Controlling Inventory Levels Using Kanbans

It is a simple fact that by controlling the number of production kanbans—whether they be cards, containers, or some other signaling mechanism—organizations can control the amount of inventory in the system. Consider our previous example. Work center A could not produce unless it had a freed-up production card. As a result, the number of production cards set precise limits on the amount of inventory between work centers A and B.

While reading the last section, you may have wondered how organizations determine the number of kanbans needed to link together two process steps. The answer depends on several factors, including the lead time between the two steps being linked, the size of the containers that hold the parts, the demand level, and the stability of demand. A general formula for calculating the number of kanbans is:

$$y = \frac{DT(1 + x)}{C} \tag{13.1}$$

where:

y = number of kanbans (cards, containers, etc.)

D = demand per unit of time (from the downstream process)

T = time it takes to produce and move a container of parts to the downstream demand point

x = a safety factor, expressed as a decimal (for example, 0.20 represents a 20% safety factor)

C = container size (the number of parts it will hold)

At Marsica Industries, work cell H provides subassemblies directly to final assembly. The production manager for work cell H, Terri O'Prey, is trying to determine how many production cards she needs. Terri has gathered the following information:

D	Final assembly's demand for subassemblies from work cell H	300 assemblies per hour, on average
T	Time it takes to fill and move a container of subassemblies from work cell H to final assembly	2.6 hours, on average
x	Safety factor to account for variations in D or T	15%
C	Container size	45 subassemblies

Using Equation (13.1), the number of production cards needed is:

$$y = \frac{DT(1 + x)}{C}$$

$$= \frac{300*2.6(1 + 0.15)}{45} = 19.93, \text{ or 20 production cards}$$

Terri rounds up her answer because there is no such thing as a fractional production card. Evaluating the results, she notes that 20 production cards is the equivalent of 20 containers of subassemblies, or:

$$(20 \text{ containers}) (45 \text{ subassemblies per container}) = 900 \text{ subassemblies}$$

And in hourly terms, 900 subassemblies equals:

$$\frac{900 \text{ subassemblies}}{300 \text{ units of demand each hour}} = 3 \text{ hours' worth of subassemblies}$$

The fact that there are slightly more subassemblies than needed is due to the safety factor and the rounding up of the number of production cards.

While Equation (13.1) is useful as a starting point, another approach used by many companies is to start with more than enough kanbans. The organization then slowly removes kanbans in an attempt to uncover the "rocks," or problems (similar to Figure 13.4). At the same time, the organization will try to shorten lead times and stabilize demand levels as much as possible, thereby further reducing the need for inventory.

After nearly a year of continuous improvement efforts in work cell H, Terri O'Prey feels it is time to reevaluate the number of production cards and hence inventory in the work cell. In particular, Terri has made the following changes:

- Production lead time has been cut from 2.6 hours to a constant 1.6 hours.
- Demand from final assembly has been stabilized at 300 subassemblies per hour.
- Smaller, standardized containers that hold just 25 subassemblies are now being used.

Because production lead time (T) and demand rate (D) have been stabilized, Terri feels she can reduce the safety factor to just 4%. She recalculates the number of kanban cards to reflect all of these changes:

$$y = \frac{DT(1 + x)}{C}$$

$$= \frac{300*1.6(1 + 0.04)}{25} = 19.97, \text{ or 20 production cards}$$

Since the container size is smaller, Terri is not concerned that the number of cards has not changed. In fact, 20 production cards are now the equivalent of:

$$(20 \text{ containers}) (25 \text{ subassemblies per container}) = 500 \text{ subassemblies}$$

and

$$\frac{500 \text{ subassemblies}}{300 \text{ units of demand each hour}} = 1.67 \text{ hours' worth of subassemblies}$$

Either way she looks at it, by improving the process, Terri has been able to cut inventory significantly.

Synchronizing the Supply Chain Using Kanbans

In Chapter 12, we alluded to the idea that kanban systems can be used to synchronize the supply chain at the PAC and vendor order management levels. Put another way, kanban can be used to link supply chain partners, as well as the work centers in a factory. Suppose, for instance, that work center B in our earlier examples is located in a facility 200 miles from work center A. In this case, electronic requests for more materials would be substituted for the factory's move cards.

Figure 13.9 shows how kanban can be used to synchronize the production and movement of goods among multiple supply chain partners. You might even think of customer demand as a pull on a rope (the kanban system) that ties together all members of the supply chain. One pull at the end of the supply chain triggers movement and production down the chain.

For a kanban system to work properly, however, there must be a *smooth, consistent* pull of material through the links. Consider the supply chain shown in Figure 13.10. As we have seen, the number of kanbans linking work centers A and B is based on an understanding of the demand rate coming from B.

But what happens if the demand rate changes or there is an interruption in the flow of goods? If final assembly demand doubles, work center B may quickly use up all the material linking it with A, and subsequent shipments from B to final assembly may be slowed down as a result.

If there is an *interruption* in the flow of goods—say, within work center B—the result could be even worse: Final assembly may have to stop production, thereby stopping the pull of goods from work centers C and D as well and shutting down the entire supply chain. This is not as far-fetched as it seems; in fact, it is exactly what happened to Toyota in 1997 when the manufacturing plant for Toyota's primary supplier of brake proportioning valves—a $20 part—burned to the ground. Within hours, the Toyota final assembly plant had to shut down due to the lack of

FIGURE 13.9
Using Kanban to Synchronize the Supply Chain

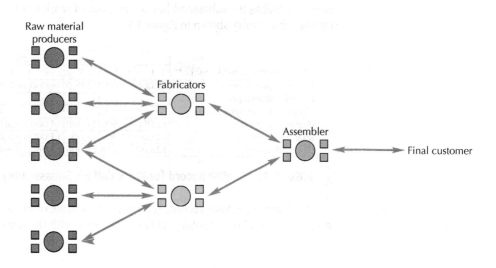

Raw material producers

Fabricators

Assembler

Final customer

FIGURE 13.10
**Work Centers A and
B as Part of a Larger
Supply Chain**

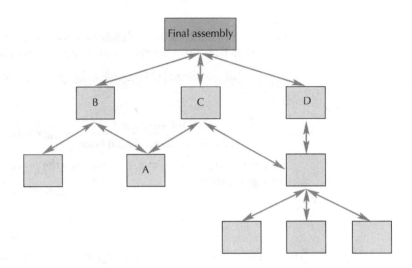

one part. The shutdown reverberated through the rest of Toyota's supply chain, with production resuming only after other Toyota suppliers started producing the missing brake parts. The point is this: For a kanban system to work properly, demand rates must be relatively stable, and interruptions must be minimized or quickly resolved.

Using MRP and Kanban Together

Some companies have found it beneficial to combine the *planning* capabilities of MRP with the *control* capabilities of kanban. In particular, MRP can be used to anticipate changes in planned order quantities over the planning horizon. This information is then used to recalculate the number of production kanbans (containers or cards) needed. Example 13.4 illustrates how the concept works.

EXAMPLE 13.4

Using MRP and Kanban Together at Marsica Industries, Part 3

The past six months have been tumultuous ones for Marsica Industries; demand levels have varied dramatically from one week to the next, as the company has taken on seasonal customers and marketing has used pricing changes to either boost or limit demand. The result for Terri O'Prey, production manager for work cell H, has been that the D values underlying her kanban calculations have been all over the place, undercutting the effectiveness of the kanban system. Terri knows that she needs some way to anticipate these changes and adjust the number of kanban production cards accordingly.

Terri also knows that the company uses MRP to estimate planned orders for components, including the subassemblies coming out of work cell H. She finds the MRP record for the subassembly shown in Figure 13.11.

** Subassembly, work cell H **		WEEK							
		1	2	3	4	5	6	7	8
Gross requirements		12,000	12,000	14,000	14,000	14,000	16,000	16,000	16,000
Scheduled receipts									
Projected ending inventory	0	0	0	0	0	0	0	0	0
Net requirements		12,000	12,000	14,000	14,000	14,000	16,000	16,000	16,000
Planned receipts		12,000	12,000	14,000	14,000	14,000	16,000	16,000	16,000
Planned orders		**12,000**	**12,000**	**14,000**	**14,000**	**14,000**	**16,000**	**16,000**	**16,000**

FIGURE 13.11 MRP Record for Work Cell H's Subassembly

Looking at the MRP record, Terri notices a couple of interesting points. First, there is no projected ending inventory. This is consistent with the Lean philosophy of having no more inventory in the system than is needed. Second, the planned orders all occur *in the same week* as the planned receipts. This is because the planning lead time for subassemblies is just 1.6 hours (Example 13.3); therefore, any orders released in a week should be completed in that week.

But the most interesting line for Terri is the planned order quantities. These tell her the total weekly demand for the subassemblies. Assuming that this demand is spread evenly across a 40-hour workweek, Terri can use the planned orders to calculate the D values for the various weeks:

$$D_{\text{weeks } 1-2} = \frac{12,000}{40 \text{ hours per week}} = 300 \text{ subassemblies per hour}$$

$$D_{\text{weeks } 3-5} = \frac{14,000}{40 \text{ hours per week}} = 350 \text{ subassemblies per hour}$$

$$D_{\text{weeks } 6-8} = \frac{16,000}{40 \text{ hours per week}} = 400 \text{ subassemblies per hour}$$

Finally, Terri can use the different demand rates and the other values from Example 13.3 to determine the number of production cards needed each week:

$$y_{\text{weeks } 1-2} = \frac{300 * 1.6(1 + 0.04)}{25} = 19.97, \text{ or } 20 \text{ production cards}$$

$$y_{\text{weeks } 3-5} = \frac{350 * 1.6(1 + 0.04)}{25} = 23.29, \text{ or } 24 \text{ production cards}$$

$$y_{\text{weeks } 6-8} = \frac{400 * 1.6(1 + 0.04)}{25} = 26.62, \text{ or } 27 \text{ production cards}$$

In practice, Terri will adjust the number of production cards by adding new cards when she anticipates that demand will go up and "retiring" freed-up production cards when she anticipates that demand will go down. But the key insight is this: Terri can use the MRP records to help anticipate needs and control production at the work cell level.

CHAPTER SUMMARY

JIT/Lean is both a business philosophy for reducing waste and a specific approach to production control. In this chapter, we reviewed the philosophical elements behind Lean and discussed how these elements fit with many of the other topics covered throughout this book, including quality management and supplier development. Even though it started out in manufacturing, the Lean philosophy has a lot to say to any organization wishing to eliminate waste.

We paid particular attention to the role of inventory in Lean environments and showed how kanban systems can be used to control the flow of materials in a Lean environment and across the supply chain. We also demonstrated why kanban systems may not be appropriate in all environments (particularly ones in which demand "pull" varies greatly) and illustrated how the planning capabilities of MRP can be combined with the control strengths of kanban.

KEY FORMULA

Number of production kanbans required (page 419):

$$y = \frac{DT(1 + x)}{C} \tag{13.1}$$

where:

y = number of kanbans (cards, containers, etc.)

D = demand per unit of time (from the downstream process)

T = time it takes to produce and move a container of parts to the downstream demand point

x = a safety factor, expressed as a decimal (for example, 0.20 represents a 20% safety factor)

C = container size (the number of parts it will hold)

KEY TERMS

Just-in-time (JIT) 410	Lean supply chain management 414	Pull system 419
Kanban system 414	Move card 418	Two-card kanban system 414
Lean 410	Muda 411	Waste 411
Lean Six Sigma 414	Production card 418	

SOLVED PROBLEM

PROBLEM

Fixing the Kanban System at Work Cell K

Because of her success in setting up a kanban system in work cell H, Terri O'Prey has been brought over to help fix the kanban system at work cell K. According to work cell K's current production manager, Tom Tucker, "We're swimming in inventory here. I thought I calculated the right number of production cards, but something must have changed."

Tom provides Terri with the information he used to determine the number of production cards:

$$\text{Assumed demand rate, } D = 260 \text{ units per hour}$$
$$\text{Lead time, } T = 2 \text{ hours}$$
$$\text{Container size} = 50 \text{ units}$$
$$\text{Safety factor, } x = 5\%$$

Tom notes, "Of course, there have been a few changes, but they're really no big deal. Demand is off slightly, down to 220 units an hour, and we've increased the container size to 100 units. But I can't see that making much of a difference."

Questions

1. Calculate the number of production cards needed, based on the original set of values given by Tom. According to the results, how many hours' worth of inventory would there be, given the original set of assumptions?
2. Now consider the changes to demand and container sizes noted by Tom. If Tom uses the *old* number of production cards, how many hours' worth of inventory would there be in the system?
3. Recalculate what the *new* number of production cards should be and estimate how many hours' worth of inventory this would equal.

Solution

Based on the old values, the number of production cards needed is:

$$y = \frac{DT(1 + x)}{C}$$
$$= \frac{260 * 2(1 + 0.05)}{50} = 10.92, \text{ or 11 production cards}$$

which is equivalent to:

$$(11 \text{ containers}) (50 \text{ units per container}) = 550 \text{ units}$$

or:

$$\frac{550 \text{ units}}{260 \text{ units of demand each hour}} = 2.12 \text{ hours' worth of units}$$

The problem, however, is that the values behind the production card calculation have changed. With a new container size of 100 units and a new demand rate of 220 units per hour, 11 production cards translates into:

$$(11 \text{ containers}) (100 \text{ units per container}) = 1,100 \text{ units}$$

or:

$$\frac{1,100 \text{ units}}{220 \text{ units of demand each hour}} = 5 \text{ hours' worth of units}$$

which is clearly too much inventory. After showing Tom the error of his ways, Terri helps him recalculate the new kanban level:

$$\frac{220*2(1+0.05)}{100} = 4.62, \text{ or } 5 \text{ production cards}$$

which is equivalent to:

$$(5 \text{ containers}) (100 \text{ units per container}) = 500 \text{ units}$$

or:

$$\frac{500 \text{ units}}{220 \text{ units of demand each hour}} = 2.27 \text{ hours' worth of units}$$

DISCUSSION QUESTIONS

1. Transportation can create value, as when an ambulance takes a patient to the hospital or a truck delivers fruits and vegetables to the grocery store. How would you differentiate between "necessary" and "unnecessary" transportation?
2. Even though waiting is a form of waste, does it always make sense to eliminate it? (*Hint*: Recall our discussion of waiting line theory in Chapter 6, and the relationship between resource levels and waiting times.)
3. Comment on the relationship between quality management (Chapter 5) and Lean. Are they the same thing, or are there some differences?
4. We noted in the chapter that kanban is not a planning tool but a control mechanism. What did we mean by that? How does the MRP/kanban example in Example 13.4 illustrate the point?
5. In what ways might a firm's suppliers improve or undermine the firm's Lean efforts? Can you think of any examples from the chapter that illustrate this idea?

PROBLEMS

(* = easy; ** = moderate; *** = advanced)

Problems for Section 13.4: Kanban Systems

1. (*) Suppose you have the following information:

    Demand rate (D) = 750 units per hour
    Lead time (T) = 40 hours
    Container capacity (C) = 1,000 units
    Safety factor (x) = 10%

    How many kanban production cards are required?

    a. 59 b. 28
    c. 30 d. 33

2. Consider the following information:

    Demand rate (D) = 200 units per hour
    Lead time (T) = 12 hours
    Container capacity (C) = 144 units
    Safety factor (x) = 15%

    a. (*) How many kanban production cards are needed?
    b. (**) How many hours' worth of demand will these cards represent?

c. (**) Suppose the container size is cut in half. Will this make any difference in the inventory levels? Show your work.

3. Consider the following information:

    Demand rate (D) = 300 units per hour
    Lead time (T) = 4 hours
    Container capacity (C) = 40 units
    Safety factor (x) = 10%

    a. (*) How many kanban production cards are needed?
    b. (**) How many hours' worth of demand will these cards represent?
    c. (**) Suppose the lead time is reduced to three hours. Will this make any difference in the inventory levels? Show your work.

4. Consider the following information:

    Demand rate (D) = 1,000 units per hour
    Lead time (T) = 2 hours
    Container capacity (C) = 250 units
    Safety factor (x) = 15%

a. (*) How many kanban production cards are needed?

b. (**) How many hours' worth of demand will these cards represent?

c. (**) Suppose the safety factor is eliminated. Will this make any difference in the inventory levels? Would this be a wise thing to do? Show your work.

5. Consider the following information:

$$Demand\ rate\ (D) = 60\ units\ per\ hour$$
$$Lead\ time\ (T) = 40\ hours$$
$$Container\ capacity\ (C) = 20\ units$$
$$Safety\ factor\ (x) = 10\%$$

a. (*) How many kanban production cards are needed?

b. (**) How many hours' worth of demand will these cards represent?

c. (**) Suppose the demand rate is doubled but the lead time is cut in half. Will this make any difference in the inventory levels? Show your work.

6. (*Microsoft Excel problem*) (***) The following figure shows a Microsoft Excel spreadsheet that calculates the number of kanban production cards needed, based on the MRP planned orders. **Re-create this spreadsheet in Excel.** Your spreadsheet should calculate new results any time a change is made to any of the highlighted cells. Your formatting does not need to be the same, but your answers should be. To test your spreadsheet, change the production lead time to 2.5 hours and the container size to 144. The number of production cards (not rounded up) for week 1 should be 6.84, and there should be 2.69 hours' worth of inventory. *Note:* To round up the kanban card calculation, use Excel's $=$ **ROUNDUP** function.

	A	B	C	D	E	F	G	H	I	J	K	L
1	Using MRP Planned Orders to Determine the Number of Kanban Production Cards Needed											
2												
3			Hours per week:	40								
4			Production lead time (T):	3	hours							
5			Container size (C):	5.0%								
6			Safety factor (x):	300								
7												
8							WEEK					
9				1	2	3	4	5	6	7		
10		Planned orders (from MRP):		15,000	16,000	15,000	15,000	14,500	14,000	13,000		
11												
12												
13			Hourly demand (D):	375	400	375	375	362.5	350	325		
14												
15	# of production cards (not rounded)			3.94	4.20	3.94	3.94	3.81	3.68	3.41		
16	# of production cards (rounded up)			4	5	4	4	4	4	4		
17												
18			Hours' worth of inventory	3.20	3.75	3.20	3.20	3.31	3.43	3.69		

CASE STUDY

Supply-Chain Challenges in Post-Earthquake Japan

Japanese automakers have long been known for the quality of their products, and especially for the efficiency of their streamlined manufacturing and supply processes. Thus, few people could have predicted how severely the destructive earthquake and tsunami that struck Japan in March 2011 would disrupt the country's entire auto industry. Matters were further complicated by the damage the quake and floodwaters caused to one of Japan's nuclear power plants, interrupting power supplies around the country and creating a dangerous radiation zone for miles around the plant.

Following the quake and ensuing floods, most automotive factories in Japan were closed for at least several weeks, bringing to a halt about 13% of worldwide auto production. Toyota, Honda, and Mazda shut down many of their parts and manufacturing plants in Japan, and Toyota also announced plans to suspend production in at least one North American plant because of parts shortages. The company said it would make plant improvements and run training programs in its other U.S. facilities while the assembly lines were idle or run operations on a part-time basis to conserve its parts inventory. Honda, Nissan, and Subaru also reduced their North American output as they anticipated and tried to deal with expected parts shortages.

Since one of the guiding principles of Lean production is to keep parts inventories as low as possible, it wasn't long before these shortages occurred. "The supply chain in the automotive industry is so fragile," said one legal advisor to the global auto industry. "It's based on just-in-time principles, where you don't have a lot of inventories built up, so you leave yourself without much margin for error when a supply interruption happens."

Industry observers predicted that about half of Japan's auto capacity would remain closed for at least eight weeks after the disaster, which would eventually put about one-third of worldwide production in jeopardy, as the effects of parts

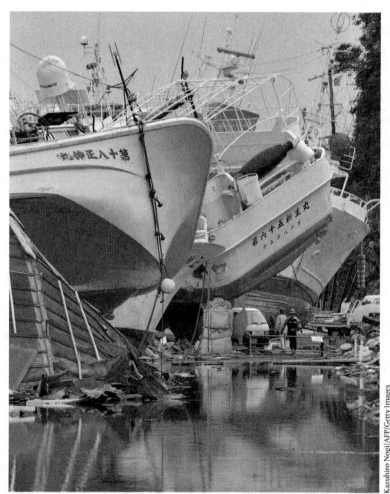

Kazuhiro Nogi/AFP/Getty Images

The disaster zone in Kesennuma, Miyagi prefecture, 100 days after a massive 9.0-magnitude earthquake and tsunami devastated the northeastern coast of Japan.

shortages made themselves increasingly felt in manufacturing facilities far from Japan. One auto industry research firm predicted that about five million cars that the industry had expected to sell in 2011 would never be made.

By spring and summer 2011, in fact, U.S. auto dealers were reporting what one called "a lot of emptiness" in their showrooms. Many logged dwindling sales as supplies fell to as little as one-fifth their normal levels, and popular cars such as the Honda Civic and Accord went out of stock. Without new cars to sell, even trade-in sales were slowing. Honda posted a 27% decline in sales for August 2011, and Toyota anticipated a dramatic 31% profit decline for the year. Although the Japanese auto industry worked hard to quickly return to full capacity, output was still not fully restored some six months after the disaster. The disaster's long-lasting ripple effects thus motivated industry executives to consider some changes in their vaunted manufacturing and supply operations. Traditionally, Toyota had used a single source for many parts that were common to more than one of its car models. Although the company locally sources about 85% to 90% of parts and materials needed for its North American manufacturing operations, a strategy that should make it less vulnerable to supply interruptions in Japan, it actually builds a larger proportion of its

vehicles in Japan than do the other automakers, so the 2011 disaster was a serious blow.

In response to these problems, Toyota's management began work to "foolproof" the supply chain so that it could recover from major interruptions in as little as two weeks. The plan had three parts. First, Toyota would increase standardization of auto parts so all Japanese carmakers could share the supply. These parts would be made in several locations to ensure uninterrupted supply. Next, the company asked its upstream suppliers of highly specialized parts, or parts that are sourced from only one location, to hold larger inventories than they had been carrying, as and opened up new options for manufacturing such parts to reduce its dependence on single sources. Finally, and perhaps most ambitiously, Toyota took steps to make each of its global regions independent of the others in terms of parts supply, so supply chain disruptions in one area will not spill over into the operations of any other areas.

Questions

1. What are some of the advantages of the supply chain used in the Japanese auto industry before the March 2011 earthquake and tsunami? What were some of its disadvantages?

2. Is Toyota's plan for a "foolproof" supply chain consistent with the Lean production philosophy? Explain.
3. Can you think of any additional ways Toyota (and its competitors in the Japanese auto industry) can improve

upon the company's plan to create a "foolproof" supply chain?
4. What impact do you think Toyota's plan will have on the way it handles relationship management in its supply chain?

Sources: Based on Chang-Ran Kim, "Toyota Aims for Quake-Proof Supply Chain," *Huffington Post*, September 6, 2011, **www.huffingtonpost.com/ 2011/09/06/toyota-aims-for-quake-pro_n_950105.html;** James R. Healey, "Honda Zapped as Nissan, VW Report Strong August Sales," *USA Today,* September 1, 2011, **http://content.usatoday.com/communities/driveon/post/2011/09/vw/1;** Mike Ramsey, "Honda Struggles with Supply," *Wall Street Journal,* August 17, 2011, p. B3; Hiroko Tabushi, "Toyota Expects 31% Profit Slump," *New York Times,* June 11, 2011, **www.nytimes.com/2011/06/11/ business/global/11toyota.html?scp=1&sq=toyota%20expects%2031%%20profit%20slump&st=cse;** Jonathan Schultz, "With Supplies Dwindling, Some Honda Dealers Foresee Long, Dry Summer," *New York Times* Wheels blog, May 4, 2011, **http://wheels.blogs.nytimes.com/2011/05/04/with- supplies-dwindling-some-honda-dealers-foresee-long-dry-summer/?scp=1&sq=with%20supplies%20dwindling,%20some%20honda%20 dealers&st=cse;** Nick Bunkley, "Toyota Plans to Reduce Production for 6 Weeks," *New York Times,* April 19, 2011, **www.nytimes.com/2011/04/20/ business/global/20auto.html;** Nick Bunkley and David Jolly, "Toyota, Struggling with Part Shortages, to Restart Car Lines," *New York Times,* March 24, 2011, **www.nytimes.com/2011/03/25/business/global/25auto.html.**

REFERENCES

Books and Articles

Blackstone, J. H., ed., *APICS Dictionary,* 15th ed. (Chicago, IL: APICS, 2016).

Ramsey, M., "Honda Struggles with Supply," *Wall Street Journal,* August 17, 2011, p. B3.

Womack, J., and Jones, D., *Lean Thinking: Banish Waste and Create Wealth in Your Corporation, Revised and Updated* (New York: Free Press, 2003).

Womack, J., Jones, D., and Roos, D., *The Machine That Changed the World: The Story of Lean Production* (New York: Harper-Collins, 1991).

Internet

Bunkley, N., "Toyota Plans to Reduce Production for 6 Weeks," *New York Times,* April 19, 2011, **www.nytimes .com/2011/04/20/business/global/20auto.html.**

Bunkley, N., and Jolly, D., "Toyota, Struggling with Part Shortages, to Restart Car Lines," *New York Times,* March 24, 2011, **www.nytimes.com/2011/03/25/business/global/ 25auto.html.**

Cremar, A., "Porsche 'Shock Therapy' Spurs VW, Lufthansa Efficiency Drive," *Automotive News Europe,* December 13, 2010, **http://europe.autonews.com/article/20101213/ ANE/101209816/porsche-%E2%80%98shock-therapy- spurs-vw-lufthansa-efficiency-drive.**

Debusk, C., and Rangel, A., "Creating a Lean Six Sigma Hospital Discharge Process," *iSixSigma.com,* September 15, 2004, **http://issuu.com/desandipan/docs/creating-a- lean-six-sigma-hospital-discharge-proce.**

Healey, J. R., "Honda Zapped as Nissan, VW Report Strong August Sales," *USA Today,* September 1, 2011, **http:// content.usatoday.com/communities/driveon/post/ 2011/09/vw/1.**

Joseph, N., "Porsche Consulting Sets Up Shop in Atlanta," Autoblog, July 21, 2011, **www.autoblog.com/2011/07/21/ porsche-consulting-sets-up-shop-in-atlanta/.**

Kim, C. R., "Toyota Aims for Quake-Proof Supply Chain," *Huffington Post,* September 6, 2011, **www.huffingtonpost .com/2011/09/06/toyota-aims-for-quake-pro_n_ 950105.html.**

Motorola University, **www.motorolasolutions.com/US-EN/ Home.**

Mullenhour, P., and Flinchbaugh, J., "Bring Lean Systems Thinking to Six Sigma," *Quality Digest,* March 2005, **www .qualitydigest.com/mar05/articles/05_article.shtml.**

Schultz, J., "With Supplies Dwindling, Some Honda Dealers Foresee Long, Dry Summer," *New York Times* Wheels blog, May 4, 2011, **http://wheels.blogs.nytimes.com/2011/ 05/04/with-supplies-dwindling-some-honda-dealers- foresee-long-dry-summer/?scp=1&sq=with%20 supplies%20dwindling,%20some%20honda%20 dealers&st=cse.**

Tabushi, H., "Toyota Expects 31% Profit Slump," *New York Times,* June 11, 2011, **www.nytimes.com/2011/06/11/ business/global/11toyota.html?scp=1&sq=toyota%20 expects%2031%%20profit%20slump&st=cse.**

"Typical Porsche: No Superfluous Parts," *Porsche Consulting,* no. 10, January 2011, **www.porsche-consulting.com/ it/stampa/porsche-consulting-the-magazine/detail/ issue-10-january-2011-4/.**

Mikeledray/Shutterstock

CHAPTER
fourteen

Managing Projects

CHAPTER OUTLINE

Introduction

14.1 The Growing Importance of Project Management

14.2 Project Phases

14.3 Project Management Tools

14.4 Project Management Software

14.5 PMI and the *Project Management Body of Knowledge* (PMBOK®)

Chapter Summary

CHAPTER OBJECTIVES

By the end of this chapter, you will be able to:

- Explain the difference between routine business activities and projects.
- Describe the five major phases of a project.
- Construct a Gantt chart or project network diagram, and use these tools to manage a project.
- Describe some of the key features and advantages of project management software.
- Describe what the Project Management Institute is, and what type of information can be found in the Institute's Project Management Body of Knowledge (PMBOK®)

HARNESSING THE NEW ZEALAND WINDS

Te Apiti Wind Farm, North Island, New Zealand

THE first wind farm to supply electricity to New Zealand's national grid, the Te Apiti wind farm produces enough clean and sustainable power for about 39,000 homes. The site was well chosen; the turbines' 115-foot-long blades take full advantage of a natural high-speed wind tunnel created by nearby Manawatu Gorge.

Te Apiti's 55 turbines, 230 feet tall, are electronically controlled and help conserve water and reduce pollution and greenhouse gas emissions by replacing the use of fossil fuels such as gas and coal for generating electricity. They also provide additional income for the farmers whose land they occupy and they even add one other benefit to the local economy: They attract some 400 groups of sightseers every week.

Despite the need to construct over 13 miles of extra-wide new roads at its remote location and install almost 25 miles of cable while adhering to the requirements of several landowners at the site, the Te Apiti facility was up and running five days ahead of schedule and within its budget of NZ$200 million, just 11 months after construction started. Its planners relied on effective project management tools and techniques to overcome challenges such as unstable terrain, streams, drop-offs in the level of the land, consistently bad weather, and a major gas pipeline running through the construction site. Perhaps most challenging of all were two unexpected rainstorms of historic proportions. These storms struck within 10 days of each other, bringing the highest flooding ever recorded for the area and destroying the main access bridge to the Te Apiti site. Contractors and staff were temporarily called away to help with the government's flood recovery efforts, and with the main water route also closed down for several weeks in the aftermath of the storms, access was limited for a time to a single route.

To meet all the project requirements, Meridian Energy Limited, which built and now operates the site, worked with its consultants and contractors from the beginning to develop a well-defined and all-inclusive project plan. Its goals were to create a robust and collaborative team culture and to promote clear communication and sound decision making. Everyone working on the site met with the rest of the team every day, and management met with all of the project vendors once a week. The results achieved all the project team's expectations. The project, the Southern Hemisphere's largest wind farm at the time it was completed, achieved an outstanding safety record over the course of 250,000 work hours. Te Apiti is now a registered "gold standard" site that diversifies the area's energy supply and showcases and helps develop the application of renewable energy in New Zealand.

Sources: Based on New Zealand Wind Energy Association, "Te Apiti Wind Farm," **www.windenergy.org.nz/te-apiti-wind-farm;** Meridian Energy, "Te Apiti Wind Farm," **www.meridianenergy.co.nz/about-us/our-power-stations/wind/te-apiti.**

INTRODUCTION

Much of this book deals with how businesses should develop and manage ongoing operations and supply chain processes. Examples include the procure-to-pay cycle, forecasting, master scheduling and MRP, kanban systems, reorder point inventory systems, and systems for tracking quality levels, to name just a few.

But in addition to these day-to-day activities, all businesses, at one time or another, must embark on projects. A **project** is "a temporary endeavor undertaken to create a unique product, service, or result."[1] Unlike other business activities, a project has a clear starting point and ending point, after which the people and resources dedicated to the project are reassigned.

Not all projects are as dramatic or large as the wind farm built by Meridian Energy. Examples of projects include developing a new product or service, making long-term process or

Project
According to PMI, "a temporary endeavor undertaken to create a unique product, service, or result." Unlike other business activities, a project has a clear starting point and ending point, after which the people and resources dedicated to the project are reassigned.

[1] Project Management Institute, *A Guide to the Project Management Body of Knowledge (PMBOK® Guide)*, 5th ed. (Newtown Square, PA: Project Management Institute, 2013).

capacity decisions, and even implementing a new software system. All of these represent non-routine activities that are vital to the survival of a business.

Projects are distinct from "typical" business activities in several ways. We've already noted that projects are nonroutine. For example, a company may schedule employees' work hours every month or reorder inventory items every week. These are routine business activities. On the other hand, projects such as moving headquarters, breaking into a new geographic market, and developing a new passenger jet may happen only once in a decade and have a significant impact on a firm's competitive position.

Second, the nonroutine nature of projects often makes them very difficult to manage. Consider a new product development project. At the start of the project, no one is quite sure what the final product will look like, how long it will take to complete, what resources will be needed, and what the final costs will be. This is not to say that developing a new product is more complex than, say, building a car, but at least the car manufacturer has an idea what it is building!

Third, projects typically require significant levels of cross-functional and interorganizational coordination—more, in fact, than routine business activities, which can often be formalized enough to be managed by a small group of people. The cross-functional and inter-organizational nature of projects presents unique organizational challenges. For example, an engineer working on a smartphone development team may have to report to two managers: his functional (engineering) manager and a project manager charged with getting the smartphone developed on time.

Fourth, a project, unlike routine activities, has a defined ending point, at which time the project is complete. Bridges are opened. New information systems are brought online. New products or services are launched. When this occurs, the people and resources involved must be assigned to new projects.

For many organizations, such as construction firms and software developers, projects actually account for the bulk of business activity. Routine business processes pale in comparison to the time and effort these firms must spend on developing new software products on budget, on time, and as bug-free as possible. The firms that succeed under these conditions typically are highly competent at managing projects.

14.1 THE GROWING IMPORTANCE OF PROJECT MANAGEMENT

Project management
According to PMI, "the application of knowledge, skills, tools and techniques to project activities to meet project requirements."

The Project Management Institute (**www.pmi.org**) defines **project management** as "the application of knowledge, skills, tools and techniques to project activities to meet project requirements."[2] However, until recently, project management was often treated more as an art than an actual management discipline; completing projects on time and on budget was often attributed primarily to good luck. And when things didn't go right (which often happened), managers wrote it off as the inevitable consequence of managing complex, nonroutine activities.

But this is no longer the case. For one thing, companies no longer accept the premise that projects are too complex to manage well. Second, professional organizations, such as the Project Management Institute, have emerged to educate practicing managers on state-of-the-art tools and techniques. As a management discipline, project management has matured.

Industry trends have also pushed project management to the forefront. Two trends of particular interest are:

- The faster pace of strategic change
- The changing role of middle management

Let's talk about each of these in turn, starting with the pace of strategic change. New product lines must be introduced more often to fight off hungry competitors. Information technology solutions that used to last 10 years are now out of date after 5, and customer and supplier networks quickly change, requiring new supply chain solutions. The result of all this

[2]Ibid.

is that companies find themselves involved in many more projects with strategic ramifications than they were involved in just a few years ago. As the number of projects increases, the case for improved project management becomes even stronger for a firm.

Project management has also received more attention as the traditional role of middle management has shrunk. Advanced information systems now handle many of the data analysis tasks that middle managers used to perform. At the same time, many companies have taken the authority and responsibility for work outcomes away from middle managers and pushed them down to direct supervisors and workers.

While the result has been a dramatic decrease in the number of middle managers, those who are left are more involved in managing projects, with their decision-making ability and flexibility put to better use. Simply put, middle managers who hope to keep their jobs, much less advance, will need to learn how to manage projects.

14.2 PROJECT PHASES

Because of the unique characteristics of projects, a whole set of tools has been developed to plan and control projects. Before we get to these tools, however, let's look at the five phases of a generic project. (You might want to compare and contrast these phases with the detailed description of the product development process in Chapter 15.) While the amount of time and resources spent on each phase will differ from one situation to the next, nearly all projects go through these phases. Figure 14.1 emphasizes two other points: the finite nature of a project and the typically high level of resources needed to both plan and carry out the project activities.

Concept Phase

Concept phase
The first of five phases of a project. Here, project planners develop a broad definition of what the project is and what its scope will be.

In the **concept phase,** project planners develop a broad description of what the project is and what its scope will be. For example, project planners might describe the project as "Launch a new online degree program" or "Open up a new support center in Brazil." Once the project has been broadly described, planners identify key resources, budget requirements, and time considerations. Key outputs of this phase include initial budget estimates, estimates of personnel needed, and required completion dates. Experience suggests that budget estimates made during the concept phase are usually accurate to ±30% compared to the actual final budget. Planners use this information not only to get an early fix on the scope of the project but also, in many cases, to determine whether a project is feasible. This is particularly important for new product or service development projects.

Project Definition Phase

Project definition phase
The second of five phases in a project. Here, project planners identify how to accomplish the work, how to organize for the project, the key personnel and resources required to support the project, tentative schedules, and tentative budget requirements.

If project planners believe the project is feasible, they proceed to the **project definition phase.** Project definition provides greater detail than the concept phase. The project definition identifies how to accomplish the work, how to organize for the project, the key personnel and resources required to support the project, tentative schedules, and tentative budget requirements. Budget estimates begin to become more exact, with a target of ± 5–10% compared to the actual final budget.

FIGURE 14.1 Five Phases of a Generic Project

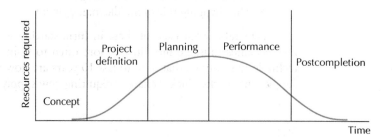

Planning Phase

Planning phase
The third of five phases of a project. Here, project planners prepare detailed plans that identify activities, time and budget targets, and the resources needed to complete each task. This phase also includes putting in place the organization that will carry out the project.

Milestone
A performance or time target for each major group of activities in a project.

The **planning phase** entails preparing detailed plans that identify activities, time and budget targets, and the resources needed to complete each task. This phase also includes putting in place the organization that will carry out the project. Firms often create project teams to perform the day-to-day tasks required to complete the project. The planning phase is particularly critical because there is a strong relationship between effective planning and successful project outcomes.

Detailed planning provides an opportunity to discuss each person's role and responsibilities throughout the project. A key part of this phase is developing performance and time targets for major groups of activities, known as **milestones.** These milestones will be used to track the progress of the project. An organization must also define how the different tasks and activities that make up the project come together to result in a completed project. The detailed plan serves as a reference that enables everyone to determine how the project is progressing at various points in time. Later we will address project planning and control tools and techniques in more detail.

Table 14.1 shows an example of some of the detail that might come out of this phase. In this example, activity group 3 of a larger project has been broken down into specific activities. In addition to an overall budget and a time milestone of July 9, 2020, the table indicates personnel assignments and responsibilities, budgets, and due dates for each of the five individual activities.

Performance Phase

Performance phase
The fourth of five phases of a project. In this phase, the organization actually starts to execute the project plan.

In the **performance phase,** the organization actually starts to execute the project plan. It is here that the value of the previous phases really becomes apparent. Specifically, effective planning increases the likelihood that actual performance outcomes will meet expectations. Project managers play a particularly important role here in coordinating and directing the work effort and in ensuring that time and performance milestones are met. Depending on the type of project, this may be the longest phase.

Postcompletion Phase

Postcompletion phase
The fifth of five phases of a project. This is the phase in which the project manager or team confirms the final outcome, conducts a postimplementation meeting to critique the project and personnel, and reassigns project personnel.

The **postcompletion phase** is the "wrap-up" phase of project management, which includes several important tasks. During this phase, the project manager or team:

- Confirms that the final outcome of the project meets the expectations of management or the customers. This usually entails a comparison of actual outcomes (time, cost, etc.) to the expected outcome established during planning.
- Conducts a postimplementation meeting to discuss the strengths and weaknesses of the project effort and personnel. As we saw in our discussion of continuous improvement in Chapter 4, an effective organization learns from its experiences.
- Reassigns project personnel to other positions or projects. One of the primary characteristics of projects as a form of work is the movement of personnel from project to project.

TABLE 14.1 Example of Detailed Project Information, Including Budget and Time Milestone

ACTIVITY GROUP 3: Build and deliver product to the customer
TIME MILESTONE: 7/9/20
BUDGET: $70,000

SPECIFIC ACTIVITY	PERSONNEL	BUDGET	DUE DATE
3.1 Complete specifications	John C.* Chester B.	$15,000	6/4/20
3.2 Complete Subassembly A	Maria G.* Tom T. Debra V.	$20,000	6/19/20
3.3 Complete Subassembly B	Philip B.* Emily W.	$24,000	6/19/20
3.4 Final assembly and testing	John C.* Chester B. Anne I.	$9,000	7/2/20
3.5 Deliver and train customer	Anne I.*	$2,000	7/9/20

*Indicates person with primary responsibility.

14.3 PROJECT MANAGEMENT TOOLS

Practitioners and academics have developed a host of tools to aid organizations in their project management efforts. Project management tools are used to plan, measure, and track a project's progress. In this section, we introduce two well-accepted tools: Gantt charts and network diagrams. These tools help managers understand what activities need to be completed, who is responsible for various activities, and when the activities should be completed. These tools also allow managers to track the time it takes to complete activities as well as costs. With the proper planning and control information, managers can take corrective actions when necessary to meet project objectives.

Gantt chart
A graphical tool used to show expected start and end times for project activities and to track actual progress against these time targets.

Gantt Charts

A **Gantt chart** is a graphical tool used to show expected start and end times for project activities and to track actual progress against these time targets. A Gantt chart therefore provides both a planning function and a control function.

EXAMPLE 14.1

Gantt Chart for the Gina3000 Project

Archideaphoto/Shutterstock

Courter Corporation makes high-end speakers that are used with home entertainment systems. Courter has designed a new speaker, the Gina3000, which is louder and more reliable than Courter's earlier model. Before Courter goes any further, however, it wants to give its customers—the home entertainment system manufacturers—a chance to test and critique the Gina3000.

Management has outlined 10 activities that must be completed before the Gina3000 speakers can be released for regular production. These 10 activities are listed in Table 14.2.

There are a couple of things to note about Table 14.2. First, some activities, such as **A** (Legal department approves prototype use) and **B** (R&D builds prototype speakers) can occur simultaneously. Courter Corporation should consider this when planning the expected time for the project's completion. Second, some activities have predecessors that must be completed beforehand. Take activity **H,** for example. Obviously, one can't test sample speakers before they have been made (activity **E**). Likewise, the speakers can't be made until the new equipment has been ordered and installed (activity **D**).

TABLE 14.2 List of Activities for the Gina3000 Project

ACTIVITY		DURATION (WEEKS)	PREDECESSORS
A	Legal department approves prototype use	2	None
B	R&D* builds prototype speakers	3	None
C	Customer uses and approves prototypes	3	A, B
D	New equipment is ordered and installed	5	C
E	Manufacturing produces sample speakers	2	D
F	R&D* writes up product specifications	3	C
G	Customer tests and approves sample speakers	3	E, F
H	QA** tests and approves sample speakers	3	E
I	Manufacturing finalizes process	3	E
J	Management approves product for regular production	2	G, H, I

*Research and Development. **Quality Assurance.

Figure 14.2 shows a Gantt chart for the Gina3000 project. For simplicity, each activity is referred to by its corresponding letter in Table 14.2. The Gantt chart provides a lot of useful information at a glance. First, according to the chart, the project should be completed by the end of week 18. Second, the chart tells us when specific activities should start and finish. Note that activity **C** has a planned start date of week 4. Why week 4? Because that is the first week in which *both* activity **A** and activity **B** (**C**'s predecessors) are finished.

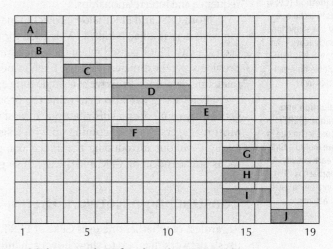

FIGURE 14.2 Initial Gantt Chart for the Gina3000 Project

As time goes on, Courter can use a Gantt chart to check its progress against the plan. In Figure 14.3, we use shading to show how much of each activity has been completed. Figure 14.3 shows that by the end of week 8, activity **F** has been completed one week ahead of schedule (i.e., the entire activity has been shaded in), while activity **D** is already two weeks late getting started (none has been shaded in). Based on this information, Courter Corporation has several options, including rescheduling the project or expediting activities to finish within the 18-week plan.

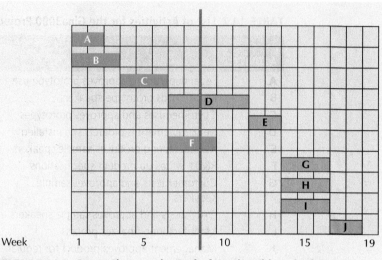

FIGURE 14.3 Gantt Chart at the End of Week 8 (blue shading indicates proportion completed)

Network Diagrams

Gantt charts have one major weakness: They fail to explicitly show precedence relationships. For example, it is unclear from Figure 14.2 or Figure 14.3 whether or not activity **F** is a predecessor of activity **G** (it is). This can be a real limitation for larger projects involving dozens or even hundreds of activities.

Network diagram
A graphical tool that shows the logical linkages between activities in a project.

Network diagrams improve on Gantt charts by visually showing the linkages between various activities. The **critical path method (CPM)** and the **program evaluation and review technique (PERT)** are two popular network-based techniques. Like Gantt charts, these techniques require the user to identify the activities that make up a project and to determine their sequence and interrelationships.

Critical path method (CPM)
A network-based technique in which there is a single time estimate for each activity. An alternative approach is PERT, which has multiple time estimates for each activity.

Both CPM and PERT allow project managers to monitor progress over time while managing costs across all activities. CPM is used for projects where there is a single time estimate for each activity. PERT is used when the time estimates are less certain and it makes more sense to provide several estimates—a most likely, a pessimistic, and an optimistic estimate. These estimates are combined to arrive at a single time estimate for each project activity.

Program evaluation and review technique (PERT)
A network-based technique in which there are multiple time estimates for each activity. An alternative approach is CPM, which has a single time estimate for each activity.

PERT users can also determine the probability of completing a project by a certain target date by using normal distribution curve statistics.[3] In reality, PERT is rarely used in practice. Most managers find that coming up with a single best estimate of an activity's time is difficult enough without introducing the added complexity of multiple estimates. We will therefore focus our attention on CPM and the use of single time estimates.

Constructing a Network Diagram

Regardless of whether one uses CPM or PERT, the underlying logic is the same. Each approach uses a network diagram to show how each individual activity relates in time and sequence to all other activities. Network diagrams show at a glance how separate activities come together to form an entire project.

Activity on node (AON) diagram
A network diagram in which each activity is represented by a node, or box, and the precedence relationships between various activities are represented with arrows.

While there are several ways to construct network diagrams, the process is much the same in both CPM and PERT. The major steps are as follows:

1. Identify each unique activity in a project by a capital letter that corresponds only to that activity.
2. Represent each activity in the project by a node that also shows the estimated time it will take to complete the activity. This style of network diagram is known as an **activity on node (AON) diagram.**

---

[3]For a detailed description of these methods, see L. Krajewski, M. Malhotra, and L. Ritzman, *Operations Management: Processes and Supply Chains*, 11th ed. (Upper Saddle River, NJ: Prentice Hall, 2015).

Critical activity
A project activity for which the earliest start time and latest start time are equal. A critical activity cannot be delayed without lengthening the overall project duration.

Network path
A logically linked sequence of activities in a network diagram.

Critical path
A network path that has the longest, or is tied for the longest, linked sequence of activities.

3. If an activity has an immediate predecessor(s), show the relationship by connecting the two activities with an arrow. The network diagram consists of all the activity nodes and arrows linking them together.
4. Determine the earliest start time (*ES*) and earliest finish time (*EF*) for each activity by performing a forward pass.
5. Determine the latest finish time (*LF*) and latest starting time (*LS*) for each activity by doing a backward pass.
6. Determine the critical activities and path(s) in the project. **Critical activities** are activities for which the earliest start time and the latest start time are equal. Critical activities cannot be delayed without lengthening the overall project duration. **Network paths** are logically linked sequences of activities in the network diagram. A path is a **critical path** if it is the longest path in the network (or tied for longest path). The duration of the project is equal to the duration of the critical path(s).

EXAMPLE 14.2

Network Diagram for the Gina3000 Project

Courter Corporation decides to follow the six steps outlined above to create a network diagram of the Gina3000 project.

Step 1. *Identify each unique activity in a project by a capital letter that corresponds only to that activity.* This has already been done in Table 14.2.

Step 2. *Represent each activity in the project by a node that also shows the estimated time it will take to complete the activity.* To illustrate, "Customer uses and approves prototypes" (activity **C**) is estimated to take 3 weeks. Courter represents this as follows:

Step 3. *If an activity has an immediate predecessor(s), show that relationship by connecting the two activities with an arrow.* Activity **A** immediately precedes activity **C**. This is shown as follows:

The same logic is used to link all the activities in the project. The result is the AON network diagram for the Gina3000 project shown in Figure 14.4. Note that there is one arrow for each predecessor relationship listed in Table 14.2.

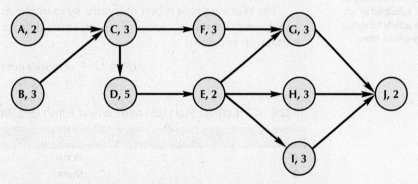

FIGURE 14.4 AON Network Diagram for the Gina3000 Project

Now consider the fact that even though activity **A** is not listed as an *immediate* predecessor for any activity except **C**, it must still be completed before all other activities, except for **B**. That is, all the activities except **B** are on a network path in which activity **A** is the first activity that must be completed. One path through the network is the sequence **A–C–F–G–J**. This path implies that **A** must be completed before **C**, **C** before **F**, and so on. Paths are the key to understanding the relationship between activities and determining the length of a project. There are a total of eight different paths in this network. Can you find all of them?

Forward pass
The determination of the earliest start and finish times for each project activity.

Earliest start time (ES)
The earliest an activity can be started, as determined by the earliest finish time for all immediate predecessors.

Earliest finish time (EF)
The earliest an activity can be finished, calculated by adding the activity's duration to its earliest start time.

Step 4. *Determine the earliest start time* (ES) *and earliest finish time* (EF) *for each activity.* This step is also known as the **forward pass** through the network. In general, the **earliest start time (ES)** is defined as follows:

$$ES = \text{earliest time by which } all \text{ immediate predecessors could be finished}$$
$$= \text{latest } EF \text{ for all immediate predecessors} \qquad (14.1)$$

Neither **A** nor **B** has any predecessors, so their $ES = 0$. But what about activity **C**? The earliest time **C** can start is based on the earliest time that *both* **A** and **B** will be finished. Because the EF for $\mathbf{A} = 2$ and $\mathbf{B} = 3$ the earliest start time for $\mathbf{C} = 3$.

The **earliest finish time (EF)** is calculated as follows:

$$EF = ES + \text{activity's duration} \qquad (14.2)$$

For activity **A**, then, $ES = 0$ and $EF = 0 + 2 = 2$ (that is, the end of week 2). For activity **C**, $EF = 3 + 3 = 6$. Table 14.3 shows the earliest start (ES) and earliest finish (EF) times for each activity in our speaker development project. There are several interesting pieces of information in Table 14.3. First, the table indicates that the entire project can be completed by the end of week 18. That is because the highest EF value for any activity in the table is 18. This finding is consistent with the Gantt chart shown in Figure 14.2.

Second, look at the earliest start times for activities **G** and **J**. Activity **G** has two immediate predecessors, **E** and **F**. Even though activity **F** can be completed as early as week 9, activity **E** won't be completed until week 13. Therefore, week 13 is the earliest we can start activity **G**. Similarly, activity **J** must wait until activities **G, H,** and **I** are *all* finished.

Backward pass
The determination of the latest finish and start times for each project activity.

Latest finish time (LF)
The latest an activity can be finished and still finish the project on time, as determined by the latest start time for all immediate successors.

Latest start time (LS)
The latest an activity can be started and still finish the project on time, calculated by subtracting the activity's duration from its latest finish time.

Step 5. *Determine the latest finish time* (LF) *and latest start time* (LS) *for each activity.* This step is also known as the **backward pass.** Calculating the LS and LF times indicates how late specific activities can be performed and still get the project done by a certain time. This step is particularly important when trying to determine what impact a delay might have on the length of a project.

Latest finish time (LF) is defined as follows:

$$LF = \text{latest time by which } all \text{ immediate successors}$$
$$\text{must be started in order to finish the project on time}$$
$$= \text{earliest } LS \text{ for all immediate successors} \qquad (14.3)$$

The **latest start time (LS)** is calculated as follows:

$$LS = LF - \text{activity's duration} \qquad (14.4)$$

The backward pass is best illustrated by example. Activity **J** has the latest EF of any activity (end of week 18). Setting the latest finish time for activity **J** equal to 18, the latest start time is as follows:

$$LS = LF - \text{activity's duration}$$
$$= 18 - 2 = 16$$

TABLE 14.3 Earliest Start (*ES*) and Earliest Finish (*EF*) Times for Gina3000 Project

ACTIVITY	DURATION	PREDECESSORS	ES	EF
A	2	None	0	2
B	3	None	0	3
C	3	A, B	3	6
D	5	C	6	11
E	2	D	11	13
F	3	C	6	9
G	3	E, F	13	16
H	3	E	13	16
I	3	E	13	16
J	2	G, H, I	16	18

The latest start time answers the question "How late can this activity be started and still complete the project on time?" Having calculated the *LF* and *LS* for activity **J,** we work backward (thus the term *backward pass*) to those activities immediately preceding **J:** activities **G, H,** and **I.** Having completed the calculations for those activities, we then work backward to activities **E** and **F.** Table 14.4 summarizes the results of the forward and backward passes.

Step 6. *Determine the critical activities and path(s) in the project.* Combined with the network diagram (Figure 14.4), the values in Table 14.4 provide Courter's management with some valuable information. First, look at activities **B, C, D, E, G, H, I,** and **J** (marked with asterisks). In each case, *ES* = *LS.* This means that the *latest* these activities can be started and still get the project done on time is *also the earliest* they can be started. Because *any* delay in these activities will cause the entire project to be late, these activities are critical activities.

Activities **A** and **F,** in contrast, are not critical activities. The amount of allowable delay, or **slack time,** is calculated as follows:

$$\text{Slack time} = LS - ES \tag{14.5}$$

For activity **A,** $3 - 2 = 1$ week of slack time; for activity **F,** $10 - 6 = 4$ weeks of slack. Now try to calculate the slack time for one of the critical activities. The answer should be zero, reinforcing the notion that critical activities cannot be delayed without delaying the entire project.

Figure 14.5 marks the critical activities in red, thereby showing the critical paths in the project. Critical paths are always the longest paths in the network, as there is no slack time in any of the activities they link together. In this case, there are three critical paths: **B–C–D–E–G–J, B–C–D–E–H–J,** and **B–C–D–E–I–J.** By adding up the times for the individual activities in each path, Courter realizes that each critical path takes 18 weeks. This result is consistent with the Gantt charts (Figures 14.2 and 14.3) and Table 14.4. A final point: While a project may have many critical paths, it must always have at least one critical path. After all, some path has to be the longest!

Slack time
The difference between an activity's latest start time (*LS*) and earliest start time (*ES*). Slack time indicates the amount of allowable delay. Critical activities have a slack time of 0.

TABLE 14.4 Results of Forward and Backward Passes on the Gina3000 Project

ACTIVITY	DURATION (WEEKS)	PREDECESSORS	ES	EF	LS	LF
A	2	None	0	2	1	3
B*	2	None	0	3	0	3
C*	3	A, B	3	6	3	6
D*	5	C	6	11	6	11
E*	2	D	11	13	11	13
F	3	C	6	9	10	13
G*	3	E, F	13	16	13	16
H*	3	E	13	16	13	16
I*	3	E	13	16	13	16
J*	2	G, H, I	16	18	16	18

*Critical activity.

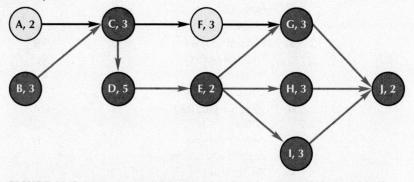

FIGURE 14.5 AON Network Diagram for the Gina3000 Project (critical activities and paths marked in red)

Crashing a Project

In many instances, the initial estimate of the time required to complete a project might be unacceptable. For high-tech products, even a few months of delay can often result in a significant loss of market share. And any city hosting the Olympics has no choice but to complete construction before the games begin; there is no room for negotiation. Alternatively, managers may be offered financial or other incentives for completing a project early.

Crashing
Shortening the overall duration of a project by reducing the time it takes to perform certain activities.

Crashing is an effort to shorten the overall duration of a project by reducing the time it takes to perform certain activities. As with the initial development of the network diagram, there is a series of steps to follow when crashing a project:

1. List all network paths and their current lengths. Mark all activities that can be crashed.
2. Focus on the critical path or paths. Working one period at a time, choose the activity or activities that will shorten all critical paths at the least cost. The one rule is this: Never crash an activity that is *not* on a critical path, regardless of the cost. Doing so will not shorten the project; it will only add costs.
3. Recalculate the lengths of all paths and repeat step 2 until the target project completion time is reached or until all options have been exhausted.

EXAMPLE 14.3

Crashing a Project at Courter Corporation

Nearly 60% of the cost of Courter Corporation's products comes from components provided by outside suppliers. As a result, management would like to:

- Develop a set of performance criteria and an evaluation system for assessing potential suppliers.
- Identify, evaluate, and select suppliers for critical components.
- Develop an IT system that will evaluate the performance of the selected suppliers on a continuous basis.

Management requires that the entire project be completed within *23 weeks*. Table 14.5 lists the various activities that must be completed. In addition to the estimated duration and predecessors for each activity, the table shows how many weeks each activity can be crashed and the crash cost for each week. For example, the expected duration of activity **B** is 6 weeks. However, for an additional $500, activity **B** can be squeezed down, or crashed, by 1 week.

TABLE 14.5 List of Activities for Supplier Selection and Evaluation Project

ACTIVITY		ORIGINAL LENGTH (WEEKS)	PREDECESSORS	NUMBER OF WEEKS ACTIVITY CAN BE CRASHED	CRASH COST PER WEEK
A	Assemble project team	2	None	—	
B	Identify potential suppliers	6	A	1	$500
C	Develop supplier evaluation criteria	4	A	—	
D	Develop audit form	3	C	1	$800
E	Perform supplier financial analysis	2	B	—	
F	Visit suppliers	8	E, D	2	$2,000
G	Compile visit results	5	F	1	$700
H	Identify needs for IT system	4	A	—	
I	Perform systems analysis and coding	10	H	2	$300
J	Test system	3	I	—	
K	Select final suppliers	2	G	—	

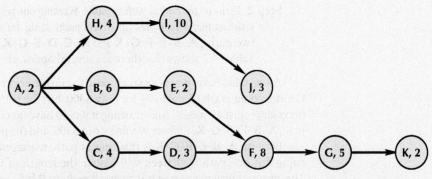

FIGURE 14.6 Network Diagram for Project

Note that not all activities can be crashed. For instance, testing of the computerized supplier evaluation system (activity **J**) and final selection (activity **K**) cannot be crashed at all.

Figure 14.6 shows the network diagram for this project. Notice that there are three paths: **A–B–E–F–G–K, A–C–D–F–G–K,** and **A–H–I–J.** Interestingly, there are *two* final activities, **K** and **J.** That is because the development of the IT system (**A–H–I–J**) is essentially independent of the supplier selection effort.

Table 14.6 contains the results of the forward and backward passes for this project. (You might want to calculate the *ES, EF, LS,* and *LF* values yourself in order to convince yourself that you understand how they were obtained.) Of the three paths, only **A–B–E–F–G–K** is critical because the activities on this path are the only ones for which *ES* = *LS*. Based on Table 14.6, we can conclude that the project will take 25 weeks.

Yet Courter management wants the project completed in *23* weeks, not 25. Can it be done, and if so, what is the cheapest way to accomplish the task? Crashing, like network development, can be divided into several steps.

> **Step 1.** *List all network paths and their current lengths. Mark all activities that can be crashed.* Table 14.5 shows the duration, crash time, and crash cost for each activity in this project. The current length of each path, therefore, is as shown in Table 14.7 (where all activities that can be crashed appear in color).

TABLE 14.6 Results of Forward and Backward Passes for Project

ACTIVITY	DURATION (WEEKS)	PREDECESSORS	ES	EF	LS	LF
A*	2	None	0	2	0	2
B*	6	A	2	8	2	8
C	4	A	2	6	3	7
D	3	C	6	9	7	10
E*	2	B	8	10	8	10
F*	8	E, D	10	18	10	18
G*	5	F	18	23	18	23
H	4	A	2	6	8	12
I	10	H	6	16	12	22
J	3	I	16	19	22	25
K*	2	G	23	25	23	25

*Critical activity.

TABLE 14.7 Network Paths for Project*

PATH	LENGTH
A–B–E– F–G–K	25**
A–C–D–F–G–K	24
A–H–I–J	19

*Activities that can be crashed appear in color.
**Critical path.

Step 2. *Focus on the critical path or paths. Working one period at a time, choose the activity or activities that will shorten all critical paths at the least cost.* We will need to shorten two paths, **A–B–E–F–G–K** and **A–C–D–F–G–K,** to meet the 23-week deadline. Table 14.7 shows that there are several options for crashing each.

As we said above, it never makes sense to crash a noncritical activity. Look at activity **I.** Courter could crash that activity for only $300, but the path it is on is already shorter than necessary—just 19 weeks. And crashing it would have no effect on the length of the critical path, **A–B–E–F–G–K.** Courter would be out $300, and the project would still take 25 weeks.

Because **A–B–E–F–G–K** is the longest path, management should start there. Shortening this one path by 1 week will reduce the length of the entire project to 24 weeks. The cheapest way to shorten it is to crash activity **B** by 1 week, at a cost of $500. The new path lengths are shown in Table 14.8. Notice that neither of the other two paths is affected because activity **B** is not on them.

TABLE 14.8 Updated Network Path Lengths

	LENGTH		LENGTH AFTER CRASHING B
A–B–E–F–G–K	25*		24*
A–C–D–F–G–K	24		24*
A–H–I–J	19		19
Crashing cost: $500.			

*Critical path.

Step 3. *Recalculate the lengths of all paths and repeat step 2 until the target project completion time is reached or until all options have been exhausted.* After activity **B** has been crashed, two paths become critical: **A–B–E–F–G–K** and **A–C–D–F–G–K.** Any further crashing efforts must consider both those paths. The next cheapest crashing option, therefore, is to crash activity **G,** at a cost of $700 (see Table 14.5). Doing so will bring down the lengths of both **A–B–E–F–G–K** and **A–C–D–F–G–K** to the required 23 weeks. Table 14.9 shows the final results.

TABLE 14.9 Final Results of Crashing Activities B and G

	ORIGINAL LENGTH		LENGTH AFTER CRASHING B		LENGTH AFTER CRASHING G
A–B–E–F–G–K	25*		24*		23*
A–C–D–F–G–K	24		24*		23*
A–H–I–J	19		19		19
Crashing cost: $500 + $700 = $1,200.					

*Critical path.

If Courter wanted to collapse the project any further, it would have to reduce activity **F** by 2 weeks, at a cost of $2,000. Crashing activity **D** wouldn't be enough because it affects only path **A–C–D–F–G–K.** And crashing activity **I** wouldn't help at all because it isn't on any critical path.

14.4 PROJECT MANAGEMENT SOFTWARE

The advent of cheap computer power has resulted in an explosion in the number of project management software packages. What we did by hand in the previous section—drawing networks, determining critical paths, crashing projects—can be done automatically, using software. These software packages enable far more sophisticated planning than anything discussed here. Nearly every package, for instance, allows users to evaluate the impact of resource constraints or to consider multiple estimates of activity time, as is done in PERT. In addition, nearly every software package offers resource utilization reports and exception reports on activities that are in danger of falling behind or becoming critical. This latter feature can be particularly valuable in managing complex projects with hundreds of activities because it highlights the critical few activities that managers need to pay attention to.

To give you a flavor for how these packages work, this section includes screenshots from one popular package, Microsoft Project. Figure 14.7 shows how we might set up the Gina3000 project (discussed in Examples 14.1 and 14.2) in Project. Compare the activities ("tasks") listed here with those in Table 14.2. As you can see from the toolbar on the left side of the screen, the software package offers some fairly sophisticated resource management tools.

Figure 14.8 shows the Gantt chart that Project generated for the project. Note the similarities to Figures 14.2 and 14.3. Microsoft Project has the added advantage of showing precedence relationships using arrows.

Figure 14.9 shows the AON diagram for the project. As with other software packages of this type, Microsoft Project automatically calculates starting and ending times and identifies the critical activities and paths. In this case, the critical activities and path are highlighted in the lighter shade. Once again, you might compare this network diagram with those we showed earlier, in Figures 14.4 and 14.5. While slightly different, they contain the same basic information. One benefit of using this software package is that it automatically updates diagrams as activities are added or deleted and as time estimates change.

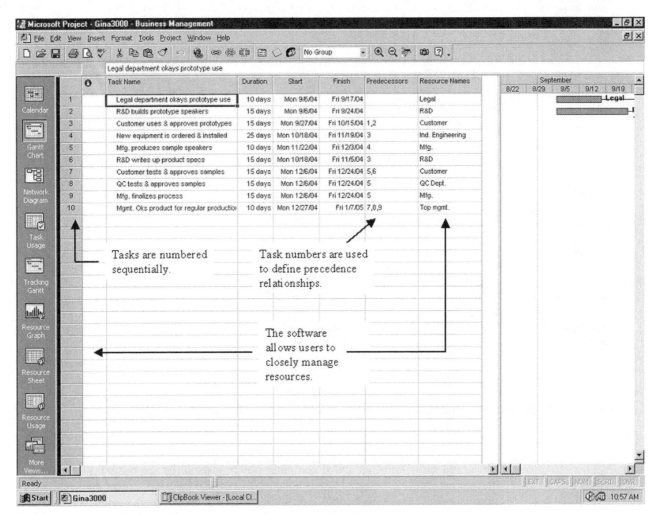

FIGURE 14.7 Entering the Gina3000 Project into Microsoft Project
Windows 10, Microsoft Corporation

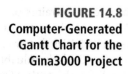

FIGURE 14.8
Computer-Generated
Gantt Chart for the
Gina3000 Project

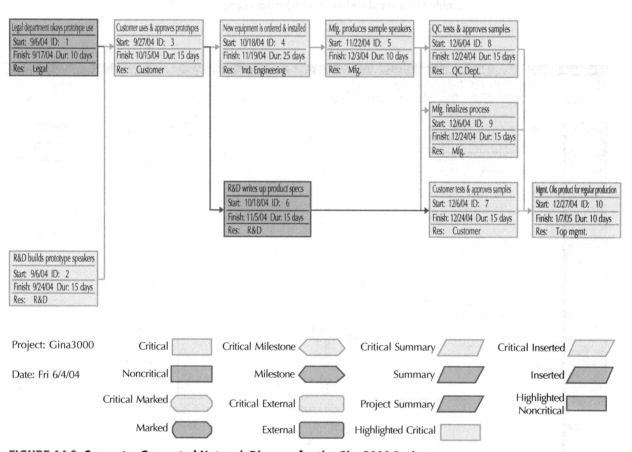

FIGURE 14.9 Computer-Generated Network Diagram for the Gina3000 Project

Even with almost unlimited computer power, it's still the responsibility of managers to make sure that project information is updated on a regular basis, particularly when activities or time estimates change frequently. Sophisticated users of project management software update project information on a weekly or even daily basis to stay on top of changes that could affect the timing or cost of a project.

14.5 PMI AND THE *PROJECT MANAGEMENT BODY OF KNOWLEDGE* (PMBOK®)

Throughout this book, we have identified numerous professional organizations dedicated to the advancement of operations and supply chain practices. The Project Management Institute (PMI) is one such organization. PMI serves the needs of project management professionals from a wide range of industries, including software development, construction, finance, and manufacturing. In addition to certification and other educational offerings, PMI also sponsors conferences, research, and special interest groups for individuals interested in various aspects of project management.

Perhaps the organization's best-known output is the *Guide to the Project Management Body of Knowledge* (PMBOK)[4] The PMBOK guide serves several needs. First, it provides a common language for discussing project management issues. Second, it identifies and disseminates generally accepted project management knowledge and practices. Third, and perhaps most importantly, it serves as a basic reference source for project management.

The guide divides the body of knowledge into two main parts. The first part defines the various business processes that organizations follow in carrying out projects. The PMBOK recognizes five major process groups: Initiating, Planning, Executing, Controlling and Monitoring, and Closing.

The second part of the PMBOK covers nine knowledge areas applicable to nearly all projects. These knowledge areas include such topics as managing the scope, quality, time, and cost of projects; managing human resources and communications between the various parties; and managing project risk. It's interesting to note that while the PMBOK deals with these knowledge areas within the context of project management, it draws heavily from other managerial disciplines such as organizational behavior and finance.

CHAPTER SUMMARY

Projects represent nonroutine business activities that often have long-term strategic ramifications for a firm. In this chapter, we examined how projects differ from routine business activities and discussed the major phases of projects. We noted how environmental changes have resulted in increased attention being paid to projects and project management over the past decade.

In the second half of the chapter, we introduced some basic tools that businesses can use when planning for and controlling projects. Both Gantt charts and network diagrams give managers a visual picture of how a project is going. Network diagrams have the added advantage of showing the precedence between activities, as well as the critical path(s). We wrapped up the chapter by showing how these concepts are embedded in inexpensive yet powerful software packages such as Microsoft Project.

If you want to learn more about project management, we encourage you to take a look at the Web site for the Project Management Institute (PMI) at **www.pmi.org.**

KEY FORMULAS

Earliest start time for a project activity (page 438):

$$ES = \text{latest } EF \text{ for all immediate predecessors} \tag{14.1}$$

Earliest finish time for a project activity (page 438):

$$EF = ES + \text{activity's duration} \tag{14.2}$$

Latest finish time for a project activity (page 438):

$$LS = \text{earliest } LS \text{ for all immediate predecessors} \tag{14.3}$$

Latest start time for a project activity (page 438):

$$LS = LF - \text{activity's duration} \tag{14.4}$$

Slack time for a project activity (page 439):

$$\text{Slack time} = LS - ES \tag{14.5}$$

---

[4]Project Management Institute, *A Guide to the Project Management Body of Knowledge (PMBOK® Guide).*

KEY TERMS

Activity on node (AON)
  diagram   436
Backward pass   438
Concept phase   432
Crashing   440
Critical activity   437
Critical path   437
Critical path method (CPM)   436
Earliest finish time (*EF*)   438

Earliest start time (*ES*)   438
Forward pass   438
Gantt chart   434
Latest finish time (*LF*)   438
Latest start time (*LS*)   438
Milestone   433
Network diagram   436
Network path   437
Performance phase   433

Planning phase   433
Postcompletion phase   433
Program evaluation and review
  technique (PERT)   436
Project   430
Project definition phase   432
Project management   431
Slack time   439

SOLVED PROBLEM

PROBLEM

Project Management at the GriddleIron

Lance Thompson is opening a new restaurant called the GriddleIron in Collegetown. The first football game of the fall is in 15 weeks, and Lance wants to be open in time to serve visiting alumni and other fans.

Table 14.10 lists all the activities that Lance needs to complete, as well as crashing options for two of the activities. How long will the project take if Lance doesn't crash any activities? Can Lance meet his 15-week deadline? If so, what will the cost be?

Solution

Figure 14.10 shows the network diagram for the GriddleIron project, while Table 14.11 shows the results of the forward and backward passes.

TABLE 14.10 Activity List for the GriddleIron Project

ACTIVITY		ORIGINAL LENGTH (WEEKS)	PREDECESSORS	NUMBER OF WEEKS ACTIVITY CAN BE CRASHED	CRASH COST PER WEEK
A	Get city council permission and permits	4	None	—	
B	Get architect to draw up renovation plans	4	A	—	
C	Hire manager	3	A	—	
D	Hire staff	3	C	—	
E	Train staff	1	D	—	
F	Select and order kitchen equipment	2	B	—	
G	Select and order dining room and bar furnishings	1.5	B	—	
H	Renovate dining area	4	G	1	$2,000
I	Renovate kitchen area	5	F	2	$1,000
J	Perform fire inspection	1	H, I	—	
K	Perform health inspection	1	H, I	—	
L	Grand opening	1	J, K		

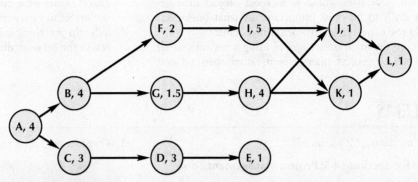

FIGURE 14.10 Network Diagram for the GriddleIron Project

TABLE 14.11 Forward and Backward Pass Results for the GriddleIron Project

ACTIVITY	EARLIEST START	EARLIEST FINISH	LATEST START	LATEST FINISH
A*	0	4	0	4
B*	4	8	4	8
C	4	7	10	13
D	7	10	13	16
E	10	11	16	17
F*	8	10	8	10
G	8	9.5	9.5	11
H	9.5	13.5	11	15
I*	10	15	10	15
J*	15	16	15	16
K*	15	16	15	16
L*	16	17	16	17

*Critical activity.

Looking at the results, we can see that there are two critical paths: **A–B–F–I–J–L** and **A–B–F–I–K–L.** The critical paths are both 17 weeks long, with the next longest paths being 15.5 weeks.

To meet the 15-week deadline, Lance must make sure that *all* paths are less than or equal to 15 weeks. Table 14.12 shows the crashing logic. First, Lance crashes activity **I** by 1 week, bringing both critical paths down to 16 weeks. Next, Lance crashes activity **I** by another week and **H** by 1 week. If Lance did not crash activity **H,** then two new paths (**A–B–G–H–J–L** and **A–B–G–H–K–L**) would become critical at 15.5 weeks, and the project would miss the deadline. The total crashing costs are $1,000 + $1,000 + $2,000 = $4,000.

TABLE 14.12 Crashing Logic for the GriddleIron Project

PATH	ORIGINAL LENGTH (WEEKS)	CRASH I 1 WEEK	CRASH I ANOTHER WEEK, AND CRASH H 1 WEEK
A–B–F–I–J–L	17*	16*	15*
A–B–F–I–K–L	17*	16*	15*
A–B–G–H–J–L	15.5	15.5	14.5
A–B–G–H–K–L	15.5	15.5	14.5
A–C–D–E	11	11	11

*Critical path.

DISCUSSION QUESTIONS

1. Visit the Web site for the Project Management Institute at **www.pmi.org.** What types of educational material are available for project managers? What types of professional certification programs are available? What do you think a professional project manager does?

2. In what businesses would you expect project management skills to be most important? In what businesses would you expect them to be least important?

3. What are the main advantages of using a network-based approach to project management rather than a Gantt chart? Under what circumstances might a Gantt chart be preferable to a network-based approach?

4. Why do you think it is important for project planners to revisit the network diagram as time goes on?

PROBLEMS

(* easy; ** moderate; *** advanced)

Problems for Section 14.3: Project Management Tools

1. Consider the following project activities:

ACTIVITY	DURATION (DAYS)	PREDECESSORS
A	3	None
B	2	None
C	6	A
D	1.5	A, B
E	2.5	C, D
F	3.5	D
G	4	E, F

a. (*) Draw the project network diagram.
b. (*) Identify all the paths through the network and their lengths.
c. (**) Identify all the critical activities and path(s). How long will the entire project take?
d. (**) Management would like to complete the project in less than 12 weeks. Management has determined that activity **C** can be crashed 4 weeks, for a total cost of $10,000. No other activities can be crashed. Will crashing activity **C** meet management's goal of less than 12 weeks? Why or why not?

2. Consider the following project activities:

ACTIVITY	DURATION (DAYS)	PREDECESSORS
A	1	None
B	2	None
C	1.5	None
D	3	A, B
E	2.5	C
F	1.5	D, E
G	4	F
H	2	F

a. (*) Draw the project network diagram.
b. (*) Identify all the paths through the network and their lengths. Are there any activities that are on *all* paths?
c. (**) Identify all the critical activities and path(s). How long will the entire project take?
d. (**) Every day the project goes on costs the company $5,000 in overhead costs. One of the managers responsible for carrying out activity **E** feels she can crash the activity by 1 week through the use of overtime. The cost would be only $2,500. Should the company do it? Why or why not?

3. Consider the following project activities:

ACTIVITY	DURATION (DAYS)	PREDECESSORS
A	4	None
B	3	A
C	7	A
D	9	A
E	8	A
F	7	B
G	6	C
H	13	C
I	4	D, E
J	12	E
K	1	E
L	5	F, G, H
M	4	I, J, K
N	5	L, M

a. (*) Draw the project network diagram.
b. (*) Identify all the paths through the network and their lengths.
c. (**) Identify all the critical activities and path(s). How long will the entire project take?
d. (**) After you complete part b and before you perform the forward and backward passes, you should already be able to tell that activities **A** and **N** are on the critical path(s). Why?
e. (**) After constructing the project network diagram, management comes up with the following information regarding how many days certain activities can be crashed and at what cost:

ACTIVITY	NUMBER OF DAYS ACTIVITY CAN BE CRASHED	CRASH COST PER DAY
C	3	$1,000
D	3	$2,500
E	2	$5,000
G	1	$1,000
H	3	$3,000
J	2	$2,000

Suppose that every day the project goes on costs the company $3,500. How many days should management crash the project? What activities should it crash? What is the new project length?

4. Consider the following project activities:

ACTIVITY	DURATION (WEEKS)	PREDECESSORS
A	4	None
B	5	None
C	7	B
D	3	A, C
E	6	B
F	6	D
G	8	D
H	4	E, G

a. (*) Draw the project network diagram.
b. (*) Identify all the paths through the network and their lengths.
c. (**) Identify all the critical activities and path(s). How long will the entire project take?
d. (**) Which activity or activities have the most slack? What are the practical implications of this slack?
e. (**) Management has determined that the project must be completed in 25 weeks or less and that "cost is no object." How many paths will need to be crashed in order to meet this goal? Which activities do not need to be considered for crashing?
f. (**) Just before starting the project, someone points out that (1) activity **A** really needs to be done before activity **C**, and (2) activity **C** needs to be completed before activity **G** can start. What is the impact on the expected length of the project?

5. Spartan Cabinets is thinking of offering a new line of cabinets. The project activities are as follows:

ACTIVITY	DURATION (WEEKS)	PREDECESSORS
A Hire workers	8	None
B Install equipment	6	None
C Order materials	3	None
D Test equipment	4	B
E Train workers	6	A, B
F Run pilot tests	5	C, D

a. (**) Identify all the paths through the network and their lengths. Which activities "start" one or more paths? Which activities "end" a path? How will those activities affect ES/EF and LS/LF calculations?
b. (**) Identify all the critical activities and path(s). How long will the entire project take?
c. (**) Suppose management of Spartan Cabinets has developed additional information regarding crashing options for the various activities:

ACTIVITY	DURATION (WEEKS)	NUMBER OF WEEKS ACTIVITY CAN BE CRASHED	CRASH COST PER WEEK
A Hire workers	8	3	$2,000
B Install equipment	6	1	4,000
C Order materials	3	1	1,000

(Continued)

ACTIVITY	DURATION (WEEKS)	NUMBER OF WEEKS ACTIVITY CAN BE CRASHED	CRASH COST PER WEEK
D Test equipment	4	2	2,500
E Train workers	6	2	5,000
F Run pilot tests	5	3	3,000

To illustrate, activity **A** can be crashed by up to 3 weeks, at a cost of $2,000 per week. Therefore, activity **A** can be 8, 7, 6, or 5 weeks long, depending on how much money Spartan Cabinets decides to spend to crash the activity. What is the cheapest way to crash the project by 2 weeks? What is the shortest time in which the project can be completed? (Assume that cost is not a concern.)

6. After graduation, you and several of your friends decide to start a new software company. As the vice president of operations, you are in charge of several production steps, including the process of recording software onto a CD. You have identified several activities that must take place before this "burn-in" process is ready to use:

ACTIVITY	DURATION (WEEKS)	PREDECESSORS
A Consult with engineering	3.5	None
B Determine equipment layout	2	None
C Install equipment	4.5	A, B
D Order materials	2	A
E Test equipment	2	C
F Train employees	3	D, E
G Perform pilot runs	2	F
H Get OSHA approval	4	E

a. (**) Draw the project network and calculate all ES, EF, LS, and LF times.
b. (**) Every week of delay in the project costs your company $3,000. Suppose you know the following: (1) Activity **G** can be crashed by 1 week, at a cost of $1,500; (2) activity **F** can be crashed by 1 week, at a cost of only $50; and (3) activity **H** can be crashed by 1 week, at a cost of $2,000. Should you try to crash the project? If not, why not? If so, how much money will the company save?

7. For this question, consider the Gina3000 project described in Examples 14.1 and 14.2 of the textbook.

a. (***) Consider Table 14.4 and Figure 14.5. Every week the project continues costs the Courter Corporation an additional $5,000 in lost profits. The quality control manager says she can crash activity **H** from 3 weeks down to 2 weeks by working overtime. Doing so would cost an additional $2,000. Should Courter do it?
b. (***) Writing up the product specifications (activity **F**) is taking longer than expected. Assuming that no other activities have been delayed or crashed, how many weeks can activity **F** be delayed without delaying the entire project?

CASE STUDY

Viva Roma!

Certe, toto, sentio nos in kansate non iam adesse.

Robert Curtis had just been hired into his first academic job as an assistant professor of classics at Topeka State University. One day in September 2020, not long after Robert had started, the department head came to talk to him.

> *Bob, I know it's a little sudden and we usually don't ask new assistant professors to handle such a task, but I'd like you to put together our summer study abroad program in Rome. Professor Wurst has done it for the past 10 years, but he won't be able to this year. Plan on about 15 to 20 students. The program usually lasts about a month, going from mid-June to mid-July, but the college is usually flexible on the exact dates. So what do you think?*

Even though he was new, Robert thought working on this project would be a great opportunity, and he started to think about what he should do next. He had never put together such a trip before, so it made sense to start by listing all the different activities that had to take place to get the trip planned in time. Robert wanted to post the complete information packet by March 31, 2021, which would give prospective students plenty of time to plan for the trip and meet the May 15 registration deadline.

The first thing Robert had to do was negotiate the exact starting and ending dates with the college, as well as make a rough estimate of the per-student costs. Specifically, Robert needed to know when the students would leave and when they would be expected to return to the United States. Robert felt he could do all this within one week.

Once Robert had these date and cost targets, he would then need to develop a daily schedule of the sites to visit, including any trips outside the Rome area (such as to Florence or Naples). Robert knew this would take a little time; museums and historical sites in Italy do not keep typical business hours, and some sites might even be closed for repair. Robert felt that this would take at least three weeks.

With a detailed schedule in hand, Robert would then have to make air transportation arrangements (one week) and local transportation arrangements (about one week) and select the pensiones to stay in during the trip (three weeks). Because Robert knew a lot of the time would be spent playing "email tag" with various people, all three of these activities could go on simultaneously.

Finally, Robert thought he would need to give himself a few weeks to finalize any loose ends. For example, he might learn that there were no rooms available during the time he wanted to schedule a side trip to Herculaneum, resulting in the need to adjust the schedule and other arrangements. With the finalized plans and costs in place, Robert would then need to develop and post the online information packet for students (one week).

Questions

1. What are the important time milestones for this project?
2. Given these time milestones, when should Robert start on the project? Draw a network diagram and determine the earliest and latest starting and finishing times for all activities. From a scheduling perspective, which activities are critical?
3. Comment on the time estimates for the various activities. Should Robert give himself more time? What are the pros and cons of doing so? Are there any pitfalls to starting too early? Where might he get good estimates of these times?

REFERENCES

Books and Articles

Krajewski, L., Malhotra, M., and Ritzman, L., *Operations Management: Processes and Supply Chains*, 11th ed. (Upper Saddle River, NJ: Prentice Hall, 2015).

Project Management Institute, *A Guide to the Project Management Body of Knowledge* (PMBOK®), 5th ed. (Newtown Square, PA: Project Management Institute, 2013).

Internet

Meridian Energy, "Te Apiti Wind Farm," **www.meridianenergy .co.nz/about-us/our-power-stations/wind/te-apiti.**

New Zealand Wind Energy Association, "Te Apiti Wind Farm," **www.windenergy.org.nz/te-apiti-wind-farm.**

Project Management Institute, **www.pmi.org.**

Project Management Institute, "New Zealand Wind Farm: Completed On-Time and within Budget Despite Record Storms," **www.pmi.org/Business-Solutions/~/media/ PDF/Case%20Study/Case_New%20Zealand%20 Wind%20Farm.ashx.**

Mikeledray/Shutterstock

CHAPTER
fifteen

CHAPTER OUTLINE

Developing Products and Services

CHAPTER OBJECTIVES

By the end of this chapter, you will be able to:

- Explain why product design is important to the success of a business.
- Describe the six dimensions of product design that are of particular interest to operations and supply chain managers.
- Describe the five phases of product and service development and explain the difference between sequential development and concurrent engineering.
- Discuss the different roles played by areas such as marketing, engineering, and suppliers during the development process.
- Describe some of the most common approaches to improving product and service designs, including the Define–Measure–Analyze–Design–Verify (DMADV) process, quality function deployment (QFD), design for manufacturability (DFM), and target costing.

CASTING A NET AROUND MALARIA

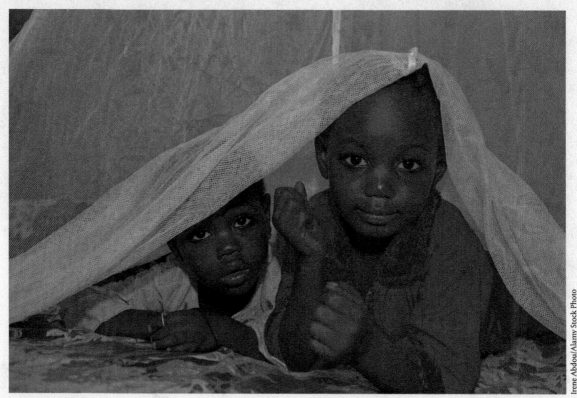

Henry Kimuyu, three, and his brother Vincent, eight, rest after school under an insecticide-treated mosquito net at their home in Nairobi, Kenya.

Since its symptoms were first reported in Chinese medical writings more than 4,000 years ago,[1] malaria has presented an enormous health challenge. Recent efforts to eradicate the mosquito-borne parasitic disease have met with some success: In 2016, the World Health Organization (WHO) reported that the number of cases fell from an estimated 244 million in 2005 to 212 million in 2015, while the estimated number of deaths due to malaria decreased from 985,000 in 2000 to 429,000 in 2015.[2] Malaria has had a disproportionately large impact in sub-Saharan Africa, where approximately 40% of public health expenditures can be traced back to the disease.

One relatively new product that has been used to fight the spread of malaria combines an old idea with state-of-the-art textiles and chemistry: bed nets impregnated with insecticides. One of the companies producing such bed nets is Vestergaard, a European company specializing in complex emergency response and disease control products. Recently, Vestergaard Frandsen introduced the PermaNet 3.0 Combination Net, which slowly releases insecticide

embedded in the yarn onto the surface of the netting. The result is a bed net that is effective at killing mosquitoes, even after multiple washings.[3]

While the PermaNet product concept is a good one, producing and then distributing the bed nets to where they are needed presents some significant operations and supply chain challenges for Vestergaard. For one thing, the prevailing price for similar bed nets is $5 to $7 a unit. Such a low price target puts significant cost pressure on operations and supply chain activities. Second, Vestergaard must build and maintain a network of suppliers and manufacturers capable of providing the needed volumes of specialized insecticides and textiles required to produce the PermaNet bed nets. A third challenge is effectively and efficiently distributing the bed nets in countries with limited transportation infrastructures and scattered populations.

While overcoming these operations and supply chain challenges is not easy, the payoff is much more than financial. As United Nations Secretary General Ban Ki-Moon wrote in the introduction to the *World Malaria Report 2010*:[4]

[1] Centers for Disease Control and Prevention, *The History of Malaria, an Ancient Disease*, **www.cdc.gov/malaria/about/history/**.
[2] World Health Organization, *World Malaria Report 2016*, **http://apps.who.int/iris/bitstream/10665/252038/1/9789241511711-eng.pdf?ua=1**.
[3] Vestergaard, *PermaNet*, **www.vestergaard.com/our-products/permanet**.
[4] World Health Organization, *World Malaria Report 2010*, **www.who.int/malaria/world_malaria_report_2010/en/index.html**.

Two years ago, I called for universal coverage of malaria-control interventions by the end of 2010, in order to bring an end to malaria deaths by 2015. The response was impressive. Enough insecticide-treated mosquito nets have been delivered to Sub-Saharan Africa to protect nearly 580 million people. . . . An additional 54 million

nets are slated for delivery in the coming months, bringing the goal of universal coverage within reach. . . . The World Malaria Report 2010 shows what is possible when we join forces and embrace the mission of saving lives.

INTRODUCTION

Vestergaard's experiences highlight some of the issues companies face when developing new products and services. But how do companies go about managing the development process, and what roles do various parties within and outside the firm play? These questions are the subject of this chapter. First, we discuss the role of product and service development in today's businesses, emphasizing the impact new and enhanced products and services have on a firm's ability to compete.

We then turn our attention to the actual process by which companies develop new products and services or modify existing ones. We pay special attention to operations and supply chain perspectives on product and service design: What are the important considerations? What role do the purchasing function and suppliers play? What tools and techniques are companies using to enhance the product development effort?

Product Design and the Development Process

Product design
The characteristics or features of a product or service that determine its ability to meet the needs of the user.

Product development process
According to the PDMA, "a disciplined and defined set of tasks, steps, and phases that describe the normal means by which a company repetitively converts embryonic ideas into salable products or services."

It's important for us to distinguish between product design and the product development process. **Product design** can be thought of as the characteristics or features of a product or service that determine its ability to meet the needs of the user. In contrast, according to the Product Development and Management Association (PDMA), the **product development process** is "a disciplined and defined set of tasks, steps, and phases that describe the normal means by which a company repetitively converts embryonic ideas into salable products or services."[5] In this chapter, we focus on how product and service design affects operations and supply chain activities and what role operations and supply chains play in the development process. We use the term *product design* to refer to the development of both intangible services and physical products. As you can probably guess, product development is by necessity a cross-functional effort affecting operations and supply chain activities, as well as marketing, human resources, and finance.

Four Reasons for Developing New Products and Services

There are least four reasons why a company might develop new products or services or update its existing ones. The first is straightforward: *New products or services can give firms a competitive advantage in the marketplace.* Consider the problem facing H&R Block a few years ago: How do you attract customers when faced with increasing competition from other tax preparation firms as well as PC-based software packages that can help people do their tax returns on their own? You do it by providing new and distinctive services such as PC-based will kits, refund anticipation loans (RALs), and a Web page that provides customers free and for-fee tax preparation software, as well as valuable information in multiple languages.

Not all product development efforts *directly* benefit the customer, however. This leads to our second reason for developing new products or services: *New products or services provide benefits to the firm.* Samsung might redesign one of its products so it has fewer parts and is easier to assemble. Even though the product might look and function exactly as before, the result is improved assembly productivity and lower purchasing and production costs. Samsung might or might not share these savings with the customer.

[5] Product Development and Management Association, *The PDMA Glossary for New Product Development*, www.pdma.org/p/cm/ld/fid=360#P.

Honda is a leader in the design and manufacture of gas-powered engines. These strengths have allowed the company to enter a wide range of markets, including automobiles, motorcycles, personal watercraft, and portable generators.

Third, *companies develop new products or services to exploit existing capabilities.* An excellent example is Honda. Honda progressed from making and selling motorcycles, to automobiles, lawn equipment, and personal watercraft. In retrospect, it is easy to see that Honda has built on its core competencies in the design and production of gas-powered vehicles. It will be interesting to see how Honda maintains its advantage as more products shift to alternative fuels.

Fourth, *companies can use new product development to block out competitors.* Consider the case of Gillette.[6] By the early 1990s, Gillette had grown tired of spending millions to develop a new razor blade, only to have competitors introduce cheaper (and poorer-quality) replacement blades within a few months. Gillette now makes a point of designing new razors so that they not only provide customers with a superior shave but are also difficult for competitors to copy. Developing new products like this requires a great deal of coordination with the manufacturing arm of the firm. Of course, a firm might have multiple reasons for developing a new product or service or for updating existing ones. But regardless of the underlying reasons, the development effort must be consistent with the strategy of a firm.

15.1 OPERATIONS AND SUPPLY CHAIN PERSPECTIVES ON DESIGN

If someone were to ask you, as a consumer, what the important dimensions of product design are, you might mention such aspects as functionality, aesthetics, ease of use, and cost. Operations and supply chain managers also have an interest in product design because ultimately these managers will be responsible for providing the products or services on a day-to-day basis. To understand the operations and supply chain perspective, think about a new electronic device. It is one thing for a team of highly trained engineers to build a working prototype in a lab. It's quite another thing to make millions of devices each year, using skilled and semiskilled labor, coordinate the flow of parts coming from all over the world, and ship the devices so that they arrive on time, undamaged, and at the lowest possible cost. Yet, this is exactly what the operations and supply chain managers at companies such as Lenovo and Apple are doing.

The interest of operations and supply chain management in *service* design is even greater. This is because the service design is often the operations process itself. To take an example from physical distribution, when a transportation firm agrees to provide global transportation services to a large customer, it has to make decisions regarding the number of trucks, ships, or airplanes required; the size and location of any warehousing facilities; and the information systems and personnel needed to support the new service.

---

[6]L. Ingrassia, "Taming the Monster: How Big Companies Can Change: Keeping Sharp: Gillette Holds Its Edge by Endlessly Searching for a Better Shave," *Wall Street Journal,* December 10, 1992.

With this in mind, the operations and supply chain perspective on product design usually focuses on six dimensions:

1. Repeatability
2. Testability
3. Serviceability
4. Production volumes
5. Product costs
6. Match between the design and existing capabilities

Repeatability, Testability, and Serviceability

Repeatability, testability, and serviceability are dimensions of product design that affect the ability of operations to deliver the product in the first place and to provide ongoing support afterward. *Repeatability* deals with the question, Are we capable of making the product over and over again, in the volumes needed? This is addressed through robust design. The PDMA describes **robust design** as "the design of products to be less sensitive to variations, including manufacturing variation and misuse, increasing the probability that they will perform as intended."[7] Product designs that are robust are better able to meet tolerance limits (see Chapter 5), making it easier for the operations and supply chain functions to provide good products on an ongoing basis.

Testability refers to the ease with which critical components or functions can be tested during production. Suppose for a moment that your company manufactures expensive electronics equipment. The manufacturing process consists of a series of steps, each of which adds parts, costs, and value to the product. If a $5 component has gone bad, you want to find this out before you assemble it with some other component or put together the final product.

Serviceability is similar to testability. In this case, serviceability refers to the ease with which parts can be replaced, serviced, or evaluated. Many modern automobiles require that the engine be unbolted from the car frame and tilted forward before the spark plugs can be changed—hardly a plus for shade-tree mechanics! On the other hand, all new cars have computer diagnostics systems that allow mechanics to quickly troubleshoot problems.

Serviceability is of particular interest to organizations that are responsible for supporting products in the field. When products are easy to service, costs can be contained, and service times become more predictable, resulting in higher productivity and greater customer satisfaction.

Production Volumes

Once a company decides to go forward with a new product or service, it becomes the job of operations and supply chain managers to make sure that the company can handle the resulting volumes. This responsibility might mean expanding the firm's own operations by building new facilities, hiring additional workers, and buying new equipment. It might also require joint planning with key suppliers.

As we saw in Chapter 3, the expected volume levels for a product or service also affect the *types* of equipment, people, or facilities needed. Highly automated processes that are too expensive and inflexible for low-volume custom products can be very cost-effective when millions of units will be made.

Product Costs

One study concluded that 80% of the cost for a typical product is "locked in" at the design stage. In other words, any effort to "tweak" costs later on will be limited by decisions that were made early in a product's life. Given the importance of costs in operations and supply chain activities,

Robust design
According to the PDMA, "the design of products to be less sensitive to variations, including manufacturing variation and misuse, increasing the probability that they will perform as intended."

Testability
The ease with which critical components or functions can be tested during production.

Serviceability
The ease with which parts can be replaced, serviced, or evaluated.

[7]Product Development and Management Association, *The PDMA Glossary for New Product Development.*

it is not surprising that operations and supply chain managers have a vested interest in addressing cost before the product design has been finalized.

For our purposes, we can think of products and services as having obvious and hidden costs. Obvious costs include such things as the materials required, the labor hours needed, and even the equipment costs needed to provide a particular service or product. These costs are usually the easiest ones to see and manage (i.e., we can track material usage, machine time, and the amount of direct labor that goes into our products or services).

Hidden costs are not as easy to track, but can have a major impact nonetheless. Hidden costs are typically associated with the overhead and support activities driven by some aspect of design. There are numerous drivers of hidden costs, but we will talk about three to make the point:

1. The number of parts in a product
2. Engineering changes
3. Transportation costs

Think about the activities that are driven by the number of parts used in a product, such as a washing machine. Engineering specifications must be developed for each part. The manufacturer must identify a supplier for each part and then place and track orders. Furthermore, the manufacturer must monitor the inventory levels of each part in its manufacturing plants and service support centers. Even if the manufacturer stops selling the washing machine after five years, it must continue to stock each part for years to come. All these activities represent hidden costs driven by the number of parts. Clearly, the manufacturer has an incentive to reduce the number of parts in a washing machine and to share parts across as many products as possible.

Engineering change
A revision to a drawing or design released by engineering to modify or correct a part.

There are also hidden costs associated with engineering changes to a product. An **engineering change** is a revision to a drawing or design released by engineering to modify or correct a part.[8] Returning to our washing machine example, suppose the manufacturer decides to make improvements to a part once the washing machine has been on the market for a few years. Suppliers, plants, and service support centers have to be notified of the change, and inventories have to be switched over from the old part to the new one. Yet the manufacturer will still have to keep track of information on both parts for years to come. Clearly, the manufacturer has a real financial incentive to design the part right the first time.

Products can also be designed to minimize transportation costs. Oddly shaped or fragile products can quickly drive up transportation costs. In contrast, products that can be shipped in standardized containers to take advantage of lower transportation rates can hold down the costs of distribution. NordicTrack engineers designed the Walk-Fit treadmill so that the electronics could be shipped to the customer separately from the treadmill. This was important because these components were made in different parts of the world. But there was another benefit as well: By separating the electronics from the treadmill, engineers allowed the bulky treadmill to be shipped at a lower per-pound rate. If the relatively fragile electronics had been included with the bulkier treadmill, the entire product would have had to be shipped at a much higher rate.

Match with Existing Capabilities

Finally, operations and supply chain managers are always concerned with how well new products or services match up with existing products or capabilities. A new product or service that allows a manufacturer to use existing parts and manufacturing facilities is usually easier to support than one that requires new ones. Similarly, services that exploit existing capabilities are especially attractive. An excellent example is the online tracking service that FedEx provides to its customers. In fact, this service was built on an existing capability supported by FedEx's internal tracking software.

---

[8]J. H. Blackstone, ed., *APICS Dictionary*, 15th ed. (Chicago, IL: APICS, 2016).

SUPPLY CHAIN CONNECTIONS

HOW HARD IS IT TO MAKE A COOKIE?

Nabisco Biscuit Co. makes cake and snack products that have become American classics, like Oreo, Chips Ahoy!, and Barnum's Animal Crackers. Another Nabisco classic is the story of the debut of its SnackWell's line of cookies and cakes. More than a year after launching the fat-free chocolate-and-marshmallow Devil's Food Cookie Cake in the early 1990s, Nabisco still couldn't meet consumer demand, setting off rumors of store rationing and fights among frenzied customers in search of a "healthy" snack. How hard could it be to make a cookie?

It turned out to be very hard indeed. Nabisco's senior director of operations services at the time claimed "the Devil's Food Cookie Cake is the hardest one we make." Because the cookie's center, unlike simpler confections, was covered with marshmallow all around and then drenched in chocolate icing, it would get stuck to a conventional conveyor belt. The solution was a "pin trolley system," invented in the 1920s, which set each cookie-cake center on a tiny upright pin mounted on a trolley.

A chain pulled the trolley along, taking four hours to cover a mile-long track winding through the bakery while the centers were coated with marshmallow and chocolate and allowed to air-dry in between. (Because the cookie was fat-free, the company couldn't chill it to shorten the drying time.) On top of having a painfully slow manufacturing process for its product, for a time Nabisco had pin-trolley equipment available in only one bakery in South Dakota. The initial shortage was so great that when it was first introduced, the cookie was sold only in the Northeast United States.

Nabisco has long since ramped up its production of the Devil's Food Cookie Cake, and over the years the product has had to prove itself against up-and-coming competitors in the low-calorie snack-food market. Nabisco's current marketing plans call for a renewed advertising campaign for the SnackWell brand, and it's a safe bet there will be plenty of Devil's Food Cookie Cakes on the shelves this time around.

Sources: Based on the company website, **www.nabiscoworld.com,** accessed September 26, 2011; Andrew Adam Newman, "Snackwell's Nudges Up the Portion Pack," *New York Times,* April 20, 2011, **www.nytimes.com/2011/04/21/business/media/21adco.html;** K. Deveny, "Man Walked on the Moon but Man Can't Make Enough Devil's Food Cookie Cakes," *Wall Street Journal,* September 28, 1993.

It may *seem* obvious that companies should consider such factors as production volumes and existing capabilities when designing new products or services. But what happens if they don't? Well, Nabisco ran into exactly this problem in 1993, when it introduced SnackWell's Devil's Food Cookie Cakes. The *Supply Chain Connections* box reveals a classic example of what can happen when the operations and supply chain perspective is not adequately considered when designing a new product.

15.2 THE DEVELOPMENT PROCESS

In the previous section, we talked about some product design dimensions of particular interest to operations and supply chain managers. But there are other perspectives to consider, including those of the final customer, marketing, engineering, and finance, to list just a few. How do firms go about designing products and services that incorporate all these perspectives? And how do they move from the idea stage to the actual launch of a new product or service? This section describes a model of the product development process and discusses the organizational roles played by different functional areas and supply chain partners.

A Model of the Development Process

All of us have experienced products or services that for some reason stood out from the competition—a tablet computer that was easier to use or more powerful than previous models, an airline seat that was more comfortable, or an online financial service that allowed us to check our portfolios and initiate trades 24 hours a day.

Good design does not happen by accident. Rather, it requires a coordinated effort supported by many individuals, both within and outside a firm. Table 15.1 offers one view of the

TABLE 15.1
Phases of Product and Service Development

FUNCTIONAL ACTIVITIES	CONCEPT DEVELOPMENT	PLANNING	DESIGN AND DEVELOPMENT	COMMERCIAL PREPARATION	LAUNCH
Engineering	Propose new technologies; develop product ideas	Identify *general* performance characteristics for the product or service; identify underlying technologies	Develop *detailed* product specifications; build and test prototypes	Resolve remaining technical problems	Evaluate field experience with product or service
Marketing	Provide market-based input; propose and investigate product or service concepts	Define target customers' needs; estimate sales and margins; include customers in development effort	Conduct customer tests; evaluate prototypes; plan marketing rollout	Train sales force; prepare sales procedures; select distribution channels	Fill downstream supply chain; sell and promote
Operations and supply chain functions	Scan suppliers for promising technologies/ capabilities	Develop initial cost estimates; identify key supply chain partners	Develop *detailed* process maps of the operations and supply chain flows; test new processes	Build pilot units using new operations; train personnel; verify that supply chain flows work as expected	Ramp up volumes; meet targets for quality, cost, and other performance goals

Source: Based on S. Wheelwright and K. Clark, *Revolutionizing Product Development* (New York: Free Press, 1992).

development process. The table divides the development process into five phases, paying particular attention to the roles played by the operations and supply chain functions, as well as by marketing and engineering.

Concept development phase
The first phase of a product development effort. Here a company identifies ideas for new or revised products and services.

In the **concept development phase,** a company identifies ideas for new or revised products and services. As Table 15.1 suggests, these ideas can come from a variety of sources, not just from customers. For example, engineering might identify a new material that can reduce the weight and cost of a product, even before marketing or the customer knows about it. The operations and supply chain functions have a role to play here as well: Purchasing personnel might look at potential suppliers to see if they have any promising new technologies or capabilities that could be turned into a new product or service.

Planning phase
The second phase of a product development effort. Here the company begins to address the feasibility of a product or service.

If a concept is approved, it will pass on to the **planning phase,** where the company begins to address the feasibility of a product or service. Customers are often brought in at this stage to evaluate ideas. Engineering might begin to identify the general performance characteristics of the product or service and the process technologies needed to produce it. Marketing will start to estimate sales volumes and expected profit margins. Operations and supply chain personnel might start identifying the key supply chain partners to be involved. Many ideas that look good in the concept development phase fail to pass the hurdles set at the planning phase. A product may be too costly to make, may not generate enough revenues, or may simply be impossible to produce in the volumes needed to support the market.

Design and development phase
The third phase of a product development effort. Here the company starts to invest heavily in the development effort and builds and evaluates prototypes.

Ideas that do clear the hurdles go on to the **design and development phase,** during which the company starts to invest heavily in the development effort. In this phase, the company builds and evaluates prototypes of the product or service. Product prototypes can range from simple Styrofoam mock-ups to fully functional units. Service prototypes can range from written descriptions to field tests using actual customers. At the same time, operations and physical distribution begin to develop detailed process maps of the physical, information, and monetary flows that will need to take place in order to provide the product or service on a regular basis (Chapter 4). They may even start to develop quality levels for key process steps (Chapter 5). The design and development phase is complete when the company approves the final design for the product and related processes.

Commercial preparation phase
The fourth phase of a product development effort. At this stage, firms start to invest heavily in the operations and supply chain resources needed to support the new product or service.

The **commercial preparation phase** is characterized by activities associated with the introduction of a new product or service. At this stage, firms start to invest heavily in the operations and supply chain resources needed to support the new product or service. This may mean new facilities, warehouses, personnel, and even information systems to handle production requirements. Obviously, this phase will go more smoothly if the new product or service can build on existing operations and supply chain systems. If new supply chain partners are required or if new technologies are needed, commercial preparation and launch can be much more difficult and expensive.

Launch phase
The final phase of a product development effort. For physical products, this usually means "filling up" the supply chain with products. For services, it can mean making the service broadly available to the target marketplace.

The last phase is the **launch phase.** For physical products, this usually means "filling up" the supply chain with products. For services, it can mean making the service broadly available to the target marketplace, as in the case of cellular service. In either case, operations and supply chain managers must closely monitor performance results to make sure that quality, cost, and delivery targets are being met and must take corrective action when necessary.

Sequential Development versus Concurrent Engineering

Sequential development process
A process in which a product or service idea must clear specific hurdles before it can go on to the next development phase.

The development model in Table 15.1 outlines a sequential development process. A **sequential development process** is one in which a product or service idea must clear specific hurdles before it can go on to the next development phase. The result is that while many ideas may be considered at the relatively inexpensive concept development phase, few make it to the commercial development and launch phases, where significant resources have to be invested. Steven Wheelright and Kim Clark of the Harvard Business School describe this process as the *development funnel.*

Concurrent engineering
An alternative to sequential development in which activities in different development stages are allowed to overlap with one another, thereby shortening the total development time.

An alternative to sequential development is concurrent engineering. As the name implies, **concurrent engineering** allows activities in different development stages to overlap with one another, thereby shortening the total development time. For example, engineering may begin to build and test prototypes (design and development phase) even before the general product characteristics have been finalized (planning phase). In contrast to a sequential development process, in which there is a clear handoff from one stage to the next, concurrent engineering requires constant communication between participants at various stages in the development effort. Figure 15.1 illustrates the idea.

Concurrent engineering helps reduce development times by forcing development teams to agree on critical product and process characteristics *early* in the development process, usually in the concept through design and development phases. These broad characteristics—costs, size, materials, markets to be served, and so on—provide clear guidance and boundaries for later activities. Returning to our engineering example, the *only way* engineers can start to build prototypes before the product characteristics are finalized is if there is *general* agreement regarding the characteristics of the new product (size, basic features, etc.). When this isn't the case, firms will need to follow a more sequential approach.

FIGURE 15.1
Concurrent Engineering

Overlapping development phase requires tight coordination, but shrinks development times.

Concept development

Planning

Design and development

Commercial preparation

Launch

Product development time

15.3 ORGANIZATIONAL ROLES IN PRODUCT AND SERVICE DEVELOPMENT

Product or service development is almost always a cross-functional effort. Table 15.1 shows how various parties contribute to the development effort in different ways. How well the different functions coordinate their efforts goes a long way toward determining the success of any development effort. Marketing, for example, might need to work with engineering to know what product features are technologically feasible. Purchasing then might help identify outside sources for needed inputs or services. Let's take a moment to discuss how different functions contribute to the development effort.

Engineering

Engineering provides the expertise needed to resolve many of the technological issues associated with a firm's products or services. Some of these issues center on the actual design of a product or service. A product engineer might be asked to design a lightweight yet durable outer casing for a new smartphone. Or a team of civil and electrical engineers might be asked to design a network of transmission towers for the relay of cell phone signals.

Other issues center on operational and supply chain considerations. Industrial engineers, for instance, might develop specifications for the manufacturing equipment needed to make the smartphone casings or transmission towers. Packaging engineers might be asked to develop shipping containers that strike a balance between cost and protection against damage.

Marketing

In most firms, marketing has primary responsibility for understanding what goes on in the marketplace and applying that knowledge to the development process. Who buys our company's products or services, and how much will they pay? Who are our company's competitors, and how do their products and services stack up against ours? How large is the market for a particular product or service? Marketing professionals use a variety of research techniques to answer such questions, including surveys, focus groups, and detailed market studies. When it comes to really understanding what customers want, many companies would be lost without marketing's input.

But marketing's role goes beyond providing information in the early phases of the development process. Marketing also has to select distribution channels, train sales personnel, and develop selling and promotional strategies.

Accounting

Accounting plays the role of "scorekeeper" in many companies. Not only do accountants prepare reports for the government and outside investors, they are also responsible for developing the cost and performance information many companies need to make intelligent business decisions. How much will a new product or service cost? How many hours of labor or machine time will be needed? The answers to these types of questions often require input from the firm's accountants.

Finance

The role of finance in product and service development is twofold. First, finance establishes the criteria used to judge the financial impact of a development effort. How much time will pass before our company recoups its investment in a product or service? What is the expected rate of return? How risky is the project? Once a company decides to proceed with the development of a product or service, it is the responsibility of finance to determine exactly how the company will acquire the needed capital.

Forma designs of Raleigh, North Carolina, improved the grips of screwdrivers. Even small changes such as this can make a big difference in the marketplace.

Designers

Designers can come from a variety of educational backgrounds—from engineering, design, and business schools, to name a few. Their role is one of the least understood aspects of the development process. One myth is that designers only do *product* design. But they do much more than that. They create identities for companies (logos, brochures, etc.), environments (such as buildings, interiors, and exhibits), and even service experiences. To make cell towers blend in with the environment, for example, designers have camouflaged the giant poles as trees or added decorative latticework.

A second myth is that designers simply make something "look good." This suggests that design is all form and no content. Yet consider an apparently simple handheld tape measure redesigned by Forma Design of Raleigh, North Carolina. As part of the redesign effort, Forma changed the tape measure so that the thumb presses against the index finger to work the tape measure's locking mechanism. Before that, users had to apply force between the thumb and *little* finger. If you try pushing your thumb against your little finger and then your index finger, you can see for yourself that the new design results in considerably less hand fatigue. Designers also work with schedules and constraints, just like other professionals. For example, in the redesign of the tape measure, Forma was not allowed to change any of the internal mechanisms.

Purchasing

Purchasing deserves special mention because it plays several important roles in product development. As the main contact with suppliers, purchasing is in a unique position to identify the best suppliers and sign them up early in the development process. Many purchasing departments even have databases of preapproved suppliers. The process of preapproving suppliers for specific commodities or parts is known as **presourcing.**

Presourcing
The process of preapproving suppliers for specific commodities or parts.

Another role purchasing plays is that of a consultant with special knowledge of material supply markets. Purchasing personnel might recommend substitutes for high-cost or volatile materials or standard items instead of more expensive custom-made parts. Finally, purchasing plays the role of monitor, tracking forecasts of the prices and long-term supply of key materials or monitoring technological innovations that might affect purchasing decisions.

Suppliers

Suppliers can bring a fresh perspective to the table, thereby helping organizations see opportunities for improvement they might otherwise miss. Teaming up with suppliers can also help organizations divide up the development effort, thereby saving time and reducing financial risks. Boeing, for instance, uses outside suppliers to develop many of the key components and subassemblies for its jets. If Boeing tried to develop a jet on its own, the project would cost considerably more money and take much longer.

Bringing suppliers into the development effort goes beyond just sharing information with them. Important suppliers should be included early in the development of a new product, perhaps even as part of the project team. The benefits of such early inclusion include gaining a supplier's insight into the development process, allowing comparisons of proposed production requirements with a supplier's existing capabilities, and allowing a supplier to begin preproduction work early.

The degree of supplier participation can also vary. At one extreme, the supplier is given blueprints and told to produce to the specifications. In a hybrid arrangement, called **gray box design,** the supplier works with the customer to jointly design the product. At the highest level of supplier participation, known as **black box design,** suppliers are provided with general requirements and are asked to fill in the technical specifications.

Black box design is best when the supplier is the acknowledged "expert." For example, an automotive manufacturer may tell a key supplier that it wants an electric window motor that costs under $15, pulls no more than 5 amps, fits within a certain space, and weighs less than 2 pounds. Given these broad specifications, the supplier is free to develop the best motor that meets the automotive manufacturer's needs.

Gray box design
A situation in which a supplier works with a customer to jointly design the product.

Black box design
A situation in which suppliers are provided with general requirements and are asked to fill in the technical specifications.

Who Leads?

Ultimately, someone or some group has to have primary responsibility for making sure the product development process is a success. But who? The answer depends largely on the nature of the development effort and the industrial setting. In high-tech firms, scientists and engineers typically take the lead. Their scientific and technological expertise is essential to developing safe, effective products that can be made in the volumes required. In contrast, at a toy producer, the technical questions usually aren't nearly as interesting as the consumers and markets themselves: What toys will be "hot" next December? How many will be sold? Marketing is, therefore, likely to have primary responsibility for managing the development effort.

15.4 APPROACHES TO IMPROVING PRODUCT AND SERVICE DESIGNS

Coordinating a product development effort while ensuring that all dimensions of performance are adequately considered is not an easy task. As a result, organizations have developed useful approaches to help accomplish these goals. The purpose of this section is to introduce you to some of the most common approaches.

DMADV (Define–Measure–Analyze–Design–Verify)

Chapter 4 introduced the Six Sigma methodology and the DMAIC (Define–Measure–Analyze–Improve–Control) approach to improving existing business processes. The Six Sigma methodology also includes a process called **DMADV (Define–Measure–Analyze–Design–Verify),** which outlines the steps needed to create *completely new* business processes or products. As with DMAIC, the DMADV process places a premium on rigorous data analysis, and depends on teams of black belts, green belts, and champions to carry it out. The five steps of DMADV are:

DMADV (Define–Measure–Analyze–Design–Verify)
A Six Sigma process that outlines the steps needed to create *completely new* business processes or products.

> Step 1. *Define* **the project goals and customer deliverables.** Since the focus is on a *new* process or product, the Six Sigma team must properly scope the project to ensure that the effort is carried out in a timely and efficient manner. What products or services do we want to provide and to whom? How will we know when we have completed the project successfully?

Step 2. *Measure* **and determine customer needs and specifications.** The second step requires the team to develop a clear picture of what the targeted customers want in terms of quality, delivery, cost or other measures of interest. Market research techniques as well as quality function deployment (QFD), which we describe shortly, are employed here.

Step 3. *Analyze* **the product or process options to meet the customer needs.** In this step, the Six Sigma team evaluates how the various options available stack up against the customers' requirements.

Step 4. *Design* **the product or process.** Here, the hard work of designing the product or process, as outlined in the "Design and Development" column of Table 15.1, takes place.

Step 5. *Verify* **the new product or process.** Finally, the team must verify the results. Does the product or process perform as intended? Does it meet the needs of the targeted customers?

Quality Function Deployment (QFD)

One of the greatest challenges firms face when designing new products or services is moving from vague notions of what the customer wants to specific engineering or operational requirements. **Quality function deployment (QFD)** is one tool that has been developed to formalize this process. First introduced in Japan in the early 1970s, QFD became very popular in the late 1980s and continues to be used by companies.[9]

Quality function deployment (QFD) ·
A graphical tool used to help organizations move from vague notions of what customers want to specific engineering and operational requirements. Also called the "house of quality."

Figure 15.2 shows a simplified example of a QFD matrix for a smartphone. This matrix is sometimes called the "house of quality," due to its obvious resemblance. The left side of the matrix lists general customer requirements and their relative importance (1–10) to the target customers. Note that these requirements are stated in terms of how the product performs, not specific characteristics. Along the top is a list of specific product characteristics. The main body of the matrix shows how each of the product characteristics does or does not support the customer requirements. As you can see, there are some potential conflicts. For example, the off-the-shelf electronics characteristic is consistent with an inexpensive unit but conflicts with customers' desires for more functionality. Ultimately, a trade-off may need to be made. Finally, the "roof" of the matrix shows synergies between some of the features. Obviously, off-the-shelf electronics conflicts with customized ones. On the other hand, a molded plastic casing and a thicker casing are two product characteristics that can easily be combined.

FIGURE 15.2
QFD Matrix for a Smartphone

[9]J. Hauser and D. Clausing, "The House of Quality," *Harvard Business Review*, 66, no. 3 (May–June 1988): 63–73.

FIGURE 15.3
Using QFD Matrices to Move from Customer Requirements to Process Specifications

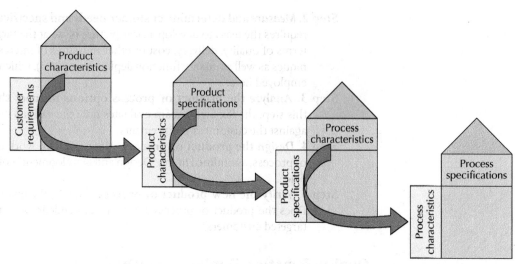

The matrix in Figure 15.3 moves the organization from customer requirements to broad product characteristics. But the process doesn't end here. The ultimate goal is to identify the specific manufacturing and service process steps needed to meet the customers' requirements. As a result, an organization may develop a series of QFD matrices that make the following logical linkages:

First matrix: Customer requirements → Product characteristics
Second matrix: Product characteristics → Product specifications
Third matrix: Product specifications → Process characteristics
Fourth matrix: Process characteristics → Process specifications

Figure 15.3 illustrates this idea.

In Figure 15.2, we identified "Rugged" as an important customer requirement and "Thicker Casing" as one product characteristic that would support this need. To move to *product specifications*, we need to translate "Thicker Casing" into more detailed information regarding the materials needed and the actual thickness value. Next, we have to describe the *process characteristics* needed to meet these product specifications regularly. This might include information on tolerance limits and acceptable process variability. Finally, we need to identify the specific manufacturing resources needed (e.g., "an injection molding device with computer controls") to support the process characteristics.

Computer-Aided Design (CAD) and Computer-Aided Design/Computer-Aided Manufacturing (CAD/CAM)

Advancements in information systems have also transformed the development process. In particular, **computer-aided design (CAD) systems** allow engineers to develop, modify, share, and even test designs in a virtual world. By doing so, CAD systems help organizations avoid the time and expense of paper-based drawings and physical prototypes.

Computer-aided design/computer-aided manufacturing (CAD/CAM) systems take the process a step further. Here, CAD-based designs are translated into machine instructions, which are then fed automatically into computer-controlled manufacturing equipment. Such systems allow for rapid prototyping and reduce the time and costs associated with producing one-of-a-kind pieces.

The "Design for . . . " Approaches

At a minimum, products and services must be designed to meet the needs of customers. But beyond this, organizations also want products and services to be easy to make, easy to maintain, virtually defect free (to reduce their costs as well as improve customer satisfaction), and environmentally sound. This has led to what can be called the "design for . . . " approaches to product

Computer-aided design (CAD) system
An information system that allows engineers to develop, modify, share, and even test designs in a virtual world. CAD systems help organizations avoid the time and expense of paper-based drawings and physical prototypes.

Computer-aided design/computer-aided manufacturing (CAD/CAM) system
An extension of CAD. Here, CAD-based designs are translated into machine instructions, which are then fed automatically into computer-controlled manufacturing equipment.

and service design. Four critical approaches are design for manufacturability (DFM), design for maintainability (DFMt), Design for Six Sigma (DFSS), and design for the environment (DFE).

Design for manufacturability (DFM) is "the systematic consideration of manufacturing issues in the design and development process, facilitating the fabrication of the product's components and their assembly into the overall product."[10] In general, the goal of DFM is to design a product that can be produced at consistently high quality levels, at the lowest cost, and, when possible, with existing processes.

Two ways in which organizations accomplish DFM are parts standardization and modularity. **Parts standardization** refers to the planned elimination of superficial, accidental, and deliberate differences between similar parts in the interest of reducing part and supplier proliferation. By standardizing and sharing parts across various products, companies can reduce the time and cost of developing new products and reduce the cost of the final product.

Modular architecture is another way in which organizations implement DFM. A **modular architecture** is a "product architecture in which each functional element maps into its own physical chunk. Different chunks perform different functions; the interactions between the chunks are minimal, and they are generally well defined."[11] To illustrate, consider the typical Microsoft-compatible PC. Suppose a PC retailer sells PCs that are assembled from the following module options:

- Four different system units
- Two different graphics cards
- Five different displays
- Three different printers

The visual functionality of the PC is contained within the graphics cards and displays, while the print functionality is contained within the printer. The remainder of the PC's functionality is within the system unit itself. What makes this product truly "modular" is the fact that the PC retailer can easily swap modules to make a different final configuration, as PCs use standard interfaces for plugging in displays, printers, and the like. In fact, the 14 modules above can theoretically be configured into $4 \times 2 \times 5 \times 3 = 120$ different combinations.

In contrast to DFM, **design for maintainability (DFMt)** is "the systematic consideration of maintainability issues over a product's projected life cycle in the design and development process."[12] Here the focus is on how easy it is to maintain and service a product after it has reached the customer. DFMt directly supports an organization's efforts to improve the serviceability of its products and services.

Design for Six Sigma (DFSS), as the name implies, seeks to ensure that the organization is capable of providing products or services that meet Six Sigma quality levels—in general, no more than 3.4 defects per million opportunities. DFSS is often mentioned in conjunction with DMADV, with DMADV serving as the process for achieving DFSS.

Finally, **design for the environment (DFE)** addresses "environmental, safety, and health issues over the product's projected life cycle in the design and development process."[13] DFE is becoming increasingly important for companies seeking to respond to both market pressures and regulatory requirements. To illustrate how companies are implementing DFE, consider some examples recently reported by Apple:[14]

- The 2014 iMac uses 0.9 watt of electricity in sleep mode, a 97% reduction from the first iMac.
- Between 2007 and 2011, Apple reduced the packaging for the iPhone by 42%.
- Even though it has a much larger screen than its 15-inch predecessor, the 2014 21.5-inch iMac required 50% less material.
- Computer displays are now manufactured with mercury-free LED backlighting and arsenic-free glass.

Design for manufacturability (DFM)
According to the PDMA, "the systematic consideration of manufacturing issues in the design and development process, facilitating the fabrication of the product's components and their assembly into the overall product."

Parts standardization
The planned elimination of superficial, accidental, and deliberate differences between similar parts in the interest of reducing part and supplier proliferation.

Modular architecture
According to the PDMA, a "product architecture in which each functional element maps into its own physical chunk. Different chunks perform different functions; the interactions between the chunks are minimal, and they are generally well defined."

Design for maintainability (DFMt)
Per the PDMA, "the systematic consideration of maintainability issues over a product's projected life cycle in the design and development process."

Design for Six Sigma (DFSS)
An approach to product and process design which seeks to ensure that the organization is capable of providing products or services that meet Six Sigma quality levels—in general, no more than 3.4 defects per million opportunities.

Design for the environment (DFE)
According to the PDMA, an approach to new product design that addresses "environmental, safety, and health issues over the product's projected life cycle in the design and development process."

[10] Product Development and Management Association, *The PDMA Glossary for New Product Development*.
[11] Ibid.
[12] Ibid.
[13] Ibid.
[14] Apple, *The Story behind Apple's Environmental Footprint*, **www.apple.com/environment/**.

Target costing (or design to cost)
The process of designing a product to meet a specific cost objective. Target costing involves setting the planned selling price and subtracting the desired profit, as well as marketing and distribution costs, thus leaving the required target cost. Also known as *design to cost*.

Value analysis (VA)
A process that involves examining all elements of a component, an assembly, an end product, or a service to make sure it fulfills its intended function at the lowest total cost.

Target Costing and Value Analysis

Cost is such an important aspect of product and service design that organizations have developed approaches specifically focused on this dimension. In this section, we talk about two of them: target costing and value analysis. In general, target costing is done during the initial design effort, while value analysis is applied to both new and existing products and services. **Target costing,** also called **design to cost,** is the process of designing a product to meet a specific cost objective. Target costing involves setting the planned selling price and subtracting the desired profit, as well as marketing and distribution costs, thus leaving the required target cost.

Value analysis (VA) is a process that involves examining all elements of a component, an assembly, an end product, or a service to make sure it fulfills its intended function at the lowest total cost. The primary objective of value analysis is to increase the value of an item or a service at the lowest cost without sacrificing quality. In equation form, value is the relationship between the function of a product or service and its cost:

$$\text{Value} = \text{function}/\text{cost} \qquad (15.1)$$

There are many variations of function and cost that will increase the value of a product or service. The most obvious ways to increase value include increasing the functionality or use of a product or service while holding cost constant, reducing cost while not reducing functionality, and increasing functionality more than cost (e.g., offering a five-year warranty versus a two-year warranty with no price increase raises the value of a product to the customer).

A common approach for implementing value analysis is to create a VA team composed of professionals with knowledge about a product or service. Many functional groups can contribute to the value analysis team, including engineering, marketing, purchasing, production, and key suppliers. Value analysis teams ask a number of questions to determine if opportunities exist for item, product, or service improvement. Some typical questions include the following:

1. Is the cost of the final product proportionate to its usefulness?
2. Does the product need all its features or internal parts?
3. Is there a better production method to produce the item or product?
4. Can a lower-cost standard part replace a customized part?
5. Are we using the proper tooling, considering the quantities required?
6. Will another dependable supplier provide material, components, or subassemblies for less?
7. Are there equally effective but lower-cost materials available?
8. Are packaging cost reductions possible?
9. Is the item properly classified for shipping purposes to receive the lowest transportation rates?
10. Are design or quality specifications too tight, given customer requirements?
11. If we are making an item now, can we buy it for less (and vice versa)?

The most likely VA improvements include modifying product design and material specifications, using standardized components in place of custom components, substituting lower-cost for higher-cost materials, reducing the number of parts that a product contains, and developing better production or assembly methods.

CHAPTER SUMMARY

Product and service development is critical to the success of many firms. Points to take away from this chapter include the following:

- Having a well-managed development process, whether it is a sequential process or one based on concurrent engineering, is crucial.
- It is important to consider operations and supply chain perspectives when developing new products and

services, including repeatability, testability, and serviceability of the design; volumes; costs; and the match with a company's existing capabilities.

As the last section of this chapter made clear, organizations have developed various tools and techniques for ensuring that the development process not only goes smoothly but also results in "good" designs.

KEY TERMS

Black box design   462

Commercial preparation phase   459

Computer-aided design (CAD) system   464

Computer-aided design/computer-aided manufacturing (CAD/CAM) system   464

Concept development phase   458

Concurrent engineering   459

Design and development phase   458

Design for maintainability (DFMt)   465

Design for manufacturability (DFM)   465

Design for Six Sigma (DFSS)   465

Design for the environment (DFE)   465

Design to cost   466

DMADV (Define–Measure–Analyze–Design–Verify)   462

Engineering change   456

Gray box design   462

Launch phase   459

Modular architecture   465

Parts standardization   465

Planning phase   458

Presourcing   461

Product design   453

Product development process   453

Quality function deployment (QFD)   463

Robust design   455

Sequential development process   459

Serviceability   455

Target costing   466

Testability   455

Value analysis (VA)   466

DISCUSSION QUESTIONS

1. In this chapter, we described several approaches to product design, including parts standardization and modularity. How do these two approaches relate to the dimensions of product design described earlier in the chapter?
2. We talked about concurrent engineering as an alternative to sequential development. What are the advantages of concurrent engineering? Under what circumstances might sequential development be preferable?
3. Consider some of the dimensions of product design that we listed as important to operations and supply chain managers. Are these dimensions more or less important than whether the product or service meets the customers'

needs? Can you think of situations in which there might be conflict between these different perspectives?
4. Consider the phases of product and service development shown in Table 15.1. Why is it important to include customers early in the development process?
5. Which type of product development effort would be better suited to concurrent engineering: a radically new product involving cutting-edge technologies or the latest version of an existing product? Why?
6. What are some of the benefits of including suppliers in the product development process? Can you think of any risks?

CASE STUDY

Design for Supply Chain Programs

Design for Supply Chain (DfSC) is a systematic method of ensuring the best fit between the design of a product throughout its lifetime and its supply chain members' resources and capabilities. Even something as simple as flattening the tops of soda cans, as beverage makers did in the 1950s, can revolutionize product development, transform transportation and inventory processes, and generate huge cost savings and increased customer satisfaction. Hewlett-Packard (HP) has been in the forefront of adopting DfSC principles, and IBM is another staunch proponent.

IBM developed a short list of DfSC principles that have helped it create products that are both competitive and supply-chain-efficient throughout their life cycles. Briefly stated, these principles are:

1. Integrate products parts and components as much as possible to reduce product assembly time.
2. Use industry-standard parts whenever possible to lower costs and simplify sourcing efforts.
3. Reduce lead times on critical components to avoid paying premium shipping fees on rush orders.
4. Design products for supply-chain-friendliness throughout their life cycle, planning for and minimizing the cost and

disruption of design and technology changes as products mature.
5. Build supply chains based on the company's strategic plan, not around the idiosyncratic requirements of specific products.
6. Use common components and modular design, thereby reducing product variability.
7. Minimize inventory costs and reduce the risk of obsolescence by building to order from common components and subassemblies, rather than building to stock.
8. Design products to give customers flexibility when ordering while keeping costs in line.
9. Use high quality parts and parts which can be quickly diagnosed to minimize warranty costs and improve after sales service.

HP similarly uses DfSC to consider the impact of its design decisions over product lifetimes, from pre-launch through production to end of life cycle, in all its business units and regions. The DfSC strategy—essentially looking back in order to see ahead—helps improve HP's relationships with suppliers, manufacturers, logistics service firms, retailers, and consumers.

To use DfSC, which it adopted in the early 1990s, HP first asks four questions about its products:

1. What makes the product a good fit for a particular supply chain?
2. Which design decisions produce that result? For example, does the product have unique parts?
3. When and why are design decisions being made, and who is making them?
4. How can the company deliver great products at higher profit margins?

Since adopting DfSC and successfully propagating its use throughout the company, HP has been able to introduce more new products faster and at lower cost. It has increased its revenues and kept customers happy. At the same time, the company has found ways to improve its inventory efficiency without offsetting risks onto its suppliers (which would damage its supply-chain relationships) or reducing the quality of product inputs (which would increase the cost of honoring product warranties as well as damaging customer relationships).

HP's six DfSC techniques are:

1. **Variety control.** Having fewer SKUs allowed the company to reduce inventory 42% and increase product availability in its PC division.
2. **Logistics enhancement.** Making an InkJet printer 45% smaller saved more than $1 per unit in logistics costs.
3. **Commonality and reuse.** While unique parts make products distinctive, they increase inventory costs and, often, time to market.

4. **Postponement.** Designing products to remain generic as long as possible during the production process, until it's known how the end user wants to customize them, saves costs.
5. **Tax and duty reduction.** These costs can be higher or lower based on the country of origin.
6. **Take-back facilitation.** Design and packaging changes can reduce both manufacturing and environmental costs.

HP estimates that DfSC techniques have saved it about $200 million per year.

Questions
1. What is the relationship between design for manufacturability (DFM) and design for supply chain (DfSC)?
2. In the chapter, we discussed parts standardization and modular architecture. How do these two approaches support DfSC?
3. You hear someone say, "DfSC sounds fine in theory, but I think it will have two negative effects. First, it will slow down the product development process because now all the areas that make up supply chain management—procurement, manufacturing, and logistics—will need to be involved. Second, it gives too much power to the supply chain functions. After all, if supply chain managers think something is too difficult to ship or too expensive to make, they may say no." What do you think? Are these legitimate concerns? How should operations managers address them?

Sources: Based on Heather E. Domin, James Wisner, and Matthew Marks, "Design for Supply Chain," *Supply and Demand Chain Executive*, December 2, 2007, **www.sdcexec.com/article/10289661/design-for-supply-chain?page=3;** Brian Cargille and Chris Fry, "Design for Supply Chain: Spreading the Word across HP," *Supply Chain Management Review*, July–August 2006, **www.strategicmgmtsolutions.com/DfSC-HP.PDF;** "Hewlett Packard's Design for Supply Chain Program," *Supply Chain Brain*, **www.supplychainbrain.com/content/industry-verticals/high-techelectronics/single-article-page/article/hewlett-packards-design-for-supply-chain-program/,** December 1, 2005.

REFERENCES

Books and Articles

Blackstone, J. H., ed., *APICS Dictionary*, 15th ed. (Chicago, IL: APICS, 2016).

Deveny, K., "Man Walked on the Moon but Man Can't Make Enough Devil's Food Cookie Cakes," *Wall Street Journal*, September 28, 1993.

Griffin, A., "PDMA Research on New Product Development Practices: Updating Trends and Benchmarking Best Practices," *Journal of Product Innovation Management* 14 (1997): 429–458.

Hauser, J., and D. Clausing, "The House of Quality," *Harvard Business Review* 66, no. 3 (May–June 1988): 63–73.

Ingrassia, L., "Taming the Monster: How Big Companies Can Change: Keeping Sharp: Gillette Holds Its Edge by Endlessly Searching for a Better Shave," *Wall Street Journal*, December 10, 1992.

Wheelwright, S., and K. Clark, *Revolutionizing Product Development* (New York: Free Press, 1992).

Internet

Apple, *The Story behind Apple's Environmental Footprint*, **www.apple.com/environment/.**

Cargille, B., and C. Fry, "Design for Supply Chain: Spreading the Word across HP," *Supply Chain Management Review*, July–August 2006, **www.strategicmgmtsolutions.com/DfSC-HP.PDF.**

Centers for Disease Control and Prevention, *The History of Malaria, an Ancient Disease*, **www.cdc.gov/malaria/about/history/.**

Domin, H. E., J. Wisner, and M. Marks, "Design for Supply Chain," *Supply and Demand Chain Executive*, December 2, 2007, **www.sdcexec.com/article/10289661/design-for-supply-chain?page=3.**

"Hewlett Packard's Design for Supply Chain Program," *Supply Chain Brain*, December 1, 2005, **www.supplychainbrain.com/content/industry-verticals/high-techelectronics/single-article-page/article/hewlett-packards-design-for-supply-chain-program/.**

Newman, A. A., "Snackwell's Nudges Up the Portion Pack," *New York Times*, April 20, 2011, **www.nytimes.com/2011/04/21/business/media/21adco.html.**

Product Development and Management Association, *The PDMA Glossary for New Product Development*, **www.pdma.org/p/cm/ld/fid=27.**

Vestergaard, *PermaNet*, **www.vestergaard.com/our-products/permanet.**

World Health Organization, *World Malaria Report 2013*, **www.who.int/malaria/publications/world_malaria_report_2013/en/.**

APPENDICES

APPENDIX I NORMAL CURVE AREAS

To find the area under the normal curve, you can apply either Table I.1 or Table I.2. In Table I.1, you must know how many standard deviations that point is to the right of the mean. Then, the area under the normal curve can be read directly from the normal table. For example, the total area under the normal curve for a point that is 1.55 standard deviations to the right of the mean is .93943.

TABLE I.1

	.00	.01	.02	.03	.04	.05	.06	.07	.08	.09
.0	.50000	.50399	.50798	.51197	.51595	.51994	.52392	.52790	.53188	.53586
.1	.53983	.54380	.54776	.55172	.55567	.55962	.56356	.56749	.57142	.57535
.2	.57926	.58317	.58706	.59095	.59483	.59871	.60257	.60642	.61026	.61409
.3	.61791	.62172	.62552	.62930	.63307	.63683	.64058	.64431	.64803	.65173
.4	.65542	.65910	.66276	.66640	.67003	.67364	.67724	.68082	.68439	.68793
.5	.69146	.69497	.69847	.70194	.70540	.70884	.71226	.71566	.71904	.72240
.6	.72575	.72907	.73237	.73536	.73891	.74215	.74537	.74857	.75175	.75490
.7	.75804	.76115	.76424	.76730	.77035	.77337	.77637	.77935	.78230	.78524
.8	.78814	.79103	.79389	.79673	.79955	.80234	.80511	.80785	.81057	.81327
.9	.81594	.81859	.82121	.82381	.82639	.82894	.83147	.83398	.83646	.83891
1.0	.84134	.84375	.84614	.84849	.85083	.85314	.85543	.85769	.85993	.86214
1.1	.86433	.86650	.86864	.87076	.87286	.87493	.87698	.87900	.88100	.88298
1.2	.88493	.88686	.88877	.89065	.89251	.89435	.89617	.89796	.89973	.90147
1.3	.90320	.90490	.90658	.90824	.90988	.91149	.91309	.91466	.91621	.91774
1.4	.91924	.92073	.92220	.92364	.92507	.92647	.92785	.92922	.93056	.93189
1.5	.93319	.93448	.93574	.93699	.93822	.93943	.94062	.94179	.94295	.94408
1.6	.94520	.94630	.94738	.94845	.94950	.95053	.95154	.95254	.95352	.95449
1.7	.95543	.95637	.95728	.95818	.95907	.95994	.96080	.96164	.96246	.96327
1.8	.96407	.96485	.96562	.96638	.96712	.96784	.96856	.96926	.96995	.97062
1.9	.97128	.97193	.97257	.97320	.97381	.97441	.97500	.97558	.97615	.97670
2.0	.97725	.97784	.97831	.97882	.97932	.97982	.98030	.98077	.98124	.98169
2.1	.98214	.98257	.98300	.98341	.98382	.98422	.98461	.98500	.98537	.98574
2.2	.98610	.98645	.98679	.98713	.98745	.98778	.98809	.98840	.98870	.98899
2.3	.98928	.98956	.98983	.99010	.99036	.99061	.99086	.99111	.99134	.99158
2.4	.99180	.99202	.99224	.99245	.99266	.99286	.99305	.99324	.99343	.99361
2.5	.99379	.99396	.99413	.99430	.99446	.99461	.99477	.99492	.99506	.99520
2.6	.99534	.99547	.99560	.99573	.99585	.99598	.99609	.99621	.99632	.99643
2.7	.99653	.99664	.99674	.99683	.99693	.99702	.99711	.99720	.99728	.99736
2.8	.99744	.99752	.99760	.99767	.99774	.99781	.99788	.99795	.99801	.99807
2.9	.99813	.99819	.99825	.99831	.99836	.99841	.99846	.99851	.99856	.99861
3.0	.99865	.99869	.99874	.99878	.99882	.99886	.99899	.99893	.99896	.99900
3.1	.99903	.99906	.99910	.99913	.99916	.99918	.99921	.99924	.99926	.99929
3.2	.99931	.99934	.99936	.99938	.99940	.99942	.99944	.99946	.99948	.99950
3.3	.99952	.99953	.99955	.99957	.99958	.99960	.99961	.99962	.99964	.99965
3.4	.99966	.99968	.99969	.99970	.99971	.99972	.99973	.99974	.99975	.99976
3.5	.99977	.99978	.99978	.99979	.99980	.99981	.99981	.99982	.99983	.99983
3.6	.99984	.99985	.99985	.99986	.99986	.99987	.99987	.99988	.99988	.99989
3.7	.99989	.99990	.99990	.99990	.99991	.99991	.99992	.99992	.99992	.99992
3.8	.99993	.99993	.99993	.99994	.99994	.99994	.99994	.99995	.99995	.99995
3.9	.99995	.99995	.99996	.99996	.99996	.99996	.99996	.99996	.99997	.99997

Source: From Richard I. Levin and Charles A. Kirkpatrick, *Quantitative Approaches to Management*, 4th ed. Copyright © 1978, 1975, 1971, 1965 by McGraw-Hill Education, Inc. Reprinted by permission.

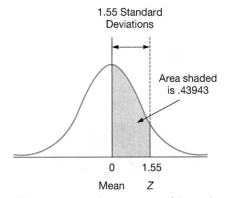

1.55 Standard Deviations

Area shaded is .43943

0   1.55

Mean   Z

As an alternative to Table I.1, the numbers in Table I.2 represent the proportion of the total area away from the mean, μ, to one side. For example, the area between the mean and a point that is 1.55 standard deviations to its right is .43943.

TABLE I.2

Z	.00	.01	.02	.03	.04	.05	.06	.07	.08	.09
0.0	.00000	.00399	.00798	.01197	.01595	.01994	.02392	.02790	.03188	.03586
0.1	.03983	.04380	.04776	.05172	.05567	.05962	.06356	.06749	.07142	.07535
0.2	.07926	.08317	.08706	.09095	.09483	.09871	.10257	.10642	.11026	.11409
0.3	.11791	.12172	.12552	.12930	.13307	.13683	.14058	.14431	.14803	.15173
0.4	.15542	.15910	.16276	.16640	.17003	.17364	.17724	.18082	.18439	.18793
0.5	.19146	.19497	.19847	.20194	.20540	.20884	.21226	.21566	.21904	.22240
0.6	.22575	.22907	.23237	.23565	.23891	.24215	.24537	.24857	.25175	.25490
0.7	.25804	.26115	.26424	.26730	.27035	.27337	.27637	.27935	.28230	.28524
0.8	.28814	.29103	.29389	.29673	.29955	.30234	.30511	.30785	.31057	.31327
0.9	.31594	.31859	.32121	.32381	.32639	.32894	.33147	.33398	.33646	.33891
1.0	.34134	.34375	.34614	.34850	.35083	.35314	.35543	.35769	.35993	.36214
1.1	.36433	.36650	.36864	.37076	.37286	.37493	.37698	.37900	.38100	.38298
1.2	.38493	.38686	.38877	.39065	.39251	.39435	.39617	.39796	.39973	.40147
1.3	.40320	.40490	.40658	.40824	.40988	.41149	.41309	.41466	.41621	.41174
1.4	.41924	.42073	.42220	.42364	.42507	.42647	.42786	.42922	.43056	.43189
1.5	.43319	.43448	.43574	.43699	.43822	.43943	.44062	.44179	.44295	.44408
1.6	.44520	.44630	.44738	.44845	.44950	.45053	.45154	.45254	.45352	.45449
1.7	.45543	.45637	.45728	.45818	.45907	.45994	.46080	.46164	.46246	.46327
1.8	.46407	.46485	.46562	.46638	.46712	.46784	.46856	.46926	.46995	.47062
1.9	.47128	.47193	.47257	.47320	.47381	.47441	.47500	.47558	.47615	.47670
2.0	.47725	.47778	.47831	.47882	.47932	.47982	.48030	.48077	.48124	.48169
2.1	.48214	.48257	.48300	.48341	.48382	.48422	.48461	.48500	.48537	.48574
2.2	.48610	.48645	.48679	.48713	.48745	.48778	.48809	.48840	.48870	.48899
2.3	.48928	.48956	.48983	.49010	.49036	.49061	.49086	.49111	.49134	.49158
2.4	.49180	.49202	.49224	.49245	.49266	.49286	.49305	.49324	.49343	.49361
2.5	.49379	.49396	.49413	.49430	.49446	.49461	.49477	.49492	.49506	.49520
2.6	.49534	.49547	.49560	.49573	.49585	.49598	.49609	.49621	.49632	.49643
2.7	.49653	.49664	.49674	.49683	.49693	.49702	.49711	.49720	.49728	.49736
2.8	.49744	.49752	.49760	.49767	.49774	.49781	.49788	.49795	.49801	.49807
2.9	.49813	.49819	.49825	.49831	.49836	.49841	.49846	.49851	.49856	.49861
3.0	.49865	.49869	.49874	.49878	.49882	.49886	.49889	.49893	.49897	.49900
3.1	.49903	.49906	.49910	.49913	.49916	.49918	.49921	.49924	.49926	.49929

APPENDIX II POISSON DISTRIBUTION VALUES

$$P(X \le c; \lambda) = \sum_{0}^{c} \frac{\lambda^x e^{-\lambda}}{x!}$$

The following table shows 1,000 times the probability of c or fewer occurrences of an event that has an average number of occurrences of λ.

Values of c											
λ	0	1	2	3	4	5	6	7	8	9	10
.02	980	1,000									
.04	961	999	1,000								
.06	942	998	1,000								
.08	923	997	1,000								
.10	905	995	1,000								
.15	861	990	999	1,000							
.20	819	982	999	1,000							
.25	779	974	998	1,000							
.30	741	963	996	1,000							
.35	705	951	994	1,000							
.40	670	938	992	999	1,000						
.45	638	925	989	999	1,000						
.50	607	910	986	998	1,000						
.55	577	894	982	998	1,000						
.60	549	878	977	997	1,000						
.65	522	861	972	996	999	1,000					
.70	497	844	966	994	999	1,000					
.75	472	827	959	993	999	1,000					
.80	449	809	953	991	999	1,000					
.85	427	791	945	989	998	1,000					
.90	407	772	937	987	998	1,000					
.95	387	754	929	984	997	1,000					
1.00	368	736	920	981	996	999	1,000				
1.1	333	699	900	974	995	999	1,000				
1.2	301	663	879	966	992	998	1,000				
1.3	273	627	857	957	989	998	1,000				
1.4	247	592	833	946	986	997	999	1,000			
1.5	223	558	809	934	981	996	999	1,000			
1.6	202	525	783	921	976	994	999	1,000			
1.7	183	493	757	907	970	992	998	1,000			
1.8	165	463	731	891	964	990	997	999	1,000		
1.9	150	434	704	875	956	987	997	999	1,000		
2.0	135	406	677	857	947	983	995	999	1,000		

Source: Adapted from E. L. Grant, *Statistical Quality Control,* McGraw-Hill Book Company, New York (1964). Reprinted by permission.

Values of c

λ	0	1	2	3	4	5	6	7	8	9	10	11	12	13	14	15	16	17	18	19	20	21	22
2.2	111	359	623	819	928	975	993	998	1,000														
2.4	091	308	570	779	904	964	988	997	999	1,000													
2.6	074	267	518	736	877	951	983	995	999	1,000													
2.8	061	231	469	692	848	935	976	992	998	999	1,000												
3.0	050	199	423	647	815	916	966	988	996	999	1,000												
3.2	041	171	380	603	781	895	955	983	994	998	1,000												
3.4	033	147	340	558	744	871	942	977	992	997	999	1,000											
3.6	027	126	303	515	706	844	927	969	988	996	999	1,000											
3.8	022	107	269	473	668	816	909	960	984	994	998	999	1,000										
4.0	018	092	238	433	629	785	889	949	979	992	997	999	1,000										
4.2	015	078	210	395	590	753	867	936	972	989	996	999	1,000										
4.4	012	066	185	359	551	720	844	921	964	985	994	998	999	1,000									
4.6	010	056	163	326	513	686	818	905	955	980	992	997	999	1,000									
4.8	008	048	143	294	476	651	791	887	944	975	990	996	999	1,000									
5.0	007	040	125	265	440	616	762	867	932	968	986	995	998	999	1,000								
5.2	006	034	109	238	406	581	732	845	918	960	982	993	997	999	1,000								
5.4	005	029	095	213	373	546	702	822	903	951	977	990	996	999	1,000								
5.6	004	024	082	191	342	512	670	797	886	941	972	988	995	998	999	1,000							
5.8	003	021	072	170	313	478	638	771	867	929	965	984	993	997	999	1,000							
6.0	002	017	062	151	285	446	606	744	847	916	957	980	991	996	999	999	1,000						
6.2	002	015	054	134	259	414	574	716	826	902	949	975	989	995	998	999	1,000						
6.4	002	012	046	119	235	384	542	687	803	886	939	969	986	994	997	999	1,000						
6.6	001	010	040	105	213	355	511	658	780	869	927	963	982	992	997	999	999	1,000					
6.8	001	009	034	093	192	327	480	628	755	850	915	955	978	990	996	998	999	1,000					
7.0	001	007	030	082	173	301	450	599	729	830	901	947	973	987	994	998	999	1,000					
7.2	001	006	025	072	156	276	420	569	703	810	887	937	967	984	993	997	999	999	1,000				
7.4	001	005	022	063	140	253	392	539	676	788	871	926	961	980	991	996	998	999	1,000				
7.6	001	004	019	055	125	231	365	510	648	765	854	915	954	976	989	995	998	999	1,000				
7.8	000	004	016	048	112	210	338	481	620	741	835	902	945	971	986	993	997	999	1,000				
8.0	000	003	014	042	100	191	313	453	593	717	816	888	936	966	983	992	996	998	999	1,000			
8.5	000	002	009	030	074	150	256	386	523	653	763	849	909	949	973	986	993	997	999	999	1,000		
9.0	000	001	006	021	055	116	207	324	456	587	706	803	876	926	959	978	989	995	998	999	1,000		
9.5	000	001	004	015	040	089	165	269	392	522	645	752	836	898	940	967	982	991	996	998	999	1,000	
10.0	000	000	003	010	029	067	130	220	333	458	583	697	792	864	917	951	973	986	993	997	998	999	1,000

APPENDIX III VALUES OF $e^{-\lambda}$ FOR USE IN THE POISSON DISTRIBUTION

Values of $e^{-\lambda}$

λ	$e^{-\lambda}$	λ	$e^{-\lambda}$	λ	$e^{-\lambda}$	λ	$e^{-\lambda}$
.0	1.0000	1.6	.2019	3.1	.0450	4.6	.0101
.1	.9048	1.7	.1827	3.2	.0408	4.7	.0091
.2	.8187	1.8	.1653	3.3	.0369	4.8	.0082
.3	.7408	1.9	.1496	3.4	.0334	4.9	.0074
.4	.6703	2.0	.1353	3.5	.0302	5.0	.0067
.5	.6065	2.1	.1225	3.6	.0273	5.1	.0061
.6	.5488	2.2	.1108	3.7	.0247	5.2	.0055
.7	.4966	2.3	.1003	3.8	.0224	5.3	.0050
.8	.4493	2.4	.0907	3.9	.0202	5.4	.0045
.9	.4066	2.5	.0821	4.0	.0183	5.5	.0041
1.0	.3679	2.6	.0743	4.1	.0166	5.6	.0037
1.1	.3329	2.7	.0672	4.2	.0150	5.7	.0033
1.2	.3012	2.8	.0608	4.3	.0136	5.8	.0030
1.3	.2725	2.9	.0550	4.4	.0123	5.9	.0027
1.4	.2466	3.0	.0498	4.5	.0111	6.0	.0025
1.5	.2231						

APPENDIX IV TABLE OF RANDOM NUMBERS

52	06	50	88	53	30	10	47	99	37	66	91	35	32	00	84	57	07
37	63	28	02	74	35	24	03	29	60	74	85	90	73	59	55	17	60
82	57	68	28	05	94	03	11	27	79	90	87	92	41	09	25	36	77
69	02	36	49	71	99	32	10	75	21	95	90	94	38	97	71	72	49
98	94	90	36	06	78	23	67	89	85	29	21	25	73	69	34	85	76
96	52	62	87	49	56	59	23	78	71	72	90	57	01	98	57	31	95
33	69	27	21	11	60	95	89	68	48	17	89	34	09	93	50	44	51
50	33	50	95	13	44	34	62	64	39	55	29	30	64	49	44	30	16
88	32	18	50	62	57	34	56	62	31	15	40	90	34	51	95	26	14
90	30	36	24	69	82	51	74	30	35	36	85	01	55	92	64	09	85
50	48	61	18	85	23	08	54	17	12	80	69	24	84	92	16	49	59
27	88	21	62	69	64	48	31	12	73	02	68	00	16	16	46	13	85
45	14	46	32	13	49	66	62	74	41	86	98	92	98	84	54	33	40
81	02	01	78	82	74	97	37	45	31	94	99	42	49	27	64	89	42
66	83	14	74	27	76	03	33	11	97	59	81	72	00	64	61	13	52
74	05	81	82	93	09	96	33	52	78	13	06	28	30	94	23	37	39
30	34	87	01	74	11	46	82	59	94	25	34	32	23	17	01	58	73
59	55	72	33	62	13	74	68	22	44	42	09	32	46	71	79	45	89
67	09	80	98	99	25	77	50	03	32	36	63	65	75	94	19	95	88
60	77	46	63	71	69	44	22	03	85	14	48	69	13	30	50	33	24
60	08	19	29	36	72	30	27	50	64	85	72	75	29	87	05	75	01
80	45	86	99	02	34	87	08	86	84	49	76	24	08	01	86	29	11
53	84	49	63	26	65	72	84	85	63	26	02	75	26	92	62	40	67
69	84	12	94	51	36	17	02	15	29	16	52	56	43	26	22	08	62
37	77	13	10	02	18	31	19	32	85	31	94	81	43	31	58	33	51

Source: Courtesy of Rand Corporation.

Acceptable quality level (AQL) A term used in acceptance sampling to indicate a cut-off value that represents the maximum defect level at which a consumer would always accept a lot.

Acceptance sampling According to APICS, "the process of sampling a portion of goods for inspection rather than examining the entire lot."

Activity on node (AON) diagram A network diagram in which each activity is represented by a node, or box, and the precedence relationships between various activities are represented with arrows.

Adjusted exponential smoothing model An expanded version of the exponential smoothing model that includes a trend adjustment factor.

Aggregate planning *See* sales and operations planning (S&OP).

Agility The ability to recalculate plans in the face of market, demand, and supply volatility and deliver the same or comparable cost, quality, and customer service.

Anticipation inventory Inventory that is held in anticipation of customer demand.

Appraisal costs Costs a company incurs for assessing its quality levels.

Assemble-to-order (ATO) or finish-to-order products Products that are customized only at the very end of the manufacturing process.

Assignment problem A specialized form of an optimization model that attempts to assign limited capacity to various demand points in a way that minimizes costs.

Assortment warehousing A form of warehousing in which a wide array of goods is held close to the source of demand in order to ensure short customer lead times.

Attribute A characteristic of an outcome or item that is accounted for by its presence or absence, such as "defective" versus "good" or "late" versus "on-time."

Available to promise (ATP) A field in the master schedule record that indicates the number of units that are available for sale each week, given those that have already been promised to customers.

Back room The part of a service operation that is completed without direct customer contact.

Backward pass The determination of the latest finish and start times for each project activity.

Bar graph A graphical representation of data that places observations into specific categories.

Batch manufacturing A type of manufacturing process where items are moved through the different manufacturing steps in groups, or batches.

Benchmarking According to Cook, "the process of identifying, understanding, and adapting outstanding practices from within the same organization or from other businesses to help improve performance."

Bill of material (BOM) According to APICS, "a listing of all the subassemblies, intermediates, parts, and raw materials that go into a parent assembly showing the quantity of each required to make an assembly."

Black belt A fully trained Six Sigma expert "with up to 160 hours of training who perform[s] much of the technical analyses required of Six Sigma projects, usually on a full-time basis."

Black box design A situation in which suppliers are provided with general requirements and are asked to fill in the technical specifications.

Booked orders In the context of master scheduling, confirmed demand for products.

Bottom-up planning An approach to S&OP that is used when the product/service mix is unstable and resource requirements vary greatly across the offerings. Under such conditions, managers will need to estimate the requirements for each set of products or services separately and then add them up to get an overall picture of the resource requirements.

Break-bulk warehousing A specialized form of cross-docking in which the incoming shipments are from a single source or manufacturer.

Break-even point The volume level for a business at which total revenues cover total costs.

Build-up forecast A qualitative forecasting technique in which individuals familiar with specific market segments estimate the demand within these segments. These individual forecasts are then added up to get an overall forecast.

Bullwhip effect According to APICS, "an extreme change in the supply position upstream in a supply chain generated by a small change in demand downstream in the supply chain."

Business process management systems (BPMS) products According to Harmon, "software tools that allow analysts to model processes and . . . then automate the execution of the process at run time."

Business process modeling tools According to Harmon, "software tools that aid business teams in the analysis, modeling, and redesign of business processes."

Business process reengineering (BPR) According to APICS, "a procedure that involves the fundamental rethinking and radical redesign of business processes to achieve dramatic organizational improvements in such critical measures of performance as cost, quality, service, and speed."

Business strategy The strategy that identifies a firm's targeted customers and sets time frames and performance objectives for the business.

Capacity The capability of a worker, a machine, a work-center, a plant, or an organization to produce output in a time period.

Causal forecasting model A class of quantitative forecasting models in which the forecast is modeled as a function of something other than time.

Cause-and-effect diagram A graphical tool used to categorize the possible causes for a particular result.

Cellular layout A type of layout typically used in group technology settings in which resources are physically arranged according to the dominant flow of activities for the product family.

Champion A senior-level executive who "owns" a Six Sigma project and has the authority and resources needed to carry it out.

Changeover flexibility The ability to provide a new product with minimal delay.

Chase production plan A sales and operations plan in which production is changed in each time period to match the sales forecast.

Check sheet A sheet used to record how frequently a certain event occurs.

Cloud computing According to a National Institute of Standards and Technology (NIST) report, "a model for enabling ubiquitous, convenient, on-demand network access to a shared pool of configurable computing resources (e.g., networks, servers, storage, applications, and services) that can be rapidly provisioned and released with minimal management effort or service provider interaction."

Collaborative planning, forecasting, and replenishment (CPFR) A set of business processes, backed up by information technology, in which supply chain partners agree to *mutual* business objectives and measures, develop *joint* sales and operational plans, and *collaborate* to generate and update sales forecasts and replenishment plans.

Commercial preparation phase The fourth phase of a product development effort. At this stage, firms start to invest heavily in the operations and supply chain resources needed to support the new product or service.

Common carrier Also known as a public carrier, a transportation service provider that handles shipments on a case-by-case basis, without the need for long-term agreements or contracts.

Competitive benchmarking The comparison of an organization's processes with those of competing organizations.

Computer-aided design (CAD) system An information system that allows engineers to develop, modify, share, and even test designs in a virtual world. CAD systems help

organizations avoid the time and expense of paper-based drawings and physical prototypes.

Computer-aided design/computer-aided manufacturing (CAD/CAM) system An extension of CAD. Here, CAD-based designs are translated into machine instructions, which are then fed automatically into computer-controlled manufacturing equipment.

Concept development phase The first phase of a product development effort. Here a company identifies ideas for new or revised products and services.

Concept phase The first of five phases of a project. Here, project planners develop a broad definition of what the project is and what its scope will be.

Concurrent engineering An alternative to sequential development in which activities in different development stages are allowed to overlap with one another, thereby shortening the total development time.

Conformance perspective A quality perspective that focuses on whether or not a product was made or a service was performed *as intended.*

Conformance quality A subdimension of quality that addresses whether a product was made or a service performed to specifications.

Consolidation warehousing A form of warehousing that pulls together shipments from a number of sources (often plants) in the same geographic area and combines them into larger—and hence more economical—shipping loads.

Constraint (a) Within the context of optimization modeling, a quantifiable condition that places limitations on the set of possible solutions. The solution to an optimization model is acceptable only if it does not break any of the constraints. (b) The process step (or steps) that limits throughput for an entire process chain.

Consumer's risk (β) A term used in acceptance sampling to indicate the probability of accepting a lot with quality worse than the LTPD level.

Continuous flow process A type of manufacturing process that closely resembles a production line process. The main difference is the form of the product, which usually *cannot* be broken into discrete units. Examples include yarns and fabric, food products, and chemical products such as oil or gas.

Continuous improvement (a) A principle of TQM that assumes there will always be room for improvement, no matter how well an organization is doing. (b) The philosophy that small, incremental improvements can add up to significant performance improvements over time.

Continuous review system An inventory system used to manage independent demand inventory. The inventory level for an item is constantly monitored, and when the reorder point is reached, an order is released.

Continuous variable A variable that can be measured along a continuous scale, such as weight, length, height, and temperature.

Contract carrier A transportation service provider that handles shipments for other firms based on long-term agreements or contracts.

Control chart A specialized run chart that helps an organization track changes in key measures over time.

Control limits The upper and lower limits of a control chart. They are calculated so that if a sample falls inside the control limits, the process is considered in control.

Core competency An organizational strength or ability, developed over a long period, that customers find valuable and competitors find difficult or even impossible to copy.

Corporate social responsibility The economic, legal, ethical, and discretionary expectations that society has of organizations at a given point in time.

Cost of goods sold (COGS) The purchased cost of goods from outside suppliers.

Cost-based contract A type of purchasing contract in which the price of a good or service is tied to the cost of some key input(s) or other economic factors, such as interest rates.

Crashing Shortening the overall duration of a project by reducing the time it takes to perform certain activities.

Critical activity A project activity for which the earliest start time and latest start time are equal. A critical activity cannot be delayed without lengthening the overall project duration.

Critical path A network path that has the longest, or is tied for the longest, linked sequence of activities.

Critical path method (CPM) A network-based technique in which there is a single time estimate for each activity. An alternative approach is PERT, which has multiple time estimates for each activity.

Cross sourcing A sourcing strategy in which a company uses a single supplier for one particular part or service and another supplier with the same capabilities for a different part or service, with the understanding that each supplier can act as a backup for the other supplier.

Cross-docking A form of warehousing in which large incoming shipments are received and then broken down into smaller outgoing shipments to demand points in a geographic area. Cross-docking combines the economies of large incoming shipments with the flexibility of smaller local shipments.

Customer relationship management (CRM) A term that broadly refers to planning and control activities and information systems that link a firm with its downstream customers.

Customs broker An agent who handles customs requirements on behalf of another firm. In the United States, customs brokers must be licensed by the Customs Service.

Cycle stock Components or products that are received in bulk by a downstream partner, gradually used up, and then replenished again in bulk by the upstream partner.

Cycle time (a) The total elapsed time needed to complete a business process. Also called throughput time. (b) For a line process, the actual time between completions of successive units on a production line.

Decision support systems (DSS) Computer-based information systems that allow users to analyze, manipulate, and present data in a manner that aids higher-level decision making.

Decision tree A visual tool that decision makers use to evaluate capacity decisions. The main advantage of a decision tree is that it enables users to see the interrelationships between decisions and possible outcomes.

Decision variables Within the context of optimization modeling, variables that will be manipulated to find the best solution.

Delivery reliability A performance dimension that refers to the ability to deliver products or services when promised.

Delivery speed A performance dimension that refers to how quickly the operations or supply chain function can fulfill a need once it has been identified.

Delivery window The acceptable time range in which deliveries can be made.

Delphi method A qualitative forecasting technique in which experts work individually to develop forecasts. The individual forecasts are shared among the group, and then each participant is allowed to modify his or her forecast based on information from the other experts. This process is repeated until consensus is reached.

Demand uncertainty The risk of significant and unpredictable fluctuations in downstream demand.

Dependent demand inventory Inventory items whose demand levels are tied directly to a company's planned production of another item.

Description by brand A description method that is used when a product or service is proprietary or when there is a perceived advantage to using a particular supplier's products or services.

Description by market grade/industry standard A description method that is used when the requirements are well understood and there is common agreement between supply chain partners about what certain terms mean.

Description by performance characteristics A description method that focuses attention on the outcomes the customer wants rather than on the precise configuration of the product or service.

Description by specification A description method that is used when an organization needs to provide very detailed descriptions of the characteristics of an item or a service.

Design and development phase The third phase of a product development effort. Here the company starts to invest heavily in the development effort and builds and evaluates prototypes.

Design for maintainability (DFMt) The systematic consideration of maintainability issues over a product's projected life cycle in the design and development process.

Design for manufacturability (DFM) The systematic consideration of manufacturing issues in the design and development process, facilitating the fabrication of the product's components and their assembly into the overall product.

Design for Six Sigma (DFSS) An approach to product and process design which seeks to ensure that the organization is capable of providing products or services that meet Six Sigma quality levels—in general, no more than 3.4 defects per million opportunities.

Design for the environment (DFE) An approach to new product design that addresses environmental, safety, and health issues over the product's projected life cycle in the design and development process.

Detailed planning and control Planning that covers time periods ranging from weeks down to just a few hours out.

Development process A process that seeks to improve the performance of primary and support processes.

Direct costs Costs tied directly to the level of operations or supply chain activities, such as the production of a good or service, or transportation.

Direct truck shipment A shipment made directly, with no additional stops, changing of trucks, or loading of additional cargo.

Distribution requirements planning (DRP) A time-phased planning approach similar to MRP that uses planned orders at the point of demand (customer, warehouse, etc.) to determine forecasted demand at the source level (often a plant).

DMADV (Define–Measure–Analyze–Design–Verify) A Six Sigma process that outlines the steps needed to create *completely new* business processes or products.

DMAIC (Define–Measure–Analyze–Improve–Control) A Six Sigma process that outlines the steps that should be followed to improve an *existing* business process.

Downstream A term used to describe activities or firms that are positioned *later* in the supply chain relative to some other activity or firm of interest. For example, sewing a shirt takes place downstream of weaving the fabric, and weaving the fabric takes place downstream of harvesting the cotton.

Dual sourcing A sourcing strategy in which two suppliers are used for the same purchased product or service.

Earliest finish time (EF) The earliest an activity can be finished, calculated by adding the activity's duration to its earliest start time.

Earliest start time (ES) The earliest an activity can be started, as determined by the earliest finish time for all immediate predecessors.

Economic order quantity (EOQ) The order quantity that minimizes annual holding and ordering costs for an item.

Efficiency A measure of process performance; the ratio of actual outputs to standard outputs. Usually expressed in percentage terms.

Electronic commerce Also called *e-commerce.* "The use of computer and telecommunications technologies to conduct business via electronic transfer of data and documents."

Electronic data interchange (EDI) An information technology that allows supply chain partners to transfer data electronically between their information systems.

Electronic funds transfer (EFT) The automatic transfer of payment from a buyer's bank account to a supplier's bank account.

Employee empowerment Giving employees the responsibility, authority, training, and tools necessary to manage quality.

Engineer-to-order (ETO) products Products that are designed and produced from the start to meet unusual customer needs or requirements. They represent the highest level of customization.

Engineering change A revision to a drawing or design released by engineering to modify or correct a part.

Enterprise resource planning (ERP) systems Large, integrated, computer-based business transaction processing and reporting systems. ERP systems pull together all of the classic business functions such as accounting, finance, sales, and operations into a single, tightly integrated package that uses a common database.

Expected value A calculation that summarizes the expected costs, revenues, or profits of a capacity alternative, based on several demand levels, each of which has a different probability.

Exploding the BOM The process of working backward from the master production schedule for a level 0 item to determine the quantity and timing of orders for the various subassemblies and components. Exploding the BOM is the underlying logic used by MRP.

Exponential smoothing model A special form of the moving average model in which the forecast for the next period is calculated as the weighted average of the current period's actual value and forecast.

External failure costs Costs incurred by defects that are not detected until a product or service reaches the customer.

First-tier supplier A supplier that provides products or services directly to a firm.

Five Ms The five main branches of a typical cause-and-effect diagram: manpower, methods, materials, machines, and measurement.

Five Whys An approach used during the narrow phase of root cause analysis, in which teams brainstorm successive answers to the question "Why is this a cause of the original problem?" The name comes from the general observation that the questioning process can require up to five rounds.

Fixed costs   The expenses an organization incurs regardless of the level of business activity.

Fixed-position layout   A type of manufacturing process in which the position of the product is fixed. Materials, equipment, and workers are transported to and from the product.

Fixed-price contract   A type of purchasing contract in which the stated price does not change, regardless of fluctuations in general overall economic conditions, industry competition, levels of supply, market prices, or other environmental changes.

Flexibility   A performance dimension that considers how quickly operations and supply chains can respond to the unique needs of customers.

Flexible manufacturing systems (FMSs)   Highly automated batch processes that can reduce the cost of making groups of similar products.

Forecast   An estimate of the future level of some variable. Common variables that are forecasted include demand levels, supply levels, and prices.

Forecasted demand   In the context of master scheduling, a company's best estimate of the demand in any period.

Forward pass   The determination of the earliest start and finish times for each project activity.

Freight forwarder   An agent who serves as an intermediary between an organization shipping a product and the actual carrier, typically on international shipments.

Front room   The physical or virtual point where the customer interfaces directly with the service organization.

Functional layout   A type of layout where resources are physically grouped by function.

Functional strategy   A strategy that translates a business strategy into specific actions for functional areas such as marketing, human resources, and finance. Functional strategies should align with the overall business strategy and with each other.

Gantt chart   A graphical tool used to show expected start and end times for project activities and to track actual progress against these time targets.

Gray box design   A situation in which a supplier works with a customer to jointly design the product.

Green belt   An individual who has some basic training in Six Sigma methodologies and tools and is assigned to a project on a part-time basis.

Group technology   A type of manufacturing process that seeks to achieve the efficiencies of a line process in a batch environment by dedicating equipment and personnel to the manufacture of products with similar manufacturing characteristics.

Hedge inventory   According to APICS, a "form of inventory buildup to buffer against some event that may not happen. Hedge inventory planning involves speculation related to potential labor strikes, price increases, unsettled governments, and events that could severely impair the company's strategic initiatives."

Histogram   A special form of bar chart that tracks the number of observations that fall within a certain interval.

Hub-and-spoke system   A form of warehousing in which strategically placed hubs are used as sorting or transfer facilities. The hubs are typically located at convenient, high-traffic locations. The "spokes" refer to the routes serving the destinations associated with the hubs.

Hybrid manufacturing process   A general term referring to a manufacturing process that seeks to combine the characteristics, and hence advantages, of more than one of the classic processes. Examples include flexible manufacturing systems, machining centers, and group technology.

Independent demand inventory   Inventory items whose demand levels are beyond a company's complete control.

Indifference point   The output level at which two capacity alternatives generate equal costs.

Indirect costs   Costs that are not tied directly to the level of operations or supply chain activity.

Industry analysis   Profiles the major forces and trends that are impacting an industry, including pricing, competition, regulatory forces, substitution, technology changes, and supply/demand trends.

Information system (IS)   According to Laudon and Laudon, "a set of interrelated components that collect (or retrieve), process, store, and distribute information to support decision making, coordination, and control in an organization."

Infrastructural element   One of two major decision categories addressed by a strategy. Includes the policies, people, decision rules, and organizational structure choices made by a firm.

Insourcing   The use of resources within the firm to provide products or services.

Internal failure costs   Costs caused by defects that occur prior to delivery to the customer, including money spent on repairing or reworking defective products, as well as time wasted on these activities.

Internal supply chain management   A term that refers to the information flows between higher and lower levels of planning and control systems within an organization.

Internet of Things (IoT)   According to *Business Insider*, "a network of internet-connected objects able to collect and exchange data using embedded sensors."

Inventory   According to APICS, "those stocks or items used to support production (raw materials and work-in-process items), supporting activities (maintenance, repair, and operating supplies) and customer service (finished goods and spare parts)."

Inventory drivers Business conditions that force companies to hold inventory.

Inventory pooling Holding safety stock in a single location instead of multiple locations. Several locations then share safety stock inventories to lower overall holding costs by reducing overall safety stock levels.

ISO 9000 A family of standards, supported by the International Organization for Standardization, representing an international consensus on good quality management practices. ISO 9000 addresses business processes rather than specific outcomes.

Job sequencing rules Rules used to determine the order in which jobs should be processed when resources are limited and multiple jobs are waiting to be done.

Job shop A type of manufacturing process used to make a wide variety of highly customized products in quantities as small as one. Job shops are characterized by general-purpose equipment and workers who are broadly skilled.

Just-in-time (JIT) A philosophy of manufacturing based on planned elimination of all waste and on continuous improvement of productivity. In a broad sense, it applies to all forms of manufacturing and to many service industries as well. Used synonymously with *Lean*.

Kanban system A production control approach that uses containers, cards, or visual cues to control the production and movement of goods through the supply chain.

Lag capacity strategy A capacity strategy in which capacity is added only after demand has materialized.

Landed cost The cost of a product plus all costs driven by logistics activities, such as transportation, warehousing, handling, customs fees, and the like.

Latest finish time (LF) The latest an activity can be finished and still finish the project on time, as determined by the latest start time for all immediate successors.

Latest start time (LS) The latest an activity can be started and still finish the project on time, calculated by subtracting the activity's duration from its latest finish time.

Launch phase The final phase of a product development effort. For physical products, this usually means "filling up" the supply chain with products. For services, it can mean making the service broadly available to the target marketplace.

Law of variability According to Roger Schmenner and Morgan Swink, "The greater the random variability either demanded of the process or inherent in the process itself or in the items processed, the less productive the process is." This law is relevant to customization because completing upstream activities offline helps isolate these activities from the variability caused by either the timing or the unique requirements of individual customers.

Lead capacity strategy A capacity strategy in which capacity is added in anticipation of demand.

Lean A philosophy of production that emphasizes the minimization of the amount of all the resources (including time) used in the various activities of an enterprise. It involves identifying and eliminating non-value-adding activities in design, production, supply chain management, and dealing with customers. Used synonymously with *JIT*.

Lean Six Sigma A methodology that combines the organizational elements and tools of Six Sigma with Lean's focus on waste reduction.

Lean supply chain management An extension of the Lean philosophy to supply chain efforts beyond production. Lean supply chain management seeks to minimize the level of resources required to carry out *all* supply chain activities.

Learning curve theory A body of theory based on applied statistics which suggests that productivity levels can improve at a predictable rate as people and even systems "learn" to do tasks more efficiently. In formal terms, learning curve theory states that for every doubling of cumulative output, there is a set percentage reduction in the amount of inputs required.

Less than truckload (LTL) shipment A smaller shipment, often combined with other loads to reduce costs and improve truck efficiencies.

Level production plan A sales and operations plan in which production is held constant and inventory is used to absorb differences between production and the sales forecast.

Life cycle analogy method A qualitative forecasting technique that attempts to identify the time frames and demand levels for the introduction, growth, maturity, and decline life cycle stages of a new product or service.

Linear regression A statistical technique that expresses a forecast variable as a linear function of some independent variable. Linear regression can be used to develop both time series and causal forecasting models.

Load profile A display of future capacity requirements based on released and/or planned orders over a given span of time.

Logistics management According to the Council of Supply Chain Management Professionals (CSCMP), "that part of supply chain management that plans, implements, and controls the efficient, effective forward and reverse flow and storage of goods, services, and related information between the point of origin and the point of consumption in order to meet customers' requirements."

Logistics strategy A functional strategy which ensures that an organization's logistics choices—transportation, warehousing, information systems, and even form of ownership—are consistent with its overall business strategy and support the performance dimensions that targeted customers most value.

Lot tolerance percent defective (LTPD) A term used in acceptance sampling to indicate the highest defect level a consumer is willing to "tolerate."

Lower tolerance limit (LTL) The lowest acceptable value for some measure of interest.

Machining center A type of manufacturing process that completes several manufacturing steps without removing an item from the process.

Make-or-buy decision A high-level, often strategic, decision regarding which products or services will be provided internally and which will be provided by external supply chain partners.

Make-to-order (MTO) products Products that use standard components but have customer-specific final *configuration* of those components.

Make-to-stock (MTS) products Products that require no customization. They are typically generic products and are produced in large enough volumes to justify keeping a finished goods inventory.

Mapping The process of developing graphic representations of the organizational relationships and/or activities that make up a business process.

Market survey A structured questionnaire submitted to potential customers, often to gauge potential demand.

Master black belt A full-time Six Sigma expert who is "responsible for Six Sigma strategy, training, mentoring, deployment and results."

Master production schedule (MPS) The amount of product that will be finished and available for sale at the beginning of each week. The master production schedule drives more detailed planning activities, such as material requirements planning.

Master scheduling A detailed planning process that tracks production output and matches this output to actual customer orders.

Match capacity strategy A capacity strategy that strikes a balance between the lead and lag capacity strategies by avoiding periods of high under- or overutilization.

Material handling system A system that includes the equipment and procedures needed to move goods *within* a facility, *between* a facility and a transportation mode, and *between* different transportation modes (e.g., ship-to-truck transfers).

Material requirements planning (MRP) A planning process that translates the master production schedule into planned orders for the actual parts and components needed to produce the master schedule items.

Maverick spending Spending that occurs when internal customers purchase directly from nonqualified suppliers and bypass established purchasing procedures.

Merchandise inventory A balance sheet item that shows the amount a company paid for the inventory it has on hand at a particular point in time.

Milestone A performance or time target for each major group of activities in a project.

Mission statement A statement that explains why an organization exists. It describes what is important to the organization, called its core values, and identifies the organization's domain.

Mix flexibility The ability to produce a wide range of products or services.

Mixed production plan A sales and operations plan that varies both production and inventory levels in an effort to develop the most effective plan.

Modular architecture A product architecture in which each functional element maps into its own physical chunk. Different chunks perform different functions; the interactions between the chunks are minimal, and they are generally well defined.

Move card A kanban card that is used to indicate when a container of parts should be moved to the next process step.

Moving average model A time series forecasting model that derives a forecast by taking an average of recent demand values.

MRP nervousness A term used to refer to the observation that any change, even a small one, in the requirements for items at the top of the bill of material can have drastic effects on items further down the bill of material.

Muda A Japanese term meaning waste.

Multicriteria decision models Models that allow decision makers to evaluate various alternatives across multiple decision criteria.

Multifactor productivity A productivity score that measures output levels relative to more than one input.

Multimodal solution A transportation solution that seeks to exploit the strengths of multiple transportation modes through physical, information, and monetary flows that are as seamless as possible.

Multiple regression A generalized form of linear regression that allows for more than one independent variable.

Multiple sourcing A sourcing strategy in which the buying firm shares its business across multiple suppliers.

Net cash flow The net flow of dollars into or out of a business over some time period.

Network design applications Logistics information systems that address such long-term strategic questions as facility location and sizing, as well as transportation networks. These applications often make use of simulation and optimization modeling.

Network diagram A graphical tool that shows the logical linkages between activities in a project.

Network path A logically linked sequence of activities in a network diagram.

Objective function A quantitative function that an optimization model seeks to optimize (i.e., maximize or minimize).

Offloading A strategy for reducing and smoothing out workforce requirements that involves having customers perform part of the work themselves.

Operating characteristics (OC) curve A curve used in acceptance sampling to show the probability of accepting a lot, given the actual fraction defective in the entire lot and the sampling plan being used. Different sampling plans will result in different OC curves.

Operations and supply chain strategy A functional strategy that indicates how structural and infrastructural elements within the operations and supply chain areas will be acquired and developed to support the overall business strategy.

Operations function Also called *operations*. The collection of people, technology, and systems within an organization that has primary responsibility for providing the organization's products or services.

Operations management "The planning, scheduling, and control of the activities that transform inputs into finished goods and services."

Optimization model A type of mathematical model used when the user seeks to optimize some objective function subject to some constraints.

Order qualifier A performance dimension on which customers expect a minimum level of performance. Superior performance on an order qualifier will not, by itself, give a company a competitive advantage.

Order winner A performance dimension that differentiates a company's products and services from its competitors. Firms win a customer's business by providing superior levels of performance on order winners.

Outsourcing The use of supply chain partners to provide products or services.

p chart A specific type of control chart for attributes that is used to track sample proportions.

Packaging From a logistics perspective, the way goods and materials are packed in order to facilitate physical, informational, and monetary flows through the supply chain.

Panel consensus forecasting A qualitative forecasting technique that brings experts together to discuss and develop a forecast.

Parent/child relationship The logical linkage between higher- and lower-level items in the BOM.

Pareto chart A special form of bar chart that shows frequency counts from highest to lowest.

Parts standardization The planned elimination of superficial, accidental, and deliberate differences between similar parts in the interest of reducing part and supplier proliferation.

Percent value-added time A measure of process performance; the percentage of total cycle time that is spent on activities that actually provide value.

Perfect order A term used to refer to the timely, error-free provision of a product or service in good condition.

Performance phase The fourth of five phases of a project. In this phase, the organization actually starts to execute the project plan.

Performance quality A subdimension of quality that addresses the basic operating characteristics of a product or service.

Periodic review system An inventory system that is used to manage independent demand inventory. The inventory level for an item is checked at regular intervals and restocked to some predetermined level.

Planning and control A set of tactical and execution-level business activities that includes master scheduling, material requirements planning, and some form of production activity control and vendor order management.

Planning horizon The amount of time the master schedule record or MRP record extends into the future. In general, the longer the production and supplier lead times, the longer the planning horizon must be.

Planning lead time In the context of MRP, the time from when a component is ordered until it arrives and is ready to use.

Planning phase (a) The second phase of a product development effort. Here the company begins to address the feasibility of a product or service. (b) The third of five phases of a project. Here, project planners prepare detailed plans that identify activities, time and budget targets, and the resources needed to complete each task. This phase also includes putting in place the organization that will carry out the project.

Planning values Values that decision makers use to translate a sales forecast into resource requirements and to determine the feasibility and costs of alternative sales and operations plans.

Portfolio analysis A structured approach used by decision makers to develop a sourcing strategy for a product or service, based on the value potential and the relative complexity or risk represented by a sourcing opportunity.

Postcompletion phase The fifth of five phases of a project. This is the phase in which the project manager or team confirms the final outcome, conducts a postimplementation meeting to critique the project and personnel, and reassigns project personnel.

Postponement warehousing A form of warehousing that combines classic warehouse operations with light manufacturing and packaging duties to allow firms to put off final assembly or packaging of goods until the last possible moment.

Preferred supplier A supplier that has demonstrated its performance capabilities through previous purchase contracts and therefore receives preference during the supplier selection process.

Presourcing The process of preapproving suppliers for specific commodities or parts.

Prevention costs The costs an organization incurs to actually prevent defects from occurring to begin with.

Primary process A process that addresses the main value-added activities of an organization.

Priority rules Rules for determining which customer, job, or product is processed next in a waiting line environment.

Process According to APICS, "a set of logically related tasks or activities performed to achieve a defined business outcome."

Process benchmarking The comparison of an organization's processes with those of noncompetitors that have been identified as superior processes.

Process capability index (C_{pk}) A mathematical determination of the capability of a process to meet certain tolerance limits.

Process capability ratio (C_p) A mathematical determination of the capability of a process to meet certain quality standards. A $C_p \geq 1$ means the process is capable of meeting the standard being measured.

Process map A detailed map that identifies the specific activities that make up the informational, physical, and/or monetary flow of a process.

Procure-to-pay cycle The set of activities required to first identify a need, assign a supplier to meet that need, approve the specification or scope, acknowledge receipt, and submit payment to the supplier.

Producer's risk (α) A term used in acceptance sampling to indicate the probability of rejecting a lot with quality better than the AQL level.

Product design The characteristics or features of a product or service that determine its ability to meet the needs of the user.

Product development process According to the PDMA, "a disciplined and defined set of tasks, steps, and phases that describe the normal means by which a company repetitively converts embryonic ideas into salable products or services."

Product family In group technology, a set of products with very similar manufacturing requirements.

Product structure tree A record or graphical rendering that shows how the components in the BOM are put together to make the level 0 item.

Product-based layout A type of layout where resources are arranged sequentially, according to the steps required to make a product.

Production card A kanban card that is used to indicate when another container of parts should be produced.

Production line A type of manufacturing process used to produce a narrow range of standard items with identical or highly similar designs.

Productivity A measure of process performance; the ratio of outputs to inputs.

Profit leverage effect A term used to describe the effect of $1 in cost savings increasing pretax profits by $1 and a $1 increase in sales increasing pretax profits only by $1 multiplied by the pretax profit margin.

Profit margin The ratio of earnings to sales for a given time period.

Program evaluation and review technique (PERT) A network-based technique in which there are multiple time estimates for each activity. An alternative approach is CPM, which has a single time estimate for each activity.

Project According to PMI, "a temporary endeavor undertaken to create a unique product, service, or result." Unlike other business activities, a project has a clear starting point and ending point, after which the people and resources dedicated to the project are reassigned.

Project definition phase The second of five phases in a project. Here, project planners identify how to accomplish the work, how to organize for the project, the key personnel and resources required to support the project, tentative schedules, and tentative budget requirements.

Project management According to PMI, "the application of knowledge, skills, tools and techniques to project activities to meet project requirements."

Projected ending inventory A field in the master schedule record that indicates estimated inventory level at the end of each time period.

Proportion A measure that refers to the presence or absence of a particular characteristic.

Pull system A production system in which actual downstream demand sets off a chain of events that pulls material through the various process steps.

Pup trailer A type of truck trailer that is half the size of a regular truck trailer.

Purchase order PO A document that authorizes a supplier to deliver a product or service and often includes key terms and conditions, such as price, delivery, and quality requirements.

Qualitative forecasting techniques Forecasting techniques based on intuition or informed opinion. These techniques are used when data are scarce, not available, or irrelevant.

Quality (a) The characteristics of a product or service that bear on its ability to satisfy stated or implied needs. (b) A product or service that is free of deficiencies.

Quality assurance   The specific actions firms take to ensure that their products, services, and processes meet the quality requirements of their customers.

Quality function deployment (QFD)   (a) A graphical tool used to help organizations move from vague notions of what customers want to specific engineering and operational requirements. Also called the "house of quality." (b) A technique used to translate customer requirements into technical requirements for each stage of product development and production.

Quantitative forecasting models   Forecasting models that use measurable, historical data to generate forecasts. Quantitative forecasting models can be divided into two major types: time series models and causal models.

R chart   A specific type of control chart for a continuous variable that is used to track how much the individual observations within each sample vary.

Randomness   In the context of forecasting, unpredictable movement from one time period to the next.

Range (R)   A key measure that represents the variation of a specific sample group, used in conjunction with sample average $(\overline{X})$.

Rated capacity   The long-term, expected output capability of a resource or system.

Reliability quality   A subdimension of quality that addresses whether a product will work for a long time without failing or requiring maintenance.

Request for information (RFI)   An inquiry to a potential supplier about that supplier's products or services for potential use in the business. The inquiry can provide certain business requirements or be of a more exploratory nature.

Request for quotation (RFQ)   A formal request for the suppliers to prepare bids, based on the terms and conditions set by the buyer.

Return on assets (ROA)   A measure of financial performance, generally defined as earnings/total assets. Higher ROA values are preferred because they indicate that the firm is able to generate higher earnings from the same asset base.

Reverse logistics system   According to APICS, "a complete supply chain dedicated to the reverse flow of products and materials for the purpose of returns, repair, remanufacture, and/or recycling."

Roadrailer   A specialized rail car the size of a standard truck trailer that can be quickly switched from rail to ground transportation by changing the wheels.

Robust design   According to the PDMA, "the design of products to be less sensitive to variations, including manufacturing variation and misuse, increasing the probability that they will perform as intended."

Rolling planning horizon   A planning approach in which an organization updates its sales and operations plan regularly, such as on a monthly or quarterly basis.

Root cause analysis   A process by which organizations brainstorm about possible causes of problems (referred to as "effects") and then, through structured analyses and data-gathering efforts, gradually narrow the focus to a few root causes.

Rough-cut capacity planning   A capacity planning technique that uses the master production schedule to monitor key resource requirements.

Run chart   A graphical representation that tracks changes in a key measure over time.

Safety stock   Extra inventory that a company holds to protect itself against uncertainties in either demand or replenishment time.

Sales and operations planning (S&OP)   A process to develop tactical plans by integrating marketing plans for new and existing products with the management of the supply chain. The process brings together all the plans for the business into one integrated set of plans. Also called *aggregate planning*.

Sample average $(\overline{X})$ A key measure that represents the central tendency of a group of samples used in conjunction with range (R).

Scatter plot   A graphical representation of the relationship between two variables.

Seasonality   A repeated pattern of spikes or drops in a time series associated with certain times of the year.

Second-tier supplier   A supplier that provides products or services to a firm's first-tier supplier.

Sequential development process   A process in which a product or service idea must clear specific hurdles before it can go on to the next development phase.

Service level   A term used to indicate the amount of demand to be met under conditions of demand and supply uncertainty.

Service package   A package that includes all the value-added *physical* and *intangible* activities that a service organization provides to the customer.

Serviceability   The ease with which parts can be replaced, serviced, or evaluated.

Single sourcing   A sourcing strategy in which the buying firm depends on a single company for all or nearly all of a particular item or service.

Single-factor productivity   A productivity score that measures output levels relative to single input.

Single-period inventory system   A system used when demand occurs in only a single point in time.

Six Sigma methodology   According to Motorola, a business improvement methodology that focuses an organization on understanding and managing customer requirements, aligning key business processes to achieve those requirements, utilizing rigorous data analysis to understand and ultimately minimize variation in those processes, and driving rapid and sustainable improvement to business processes.

Six Sigma quality A level of quality that indicates that a process is well controlled. The term is usually associated with Motorola, which named one of its key operational initiatives Six Sigma Quality.

Slack time The difference between an activity's latest start time (*LS*) and earliest start time (*ES*). Slack time indicates the amount of allowable delay. Critical activities have a slack time of 0.

Smoothing inventory Inventory that is used to smooth out differences between upstream production levels and downstream demand.

Smoothing model Another name for a moving average model. The name refers to the fact that using averages to generate forecasts results in forecasts that are less susceptible to random fluctuations in demand.

Spend analysis The application of quantitative techniques to purchasing data in an effort to better understand spending patterns and identify opportunities for improvement.

Spot stock warehousing A form of warehousing that attempts to position seasonal goods close to the marketplace. At the end of each season, the goods are either liquidated or moved back to a more centralized location.

Standard output An estimate of what should be produced, given a certain level of resources.

Statement of work, or scope of work (SOW) Terms and conditions for a purchased service that indicate, among other things, what services will be performed and how the service provider will be evaluated.

Statistical quality control (SQC) The application of statistical techniques to quality control.

Strategic planning Planning that takes place at the highest levels of the firm, addressing needs that might not arise for years into the future.

Strategic quality plan An organizational plan that provides the vision, guidance, and measurements to drive the quality effort forward and shift the organization's course when necessary.

Strategy A mechanism by which a business coordinates its decisions regarding structural and infrastructural elements.

Structural element One of two major decision categories addressed by a strategy. Includes tangible resources, such as buildings, equipment, and computer systems.

Supplier relationship management (SRM) A term that broadly refers to planning and control activities and information systems that link a firm with its upstream suppliers.

Supply chain A network of manufacturers and service providers that work together to create products or services needed by end users. These manufacturers and service providers are linked together through physical flows, information flows, and monetary flows.

Supply chain management The *active* management of supply chain activities and relationships in order to maximize customer value and achieve a sustainable competitive advantage. It represents a conscious effort by a firm or group of firms to develop and run supply chains in the most effective and efficient ways possible.

Supply Chain Operations Reference (SCOR) model A framework developed and supported by the Supply Chain Council that seeks to provide standard descriptions of the processes, relationships, and metrics that define supply chain management.

Supply management The broad set of activities carried out by organizations to analyze sourcing opportunities, develop sourcing strategies, select suppliers, and carry out all the activities required to procure goods and services.

Supply uncertainty The risk of interruptions in the flow of components from upstream suppliers.

Support process A process that performs necessary, albeit not value-added, activities.

Sustainability Performing activities in a manner that meet the needs of the present without compromising the ability of future generations to meet their needs.

Swim lane process map A process map that graphically arranges the process steps so that the user can see who is responsible for each step.

Tactical planning Planning that covers a shorter period, usually 12 to 24 months out, although the planning horizon may be longer in industries with very long lead times (e.g., engineer-to-order firms).

Takt time In a production line setting, the available production time divided by the required output rate. Takt time sets the maximum allowable cycle time for a line.

Target costing (or design to cost) The process of designing a product to meet a specific cost objective. Target costing involves setting the planned selling price and subtracting the desired profit, as well as marketing and distribution costs, thus leaving the required target cost. Also known as *design to cost.*

Target service level (SL_T) For a single-period inventory system, the service level at which the expected cost of a shortage equals the expected cost of having excess units.

Target stocking point (*TS*) For a single-period inventory system, the stocking point at which the expected cost of a shortage equals the expected cost of having excess units.

Team members Individuals who are not trained in Six Sigma but are included on a Six Sigma project team due to their knowledge or direct interest in a process.

Testability The ease with which critical components or functions can be tested during production.

Theoretical capacity The maximum output capability, allowing for no adjustments for preventive maintenance, unplanned downtime, or the like.

Theory of Constraints (TOC) An approach to visualizing and managing capacity which recognizes that nearly all products and services are created through a series of linked processes, and in every case, there is at least one process step that limits throughput for the entire chain.

Third-party logistics provider (3PL) A service firm that handles all of the logistics requirements for other companies.

3D printing An additive manufacturing process that creates a physical object from a digital design.

Tiered workforce A strategy used to vary workforce levels, in which additional full-time or part-time employees are hired during peak demand periods, while a smaller permanent staff is maintained year-round.

Time series A series of observations arranged in chronological order.

Time series forecasting model A quantitative forecasting model that uses a time series to develop forecasts. With a time series model, the chronology of the observations and their values are important in developing forecasts.

Top-down planning An approach to S&OP in which a single, aggregated sales forecast drives the planning process. For top-down planning to work, the mix of products or services must be essentially the same from one time period to the next *or* the products or services to be provided must have very similar resource requirements.

Total cost analysis A process by which a firm seeks to identify and quantify all of the major costs associated with various sourcing options.

Total cost of quality curve A curve that suggests that there is some optimal quality level, Q*. The curve is calculated by adding costs of internal and external failures, prevention costs, and appraisal costs.

Total quality management (TQM) A managerial approach in which an entire organization is managed so that it excels in all quality dimensions that are important to customers.

Trade-off A decision by a firm to emphasize one performance dimension over another, based on the recognition that excellence on some dimensions may conflict with excellence on others.

Transportation inventory Inventory that is moving from one link in the supply chain to another.

Trend Long-term movement up or down in a time series.

Two-card kanban system A special form of the kanban system that uses one card to control production and another card to control movement of materials.

Upper tolerance limit (UTL) The highest acceptable value for some measure of interest.

Upstream A term used to describe activities or firms that are positioned *earlier* in the supply chain relative to some other activity or firm of interest. For example, corn harvesting takes place upstream of cereal processing, and cereal processing takes place upstream of cereal packaging.

Value analysis (VA) A process that involves examining all elements of a component, an assembly, an end product, or a service to make sure it fulfills its intended function at the lowest total cost.

Value index A measure that uses the performance and importance scores for various dimensions of performance for an item or a service to calculate a score that indicates the overall value of an item or a service to a customer.

Value perspective A quality perspective that holds that quality must be judged, in part, by how well the characteristics of a particular product or service align with the needs of a specific user.

Variable costs Expenses directly tied to the level of business activity.

Virtual supply chain A collection of firms that typically exists for only a short period. Virtual supply chains are more flexible than traditional supply chains, but they are also less efficient.

Volume flexibility The ability to produce whatever volume the customer needs.

Waiting line theory A body of theory based on applied statistics that helps managers evaluate the relationship between capacity decisions and important performance issues such as waiting times and line lengths.

Warehouse and transportation planning systems Logistics information systems that support tactical planning efforts by allocating "fixed" logistics capacity in the best possible way, given business requirements.

Warehouse management and transportation execution systems Logistics information systems that initiate and control the movement of materials between supply chain partners.

Warehousing Any operation that stores, repackages, stages, sorts, or centralizes goods or materials. Organizations use warehousing to reduce transportation costs, improve operational flexibility, shorten customer lead times, and lower inventory costs.

Waste According to APICS, in the JIT/Lean philosophy, "any activity that does not add value to the good or service in the eyes of the consumer."

Weighted center of gravity method A logistics decision modeling technique that attempts to identify the "best" location for a single warehouse, store, or plant, given multiple demand points that differ in location and importance.

Weighted moving average model A form of the moving average model that allows the actual weights applied to past observations to differ.

$\overline{X}$ chart A specific type of control chart for a continuous variable that is used to track the average value for future samples.

Yield management An approach that services commonly use with highly perishable "products," in which prices are regularly adjusted to maximize total profit.

INDEX